REGIONAL INTEGRATION AND TRADE LIBERALIZATION IN SUBSAHARAN AFRICA

Volume 1: Framework, Issues and Methodological Perspectives

REGIONAL INTEGRATION AND TRADE LIBERALIZATION IN
SUBSAHARAN AFRICA

VOLUME 1: FRAMEWORK, ISSUES AND METHODOLOGICAL
PERSPECTIVES
Edited by Ademola Oyejide, Ibrahim Elbadawi and Paul Collier

VOLUME 2: COUNTRY CASE-STUDIES
Edited by Ademola Oyejide, Benno Ndulu and Jan Willem Gunning

VOLUME 3: REGIONAL CASE-STUDIES
Edited by Ademola Oyejide, Ibrahim Elbadawi and Stephen Yeo

VOLUME 4: SYNTHESIS AND REVIEW
Edited by Ademola Oyejide, Benno Ndulu and David Greenaway

Regional Integration and Trade Liberalization in SubSaharan Africa

Volume 1: Framework, Issues and Methodological Perspectives

Edited by

Ademola Oyejide
Professor of Economics
University of Ibadan, Nigeria

Ibrahim Elbadawi
Research Coordinator
African Economic Research Consortium, Nairobi

and

Paul Collier
Professor of Economics
University of Oxford, and
Director, Centre for the Study of African Economies

First published in Great Britain 1997 by
MACMILLAN PRESS LTD
Houndmills, Basingstoke, Hampshire RG21 6XS and London
Companies and representatives throughout the world

A catalogue record for this book is available from the British Library.

ISBN 0–333–66104–4

First published in the United States of America 1997 by
ST. MARTIN'S PRESS, INC.,
Scholarly and Reference Division,
175 Fifth Avenue, New York, N.Y. 10010

ISBN 0–312–17321–0

Library of Congress Cataloging-in-Publication Data
Regional integration and trade liberalization in subsaharan Africa.
v. <1   > ; cm.
Includes bibliographical references and index.
Contents: Vol. 1. Framework, issues and methodological
perspectives / edited by Ademola Oyejide, Ibrahim Elbadawi and Paul
Collier
ISBN 0–312–17321–0 (v. 1)
1. Africa, Sub-Saharan—Economic integration.   2. Africa, Sub
-Saharan—Economic policy.   3. Africa, Sub-Saharan—Foreign economic
relations.   I. Oyejide, T. Ademola.   II. Elbadawi, Ibrahim.
III. Collier, Paul.
HC800.R448   1997
337.67—dc21
                                                              96–49387
                                                              CIP

This book is printed on paper suitable for recycling and made from fully managed and
sustained forest sources.

10   9   8   7   6   5   4   3   2   1
06   05   04   03   02   01   00   99   98   97

Printed and bound in Great Britain by
Antony Rowe Ltd, Chippenham, Wiltshire

This series on *Regional Integration and Trade Liberalization* in SubSaharan Africa is dedicated to

Gerry Helleiner

Gerry was instrumental in the creation of the African Economic Research Consortium (AERC), first as a member of the committee which lent guidance to the activities of projects, and then as a member of the first advisory committee of the AERC. From the beginning, he dedicated his time and effort to make this innovative concept a reality. Since then he has continued to support the interests of the Consortium at every opportunity.

Professionally and intellectually, Gerry has been a great supporter of development in SubSaharan Africa through his research and teaching activities in Nigeria and Tanzania. He has been a top economic adviser in several countries worldwide, often holding the title 'Wise Man'. We shall always be grateful to him for drawing the attention of the international community to the plight of SubSaharan Africa's development.

Contents

List of Figures   ix

List of Tables   x

Notes on the Contributors   xii

List of Abbreviations   xv

1   Introduction and Overview
Ademola Oyejide, Ibrahim Elbadawi and Paul Collier   1

2   Review of Theoretical Developments on
Regional Integration
Richard E. Baldwin   24

3   Macroeconomic Harmonization, Trade Reform and
Regional Trade in SubSaharan Africa
Stephen A. O'Connell   89

4   Regional Integration in SubSaharan Africa:
A Review of Experiences and Issues
William Lyakurwa, Andrew McKay,
Nehemiah Ng'eno and Walter Kennes   159

5   The Impact of Regional Trade and Monetary Schemes on
Intra-subSaharan Africa Trade
Ibrahim Elbadawi   210

6   Regional Integration and the Bias Against Agriculture and
other 'Disadvantaged' Sectors in SubSaharan Africa
Dean A. DeRosa   256

7   Evaluating Trade Liberalization:
A Methodological Framework
Paul Collier, David Greenaway and Jan Willem Gunning   306

8   Trade Liberalization and Regional Integration in Africa
Charles D. Jebuni   353

9   The Uruguay Round and SubSaharan Africa's
     Trade Policies
     Piritta Sorsa   370

10   Changing Political and Economic Conditions for
     Regional Integration in SubSaharan Africa
     H.M.A. Onitiri   398

11   Regional Integration in a SubSaharan Africa:
     Dead End or a Fresh Start?
     Jeffrey Fine and Stephen Yeo   428

Index   475

List of Figures

2.1   The well known tariff analysis diagram   30
2.2   Impact of protection on exporting country   34
2.3   Trade creation and trade diversion   37
2.4   An example of rules of origin   39
2.5   Quotas versus tariffs with imperfect competition   43
2.6   The pure profit effect   45
2.7   The U-shaped relation of concentration and openness   53
2.8   A schematic diagram of hub-and-spoke trade ties (left)
      and concentric circles (right)   55
2.9   The marginalizing tendencies of hub-and-spoke   56
2.10 Induced capital formation in the Solow model   59
3.1   Trade policy for external balance   92
3.2   General equilibrium effects of endogenous trade policy   97
3.3   Trade controls and macroeconomic consistency   104
3.4   Real effective exchange rate decompositions (a) 11 CFA
      countries (b) 15 non-CFA, non-CMA countries   131
5.1   Rates of change on intra-bloc trade flows 1980–4
      and 1986–90 (a) Value (b) % of total trade   220
5.2   Evolution of trade: region versus the rest of the
      world (a) SSA (b) ASEAN   232
6.1   Equilibrium under free trade and protection   264
6.2   Equilibrium under a regional trading arrangement   278
7.1   Import distortions   307

List of Tables

3.1 African monetary arrangements and associated trade
arrangements to 1993   113
3.2 Membership of monetary and trade arrangements in
Table 3.1   114
3.3 Macroeconomic divergence in the
East African Community   116
3.4 Inflation in selected country groups   118
3.5 Parallel premiums, fiscal deficits and inflation   130
3.6 Measures of openness   138
3.7 Intra-African exports as a share of total exports   140
4.1 Economic indicators for SSA   177
4.2 Regional integration arrangements among SSA countries:
membership, objectives, instruments and achievements   178
4.3 Economic indicators for regional groupings in SSA   182
4.4 Share of trade intra-regional exports and imports and
world exports and imports by trading schemes in selected
years (1970–91) (%)   184
4.5 Manufacturing output and exports for regional
groupings in SSA   186
4.6 Summary of membership of regional trade arrangements
in SSA   204
5.1 Selected economic indicators and intra-bloc
trade flows 1980–4 and 1986–90   211
5.2 Gravity model estimates: SSA and other low-income
countries (averages 1980–4 and 1986–90)   222
5.3 The marginal contribution of RI schemes and exchange
rate policy in the determination of bilateral trade flows:
1980–4, 1986–90 (derived elasticities)   225
5.4 Characteristics of different types of monetary integration   235
5.5 Costs and benefits of different forms of monetary
integration   236
5A.1 Reporter and partner countries in the sample   243
5A.2 Gravity model estimates: SSA and other low-income
countries (averages 1980–4 and 1986–90)   245
5A.3 Gravity model estimates: SSA and other low-income
countries (averages 1980–4 and 1986–90)   246

5A.4 Gravity model estimates: SSA and other low-income
      countries (averages 1980–4 and 1986–90)   248
6.1   Organizations for economic co-operation in developing
      regions   259
6.2   Indicators of fundamental economic factors, 1989   261
6.3   Import restrictions in SSA countries, 1987 (%)   266
6.4   Import restrictions in SSA countries by
      traded goods category, 1987 (%)   270
6.5   Price elasticity values   273
6.6   Effects of import liberalization in SSA countries   274
6.7   Manufactures for accelerated trade liberalization under the
      AFTA plan and ASEAN import restriction   284
6.8   The ASEAN trade simulation model: product categories,
      elasticity of substitution values, and country coverage 288
6.9   Changes in economywide variable, international trade,
      and economic welfare   290
7.1   Components of liberalization episodes:
      the Papageorgiou *et al.* study   310
7.2   Components of liberalization in 11 developing countries:
      the Whalley study   312
7.3   Trade policy reform proposals in 40 SAL countries   314
7.4   Performance of GDP (real annual rate of growth)   343
7.5   Export performance (real annual rate of growth)   344
7.6   Composition of results on effectiveness of SALs   347
8.1   Comparison between some characteristics of
      SSA grouping and some other regional groupings
      in the world, 1970–90   355
8.2   Intra-African exports by commodity   357
8.3   Exports by Africa to and from the countries listed   360
8.4   Imports by Africa to and from the countries listed   361
9.1   Summary of Uruguay Round (UR) commitments in
      agriculture and industry   374
9.2   Summary of main obligations for SSA from
      WTO agreements   381
9.3   Overview of initial commitments in services by sector 386
9A.1 GATT status of SSA countries   391

Notes on the Contributors

Richard Baldwin is Professor of Economics at the Graduate Institute of International Studies, Geneva with expertise in International Economics.

Paul Collier is Professor of Economics, Director of CSAE, visiting Professor at the Kennedy School of Government and an associate of HIID, Harvard University, Professor associate of CERDI, Université d'Auvergne; associate of the Tinbergen Institute, Amsterdam; and Fellow of the CEPR, London. He works on a wide range of macroeconomic, microeconomic and political economy topics concerned with Africa. He is on the African panel of the Social Science Research Council, New York; on the Council of DIAL, Paris and is a consultant for the World Bank, the European Commission, SIDA, the ILO and ODA.

Dean A. DeRosa is chairman of ADR International Ltd, a consulting firm specializing in international trade and development economics based in Falls Church, Virginia, USA. He was formerly research fellow at the International Food Policy Research Institute, senior economist at the International Monetary Fund and Asian Development Bank, and economist at the US Department of the Treasury. In recent years, his research on international trade relations and economic policy has focused on regional trading arrangements among developing countries.

Ibrahim Elbadawi is currently on leave from the Research Department of the World Bank which he joined in 1989, and is working as the research coordinator of the African Economic Research Consortium in Nairobi. He has a PhD in economics and statistics and his fields of specializations are in the areas of exchange rate economics, structural adjustment, macroeconomic policy and agriculture, international migration and remittances, and economic growth. Regionally, his main research is on subSaharan Africa.

Jeffrey C. Fine is an independent consultant based in Ottawa, Canada. His long-standing involvement in subSaharan Africa has covered such issues as economic integration, longer term prospects for growth, trade policy, investment in human resources, and the strengthening of higher education and research. Mr Fine played an instrumental role in the establishment of the African Economic Research Consortium and served as its executive director from 1988 to 1994.

Jan Willem Gunning is Professor of Development Economics at the Free University, Amsterdam. He is also professor at CERDI, University of Auvergne, member of the Centre for the Study of African Economies, University of Oxford and managing editor of the *Journal of African Economies*. His specialities are trade policy and general equilibrium modelling.

Charles Jebuni is a lecturer at the University of Ghana, Legon but is currently on sabbatical at the National Policy Research Institute in Accra, specializing in International Economics.

Walter Kennes is head of sector regional integration and programming in the Directorate General for Development of the European Commission, Brussels, Belgium. He joined the European Commission in 1984, dealing mainly with conceptual tasks and projects related to food aid and food security, the social dimension of adjustment and regional economic integration among developing countries.

William Lyakurwa is training coordinator with the African Economic Research Consortium in Nairobi. He was formerly Senior Trade Promotion Adviser with the International Trade Centre (UNCTAD/GATT) and Associate Professor of Economics at the University of Dar es Salaam, Tanzania. He holds a BA and MA from the University of Dar es Salaam and a PhD from Cornell University, Ithaca, New York.

Andrew McKay is currently a lecturer in economics at CREDIT and Department of Economics, University of Nottingham. His area of specialty is in development economics with special reference to Africa, income distribution and poverty, international trade.

N.K. Ng'eno is lecturer at the Department of Economics, at the University of Nairobi. His area of specialty is in international economics and macroeconomic theory. He is also currently on secondment to the Government of Kenya as Chief Economist, Cabinet Office, Office of the President.

Stephen A. O'Connell is currently Associate Professor of Economics at Swathmore College. His area of specialty is open economy macroeconomics, macroeconomic policy in subSaharan Africa, including African central banking and monetary policy and parallel foreign exchange markets and illegal trade and macroeconomic effects of foreign aid. Previous positions include Visiting Researcher at Centre for Study of African Economies, Oxford University, Lecturer and Research Associate at University of Dar es Salaam; Research Associate at the University of Nairobi; and Assistant Professor of Economics at University of Pennsylvania.

H.M.A. Onitiri was formerly professor of Economics, at the University of Ibadan and long-time consultant with UNECA, specializing in political economics.

Ademola Oyejide is Professor of Economics and Director of the Trade Policy Research and Training Programme at the University of Ibadan, Nigeria. His major area of expertise is international economics, with a special interest in trade policy and regional integration. He has been a member of the United Nations Committee for Development Planning, and has consulted for the World Bank. He has also been on the Advisory Committee of the African Economic Research Consortium, for whom he is currently directing a research project on regional integration and trade liberalization.

Piritta Sorsa is currently at the International Monetary Fund, Geneva Office.

Stephen Yeo is deputy director of the Centre for Economic Policy Research (CEPR) in London, having studied at McMaster University and Essex University and taught at the London School of Economics. He has acted as an adviser to a number of organizations, including the Bank of England, the Eurasia Foundation, the Ford Foundation and the United Nations Economic Commission for Africa.

List of Abbreviations

ACP	Africa–Caribbean–Pacific
AFTA	Asean Free Trade Area
ASEAN	Association of Southeast Asian Nations
BEAC	Banque des Etats de L'Afrique Centrale
CACM	Central American Common Market
CEAO	Economic Community of West Africa
CEEC	Central and Eastern European Countries
CEPGL	Economic Community of the Great Lakes Countries
CEPR	Centre for Economic Policy Research
CMA	Common Monetary Area
COMESA	Common Market for Eastern and Southern Africa
EAC	East African Community
EC	European Community
ECA	UN Economic Commission for Africa
ECOWAS	Economic Community of West African States
EU	European Union
GATS	General Agreement on Trade in Services
GATT	General Agreement on Tariffs and Trade
ISI	Import Substitution Industrialization
LAFTA	Latin American Free Trade Association
MFN	Most Favoured Nation
NAFTA	North American Free Trade Association
OAU	Organization for African Unity
OECD	Organization for Economic Cooperation and Development
PTA	Preferential Trade Area
RI	Regional Integration
SADC	Southern African Development Community
SACU	Southern African Customs Union
SSA	SubSaharan Africa
UDEAC	Central African Customs and Economic Union
UEMOA	Economic and Monetary Union of West Africa

1 Introduction and Overview

Ademola Oyejide, Ibrahim Elbadawi and Paul Collier

This chapter contains a review of a set of ten papers focused on conceptual and methodological issues related to subSaharan Africa's regional integration and trade liberalization. Though designed to be self-contained, this volume also sets the stage for three subsequent ones on country-specific trade liberalization experiences (vol. 2); and regional integration experiences (vol. 3) in addition to a synthesis volume (vol. 4). All four constitute the product of the collaborative project on 'Regional Integration and Trade Liberalization in SubSaharan Africa', sponsored by AERC and other collaborating institutions. Three of the ten chapters contained in this volume are concerned with theoretical and methodological issues at the conceptual level; five address the articulation of this conceptual framework for a pan-African analysis of regional integration (trade, monetary and sectoral), trade liberalization experiences, and the possible consequences for African international trade of the new GATT agreement; and, finally two chapters offer some future options.

1.1 REGIONAL INTEGRATION: THEORY AND DEBATE

The chapter by Baldwin (Chapter 2) and that by O'Connell (Chapter 3) provide complementary analyses of what might be expected from African regional integration. Baldwin focuses on economic theory, reviewing both the original, second-best theory of regional integration, and the more tangential insights from the recent revivals in analytic economic geography and endogenous growth theory. O'Connell provides a comprehensive analytical framework based on a small open economy model, which allows systematic analysis of the relationships between exchange rate policy, fiscal policy and trade policy in African countries. Three important conclusions came out of O'Connell's research: the dominance of macroeconomic policy consideration in the evolution of Africa's trade regimes; that the degree of monetary integration has been a key factor differentiating Africa's macroeconomic landscape; and, that currency convertibility for current account purposes is essential, although more for overall trade than for regional trade in particular.

O'Connell's last two analytical thrusts, which relate to the debate on the linkages between monetary and trade integration in subSaharan Africa, constitute a different contribution from that of Baldwin's to the debate on the efficacy of regional integration in subSaharan Africa. A further discussion on this issue will follow. The implication of O'Connell's first conclusion regarding the centrality of macroeconomic consideration in Africa's trade liberalization, will be addressed later in this chapter in the context of the review of the paper by Collier, Greenaway and Gunning (Chapter 7).

While, on the whole, the static reallocation effects to be expected from regional integration may be small, Baldwin and O'Connell both suggest that the dynamic and other effects of regional integration do matter. However, our review of the debate begins with the static effects.

The second-best theory of regional preferential trading predicts that any effects at the regional level from African regional schemes would be very small. As shown by Foroutan and Pritchett (1993) using a gravity model to simulate trade flows between African countries in the absence of trade restrictions, the scope for inter-country trade within Africa is intrinsically modest. The regional welfare effects from inducing these flows through preferential trade policy are small percentages of these small percentages, and since some of the effects are negative, the net effects may not be positive. Further, while the regional level effects are tiny, the effects on individual countries can be large because of inter-country redistributions. Second-best theory thus predicts that the politics of regional integration in Africa could be a nightmare: approximately a zero-sum game played for high stakes, with consequently little incentive for co-operation. An implication of this is that in Africa the trade policies of neighbouring countries may be unimportant, except to the extent that they involve big divergences in policy towards non-regional partners which, in turn, produce major spill overs. A shrewd government should therefore focus upon getting its national policies right once any attempt to link national policy with those of neighbouring countries could grossly complicate policy formulation and implementation with little offsetting pay-off.

However, a different type of evidence comes from recent studies on regional spillovers in growth effects. Chua (1993) and Easterly and Levine (1994) find that neighbours matter. If neighbouring countries grow rapidly that appears to assist national growth, even in Africa. These results are as yet tentative and might, for example, turn out to be accounted for by inadequate correction for fixed effects. However, to the extent that they are correct, they appear to sit uncomfortably with the conclusion that neighbours are unimportant. The major contributions of the Baldwin and the O'Connell chapters are to explore two alternative approaches to resolving this apparent conflict.

Baldwin devotes most of his review to recent innovations in economic theory which have implications for regional integration. First, he considers the 'new economic geography' in which location decisions are based upon the interplay of internal economies of scale and 'trade costs'. Trade costs can be thought of as all the costs which increase with distance between the producer and the customer, both transport costs and information costs such as language and cultural impediments to ease of transactions. High trade costs within Africa can lead to a 'hub and spoke' trade pattern in which the activities which have powerful scale economies, such as manufacturing, are located in the European 'hub'. No 'spoke' African country has a sufficiently large market to warrant the location of production in it unless trade costs within Africa can be reduced. This model, which departs from the second-best approach by the introduction of economies of scale and location-specific costs, provides a rationale for African regional integration in the context of North–South integration. The 'spokes' should be joined up, but not severed from the 'hub'. Baldwin also shows that the effect of reducing intra-regional trade costs on industrial location might not be monotonic. If, as in much of Africa, intra-regional trade costs are initially very high, then small reductions can be expected to increase the regional concentration of production, whereas large reductions might not do so. Hence, the small-step integration efforts which have characterized many of the previous regional integration processes in Africa may have generated greater inter-government conflict than would have been the case with more sweeping liberalization. While the insights of location theory are evidently pertinent for African regional integration, the framework is not of obvious help in resolving the conflict set out above. The most distinctive contribution of Location Theory is probably its insight that the good performance of a neighbour can actually be damaging as activities relocate there to benefit from its larger market and so save on trade costs. Although such a result is far from inevitable in location models, it nevertheless suggests that the approach is at a disadvantage in offering fresh insights into why the spillover effects of neighbours are positive even if trade is modest.

The second area discussed by Baldwin is endogenous growth theory. He reviews the literatures by which the return to investment in the aggregate becomes constant because of either the creative destruction of innovation or the spillover effects of human capital accumulation on the productivity of physical and human capital. He then investigates what would be the impact of trade liberalization in these models. The result is unambiguously that greater openness increases growth. The increased international sharing of knowledge which is associated with increased openness lowers the costs of innovation and so stimulates investment in innovation, thereby raising growth. Further, the redundancy implied by autarky, whereby the same discovery may be made in several countries, each time at a cost, is avoided. A further stimulus is provided by the increased competition to which domestic firms are exposed by international trade. Local monopolies benefiting from protection might have the resources to innovate, but they lack the incentive to do so because their market is not under threat from other innovating firms. Opening to international trade enables governments to introduce a competitive structure in markets which when closed support only monopoly. A final growth enhancement due to international trade is that it enables countries in which innovation is high cost, for example because human capital is expensive, to import innovations from countries in which costs are lower. However, all these growth gains apply quite generally to the opening up to trade, rather than being specific to regional trade. They lead Baldwin to the conclusion that regional integration is best pursued in the context of global liberalization. The one area in which he identifies a specific role for regional co-operation is with respect to investment terms to be offered to foreign footloose companies. If countries liberalize regionally but do not co-ordinate on investment terms, then each government is in effect able to sell the right to the regional market. Competition between governments will thereby force the price down to zero. Hence, to the extent that governments wish to tax foreign investors, they need to co-ordinate their rates of tax. While this is potentially important, in recent years foreign investment into Africa has been so small that co-ordination to raise tax rates on foreign investors can hardly be considered a pressing priority.

The theories reviewed by Baldwin thus provide a dynamic case for African trade liberalization, but not specifically a regional focus to that liberalization, except to the extent that regional liberalization should accompany global liberalization to avoid hub-spoke effects. On the other hand, O'Connell – focussing on the possible role of monetary integration in providing an institutional underpinning for convertibility and trade openness – advances a new argument which reaches a complementary conclusion but additionally provides some insight into our initial puzzle as to why neighbours might matter.

After a brief review of monetary integration as a background, O'Connell explores two main views of the linkages between monetary integration and regional trade. In one view, the potential gains from regional trade provide a central – if not the central – rationale for increases in monetary co-operation between regional partners. This view was characteristic of the classic literature on optimum currency areas, which took the existence of substantial gains to enhanced regional exchange as axiomatic and focused on the costs of monetary union. However, O'Connell discounts this view on grounds along the lines of the second-best theory of regional preferential trading reviewed above. He argues that regional trade is unlikely to be an important engine of African growth in the near term. African countries lack the income levels and structural complementarities that would generate large gains from regional specialization, whether within or across industries.[1] This leaves the second view, which argues that the main purpose of monetary integration is to contribute to investment and growth by helping to enforce the *policy restraint* necessary for macroeconomic stability. In a similar vein to Fine and Yeo (see the sub-section on options below), albeit with a more precise attention to the role of currency convertibility, O'Connell borrows from Collier's (1991) 'agency of restraint' paradigm to support monetary integration from this second perspective.

O'Connell argues that the establishment of convertibility for current account purposes is extremely important for Africa's international trade, and is probably relatively more important for non-traditional trade – including regional trade in locally-manufactured goods – than for trade in traditional products with hard-currency partners outside Africa. Clearly this argument for convertibility is a non-discriminatory one. Furthermore, he argues that convertibility does not even require co-operation, let alone monetary integration. It does require, however:

(1) at least in the short run, a willingness to abandon the use of the exchange rate as a nominal anchor (and/or a mechanism for delivering rents to favoured groups); and
(2) over the longer run, a willingness to exercise the fiscal restraint consistent with low inflation.

The rationale for monetary integration derives from its role as a relatively more credible institutional mechanism for enforcing both requisites of sustained exchange rate unification. Monetary integration can help underpin convertibility and trade openness, through its advantages over macroeconomic policy conditionality enforced by international financial institutions (IFIs) or bilateral donors – or home-grown versions of the same institutional reforms, for that matter – as an 'agency of restraint' over the medium to long term.[2] As pointed out above this terminology is Collier's (1991), who also argues that the vertical and horizontal links in the CFA zone generate a 'participatory, supra-national agency of restraint' with major advantages over the essentially alien, unidirectional, and unreliable conditionality of donors and the IFIs.

Both Baldwin and O'Connell provide a case for African liberalization *vis-à-vis* the world market. The question is whether in this context regionalism is a distraction which will absorb the attention of politicians from much more important subjects because of its glamour, or whether it has a substantial economic rationale. The case for an active regional integration policy which these chapters make is, in essence, threefold. First, regional liberalization should accompany global liberalization to avoid 'hub–spoke' effects. Second, by providing a credible 'supra-national agency of restraint', monetary integration linked to a Northern anchor may underpin a more open trade regime, by supporting a more competitive real exchange rate and releasing trade policy from a preoccupation with external balance. Third, policy liberalization should be regionally reciprocal, with Northern participation, to enhance the credibility of the reform process.

1.2 TRADE LIBERALIZATION: ISSUES, METHODOLOGIES, CONSEQUENCES

The paper by Collier, Greenaway and Gunning (Chapter 7) undertakes the task of analysing three major issues: measuring trade policy and identifying liberalization episodes; measuring trade liberalization incredibility and its consequences; and evaluating the effects of trade liberalization. In our view while the methodologies proposed in relation to the first two issues are not only creative but lend themselves to fairly unambiguous interpretation, the last issue is problematic. The authors acknowledge that evaluation of the effects of liberalization is inherently demanding for at least four reasons. First, one would need to evaluate performance under liberalization relative to a counterfactual scenario of what would have been the situation in the absence of liberalization. Second, the evaluation of the trade liberalization effects must also account for other components of the reform package, especially exchange rate policy reforms, in addition to changing external conditions. Two further complications relate to the issue of timing – how long should a liberalization programme have been in place before its evaluated? and what performance criteria should be used for evaluation? In both of the last two cases the authors provide a convincing answer. In the first case one has to study the nature of the programme in terms of its ingredients, the circumstances in which it was implemented, whether it was single or multi-staged, and so on. In the second case it is clear that the evaluation should analyse the impact on overall economic performance such as exports, investment and growth, rather than target indicators (such as reducing the nominal tariff to 10 per cent for example).

Therefore, as in the context of the literature on the impact of structural adjustment on economic performance, the discussion suggests that overcoming the first two complications discussed above is the real challenge in attempting to evaluate the effects of trade liberalization. The problem of proper attribution of effects is made all the more difficult by the very compelling analysis made by O'Connell. He argues that, until recently, the stance of trade policy in many African countries, and particularly the evolution of that stance over time, was largely a macroeconomic phenomenon. Changes in the structure of effective protection were driven primarily by balance of payments considerations rather than by conventional considerations of resource allocation. This implies that policies normally construed as primarily macroeconomic in character – like exchange rate unification – had strong effects on the domestic relative prices of traded goods. It follows that any chronology of trade policy developments or search for trade liberalization episodes must pay close attention to macroeconomic developments and their implications for exchange rate policy and exchange controls. It also follows that domestic price data are essential in determining the actual stance of trade policy, since tariffs were inframarginal for much of the post-independence period.

The same sentiment is also echoed at a broader level in the context of liberalization experiences in developing countries, where it is argued that the impact of import liberalization on export growth has usually been overestimated, because under conditions of severe external imbalances, trade policies – especially import controls – become a substitute for exchange rate policy as a means for restoring the current account balance. As such, import controls in this situation are an endogenous macroeconomic (and not trade) policy instrument. Therefore, in these situations the initial positive and usually strong impact on export of tariffication and elimination of quantity controls should be counted as a macroeconomic rather than trade effect (for example, see Rodrik, 1992).[3] Even in the case of the Western African members of the two currency unions (CFA), where macroeconomic considerations were generally less important in determining the stance of trade policy, the commitment to fixed exchange rate may well have raised the cost of trade liberalization (O'Connell).

Despite its shortcomings, the 'modified-control-group' approach – which allows for estimating a counterfactual, endogenizing the decision to undertake reforms as well as accounting for changing external conditions and other policy stances – offers the best option. However, this approach is most suited for cross-sectional analysis, where in the context of the structural adjustment literature (for example, Corbo and Rojas, 1991; Elbadawi, 1992) the analysis is based on a sample of reforming and non-reforming countries. Even though this approach is applicable at the country-specific level, time series data requirements are likely to make it of limited value for the evaluation of country-specific liberalization experiences. Perhaps due to this consideration Collier *et al.* were inclined to propose, albeit with some qualifications, the simple before-and-after approach adopted by Papageorgiou *et al.* (1991) in their seminal analysis of trade liberalization in developing countries. However, in view of the above discussion on the centrality of macroeconomic consideration in shaping Africa's trade regimes and the general, erroneous tendency to attribute the effects of macro-economically-oriented reforms to trade liberalization, considerable caution is urged when using the before-and-after approach.

1.3 EXPERIENCES

The chapter by Lyakurwa, McKay, Ng'eno and Kennes (Chapter 4) provides a review of issues and experiences related to regional integration in subSaharan Africa, while Jebuni's chapter (Chapter 8) is mainly concerned with addressing the relationship between trade liberalization and regional integration and their relative role in enhancing intra-African trade. DeRosa (Chapter 6) and Elbadawi (Chapter 5), on the other hand, address more specialized topics in the context of regional integration in subSaharan Africa. DeRosa focuses on the impact on agriculture of a regional integration-based liberalization relative to the effect due to non-discriminatory trade liberalization, while Elbadawi uses a gravity model to assess the impact of African regional/monetary integration schemes on African regional and international trade flows, and to draw comparisons with other non-African regional schemes. The paper by Sorsa analyses the possible impact of the Uruguay Round on Africa's trade prospects by focusing on subSaharan Africa's own market access commitments in the Uruguay Round and the nature of the constraints on subSaharan African policies set by the Uruguay Round.

Regional Integration Experiences in SubSaharan Africa

The main objective of Lyakurwa *et al.* was to evaluate the regional integration experiences in subSaharan Africa and to propose some researchable issues for the consideration of the regional case studies. To develop a set of principles for organizing their analysis, the authors started with a review of some key theoretical and methodological issues, including the case for regional integration (both the static and dynamic aspects); economic geography, and regional integration and outward orientation. In addition, to provide a comparative framework for the analysis, they also reviewed regional integration experiences in Asia, Europe and Latin America.

As they point out in their theoretical review, the arguments for regional integration do not lend themselves to unambiguous conclusions. Even in a simple Vinerian model, the desirability of an integration scheme depends on the balance of opposing forces, in this case trade creation and trade diversion. Moving to a more general static framework, such as that of Collier (1979), only heightens the complexity. As shown by Baldwin, the case for regional integration, especially in the context of export promotion strategy, becomes stronger when dynamic factors are taken into consideration. However, in practice whether or not this can be realized depends on the extent to which economies of scale and international competitiveness are achieved as a result, and on the feasibility of setting up a compensation scheme. This issue is a key one, given the likelihood that an effective regional integration will result in geographic concentration within the integrating region, as suggested by the recent insight from economic geography (for example, Krugman, 1991 a,b,c). The above arguments however, have not so far been borne out by the experiences of regional integration schemes in subSaharan Africa (Lyakurwa *et al.*; Elbadawi; Jebuni).

Lyakurwa *et al.* and Elbadawi provide analysis of the experiences of various regional integration schemes in subSaharan Africa. A summary of the salient features of these schemes follows.

A rather varied menu of regional integration schemes spans almost the entire space of subSaharan Africa. The stated objectives of these schemes range from co-operation between neighbouring states in a limited set of policy areas as in the case of the Southern African Development Co-ordination Conference (SADCC), to complete trade and monetary integration (for example, Communauté Economique de l'Afrique de l'Ouest (CEAO) and the Customs and Economic Union of Central Africa (UDEAC)), or to currency union and capital and labour market integration as in the case of the Southern Africa Customs Union (SACU). More recent developments aimed at reforming and further deepening of these schemes include: the accession of South Africa to SADCC to form the Southern African Development Community (SADC); the transformation of the Preferential Trade Area for Eastern and Southern Africa (PTA) into the Common Market of Eastern and Southern Africa (COMESA); the integration of CEAO with the West African Monetary Union (UMOA) in a new block, the Economic and Monetary Union of the West African States (UEMOA), that as before will be externally anchored by France; and preparation for similar arrangements for francophone Central Africa, through the merger of the Central African Monetary Union (BEAC) and UDEAC and the revival of the defunct East African Community.[4] There is a further, but at this stage conjectural, arrangement involving the extension of SACU to include other countries in Southern Africa. Another major distinguishing characteristic stems from the extent of geographical coverage of the scheme. For example, the Economic Community of the West African States (ECOWAS) and the Preferential Trade Area for Eastern and Southern African States (PTA) represent the vision of the UN Economic Commission for Africa (ECA), which argues that regional grouping in Africa should comprise a large number of countries in order to allow development of sufficiently large internal market, necessary to support the process of Africa's industrialization.[5] On the other hand, the rest of the schemes are based on a strategy of promoting regional objectives among a smaller and hopefully more homogenous neighbouring countries.

A brief review of the literature on African economic integration reveals a record of failures and unfulfilled expectations. The failures of these schemes can at least be partially explained by the own characteristics and the constraints they face (see Lyakurwa *et al.*; Fine and Yeo; and Elbadawi in this volume; Langhammer and Hiemenz, 1991; and Foroutan, 1993, for more details on the experiences of regional integration schemes in subSaharan Africa and other developing regions).

In this context, one can distinguish between two very different reasons for the lack of success of African regional integration schemes; one is a lack of real potential benefits, and the other is a lack of implementation. Several recent appraisals suggest that the second reason is probably more important (see Kennes, 1994 and Commission of the European Communities, 1995).

Intra-African Trade: The Relative Roles of Non-Discriminatory and Preferential Trade Liberalization

Jebuni (Chapter 8) observes that despite the mushrooming of regional integration schemes in subSaharan Africa, including some with extremely ambitious integration objectives, most assessments of these schemes, however, conclude that they have failed to increase intra-union trade flows. In addition to citing the evidence by Foroutan (1993), the author reviewed a wide range of evidence corroborating this conclusion (for example, Mansoor and Intoai, 1991; Lipumba and Kasekende, 1991; Ariyo and Raheem, 1991). As possible explanations of the failure of these arrangements he then quotes Foroutan, who identifies the key problems as, 'the structural characteristics of the subSaharan Africa economies, the pursuit of import substitution policies, and the very uneven distribution of costs and benefits of integration arising from economic differences among partner countries. . .'. The paper also cites further evidence on the inward-orientated trade policies partially blamed for preventing any meaningful trade integration in subSaharan Africa. For example it was estimated that 74–85 per cent of import tax was shifted to the export sector (Jebuni *et al.*, 1992), while Oyejide (1986) obtained an estimate of about 55–90 per cent for Nigeria. Also DeRosa studied net protection for agricultural exports in a large sample of African countries, using simulations with a simple partial equilibrium model of trade and real exchange rate adjustment. He found that protection reduced the value of exports from these countries by between 15 and 33 per cent per annum and inhibits export diversification.

A further evidence documented by Jebuni is that intra-African trade is dominated by trade in manufactures and foods (that is, non-traditional exports). For example, between 1985 and 1989, the combined share of manufacturing and food in intra-African exports averaged more than 55 per cent (Table 8. 2). Jebuni provides an interpretation for this trade structure by appealing to the extended version of the Heckscher–Ohlin theory (for example, Krueger, 1977; Baldwin, 1979) which suggests that it is natural for a country to export labour-intensive products to countries relatively more endowed with capital, while exporting capital-intensive goods to countries characterized by more labour-intensive economies. Clearly this analysis suggests that comparative advantage changes as the country develops (Jebuni also cites empirical evidence supporting this hypothesis).

The implication of the above analysis is that non-traditional exports will be the main comparative advantage exports suited for intra-African trade. Yet this type of exports remains the most negatively impacted by national protective measures. With this as a background, Jebuni concludes that, 'preferential/discriminatory trade liberalization within the context of import-substitution with high protection does not generate the type of competition required to induce firms to export.' On the other hand he cites both country-specific and Africa-wide evidence suggesting that intra-African trade has in fact increased with openness. For example, between 1987–92 intra-African exports increased by more than 75 per cent,[6] while it declined during the first half of the 1980s. Also evidence from Zimbabwe, Ghana and Turkey shows that stiff competition within the domestic market tends to induce firms to export.

Jebuni's ultimate conclusion is that general/non-discriminatory trade liberalization is more likely to increase regional integration in terms of trade integration than preferential/discriminatory trade liberalization schemes among African economies. This view is largely consistent with DeRosa's analysis which focuses on the sectoral implications of discriminatory preferential trade arrangements.

Sectoral Aspects of Regional Integration and Trade Liberalization

DeRosa (Chapter 6) highlights important sectoral aspects of regional integration in subSaharan Africa, emphasizing especially the implications for agriculture – the mainstay of the region's economy. Using the framework of Heckscher, Ohlin and Samuelson (HOS) model, the author draws the deleterious implications for agricultural exportables (and other disadvantaged tradable sectors for that matter) of restrictive trade regimes. He then provides evidence to establish the relevance of the HOS model based on analysis of the nominal protection for a broad sample of African countries, based on some of his previous work (DeRosa, 1992). He then uses simulations results from the cited previous work to analyse the effects of liberalization on agriculture in subSaharan Africa. His results show that not only African agriculture will substantially respond to liberalization, but that non-traditional exports will experience even greater proportional expansion. Starting with trade liberalization as a necessary condition for a viable agriculture, especially for a dynamic and diversified agricultural export sector, the author analyses the merit of regional integration in enhancing trade liberalization relative to non-discriminatory multilateral liberalization. Again he uses an extended version of the (HOS) neoclassical model, but also some quantitative estimates for the new free trade area among the members of the Association of the South-east Asian Nations (ASEAN), to analyse the relationships between regional integration and trade liberalization, and to draw possible implications for subSaharan Africa.

DeRosa's analytical and quantitative analyses suggest that the disincentives to production and trade in agriculture, and other sectors with strong potential for comparative advantage in international trade, would be reduced under regional economic arrangements, but to an extent that is substantially less than under 'open regionalism' or non-discriminatory trade liberalization. The former policy emphasizes the pursuit of expanded trade relations on a non-discriminatory basis, to the point of undertaking trade liberalization unilaterally (Arndt, 1993). Effectively, regionalism in this case is much more concerned with external economic policy co-ordination and regional co-operation than with attempting to enhance regional trade directly, especially when the latter objective requires discriminatory trade policies. Even though the ASEAN was not designed to actively promote trade, the evidence provided by DeRosa and Elbadawi suggests that it has been a strong trade-creating block, partly because of its features of 'open regionalism'.

The message for subSaharan Africa is that in addition to fostering possible dynamic gains, 'open regionalism' in the style of the ASEAN could help avert a biased structure of incentives against agriculture, and hence allow the sector to play its leading role as an engine of growth for the economies of the region. However, to the extent that macroeconomic considerations have been dominant in shaping Africa's trade regimes as shown by O'Connell, macroeconomic policy stance could effectively determine the feasibility of 'open regionalism' in subSaharan Africa.

The Effectiveness of Regional Trade/Monetary Schemes

In Chapter 5 Elbadawi is concerned with formally modelling the determinants of regional and international African trade in the context of an extended traditional 'gravity model'. In addition to controlling for the standard factors that reflect absolute trade potential in a given country and the factors that affect the trade attraction between any two trading partners, the paper's model also accounts for the following potential determinants:

(1) the effects of the regional integration schemes (including currency unions) in subSaharan Africa and in other regions pertaining to the other countries in the sample;
(2) the trade diversion (or creation) effects of the regional integration schemes;
(3) the further marginal effects of these schemes after controlling for real exchange rate volatility and real exchange rate overvaluation.

After controlling for the traditional gravity variables and exchange rate policy, Elbadawi's results suggest three fundamental conclusions on the effects of regional schemes in subSaharan Africa and other developing countries. First, by and large the experience of regional integration in subSaharan Africa has been a failure. However, the results also show that the African experience is by no means unique and there are parallels to it in other developing regions (namely Latin America). Second, the ASEAN has significantly enhanced both intra-regional as well as inter-regional trade, even though it was not explicitly designed to be a deliberate trade creating scheme. Third, the two monetary unions (CEAO, UDEAC), especially CEAO, have displayed extreme patterns of performance, where their effects on both intra-scheme and inter-scheme trade flows have been very positive (negative) and substantial during the first (second) half of the 1980s.

Elbadawi devotes considerable attention to the interpretation of the above results by relating it to the characteristics of these schemes and the development paradigm upon which they were initiated. In this connection, he reviews Fine and Yeo's critique of the African schemes and their proposal of an alternative approach to regional integration (Chapter 9). They argue against renewed regional integral efforts in subSaharan Africa along the traditional lines, where the existing regional schemes are called upon to attempt directly promoting regional trade despite repeated failures. In their view, these schemes are inappropriately structured, since they were designed to pursue the now ill-fated and out-moded import-substitution development strategy. They propose a new paradigm for regional integration in subSaharan Africa inspired by the experiences of post-Second War Europe and the recent 'miracle' experience of East Asia. They propose that regional integration initiatives in subSaharan Africa should be designed to achieve the twin objectives of fostering national policy credibility, and rapid physical and human capital accumulation – the latter being initially triggered by enhanced direct foreign investment and by saving and investment surges within the region in subsequent stages. They provide an exhaustive review of the evidence linking regional integration to these two objectives, which are now being accepted as the two main fundamentals behind East Asia's economic miracle. The key element of this strategy adopts the Collier (1991) and Collier and Gunning (1993) proposal of 'participatory supranational agencies of restraint' in which national economic policy will be tied in a reciprocal threat-making arrangement to a Northern anchor (the European Union).

Finally on the role of the CFA monetary unions of West Africa (both the UEMOA and the prospective successor to BEAC) Elbadawi's analysis suggests that the success of these unions in enhancing bilateral trade within and outside the schemes depends on three prerequisites. First, respecting static macroeconomic balances (especially fiscal balance) on a sustained basis is essential for ensuring a positive outcome in terms of economic performance (including trade performance) of the fundamental policy trade-off facing the zone (that is, abdication of the exchange rate as an instrument of national policy in return for monetary stability); second, it is necessary to reform the inherently trade-impeding zone-wide distributional/allocational arrangements before the potentially positive effects on trade of the zone monetary discipline can be realized; and third, a favourable external environment is needed, especially a reversal or moderation of the French franc appreciation *vis-à-vis* the US dollar and the worsening terms of trade for primary commodities. However, the author conjectures that given the recent and anticipated future appreciation of the French franc *vis-à-vis* the US dollar, the continued pegging of the CFA franc to it is bound to generate problems for the zone in the not too distant future, despite the recent huge devaluation of the CFA franc in 1994.

The Uruguay Round and Africa's International Trade

In Chapter 9 Sorsa turns to African experience in international trade policy co-ordination through the Uruguay Round of the GATT. Whereas some concern has been expressed that African governments will find their commitments burdensome, Sorsa shows that to a large extent Africa was a non-participant. Apart from South Africa few African governments made substantial liberalization commitments on border protection in agriculture, industry or services. Partly, this reflected a bias in GATT against coverage of the most common African trade distortions.

For example, whereas the reduction in agricultural subsidies formed an important component of the negotiations, the reduction in agricultural export taxation, which would have been more pertinent for Africa, was not covered. Whereas the major loophole in developed country liberalization – 'voluntary' export restraints and related QRs – were negotiated away, the major African loophole, trade restrictions 'justified' on balance of payments grounds, remains. However, even with these limitations the round created direct opportunities for binding tariff rates not to exceed newly liberalized rates. African governments generally did not take up these opportunities. As a result, progress in non-preferential trade liberalization will continue to depend upon unilateral government actions. As discussed below, one major difference between such liberalization and GATT round agreements is that there is no lock-in. One of the themes of this study is that trade liberalizations which have only limited credibility generate limited investment responses. Hence, the missed opportunity for increasing credibility may have been costly. Rather than treating the GATT (and its successor WTO) as a source of costly commitments to be avoided, Sorsa argues that African governments should have attempted to shift the agenda towards their own concerns including the establishment of credible commitments.

1.4   OPTIONS

Among the future trade policy options for African governments two polar strategies can be distinguished: the unilateral freeing of trade on a non-preferential basis versus the creation of a Pan-African economic area with a central decision structure for co-ordinated and reciprocally preferential policies. Before considering intermediate options we will set out these polar positions, each of which has some intuitive common-sense appeal.

The former takes as its basic insight the notion that Africa consists of small, open economies and that for such economies unilateral free trade is Pareto efficient. At present, despite considerable reductions in trade barriers over the past decade, most African countries still impose fairly high barriers through tariffs and export taxes or through managed exchange rate arrangements. The future agenda on this view is therefore continued unilateral reductions in these barriers. The coordination of such unilateral government decisions would be of no value and would be costly because progress would be at the pace of the slowest and because international negotiations would tie up high level personnel in glamorous but futile meetings. On this view trade restric-tions are a policy error and in correcting that error a government should have little interest in whether other governments continue with the mistake. Jebuni's chapter in this volume adds a further twist to this argument. Even if increased African integration is seen as intrinsically desirable, it is best achieved as an automatic by-product of the unilat-eral reduction of trade barriers. He shows that since 1987, when Afri-can governments embarked upon the unilateral, non-preferential freeing of trade, African intra-regional trade has expanded more rapidly than its other international trade whereas previously it was in decline.

Onitiri, in Chapter 10 is almost diametrically opposed to this view of future policy. The future trade policy of Africa should resemble that of North America and Europe by intensively negotiating a re-gional trading bloc: the African Economic Community. As between the NAFTA and EU models Onitiri clearly favours the latter. Whereas NAFTA has no central secretariat, being simply a treaty between gov-ernments, the AEC would, like the EU, have a headquarters, a secre-tary general, and indeed all the trappings of an international organization, based around the existing Pan-African institutions, the OAU, the ECA and the ADB. The benefits of such regional co-ordination on this view include, but extend well beyond, trade policy and the integration of markets. Onitiri emphasizes the integration of production, the harmo-nization of fiscal and monetary policies, and conflict resolution proce-dures between neighbours. Thus, over a whole range of policies, action at the national level would be transferred to the Pan-African level.

To what extent are these visions genuinely alternatives? In one sense they are clearly incompatible. African governments can either reduce trade barriers unilaterally and non-preferentially or through co-ordinated reciprocal preferences. The more a government reduces its trade barri-ers non-preferentially the less it can offer preferentially. If it is in the midst of lengthy negotiations with other governments on tariff levels it is in no position to reduce tariffs unilaterally. An African Economic Community would involve a common external tariff, but unilateral trade liberalization conducted at radically different speeds by different gov-ernments according to their domestic political circumstances is likely to widen rather than narrow the current disparities between national tariff structures, making the task of harmonization on a common rate more difficult. Faster, unilateral trade liberalization is therefore likely to slow down what would already be a slow process of harmonization. However, there are some respects in which Pan Africanism and uni-lateralism could be complementary. As Baldwin and Fine and Yeo argue, regional trade preferences become less diversionary and therefore less costly as the overall level of trade protection is reduced. If in the past African regional integration attempts have failed politically because of the high cost of these diversion effects, the political obstacles to preferential integration may be reduced by the unilateral freeing of trade. Further, many of the gains from Pan-African co-ordination identified by Onitiri need not involve preferential trade policy. Fiscal and monetary harmonization, or agreements of region-wide environmental policies, do not require preferential tariffs and previous attempts to base regional economic co-ordination on trade policy, where there are usually some clear losers, may have handicapped attempts to co-ordinate in areas where potentially all participants can gain. The EU and NAFTA may indeed be viewed as instances of such gains since the margin of tariff preference which they provide to their members is very low. Just as Jebuni can argue that unilateral trade liberalization is necessary to achieve regional integration, so Onitiri might argue that African policy co-ordination in some areas is necessary for African economies to succeed in world markets beyond the narrow base of traditional exports.

Whereas Pan Africanism intrinsically involves inter-government co-ordination, trade liberalization can be unilateral. However, non-African governments have in fact achieved most of their trade liberalizations through multinational co-ordination. The latest round of these negotiations, the Uruguay Round, involved little African participation with the exception of South Africa, as discussed by Sorsa. She shows that the so-called 'burden' of commitments made by African governments was in fact very light. Have African governments been missing something by this reluctance to participate, or does the argument set out above apply with even greater force: co-ordination would merely slow down what can as readily be achieved by unilateral government action? The argument for co-ordinated as opposed to unilateral liberalization is twofold. First, a government might thereby persuade other governments to improve access to their markets in return for improved access to its own market. African access to developed country markets is far from being unrestricted and indeed has in some respects become less open over the past two decades.[7] During this period, to the extent that African governments have concerned themselves with international trade negotiations outside the continent, they have sought non-reciprocated trade concessions, the so-called 'S and D' − special and differential. Arguably, by deciding not to take the line of reciprocity, African governments have placed themselves in a weaker negotiating position.

The second argument in favour of co-ordinated liberalization is that by setting national decisions in the context of a web of reciprocal deals the national decisions thereby acquire greater commitment and so greater credibility. As discussed by Sorsa, the key negotiations in the Uruguay Round concerned not just liberalizations but 'bindings', that is undertakings by governments not to set tariffs above certain levels. Bound tariff reductions lock the government in to liberalization in a way which unilateral liberalizations do not. This is of particular importance to Africa because for liberalization to generate an investment response the private sector must be assured that it is credible in the long term and is not just a short-term response to donor pressure. Only South Africa has used the Uruguay Round to make such binding commitments at a meaningful level. Zimbabwe, which also took part in the round, bound its tariffs at a level so far above its actual tariff rates as to leave the government a large degree of freedom for the reversal of its recent liberalization. Perhaps the limited participation by African governments in the Uruguay Round was therefore a missed opportunity to lock into the previous unilateral liberalizations. Because such multinational negotiating rounds are infrequent, Africa will have to wait perhaps for a decade for the next opportunity.

Fine and Yeo, in Chapter 11, take up the theme of policy lock-in, as provided by the GATT commitments on bindings, but in the context of regional rather than global policy co-ordination. They thus return to the political agenda of African co-operation espoused by Onitiri but place emphasis upon a different type of benefit. Regional reciprocal trade agreements can help to create a web of reciprocal deals and threats, as with the GATT rounds, which increase the penalties of policy reversal and so reduce its likelihood. However, Fine and Yeo argue that to date reciprocity confined only to African governments has not provided a sufficient cost of default to deter non-compliance. They propose that the regional agreements should be extended to include developed country participants of which the most obvious, though not the only, candidate would be the European Union. The NAFTA model, which Onitiri sees as a *continental* trade bloc, and therefore corresponding to an African Economic Community, Fine and Yeo see as a *North–South* trade bloc, and therefore corresponding to an Africa–EU relationship. They see the advantages of such a bloc as threefold. First, it would improve access to Northern markets for African non-traditional exports in a way that has not satisfactorily been achieved by 'S and D'. Second, the penalties consequent upon an African government reversing its trade liberalization would be sufficiently severe that there would be credible policy lock-in: African investors could commit themselves instead of remaining liquid. Third, the increased penalties of reversal would secure *intra-regional* liberalization where in the past it has failed. This third argument bears some similarity to the Jebuni proposition that African regional integration can be achieved by unilateral non-preferential trade liberalization. In both cases the objective of African integration is achieved not by head-on intra-African trade negotiations but as the by-product of some other process. The difference between the Fine and Yeo approach and that of Onitiri is exemplified in their conflicting attitudes to the recently formed West African Economic and Monetary Union (UEMOA). Fine and Yeo see it as a model for other African regional agreements, with the role of France in UEMOA being replaced by a larger entity such as the EU. Onitiri sees the formation of UEMOA as a potentially confusing element in the negotiations needed to forge a Pan-African economic community, both because it creates yet another sub-continental institution and because of the involvement of a non-African participant. The menu of options for future trade policy thus includes both unilateralism and co-ordination. Co-ordination can take the radically different forms of participation in the World Trade Organization or the creation of a continental preferential trading bloc. In between, is the proposal of Fine and Yeo that coordination should be both regional and extra-regional, building for Africa a North–South bloc in the spirit of NAFTA.

Notes

1. Nevertheless this view has considerably influenced regional integration initiatives in and outside Africa. O'Connell notes that, 'Regional trade promotion was an important objective in most stages of European monetary integration in the postwar period, and the notion of accelerated development through increased regional trade appears central to the UN Economic Commission for Africa's (ECA) vision for its African sub-regions and ultimately for Africa as a whole'.
2. O'Connell characterized multilateral and bilateral-based macroeconomic conditionality as one of 'restraint without cooperation'. He observes that traditional macroeconomic conditionality is not designed to obtain macroeconomic restraint over anything but the short term. However, he suggests that, 'this situation has clear advantages over the opposite extreme of "cooperation without restraint" epitomized by the regional clearing mechanisms that cover most of Africa and the (less prevalent) bilateral countertrade agreements between regional partners'.
3. This view is corroborated by Ndulu and Semboja (1994), who estimated the contribution of macroeconomic reform and import liberalization to

manufacturing export growth in Tanzania by estimating a two equation model consisting of a first equation on the determinants of manufacturing exports which includes the real exchange rate among others, and a second equation specifying the real exchange rate as a function of long-term fundamentals (which include the trade regime) as well as the short-run macroeconomic influences (such as the rate of growth of money supply). The result of their decomposition analysis show that, over several episodes during the last two decades (1970–9, 1980–5, and 1986–90) the effects of macroeconomic policy in Tanzania on manufacturing export growth has been at least ten times the effect due to import liberalization.

4. In terms of membership, the mergers in francophone West Africa are not that consequential: CEAO and UMOA are almost identical in terms of member countries, since the former includes in addition to Mauritania all the members of the latter except Togo (Togo and Guinea are observers in CEAO); and UDEAC is identical to BEAC.

5. According to this view, no more than four such regional groupings should exist in Africa: North, West, Central, and East and South. Thus the PTA, like its counterpart in the Western Africa, ECOWAS, received the active support of the ECA (for example, Foroutan, 1993).

6. This may be an overestimate since some of it may represent an 'officialization' of previously illegal trade, in response to trade and exchange rate liberalization.

7. For a recent account of the deterioration in developing countries' access to developed country markets see Page (1994).

References

Ariyo, A. and M.I. Raheem (1991) 'Enhancing Trade Flows within the ECOWAS sub-Region: An Appraisal and some Recommendations', ch. 23 in A. Chhibber and S. Fischer (eds), *Economic Reform in Sub-Saharan Africa* (Washington DC: World Bank).

Baldwin, R. (1979) 'Determinants of Trade and Foreign Investment: Further Evidence', *Review of Economics and Statistics*, 61: 259–66.

Chua, H. (1993) 'Regional Spillovers and Economic Growth', Centre Discussion Paper no. 700, Economic Growth Center, Yale University.

Collier, P. (1979) 'The Welfare Effects of Customs Unions: An Anatomy', *Economic Journal*, 89: 84–95.

—— (1991) 'Africa's External Economic relations: 1960–90', *African Affairs*, 90 (360): 339–56.

—— and J. Gunning (1993) 'Linkages Between Trade Policy and Regional Integration', paper presented at an AERC conference on *Trade Liberalization and Regional Integration in SSA*, Nairobi, Dec.

Commission of the European Communities (1995) 'European Community Support for Regional Economic Integration Effects Among Developing Countries', Communication from the Commission, COM (95) 219, 16 June 1995 (Brussels).

Corbo, V. and R. Rujas (1991), 'Country Performance and Effectiveness of

World Bank – supported Adjustment Programs', Policy Research Working Paper no. 623, World Bank (Mar.).

De Rosa, D.A. (1992) 'Protection and Export Performance in Sub-Saharan Africa', *Weltwirtschaftliches Archiv*, 128 (1): 88–124.

Easterly, W. and R. Levine (1994) 'Africa's Growth Tragedy', an invited paper presented at the bi-annual Research Workshop of the African Economic Research Consortium, Nairobi, 29 May.

Elbadawi I. (1992) 'World Bank Adjustment Lending and Economic Performance in Sub-Saharan Africa in the 1980s: A Comparison of Early Adjustors, Late Adjusters, and Non-Adjusters', Policy Research Working Paper no. 1001 (The World Bank).

Foroutan, F. (1993) 'Regional Integration in Sub-Saharan Africa: Past Experience and Future Prospects', in J. de Melo and A. Panagariya (eds), *New Dimensions in Regional Integration* (Cambridge University Press).

—— and L. Pritchett (1993) 'Intra Sub-Saharan Trade: Is it Little?', *Journal of African Economies*, 2 (1): 74–105.

Jebuni, C.D., A. Oduro, Y. Asante and G.K. Tsikata (1992) *Diversifying Exports: A supply Response of Non-Traditional Exports to Ghana's Economic Recovery Programme* (London: Overseas Development Institute).

Kennes, W. (1994) 'The European Union and Support for Regional Economic Integration in Africa' mimeo (Brussels: European Commission).

Krueger, A.O. (1977) 'Growth Distortions and Patterns of Trade among Many Countries', *Princeton Studies in International Finance*, 40.

Krugman P.R. (1991a) *Geography and Trade* (Leuven: Leuven University Press and Cambridge, Mass.: MIT Press).

—— (1991b) 'History and Industry Location. The Case of the U.S. Manufacturing Belt', *American Economic Review*.

—— (1991c), 'Increasing Returns and Economic Geography', *Journal of Political Economy*.

Langhammer, R. and U. Hiemenz (1991) 'Regional Integration Among Developing Countries: Survey of Past Performance and Agenda for future Policy Action', Occasional paper no. 7 (Washington DC: UNDP–World Bank Trade Expansion program, World Bank).

Lipumba, H.H.I and L. Kasekende (1991) 'The Record and Prospects of the Preferential Trade Area for Eastern and Southern African States', ch. 22 in A. Chhibber and S. Fischer, *Economic Reform in Sub-Saharan Africa* (Washington DC: World Bank).

Mansoor, A. and A. Inotai (1991) 'Integration Efforts in Sub-Saharan Africa: Failures, Results and Prospects – a Suggested Strategy for Achieving Efficient Integration', ch. 21 of A. Chhibber and S. Fischer (eds), *Economic Reform in Sub-Saharan Africa* (Washington DC: World Bank).

Ndulu, B. and J. Semboja (1994) 'The Development of Manufacturing for Exports in Tanzania: Experience, Policy and Prospects', forthcoming in G. Helleiner (ed.), *The Transition to Manufacturing for Export in the Developing World: Problems and Possibilities* (Helsinki: WIDER).

Oyejide, A.T. (1986) *The Effects of Trade and Exchange Policies on Agriculture in Nigeria*, Research Report no. 555 (Washington DC: IFPRI).

Papageorgiou, D., M. Michaely and A. Choksi (1991) *Liberalising Foreign Trade*, 7 vols (Oxford: Basil Blackwell).

Page, S. (1994) *How Developing Countries Trade* (London: Routledge).

Rodrik, D. (1992) 'Closing the Productivity Gap; Does Trade Liberalization Really Help', in G. Helleiner (ed.), *Trade Policy Industrialisation and Development, New Perspectives* (Oxford: Clarendon Press).

2 Review of Theoretical Developments on Regional Integration*

Richard E. Baldwin

2.1 INTRODUCTION

Regional integration is once again a topical issue, due mostly to policy changes in Europe and North America. With the 1992 Single Market programme nearly completed and the Maastricht Treaty ratified, European integration is expanding its breadth through enlargement to the North and the East. After a difficult start, the United States is now the centre of its own regional integration effort. The drive to formal market integration in a third natural bloc, East Asia, has been weak to date and holds little promise for the near future. Nonetheless, intra-Asian trade and investment flows are growing by leaps and bounds, so one may speak of a *de facto* trading bloc even if no *de jure* bloc is on the horizon.

The importance of this trend for Africa and for the world cannot be understated. Europe and North America each account for about a third of global economic activity. Closer trade and monetary integration within these two regions alone will alter international economic relations throughout the world. Already we see the global trading system sliding away from multilateralism. If the rules-based multilateral trading system is eroded by regionalism, it will be the world's small economies that suffer the most. To use a perhaps unfortunate analogy, the fact that the USA and the USSR had nuclear arms kept the peace between the large blocs. It did not, however, keep the USA from invading small countries like Panama and Grenada, nor did it keep the Soviets from invading Afghanistan.

In the same way, the dire economic consequences of a trade war between major blocs is likely to deter such an outcome. Without strong,

* I wish to thank Ademola Oyejide, Andre Sapir, Sophie Huang, Rikard Forslid and Peter Johns for comments and suggestions.

well-respected multilateral trade rules, domestic protectionist pressures in the large trade blocs may lead to harmful trade policies toward smaller economies. This possibility should be of particular concern to African economists, since in 1991 $60.8 bn of Africa's $82.6 bn of exports went to either the EU ($45.8 bn) or the US ($15 bn). Moreover, these aggregate numbers hide the fact that the EU market is even more important for certain African countries.

In addition to these global trends, Africa has special reasons for being interested in regional integration. To quote Foroutan (1993):

> The appeal of some form of regional integration in subSaharan Africa (SSA) is almost intuitive. The SSA countries are very small in economic terms. In 1989, the GNP of all SSA countries put together was approximately equal to that of Belgium ... Imagine subdividing Belgium into forty something independent countries, each with its own isolated goods and factor markets, a different public administration, currency, language, fiscal and monetary authorities, army, plus a very inefficient intercountry transport network. Economists would contend that the welfare of individuals would surely be reduced.

Despite the force of this sort of argument, virtually all regional integration efforts have failed in SSA. Foroutan puts the blame for this lack of success on the structural characteristics of the SSA countries and their import-substitution policies. He suggests, however, that regional trade integration pursued in tandem with general economic liberalization, trade liberalization in particular, could provide an enabling environment for SSA producers that begins to compete in world markets.

As an additional point, I would suggest that the successive multilateral trade talks and various bilateral agreements between individual SSA nations and the EU or the USA have created a 'hub-and-spoke' arrangement. That is, since barriers to intra-SSA exports remain very high, but barriers to SSA–EU and SSA–US exports are low, a schematic diagram of SSA trade arrangements would resemble an old-fashioned wagon wheel. Trade among the 'hub' countries (the North) and between the hub and the SSA countries (at least for exports from the SSA) is quite free, but trade among SSA nations (the 'spokes') is not.

The purpose of this chapter is simple: to review and critique both old and new theory on regional integration. Readers will soon realize (and I freely admit) that my comparative advantage lies in the review and critique part. I am not a specialist on Africa and as such my ability to assess the relevance of the theory is limited. For this same reason,

I draw heavily on the European experience for examples. I hope that this chapter provokes economists who know much more about Africa than I to assess what parts of the theory are most relevant to SSA.

This chapter has five sections after the introduction. Section 2.2 presents a general framework that is useful for organizing the various effects of regional integration. It shows that the effects of regional integration can be divided into allocation effects and accumulation effects. These correspond to the more traditional classifications of static and dynamic. However, since there has been a great deal of confusion over what is meant by dynamic (some authors consider a change in scale economies to be a dynamic effect), we introduce a new labelling system to keep a clean separation of effects. Section 2.3 looks at the impact of integration (and liberalization in general) on the efficiency with which resources are allocated in an economy. This contains the standard, well-known analyses such as the classical trade-creation and trade-diversion diagram. It also covers some of the newer insights that were developed in various studies of the impact of closer European integration.

Section 2.4 looks at the effects of integration on the location of economic activity. These location effects appear to be spatial allocation effects from the perspective of the whole region, however, they appear mainly as accumulation effects from the point of view of the individual nation or locale. Thus, to avoid confusion, locational effects are given their own heading. This section deals with the emerging literature on economic geography. As market integration dissolves economic barriers between nations, national boundaries no longer provide the most natural units of analysis; economic geography focuses instead on economic concentrations. Using tools developed to study the trade effects of imperfect competition and scale economies, the 'new' location theory has focused mainly on the location effects of trade liberalization. This approach promises to advance our understanding of how market integration affects migration of labour and capital, uneven regional development and industrial concentrations.

Section 2.5 considers accumulation or growth effects. This section covers the traditional neoclassical growth models as well as the new endogenous growth models in which long-run growth rates are determined endogenously. The theory focuses on the theoretical and empirical link between market integration, growth and convergence. The section also includes some discussion concerning the empirical measurement of such effects.

2.2 AN ORGANIZING FRAMEWORK

One of the most important tasks of a literature review is to structure the literature. As it turns out, it is fairly easy to provide a formal organizing framework for regional integration literature. The framework considered here is far from completely general, however, and as shown in the appendix it can be extended to include many other issues.

An integration effort that removes barriers on trade with regional partners will, in general, change the prices faced by domestic firms and consumers, change world prices (for large countries), and change the volume of imports and exports to and from the partner countries and the rest of the world. Moreover, the liberalization may change the amount of rents earned by domestic imperfectly competitive firms, change the exploitation of scale economies by domestic firms, change the variety of goods available and, finally, lead to various growth effects. To summarize these eight effects, we can write:

Welfare change = (terms of trade) | (volume of trade) + (trade rents)
+ (pure profit) + (scale) + (variety)
+ (capital formation) − (forgone consumption)
+ (technological spillovers)   (2.1)

This framework is derived more formally in the appendix to this chapter, pp. 83–6.

The first two rows of effects may be called allocation effects since these concern the reallocation of resources. In the first row are the effects that can occur when one assumes perfect competition and constant returns to scale. The second row involves effects that are possible under imperfect competition and increasing returns to scale. The last two rows are growth effects, or accumulation effects. That is, a liberalization may induce capital formation (or capital destruction), be it human capital, physical capital or knowledge capital. In all cases, the welfare gains are substantially offset since consumption must be forgone in order to build up the extra capital (or increased if capital is destroyed). If the capital is financed by borrowing, then the reduced consumption is delayed until the debt is repaid. The final effect concerns technological spillovers. It is often asserted that human, physical and/or knowledge capital formation leads to spillovers. That is, the social rate of return to such investment exceeds the private return. The possibility of this type of wedge between the private and social rate of return to capital is captured by the term in the last row.

This formula is far from completely general. Interested readers can easily extend the approach to include virtually any effect. Any factor, such as adjustment costs, that drives a wedge between income and expenditure would enter in the same way as dI. Any factor that affects the stock of wealth – environmental damage or changes in the value of vintage capital, for example – could be included by using a slightly different form of the indirect utility function (full intertemporal indirect utility functions include current wealth) and/or putting environment variables, such as emissions, in the cost functions. Changing these would create additional terms. Considerations of income distribution could be incorporated by using an indirect social welfare function that included a Gini coefficient instead of using the indirect utility function for a representative consumer. One could also include an X-inefficiency term in the cost functions. All sorts of price wedges, such as a wedge between factor rewards and marginal products, could be introduced in the same way as the wedge in traded goods prices was introduced.

2.3 ALLOCATION EFFICIENCY EFFECTS

Every economy must allocate its resources to the production of goods and then must allocate the produced goods among its citizens. In a market economy, these allocations are the outcome of innumerable decisions made primarily by private citizens acting in their own best interest. However, an allocation based on selfishness cannot possibly be good for a society, unless it is restrained and co-ordinated by some mechanism. Competition among firms facing market-determined prices is the dominant restraining and co-ordinating force in a market economy. Competition among private producers ensures that market prices broadly reflect the cost of the resources used in making, distributing and marketing goods. When consumers or firms decide to buy a particular good, they are implicitly 'voting' on the allocation of productive resources. Their demand directs resources to the production of that good. In this sense, market-determined prices are extremely important signals between consumers and producers.

Barriers that hinder competition among firms and/or constrict consumers' ability to choose among goods distort these market signals. Consequently they tend to worsen the allocation efficiency of an economy. When competition is restrained, by government policies or collusion, self-interested firms naturally take advantage of this by raising prices above costs. This reduces the efficiency of the economy with the result that prices do not reflect the true costs of production, which typically leads to an inefficient allocation of resources. Government policy that interferes with market pricing similarly reduces efficiency, since such interference garbles the price-based communication among producers and between producers and consumers. Thus even if competition checks the behaviour of self-interested firms, garbled prices get translated into a garbled and inefficient allocation of the nation's resources.

Government-imposed barriers to international transactions are extremely commonplace. These barriers hinder international competition among firms and distort the market determination of prices. As such, they typically reduce the efficiency with which the market allocates resources. This section explores in more detail several channels through which barriers reduce the efficiency of resource allocation in a market economy.

Allocation Effects in Competitive Industries

We start with the most basic analysis. Although this analysis is well-known, we review it to fix ideas and introduce notation. In particular, we wish to introduce a distinction between trade barriers that create rents (tariffs, quotas, and so on) and barriers that simply raise the real cost of trade (excessive red-tape delays, and so on).

Standard Analysis of Unilateral Trade Barrier Reduction for a Small Country

Barriers that raise the cost of importing foreign goods artificially distort the relative prices of domestic and foreign goods. This harms economic efficiency. The classic analysis of these effects, assuming that changes in protection have no impact on world prices, is shown in Figure 2.1. In terms of the organizing framework in eq. (2.1), we are considering only the volume of trade effect and the trade rents effect.

To be concrete, consider a country's market for electric stoves. To keep things simple, suppose that the domestic economy is small enough so that its demand for stoves will not affect the world price (i.e., the import supply curve is flat at the world price of P^2) and domestic and imported stoves are perfect substitutes. Import barriers of all types raise the local consumer price of imported goods above the international price. The figure shows the case where a trade barrier has increased the local price of imports from the world price P^2 to P^1. We consider the impact of removing this barrier.

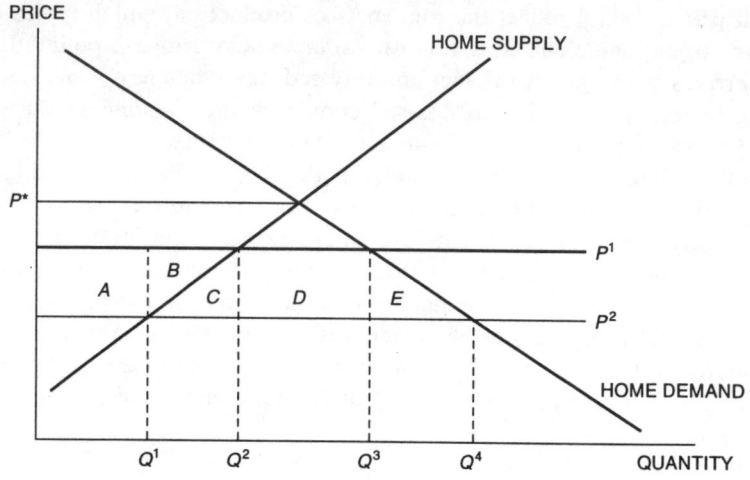

Figure 2.1 The well known tariff analysis diagram

There are four positive effects of this price fall:

- The price of domestically produced stoves also falls to P^1 since domestic stoves cannot compete with imports at a higher price and there is no reason to sell them for less.
- The domestic price fall reduces domestic production from Q^2 to Q^1.
- The lower price of imports and domestic stoves increases consumption from Q^3 to Q^4.
- The combination of lower domestic output and higher domestic consumption increases imports from Q^3-Q^2 to Q^4-Q^1 since imports identically equal consumption minus production.

Welfare analysis The well-known analysis in Figure 2.1 is valid for any trade barrier that introduces a wedge between international and local prices. However, when we turn to the welfare analysis, a sharp distinction must be made between trade barriers where the trade rents (i.e., the rent created by buying imports at the world price and reselling them at the higher domestic price) are captured domestically and those where they are captured by foreigners. Of course, for many real-world policies trade rents may be shared between foreigners and domestic residents. Additionally, we must realize that some trade barriers create no rents at all. They create a wedge between domestic and world prices by raising the real cost of importing goods. For example, barriers such

as excessive red-tape restrictions and bogus industrial standards introduce a gap between world and local prices, but this gap is not pocketed by anyone. Rather, it represents the cost of real resources that
must be devoted to overcoming the barriers. We call these cost-creating barriers as opposed to rent-creating barriers.

Rent-creating barriers   The classic example of a rent-creating barrier
is a tariff. In this case, all trade rent is captured domestically, so there
is no trade rent effect. That is to say, in terms of eq. (2.1), there is
only one net effect of liberalization, namely the volume of trade effect.
This net effect is composed of three gross welfare effects:

(1) The government loses revenue equal to imports times the tariff,
    that is, area D.
(2) Consumers gain since they pay less for stoves. The gain consists
    of two parts: (a) the price reduction, P^1-P^2, times all the stoves
    they bought at the old price, that is, areas $A + B + C + D$; and
    (b) area E, which equals what consumers would pay to have the
    right to buy the extra stoves $Q^4 - Q^3$ at the world price.
(3) Domestic producers lose from the lower price. The loss consists
    of two parts: the price fall times the number of stoves they sold at
    the old price (area A), + area B, which is the profit they used to
    make selling the extra stoves $Q^2 - Q^1$ at the old price.

The loss to the government and firms are less than the gain to consumers. Adding up the gains and losses to all domestic residents, the
country as a whole gains by the area $C + E$. This is the pure gain due
to allocation inefficiencies induced by the tariff. These are called Harberger
triangles or the volume of trade effect. Area C represents the gain due
to the initial inefficient allocation of domestic resources. The country
was using resources that are worth P^1 to make stoves when it could
have bought the stoves at a cost of P^2 on the world market. Area E
represents the initial allocation inefficiency on the consumers' part.
The tariff distorts prices so consumers do not face the true cost of
stoves. Consequently, they allocated their expenditures inefficiently,
buying too few stoves as opposed to other goods.

Quantitative restrictions, such as import quotas and voluntary export
restraints, constitute another major type of rent-creating barrier. Removing a quota that reduced imports to $Q^3 - Q^2$ would have the effect
of lowering the price of imports to P^1 and would therefore have the
same positive effects as the tariff studied above. Indeed, if the quota is

enforced by an import licensing scheme, and the government sells the licences at a price that just equals the gap between local and international prices, the welfare effects will be identical. In fact, if the government gives away the licences to domestic citizens or firms, the net welfare will still be the same. The difference would be that the rent (area D) would be pocketed by a private citizen or firm instead of by the treasury.

In some cases, however, it is a foreign firm or foreign government that holds the rights to the trade rents. Indeed, throughout the industrialized world it is extremely common for trade barriers to be arranged so that the wedge is earned by foreigners. One reason for this is that the rent is used as a carrot to soothe the anger of foreign companies and governments with having a trade barrier imposed. Examples of this are voluntary export restraints (VERs), price-raising arrangements made to avoid dumping duties and international cartelization of markets such as textiles and clothing (the Multi-Fiber Agreement) and steel. In all these cases the net gain to the country of liberalization is even greater, since less of the gain to domestic consumers is offset by losses to other domestic interests. Specifically, the total static gain from liberalization is $C + D + E$. Thus the area D is a measure of the trade rents effect mentioned in equation (2.1).

It is important to note that the primary effect of the tariff is to redistribute money from consumers to domestic firms and the treasury. Indeed, it is easy to show that a 10 per cent tariff is exactly like a 10 per cent sales tax plus a 10 per cent subsidy to domestic producers. In this sense, tariffs are an inefficient means of taxing citizens and subsidizing domestic production.

Cost-creating barriers Some trade in Africa is subject to a host of seemingly minor policies that increase the real cost of importing and exporting goods, especially manufactured goods. When trade barriers entail higher real trade costs, the area D is not gained by anybody. Trade just becomes more difficult, so resources that were previously devoted to making useful goods and services must be diverted to overcoming such barriers. Typical examples of such policies are complicated and slow customs procedures and unnecessary delays in the verification of industrial and health standards, as well as the imposition of spurious health, environment or industrial requirements. Similarly, some countries make it difficult and expensive for importers to obtain licenses or foreign exchange for importing. The net cost to the nation of imposing this sort of barrier is again $C + D + E$.

One of the most important types of such barrier involves industrial and health standards that are chosen at least in part to restrict imports. For example, some countries refuse to accept safety tests performed in foreign countries, even in highly industrialized nations. This forces importers to retest their products in the local country. In addition to raising the real cost of imported goods, this sort of barrier delays the introduction of new products. While this clearly harms consumers, domestic producers may benefit since it may give them time to introduce competing varieties.

A related set of cost-raising barriers consists of unusual industrial, health and environmental standards. These are standards that differ from internationally recognized norms. The net effect is to protect domestic producers or service providers. Domestic firms design their products with these standards in mind while foreign firms, for whom the domestic market may be relatively unimportant, are unlikely to. Bringing imported products into conformity raises the real cost of imports.

One reason this sort of barrier is so common is that the government agencies charged with formulating and enforcing standards are often 'captured' by special interest groups representing the industries they are supposed to regulate. That is, domestic firms and service providers who gain from having standards that reduce import competition often play an important role in setting the standards. For example, even if the government formally decides on standards, a domestic industry association often suggests or approves the standards.

Of course, nations do need health, environmental and industrial standards. One solution to the problem of setting standards without unduly restricting international trade and competition is to participate in international groups that establish standard regulations. Another, which the EU Single Market Programme adopted for many issues, is that of mutual recognition. Under this principle, products that have been approved under the rules of any EU country will be accepted as approved in all EU markets.

Standard Effects of Import Barriers on Exporters

So far we have focused on the domestic impact of domestic trade barriers. The opposite side of the equation – the impact of trade barriers on the exporter's country – is our next subject. As before, we make simplifying assumptions to highlight the economic logic. Specifically, we assume that there are only two countries, labelled country 1 and country 2. Figure 2.2, which shows the markets in countries 1 and 2

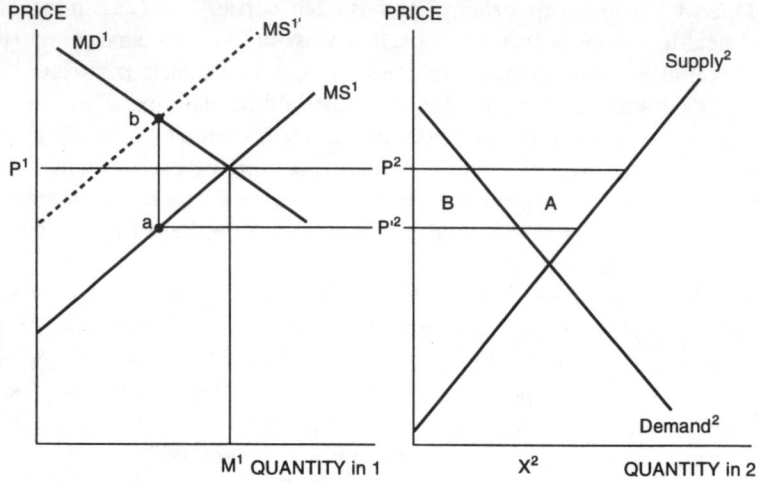

Figure 2.2 Impact of protection on exporting country

for electric stoves, assumes that 1-made and 2-made stoves are indistinguishable to consumers. The right diagram shows country 2's supply and demand curves. For prices above the intersection of its supply and demand, country 2 has an excess supply of stoves that it will export. In the left diagram the MD curve shows country 1's import demand (this is simply country 1's total demand curve minus its supply curve), and MS shows the import supply curve. Supposing that initially there is free trade in stoves between the two countries, MS is also country 2's export supply curve. The free trade equilibrium prices and quantities are shown as P^1, M^1, P^2 and X^2. Notice that P^1 equals P^2 due to free trade.

Next consider the impact on country 2 of a rent-creating import barrier imposed by country 1. To be specific, suppose country 1's government imposes an import tariff equal to the distance between points 'a' and 'b' in the diagram. The import tax can be represented as a shift back in the MS curve, since each level of local price in country 1 corresponds to a lower level of imports. The net effect is a wedge between the price of stoves in countries 1 and 2. This drives down the price received by country 2's exporters. As a consequence, its producers and consumers face a lower price for stoves. The positive effects of these price changes are straightforward. Consumption and imports in country 1 fall and domestic production rises. Production and exports in country 2 fall, while consumption rises. Using the analysis above it is easy to see that producers based in country 2 lose more than its consumers and government gain: namely, the lower prices harm its producers by the area $A + B$. Country 2's consumers gain from lower prices by the area B. Country 2's net loss is therefore equal to A.

It is easy to use this diagram to analyse the impact of a wide variety of import restricting policies on the welfare of exporting countries.

Standard Analysis of Geographically Discriminatory Barriers

When a country maintains geographically discriminatory trade barriers – for instance when Kenya maintains higher barriers against imports from Nigeria than it does against imports from France – the analysis gets slightly more complicated. The reason is that change in the discriminatory barrier may lead domestic importers to switch suppliers. Since different suppliers may charge different prices, this supply-shifting can end up changing the price the country pays for its imports. In terms of equation (2.1), this ends up looking like a change in the world price.

Take the case of a discriminatory tariff. A domestic importer wishing to buy a good from abroad usually searches for the lowest priced good that meets her needs. Broadly speaking, this search is in the national interest since it reduces the cost to the nation of acquiring the good. If the home government imposes different tariff rates on the imports from different countries, the prices that guide the importer's search will be warped. Consequently, the importer will not necessarily buy from the lowest cost producer; she will buy from the country whose price plus the relevant tariff is lowest. The tariff distorts the price signals, so the private importer's choice may be misguided from the social point of view. Another way to say this is that importers face a price that equals the true cost to the nation plus the tariff. Since the tariff gets paid to the home government, it is not a true cost to the nation. Thus lower tariffs against only certain countries' goods may actually lead importers to switch from low-cost foreign suppliers to high-cost foreign suppliers. From the national standpoint, this 'trade diversion' constitutes a loss. This loss mitigates and may reverse the usual gains from liberalization.

Figure 2.3 shows the analysis for any barrier that raises the price of imports in a geographically discriminatory manner. The figure considers the case of two potential sources of imports, country A and country B. To set the stage, suppose that initially the home country imposes a trade barrier that raises the local price of all imports above the inter-national price by 'T' dollars as shown in the figure. As before, we suppose the country is small enough to face a flat import supply curve from all countries. Clearly it would cost home consumers $P^A + T$ to import from country A and $P^B + T$ to import from B, so all imports would come from B. Competition from imports fixes the price of local goods at $P^A + T$, and imports at $Q^3 - Q^2$.

Next suppose the home country signs a free trade agreement with B but not with A. This discriminatory liberalization artificially changes the relative competitiveness of goods from countries A and B. Indeed, now goods from B cost P^B while goods from A cost $P^A + T$. Quite naturally, home consumers will divert all of their import demand from A to B. There are four positive effects:

- The preferential liberalization increases competition from imports and thereby forces down the price of locally made goods to P^B.
- Some high-cost home production is replaced by lower cost imports. This amount is equal to $Q^2 - Q^1$.
- Imports from country B are entirely replaced by imports from country A.
- Consumption rises to Q^4.

Welfare analysis Again, welfare analysis requires us to distinguish between rent-creating and cost-creating barriers. The simplest rent-creating policy is that of a government tariff. In this case, the government loses all tariff revenue due to the switch of import sources. This loss equals $D + F$. The lower price benefits home consumers by an amount equal to $A + B + C + D + E$, and domestic producers are harmed by $A + B$. The net impact on the home country's welfare equals the two trian-gles $C + E$ − the rectangle F. This amount may be positive or negative.

Traditional analysis classifies the welfare effects of a discriminatory tariff into 'trade creation' and 'trade diversion'. The cost of trade di-version, area F, stems from the fact that after the discriminatory liber-alization, the country buys from a higher-cost international supplier. The trade creation gains, areas $C + E$, are exactly equal to the gains we saw from the tariff cut above. The source of the gain is also ex-actly the same, consisting of a reduced producer distortion (area C) and a reduced consumer distortion (area E).

The fact that a country can lose from a discriminatory tariff liberali-zation has spawned a vast theoretical literature. This has identified many rules of thumb about when discriminatory liberalization is likely to increase national welfare. Perhaps the most enduring and most intui-tive of these concerns the fraction of total imports that come from

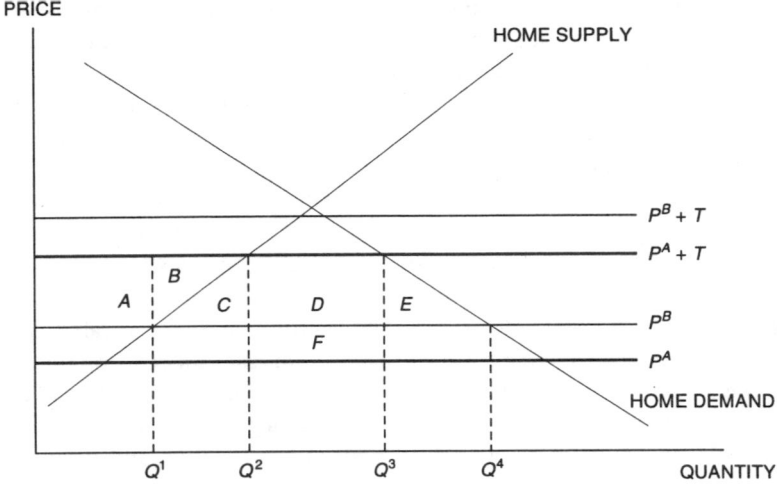

Figure 2.3 Trade creation and trade diversion

other members of the preferential trading area. It is easy to understand this using Figure 2.3. In this case, the home country initially imports none of the good from the country with which it signs the free trade agreement. Consequently, the discriminatory tariff cut could, and in this case did, lead home consumers to switch from a low-cost supplier to a high-cost supplier. This opened the door to a possible welfare loss from the bilateral free trade agreement. For comparison, suppose instead that the free trade deal were signed with country A. Since A was already the low-cost supplier, there is no possibility that tariff discrimination would force home consumers to switch to higher-cost suppliers. Consequently, the liberalization would unambiguously make the home country better off.

Actual trade between countries is made up of thousands of products, so to be complete one would have to go through thousands of diagrams like Figure 2.3 to check whether the home country would gain or lose from a preferential trade arrangement. An obvious shortcut, however, is simply to look at how much trade the home country does with its intended partners. If it already imports a great deal from its partners, then it is likely that the partners were the low-costs suppliers even before liberalization. Consequently, discriminatory tariff cuts on imports from these countries are likely to lead to little switching from low-cost to high-cost producers. Plainly this rule of thumb is not infallible.

We have assumed that the gap was caused by a home government tariff. However, many import barriers raise the local price above foreign prices, but do not generate revenue for the home government. For instance, many governments strike deals with foreign firms limiting the amount of goods that they will sell in the home market, or forcing foreign firms to raise their prices to avoid antidumping duties. In such cases, it is the foreigners who earn the profit equal to the area $D + F$ prior to liberalization. Thus when a discriminatory tariff reduction destroys these profits, there is no loss to the home country to offset the gains of lower prices. The gain from liberalization is $C + D + E$.

Removing cost-raising barriers The welfare analysis is also quite different when considering trade barriers that impose real costs on imports. If the price wedge T was due to, say, excessive bureaucratic delays, then eliminating the barrier in a discriminatory manner (namely, only against imports from B) would have all of the positive and normative effects mentioned above except the one dealing with government revenue. Consequently, the liberalizing nation gains as a whole, even though trade is diverted. The size of the gain is $C + D + E$.

These last two results are quite important since, as we mentioned above, many trade barriers are either of the cost-raising type or the rent-creating type in which foreigners get the rents. It would seem that trade within Africa has been hobbled by a very long list of cost-raising barriers. For instance the transportation system for intra-African trade is less developed than the one for extra-regional trade. The same is true of telecommunications and postal services. The implication is that removing cost-raising barriers on a regional – as opposed to multilateral – basis cannot lead to a worsening of welfare due to trade diversion.

The Cost of Rules of Origin

Any preferential trade agreement requires 'rules of origin' that specify how customs officials determine where particular products are from in order to know which trade barriers to apply. The absence of such rules would create an incentive to reroute trade artificially in order to avoid trade barriers. For instance, consider a free trade area between a country that imposes a high tariff on Taiwanese radios and one that imposes a low tariff on Taiwanese radios. An importer based in the high tariff country might attempt to avoid the high duty by importing the radio into the low tariff country and then re-exporting it into her own country duty free. Rules of origin are needed to prevent this 'trade deflection'. Rules of origin can be very complicated. For instance the main body of the Interim Agreement between Poland and the EU fills thirteen pages; Protocol 4, which describes how to determine whether a product originates in Poland or the EC, is over sixty pages long with all of its annexes. The rules of origin become more complicated as countries' trade arrangements become more complicated (see Figure 2.4).

Rules of origin can significantly affect the allocation efficiency effects of a preferential trade agreement, although the economic impact varies greatly depending upon the exact wording of the rules. None the less, it is clear that these rules, together with the preferential access embodied in a preferential trade agreement, tend to protect producers

---

One of the most common forms of rules of origin is based on the concept of 'change in tariff heading.' According to this concept, an article completed in one country from materials originating in another is said to originate in the second country if the processing was sufficient to change the tariff classification of the article. Another popular concept, which is often combined with change of tariff heading, involves minimum value added. That is, for a product to be considered as originating from country A, a certain percentage of its final value (often at least 40 per cent) must have been added in country A,

Before the European Economic Area agreement, trade between EFTA States and EC States was governed by individual bilateral free trade agreements; one between each EFTA and the EC. Additionally EFTA was a free trade area itself, so trade in manufactured products was duty-free among EFTAs. Since each EFTAn maintained different tariffs against third countries, a complicated set of origin rules was imposed to prevent tariff circumvention. Consider, for example, an Austrian-based firm that wished to get duty-free treatment for its exports to the EC. To do so, the firm would have to prove that its product originates in Austria. According to the rules, its product originated in Austria only if it fulfils one of the following criteria.

(1) It is wholly produced in Austria.
(2) It is produced with materials from third countries, provided that:

- *all* materials, parts and components imported from countries not member of EFTA or the EC are classified under 4-digit Customs Co-operation Council Nomenclature (CCCN) headings that are different from that of the final product; and
- for certain finished products, additional limitations restrict the value of inputs from non-EFTA, non-EC sources.

To fulfil these conditions, the exporter must maintain up-to-date and accurate records of:

- the tariff classification of all materials imported from non-EFTA, non-EC countries and the tariff classification of all its finished products;
- the tariff classification and origin of all products imported from subcontractors in other EFTA or EC countries; and
- the value of materials imported from non-EFTA, non-EC nations that are of the same tariff classification as the finished product.

This information is based on Herin (1986).

Figure 2.4 An example of rules of origin

of intermediate materials and components. They may also unintentionally harm the interests of third countries. For instance, consider a manufacturer of products that fall under the Harmonized System heading number 8208 (knives and cutting blades for mechanical appliances). Suppose that prior to Poland's free trade agreement with the EC, the manufacturer imported some components from, say, Lithuania. Under the free trade agreement, the Polish manufacturer's product is granted preferential access to the EC only if at least 40 per cent of its value is added in either Poland or the EC. This restriction may induce the Polish firm to switch from the Lithuanian supplier to a higher-cost EC-based supplier in order to meet the 40 per cent value-added rule.

A common provision aimed at reducing this artificial switching of suppliers induced by rules of origin is called 'cumulation'. Continuing to use our Polish example, a cumulative system would require that at least 40 per cent of the value of the final product be added in Poland, or any other country (such as the Czech Republic and Hungary) with which the EC had a similar preferential trade agreement.

Rules of origin can impose a heavy administrative cost on exporters and importers and lead to an artificial distortion of the trade pattern. Herin (1986) documents the cost of the rules of origin for intra-EFTA and EFTA-EC trade. He found that these rules were so complex that many EFTA-based and EC-based exporters preferred to pay the higher, non-preferential tariff rather than incur the administrative costs necessary to qualify for zero-tariff treatment under the EC–EFTA free trade agreements. Specifically, in 1984 a fifth of the EC's exports to EFTA and a fourth of EFTA exports to the EC were subject to the non-preferential tariff.

Inside a customs union like the EC, none of these rules are necessary for intra-EC trade, at least in principle. However, even though the EC-12 have had common external tariffs, they have until very recently maintained national quotas on some non-EC imports. (The cases of Italian quotas on Japanese autos and French quotas on Latin American bananas have been much reported in the press.) In order to enforce these quotas, time-consuming customs procedures were necessary. The example of bananas shows how complicated trade arrangements can lead to hidden costs. France, which maintains preferential trade arrangements with its former colonies, discriminated against bananas imported from Latin America. Germany, however, bought most of its bananas from Latin America since they are the low-cost producers. France had to maintain custom surveillance to prevent cheap bananas from slipping across the German border.

Allocation Effects in Imperfectly Competitive Industries

International trade in goods typically increases competition in local markets. Import protection, by contrast, typically decreases competition. Since competition is the central pillar of market economies, the pro-competitive effect of trade liberalization is an important channel through which liberalization increases allocation efficiency. The pro-competitive effect occurs when trade liberalization intensifies competition between foreign and domestic firms and thereby restrains anti-competitive behaviour both domestically and abroad.

Traditional Analysis: the Positive Effects

The domestic market of a small country may not support a large number of firms, especially in industries in which scale economies are important. This can cause problems since small numbers of firms tend to collude and exploit consumers by raising prices. Competition from imports is an important means of restraining the monopoly power of domestic firms. The traditional analysis of import competition on the competitive behaviour of domestic firms is illustrated below.

Domestic monopolist and import competition with homogeneous products Consider the case of a domestic monopolist in a country where imports are initially forbidden. It is well known that a monopolist will restrict sales in order to raise prices and profits. In particular a monopolist chooses sales at the level where the extra revenue from selling one more unit just equals the extra cost of producing it. It is useful to breakdown the extra revenue (namely, marginal revenue) into its direct and indirect components. The direct effect is the price that the firm receives for the extra unit it sells. The indirect effect is the extent to which the extra sale marginally depresses the market price, thereby reducing the revenue the firm receives on all of its sales. The fact that firms with market power take account of this indirect effect is what leads to economically inefficient pricing. Were it not for the indirect effect the firm would set price equal to marginal cost, and consumers would then face the true cost of the good. As we shall see, the crucial impact of import competition on the monopoly pricing of domestic firms concerns the indirect effect.

To study the impact of import competition on the monopolist's position, suppose that imports are allowed. In this simple example, competition from imports completely wipes out the indirect effect. If consumers have unlimited access to imports at the world price, all the monopolist's price-setting power is destroyed. The monopolist cannot charge a higher price since she would lose all her customers to imports. Moreover, there is no reason for her to charge less, so the international price becomes the domestic price. These two facts combine to remove the indirect effect mentioned above. Since the international price is the true cost to the country of making or consuming the good, pricing efficiency is restored. Imposing a tariff will raise the domestic price to the international price plus the tariff. The tariff means that consumers no longer face the true cost of the good, so an inefficient allocation of resources results. None the less, the unrestricted ability of consumers to import destroys the monopoly power of the domestic firm.

As in the section on MFN tariffs, the positive analysis for a tariff and other rent-creating barriers is fairly similar. However, the welfare impact depends in an important way on who gets the rents (if any) created by a trade barrier. Since there is nothing essentially different between the perfect and imperfect competition cases on this point, we do not repeat the welfare analysis.

Imperfect substitutes Our example clearly illustrates the pro-competitive effect of imports. However, it is quite unrealistic. Import competition rarely completely destroys a domestic firm's ability to set prices. Figure 2.5 shows the more general case where imports are an imperfect substitute for domestic goods, so consumers' ability to buy imports still leaves the domestic firm some price-setting freedom.[1]

The demand curve and corresponding marginal revenue curve for home goods are shown as D and MR for a given tariff on imports. As usual, the home firm would sell Q units at a price of P. If the tariff on imports is lowered, foreign goods will be sold at a lower price, inducing some of the domestic firm's customers to switch to imports. Consequently, the demand for home goods at any price is reduced. This is shown as a shift of D to D'. Normally this will also shift the marginal revenue curve to MR'. The net result will be lower prices of imports and domestic goods. More to the point, the market power of the domestic firm will be reduced. By market power, we mean the extent to which the home firm charges a price that exceeds marginal cost. Clearly, in this example the domestic firm's mark up is reduced (the price is lower but marginal cost is constant). This leads to lower prices and output of the home goods, with the usual impact on profits and consumer welfare. Namely, the price reduction creates greater benefits for domestic consumers than losses to domestic producers. Furthermore,

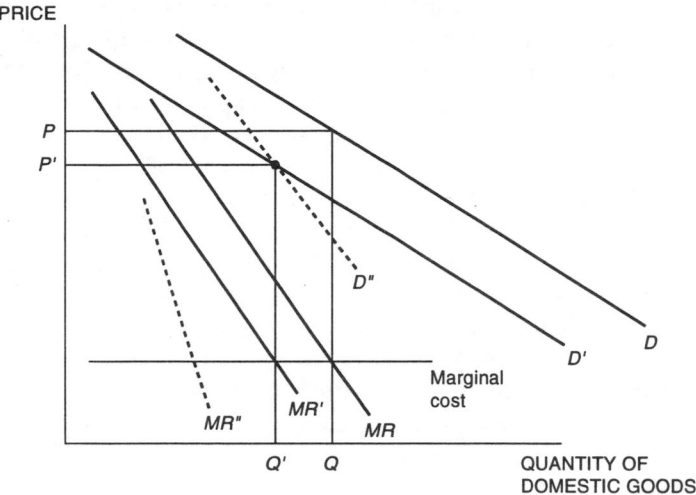

Figure 2.5 Quotas versus tariffs with imperfect competition

since prices more closely reflect true costs, the efficiency with which resources are allocated is improved.

Non-equivalence of tariffs and quantitative restrictions Next consider the effects of reducing imports through the use of a quantitative restriction such as a quota instead of a tariff. In Figure 2.5, the demand curve with a quota intersects the demand curve for tariff at Q'. The reason for this is simple. If the home firm charged P' with the quota, the local price of imports would be just the same as the local price with the tariff. Consequently, the amount of home good demanded at P' would be the same as under the tariff, namely Q'.

Notice, however, that the D'', demand curve facing the home firm when the restriction is a quantitative restriction, is steeper than it is for a tariff. To understand the reason for this, think about what a quota is. If the domestic firm raises its price, some consumers may wish to switch to the imported goods. With a tariff, their switching will not bid up the price of imported goods too much, so many will switch. However, with a quota the increased demand stemming from switching consumers will bid up the price of the limited quantity of imports permitted under the quota. Of course this higher price of imported goods will discourage some domestic consumers from switching. The bottom line is that if the domestic firm raises its price, it will lose fewer sales with a quota than it will with a tariff. Graphically this means the demand curve is steeper. The implication of the steeper demand curve is that the corresponding marginal revenue curve MR'' is to the left of the marginal revenue curve with a tariff. Clearly this will lead to a higher domestic price than under the tariff.

The key result here is the comparison of impact of tariffs and quotas on market power of local firms. Here we saw that a tariff and a quota that limited imports equally led to different prices of the domestic substitute. In particular, the quota led to higher prices than the tariff.

The intuition for this result is the same as before. With a tariff, consumers always have the alternative of importing. With a quantitative restriction, they have the alternative only for the fixed number of imported goods permitted. Thus with a quantitative restriction, the domestic firm does not face import competition on the margin.

The Normative Effects

Equation (2.2) – see p. 58 – shows that there are three additional welfare effects in the case of imperfectly competitive industries facing non-increasing returns to scale: the pure profit effect, the scale effect and the variety effect.

Pure profit effect   Consider first the pure profit effect. This may arise when the pre-liberalization domestic price exceeds domestic average costs. It interacts with the volume of trade and trade rents effects in a subtle way. Figure 2.6 helps us sort out the consequences assuming the small country case (world supply curve is flat) and a domestic monopolist facing constant returns to scale (so her supply average cost curve is flat). The figure shows the domestic market for a single good whose pre-liberalization price and domestic production is p_0 and X_0 respectively (we do not explain why X_0 is the equilibrium output in the diagram, but it is where the marginal revenue and marginal cost intersect). Suppose a tariff reduction lowered domestic prices from p_0 to p_1. Moreover, to fix ideas, suppose that there is no change in domestic output. The gross welfare effects of this are simple. The price reduction raises consumer surplus by the areas $A + B + C + D$. The price fall lowers tariff revenue by C and domestic profits by $A + B$. Thus the net welfare effect (this is the volume of trade effect) is D. Now suppose, instead, that the price fall induced the domestic monopolist to reduce output from X_0 to X_1. In this case, there are two additional gross effects. Imports rise, so tariff revenue rises by the area $G + H$

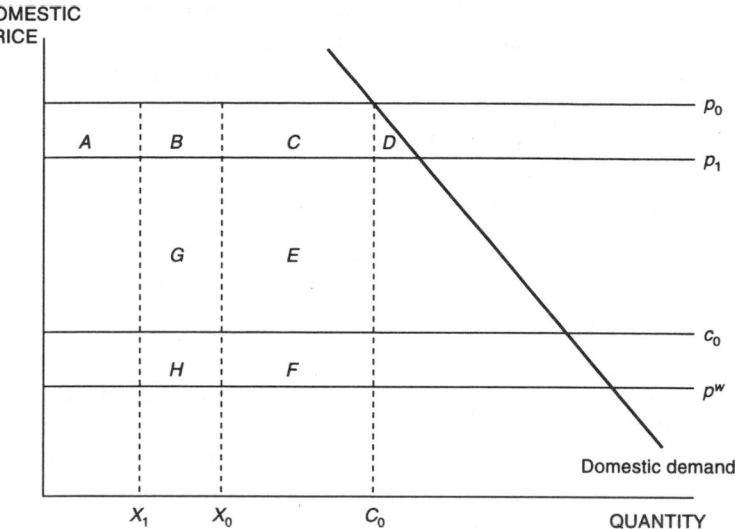

Figure 2.6 The pure profit effect

and the fall in domestic output further reduces profits by *G*. Thus we have a new net welfare effect, equal to *H*. This is the pure profit effect. Intuitively it arises since the liberalization leads to the replacement of expensive domestic production by lower cost imports (c_0 is above p^w).

In this example, we have made two key assumptions: liberalization reduced domestic output (this need not be the case in an imperfectly competitive industry) and c_0 is above p^w. Interested readers can use a diagram like Figure 2.6 to work out what would happen if c_0 were below p^w and/or liberalization raised domestic output.

Scale and variety effects　These effects are quite easy to understand. Protection of an imperfectly competitive industry may result in the existence of too many firms, each operating at an inefficient scale of production. Liberalization, including regional liberalization, may force a rationalization of industries. That is, some firms may close so that the remaining firms can operate at a more efficient scale of production. The variety effect is even more direct. Opening up to international trade and investment is likely to increase the variety of goods available to domestic consumers. In general, this increases welfare. When domestic consumption comes from firms, this variety effect may have an extra effect on costs. That is, if liberalization gives domestic firms a wider choice of intermediate products and capital goods, they are better able to choose the variety that best suits their needs. This can raise productivity.

These two effects proved to be quite important quantitatively in the case of European regional integration. The reason is that most of intra-European trade consists of two-way trade in similar products in which scale economies are important.

2.4 LOCATION EFFECTS

Trade, investment and migration barriers influence location of productive activity. Consequently, one very important – but much neglected – aspect of integration is the effect of a trade arrangement on the region's economic geography. Data in Europe, for instance, show a very strong link between peripherality and per caput income levels. Of course, peripherality is a relative concept, so one needs to be careful. (Is Iceland on the outskirts of Europe or conveniently placed between the European and North American markets?) Nevertheless, it is probably fair to say that Switzerland is more centrally located than Ireland, Greece and Portugal. Furthermore, it is pretty easy to believe that being right in the middle of Europe's industrial heartland gives Swiss industry an edge not enjoyed by Irish industry. In fact, if one takes seriously the technological spillover stories from the new growth theory, this advantage may lead to differences in long-run growth rates as well as average income levels.

In subSaharan Africa (SSA) locational effects have also proved to be important. For instance, Foroutan (1992) states that a common reason for the failure of regional integration in SSA is that it 'raises concern among the poorest SSA countries that the removal of barriers to trade may cause the migration of the few industries they possess to industrially more advanced countries.' If it is true that regional integration always causes relocation and this relocation is politically unacceptable, then one might think of designing integration schemes in a way that will reduce location effects. For instance, an asymmetric phase-out of tariffs (more industrialized nations reduce tariffs faster than less industrialized countries) might help.

Krugman–Venables Theory

Paul Krugman, Tony Venables and others have recently developed a set of tools that help us think systematically about how policy can affect the agglomeration of economic activity on a very large scale. The tools address two fundamental questions: why and where do industries concentrate geographically? This 'new location theory' is quite distinct from the classic approach. Alfred Marshall listed three main reasons why industries concentrate in geographically small areas: labour market pooling, supply of non-traded intermediate goods and technological spillovers. Krugman in his excellent little book, *Geography and Trade*, argues that these three effects best explain fairly small economic concentrations such as a single city or small cluster of cities.[2] The location of economic activity, at least in industrialized countries, displays a much grander pattern. For instance the concentration of industrial activity currently seen in Northern Italy covers hundreds of kilometres. This very large-scale agglomeration suggests that there are much broader forces governing economic geography.

Basic Analytic Framework

The basic approach to understanding this grand scale of agglomeration relies on two economic forces: (1) increasing returns to scale in production that are internal to the firm, and (2) trade costs. Note that technology-based externalities – for example knowledge spillovers, non-traded intermediates – are not part of this approach. In fact, they are assumed away in order to sharpen the focus of the analysis. We turn first to the role of scale economies and trade costs; since these are at the very heart of the theory, it is worth discussing them in more detail.

Increasing returns simply means that average costs fall as the scale of production rises. There are many reasons for this, but the most common and intuitive is fixed costs. If selling their goods requires a firm to build a factory, undertake R&D, invest in advertisement or establish a marketing and after-sales service network, then the firm faces falling average costs. The costs of any or all of these items are substantially fixed. That is, even if the firm fails to sell a single unit of output, it must still pay for the set-up costs.

The notion of trade cost is less well established. The classic trade cost is the expense of shipping a product from the point of production to the point of sale. However, we should not limit ourselves to this. Transport cost is only the tip of the iceberg: modern business involves much more than making goods and loading them on a truck. To take a very concrete example, let us consider what it would require to sell fresh pasta in Western Europe, supposing the product is made in Italy. Most food in Europe is sold through local supermarkets and small shops, so the pasta-maker must somehow get the goods on the shelves of these stores. How does this occur? The pasta-maker must have a sales force that goes out and tells the local stores about the pasta and tries to convince them that they should order some because they will make money selling it. This must be done in the local language. In order to prevent chaos in this selling effort, the pasta-maker must have a marketing staff that directs the effort throughout Europe. Moreover, the necessary information flow is not one-way. The pasta-maker has to find out about consumers' ever changing likes and dislikes concerning every aspect of the product: package size, spiciness, ingredients, how long the product must stay fresh, and so on.

The point of this whole discussion is to bring out the importance of distance. All of the activities mentioned typically get harder and harder – and therefore more and more expensive – the further away consumers are from the headquarters in Italy. The financial cost and time demand of travelling, the difficulty and cost of communicating between different cultures and languages are all part of trade costs. Obviously this is a special case, but the point is general. Trade costs involve much, much more than shipping the product.

Why Location Matters

Scale economies force firms to think about where to locate. Trade costs make the location a significant issue. If average production costs fall with the scale of production at a particular location, then firms face a serious trade-off in their location decision. Concentrating productive capacity lowers average costs but raises the costs of selling output to dispersed customers. The point can be made crystal clear by considering the converse case of constant returns to scale with small trade costs. In this case the firms' optimal location decision of firms' is trivial, but ridiculous. To avoid even tiny transport costs each firm would place a small amount of manufacturing capacity right next to each of its customers. Every consumer would have a scaled-down model of all manufacturing plants located in her own garden! The absence of scale economies implies that this other-worldly distribution of economic activity would be just as efficient as the massive concentration that we observe in the modern world.

Before preceding to how all this affects location, a side comment is in order. The first is that once we open the door to increasing returns to scale, we must deal with imperfect competition. If average cost falls with output, there is a strong tendency for a small number of firms to dominate. In such cases it is quite unlikely that they would act in a perfectly competitive manner. Thus, imperfect competition will necessarily be involved in the Krugman–Venables framework. Imperfect competition *per se* does not play an active role in the framework, but it is an unavoidable aspect of the models.

Equilibrium Location of Industry

We now turn to the core mechanism of the Krugman–Venables framework. Firms facing scale economies would prefer to concentrate production. Other things (for example production cost) being equal, firms would want to locate near the biggest market to reduce trade cost as much as possible. This line of reasoning starts to turn circles on itself. For many sectors, industry is its own best customer. Thus firms want to be where other firms are located. Firms that sell goods directly to consumers face a similar circularity. Their customers are located where the jobs are and the jobs tend to be concentrated where firms are located. Accordingly there is a mutually amplifying interaction between transport-costs-avoidance and market size determination. Firms' desire to be near customers tends to concentrate demand for intermediate and final products. And this agglomeration of firms' and workers' purchasing power tends to attract more firms.

Thus there is a circular mechanism involving transportation-costs-avoidance (firms' wish to be near large markets) and market size (firms' location decisions influence market size). We refer to this as 'circular causality'.

An illustration To illustrate circular causality, imagine a country in which there are only two locations (the coast and the interior), only two economic activities (farming and manufacturing) and only two types of labourers (farmers and workers). Farmers are assumed to be tied to their land and are divided evenly between the two locations. Manufactured goods can be made on the coast or in the interior, but setting up a factory involves a large fixed cost. In an established factory, the labour required to produce manufactured goods rises linearly with the output. Furthermore, a firm located in one locale must incur some costs to sell to consumers located in the other. Finally, suppose that demand for manufactured goods in each locale is proportional to its population of farmers and industrial workers.

If the fixed cost is large enough, then each firm will want to have only one factory, so its choice is to locate on the coast or in the interior. Given the transport costs, it wants to locate in the region with the higher population. But in our simple model, the population in the two regions differs only by the number of industrial workers (farmers are assumed to stay on their land). The question of how many workers are in each region, though, depends upon the location decision of all firms. There are two stable outcomes: all industry located on the coast, or all located in the interior.

The outcome has implications for real wages. By assumption, the labour of farmers and workers cannot be substituted, so the location of industry will not affect farmers' physical marginal productivity; this depends only on the ratio of farmers to land. However, the location of industry affects farmers' real wages through the price of industrial goods. Due to trade costs, industrial goods are more expensive in the region without industry. Higher prices mean lower real wages, so farmers should be concerned about industry location. Workers' wages are of course equal no matter which region the industry ends up in since they will be living near industry.

So far we have stacked the model towards spectacular outcomes. All the industry ends up in one region or the other. Imagine that only half of the industrial workers in each region are mobile. In this case, the industrial wages in the two regions will adjust to prevent complete concentration. To work through this assertion, suppose instead that all industry moves to the coast, taking with it half of the interior's workers. The remaining interior workers will have nothing to do. As a result, it is very likely that they will be willing to work for a lower wage than that earned by coastal workers. If trade costs are not too high, the low wages in the interior will attract some firms back to the interior. In fact, that difference in wages will have to be large enough to offset the trade cost disadvantage incurred by the firm that chose to locate in the small interior market.

Of course, the simple model leaves out many realistic effects, but it serves the purpose of illustration. The future research agenda for economic geography is vast, both on a theoretical and empirical level. The question of what regional integration does to industrial concentration is important, but as yet not well understood. Even more detailed questions such as what are the best policies in order to help disadvantaged regions, are even more pressing (at least in Europe) but are even less well understood. There is a great deal of informal reasoning and 'common wisdom' (for example, the central government should build more physical infrastructure such as roads and telecommunications systems, and promote more investment in human capital by building and improving schools). In fact, these policies have failed dismally in some cases (Southern Italy), but enjoyed mild success in others (Ireland and Portugal).

Multiple equilibriums   This simple example shows us two very important and very general results. First, note that we have not assumed any of Marshall's externalities. There are no technological spillovers or advantages from labour pooling. Thus it is understandable why concentration of industrial activity occurs in industries with such different technologies as financial services and automobiles. Second, in general we have multiple stable equilibriums. Thus, history can matter. Another implication of this is that temporary policies can, by shifting the economy between stable equilibriums, have effects that last even after the policy has been discontinued (it is fashionable to call this effect 'hysteresis').

Expectations matter   The simple story above avoided the issue of time and therefore questions of firms' expectations. But this should not prevent us from realizing that location decisions are often very expensive to reverse. Building a factory or locating a headquarters in a particular place generally entails a commitment of ten to thirty years. Consequently, location decisions will typically be made with an eye to future policies and conditions, not just current circumstances. A key point is that future policy, and therefore uncertainty about future policy, can have important effects on location. Indeed, expectations may be at least as important as current policy.

Location is one of the areas of economics where self-fulfilling expectations may play an important role. We saw that multiple stable equilibriums are endemic to location models. The question of which equilibrium the economy ends up at has not been answered. It would be natural to suppose that industry would flock to the region with a head start in industrialization. Some reflection on the decision process of firms, however, reveals that this need not be the case. If all the firms believe, for some reason or another, that a particular region will become the centre, then that is where the centre will be. The beliefs become a self-fulfilling prophecy.

Small policy changes may have large effects   Another implication of multiple equilibriums and the importance of expectations is that seemingly small policy changes may have large effects on industrial concentrations. Think about the original simple story of two identical regions. Initially this is a knife edge model. Any slight advantage accruing to one locale will tend to divert all industry to that locale. Thus policy changes that seem small may lead to massive relocation. Moreover, the same policy may have entirely different effects before and after the concentration question has been resolved. In equilibrium, firms are not just indifferent to locating in the two places; they definitely prefer to be where all the others are. The circular causality of location provides the 'winner' with some breathing space. For instance, Germany already has a massive concentration of industry, making it a very attractive place to locate. Accordingly, the German government can impose taxes and regulations (up to some limit) on firms located in Germany without causing massive relocation. A new region that wishes to attract industry does not have this luxury.

The political economy of location   A slight extension of this model helps us to apply this reasoning to real world concerns and develop some political economy arguments. 'Farmers' was a shorthand for productive factors that do not move. Land is another obvious one. More generally, certain types of workers are more likely to move than others. This is true for international migration. It also holds for migration between regions within a country. For instance, highly skilled workers tend to move around more, even within a single country. Indeed, one could imagine a whole range of factors marked by varying degrees of mobility, as measured by the wage gaps workers would tolerate without moving. The logic of the simple example suggests that these highly mobile factors – capital, technology and highly skilled workers – will not care very much where the concentration takes place. The less mobile factors will. If the less mobile workers and factors – land, farmers and medium-skilled workers – tend to be the low-paid factors, then industry relocation will take on the tone of a rich versus poor debate. This is what has happened in Europe.

Trade Arrangements and Location Effects

The U-shaped Relationship of Trade Costs and Concentration

Krugman and Venables (1989) show that the link between trade barriers (or trade costs more generally) and industry location is not sim-

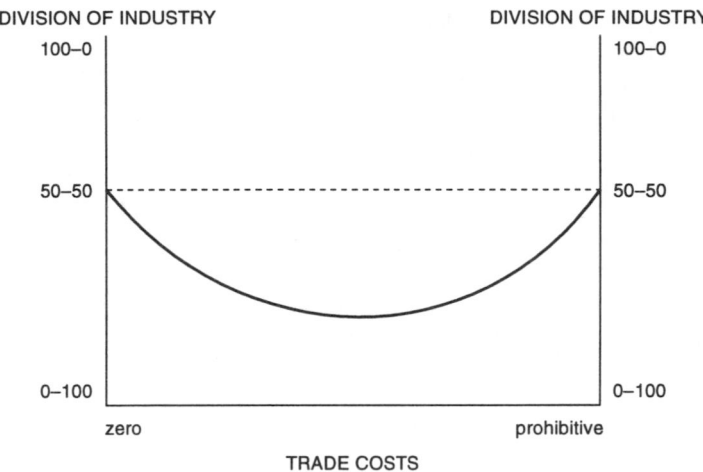

DIVISION OF INDUSTRY

100–0

50–50

0–100

zero

DIVISION OF INDUSTRY

100–0

50–50

0–100

prohibitive

TRADE COSTS

Figure 2.7 The U-shaped relation of concentration and openness

ple and monotonic. The easiest way to see this is to consider two identical countries under two extreme cases: prohibitive trade costs and no trade costs. With no trade costs, the circular causation discussed above does not operate. Firms would tend to spread out in search of low cost immobile factors, such as land. Starting from this pole a slight rise in trade barriers would lead to increased concentration. The opposite occurs at the other extreme. If trade costs are initially prohibitive, location will be decentralized since firms will be forced to produce locally. If trade barriers fall to just below the prohibitive level, the circular causation kicks in and some firms will relocate in search of bigger markets (see Figure 2.7).

More generally, consider one small region and one large region that are separated by prohibitive barriers. In order for producers in the small country to cover their fixed costs with lower sales, prices must be higher in the small country than in the large one. As the barriers come down, trade tends to narrow this price gap, thereby driving some firms in the smaller market to relocate to the big market. Not all firms leave, however, since the reduced competition in the small countries means increased market share for remaining firms. Moreover, the centralizing force is also mitigated by wage differences, presuming that some labour is immobile. Thus, a growing unevenness in dispersion is accompanied by increasing wage differentials. This latter fact means that there is a tension between a firm's desire to be in the low-wage region, and its desire to avoid trade costs. That is, locating in the big market mini-mizes trade costs, but maximizes wage costs.

This negative relationship between even industrial dispersion and trade costs (lower costs–more uneven dispersion) continues only so far. At some point the negative relationship turns around. If trade costs continue to fall, location in the small market looks better and better. The trade-cost disadvantage fades and the wage-cost advantage rises. At some point firms move from the large market back to the small one. In doing this, they drive the small-country wages back up to-wards the big-country wages. Once we get to zero trade costs, we are back to the even distribution, but now wages are as high in the small country as they are in the large country.

Political Economy of Shock Treatment Liberalization

It is interesting to apply this analysis to the political economy of lib-eralization. Suppose initially that countries in a region of the world impose quite high tariff and non-tariff barriers on intra-regional trade. This line of reasoning suggests that a gradualist approach to market opening may be self-defeating. As the barriers begin to come down, the industrial profits and wages in the smaller countries fall and those in the bigger countries rise. Moreover, relocation of industrial activity would show up as investment-led growth in the big market and invest-ment-led recession in the smaller markets.

Of course, consumers in the small country gain from lower prices and the increased choices provided by imports. However, in politics consumers' voices are often ignored. It is manifest that anti-liberaliza-tion forces in the small markets would gain strength. They would op-pose further liberalization and, depending upon the balance of political power, industrial firm owners and workers in the small country might well reverse the liberalization. At least in theory, none of this would happen if the countries jumped straight to zero trade costs. Even if this is not possible, jumping close to free trade would mean that small-region industrial workers would support slightly more liberation and would oppose slightly more protection, as long as the decision was restricted to marginal changes in policy.

Investment Deterring Aspects of Hub-and-Spoke FTAs

The actual trade relations of SSA countries can be classified as a 'hub-and-spoke' arrangement. This name comes from the way in which a schematic diagram of Africa's trade ties resemble an old wagon wheel

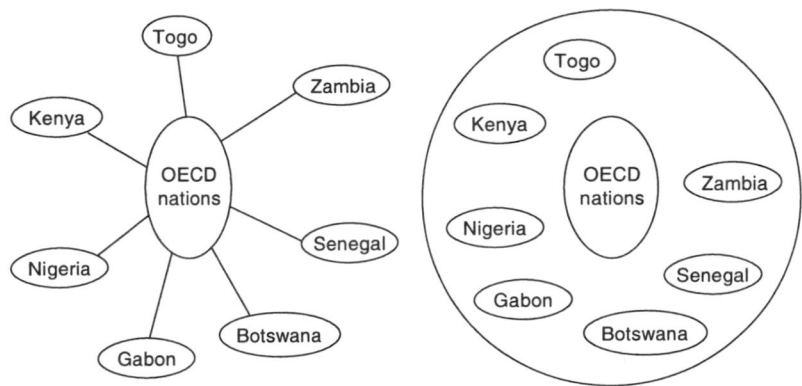

Figure 2.8 Schematic diagram of hub-and-spoke trade ties (left) and concentric circles (right)

(Figure 2.8). Europe and North America are the 'hub' (or centre of the wheel) and the African nations are the spokes. The key feature of a hub-and-spoke arrangement is that trade between the hub and each spoke is easier than trade among the spokes. In this subsection, we argue that the hub-and-spoke trade arrangements exert a marginalizing effect on African economies.

The marginalizing tendencies of hub-and-spoke trade arrangements can be illustrated with a numerical example. Figure 2.9 shows a hypothetical case, which intentionally puts to one side several important issues. Imagine there are three locations being considered as the site for a new manufacturing facility: England and two West African sites, one in Nigeria and one in Ghana. For simplicity, assume the firm expects total sales of its output to each market to be fixed, with 75 per cent sold in the UK and 12.5 per cent sold in each African country. (This simplification lets us divorce cost considerations from demand considerations.) Imagine the unit production costs would be 10 if the plant is located in the UK, 8 if the plant is located in either African nation and 15 if three separate plants must be built. Economies of scale explain the high cost of dividing up production; lower African unit labour costs explain why the UK location means higher production costs. Suppose initially that the unit trade costs amounted to 6 for all three trade flows: the two African–UK bilateral trade flows and the intra-African trade flow. Unit trade costs within any of the three markets are normalized to zero.

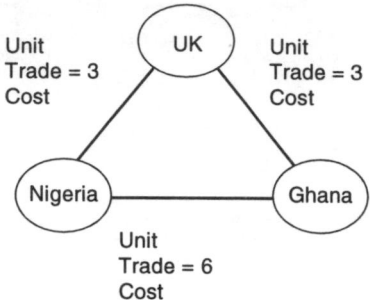

Unit Production Costs: 10 in UK, 8 in Nigeria or Ghana

Figure 2.9 The marginalizing tendencies of hub-and-spoke

Clearly the manufacturer will locate the factory where the sum of production and trade costs is minimized. It is easy to calculate that with even trade costs, the UK is the cheapest place to put the factory. The average cost in either African location is 13.25 – 8 for production plus an average trade cost of $(\frac{3}{4})*6 + (\frac{1}{8})*0 + (\frac{1}{8})*6$. This surpasses the UK location costs of 11.5. The high unit production cost in the EC is more than offset by the lower average trade cost. The point is that the savings on trade costs (recall that three-quarters of the customers are located in the UK) outweigh the higher production costs.

Next, suppose that various liberalization schemes lower the cost of trade between the UK and Africa, but not on intra-African trade. In particular, suppose the North–South per unit trade costs become 3, while the South–South unit costs remain at 6. Arithmetic shows that the average unit cost of locating the plant in the UK is still lower (10.75) than locating in either Nigeria or Ghana (11 each). Although the trade liberalization lowers North–South trade costs, trade costs within the UK are lower yet, so there is still some market size effect favouring the UK location. Location in the UK confers preferential access to all three markets, not just two.

Lastly, consider the impact of eliminating the hub-and-spoke system by reducing intra-African trade costs to the same level as the North–South trade costs. This would result in a 'concentric circles' arrangement (Figure 2.8). That is, all the countries in the outer circle would have approximately equal trade costs with all nations in their own circle and as well as with all the nations in the hub. Nations that are in the hub may enjoy even lower trade costs with each other. Here we see that total unit costs of locating in Nigeria or Ghana are lower (10.625) than the unit costs of locating in the UK (10.75). Even though location in the UK implies zero trade costs for 75 per cent of the manufacturer's sales, the lower African production costs finally become the dominant issue.

Of course this simple illustration is not general, and we do not mean to say that filling in the gaps between 'spokes' will lead to a tidal wave of foreign investment into Africa. Nevertheless, the basic message is clear. Hub-and-spoke FTAs have a tendency to marginalize the spoke economies, since production facilities located in the spokes have artificially lower market access than factories in the hub. Consequently, hub-and-spoke FTAs render an artificial deterrent to investment in the outer economies. Filling in the gaps with spoke–spoke FTAs removes this policy-induced investment deterrent.

2.5 ACCUMULATION (GROWTH) EFFECTS

Policy-makers and economists generally believe that economic integration is an engine of growth. The basic link between integration and growth is simple to describe: It is dictated by the logic of growth. Growth in per caput output requires the accumulation of some factor of production (using the term broadly to include knowledge capital, that is, the stock of knowledge, as a factor of production). Consequently, international trade arrangements affect growth by affecting the accumulation of factors. Most accumulation of productive factors is intentional and is called investment. Accordingly, we can say that trade affects growth mainly via its effect on investment in human capital, physical capital or knowledge capital. The qualification 'mainly' is necessary since trade may also affect unintentional accumulation. For instance, by speeding the international dissemination of technological progress, trade may hasten growth without directly affecting investment.

Growth effects fall naturally into two categories: medium-term and long-term. An instance of medium-term effects is that of induced physical capital formation. For all the reasons documented above, closer integration improves the efficiency with which productive factors are combined to produce output. As a side effect, this efficiency gain makes the region a better place to invest, so more investment occurs. The result is that the initial efficiency gains are boosted by induced capital formation. While the above-normal capital formation is occurring, the economies experience a medium-term growth effect; it is only medium-term because it will eventually peter out. As the amount of capital per worker rises, the marginal incentive to invest in more capital diminishes and eventually the above-normal capital formation stops. A good example of this is the investment boom that Spain experienced around the time of its accession to the EU.

Long-term growth effects involve a permanent change in the rate of accumulation, and thereby a permanent change in the rate of growth. It is much harder to find examples of this. Besides, the economics of it are necessarily more complicated, as we shall see below.

Medium-term Accumulation: Induce Capital Formation

Neoclassical growth literature, started by Solow (1956), provides a simple way for thinking about the medium-term growth effects of trade liberalization. The Solow model provides the simplest way of determining the capital stock at any point in time. Specifically, it assumes that the fraction of output invested is constant and that all investment comes from domestic sources. The next assumption concerns the relationship between capital and output. A nation's aggregate output is related to its supplies of productive factors and the level of technology according to:

$$Y_t = A_t K_t^\alpha L_t^{1-\alpha} \tag{2.2}$$

where the factors of production are physical capital (K) and labour (L) and the variable A is total factor productivity, that is, knowledge capital. Finally, it is assumed that a constant fraction of the capital stock depreciates each year.

To understand growth in this model, it is first necessary to understand how the level of the capital stock is determined. Figure 2.10 assists in this task. Both L and A are assumed constant to simplify things. The Y/L^* curve is concave due to the assumed diminishing returns to capital holding L constant. The depreciation/L schedule is straight since the amount of depreciation per worker increases linearly with the level of the capital stock. The Savings/L curve has a shape similar to that of the Y/L curve since savings is a constant fraction of output.

Noteworthy things occur at intersections or tangencies in economics diagrams. Since there are no tangencies in this one, the equilibrium capital–labour ratio must be where the Savings/L and the Depreciation/L curves cross, that is, K/L^*. The reason is simple: if the capital–labour ratio were lower, the savings per worker would exceed the depreciation per worker. This would cause the level of the capital stock

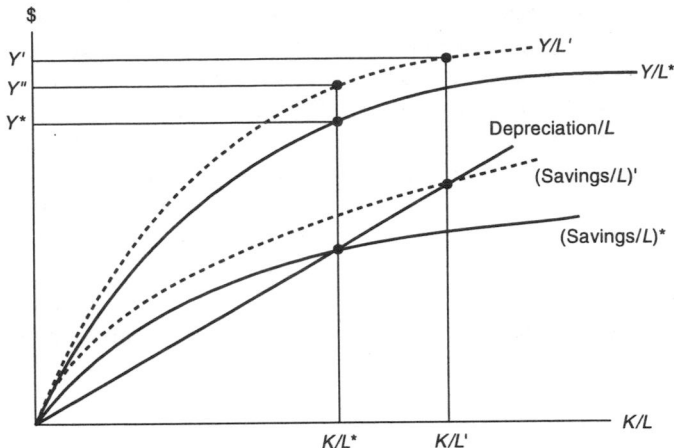

Figure 2.10 Induced capital formation in the Solow model

to rise compared with the labour force. If the capital–labour ratio were higher, the reverse would be true. This sort of equilibrium in a dynamic model is called a 'steady state' since it is the state of the model where motion stops. In this case, the 'state' is K/L and the 'motion' is a rise or fall in K/L.

Trade and Growth Effects

The simple medium-term growth effects can be illustrated with Figure 2.10. Consider a liberalization program for which the allocation efficiency effects have been estimated. For example, suppose it has been estimated that a particular programme would increase GDP by, say, 1 per cent. The way this is usually calculated is by totting up all of the static allocation effects. In other words, they calculate the impact assuming there will be no change in the capital stock. However, the only way Y can rise by 1 per cent without an increase in K or L is for A to rise by 1 per cent. In Figure 2.10, this corresponds to a shift up in the Y/L curve to Y/L'. With a constant investment rate, this would directly boost per caput savings to Savings/L'.

The estimated allocation effect is the output increase that would occur without any change in the capital–labour ratio, that is, Y'' minus Y^*. But clearly this is an incomplete analysis, since the old steady-state capital–labour ratio is no longer valid. As the K/L ratio rises towards the new steady-state level, there will be a knock-on increase in GDP per capita. This knock-on effect is the medium-run growth effect, that is, the induced capital formation effect. Its eventual impact on GDP is the difference between Y'' and Y'.

The induced capital formation effect argues that market integration should coincide with investment-led growth. After all, an increase in integration that is large enough to have a noticeable economy-wide impact is also likely to boost the productivity of the capital stock. The resulting faster accumulation of capital, that is, induced-capital formation, will provide the economy with more resources, thus augmenting the output gains due to increased static efficiency. The same sort of pro-investment effect could induce a higher rate of investment in human capital and knowledge capital as well.

Measuring Dynamic Effects with the Aggregate GDP Approach

The aggregate GDP approach does much violence to the details of the composition of output. After all, it is somewhat blunt to talk about output as if the economy produced only one good. Counterbalancing this, however, is the fact that (2.2) is widely used; more to the point, its simple structure allows us to use estimates of the static efficiency gains from market integration to measure the dynamic effects. That is, if the economy is to produce, say, 1.5 per cent more output with the same amount of inputs, then it must be that the path of A in (2.2) shifts up by 1.5 per cent. As it turns out, this is sufficient to back out the implied dynamic effects. Specifically, differentiating (2.2) with respect to A and gathering terms, we see that:

$$\%\Delta\text{GDP} = (\%\Delta A)(1 + \frac{\alpha}{1-\alpha}) \qquad (2.3)$$

where $\%\Delta$ means 'percentage change in'. This is the sum of the static efficiency effect and the induced capital (human and physical) formation effect.

Adjustment period   It will take decades to reach the new higher steady-state GDP, since even if the static efficiency gains are rapidly phased in, factor accumulation takes time. A simple approximation (assuming a constant savings rate) allows us to gauge how much time. Using (2.2) and the conditions that relate the capital stock to investment and depreciation, the dynamics around the steady state can be approximated by:

$$\frac{dY/Y}{dt} = (n + \eta + \delta)(1 - \alpha)(lnY^* - lnY_t) \qquad (2.4)$$

where Y^* is the new steady-state level of per capita output. That is to say, per capita GDP rises towards its new steady state in a way that closes a certain per cent of the gap between the current level and the steady-state level each year. This certain percentage equals $(n + \eta + \delta)$ $(1 - \alpha)$, where n is the population growth rate, η is the rate of productivity advance and δ is the depreciation rate. Thus during the transition, Y/L and K/L should grow faster than their long-run rates, with K/L further above its trend than Y/L. This comes from the fact that Y/L is driven by faster than 'normal' accumulation of factors, but the transmission is muted since α is less than unity.

Note that this approximation implies that the adjustment process is not linear. Rather, the extra growth is heavily front-loaded. To illustrate this point, take α to be two-thirds, δ to be 13 per cent per annum and a total factor productivity growth (namely, η) to be 2 per cent per annum. This generates $\alpha(n + \eta + \delta)(1 - \alpha)$ equal to 5 per cent, implying a half-life of about fourteen years.

The transition time that we get assuming a constant investment rate is shorter than that obtained when we allow intertemporal optimization. When we allow re-optimization on the saving rate, citizens understand that they will be wealthier in the future. This makes them feel wealthier today, and so increases consumption somewhat today. This reduces the saving rate and thereby postpones attainment of the new steady state.

Output is not welfare In studying the induced capital accumulation effect, it is critical to bear in mind the fact that extra output is not a measure of extra welfare. Citizens must forgo consumption to accumulate the extra capital. Thus the increase in future consumption is largely and perhaps entirely offset by the necessary forgone consumption during the transition path. This point is clear from eq. (2.1). The increase in the value of factor supplies is offset by the investment necessary. There is still room for welfare gains, however, from two sources. First, for non-marginal changes there will be small gains and if the public rate of return on investment exceeds the private rate, then positive accumulation will have positive welfare effects. Baldwin (1992a) shows more formally that the welfare effects depend on the wedge between the social and private return to capital, and provides some numerical estimates of the welfare effects of the 1992 programme. The general finding is that welfare effects stemming from induced capital formation are more than an order of magnitude smaller than those stemming from the static effects.

Problems with the Aggregate GDP Approach

The estimates of dynamic effects that come from the aggregate GDP approach are very rough and do not reach the high standards of empirical rigour attained in many other branches of economics. These calculations are really nothing more than an illustration of the common-wisdom propositions that growth effects may easily be more important than static effects. Indeed it is probably best to think of them as merely suggestive. Samuel Johnson's quip about a dog walking on its hind legs is an apt way to summarize the point of these rough calculations: the interest lies not in that it is done well, but rather that it is done at all.

Assuming the existence of an aggregate output function, such as equation (2.2), allowed an easy and transparent estimate of medium-run dynamic effects. The aggregate GDP approach has many limitations, however, which must be kept in mind. The limitations stem from two sources. First, GDP functions generally do not have a well-specified micro-foundation, unless very restrictive assumptions are made. The second, and more practical, is that integration does not affect all sectors equally. Consequently the static efficiency gains may be biased towards sectors that are intensive in the use of human or physical capital. Such biases, however, invalidate the procedure we used to back out the initial change in marginal products from existing estimates of total static gains. To see this, recall that the rough calculation above required us to assume that the liberalization raised the marginal productivity of all factors proportionally. That is to say, we viewed the static efficiency effect as a Hicks-neutral technological change.

To give an illustration of the importance of this shortcoming, we consider the medium-run growth effects of the EC's 1992 programme. Although the ongoing integration of the EC is extremely broad, it does not affect all sectors and it does not affect all sectors equally. For example, the pro-competitive effect should have more impact on industries with increasing returns to scale than on the constant-returns-to-scale sector; the reduction in trade cost should affect traded goods more than untraded goods. The mobility of labour existed for many years in the EC, but harmonization of standards and mutual recognition of professional qualifications will boost mobility of certain types of labour more than others. The European Union and the removal of capital controls should encourage capital mobility more than labour mobility. The fact that certain EC economies were always more open and integrated than others before the 1992 programme, also implies that the monetary and economic union will have different impacts on different countries. Of course many more such examples exist. The fact that European integration does not affect all sectors and all countries equally is likely to have important implications for quantitative estimates. This is especially true for the induced capital formation effects since the reforms may boost the productivity of certain factors more than others. Given that the static efficiency impact of the 1992 programme will almost surely fall more heavily on traded goods and scale-economy goods, the Stolper–Samuelson theorem suggests that the rewards to physical and human capital might rise *more* than the average amount.

Ceaseless Accumulation: the 'New' Growth Theory

Continual output growth per person requires the continual accumulation of factors of production. In the Solow model, and the neoclassical model more generally, this ceaseless accumulation takes the form of productivity-boosting knowledge. However, in the Solow model the rate of productivity growth is taken as given. The model does not attempt to address its determinants. Consequently, it would be entirely futile to use this framework to organize our thinking about the long-term growth effects of trade arrangements. The big contribution of the 'new' growth theory, which many view as having started with Romer (1983, 1986), is to endogenize the ceaseless accumulation of factors. Since accumulation is the key focus, the best of these models concentrate on specifying the micro-foundations of accumulation. In particular, they carefully lay out the private costs and benefits to investing in more capital, more skills or more technical progress. Precisely because endogenous growth models delve into the private costs and benefits of accumulation, they permit consideration of a much wider range of economic channels by which trade affects growth.

Basic Logic of Endogenous Growth Models

Before turning to the ways in which trade arrangements can affect long-term growth, we address the logic of endogenous growth theory and briefly review several important models.

The key to endogenizing output growth is to endogenize investment. To do this convincingly, one must lay out the micro-foundations of individuals' investment decisions. Whatever the details of these micro-foundations, the bottom line will be that the rate of investment depends on the costs and benefits of investing. Now clearly, if the rate of investment is to remain constant in the long run, then the private net return on new investments should also remain constant in the long run. This brings us to the first crucial aspect of an endogenous growth model. The necessity for the real return to investment is to be non-diminishing in the capital stock.

To see this point more clearly, consider the relationship between the private return to investment and the economy's capital–labour ratio. In the Solow model, the return to investment declined as the capital–labour ratio rose due to diminishing social returns to capital (holding the labour forces constant). Clearly, this situation will not be marked by continuous growth. Growth will slow as the rising capital–labour ratio forces downwards the return to investment. By contrast, if there are increasing returns to capital, we should see the return to investment increase as the capital–labour ratio rises. Since investors will want to do more and more investing as the private return rises, this situation will correspond to an ever-rising rate of growth. Since continually rising growth rates are not among the world's problems, we ignore this case.

At the denouement of several Sherlock Holmes novels, the great detective remarks that if one has eliminated all possible answers to a problem except one, the remaining possibility, however unlikely, must be the solution. Applying this reasoning leads us to conclude that continuous growth requires that the returns to capital be exactly constant. The point is quite general. Ceaseless growth requires ceaseless accumulation and ceaseless accumulation requires that the return to accumulation does not fall as the capital stock rises.

As it turns out, this requirement places a big stumbling block in the path of builders of endogenous growth models. A constant marginal return to investment implies a private return to investing that is unrelated to the amount of investment that has been done. That means that private investors think that the gap between the cost of investing and the benefit to investing is constant no matter how much investing they do. This is a problem since it implies that private investors' demand for capital is not well-behaved. 'Not well-behaved' means that, depending upon the relationship between the cost and benefit of investing, private investors will want to do no investing or an infinite amount of investing, or will be entirely indifferent to how much investing they do. If the cost exceeds the return, no one will invest. If the return exceeds the cost, everyone will wish to invest an infinite amount. If the cost equals the return, then no one will care how much they invest. The rate of investment and therefore the rate of growth is either zero, infinite or undetermined by the actions of investors. It should be plain this type of set-up is not going to be much good for studying the determinants of growth or the growth effects of various government policies. Three important lessons should be learned from this:

- the growth rate of output depends upon the rate of accumulation of factors, that is, the rate of investment;
- to make the rate of GDP growth endogenous, it is necessary to endogenize the rate of investment. In a market economy, this means detailing the cost and benefits of investment faced by private, self-interested investors; and
- continual growth requires that the return on investment is not diminishing in the capital stock.

To go beyond this shallow model of growth, we are going to want the decision of private investors to be well-behaved. This requires that each private investor perceive her personal return to investing to be diminishing in her own level of investment. This requirement leads us to the following important conclusion. If the private investment decision is to be well-behaved, there must be a 'wedge' between the public and private return to investment that implies the private return is perceived as diminishing as the capital stock rises, but social or economy-wide return is not. We now turn to several more sophisticated endogenous growth models. Notice that each model displays two critical features: (1) a wedge between the private and public (that is, aggregate) rate of return to investment, and (2) a public rate of return that is not diminishing in the aggregate capital stock.

Three Main Varieties of the 'New' Growth Models

There are many ways of classifying the numerous models of endogenous growth that now exist. I find it most useful to sort them into piles according to which type of factor they assume to be accumulating: physical capital, human capital or knowledge capital. This brings to the fore a pivotal distinction between primary factors, which do not accumulate (or accumulate for reasons that are not addressed in the model), and factors that do accumulate. Most models take labour and land as primary factors ('non-reproducible factors' is an equivalent term for primary factors). Several models allow more than one type to accumulate; however, even in these, one factor usually plays the dominant role, at least in the motivation of the model.

Knowledge capital   Robert Solow taught us long ago that technical progress is the driving force behind long-term per caput income growth. The first category of new growth theories picks up on Solow's insight by endogenizing technical progress. Technical progress is nothing other than knowledge creation, and ceaseless technical knowledge leads to a continually rising stock of knowledge. To stress the similarities with the other models, technical progress can be thought of as the accumulation of productivity-boosting 'knowledge capital'.

In the earliest of these models (Romer, 1983, 1986), the micro-foundations of knowledge creation and knowledge spillovers were somewhat vague. Private firms, which are assumed to be small compared with the whole economy, individually face diminishing returns to their investments in knowledge creation. Yet from an economy-wide perspective the rate of return to investment does not fall due to technological spillovers in production. That is, the productivity of an investment that a firm installs today depends positively upon how much investment has been done in the past. The reason this is so was not fully explained in Romer's early models. The cumulative action of many small firms raises the economy-wide capital stock, and thereby continually prevents the private return on investment from falling. Here the wedge between private and social return to investment relies on technological spillovers in the output sector. These models have the attractive feature that firms' investment decisions are well-behaved, since the technology spillover introduces a public–private wedge. As a result, the amount of investment that private firms wish to make responds sensibly to changes such as tax incentives, trade liberalization, and so on.

A set of more recent models focuses more explicitly on the micro-foundations of innovation, that is, the decisions by firms to invest in productivity-boosting innovations. In these models, private firms invest in knowledge creation because it provides them with an edge over other firms. The profit earned in exploiting this advantage provides a return on the knowledge-creation investment. From the economy-wide point of view the net result of this profit-motivated activity is output growth. That is to say, the economy's primary factors produce more and more output each year due to this endless stream of innovations. In these models, private knowledge-creation has an unintentional side effect – a contribution to the public stock of knowledge. The models assume that this unintentional spillover feeds back into the economy by raising the productivity of resources employed in innovating. This unintentional side effect creates the private-versus-social wedge in these models. Thus, unlike the early models, knowledge spillovers affect the productivity of resources located in the innovation sector instead of the output sector.

Another common feature of these models is their assumption (explicitly or implicitly) that there is a 'production function' for knowledge that specifies the relationship among primary resources devoted to innovation, the existing stock of innovations and the discovery of innovations. I find it useful to think of the production function for innovations as a great book in the sky with an infinite number of pages. Each page contains the blueprints for a new product or a new innovation. Everyone in the economy knows about the book and all know the quantity of primary resources needed to read the pages. Whoever reads a page first gets an infinite patent on the innovation on that particular page. Though it costs real resources to read a page, doing so provides a continual stream of profits from exploitation of the resulting patent.

There are two sub-varieties of these innovation models: product-innovation models and process-innovation models. In the production innovation models, output growth is driven by a constant flow of product innovations that raise primary factor productivity. The new products are interpreted as intermediate goods, so the productivity-raising effect is interpreted as reflecting the manner in which a finer division of labour permits greater specialization and efficiency. Development of a new variety yields the developer an infinite life patent; it also contributes to the public stock of knowledge due to the non-appropriability of some of the newly created knowledge. The patent affords the developer a return on her R&D investment; the knowledge spillovers feed back into innovation by lowering the development cost of additional new products. Thus, although new products garner progressively smaller market shares (and profits) due to the progressively larger number of competitors, they can be developed at a progressively lower cost. Given proper assumptions on the magnitude of the knowledge feedback, the result is a time invariant rate of return on labour invested in R&D activity. This leads profit-motivated firms to invest a constant fraction of the economy's primary resources in production development, thereby resulting in a constant flow of new products and constant income growth.

Technological spillovers in innovation create a wedge between the private and public returns to innovation investment. To use the great-book-in-the-sky parallel, the usefulness of the blueprint on each page is the same, however the information on each page is encoded. Though it takes time to decipher the blueprint on each new page, the amount of time shrinks with each new page turned, since innovators learn from past decoding experiences. In this analogy, the spillover is that everyone learns all the past decoding lessons free.

A separate line of thought has been pursued by the process-innovation models.[3] Unlike the product-innovation models, these innovations may drive some existing firms out of business. The reason is simple. Instead of creating a new product that can be sold side-by-side with existing products, process innovations allow the innovator to make existing products more cheaply. This means the owner of the innovation may find it worth while to charge a price that drives her competitors out of business. The profits earned by the innovator from exploiting this edge compensate her for the R&D costs. However, even as the most recent innovator is luxuriating in profits, other firms are developing processes that have even lower manufacturing costs. When one of them succeeds, the previous ruler-of-the-hill is deposed. This ceaseless search for cost-lowering innovations leads to a ceaseless accumulation of knowledge and drives manufacturing productivity ever higher. 'Creative destruction' is the term that Schumpeter (1942) used to describe the process.

As with product-innovation models, the private-versus-social wedge in these models appears in the innovation sector. However, the technology spillover takes a different form. The 'production function' for innovations does not change in the sense that the amount of resources necessary to obtain a new innovation does not change. What does change is the nature of the resulting innovation. Each new innovation is clearly better than the last. There is a spillover in that each new innovator gets to start working directly on the frontier of knowledge. Using the great-book comparison, the page-reading cost (in terms of primary resources) does not change, but the usefulness of the blueprint increases with every page. The technological spillover is like assuming that each innovator gets to read all the previously-turned pages free, so that they do not have to re-invent the wheel.

One model in the process-innovation vein, which is especially important for understanding real-world process innovation, is the 'quality ladders' of Grossman and Helpman (1991). This is a model where each subsequent page of the great-book reveals a process that allows the page-turner to raise the quality of her product without raising the manufacturing cost. This is important to understanding modern technical progress since for many innovative industries, such as personal computers and consumer electronics, it is difficult to classify advances as product innovations or process innovations. Take the example of portable radios. Electronic firms make more or less the same products using more or less the same process, but each year the radios are clearly superior – lighter, more durable, more powerful, with better sound, and so on.

Political economy of creative destruction   The notion of creative destruction is extremely important in understanding how an economy directed by selfish motives can year after year produce more and more from the same primary factors. Each time a new product or process is developed, part (or all) of the value of previous inventions is destroyed. Schumpeter wrote:[4]

> The fundamental impulse that sets and keeps the capitalist engine in motion comes from the new consumer goods, the new methods of production or transportation, the new markets, . . . [This process] incessantly revolutionizes the economic structure from within, incessantly destroying the old one, incessantly creating a new one. This process of Creative Destruction is the essential fact about capitalism. (Cited in Aghion and Howitt, 1990)

Since most economists would agree with Schumpeter's assessment, it is worth considering the political economy of creative destruction. Many existing firms and industries wield political influence that far exceeds their numbers or even their weight in the economy. This fact is often cited as an explanation of why nations so frequently adopt import barriers that help the few at the expense of the many. The same fact, however, would suggest that existing firms may very well attempt to stifle technical progress. After all, technical progress will threaten their current position in the market. The current leaders have knowledge that gives them an edge over other firms. Like any good owner of capital, these firms will resist a move to increase competition. Unfortunately, resisting competition in this context means resisting the introduction of new technology. Thus selfish firms, left to their own devices, will attempt to stifle the economy's growth by suppressing the introduction of new technology. That is, the existing firms might be quite capable of matching the technical progress and thereby maintaining their positions, but clearly they would rather not have to do so. Thus just as competition was essential to an efficient static allocation of resources, competition or at least the threat of competition is a necessary condition for technical progress.

Another of Schumpeter's ideas – the trade-off between dynamic and static efficiency – is closely related to this, yet it is widely misunderstood. Schumpeter pointed out that innovation is costly and so a firm must expect to earn what might appear to be above-normal profit to compensate it for its knowledge creation investment. Though above-normal profits might be considered inefficient from a static point of view, they are necessary for dynamic efficiency (that is, optimal investing in knowledge creation). This trade-off, however, is widely misunderstood to justify market power on behalf of existing firms and government policies that protect such market power. A closer look, however, reveals no such trade-off. What is needed is that innovators earn a fair return on their knowledge capital. If we properly account for all inputs, including knowledge capital, a dynamically efficient economy does not require 'above-normal profits'.

This point is especially important in the context of Central and Eastern Europe. In an attempt to promote domestic industry, government may strive to protect existing firms from competition, the idea being that protection would raise the return to introducing productivity-enhancing technology and thereby promote technical progress and growth. The weak link in this chain of reasoning is the last one. Unless existing firms are threatened by new technologies, they have very little incentive to invest continually in new productivity-boosting knowledge.

Human capital   Lucas (1988) opened a new line of thinking in the endogenous growth literature by focusing on the contribution of human capital to GDP growth. Human capital is the skill of workers. It is considered capital since skill embodied in workers can produce a flow of service for an extended period, just as a capital good can. Models that focus on human capital accumulation do not differ in their fundamental economic structure from the models already discussed. The basic logic of ceaseless accumulation must be respected. In particular, the economy-wide rate of return on investing in human capital cannot be forever falling or rising. Moreover, to assure the well-behaved nature of the self-interested investment decisions of private citizens and firms, the models must have some way of introducing a wedge between the private and social (that is, economy-wide) rates of return.

We start with a trivial relabelling. First, it is obvious that by calling it 'capital' instead of 'human capital', we could interpret the first endogenous growth models presented above as showing that the human capital can be a source of growth. What is interesting about models that focus on human capital is that they provide a particularly convincing story behind the existence of the private–social wedge. People invest in raising their skill level because they anticipate that there will be a lot of capital that will allow them to turn high skill levels into high salaries. Likewise, firms invest in new plant and equipment because they expect there to be a lot of skilled workers around to make the factories turn a profit. The wedge exists since undertaking the investments in human capital does not take account of the output-boosting effect of the capital formation that their actions will induce.

One interesting application of this approach is to understand the spectacular growth experienced by Japan and Germany after the Second World War. In both cases, the economies suffered a large loss of physical and human capital, though the loss in physical capital was by far the larger of the two. Given the implications of diminishing re turns to K and H taken separately, this means that the postwar economies of Japan and Germany were extremely good places to invest physical capital. They had lots of human capital compared with physical capital, so the return on physical capital was extraordinarily high. Following the usual logic that a high rate of return attracts a high rate of investment, the theory predicts that Japan and Germany should have experienced above-normal growth during this period. Moreover, the growth should have been investment-led.

Physical capital The least popular variety of the new growth models focuses on physical capital accumulation as the engine of growth, although as we saw above, physical capital appears in many models. One of the few articles to take this approach seriously is Romer's (1987), which is appropriately titled, 'Crazy Explanations for the Productivity Slowdown'. The verbal arguments in the model make it clear that what is really being assumed is that physical capital faces non-diminishing returns because of the technology that is embodied in capital. The unpopularity of the models stems from empirical evidence rather than theoretical objections. Many economists have attempted to measure the aggregate output elasticity of the aggregate capital stock, both the social rate of return and the private rate of return. All these studies find diminishing returns to physical capital. The main conclusion for this line of thinking is a negative result. The accumulation of physical capital is not to be considered a driving force of growth. Rather, its continual accumulation is either a side effect of the accumulation of productivity-boosting knowledge, or its importance is intertwined with some other factor such as human capital.

Long-run Growth Effects of Trade Arrangements

After all these preliminaries, we are finally ready to discuss the permanent growth effects of trade arrangements. One of the surest lessons of growth theory is that sustained GDP growth requires sustained productivity growth and sustained productivity growth requires continual accumulation of knowledge. This line of reasoning directs us to investigate the impact of international market opening on the private return to innovation. An international version of the Romer model proves to be a useful workhorse for this task. Consider a world with two countries (call them home and foreign) that are both identical to the model described above.

Market size, competition and knowledge spillover effects   In our first thought-experiment, each country is initially closed. The experiment is what will happen when free trade in intermediary goods is permitted. To keep effects separate, we assume for the moment that there are no international spillovers of knowledge. To use the great-book-in-the-sky analogy, home and foreign innovators do not learn from each others' past decoding experiences, only from domestic experiences.

Having done most of the spade work, we jump right to the heart of the matter: the benefit and cost of innovating in the integrated world equilibrium as opposed to the benefit and cost in autarky. Since the developer of a new intermediate good will receive a share of world consumption expenditure in every period (recall each innovation has an infinite-lived patent), the value of having a patent – and therefore the value of innovating – will be affected in two conflicting ways. On one hand the access to a larger market boosts the profitability of innovation, while on the other hand the increased competition from existing foreign innovations dampens the R&D profitability. In general we cannot say what the net effect would be.

Now consider the impact on the value of innovating. Suppose that we could open international flows of knowledge without opening trade. While this is highly unlikely to happen in the real world (except via espionage), it is a convenient thought-experiment. The effect would be a decrease in the cost of innovation in both countries. Clearly this would boost the private return to innovation, draw more resources into innovation and thereby stimulate long-run growth. In terms of the great-book metaphor, this would be like foreign and domestic innovators swapping tips on how to decode the blueprints more quickly. Since it is entirely possible that this exchange would make both groups into faster decoders, it would lower the cost of investing in innovation.

Putting the three effects together eliminates all the ambiguity. Opening trade between two previously closed, identical economies definitely raises growth rates in both countries.

As a note, we should mention the redundancy effect. In a model with more structure on the innovation technology, the exact ordering of intermediate goods development may lead to a substantial overlap in home and foreign varieties without international trade. Thus, an additional effect of trade on growth is to prevent redundant R&D efforts. The next subsection, however, argues that rivalry in R&D is not all bad for the rate of innovation.

Pro-competitive effects on innovators In the above discussion, import competition by itself was an anti-growth effect since it reduced the profitability of innovation. This does not match informal analyses that argue import competition boosts growth by disciplining domestic firms – forcing them to quicken their pace of innovation in order to match international competition. The critical distinction is between competition among innovations and competition among innovators.

To build understanding of the pro-growth effect of import competition, consider a static set-up. Suppose a firm has a monopoly on innovation in its industry. Say that its profits would be a positive number Π^N if it does not innovate and $\Pi^I - F$ if it does (F is the cost of the innovation). The profit-motivated firm innovates only if $\Pi^I - F$ is greater than Π^N. Note that $\Pi^I - F > \Pi^N > 0$. It may very well happen that even though innovation is profitable ($\Pi^I - F > 0$), the monopolist prefers to stay with the old technology and thus avoid the R&D costs. Contrast this with the other extreme assumption of free entry into innovation. In this instance, the firm does not have the luxury of comparing the innovation and no-innovation profits. If the incumbent does not innovate, someone else will. Thus innovation occurs whenever it is profitable.

It should be obvious that the threat of innovation by foreign firms will move the situation for the monopoly-innovator case towards the perfect-competition case. In this manner, import competition can spur innovation and growth. Note that the competition here is not among innovations; it is among innovators.

Several policy conclusions stem from this thinking.[5] In the modern world, innovation is done by established firms. Since there are many barriers to entry, innovation activity itself is marked by imperfect competition. The fact that competition or even the threat of competition from foreign firms changes the rate of innovation of existing firms is important. For instance, evidence that a particular liberalization has driven some innovative firms out of business cannot be used to argue that innovation in the country has slowed. It is entirely possible that import competition raises the rate of innovation of remaining firms enough to result in a higher economy-wide progress.

Trade in intellectual property rights, even without trade in goods, can have a similar pro-growth effect. That is, even if a domestic firm has a monopoly on domestic innovation, the ability of potential rivals to purchase foreign technology will put pressure to innovate faster. Since foreign technology often comes bundled with direct investment, foreign direct investment may stimulate productivity growth of domestic firms.

Innovation and international capital market integration   The oft-repeated sentence, 'Investment is the key to growth', suggests that in as far as trade arrangements affect financial markets, they may affect the rate of investment and therefore long-run output growth. In the simple Romer model described above, we introduce a wedge intended to be a reduced-form measure of capital market imperfection. If international integration ameliorates the capital market imperfections and thus the wedge, the result will be faster growth.

Take the example of an inefficient financial sector – inefficient in the sense that it creates a big spread between the return earned by savers and the cost of funds available to investors. The big spread might be the result of backwards banking technology, or it might simply result from monopoly power in the banking sector. Whatever the cause, competition from foreign financial firms has the potential to narrow the gap between interest rates facing savers and investors. Consequently reducing the intermediation wedge will raise the equilibrium quantity of resources devoted to innovation and the GDP growth rate.

Another example involves risk. Individual savers who cannot diversify their wealth are more risk-averse towards new investments than when they are well diversified. The point is that when one's wealth is spread out over many assets, the bad performance of some tends to be offset by the good performance of others. Thus diversification allows people, and banks, to be less concerned about the variability of any single investment; instead, they focus more on average returns. The net effect is to lower the risk premium demanded on investments. This translates into a lower cost of capital to innovators and a faster rate of innovation. International market opening, such as is going on in the East, may lower the cost of capital by lowering risk premiums. Moreover, allowing foreign financial firms to participate in the creation of capital markets can also spur investment in knowledge creation.

Growth effects of comparative advantage in R&D   A fundamental gain from trade stems from the fact that it allows countries to specialize in what they do well and trade for the rest. The same goes for innovation. If knowledge spills over internationally, then by allowing some countries to focus on innovation and others on production, trade may raise all growth rates. Clearly no small country could maintain a high standard of living if it had to be self-sufficient in innovation. Think of the fraction of national resources that would have to be diverted into research and development if every improved process and every new product had to be developed at home.

Poverty traps, take-offs and the big push   The growth rates of countries display striking and persistent differences.[6] Some countries seem to be on a high growth path for decades at a time, others limp along at 1 to 2 per cent per year and yet others seem to be struck with zero or even negative growth rates. This real-world fact has spawned several new growth models to account for it. The basic feature of all such models is multiple equilibrium growth paths. That is, there will be a stable equilibrium in which very few of the economy's primary resources are devoted to accumulation and one (or more) in which a good deal of resources are devoted to accumulation. The former is the poverty trap and the latter is the medium-growth track. A take-off happens when something occurs to shift the economy from the low-growth stable equilibrium to medium-growth equilibrium. The 'big push' made famous by Rosenstein-Rodan (1943), is one example of something that will shift the economy between growth paths.

The formalization of such ideas is generally pretty tricky. One convincing model of this phenomenon is Azariadis and Drazen (1990). The basic idea can be seen with a slight modification of the human capital model described above. Suppose the relationship between the growth of human capital and the amount of time spent in training or education depends on the initial level of human capital. In particular the higher the starting level of human capital, the more efficient the accumulation process. However, efficiency increases only up to a limit. The economics of this assumption is very appealing. The effectiveness of schooling and training in a country depends in part on the general level of education and skill that already exists. If everybody in a child's family already knows how to read, the child can easily get help at home. This makes the child's time at school more efficient. The same story applies to on-the-job training. If a worker's colleagues are all very highly skilled, the firm may find it much easier to train new workers and raise the skill level of the existing workforce. Of course there are limits to this sort of spillover and they may be most important at very low levels of skill.

This small modification can create a poverty trap. With a very low level of human capital, the cost of acquiring skills will be very high, so the return on investing in skills may be quite low. As a result, it may exceed people's willingness to forgo consumption today to invest in skill formation. In this case, there is no accumulation of human capital and therefore no growth. This is a stable equilibrium since if no one finds it worth while to invest, the situation will never change. Clearly a 'big push' would be needed to boost the initial level of human skill to lift the economy out of the zero-growth equilibrium, or poverty trap. Once the level got above a certain cut-off point, a 'take-off' would occur. Privately motivated investment in skills would continue. The result would be a rising rate of growth that converged at a steady level.

This process could be exactly reversed by the opposite of a 'big push', which we might call a 'big drag'. For instance, suppose a shock of some sort causes a big reduction in the level of human capital. The result could be a halt in the private accumulation of growth. In our simple model, skills never depreciate, so output does not actually fall. In the real world, however, a workforce may experience a declining skill level that would lead to negative output growth.

2.6 POLITICAL ECONOMY EFFECTS

Politics is almost always the driving force behind the creation of, and the success or failure of, regional integration initiatives. It is therefore worth considering political economy effects.

Political Economy Theory

Economics is labelled the dismal science because of its gloomy view of human nature. Economists take it as axiomatic that greed governs human behaviour and that the consumption of goods and services is the object of this greed. That is to say, people work, save and vote to maximize their own well-being. Economists also apply this dismal approach to politics, assuming that greed governs politicians' behaviour. However, it is assumed that power, rather than consumption, is the aim of policy-makers' greed. Power in this context is the probability of getting or staying elected. This is an oversimplification, but it is didactic. By ignoring many confounding considerations, one can get quickly to the core logic of political economy. With this in hand, complications can be introduced without swamping the analytic framework. The alternative approach of admitting from the start that everything affects everything can result in muddled reasoning.

Once might think that a government, which is concerned only with power and is elected by voters who care only about consumption, would choose policies that maximized the material welfare of the electorate. While this might be true in some utopian society, it is never so in the real world. The trouble is that any political system distorts politicians' view of the welfare of the electorate. The most important of these political distortions involve the costs that voters face in obtaining information about the nature and effect of policies, the cost of voting and the cost of organizing an effective political force. Because of these distortions, politicians' quest for political support is very frequently at odds with the maximization of national welfare. The political system is a prism through which the government looks when trying to judge how its actions will affect the economy.

This application of the dismal science to politics is called the endogenous policy approach, since it presumes that policy is endogenous to (that is, determined by) the economic system. Many prevalent traits of trade policy throughout the world can be understood with this approach. For instance, in virtually every country in the world, cheap imports are condemned. From the point of view of national welfare, this is ludicrous. Quite simply, consumers benefit and producers lose from cheaper imports, but the consumers' monetary gains outweigh the losses of the firms. All becomes clear when one realises that elected governments do not care about national welfare. They care about political support. Because consumers are rarely organized into an effective political force, and because domestic firms and labour unions usually are, the losses of consumers are heavily discounted by the body politic. This is the prism of politics.

Another very common feature of protection is accounted for by an extension of this reasoning. In nearly all industrialized countries, tariff rates follow a pattern that is called 'tariff escalation'. That is, tariffs on primary and intermediate products are generally lower than tariffs on consumers goods. The reason is that the 'consumers' of primary and intermediate goods are firms. For such goods, both domestic producers and domestic consumers are organized, so the government tends to grant less protection.

To apply this approach to trade arrangements, the pure-greed motivation of policy-makers needs to be amplified. We need to assume that certain policy choices are made for reasons that are determined outside the political-economic system.[7] It is these events that are the ultimate cause of the changes in trade arrangements and changes in more detailed policies that follow from the trade arrangement changes.

Asymmetric Lobbying Effects

The political economy forces driving this domino effect are strengthened by a peculiar tendency of special interest groups; they usually fight harder to avoid losses than they do to secure gains. In this light it is important to note that joining the regional integration in Europe would allow firms based in non-member countries to avoid damages as well as to win new commercial opportunities. While there may be many explanations for this asymmetric phenomenon, a simple economic interpretation based on unrecoverable investments ('sunk costs', in economists' jargon) seems to fit the facts. Entry into most industries and markets involves large unrecoverable investments in product development, training, brand name advertisement and production capacity. In such situations, established firms can earn positive profits without attracting new firms, but only in as far as these profits constitute a fair return on the entry investments. A more technical way of saying this is that sunk costs create quasi-rents.

Take it as given that a particular export industry has already incurred the sunk costs. Consider the industry's incentive to lobby. If a country's exporters obtain additional access to foreign markets, their sales and profits will typically rise. The increase in pure profit, however, will attract new competition, so the size of the gains must be limited. In the extreme, entry continues until all pure profit disappears. Correspondingly, the incentive to lobby for new export opportunities will be limited, and in the extreme will disappear altogether. That is to say, lobbying in a successful industry attracts entry that offsets the benefits of the lobbying. Next consider the reaction of an established firm to an unanticipated policy change (such as a trade liberalization) that would reduce its relative competitiveness and profitability. To be concrete, suppose that the change would wipe out half its quasi-rents, so it is earning a below-market return on its sunk capital. Since it would not actually be losing money, the firm would not shut down. More to the point, the firm should be willing to spend up to half its quasi-rents on lobbying for membership, if doing so would reverse the loss of relative competitiveness. Finally, as long as the lobbying merely restores profitability to a normal market rate, no new entrants would be attracted. Consequently, the benefit to lobbying is greater in industries that are in trouble than it is in industries that are doing well.[8] A more colloquial way of expressing this is that losers lobby harder than winners.

Political Economy of Trade Negotiations

Exports are good and imports are bad, according to mercantilistic thinking.[9] This reasoning has been thoroughly debunked and most policy-makers denounce it in public speech. Nevertheless, mercantilism is still the paramount force behind trade liberalization. Politically powerful export industries in search of new export markets compel their governments to negotiate trade deals. For the export industries, access to foreign markets is the prize. For the government, the political support of exporters is the reward. The cost, as far as politicians are concerned, consists of having to allow foreigners access to the domestic market. Reciprocal liberalization angers domestic import-competing industries. This is a cost to governing politicians since the import-competing industries may reduce political support for the government, or they may increase their support for the political opposition. Domestic consumers, who benefit directly from liberalization, carry little political weight since they are almost never organized.[10] In short, from the politicians' point of view exports are good and imports are bad.

This notion is commonly expressed in more sophisticated language. Political leaders often say that trade is good because trade creates jobs. This is utter nonsense from the medium-run or long-run economic perspective. An increase in exports may temporarily create more jobs when the economy is in a recession; in the long run, however, unemployment is determined by the structure of the labour market. By altering the allocation of a nation's resources, trade may change the types of jobs that are available. Trade does not, however, alter the number of jobs available in the long run. Political leaders are right in saying trade is good, but they point to the wrong reason. Trade is good because it improves the allocation of domestic resources and stimulates growth.

The Political Economy Juggernaut

Given the pre-eminence of this mercantilistic thinking among policy-makers, international negotiation based on an exchange of market access is a stroke of genius. In chasing the mirage of job creation, governments end up choosing policies that benefit their nations. More precisely, insisting that market access be exchanged reciprocally arrays the political power of exporters against the political power of protectionists. The result is a political economy juggernaut. Growth throughout the world makes access to foreign markets increasingly attractive. This leads exporters continually to push their governments to negotiate further market opening deals. As growth continues, fostered by international market opening, the juggernaut rolls forward, slowly but surely grinding down trade barriers.

This sort of effect requires that export interests be powerful politically and that they be interested in bargaining down foreign barriers. In subSaharan Africa, however, the bulk of exports are primary products for which trade barriers are already fairly low. Thus, there have been no powerful export lobbies challenging the political power of import competing industry.

Mercantilistic Law of the Jungle

The problem with this mechanism is that it may create a sort of law of the jungle. Since market access is the currency of exchange, countries with big markets can afford to buy lots of preferential access. Countries with small markets cannot, or worse yet, may be coerced into lopsided agreements. The genius of the GATT was to civilize this law of the jungle without subverting the political economy forces underpinning it. The trick was to strap the principle of unconditional most-favoured-nation (MFN) on to the back of the juggernaut.[11] The result is that pro-liberalization exporters in the big markets end up opening markets worldwide for all nations, large and small.

Political Economy of Hub-and-Spoke Bilateralism

Earlier, we argued that the political economy of trade negotiation is a happy coincidence of mistakes.[12] From a political perspective, exports are good and imports are bad. A more subtle expression of this idea is the trade is good because trade creates jobs. No matter how it is expressed, this idea is nonsense from the medium-run or long-run economic perspective. Be that as it may, the important fact is that this mistaken reasoning points governments in the right direction. It leads them to conduct trade negotiations based on an exchange of market access. Specifically, since exports are good and imports bad, if country A wants better access to country B's markets, then country A is expected to 'pay' for this market access by opening its own market to B's exports.[13]

Usually, the market opening that result from this mistaken reasoning is good for all nations involved. A drawback of this mechanism, however, is that it may create a sort of law of the jungle. That is, with market access as the currency of exchange, big countries are rich and small countries are poor. The rules of the GATT correct this imbalance with the principle of most favoured nations (MFN) treatment. However, when it comes to negotiating regional trade arrangements, MFN does not apply, so the law of the jungle may prevail.

Political economy forces created by an application of this law of the jungle support hub-and-spoke bilateralism. Take a country like the Czech Republic. On the pro-liberalization side, Czech exporters have a large interest in the EU market, but only a minor interest in the market of, say, Estonia. On the anti-liberalization side, Czech import-competing industries dislike imports whether they come for the EU, Estonia or elsewhere. Now consider the lineup of political forces inside the Czech Republic. Czech exporters are willing to fight quite hard for market opening with the big EU market. They are willing to fight much less hard for market opening with Estonia. In other words, there are strong political forces backing market opening with the 'hub' but very little support for market opening with other 'spokes'. Since Czech protectionists simply want to reduce import competition from any source, the protectionists are likely to win when it comes to blocking spoke–spoke liberalization, though they lose when it comes to hub–spoke liberalization.

An interesting add-on effect may occur if foreign investment from the hub is important in the spoke economies. To attract foreign investors, the spoke governments may promise protection from imports. Moreover, given a credible trade agreement with the hub, it is much easier for the spoke government to promise long-term protection against imports from other spoke economies. If this sort of pandering-for-investment protectionism becomes quite common, the spoke economies may end up 'Balkanized'. That is, foreign multinationals may be enticed into locating inefficiently small production facilities in each spoke economy. Having done this, the multinationals may become a new anti-liberalization force. Companies from the hub that have invested in inefficiently small facilities in several spoke economies may resist efforts to liberalize spoke–spoke trade. This may make the hub governments more reluctant to take any initiative in redressing hub-and-spoke bilateralism.

Why FTAs Between Developing Nations Usually Fail

If some idiosyncratic event stirs a great wave of enthusiasm for brother-hood among the spoke economies, politicians in these countries may sign agreements promising to open spoke–spoke trade. Yet once the headlines fade and the enthusiasm wanes, the drab politics of protectionism usually reasserts itself. Promises are broken, or never fulfilled, and the expected liberalization never appears. Moreover, since protectionist forces reappear in both spoke economies, the broken promises are generally accepted without protest. Note how different the situation is for spoke–hub trade arrangements. Exporters in both the hub and the spoke (but especially those in the spoke economies) care a good deal about access to each others' markets. Accordingly, exporters would raise their voices if promises were not kept. That is to say, the same sort of backsliding that is common in spoke–spoke agreements will not be tolerated in hub–spoke trade deals.

The 'Passing Parade' Pandering Problem

Some competition among SSA governments for foreign direct investment is probably a healthy thing for all parties. Inward investment is promoted by policies such as guaranteed profit remittances, property rights assurances (especially for intellectual property rights) and an absence of trade-related investment measures such as export requirements and local content rules. Although this is well understood, governments throughout the world often do not adopt such policies for domestic political reasons. Competition for foreign direct investment is an effective way of ensuring that they stick to FDI policies that are in their best interest anyway.

However, too much competition among SSA policy-makers could lead to an inferior, non-cooperative outcome. The basic problem can be exemplified with the so-called 'passing parade' parable. Imagine a crowd gathers to watch a parade. As the parade passes, people in the front stand on their toes to see better, thus forcing all those behind them also to stand on their toes. In the end, most see no better than before, but all have to stand on their toes.

In SSA, potential investors, foreign and domestic alike, have an incentive to ask for import protection as a condition for making their investments. However if all nations succumb to this pandering and erect trade barriers to attract investment or retain jobs, they could all end up 'standing on their toes' without results. This destructive competition could backfire. Each country's un-coordinated pandering to foreign investors could lead to trade barriers that lower the overall attractiveness of the region, thus resulting in less investment in each country.

2.7 CONCLUDING REMARKS

This chapter is meant to provide an accessable review of old and new theory of regional integration. Having read it, readers will understand that the literature is vast and occasionally very difficult. Despite the length of the chapter, I have not been able to deal with all of the theory. For instance, I have not touched on most of the traditional approaches to measuring the effects of a regional integration. I am not a specialist on subSaharan Africa, so this paper has made only superficial efforts at assessing the relevance of the various effects for African regional integration. It is my hope that this chapter will stimulate thinking among economists who know much more about Africa to apply and extend the relevant parts of the theory.

APPENDIX 2A: A FRAMEWORK FOR EMPIRICAL TRADE POLICY ANALYSIS

To introduce the framework, we must first provide a brief explanation of the economy's demand side and supply side.

The Demand Side

Consider a nation whose welfare can be summarized by a single utility function. This so-called representative consumer approach submerges many important considerations (especially concerning income distribution), but it does provide an easy way of summarizing the impact of regional integration on national welfare. This notional individual consumes all goods and receives all income. The traditional approach takes utility as dependent upon the consumption of goods. However, it is equally possible to show that the utility of maximizing consumers depends upon prices and total expenditure on consumption using the so-called indirect utility function. (In the usual budget-line and indifference curve diagram, it is clear that all changes in utility are caused by relative price changes and/or income changes.) As it turns out, it is easier to use this indirect utility function for analysing policy changes. The reason is that it is typically easier to observe price and income changes than changes in the consumption of individual goods.

More formally, we write the consumer's indirect utility function for a single period as: $V(p,n,E)$, where p and n are the domestic goods price vector and the vector of the number of varieties available in each sector. The symbol E stands for total expenditure for the current period.

The Supply Side

There are really three sets of questions that must be settled by the supply side: how much of which factors will be used to produce the various goods, how much will the factors be paid and what prices will firms charge for these goods. Of course in equilibrium the answers to these questions will be influenced by the demand side. The standard approach to answering these questions from the supply side is to start out with production functions and factor supplies. However, it is much more convenient to start with cost functions instead of production funtions. If firms are maximizing profits, then we can just as well represent that supply side with average cost functions. For any given level of output, the factor demands are chosen to minimize costs. This answers the first set of questions. Using the cost function and our knowledge of the behaviour of firms, we can answer the last set of questions, that is, what prices will be charged. For perfectly competitive firms, price equals marginal costs. For firms with market power, price is set so that marginal revenue equals marginal costs. To answer the middle set of questions – how much are factors paid – we need to know more about the structure of factor markets. If they are competitive, then factors are paid their marginal products. If they are not, then there will be a wedge between the marginal product and factor rewards. If the factors have market power (for example, unionized labour, or rationed capital), then factor prices exceed the marginal product. If the firms have monopsony power in factor markets, then the factor prices are below their marginal products.

More formally, production technology is given by a vector of average cost functions, c. For a typical firm in a typical sector (sector i), this is shown by the average cost function $c(w,x,v)$, where w is the vector of domestic factor prices, x is the firm's output and v is the vector of domestic factor supplies. The inclusion of x allows for scale economies and diseconomies at the firm level. The inclusion of v allows for technological spillovers of the kind used in endogenous growth models. We define factors broadly, so knowledge capital is considered a factor. Thus the inclusion of factor supplies in the average cost function allows for technological progress based on knowledge creation.

The Impact of Price and Expenditure Changes

Suppose, for the sake of argument, that we knew how a particular regional integration scheme would change consumer prices. To keep things really simple, suppose that only one consumer price fell. Using these data, it would be quite simple to pin down the welfare effects on our representative consumer. The price fall would boost welfare (consumer surplus would rise by an amount that is closely related to the initial level of consumption). However, the price change might very well affect income as well. In particular, it might lower government revenue (recall that the representative consumer receives all income in the economy including government revenue) and it might lower profits of domestic firms producing a competing product. The last consideration involves the difference between incomes and expenditure on consumption. Since the representative consumer is doing all the investing in this economy, the change in income may not be translated one-to-one into a change in consumption expenditure.

More formally, we can capture the impact of the price and income changes by totally differentiating the indirect utility function. Totally differentiating the indirect utility function and dividing through by the marginal utility of income in order to convert units from utils to real dollars, we have:

$$\frac{V}{P} / \frac{V}{E} = \Sigma_i\{(-C_i)dp_i + (\frac{V}{n_i} / \frac{V}{E})dn_i\} + dE$$

where C_i is domestic consumption of good i (capital C is consumer, small c is cost) and p_i is the domestic consumer price. The total differential of expenditure (that is, dE) is simply, $dY - dI$, where I is current investment and Y is current income. Income consists of factor payments and rents (domestic monopoly rents and trade-barrier rents that are captured domestically):

$$Y = \Sigma_j w_j v_j + \Sigma_i[\phi_i(p_i^w - p_i)M_i + (p_i - c_i)X_i]$$

where X_i, M_i and p_i^w are the domestic output (some of all firms' output in a sector), the imports and the world price of good i. The variable ϕ_i indicates how much of the rent from import barriers is captured domestically (rather than by foreigners). For sectors where foreigners get all the rent, or the barrier is of the cost-raising type so no one gets the rents, the corresponding elements are zero.

To capture all the effects of a regional integration on income, we totally differentiate income. The result, using Shepard's lemma to simplify (this states that the derivative of the cost function with respect to wages equals factor demands), is:

$$dY = \Sigma_i\{(p_i - c_i)dX_i + X_i dp_i - X_i(\frac{c_i}{x_1} dx_i + \frac{c_i}{v_1} dx_i$$
$$+ \phi_i(p_i - p_i^w)dM_1 + \phi_i M_i dp_i - \phi_i M_i dp_i^w + (p_i - p_i^w)Md\phi_i\}$$

where the possibility of ϕ changing reflects the possiblity of switching between various forms of protection. The summation over i indicates summation over all goods. The summation over j indicates summation over all factors.

Finally, we must combine the direct impact of price changes on utility with its indirect effect on income. This is accomplished using two facts: dE equals

$dY - dI$, and balanced trade implies investment must equal domestic savings. The result is:

$$dV/V_E = \Sigma_i\{(\phi - 1)Mdp - \phi Mdp^w + (p - p^w)Md\phi + \phi(p - p^w)dM$$
$$+ [(p - c)]dX + X(-c_x)dx\}$$
$$+ \Sigma_j\{X(-c_v)dv + (wdv - dI)\}$$

This corresponds to the various effects listed in equation (2.1).

Notes

1. Helpman and Krugman (1989) provide a very readable presentation of these and related issues. The presentation in this subsection draws heavily on their work.
2. MIT Press, 1991.
3. A little known article, Krugman (1988) later published in Krugman (1990), first outlined this approach. The basic modelling framework in Krugman (1988) comes from Sheilfer (1986).
4. Note that literary styles do not seem to be governed by a quality ladder. Modern economists rarely approach the eloquence of the great neoclassical economists.
5. See Baldwin (1992b) for a more thorough working through of the pro-growth effects of import competition.
6. This subsection draws heavily on Azariadis and Drazen (1990).
7. Sufficiently torturous reasoning can often be used to explain even these 'exogenous' choices. Since understanding, not intellectual purity, is the goal, certain choices are just taken as given.
8. See Baldwin (1992b) for details.
9. Mercantilism is an economic doctrine from the seventeenth and eighteenth centuries.
10. An important exception is when the consumer is industry. That is, when it comes to imported intermediate goods, the domestic consumers and domestic producers are both industries.
11. The principle of unconditional most favoured nation (MFN) treatment in the context of negotiation means that countries must open up their markets to all countries with MFN status when they offer to open it up to any country. Perhaps a better term would be non-discrimination.
12. This is just a convenient way of expressing the notion that the politics and economics of trade negotiations are mismatched. Governments are not mistaken, they are simply interested in maximizing political support rather than national welfare. The happy coincidence is that higher national welfare is a by-product of the political optimization.
13. Note that import liberalizations are called 'concessions' by trade negotiators. This is crazy from the point of view of national welfare, since the concession boosts the welfare of the conceding nation. Indeed it may help the conceding nation more than the country that wins the concession.

References

Aghion, P. and P. Howitt, (1990) 'A model of growth through creative destruction', NBER Working Paper no. 3223, *Econometrica*, 60 (2): 323–51.

Azariadis, C. and A. Drazen, (1990) 'Threshold Externalities in Economic Development', *Quarterly Journal of Economics*, 105 (2): 501–26.

Baldwin R. (1989) 'Growth Effects of 1992', *Economic Policy*, 9: 247–82.

—— (1992a) 'Measurable Dynamic Gains from Trade', *Journal of Political Economy*, 100 (1): 162–74.

—— (1992b) 'On the Growth Effects of Import Competiton', NBER Working Paper no. 4045.

—— and A. Venables (1993) 'International migration, capital mobility and transitional dynamics', *Economica*, 61 (243): 285–300.

Barro, R. (1991) 'Economic growth in a cross-section of countries', *Quarterly Journal of Economics*, 106: 407–43.

—— and X Sala-i-Martin (1990) 'Economic growth and convergence across the United States', NBER Working Paper no. 3419.

Brown, D. (1992) 'The impact of a NAFTA: applied general equilibrium models', *Brookings Papers on Economic Activity* (Washington, DC: Brookings Institute).

Caballero, R. and R. Lyons (1989) 'Increasing returns and imperfect competition in European industry', *European Economic Review*, 34 (4): 805–26.

Cohen, D. (1992) 'Tests of the "convergence hypothesis": a critical note', CEPR DP 691.

Commission of the European Communities (1988) 'The Economics of 1992', *European Economy*, no. 35 (known as the Cecchini Report).

Flam, H. (1992) 'Product markets and 1992: full integration, large gains?', *Journal of Economic Perspectives*, 6 (4): 7–30.

Foroutan, F. (1993) 'Regional Integration in Sub-Saharan Africa: Past Experience and Future Prospects', in J. de Melo and A. Panagariya (eds), *New Dimensions in Regional Integration* (Cambridge University Press).

Gasiorek, M., A. Smith, and T. Venables (1992) 'Completing the internal market in the EC: factor demands and comparative advantage', in L.A. Winters and A.J. Venables (eds), *European Integration: trade and industry* (Cambridge University Press).

Grossman, G. and E. Helpman (1991) *Innovation and Growth in the World Economy* (Cambridge, Mass.: MIT Press).

Haaland, J. and V. Norman (1992) 'Global Production Effects of European Integration', in L.A. Winters and A.J. Venables (eds), *European Integration: trade and industry* (Cambridge University Press).

Hall, R. (1989) 'Increasing returns: theory and measurement with industry data', Standford University mimeo.

Helpman, E. and P. Krugman (1989) *Trade Policy and Market Structure* (Cambridge, Mass.: MIT Press).

Herin, J. (1986) 'Rules of Origin and Differences Between Tariff Levels in EFTA and the EC', EFTA Occasional Paper no. 13.

Jaffe, A. (1986) 'Technology opportunity and spillovers of R&D: evidence from firms' patents, profits and market value', *American Economic Review*, 76 (5): 984–1001.

Krugman, P. (1988), 'Endogenous Innovation, International Trade and Growth', published in P. Krugman (ed.), *Rethinking International Trade* (Cambridge, Mass.: MIT Press).

—— (ed.) (1990) *Rethinking International Trade* (Cambridge, Mass.: MIT Press).

—— (1991) *Geography and Trade* (Cambridge, Mass.: MIT Press).

—— and A. Venables (1989) 'Integration and Competitiveness of Peripheral Industry', in C. Bliss and J. Braga de Macedo (eds), *Unity with Diversity in the European Community* (Cambridge University Press).

Lipsey, R. (1960) 'The Theory of Customs Unions: A General Survey', *Economic Journal*, 70: 496–513.

Lucas, R. (1988) 'On the mechanics of economic development', *Journal of Monetary Economics*, 22 (1): 3–42.

Mankiw, G., D. Romer and P. Weil 'A contribution to the empirics of economic growth', *Quarterly Journal of Economics*, 107 (2): 407–37.

Maddison, A. (1987) 'Growth and slowdown in advanced capitalist economies: techniques of quantitative assessment', *Journal of Economic Literature*, 25 (2): 649–98.

Romer, P. (1983) 'Dynamic competitive equilibria with externalities, increasing returns and unbounded growth', PhD thesis, University of Chicago.

—— (1986) 'Increasing returns and long run growth', *Journal of Political Economy*, 94 (5): 1002–37.

—— (1987) 'Crazy Explanations for the Productivity Slowdown', *NBER Macroeconomic Annual* (Cambridge, Mass.: MIT Press) pp. 163–202.

—— (1990) 'Endogenous Technological Change' *Journal of Political Economy*, 98 (5): 571–1102.

Rosenstein-Rodan, P. (1943) 'Problems of Industrialization of Eastern and Southeastern Europe', *Economic Journal*, 53: 202–11.

Schumpeter, J. (1942) *Capitalism, Socialism and Democracy* (New York: Harper).

Sheilfer, A. (1986) 'Implementation Cycles', *Journal of Political Economy*, 94 (6): 1163–90.

—— M.A.M. Smith, T. Venables and M. Gasiorek (1992) '1992: Trade and Welfare – A general equilibrium model', CEPR discussion paper.

Solow, R. (1956) 'A contribution to the theory of economic growth', *Quarterly Journal of Economics*, 70: 65–94.

Venables, A. and M.A.M. Smith (1988) 'Completing the Internal Market in the European Community: Some Industry Simulations', *European Economic Review*, 32: 1501–25.

3 Macroeconomic Harmonization, Trade Reform, and Regional Trade in SubSaharan Africa

Stephen A. O'Connell

3.1 INTRODUCTION[1]

This chapter explores the influence of the macroeconomic policy environment on African international trade. The topic is broad, and the emphasis is on those aspects that intersect the central themes of the joint AERC/CEPR project – trade reform and regional integration. This chapter has three general objectives. The first is to assist in the identification and interpretation of important trade liberalization episodes by providing an analytical account of the linkages between exchange rate policy, fiscal policy and trade policy in African countries. The second is to provide basic background on African monetary integration and its linkages with international trade. The experience with monetary integration is relevant not only as a source of comparative material – has monetary integration been more or less successful than trade integration, and why? – but also as a key dimension of the macroeconomic policy environment that has influenced trade policy, whether towards regional or external partners. The final objective is to assess the impact on trade reform and regional trade of various forms of macroeconomic 'harmonization' that are less formal or less thorough than exchange rate or currency union. These include the general drift towards more flexible exchange rates or the co-ordination of national pricing policies on extra-African trade.

The chapter is lengthy and a road map may be useful. Section 3.2 provides an analytical framework for thinking about the relationships between exchange rate policy, fiscal policy and trade policy in African countries. The main thrust of this section is to emphasize the close links between trade policy and other aspects of macroeconomic policy in SSA. The section serves as background for the remaining discussion and can be skimmed or skipped altogether by readers familiar with the literature in this area. Section 3.3 provides an overview of the African experience with formal monetary integration and outlines the relationship between regional groupings aimed at monetary co-operation and groupings aimed primarily at regional trade promotion. Section 3.4 then considers the implications for trade reform of macroeconomic harmonization achieved in a piecemeal fashion, through country-by-country efforts at stabilization or structural adjustment or through institutions like regional clearing mechanisms that impose little discipline on members. Section 3.5 briefly examines the evidence on African trade patterns, both external and regional, and their relationship with the macroeconomic environment and with monetary integration in particular. Section 3.6 concludes the chapter with a summary of the main points.

3.2   CONVERTIBILITY, PROTECTION, AND FISCAL POLICY

Of all the forms of economic integration, joint action to promote regional trade has attracted the most attention in SSA in the period since independence. Despite a proliferation of formal agreements for regional trade liberalization, however, intra-African trade remains small as a share of the total trade of African countries and may even be smaller than it was around the time of independence (Berg, 1985; and Foroutan, 1993).

Among the most often cited constraints to greater intra-African trade is the inhospitable macroeconomic environment associated with overvalued exchange rates and non-convertible currencies (Berg, 1988; and Ariyo and Raheem, 1991). In drawing an analytical framework for studying the macroeconomic origins of non-convertibility and its implications for trade policy, whether towards regional or external partners, there are two main points to make. The first is that trade openness can be undercut not only by import-substituting industrialization but also by the subordination of trade policy to fiscal or external balance considerations. This has important implications for trade liberalization, since if trade restrictions or exchange controls are macroeconomically motivated, a trade liberalization that is pursued on efficiency grounds may fail in the absence of complementary macroeconomic policy adjustments. The second point is that a desire to protect international reserves leads to a strong bias towards quantitative import restrictions in preference to import tariffs; outside of the CFA zone, such restrictions were often imposed through foreign exchange rationing. The extension of exchange controls to the current account blurs the distinction between exchange rate policy and trade policy, with the result that policy changes like exchange rate unification may have more powerful implications for the stance of trade policy than does a liberalization of tariff rates.

Much of what appears here will be familiar (see for example Bevan *et al.*, 1990; Collier, 1989; Corden, 1987 and 1993; Khan and Lizondo, 1987; and Kiguel and O'Connell, 1995). The objective is to give a reasonably self-contained account that brings together various strands of the literature and which can serve as background for the rest of the chapter.[2]

The appendix contains a simple analytical model of a small open economy, drawing on Khan and Lizondo (1987). The real side uses the 1–2–3 structure of Devarajan *et al.* (1993), in which imports and domestic goods are consumed and exports and domestic goods are produced. Private spending is a constant-velocity function of financial wealth, and when foreign assets are available the demand for domestic money depends on portfolio choice between domestic and foreign assets and is determined by the differential return on these assets. Long-run equilibrium is characterized by the simultaneous achievement of internal balance, external balance and 'asset balance', the latter being a state in which total private financial wealth is constant. Short-run dynamics come from slow adjustment of domestic wages and prices, gradual changes in money supply from external imbalances or fiscal deficits and, in the presence of a foreign exchange black market, gradual changes in foreign asset holdings through illegal trade.

Internal Balance, External Balance and Asset Balance

Using M, X and D to denote imports, exports, and domestic goods, respectively, Figure 3.1 plots the real exchange rate for exports, $e \equiv P_D/P_X$, against real money balances, $h \equiv H/P_X$, in a version of the familiar internal balance/external balance diagram. The real exchange rate summarizes the relative incentives for producing for the domestic and foreign markets, while real money balances tie down private spending (assume for the present that the private sector holds no foreign assets).

The internal balance schedule (IB) is the set of points at which the labour market clears at full employment and the market for domestic goods (where output is demand-determined) also clears. Under the simplifying assumption of constant expenditure shares, IB takes the form:

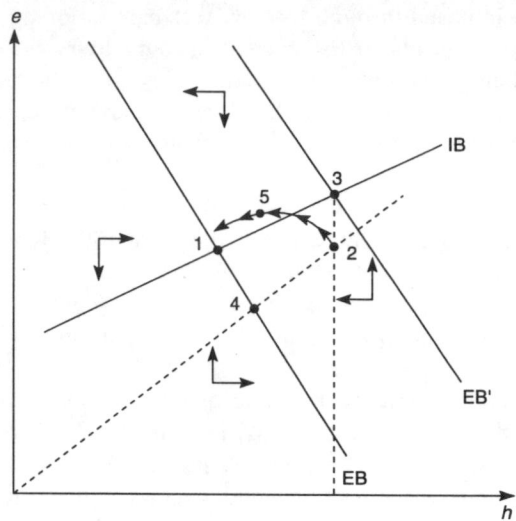

Note: A tightening in the stance of trade policy shifts EB outwards to EB'.

Figure 3.1   Trade policy for external balance

$$D_D(e, h) + G_D = S_D(e) \qquad (3.1)$$
$$\;\;\;-\;\;+\qquad\qquad\;+$$

where D_D and G_D are the private and government demands for domestic goods. S_D is the supply of domestic goods that would prevail if all labour not employed in the export sector were absorbed in the domestic goods sector.[3] The signs of partial derivatives are indicated below the equation. IB is upward-sloping because a rise in real balances increases spending on domestic goods, requiring a real appreciation to shift labour into the production of domestic goods. To the right of IB, real wealth (and thus real spending) is greater than the full-employment level, given the real exchange rate. Output is unsustainably high and upward pressure on wages feeds through to the price of domestic goods and pushes up the real exchange rate. To the left of IB, real spending is low and wages and the real exchange rate are falling due to under-employment. Under the assumption of constant expenditure shares, IB is flatter than a ray from the origin, implying that a nominal devaluation (which is a move inward along such a ray) is expansionary in the short run.[4] With rapidly adjusting domestic wages and prices, the economy remains near the IB schedule.

The external balance schedule (EB) is the set of points along which the current account (net of foreign grants) is zero. Since there are no capital flows, this is also the schedule along which international reserves are fixed. EB takes the form:

$$\tau^*[D_M(\theta\tau^*, h) + G_M - a_M] = S_X(e) \qquad (3.2)$$
$$\underset{-}{}\ \underset{+}{}$$

where D_M, G_M, a_M and $\tau^* \equiv P_M^*/P_X^*$ are the private and government demands for imports, foreign assistance measured in terms of imports and the world terms of trade, respectively, and θ is the 'stance of trade policy', defined below. EB is downward-sloping because a rise in real balances increases imports and requires a real depreciation to restore the trade balance. To the right of EB, the balance of payments is in deficit and international reserves are falling; to the left, it is in surplus and reserves are rising. These changes in reserves feed through to domestic money stock through the balance sheet of the central bank. If the central bank does not intervene and allows the exchange rate to float freely, the economy remains on EB continuously.

A third and final balance schedule operates in the background in Figure 3.1. This is the asset balance (AB) schedule, which gives the set of points along which the private stock of wealth is not changing. Since real money balances change either through fiscal deficits (which expand domestic credit) or through current account surpluses (which add to international reserves), the AB schedule takes the form:

$$d - a - \pi_E{}^h - \left(\frac{E}{P_x}\right)\dot{r}^* \qquad (3.3)$$

where d and a are the real fiscal deficit excluding foreign grants and foreign grants, both measured in terms of exports ($d \equiv D/P_X$, where D is the deficit in domestic currency terms, and $a \equiv EP_M^*a_M/P_X$), π_E is the rate of crawl of the nominal exchange rate, and $\dot{r}^*$ is the net accumulation of international reserves measured in foreign exchange.[5] Asset balance therefore holds when the government's domestic financing requirement is fully covered by the inflation tax and the depletion of international reserves. Since a rise in real balances reduces the growth of real money supply through both channels, real balances are falling to the right of AB and rising to the left.

We begin by assuming that the government pegs the exchange rate and maintains a zero domestic borrowing requirement. The AB schedule is then *identical* to the EB schedule, and we can proceed in the familiar internal balance/external balance framework.

Protection for External Balance

The relative price that influences the private demand for imports in the external balance schedule (eq. (3.2)) is the domestic price of imports in terms of exports, $P_M/P_X \equiv \theta\tau^*$. This relative price has two components. One is τ^*, which is exogenous since the country is small in world markets. The other is the 'relative protection coefficient', θ, which summarizes the stance of trade policy and is very much under the control of policy. Defining q as the implicit tariff applying to imports and t_x as the export tax rate, θ is given by:[6]

$$\theta \equiv \frac{P_M/EP_M^*}{P_x/EP_M^*} = \frac{1+q}{1-t_x} \tag{3.4}$$

For the moment, assume that import controls are limited to *ad valorem* tariffs, so that q is equal to the import tariff rate t_M. The stance of trade policy is therefore fixed and equal to $\theta = (1 + t_M)/(1 - t_x)$. In this case, eqs (3.1) and (3.2) uniquely determine the levels of real money balances and real exchange rate for exports that are consistent with internal and external balance. In Figure 3.1, long-run equilibrium holds at point 1.

Suppose now that a rise in the money supply moves the economy momentarily to a point like 2, where there is over-employment and a payments deficit. There is a standard menu of policy choices for restoring long-run equilibrium starting at point 2. One approach is to solicit an increase in aid or commercial capital inflows (the latter would enter the EB schedule symmetrically with aid). This shifts the EB schedule upwards, supporting higher real wealth and a more appreciated real exchange rate at a point like 3. The external inflow 'validates' the higher level of private spending, but does so by drawing down the goodwill of external donors or future generations; it is likely to be a temporary solution at best. Another approach is to float the exchange rate. The nominal exchange rate does not enter the IB or EB schedules, so the long-run equilibrium is invariant to the exchange rate regime (provided the exchange rate is unified). But the money supply and price of domestic goods are predetermined in the short run, so changes in the level of the nominal exchange rate have the effect of moving both e and h inward along a ray from the origin. An immediate depreciation therefore takes us to point 4 and then along EB to 1 as labour market pressures drive wages up. This is an inflationary adjustment pattern: at point 1 all prices and wages will have increased in proportion to the original increase in nominal money.

The authorities can also accomplish a major portion of the adjustment through a one-shot devaluation (to point 4 or thereabouts). Resistance to devaluation was deeply imbedded in African policy-making by the late 1960s, however. The model gives some credence to inaction in the face of elasticity pessimism and other beliefs (or political constraints) variously expressed by policy-makers:

(1) if export supply and import demand elasticities are low (economies are 'rigid'), the IB schedule is steep and devaluation is more likely to be contractionary on impact; and
(2) a devaluation reduces real wages, potentially provoking political unrest and cost-push inflation (given the stance of trade policy, e is directly proportional to the real consumption wage here[7]).

If external financing and devaluation are ruled out and convertibility is maintained, the central bank starts to lose reserves at point 2. Private wealth and spending fall, and adjustment takes place automatically along a trajectory like the one through point 5, ending at point 1. The adjustment pattern involves a contractionary phase during which the the real exchange rate first appreciates under the pressure of excess demand and then depreciates as unemployment emerges and domestic prices fall; and it requires policy-makers to finance a temporary balance of payments deficit. While the output loss from contraction is small when wages and prices are highly flexible, the international evidence (ranging from the British experience in the inter-war years to the protracted recessions in the UMOA countries starting in the early 1980s and the BEAC countries starting in the mid 1980s) suggests that the transition periods associated with real exchange rate over-valuation can be extended and difficult. A central bank that is politically constrained – or simply illiquid – may seek a fourth option.

The fourth option (relative to financing, devaluation or contraction) is to impose what Bevan *et al.* (1990) call an 'endogenous trade policy'. By tilting the overall structure of protection towards the import sector – raising θ – the government can improve the long-run trade balance at any level of private spending, shifting the EB schedule up until it goes through point 3.[8] The pressure of over-employment at point 2 then drives up wages and the prices of domestic goods, leading to an adjustment from point 2 to a new long-run equilibrium at point 3. To summarize:

*Point 1:   A tightening of trade restrictions can substitute for external
financing, devaluation or domestic contraction in resolving a monetary
disequilibrium associated with excessive real balances. This adjustment
pattern permanently lowers trade volumes relative to the other options.*

Since the current account must be balanced in the long run, trade volumes decline on both the import and export side (the decline in export
volume follows from the real appreciation in Figure 3.1). The financing option can protect import volumes, but this effect is temporary
unless the financing comes as a permanent increase in aid.[9]

Figure 3.2 shows the analysis in Figure 3.1 in a general equilibrium
diagram, under the assumptions that government spending and aid are
zero.[10] As with any departure from free trade in an otherwise non-
distorted small open economy, the endogenous trade policy lowers the
steady-state welfare of the private sector. From a political economy
viewpoint, this efficiency loss may well exert only a limited impact on
policy formation. The two diagrams are easily manipulated to 'rationalize'
a leaning towards endogenous trade policy in the face of other sources
of external balance problem, like a collapse in the terms of trade.

The necessary condition for a point like 3 to be reached through
trade policy alone is that the effective protection of imports increases
relative to that of exports. By Lerner symmetry, this can be accomplished either through an increase in import protection or through an
increase in export taxation, or both. Whatever the combination of trade
policies leading to the increase in θ, trade volumes are lower at point
3 than they are at point 1, both on the export side and on the import
side. Real balances are permanently higher, measured in terms of exports; but they are lower in terms of the domestic price level (this real
balance effect is essential in rendering the new equilibrium sustainable). The conclusion is straightforward: the refusal to devalue in the
face of persistently expansionary macroeconomic policy leads to a
combination of real appreciation and increased trade restrictions, and
to a decline in trade volumes.

Since it is only θ that enters the balance schedules (and not t_M, q or
t_X separately), it makes no difference for the long-run equilibrium whether
the required tightening of trade policy is achieved through taxes or
quantitative restrictions on trade, or whether these policies work through
the import or export side. All forms of trade restriction are perfect
substitutes in their long-run effects on external balance. These policies
have very different effects in the short run, however. First of all, an
increase in import protection improves the balance of payments, while

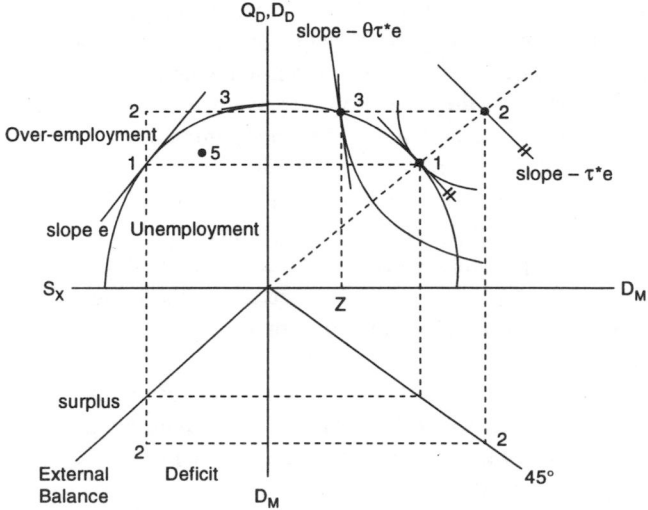

Note: An import quota of size Z avoids contractionary adjustment through point 5.

Figure 3.2   General equilibrium effects of endogenous trade policy

an increase in export taxes, which shifts the temporary equilibrium outwards on a ray from the origin, worsens it. It is not surprising, therefore, that when trade policy is mobilized for external balance purposes, the instruments of choice are import restrictions (Corden, 1993). Second, quantitative restrictions are superior to taxes for insulating reserves from shocks to foreign prices or speculative behaviour by the private sector. The need to protect international reserves therefore leads to a strong bias in favour of *convertibility restrictions* on the current account, in the form of import quotas or foreign exchange rationing. Under convertibility restrictions, the implicit tariff q adjusts *automatically* to the excess demand for imports, leaving less uncertainty about the central bank's foreign exchange outlays. In the limit, reserve losses can be kept to zero along the entire adjustment path by directly rationing foreign exchange for imports. In this case, dynamic adjustment takes place vertically from point 2 to point 3 in Figure 1, with the EB schedule shifting up smoothly in response to the tightening import quota implied by declining exports.

The scenario depicted here was played out in many African coun tries in the period from 1970 to 1985. As we shall see, trade policy in the CFA countries was subordinated to external balance less than in the rest of Africa. The arrangements of the zone made it less likely that countries would develop serious imbalances in the first place; but equally importantly, they ruled out the use of exchange controls, which became a major instrument for the endogenization of trade policy in much of the rest of Africa.

It is important to emphasize that the stance of trade policy, as summarized by θ, is entirely determined by convertibility restrictions when they are binding. Thus while tariffs may exist at point 1, they are infra-marginal at point 3. The import control regime is the primary determinant of the level of effective protection:

Point 2:   When trade controls are motivated by balance of payments considerations, the trade policy stance is determined by exchange controls and other quantitative restrictions at the margin, rather than by import tariffs and export taxes.

This implies that measures of openness that ignore the tightness of the exchange control regime – such as nominal or effective tariffs, or the share of commodities covered by import licensing requirements – may be highly misleading when the stance of trade policy is driven by considerations of external balance.

Protection for Fiscal Balance

Developing countries depend on trade taxes for revenue to a significantly higher degree than do developed countries (Gemmel, 1993 and Greenaway and Milner, 1991); this dependence is even higher on average in SSA than in other low-income developing countries. Other things being equal, a heavy reliance on trade taxes produces a more closed economy, and a more appreciated real exchange rate for exports, than if other revenue sources were used:

Point 3:   If convertibility restrictions are not binding, a substitution of trade taxes for lump-sum taxes tightens the stance of trade policy (that is, raises θ), appreciates the real exchange rate for exports, and lowers trade volumes.

The tax substitution described here is precisely the policy combination illustrated in the shift from point 1 to point 3 in Figures 3.1 and 3.2 (since there the deficit was held fixed).

The Revenue Motive and the Structure of Trade Intervention

When the revenue motive is important, the structure of trade intervention will be substantially influenced by the different revenue potency
of alternative trade policy instruments. There are three implications
here. First, relatively low costs of collection and enforcement made
the non-diversified primary export sectors in SSA an important source
of fiscal revenue in the colonial period. This role was expanded in the
1960s as newly independent governments sought revenue to meet an
expanded development agenda (Bates, 1981). But export taxes worsen
the balance of payments in the short run. If this effect is not neutral-
ized by devaluations of the official exchange rate, the desire to protect
reserves may produce a complementarity between export taxes and
quantitative import restrictions. The expansion of export taxes starting
in the mid-1960s thus provided an independent impetus to the subsequent proliferation of quantitative restrictions on the import side. This
is particularly true outside of the CFA zone, where central banks faced
a tight balance of payments constraint.

Second, quantitative restrictions reduce trade tax revenues, while trade
taxes may increase them. In contrast with the external balance motive
for protection, therefore, the fiscal motive creates a distinction between taxes and quantitative restrictions even in the long run. To push
this a bit further, let $\theta_R \equiv (1 + t_M)/(1 - t_X)$ be the trade policy term
that is relevant for revenue. The overall stance of trade policy, $\theta =
(1 + q)/(1 - t_X)$, exceeds θ_R whenever convertibility restrictions are
binding. Disaggregating the fiscal deficit into its spending and revenue
components, using t to denote revenue from sources other than trade
taxes, and setting a to zero, the fiscal deficit can be written (see the
appendix):

$$d = eG_D - t - \theta_R \tau^* D_M(\theta \tau^*, h) - (\frac{t_x}{1 - t_x}) \dot{r}, \quad \theta_R \leq \theta \quad (3.5)$$

In a long-run equilibrium (where $\dot{r}^* = 0$), trade taxes enter only through
the third term on the right-hand side. When convertiblity restrictions
are not binding $(\theta = \theta_R)$, this term generates a 'Laffer curve' along
which a tightening of trade policy increases the revenue yield from
any volume of imports and exports, but also reduces the tax base by
reducing trade volumes.[11] Revenue therefore rises with an increase in
θ_R if and only if the price elasticity of demand for imports is below
unity. When convertibility restrictions are binding, so that $\theta > \theta_R$, a

rise in trade taxes has *no* effect on domestic relative prices and trade volumes. Revenue unambiguously rises with higher trade taxes, and there is no effect on external balance since θ is unchanged. A tightening of binding quantitative restrictions, in contrast, always reduces revenue by shrinking the tax base.

Finally, note that a high degree of existing dependence on trade taxes may substantially reduce the revenue yield of further increases, even before the yield becomes negative on the margin. This imposes a limit on the use of trade taxes for fiscal purposes that is additional to the microeconomic deadweight losses associated with restricting trade in a small economy.

Multiple Exchange Rate Equivalencies

Though we have been thinking of t_M and t_X as tax rates, there is a tight equivalence between trade taxes and departures from unified nominal exchange rates for current account transactions. A given stance of trade policy can be obtained either through trade interventions or through the assignment of different exchange rates to different categories of transaction. Thus a system of multiple exchange rates in which foreign exchange is purchased from exporters at a lower price than it is sold to importers amounts to a combination of import tariff and export tax. The equivalence extends to the consolidated fiscal accounts as well – and therefore to the AB schedule – once one includes the quasi-fiscal gains or losses from central bank intervention at multiple exchange rates.

The most common form of multiple exchange rate regime in SSA has been a black market system in which the bulk of export transactions and a subset of import transactions are assigned to an officially managed exchange rate (or set of rates), while all remaining transactions are (implicitly) assigned to a freely-floating illegal parallel rate. In such a system the central bank typically intervenes only at the official exchange rate(s), if at all; more typically, it runs an endogenous trade policy in which officially remitted export proceeds are devoted first to government import requirements and then, as a residual, to private sector imports. The equivalencies discussed here continue to hold, in the sense that relative to the counter-factual of unified exchange rates, the gap between the parallel and official exchange rates generates both relative price effects that alter the stance of trade policy and revenue effects that alter the AB schedule.

Illegal Trade and the Stance of Trade Policy

Trade restrictions drive a wedge between the domestic and international prices of traded goods, and in doing so provide incentives for illegal trade (Bhagwati and Hansen, 1973 and Pitt, 1981). Illegal trade has three main impacts: it liberalizes the trade regime, shifts income from the public to the private sector, and wastes resources. The focus here is on the first two effects.[12]

The first effect of illegal trade is to liberalize the trade regime.[13] If the costs of illegal trade were zero, trade taxes and convertibility restrictions would be completely ineffective and free trade would prevail regardless of the official stance of trade policy. Since illegal trade is costly, the liberalization it implies is always incomplete. The existence of such trade none the less forces a distinction between the 'official' stance of trade policy – the value of θ that would prevail if all trade restrictions were perfectly enforced – and the 'actual' stance, which will typically be more liberal.

The tendency of illegal trade to liberalize the actual stance of trade policy is illustrated by two of the centrally important forms of illegal trade in SSA: under-invoicing to avoid trade taxes, and smuggling or under-invoicing to supply the domestic market for quota-constrained imports. Pitt (1981) shows that if perfectly competitive importers and exporters are able to reduce their trade tax bills by under-invoicing, these tax savings will be passed on to domestic producers and consumers in the form of a 'price disparity' on both goods. The domestic price of imports will be below the tariff-inclusive world price, and the domestic price of exports will be above the net-of-tax world price; θ falls relative to its official value. Alternatively, suppose that import smuggling or under-invoicing is the result of convertibility restrictions that create a quota rent on imports in the domestic market. The inflow of additional imports will drive down the quota rent in the same way as the relaxation of a perfectly enforced quota would do. In an equilibrium with balanced (legal and illegal) trade: (1) total imports and exports will be higher; and (2) the actual stance of trade policy (as summarized by θ) will more liberal, than if enforcement were perfect (O'Connell, 1991).

Illegal trade therefore creates a slippage between trade policy instruments and trade policy effects. However, as long as illegal trade takes place subject to increasing marginal costs, changes in tariffs and convertibility restrictions retain some influence over the actual stance of trade policy:

Point 4:   *When there is illegal trade, the actual stance of trade policy is more liberal than the official stance. As long as illegal trade is subject to increasing marginal costs, however, a tightening of the official stance results in a tightening of the actual stance.*

In the absence of revenue effects, therefore, illegal trade weakens but does not remove the role of trade restrictions in securing external balance. In terms of the IB and EB schedules, illegal trade operates entirely in the background, creating a slippage between changes in trade policy instruments and changes in the actual stance of trade policy. Higher tariff and/or export tax rates, or tighter import quotas, are required to achieve the same real exchange rate for exports and support the same level of real spending. But a tightening of trade restrictions still shifts EB upwards and can substitute for fiscal adjustment or other more painful measures.

Revenue effects can be substantial, however, and may seriously undercut the use of trade policy for external balance. The problem is that because trade tax revenue is only collected on *official* trade flows, illegal trade tends to increase the elasticity of the trade tax base to changes in θ. Increases in θ push a larger *share* of total trade underground, thereby lowering official trade volumes by more than they lower actual trade volumes. Revenues therefore fall by more when convertibility restrictions are tightened; when such restrictions are not binding, revenue-maximizing tariff and export tax rates are lower than they would otherwise be, making it more likely that a rise in these rates will reduce revenue. These effects are likely to be larger in the long run than the short run, since increases in illegal trade require investment in information, clandestine relationships and transport technology.

This brief discussion of illegal trade suggests a variety of cautions for interpreting developments in the external sector. The first is that standard measures of the official stance of trade policy, such as nominal tariff rates, are imperfect proxies for the actual policy stance even in the absence of quantitative restrictions. The second is that changes in the enforcement effort can alter the actual stance of trade policy even with no change in the official stance. The third is that illegal trade may produce a marked disparity between overall trade volumes and officially measured trade volumes. This may not be damaging for empirical work (for example, estimating aggregate export supply functions) if the official share of overall trade is constant. It will produce misleading results, however, if policy changes that alter the share are not held constant. The export supply response to real exchange changes, for example, will tend to be overestimated if the regression leaves out a measure of the incentives for export smuggling. Part of the apparent price response of official exports will in fact represent an 'officialization' of previously smuggled exports, rather than a true aggregate export response. (Kamin 1993 provides evidence.)

Fiscal Deficits, Inflation and Macroeconomic Consistency

We have now seen that there may be strong pressures to mobilize trade policy for fiscal or external balance, with adverse effects on trade volumes. In Figures 3.1 and 3.2, the external balance problem was essentially short-run in nature; what motivated trade restrictions was an unwillingness either to lose a finite amount of reserves and sustain a period of unemployment, or to implement a one-shot devaluation. This section endogenizes the money supply and examines the external balance problem that emerges in a managed exchange rate regime when the authorities run large fiscal deficits while attempting to retain a 'nominal anchor' role for the official exchange rate. The basic point is apparent in the asset balance schedule (Eq.(3.3)). When the private sector is in asset equilibrium, the portion of the fiscal deficit (net of grants) that is not financed by the inflation tax will be financed by a depletion of international reserves *on a continuing basis*. The unsustainability of such a situation implies a tight consistency requirement between the exchange rate regime and the fiscal deficit: if the domestic financing requirement is positive and convertibility is to be maintained, the exchange rate must depreciate rapidly enough to reconcile a stable real exchange rate with a money growth rate – and accompanying inflation rate – sufficient to finance the fiscal deficit via the inflation tax.[14]

The consistency requirement is illustrated in Figure 3.3, which assumes that both the fiscal deficit (net of grants) and the rate of crawl of the exchange rate are constant and positive (the analysis also goes through with zero inflation; see Khan and Lizondo, 1987). With a positive rate of crawl the AB schedule becomes steeper than EB; the two schedules cross at point 1, where the inflation tax exactly covers the deficit. Now consider a cut in lump-sum taxes that raises the fiscal deficit, shifting the AB schedules to the right through a point like 2. At point 1, real balances begin to rise at the rate of the fiscal deficit. If convertibility is maintained, the balance of payments goes into deficit, reducing the rate of money growth, which none the less remains positive because

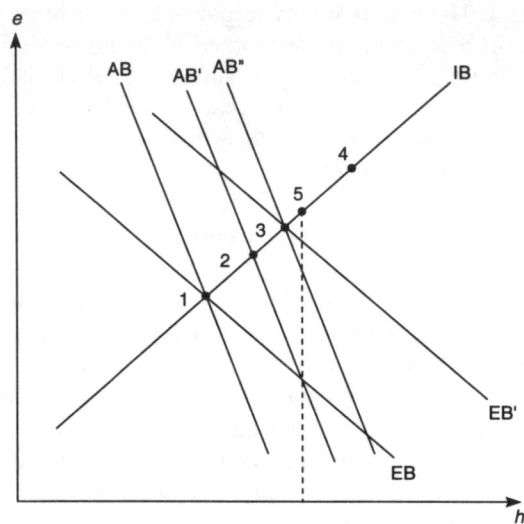

Note: A tightening of trade policy with unchanged fiscal deficit restores equilibrium at point 5. With a favorable revenue effect, equilibrium is at point 3.

Figure 3.3   Trade controls and macroeonomic consistency

of the fiscal deficit. Adjustment leads eventually to point 2, where real balances are stationary but international reserves are falling at the rate of the fiscal deficit.

The situation at point 2 is unsustainable, and some mechanism for closing the gap between the AB and EB schedules is required to restore macroeconomic consistency. A fiscal adjustment would clearly do the job; as pointed out by Khan and Lizondo (1987), this can take the form of an increase in lump-sum taxes or a cut in government spending either on domestic goods or on imports. With the exception of the cut in G_M, which leaves the real exchange rate unchanged, these policies depreciate the real exchange rate (and therefore increase trade volumes) as part of the adjustment. Another policy is to float the exchange rate. In this case, the short-run equilibrium jumps immediately to the EB schedule and remains there, and the long-run equilibrium at point 1 is obtained through an endogenous increase in inflation tax revenue that shifts AB to the left. The authorities must therefore accept a permanent rise in inflation. An alternative with the same long-run properties is to retain a managed exchange rate but increase the rate of crawl of the exchange rate to the long-run equilibrium rate in the floating system. As indicated in Figure 3.3, with positive inflation the AB schedule becomes steeper than EB.

As before, however, fiscal adjustment is painful, and governments in SSA were reluctant to abandon a potentially valuable nominal anchor by floating the exchange rate or increasing its rate of crawl. We briefly consider three alternatives here:

Point 5: *Trade taxes, quantitative import restrictions and capital controls are all capable, under certain conditions, of resolving otherwise inconsistent choices of fiscal policy and the rate of crawl of the exchange rate.*

Point 5 is deliberately vague because it would take a separate paper to work out the full set of conditions, including the forward-looking dynamics that enter through portfolio choice. A valuable start in this direction appears in Bevan *et al.* (1990, appendix to ch. 2), and this is an interesting area for further work. The point is simply that the role of trade restrictions and exchange controls in avoiding unpalatable *short-run* adjustment problems is not necessarily undercut when the fundamental adjustment problem is *long-run* in nature. To see this, consider the impact of the three alternative policies on the balance schedules.

The impact of an increase in trade taxes depends on whether convertibility restrictions are binding or not. If they are not, a rise in θ_R improves the trade balance and shifts both AB and EB upwards by equal amounts. As long as the economy is on the good side of the trade tax Laffer curve, fiscal revenues rise, and the AB curve falls back down to some degree. The two curves meet at a new long-run equilibrium at a point like 3. If convertibility restrictions *are* binding, trade volumes are independent of the tax rates, so the trade balance is unchanged; as there is no Laffer curve, AB unambiguously shifts back to the left. Equilibrium is restored at point 1; in effect, the convertibility restrictions have increased the fiscal potency of trade taxes by converting them into lump-sum taxes on the margin.[15]

Given the role of revenue effects here, it is tempting to conclude that trade restrictions that do not increase revenue – like a tightening of exchange controls on current account transactions – cannot resolve an inconsistency between fiscal policy and the rate of crawl. But any trade restriction that improves the trade balance on the margin will increase the sustainable level of financial wealth (measured in terms of exports). The latter effect increases the base for the inflation tax, potentially restoring consistency at an unchanged inflation rate.[16] In Figure 3.3, a tightening of convertibility restrictions that raises θ can produce a long-run equilibrium at a point like 4 provided the adverse revenue effect associated with lower trade volumes is not too large (with unchanged fiscal deficit, the equilibrium would be at point 5).

Capital Controls and Foreign Exchange Black Markets

Finally, consider the role of exchange controls on the capital account. We noted above that when the central bank faces a liquidity problem the preferred instrument for endogenous trade policy is direct rationing of foreign exchange for imports. Such a scheme *presupposes* controls on the acquisition or use of foreign currency for portfolio purposes, and indeed tight controls on the capital account were characteristic of most countries outside the CFA zone by the early 1970s.[17] These controls played a number of roles, but an important one was to enhance the government's revenue base by creating a captive demand for the government's domestic liabilities.[18] Effective capital controls simultaneously raise the demand for the government's domestic liabilities (including the monetary base) and reduce the degree of substitutability between these and foreign financial assets. The first effect increases the inflation tax revenues associated with any inflation rate, allowing the government to finance a larger fiscal deficit without an increase in inflation. A tightening of capital controls may therefore seem an attractive way of reconciling larger fiscal deficits with a non-accommodative policy towards the official exchange rate. The second effect increases the revenue-maximizing inflation rate (Adam, *et al.* 1993) and the revenue yield from increased inflation on the margin. By encouraging greater reliance on the inflation tax, this may have played the indirect role of enhancing the effectiveness of current account restrictions in resolving macroeconomic inconsistencies.

Incorporating asset substitution introduces forward-looking dynamics, the possibility of an inflation-tax Laffer curve and, in the presence of capital controls, a foreign exchange black market. There are two observations on accommodating these features in the analytical framework. First, when the exchange rate is unified, the rate of crawl is fixed, and the capital account is open, the IB/EB/AB analysis goes through unchanged. The basic reference is Khan and Lizondo (1987); this is an appropriate framework for thinking about the CFA countries. Second, when capital controls and black markets are added to models of the type studied here, they are likely to affect the dynamics more than the steady states. Across steady states, an exchange control system acts like a set of taxes or quotas on trade transactions, generating fiscal and resource allocation effects very similar to those studied above. While a unified treatment of dynamics and steady states, and fiscal effects and resource allocation effects, has yet to be worked out, many of the basic elements are available in the literature (Lizondo, 1991; Morris, 1995; O'Connell, 1992; and Pinto 1989).

Liberalizing Macroeconomically Motivated Trade Restrictions

If trade restrictions retain any leverage over the actual stance of trade policy, removing these restrictions will generally not be feasible unless accompanying policy adjustments are carried out. The first reason for this is that a loosening of import restrictions worsens the balance of payments in the short run. Liberalization is therefore likely to be aborted if the central bank lacks reserves, and any suspicion of liquidity problems will produce speculative behaviour by the private sector that may rapidly deplete such reserves as are available. This short-run external balance problem brings out a strong complementarity between trade liberalization and devaluation, a point emphasized by Collier (1991) and documented for developing countries by Corden (1993):

Point 6: *A removal of macroeconomically-motivated convertibility restrictions is likely to be aborted if the balance of payments is not protected in the short run by an accompanying devaluation.*

The second reason for accompanying macroeconomic adjustments comes from effects that operate more gradually through the fiscal accounts and trade balance. As we saw above, trade controls, or better yet, a combination of capital controls and foreign exchange rationing for imports, were capable under certain conditions of resolving an inconsistency between fiscal policy and exchange rate policy. If they are indeed playing this role, a restoration of convertibility brings the underlying inconsistency back into the open, eventually producing a persistent combination of fiscal and payments deficits. Once again an accompanying exchange rate policy can neutralize this long-run effect, but this time it is the *rate of crawl* of the exchange rate, rather than its level, that ultimately matters, since an inflation tax problem is at the core of the unsustainability. A sustainable removal of convertibility restrictions in this case (which reduces θ permanently and has an unfavourable long-run effect on the balance of payments) requires some combination of a fiscal contraction and a rise in the rate of crawl of the exchange rate. Moving to a higher rate of crawl does not obviate the need for a one-shot devaluation up front, since the adverse short-term effect on the balance of payments is still there; but the likelihood of damaging speculation in the short run is apt to depend substantially on whether the long-run balance of payments effect is indeed favourable or unfavourable.

Exchange Rate Unification as Trade Policy

Many countries in SSA initiated reforms in the early-to-mid 1980s that were designed to reduce the premium between the parallel and official exchange rates. The analysis above interprets exchange controls applied to the current account as macroeconomically-motivated trade restrictions. It follows that exchange rate unification, which typically began with a liberalization of import rationing systems and export remittance requirements, amounted to trade liberalization.

Point 7:   *When exchange controls have permeated the current account, a restoration of convertibility for current account purposes implies a trade liberalization.*

There is extensive evidence that the domestic prices of imports and import-substitutes under foreign exchange rationing schemes tend to be driven by the parallel exchange rate, since imports can only enter the country illegally at the margin (Kiguel and O'Connell, 1995). Export prices, in contrast, are often more tightly tied to the official rate, because output is exported at the margin through official channels (for example, marketing boards), where the seller's net revenue is constant, rather than to parallel markets (where net revenue falls as the scale of costly illegal activity rises). The relative import protection coefficient – giving the divergence between the foreign and domestic terms of trade – therefore tends to be positively correlated with (one plus) the parallel premium in the long run. In this case, changes in the average value of the premium over time give a rough indication of changes in the actual stance of trade policy.[19]

Macroeconomics of Protection: Summing Up

The central theme of this section is that policy-makers in SSA have faced strong pressures to subordinate trade policy to fiscal or external balance. Under these conditions, unilateral trade liberalization amounts to a move to an unsustainable counter-factual. It is likely to be incompatible unless accompanied by an adjustment of the fiscal fundamentals and/or a move to an accommodative exchange rate policy that allows a rise in the rate of inflation.

A desire to insulate reserves implies a preference for quantitative restrictions over tariffs. Thus in much of SSA before the mid-1980s, and particularly outside the CFA countries, trade policy became endogenous, with the quantity of available import licences varying with officially remitted export revenues. In many countries, the authorities implemented trade controls by extending pre-existing capital controls to the current account. The black market premium therefore came to reflect not only the short-run excess demand for foreign exchange for portfolio purposes but also the underlying tightness of the import rationing regime. In such situations, exchange rate unification for current account purposes – meaning a removal of convertibility restrictions on current transactions – lowers the domestic price of imports relative to exports and is equivalent to a standard trade liberalization. This blurs the distinction between exchange rate policy and trade policy (and underscores the inadequacy of tariff-based measures of trade openness).[20]

The discussion in this section does not add up to a macroeconomic endorsement of exchange controls or import quotas. The associated microeconomic distortions are substantial. Recent empirical works using the black market premium as a summary measure of government distortions find that increases in long-period averages of the premium – which, as we saw above, are correlated with the tightness of restrictions on the trade account – are associated with significant reductions in economic growth (Barro and Lee, 1994). On the theoretical side, recent work by Romer (1994) suggests that when technological improvements come in the form of differentiated imported inputs, the welfare costs of trade restrictions may be orders of magnitude larger than the traditional Harberger triangles. But policy is often influenced by calculations of temporary advantage, and controls that are justifiable on temporary grounds may be politically difficult to reverse. The analysis therefore helps to explain why many countries in SSA adopted them in the 1960s and then extended them into the current account in the 1970s. The macroeconomic motivations emphasized here are in addition to the advantages of quantitative controls in delivering rents to favoured government clients, a motivation emphasized strongly by Bates (1981) and others.

Why then did many countries finally liberalize trade and exchange regimes? Experience suggests that the extra degree of policy freedom granted by exchange controls is limited, since their effectiveness is a declining function of their severity and the length of time they have been in place (Kiguel and O'Connell, 1995). In terms of the model analysed above, a combination of adverse external developments, fiscal mismanagement and increased sophistication at evading controls by the private sector can convert a sustainable policy package into one that is unsustainable. By the early 1980s, conditionality packages added an additional strong impetus for reform by tying external inflows to policy reform.

With these points as background, the remainder of this chapter focuses on the linkages between the *regional* macroeconomic environment and Africa's trade. The next two sections present an overview of African arrangements for formal monetary integration and a discussion of the non-coordinated moves towards convertibility that occurred outside of the African monetary unions since the mid-1980s.

3.3   AFRICAN MONETARY INTEGRATION

African monetary integration has had its advocates, both within and outside Africa, throughout the post-independence period. The Organization of African Unity and the UN Economic Commission for Africa see monetary union as the capstone of an integration process that began in the mid-1970s with the signing of regional protocols aimed at granting regional tariff preferences, harmonizing of external tariffs and liberalizing factor movements. The goal seems increasingly lofty as the original OAU/ECA target year of 2000 approaches, given the limited progress on these earlier objectives (Berg, 1985, 1988).[21] Other views, however, have if anything been more urgent. Mundell, writing in 1972, argued that the immediate adoption of a common currency was 'the quickest way of untying – cutting – the Gordian knot' of African underdevelopment (p. 57). More recently, Frimpong-Ansah (1994) has advocated further monetary integration in West Africa, not as the culmination of other efforts in goods and factor markets but as a precondition for their success. Collier (1991), Cobham and Robson (1994) and Guillaumont and Guillaumont (1989) point to the macroeconomic stability of the currency unions of the CFA zone and argue that the EC monetary union, if it goes forward, offers a unique opportunity for these unions to be strengthened and for other African unions to be formed.

'Monetary integration' is usually taken to imply mutually fixed exchange rates and full convertibility on both current and capital account between member countries. The polar cases of monetary integration are *informal exchange rate unions*, in which central banks agree to limit fluctuations in cross-exchange rates without the help (or constraint) of a centralized co-ordinating agency, and *full monetary unions* (or *currency unions*), in which members share a common currency and central bank. *Formal exchange rate unions* constitute an intermediate case in which a central agency co-ordinates exchange rate policy but national central banks remain autonomous in other respects. Given the mutual incompatibility of fixed exchange rates, free convertibility and independent national monetary policies, an important common feature of arrangements seeking to enforce the first two elements is the acceptance of some degree of harmonization between national monetary policies.

In this paper, the broader term 'monetary co-operation' will be used when including *clearing unions* (or payments unions) in the discussion. In a clearing union, each country is responsible, in convertible currency and at regular intervals, only for its accumulated balance *vis-à-vis* the union. Clearing arrangements are prevalent in subSaharan Africa and clearly involve some degree of co-operation between member central banks. A key difference between clearing unions and formal monetary integration schemes is that the former impose much milder restraints, if any, on the monetary and exchange rate policies of member countries.

An overview of African monetary integration reveals three main points. First, while Africa's postwar history presents a varied menu of formal monetary arrangements, the configuration of institutions that exists today is largely the legacy of choices made at independence. Second, restricting attention to arrangements that exercise a meaningful influence on domestic macroeconomic policy – call these 'restraining arrangements' – the three that survive all involve a relationship with an external anchor country (here treating South Africa as external) that dominates the bilateral relationship between subSaharan partners. Third, monetary integration has clearly delivered low inflation in Africa but it is difficult to draw unambiguous conclusions about its overall net benefits. This section begins by developing these points, and then discusses the linkages between monetary integration and trade.

A Varied Menu

Africa's post-independence experience with monetary arrangements runs the gamut from regional clearing arrangements to full monetary unions. Table 3.1 provides a summary and shows the relationship between the monetary arrangements and formal agreements aimed primarily at regional trade liberalization.[22]

Before independence, countries were united in their common dependence on colonial currencies and institutions. This implied the maintenance of fixed exchange rates *vis-à-vis* other members of the franc zone or sterling area, and tended to be associated with the free movement of capital within these areas as well. For many countries, the colonial arrangements extended to the sharing of a common currency and monetary authority, as in the East African Community, the Federation of Rhodesia and Nyasaland and the Central and West African members of the franc zone.

The prospect of political independence forced a decision on the relationship between political sovereignty and monetary sovereignty. Among the African members of the franc zone, independence saw little change beyond the transfer of responsibility for the currency issue from the Caisse Centrale de la France d'Outre-Mer to two regional central banks. These central banks each issued a version of the CFA franc tied to the French franc with a convertibility guarantee from the French Treasury.[23] In Southern Africa, Botswana, Lesotho and Swaziland made a similar choice, formalizing their long-standing monetary ties with South Africa in the Rand Monetary Area agreement of 1974. There were defections in each case; Djibouti, Guinea, Mali, Madagascar and Mauritania all established independent currencies and left the franc zone between 1949 and 1973 (Mali rejoined in 1984), and Botswana left the Rand Monetary Area in 1975. But for the seven members of UMOA, six members of BEAC and three members of the CMA (Namibia having joined on independence), the underlying monetary relationships have changed very little from those of the colonial period. These countries have maintained both dimensions of their monetary integration – a strong vertical relationship with France or South Africa, as well as a continuing horizontal integration with regional partners.

The anglophone countries, in contrast, and most countries outside of the anglophone or francophone ambit (for example, Angola, Mozambique, Zaire), adopted national currencies and central banks at independence or soon thereafter, typically with controls on capital movements *vis-à-vis* the former colonizing power. The break with colonial institutions operated on the horizontal dimension as well as the vertical. Thus while there was discussion of placing the union administered by the East African Currency Board on an African footing, the desire for monetary independence was sufficiently strong that Kenya, Tanzania and Uganda set up their own central banks in 1966. In the Federation of Rhodesia and Nyasaland, the Central African Currency Board had already, in 1956, been replaced by a shared central bank. Discussions of

Table 3.1   African monetary arrangements and associated trade
arrangements to 1993

Monetary arrangement	No.[a]	Membership	Trade arrangement	No.[a]
Regional Clearing				
PTACH (1983)	16	identical to	PTA (1981–)[b]	16
		overlaps with	COMESA (1993–)	16
		overlaps with	SADC (1992–)[c]	11
WACH (1975–)	15	subset of	ECOWAS (1975–)	16
Informal Exchange Rate Union				
EACA (1966–77)	3	identical to	EAEC (1966–77)	
Formal Exchange Rate Union				
CMA (1974–)[d]	4	subset of	SACU (1910–)	5
		overlaps with	PTA (1981–)[b]	
		overlaps with	COMESA (1993–)	
		overlaps with	SADC (1992–)[c]	
Fully Currency Union				
UMOA (1962–)[e]	7	overlaps with	CEAO (1974–)[f]	7
		subset of	ECOWAS (1975–)	
BEAC (1972–)[e]	6	identical to	UDEAC (1966–)	
		subset of	CEEAC (1983–)	10

Notes: For a more complete (though somewhat dated) list of regional organizations
involved in trade integration, see Berg (1988).
[a] Membership lists are given in Table 3.2.
[b] PTA began operations in 1984.
[c] Formerly SADCC (Southern African Development Co-ordination Conference, formed
in 1979); while SADC was not primarily a regional trade arrangement, SADCC's
ambitions in this area are as yet unclear.
[d] The CMA agreement (1986) was a modification of the pre-existing Rand Monetary
Area (RMA) agreement covering the same countries.
[e] The table ends in 1993 and therefore excludes the UEMOA (Union Économique et
Monétaire Quest-Africaine) and CEMAC (Communauté Économique et Monétaire de
l'Afrique Central), both formed in 1994 and effectively replacing UMOA and BEAC/
UDEAC.
[f] CEAO was formed out of the former UDEAO (Union Douaniére et Économique de
l'Afrique de l'Quest).

Sources: Foroutan and Pritchett (1993); Berg (1988) *Keesing's Record of World Events*,
various issues.

continued monetary union were overcome by the emerging political
wedge between Zambia and Malawi, on the one hand, and Rhodesia
on the other. All three countries introduced their own currencies soon
after the independence of Zambia and Malawi.

Although the treaties underlying the ECA's major regional groupings for economic co-operation call for improved fiscal and monetary
co-ordination among member countries, developments in formal monetary

Table 3.2   Membership of monetary and trade arrangements in Table 3.1[a]

Monetary arrangements

BEAC (Banque des États de l'Afrique Centrale): Cameroon, Central African
Republic, Chad, Congo, Equatorial Guinea (from 1985), Gabon – the
BEAC and associated trade arrangement UDEAC were effectively
replaced in 1994 by the newly-created CEMAC (Communauté
Économique et Monétaire de l'Afrique Central), with identical
membership.

CMA (Common Monetary Area): Lesotho, Namibia, South Africa,
Swaziland – this was the Rand Monetary Area from 1974 to 1986

EACA (East African Currency Area): Kenya, Tanzania, Uganda

PTACH (PTA Clearing House)

UMOA (Union Monétaire Quest Africaine): Benin, Burkina Faso, Côte
d'Ivoire, Mali (since 1984), Niger, Senegal, Togo – effectively replaced
in 1994 by the newly-created UEMOA (Union Économique et Monétaire
Quest Africaine), with identical membership.

WACH (West African Clearing House): ECOWAS minus Cape Verde

Trade arrangements

CEAO (Communauté Économique de l'Afrique de l'Quest): UMOA plus
Mauritania, minus Togo (Guinea and Togo are observers); CEAO is a
subset of ECOWAS.

CEEAC (Communauté Économique des États de l'Afrique Centrale): BEAC
plus Burundi, Rwanda, Sao Tome and Principe, Zaire

COMESA (Common Market for Eastern and Southern Africa): Eritrea,
Ethiopia, Kenya, Lesotho, Madagascar, Malawi, Mauritius, Mozambique,
Namibia, Rwanda, Sudan, Swaziland, Tanzania, Uganda, Zambia,
Zimbabwe

EAEC (East African Economic Community): membership identical to East
African Currency Area

SACU (South African Customs Area): CMA plus Botswana

ECOWAS (Economic Community of West African States): UMOA plus
Cape Verde, The Gambia, Ghana, Guinea, Guinea-Bissau, Liberia,
Mauritania, Nigeria, Sierra Leone

PTA (Preferential Trade Area for Eastern and Southern African States):
Burundi, Comoros, Djibouti, Ethiopia, Kenya, Lesotho, Malawi,
Mauritius, Rwanda, Somalia, Sudan, Swaziland, Tanzania, Uganda,
Zambia, Zimbabwe

SADC (Southern African Development Community): Angola, Botswana,
Lesotho, Malawi, Mozambique, Namibia, Swaziland, South Africa [joined
in 1994], Tanzania, Zambia, Zimbabwe

UDEAC (Union Douaniére et Économique de l'Afrique Centrale):
membership identical to BEAC (replaced in 1994; see BEAC above)

Note: [a] Memberships evolve over time, and these data are therefore subject to
error.

Sources: Foroutan and Pritchett (1993); Berg (1988); *Keesing's Record of World
Events*, various issues.

integration have on the whole been minor since the disintegration that took place outside of the francophone area at independence. Regional clearing arrangements (see Section 3.4) are the exceptions that prove the rule: though of post-independence vintage, they are the least demanding version of integration, excercising virtually no influence over the exchange rate or monetary policy of the member countries.

Monetary Stability and the External Dimension

Any meaningful arrangement for the fixity of nominal exchange rates – in which the official exchange rate continues to serve as the marginal price of foreign exchange in the domestic economy – requires some degree of harmonization between domestic inflation rates and the inflation rates of partner countries. This does not require explicit co-operation; it can be the result, for example, of independent decisions to peg to the currency of a common third-party or a currency basket. For African countries, the fundamental requirement is restraint of government domestic borrrowing, since in the absence of well-developed domestic bond markets, the banking system – and thus money growth – is the only source of domestic financing.

The East African Community provides a clear example of the incompatibility of divergent national monetary policies, mutually fixed exchange rates and an open trade and payments regime.[24] Initially the three countries operated an informal exchange rate union, with national currencies circulating at par, common external capital controls and free movement of capital within the union.[25] Moreover, the Treaty for East African Co-operation prohibited quantitative restrictions on intra-community trade, replacing them with tariffs. The central banks consulted heavily over the sterling devaluation of 1967, and later over the dollar devaluation of 1971 and the move to generalized floating in 1973, in each case taking a joint course of action that maintained relative parities. But macroeconomic policies had already diverged substantially by the early 1970s (Table 3.3), undermining convertibility within the union. Capital flight led the Tanzanian government to extend exchange controls to Kenya and Uganda in 1971. Official parities remained in line until 1979 – temporarily surviving the breakup of the Community in 1977 – but the inertia was superficial. By the mid 1970s the exchange rate had become 'the only common element of [macroeconomic] policy' (Bank of Kenya, p. 56). Although this gave the common parity an increasing symbolic importance, it was resistance to devaluation on purely nationalistic grounds that explained the lack of unilateral action

Table 3.3   Macroeconomic divergence in the East African Community

	1966–9	1970–3	1974–7	1978–81
Growth rates				
Domestic credit				
Kenya	12.9[a]	29.0	23.4	21.6
Tanzania	20.0[a]	19.9	32.1	32.7
Uganda	16.8[a]	30.2	24.5	50.4
Consumer prices				
Kenya	1.7	5.2	15.8	12.6
Tanzania	13.6	6.5	15.8	20.0
Uganda	2.5	11.3	53.5	78.3
End-of-period values				
Official exchange rate (local currency/$)				
Kenya	7.14	6.90	7.95	10.29
Tanzania	7.14	6.90	7.96	8.32
Uganda	7.14	6.90	7.95	85.15
Parallel premium (%)				
Kenya	36.6[b]	41.3	2.5	21.5
Tanzania	46.4[b]	94.9	89.1	192.7
Uganda	41.5[b]	124.1	642.1	246.5

Notes:
[a] End-1966 to end-1969
[b] December 1970

Sources: Domestic credit, consumer price index, and official exchange rate from IMF, *International Financial Statistics Yearbook, 1992*; consumer price index for Uganda, 1965–77 from IMF, *IFS Special Supplement on Prices, 1981*, and 1977–80 from East African Community statistics. Parallel exchange rates from *World Currency Yearbook*, various years. Growth rates are calculated from end-to-period to end-of-period.

in the face of policy divergence. Official exchange rates diverged with Tanzania's 10 per cent devaluation of January 1979 and Uganda's massive devaluation of the same year.

The flip side of the proposition that successful exchange-rate union *requires* some degree of macroeconomic harmonization is the proposition that adoption of an effective mechanism for enforcing such a union will enhance the macroeconomic stability of the less stable partners. This *restraining* role of monetary union is normally thought of as requiring the surrender of monetary leadership to a dominant and stable anchor country. Restraint may also operate on the horizontal dimension, at least in principle; for example, rules that require consensus between partners may build in a bias towards conservatism by granting any member whose interests are not served by a proposed policy change – such as devaluation – an effective veto (Mundell, 1972). In either case, effective restraint delivers macroeconomic stability through two channels: by lowering fiscal deficits, it reduces the pressure for monetary finance, and by lending credibility to central bank claims that it will not accommodate the inflationary expectations of the private sector, it reduces both expected and actual inflation. The first of these channels is evident in the linkage between inflation and fiscal deficits explored in section 3.2 above; the second is the theme of the extensive literature on the time consistency of monetary policy.[26]

In practice, the examples of successful monetary integration in Africa – BEAC, UMOA and CMA – have all been characterized since their inception by strong vertical ties between regional partners and a dominant anchor country. Thus in the francophone monetary unions, countries share a central bank on which the majority of the board is African, but convertibility of the currency is guaranteed by the French treasury, and the French government exerts strong leverage over monetary and exchange rate policy. In the Rand Monetary Area, Lesotho and Swaziland maintained a fixed parity with the South African rand and effectively ceded full control over monetary and fiscal policy to their larger partner. To the degree that central banks in these arrangements act as 'agencies of restraint' on fiscal deficits and monetary growth (in the terminology of Collier, 1991), an important dimension of their restraining influence is external to the participating African partners.

Tying successfully to a relatively low-inflation partner has clearly delivered low inflation in the CFA zone and CMA. CFA inflation was roughly a third, and CMA a half, of inflation in the rest of subSaharan Africa in the two-decade period from 1970 to 1990 (Table 3.4). Over long periods, inflation rates in both the CFA and the CMA countries have not diverged dramatically from those of the relevant anchor country. Particularly for the CFA countries, this has meant significantly lower average inflation than elsewhere in Africa, including among the members of the postwar franc zone who chose not to participate in regional monetary unions. France has been a lower-inflation anchor than has South Africa; indeed, Botswana's defection from the RMA in 1975 allowed that country to choose significantly lower inflation than South Africa over the entire decade of the 1980s.

In both CMA and the CFA zone, however, strains between the anchor and other partners have contributed to some weakening of the vertical relationship. The French support of German high-interest rate policy in the EMS contributed to real appreciation in the CFA zone in the

Table 3.4   Inflation in selected country groups

Group	N	1971–75	1975–80	1980–85	1985–90	1971–90
BEAC	5	9.3	11.0	10.0	1.8	7.5
UMOA	7	10.4	11.7	7.4	0.2	7.1
Mali		9.4	9.7	8.1	1.3	7.0
CFA zone	11	9.9	11.4	8.6	0.9	7.3
France		9.5	10.8	9.4	3.2	8.1
CMA	2	n.a.	14.3	14.2	13.2	n.a.
South Africa		10.3	11.9	14.0	15.3	13.0
Other SSA	19	13.2	18.3	21.3	32.8	21.1
of which:						
Nigeria		13.2	16.2	19.2	24.0	18.4
Madagascar		10.3	9.2	20.0	15.3	13.8
Botswana		10.2	13.6	7.9	16.1	12.0

Notes: N denotes number of countries used in calculation. CPI used when available; otherwise GDP deflator. UMOA calculations include Mali from 1985. BEAC excludes Equatorial Guinea. Other SSA includes Botswana, Burundi, Cape Verde, Ghana, Guinea-Bissau, Madagascar, Malawi, Mauritius, Nigeria, Rwanda, Sao Tome and Principe, Seychelles, Sierra Leone, Somalia, Sudan, Tanzania, Zambia and Zaire.

Source: World Bank, *World Tables*.

late 1980s and early 1990s. This exacerbated the external difficulties that had emerged first in UMOA in the early 1980s and then spread to BEAC with the zone-wide terms of trade collapse of the second half of the 1980s. Devaluation of the CFA franc had long been favoured by the IMF and World Bank, against French resistance, but this resistance meant underwriting increasing zone-wide external imbalances. After maintaining an unchanged parity against the French franc since 1948, the CFA countries devalued by 50 per cent against it in January 1994.

In CMA, South Africa's political transition raises uncertainties about the course of macroeconomic policy and the new government's view of its own interests in SACU and CMA. Monetary and trade policy in these organizations has always been set with little reference to the interests of the smaller members (Chipeta and Davies, 1993). Already in 1985, South Africa's debt standstill crisis had led to the temporary closure of South African foreign exchange markets and the re-introduction of a dual exchange rate system, with separate exchange rates for commercial and financial transactions; it was largely in response to a sense of diverging national interests over monetary and exchange rate policy that Lesotho and Swaziland obtained a renegotiation of the RMA agreement in 1986. In the new Common Monetary Area, Swaziland withdrew legal tender status of the rand and secured the right to operate its own exchange rate policy (Davies *et al.*, 1993). Although the modifications embodied in the CMA allow more latitude to the smaller members, they are essentially granted a reactive role rather than a consultative one with respect to South Africa's policy decisions.[27]

In both the CFA zone and the CMA, changing relationships with the anchor country hold the possibility of greater flux in these agreements in the next five years or so than in any similar period since their initiation. A natural question is whether loss of the vertical relationship is likely to be fatal for monetary stability in the subSaharan partners. There is little hope, at least in the short to medium run, for the restraining role to be taken up by large regional partners. Within UMOA and BEAC, the large partners (Côte d'Ivoire and Cameroon) have been the most overvalued. Outside of the currency arrangements, the obvious regional 'poles' in terms of economic size and level of development are Zimbabwe and Nigeria, but these countries have serious stability problems of their own.[28] The question is therefore whether restraint can operate successfully on the horizontal level. The EAC experience offers a clear cautionary note on this score, as does the problem in principle of the free-rider, whereby each member of a union has an incentive to over-exploit the discipline exercised by other members. A more promising solution, as urged by Cobham and Robson (1994), Collier (1991) and Guillaumont and Guillaumont (1989), is the replacement of weakening vertical ties with new ties between African unions and similar bodies in the developed countries, like the EMS. Collier (1991) discusses the wisdom of this solution, as opposed to one in which countries rely for restraint on internal mechanisms, such as legislatively independent central banks, or bilateral external mechanisms, such as IMF conditionality.

Costs and Benefits of Exchange Rate Union: Optimum Currency Area Arguments and the CFA Zone Experience

Proponents of further monetary integration in Africa cite two benefits in the form of (1) regional trade promotion and (2) macroeconomic stability. The benefits for regional trade are associated with the maintenance of mutual convertibility for current account purposes at stable cross-rates within the union. It is important to separate these two aspects of what might be called 'harmonization' of regional exchange regimes. The optimum currency area literature that followed Mundell's classic (1961) article assumed that exchange rates were *already* convertible for current account purposes. In this literature, the largely implicit 'microeconomic' benefits of currency union had to do with lowering the costs associated with currency conversions and reducing the variability of bilateral nominal (and therefore real) exchange rates. These benefits require explicit co-ordination and little is known even now about their precise nature or magnitude (see further discussion below).[29] Mutual regional convertibility, on the other hand, can be achieved through adoption of macroeconomic policies that support convertibility with external currencies – something that in principle can be achieved unilaterally, on a regionally non-coordinated basis.

Macroeconomic stability is enhanced by union membership to the degree that participation provides a better restraint on national monetary and fiscal policies than available alternative mechanisms. The benefits of macroeconomic stability are potentially many, ranging from the avoidance of 'shoe-leather' costs of high inflation to the provision of a more hospitable environment for private investment and enhanced effectiveness of government policy. The analysis in section 3.2 suggests that a potentially important additional benefit is the support of an open trading regime and avoidance of the inefficiencies associated with illegal trade. The trade linkage is discussed further in the next section. The remainder of this section focuses on the macroeconomic *costs* of exchange rate or currency union, which have been the main preoccupation of the literature since Mundell (1961).

The costs of exchange rate union relate to the loss of national control over the nominal exchange rate (and thus over monetary policy, which is endogenous under a managed exchange rate with convertibility). Recalling section 3.2, this means the loss of an instrument that is capable of addressing real exchange rate misalignment in the short run and accommodating the government's seigniorage requirement over the longer term. Mundell (1961) emphasized the first of these costs, focusing on the use of a nominal devaluation to cut short the contractionary adjustment to a regional demand shift under wage/price stickiness. The regional nature of this particular external shock is not important here; what matters is that the shock has an asymmetric effect across partners, leading to divergent desired adjustments in national exchange rates. In subSaharan Africa, the key external shocks are not regional demand shifts but divergent movements in the terms of trade of individual countries. As indicated in section 3.2, a persistently adverse terms of trade movement produces a contractionary adjustment pattern that can be shortened through a credible one-shot devaluation, provided any necessary accompanying fiscal adjustment is made.

The second degree of freedom lost through forsaking the nominal exchange rate is the ability to choose an inflation rate different from that of trading partners. This is a two-edged sword, since the inability of a non-credible central bank to anchor private sector expectations is one of the primary arguments for joining a union. But holding credibility issues aside, both optimum tax arguments and political economy arguments suggest that the preferred share of seigniorage in overall revenue varies considerably from country to country.[30] Thus a country with weak administrative capability may find that a commitment to low inflation implies either an overly distorting reliance on other easily collectible taxes – such as those on external trade – or a sub-optimal level of public expenditure.

Given these costs and benefits, the literature on optimum currency areas has tended to suggest that natural currency areas encompass partners with the following features:

- similar exposure to external shocks (implying less need for divergent exchange rate adjustments);
- relatively diversified production bases and wealth portfolios (implying less exposure to external shocks in general);
- relatively high degrees of wage/price flexibility (implying shorter periods of real exchange rate misalignment);
- substantial pre-existing trade links (implying relative ineffectiveness of intra-union real exchange rate movements in achieving external adjusment in any case);
- high intra-union labour mobility (as a substitute for the exchange rate changes that would be required in response to asymmetric shocks);
- similar underlying seigniorage requirements (implying less need for divergent inflation rates); and
- greater asymmetry of credibility (implying greater scope for the 'borrowing' of credibility by the weaker partner[s]).[31]

As pointed out by Cobham and Robson (1994), the CFA countries – and most other African countries for that matter – are not natural partners by most of these criteria.[32] The CMA countries are stronger candidates in principle, given the high historical mobility of labour between the smaller members and South Africa (though this has fallen substantially since the early 1970s) and the high degree of trade dependence of the smaller members on South Africa.

The benefits of macroeconomic stability appear to provide the strongest argument in favour of the African currency unions (and suggest again that restraint operating in the vertical dimension is an essential part of their logic). But do these benefits exceed the costs of losing the exchange rate instrument? Table 3.3 provides one rough measure of the stability afforded by zone membership: within SSA, inflation was roughly 14-points lower inside the zone than outside over 1971–90. Using stylized parameters for SSA, Devarajan and Rodrik (1992) argue that a 14-point reduction in inflation is not worth the output lost through inability to respond to terms of trade shocks. The calculation takes a narrow view of the benefits of macroeconomic stability, however, and one can appeal to a broader empirical literature on the relative economic performance of the CFA countries, both within Africa and more broadly in comparison with developing countries.[33] Early contributions emphasized the superior performance of the CFA countries between 1960 and 1980 with respect to growth and and number of other measures (Guillaumont and Guillaumont, 1988 and Devarajan and de Melo, 1987). The relative performance of the CFA countries started to deteriorate in the early 1980s (Devarajan and de Melo, 1991; and Elbadawi and Majd, 1992), however, and the contraction of output in the early 1990s was disastrous. There is some (limited) evidence that output has been more variable in the zone than outside, as would be expected given the role of the nominal exchange rate in facilitating adjustment to external shocks (Boughton, 1991).[34]

Overall, the jury is still out on the net costs and benefits of participation in the CFA currency unions. While there are clear benefits on the inflation front, there is also broad agreement that lack of the exchange rate instrument imposed major costs on the zone in the 1980s and 1990s. It is important to bear in mind three points in drawing lessons from the recent difficulties of the CFA countries. First, a commitment to union-wide exchange rate policy is, in principle, separate from either the choice of an anchor or the choice of relationship to the anchor (fixed parity, adjustable peg, crawling peg). The French franc has been a somewhat unfortunate anchor since the mid 1980s, as its appreciation against the dollar, and more recently within Europe, has contributed to the real effective appreciation in the CFA countries. A peg to the SDR or the ECU might have served better over this period, and in any case an earlier devaluation would have been superior to the delayed one that was implemented.

Second, any indictment of the zone's institutions (including but not limited to the choice of peg) based on the post-1980 experience must also encompass the relatively favourable earlier performance of the zone. It is conceivable, for example, that use of the exchange rate instrument in the early 1980s – or more particularly, before the unprecedented zone-wide decline in the terms of trade starting in the mid 1980s – would have opened the door for an evolution of policy associated with higher inflation, suspension of the convertibility guarantee from France, a proliferation of exchange controls, chronic capital flight, intermittent maxi-devaluations and lower growth. It is too early to tell whether pressures of this sort are emerging now that the zone has devalued for the first time in over forty years. What does seem clear is that France now prefers a weaker relationship with the countries of the zone and that the monitoring role is to some degree being shifted to the IMF – an institution whose role is at best essentially curative rather than preventative.

Third, the experience of the CFA countries illustrates rather dramatically that the question of whether membership in a monetary union will help the authorities commit to low inflation is quite separate, at least over extended time periods, from the question of whether such membership will prevent the emergence of internally-generated national macroeconomic imbalances and exchange rate overvaluation.[35] The distinction between macroeconomic stability (in the sense of low inflation and stable relative prices) and macroeconomic distortion (in the sense of real overvaluation) is useful here and comes through clearly in the analysis in section 3.2. There, the same inflation rate (for example, zero) could be associated with widely divergent stances of trade policy (0) and degrees of distortion of relative production incentives between the domestic and export markets (e). The distinction between stability and distortions becomes important if the mechanism that underpins stability – commitment to a fixed exchange rate – makes it more difficult to correct distortions once they emerge.[36]

Based on the experience of the CFA zone, therefore, the cost-benefit calculus of participation in African monetary unions is unclear. At bottom, the key question is that suggested by Boughton (1991): can the benefits of exchange rate flexibility for external adjustment be obtained while retaining the credibility of monetary policy that is associated with the current arrangements of the zone? The possibility of separating the 'agency of restraint' role from the choice of peg or the flexibility of peg is behind recent suggestions that European monetary union, should it occur, might offer a unique opportunity for the CFA countries to combine a maxi-devaluation with a shift in the peg from the

FF to the ECU, while retaining a monitoring role for France or the European Central Bank via an exchange-rate guarantee (for example, Guillaumont and Guillaumont, 1989; Cobham and Robson, 1994; and Collier, 1991). Nor has the continent experimented (outside of the Common Monetary Area) with arrangments that exercise even tighter control over member fiscal policies than the CFA unions, though this may be required to prevent severe internal difficulties even under an optimal union peg.

Monetary Integration and Trade Openness

This section addresses more explicitly the somewhat complex relationship between monetary integration and trade. Such a relationship can operate either through the effect of monetary integration on trade policy choices – that is, on the incentives to maintain an open policy regime or to liberalize pre-existing trade barriers – or through the effect of monetary integration on the private gains from regional trade for given policy settings. These two channels are considered in turn.

We saw in section 3.2 that the requirements of external sustainability and fiscal sustainability bring out a strong substitutability between exchange rate policies and trade controls.[37] The substitutability is strongest when fiscal policy is over-expansive and inflexible, since this is when revenue needs and pressures for overvaluation are most acute. In these situations, liberalization without devaluation or a major fiscal contraction may be rendered incompatible by the adverse balance of payments effect (Collier, 1991). And even if domestic policies are in line, achieving the real depreciation that accompanies trade liberalization may require a lengthy contraction of employment and output. Rodrik (1993) suggests that the latter cost may be minor for members of currency unions, since the credibility of a union-wide central bank increases the flexibility of nominal wage settlements in the private sector, allowing real wage adjustments to occur with a smaller disturbance to internal balance. But the recent experience of the zone suggests that wage/price inflexibility remains a substantial problem there.

The short-run macroeconomic costs of liberalization under a fixed exchange rate can therefore overwhelm the long-run benefits, if political considerations give policy-makers a high discount rate. If reserves are pooled, the underlying balance of payments constraint may be softened somewhat by the ability to draw on the joint reserves of the union, but it seems likely that the net effect of monetary integration is to discourage non-discriminatory trade liberalization. The policy bias against a co-ordinated liberalization *vis-à-vis* regional partners is somewhat weaker than the bias against unilateral liberalization, since each member's liberalization is transmitted postively to the balance of payments of regional trading partners. But there is a bias towards making such regional integration import-substituting and isolationist.

Fixed exchange rates therefore tend to discourage trade liberalization, particularly when the stance of trade policy is motivated by external balance problems. But this probably gets things backwards. If a central feature of monetary integration is greater macroeconomic discipline, it is less likely that trade policies will have to be geared towards containing macroeconomic pressures in the first place. The exchange rate guarantee that is part of the CFA arrangement has a similar effect, making the use of temporary quantitative restrictions less likely and therefore enhancing openness over the longer run by avoiding the political lock-in effect that is sometimes associated with such restrictions. In the end, the nature of the policy linkage between monetary integration and trade integration depends a great deal on the overall macroeconomic environment. When imbalances are large, fixity of the exchange rate discourages liberalization and may even encourage the adoption of quantitative restrictions that tighten the trade regime. On average, though, imbalances are likely to be less severe and trade policy less likely to be subordinated to them.

Arguments about the macroeconomic benefits of union membership have to be made carefully. We have noted that union membership should help underpin openness; we will see below that the evidence is ambiguous. Moreover, it matters how the discipline is achieved; in the CFA zone, for example, it is not clear that the discipline inherent in the vertical relationship with France can be reproduced in a purely horizontal relationship with regional partners. Finally, the ultimate issue is not whether currency union (with or without an external partner) helps to underpin trade openness, but whether it does so at less cost than other available mechanisms. There *are* other mechanisms available; the next section gives a brief overview of the non-coordinated movements towards macroeconomic stability and convertibility that have taken place outside the CFA zone.

The literature on optimum currency areas takes it for granted that a reduction in real exchange rate volatility between two trading partners will promote trade between those partners. Both theory and evidence are mixed on this proposition, however. In the absence of risk aversion or irreversibilities, for example, standard microeconomic theory appears to take nearly the opposite view. The possibility of substitution in response to price movements means that risk-neutral producers and consumers can capitalize on favourable price movements and limit the damage from unfavourable price movements of equal extent. Thus an increase in relative price variability (for a given mean) makes them better off and should encourage an increase in trading activity, not a decrease.[38]

On the theoretical side, sufficient risk aversion can overcome the attraction of volatility, so that a decrease in volatility spurs an increase in trade.[39] It seems clear that producers and traders engaged in official African external trade face very substantial policy-induced uncertainty about the relative prices and transactions costs they are likely to face. This is particularly true when trade and exchange rate policy becomes a tool of macroeconomic management, as it has in particular outside of the CFA zone. The large potential magnitude of policy uncertainty and the lack of institutions for handling risk therefore suggest that risk aversion may be an avenue through which volatility matters for African regional trade. Greater stability would be expected to increase the overall volume of trade and also shift trade patterns from unofficial to official channels.

Recent work on irreversible investment suggests another channel through which uncertainty about trade and exchange regimes may penalize trade, even when participants are risk-neutral (Dixit and Pindyck, 1994). The central point here is that a mean-preserving spread in the future output price increases the option value of irreversible investments. The result is an increase in the rate of return that is required to induce investment in the current period (the 'hurdle rate'). While the effects of irreversibility on the long-run capital stock are unclear, a reduction in volatility would crowd in investment in trading capacity in the short run by reducing the value of waiting to invest. This effect would be particularly biased in favour of larger-scale projects designed to operate through legal, official channels.

On the empirical side, there is surprisingly little evidence that the stabilizing of bilateral real exchange rates through exchange rate union or more thorough monetary integration increases trade. There are extremely small effects of exchange rate volatility in gravity equations for regional trade in the European Community. But this is in a setting in which convertibility already holds for current account purposes. The evidence for developing countries is mixed. Medhora (1990), for example, finds no effect of exchange rate volatility on UMOA imports over 1976–82, either aggregate or the regional share, while Caballero and Corbo (1989) and Bahmani-Oskooee and Ltaifa (1992) provide evidence for developing countries suggesting that real exchange rate volatility indeed dampens (aggregate) exports. There is ample room for further empirical work in this area. It bears emphasizing that some of the important effects of exchange rate uncertainty may have their greatest effect on the margin between legal and illegal trade rather than on aggregate trade.

3.4 PIECEMEAL PATHS TO MACROECONOMIC HARMONIZATION

The maintenance of an open trading regime depends on mutual accommodation of fiscal and exchange rate policy. If convertibility for current account purposes is to be maintained with mutually fixed exchange rates, what is required is harmonization of partner inflation rates, which in turn requires the harmonization of fiscal deficits net of external financing.[40] In African currency unions the required restraint has generally operated in the vertical dimension. This section briefly examines two alternative paths towards enhanced regional convertibility. The first, regional clearing, involves regional co-operation aimed at the symptom rather than the cause of non-convertibility. The second, unilateral stabilization and liberalization, goes to the root sources of non-convertibility but does so on a non-coordinated, non-cooperative basis and has not (as yet) involved a commitment to a fixed exchange rate.

Co-operation without Restraint: Regional Clearing

The primary economic rationale for the PTA Clearing House (and its older cousin, the West African Clearing House) is to enhance regional trade by economizing on the use of convertible currencies. In effect, the arrangement converts debits and credits that net out across the union into legal tender for settling intra-union bilateral imbalances. These arrangements reflect a judgement that the world financial system provides inadequate multilateral clearing of regional payments in Africa. In this respect their motivation is similar to that of the postwar European Payments Union and the Multilateral Clearing Arrangement that operated in the Council for Mutual Economic Assistance starting in the late 1950s. In the latter cases, however, the massive inadequacy of existing payments mechanisms was apparent; in Europe this was due to the collapse of international banking during the Depression and the

Second World War, and in the Soviet Bloc for similar reasons plus its political disengagement from the West.

Within Africa, the case is more complicated. Holding regional trade patterns fixed, the more creditworthy members have the option of clearing their balances more efficiently through the world banking system, while the others are not able to do so precisely because they are not creditworthy. On top of this, *all* members (even the creditworthy ones) have an incentive to free-ride on any credit provided by the system on more generous terms than available in the world financial markets. It is therefore difficult to make a *prima facie* case that regional clearing removes an important constraint to regional trade, or that it should substantially enhance the liquidity of member countries. Moreover, by addressing the symptom rather than the cause of lack of convertibility, the arrangement has tended to be undercut by competing palliatives – like export retention schemes that encourage exporters to invoice in hard currencies even in regional markets – undertaken at the national level (Lipumba and Kasekende, 1991).

In terms of the more modest goals of efficiency and institutional credibility, the PTACH has enjoyed greater success than the WACH, handling an increasing share of officially measured regional trade and enjoying some reduction in the ratio of net balances (payable in convertible currency) to gross flows (Berg, 1988).[41] The WACH has been particularly hampered by the dramatic asymmetry between the BEAC members, whose trade is already conducted in the convertible CFA franc, and the ten non-CFA members, some of whom (for example, Ghana, Sierra Leone) suffered from persistent central bank illiquidity through much of the 1970s and early 1980s (Frimpong-Ansah, 1990).

Restraint without Co-operation: Stabilization and Structural Adjustment

A potentially more powerful source of macroeconomic harmonization is the conditionality imposed by the IFIs and bilateral donors since the early 1980s. Conditionality-led stabilization and structural adjustment programmes employ a mix of strategies for imposing monetary restraint. In the 1990s, they have gone beyond the traditional targeting of domestic credit to imposing cash budgets on government, reforming domestic banking systems, redrafting national legislation to enhance central bank independence, externalizing customs revenue assessment and collection, and liberalizing the capital account. These arrangements reproduce the strong vertical dimension of African monetary unions, but with an essentially 'alien' vertical partner; moreover, they lack the horizontal dimension of regional co-operation since agreements are concluded bilaterally on a piecemeal, non-coordinated basis. Collier (1991) argues that these flaws seriously undercut their potential as a basis for durable restraint in the longer term.[42]

The objections notwithstanding, how much harmonization of macroeconomic policy has taken place unilaterally since the early 1980s, and in what respects? We will look first at exchange rate policy and then at inflation and fiscal deficits.

Exchange Rate Activism

The most substantial gains in terms of macroeconomic harmonization since the mid 1980s are with respect to the degree of real overvaluation of national currencies and the degree of flexibility of nominal exchange rates. Countries outside the CFA zone and CMA have broadly shifted from exchange rate passivity to exchange rate activism. The shift represents at least a temporary retreat from exchange controls as the primary tool for external balance. The adjustment is unmistakable, as shown in the first column of Table 3.5, which gives the median parallel premium on foreign exchange from 1970 to 1993 for eleven countries outside of the CFA zone and CMA. The premium increases from 40 per cent in the early 1970s to nearly 200 per cent in 1983, dropping only temporarily in the commodity boom of the late 1970s. After 1983, it falls precipitously, stabilizing between 20 per cent and 30 per cent by 1990.

The second feature is a clear shift from the use of the exchange rate as an anchor for domestic prices – a role that had long since been discredited in many cases through the increasing weight of parallel exchange rates in domestic price determination (Chhibber and Shafik, 1991 and Kiguel and O'Connell, 1995) – to its active use in avoiding real exchange rate overvaluation.[43] Underlying this change, at least in principle, is the reassertion of fiscal and monetary restraint as the primary anchor of price stability.

Improvements in export performance and the trade balance were a central target of structural adjustment programmes, leading to a prominent role for real exchange rate depreciation. Figures 3.4(a) and 3.4(b) show the dramatic difference between the CFA countries and the rest of SSA (excluding CMA) in how – and when – the required real depreciation was achieved. The figure decomposes the trade-weighted real effective exchange rate into the effective nominal exchange rate and the ratio of domestic to foreign price levels.[44] Outside the zone, internal demand

Table 3.5   Parallel premiums, fiscal deficits and inflation

Year	Median parallel premium, 11 non-CFA countries (%)	Fiscal deficit excluding grants				Dispersion of inflation	
		Average		Dispersion			
		CFA	15 Other	CFA	15 Other	CFA	11 Other
1970	41	n.a.	n.a.	n.a.	n.a.	n.a.	n.a.
1971	43	n.a.	n.a.	n.a.	n.a.	n.a.	n.a.
1972	41	n.a.	n.a.	n.a.	n.a.	3.9	6.1
1973	50	n.a.	n.a.	n.a.	n.a.	3.6	6.5
1974	38	n.a.	n.a.	n.a.	n.a.	5.6	8.6
1975	67	n.a.	n.a.	n.a.	n.a.	7.4	9.6
1976	147	n.a.	n.a.	n.a.	n.a.	10.0	19.8
1977	109	n.a.	n.a.	n.a.	n.a.	8.0	26.7
1978	87	n.a.	n.a.	n.a.	n.a.	3.7	17.3
1979	72	n.a.	n.a.	n.a.	n.a.	3.7	22.5
1980	94	7.4	10.3	7.1	6.8	3.0	23.0
1981	108	6.8	11.7	7.9	3.5	5.6	24.3
1982	159	7.0	10.9	8.1	3.8	4.0	11.0
1983	192	8.9	9.6	7.6	4.7	4.8	29.5
1984	100	7.5	8.1	6.0	4.9	6.8	22.5
1985	117	7.3	8.3	5.1	4.7	6.0	19.8
1986	136	8.7	9.0	4.5	7.6	6.6	26.3
1987	50	11.0	9.9	3.6	6.2	3.3	43.2
1988	60	10.7	9.1	4.5	6.1	4.7	26.0
1989	33	9.4	8.1	3.7	5.2	4.7	37.2
1990	23	8.1	8.9	3.5	6.8	3.8	53.5
1991	27	8.2	8.9	4.6	6.7	n.a.	n.a.
1992	19	n.a.	n.a.	n.a.	n.a.	n.a.	n.a.
1993	30	n.a.	n.a.	n.a.	n.a.	n.a.	n.a.

Notes: The country groups were based on data availability. *Parallel premium*: Ghana, Guinea, Kenya, Malawi, Mauritania, Mozambique, Nigeria, Tanzania, Uganda, Zambia, Zimbabwe. *Inflation dispersion*: CFA data include all CFA countries except Equatorial Guinea. '11 Other' comprises Burundi, Ghana, Kenya, Malawi, Mauritania, Nigeria, Rwanda, Sierra Leone, Tanzania, Zambia, and Zimbabwe. *Fiscal data*: CFA data exclude Chad and Equatorial Guinea; '15 Other' comprises Burundi, The Gambia, Ghana, Kenya, Madagascar, Malawi, Mauritania, Mozambique, Nigeria, Rwanda, Sierra Leone, Tanzania, Uganda, Zambia and Zaire. Dispersion measured by standard deviation.

Sources: Parallel premiums: *World Currency Yearbook* and IMF, *International Financial Statistics*, various issues. Fiscal data provided courtesy of K. Nashashibi (the data set is used in Nashashibi and Bazzoni (1993)). Inflation data from IMF, *International Financial Statistics*.

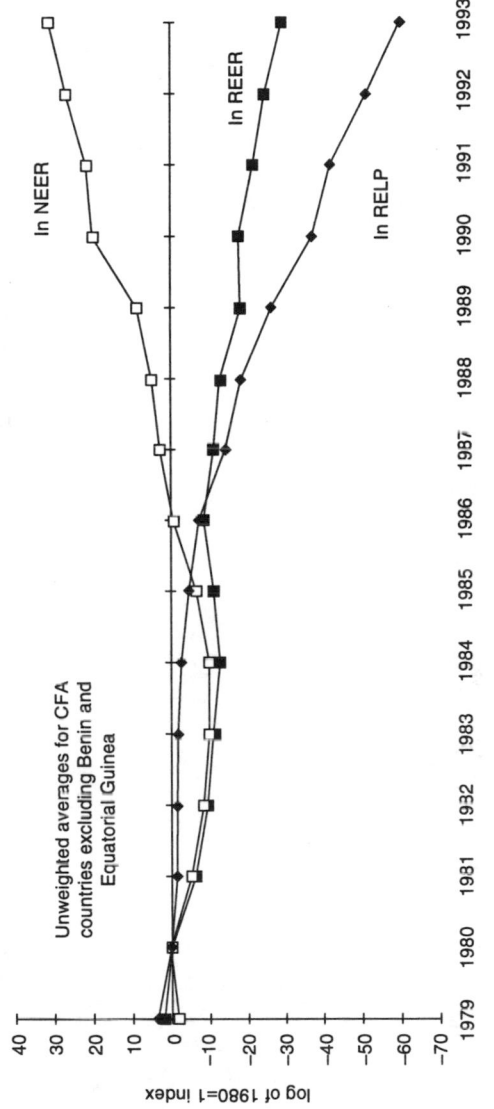

Figure 3.4a   Real effective exchange rate decompositions, 11 CFA countries

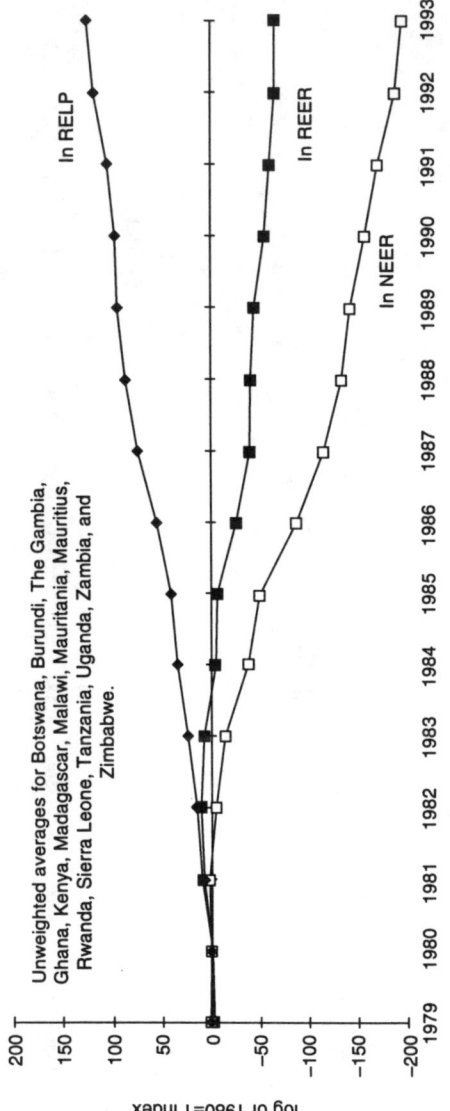

Figure 3.4b Real effective exchange rate decomposition, 15 non-CFA, non-CMA countries

pressures in the early 1980s are evident in the rise in domestic prices relative to foreign prices. In the absence of exchange rate adjustment, this produced a real appreciation that continued a trend established in the mid 1970s. Nominal devaluations were then used to bring down the real exchange rate, particularly between 1985 and 1987. That they succeeded in doing so on a persistent basis is not because domestic demand contraction subsequently lowered inflation dramatically relative to foreign levels. On the contrary, domestic inflation continued to exceed foreign inflation, but this was accommodated by continued nominal depreciation, thus helping to prevent the re-emergence of overvaluation.

Within the CFA zone, in contrast, inflation differentials tended until the mid 1980s to be small, so that movements in the real exchange rate were largely driven by exogenous developments in the nominal effective exchange rate. Between 1980 and 1985, the CFA countries benefited from the substantial depreciation of the French franc against the US dollar. Starting in 1985, however, movements in the nominal effective exchange rate turned decisively against competitiveness in the zone, a process that accelerated in the late 1980s with the appreciation of the Deutsch mark and the French policy of *franc fort*, which in combination with the fixed parity against the French franc effectively put the African countries of the CFA zone on a Deutsch mark standard. Attempts to achieve a depreciated real exchange rate therefore had to rely on dramatic reductions in domestic inflation relative to foreign inflation – at a time when inflation in the industrial countries had already fallen to low levels. The efforts at internal adjustment are evident in the massive fall in domestic prices relative to foreign prices between 1984 and 1993. The counterpart to this contractionary adjustment was a decade-long recession that reduced incomes per caput by well over 30 per cent, and given the continued adverse movements of the nominal effective rate, the final result was an average real depreciation of less than 30 per cent relative to the 1980 level. For the larger countries of the zone, the real depreciation was almost certainly inadequate given the pre-existing overvaluation and the deterioration of the terms of trade that began in the mid 1980s. The 50 per cent devaluation of January 1994 is not shown; it represented a final acknowledgement of the inadequacy of the internal adjustment mechanism, at least for the larger countries of the zone.

Inflation and Fiscal Deficits

Although the cross-country dispersion of inflation rates remained low within the CFA zone throughout the 1980s, the dispersion increased markedly outside the zone, at least through 1990 (Table 3.5). The result is not surprising. Whereas tight conditionality was imposed on the monetary financing of fiscal deficits throughout subSaharan Africa in the 1980s, part of the point of increased exchange rate flexibility outside of the CFA zone (and CMA) is that temporary failure on this front need not produce a real appreciation with damaging effects on external competitiveness. Thus countries may choose divergent inflation rates on public finance grounds, or they may prefer similar rates but face divergent traditions of policy failure (Zambia, Uganda) or policy continuity (Ghana, Tanzania) that alter the costs of achieving desired targets in the short run. In either case, exchange rate policy is increasingly geared towards accommodating fiscal and monetary outcomes in the interest of overall competitiveness, rather than providing a nominal anchor.

Table 3.5 shows average fiscal deficits (unweighted, central government, excluding grants) in 11 of the 13 CFA countries and 15 countries in the rest of subSaharan Africa (excluding CMA) for the period from 1980 to 1991. Deficits fell on average during the 1980s outside of the CFA area, and rose slightly within the CFA zone. The increase within the CFA zone was driven mainly by large inceases in the oil-exporting countries of BEAC; UMOA and the non-CFA countries were virtually identical in achieving modest reductions in the deficit over the decade. Trends in the cross-country dispersion of fiscal deficits (measured by the yearly standard deviation) follow the reverse pattern: dispersion falls markedly in the CFA zone, as the oil-exporting countries move from surpluses in the early years to deficits in the order of 10 per cent of GDP in the later years, while it increases markedly outside of the zone. There is very little evidence here of a convergence of fiscal positions in SSA.

Liberalization and Devaluation without Co-ordination

National movements towards convertibility have been fitful and unco-ordinated, so that what may eventually constitute regional convergence has meant dramatically divergent policies in the short run. These short-run divergences make the costs of non-coordination seem dramatic whether or not there are large benefits from explicit co-ordination in the longer run. The interface between the CFA or CMA countries and neighbouring countries implementing substantial real devaluations became a particular locus of policy spillovers beginning in the early 1980s, and the same process is now running in reverse with the recent CFA devaluation.

Section 3.2 provided a framework for thinking about the spillover effects of partner trade and exchange rate policies. In a unified exchange rate regime, a devaluation is beggar-thy-neighbour; it reduces domestic costs in foreign currency terms and imposes the equivalent of a temporary terms of trade shock on the partner. Trade liberalization, in contrast, has positive spillover effects, the counterpart to the deterioration in the domestic trade balance being an improvement for the partner. Exchange rate unification is more complicated. We saw in section 3.2 that unification for current account purposes implies a trade liberalization. The up-front devaluations that typically accompany exchange rate unification are therefore what Collier (1991) calls 'trade-liberalizing devaluations', designed to allow a loosening of restrictions without an excessive loss of reserves. The devaluation mutes the short-run positive transmission of the trade liberalization, but the longer-run spillover should be positive. When trade and exchange controls have been severe, additional transmission effects come from a reduction in the transactions costs associated with illegal trade.

Do these regional spillover effects add up to a major co-ordination problem in achieving current account convertibility on a regional basis? The answer seems plainly to be no, since many African countries have succeeded in moving toward convertibility on a non-coordinated basis. Should exchange rates be more closely co-ordinated? Again the answer seems to be no, given the diverse starting points in terms of degrees of overvaluation and the continuing role of exchange rate adjustments in reconciling diverse national inflation rates with the maintenance of more open trading regimes. This is not to say that consultation on exchange rates is not valuable, particularly by the larger countries whose policies have an asymmetrically strong effect on smaller regional partners. But the case for explicit co-ordination of exchange rates appears weak.

External Tariffs and Export Taxes: Co-ordination or Competition?

There is a stronger case for co-ordination of national tax rates on goods traded with common external partners.[45] Analysts agree that in the mid

1980s, unrecorded trade between countries in subSaharan Africa (excluding South Africa) was roughly of the same order of magnitude as recorded trade, perhaps 6 or 7 per cent of GDP (*Applied Development Economics*, 1988). A non-trivial share of this trade involves arbitrage between different national price structures for goods traded with common external partners. This pattern is as old as the underlying tax differentials: Hopkins (1973) cites the diversion of French-area groundnuts through British Gambia to avoid Senegal's export duty before 1855. More recently, Tanzanian and Ugandan coffee has fetched a higher price if smuggled across the Kenyan border, Ghanaian cocoa has for extended periods been worth much more if sold to the marketing authority in Côte d'Ivoire, and subsidized Nigerian oil, meant for the domestic market, has been sold profitably in neighbouring Togo. The point applies to manufactured goods as well (see, for example, Deardorff and Stolper, 1990; Berg, 1985; and Azam, 1991): Togo's relatively low tariff on automobile imports generates a stream of imports destined for the higher-tariff, higher-price Nigerian market, and Nigeria's ban on cigarette imports generates high profits for smuggling of cigarettes from Niger.

This unrecorded trade survives primarily because the internal borders separating African neighbours are more difficult to police than the major ports and railway lines that serve its external trade (it is the illegal counterpart to the legal 'trade deflection' within a free-trade area in response to divergent commercial policy towards the exterior that was analysed by Balassa [1961]). Such trade has potentially large spillover effects, most obviously on the revenue from trade taxation, but also on foreign exchange proceeds from exports and the degree of protection granted to domestic producers of import-competing goods. These spillover effects provide a case for regional co-ordination – somewhat ironically, with the objective of avoiding damaging 'tariff competition' (Johnson, 1987) on external trade. If countries balance a revenue objective against the costs of distorting production and consumption decisions, for example, the non-coordinated equilibrium will have external tariffs and export taxes that are too low, because each country ignores the positive revenue spillover for regional partners of an increase in its own tariff rate; moreover, the revenue and protection spillovers associated with external trade may become a focus of policy conflict that reduces legitimate regional trade. In such an equilibrium a co-ordinated increase in tariffs on external trade would make all partners better off.

It is important to emphasize that the case for *co-ordination* of national policies towards external trade is more general than the case for a common external tariff or export tax; the latter is likely to be optimal only under strong symmetry assumptions or in the presence of a costless mechanism for redistributing revenues among participants. And as in the case of exchange rate consultation, the case for mutual *consultation* is more general than the case for formal co-ordination. Given the height of African trade barriers, it would be difficult to argue that many African governments have been trapped in a tariff competition of the type described above (Senegal and The Gambia are possible exceptions). It is more likely that fiscal planning has simply been undermined by inadequate consideration of cross-border tax arbitrage and by the adoption of costly and ineffective ways of handling it when it becomes apparent.

3.5 MONETARY INTEGRATION AND AFRICAN TRADE

We saw in section 3.3 that the African monetary landscape remains today – in terms of formal cooperation – largely the legacy of choices made at independence. These choices were highly divergent, with the fifteen members of three African currency unions choosing to formalize tight relationships dating from before independence, and other countries dissolving these same relationships and embarking on independent monetary policies. This is in contrast to the situation with regional trade promotion, where the period since independence has seen a proliferation of agreements all generally aimed at increasing regional linkages. This section briefly looks at the empirical evidence on African trade; it first examines the general openness of African economies and then the patterns of intra-African trade.

Openness

African economies in the 1970s and 1980s were more inward-looking on average than those of Asia or Latin America. This can be confirmed by looking either at the height and prevalence of official trade barriers (for example DeRosa, 1992) or by comparing trade volumes or relative prices to those that would prevail under free trade (for example, Dollar, 1992; Guillaumont *et al.*, 1988; and Leamer, 1988). Section 3.2 suggested that the latter approach is particularly important in SSA, where the stance of trade policy has been endogenized by heavy use of quantitative restrictions and exchange controls, and where illegal trade is substantial.

Table 3.6   Measures of openness

Group	*Dollar (1992) for 1976–85*			*DeRosa (1992) for 1987*		
	N	Distortion	Variability	N	Import charges	NTBs
UMOA	7	151	0.07	4	46	49
BEAC	5	169	0.09	3	38	51
CMA	2	133	0.15			
Other SSA	25	170	0.18	16	30	91
Non-UMOA ECOWAS	7	205	0.21	n.a.	n.a.	n.a.
All SSA	39	164	0.15	n.a.	n.a.	n.a.
Asia	16	86	0.01	n.a.	n.a.	n.a.
Latin America	24	114	0.22	n.a.	n.a.	n.a.
Europe/Middle East	12	104	0.15	n.a.	n.a.	n.a.
All LDCs	n.a.	n.a.	n.a.	n.a.	20	40

Notes: Group data are unweighted averages over N countries. From Dollar (1992): *Distortion* is calculated as the ratio of the domestic price of a standardized consumption basket, converted to US dollars at the official exchange rate, to the US price for that basket. *Variability* is the coefficient of variation of distortion. From DeRosa (1992): *Import charges* include all customs and sales tax charges on imports, as a percentage of customs value. *NTBs* are the shares of total imports covered by non-tariff barriers (for example, quotas, or foreign exchange rationing). The data for All LDCs are from footnote on p. 102.

Source: Columns 2–4: author's calculations based on data in Dollar (1992). Columns 5–7: author's calculations based on UNCTAD data compiled by DeRosa (1992).

The first three columns of Table 5.6 report a price-based measure of outward orientation calculated by Dollar (1992). Using annual data for 97 developing countries over the period 1976–85, Dollar calculated the ratio of the domestic price of a fixed consumption basket to the US price converted at the official exchange rate, and regressed these country–year price ratios on measures of economic structure. The residuals from this regression were then used as a measure of the degree to which the trade and exchange rate regime was distorted in favour of producing for the domestic market rather than for exports. In effect, Dollar was calculating the influence of policy on the real official exchange rate for exports (our e in Section 3.2). The column labelled 'distortion' shows 10-year averages for various country groups. African countries have by far the strongest tilt of incentives in favour of producing for the domestic market. This inward orientation is the result not only of import-substituting industrial strategy but also, as we have seen, of the subordination of sectoral policy to the need for macroeconomic balance starting in the early 1970s.[46]

In Table 3.6 the column labelled 'variability' shows the coefficient of variation of the distortion index and provides further confirmation of the analysis in section 3.2. In particular, while Africa is the most inward-orientated region by a large margin, it is economically less volatile on average than Latin America and indistinguishable in terms of volatility from the developing countries of Europe and the Middle East. A number of individual African countries have a combination of relatively severe distortion and substantial stability (Cameroon, Central African Republic, Congo, The Gambia, Côte d'Ivoire, Niger and Zimbabwe). While this might at first glance seem an implausible combination of features, the earlier analysis suggests that a restrictive trade regime can be mobilized to 'validate' an otherwise untenable combination of nominal wealth and the official exchange rate – and that the result is precisely a real appreciation and distortion of production incentives away from exportables.[47]

The price data in Table 3.6 can in principle shed light on the effect of monetary integration on trade openness. Within Africa, UMOA emerges as unusually open, while BEAC is essentially indistinguishable from the rest of SSA. This result is broadly corroborated by calculations of effective rates of protection in Greenaway and Nam (1988) and by the extensive investigations of export performance (controlling for economic structure) in Guillaumont and Guillaumont (1988), Guillaumont *et al.* (1988), and Leamer (1988).[48] In terms of volatility, the CFA countries have less than half the instability of African countries outside the zone.

Measures of the official trade and exchange rate regime, such as those reported by DeRosa (1992), find higher nominal tariffs and a greater prevalence of non-tariff barriers in SSA than in other developing countries (see cols 5–7 in Table 3.6), even in 1987 after a broad movement towards trade liberalization was already well under way in SSA. The structure of protection in CFA countries is less tilted towards quantitative restrictions than in the rest of SSA, suggesting that the revenue motive has been relatively more important, and the liquidity motive relatively less important, in explaining the evolution of trade policy in the CFA countries compared with the rest of SSA. This is consistent with the greater liquidity and macroeconomic discipline associated with the exchange rate guarantee from France, and possibly also with the restraint on seigniorage revenues implied by the commitment to low inflation and an open capital account.[49]

Table 3.7   Intra-African exports as a share of total exports

Region and group	Share of intra-group exports in total exports			Exports to SSA as % of total exports	
	1970	*1980*	*1990*	*1980*	*1990*
West Africa					
ECOWAS[a]	2.9	3.5	5.7	3.6	6.4
CEAO	6.3	8.9	10.5	13.2	15.0
MRU	0.2	0.5	0.1	0.9	2.9
Central Africa					
UDEAC	4.8	1.6	3.0	2.1	5.9
Eastern and Southern Africa					
PTA[b]	18.0	7.6	5.9	(8.4)	7.6
Total SSA	n.a.	n.a.	n.a.	2.8	6.0

Notes:
[a] ECOWAS incudes the CEAO and MRU countries plus Cape Verde, The Gambia, Ghana, Guinea, Bissau, Nigeria and Togo.
[b] The PTA was established in 1981 and began operations in 1984.

Source: Foroutan and Pritchett (1993).

Intra-African Trade

Data difficulties are particularly severe in regional trade patterns, since a large share of intra-African trade is not captured in the official statistics (Berg, 1985). With this caveat in mind, Table 3.7 (from Foroutan, 1993) shows officially measured intra-group and intra-African exports as a share of total exports for selected regional groupings in Africa. Of the two monetary unions for which trade data are available, CEAO (the virtual equivalent to UMOA) has much higher intra-union trade, and UDEAC (equivalent to BEAC) very slightly lower, than the rest of subSaharan Africa. Intra-PTA trade, while higher than intra-African trade in general, was actually lower in 1990 than it was before the PTA began operations in 1984.

Comparisons within ECOWAS are somewhat more revealing because they control to some degree for the fact that efforts at monetary integration have typically been accompanied by simultaneous efforts at trade integration (for example, the PTA is simultaneously a payments union and, in theory, an emerging free trade area). The fact that intra-CEAO trade is so much higher than intra-ECOWAS trade suggests some role for the CFA arrangements in facilitating intra-regional trade. We have seen that monetary union may have made the emergence of endogenous trade restrictions less likely, and that it may have increased the gains from intra-union trade by stabilizing real exchange rates and reducing transactions costs. The fixity of the exchange rate would have tended to discourage trade liberalization *vis-à-vis* external partners, other things being equal, but this constraint would operate less severely for a co-ordinated liberalization with regional partners.

An obvious weakness of the data in Table 3.6 is that they do not control for economic structure. Foroutan and Pritchett (1993) remedy this by estimating a gravity model of bilateral non-oil trade flows between fifty-three developing countries in 1980–2 and then assessing African trade patterns relative to norms appropriate for the structural characteristics of African countries. They find that although there are large country-by-country discrepancies, the regional trade of African countries is close to what is predicted by the model on average. Low levels of intra-African trade therefore appear to be explained by structural factors like low income and large intra-country distances rather than by a peculiar bias against regional trade. Foroutan and Pritchett also find that trade between CEAO members is significantly higher than the gravity model predicts, and that dummy variables for ECOWAS and UDEAC are statistically insignificant (and in the case of UDEAC even negative), confirming the broad findings above.

The gravity model is a promising vehicle for further empirical work on the issues raised in this paper (see for example Ogunkola, 1993). Three central issues are whether:

(1) monetary integration has a major effect on trade openness;
(2) exchange controls have a major effect on trade openness; and
(3) the effects of monetary integration or exchange rate unification are particularly favourable to regional trade as against external trade.

The first question is difficult to answer in part because monetary integration schemes overlap with trade integration schemes. Thus CEAO is unusually open regionally, and UDEAC is typical or even closed. What do we conclude about the common feature of CFA zone membership that applies to nearly all members of these two unions? One approach would be to control for real exchange rate volatility between partners, since greater exchange rate stability is particularly associated with monetary integration.

The second issue could be approached by using a long average of the parallel foreign exchange premium. The theory in section 3.2 suggests that persistently large premiums should be associated with lower trade, whether regionally or otherwise. Entering this variable could help make precise the contribution of monetary integration above and beyond the maintenance of unified exchange rates for current account transactions. It might also help to clarify the divergent performance of CEAO and UDEAC, since major countries in the latter group trade heavily with Zaire and Nigeria, two countries where currencies are non-convertible and an unusually large portion of trade is probably unrecorded.

Both this variable and the exchange rate volatility variable could be interacted with the regional trade dummy variable to get a handle on the third issue, whether the macroeconomic effects operate particularly strongly in favour of – or against – regional trade.

3.6 CONCLUSIONS

This paper has covered a lot of ground, and this concluding section summarizes the main points.

With respect to trade reform, we have seen that until recently the stance of trade policy in many African countries, and particularly the evolution of that stance over time, was largely a macroeconomic phenomenon. Changes in the structure of effective protection were driven primarily by balance of payments considerations rather than by conventional considerations of resource allocation. This implies that policies normally construed as primarily macroeconomic in character, such as exchange rate unification, had strong effects on the domestic relative prices of traded goods. It follows that any chronology of trade policy developments or search for trade liberalization episodes must pay close attention to macroeconomic developments and their implications for exchange rate policy and exchange controls. It also follows that domestic price data are essential in determining the actual stance of trade policy, since tariffs were inframarginal for much of the post-independence period.

Macroeconomic forces were generally less important in determining the stance of trade policy among the African members of currency unions. In the CFA countries, however, a commitment to fixed exchange rate may well have raised the cost of trade liberalization. The relationship between monetary integration and trade reform is complex; the greater macroeconomic discipline associated with membership helps countries maintain open trading regimes, but the loss of the exchange rate instrument at the national level makes the transition to a liberalized regime more difficult.

The degree of monetary integration is one of the key features differentiating the macroeconomic environments of African countries, and there are three main points to consider in an overview of the African experience with monetary integration:

- The experience is varied, and includes examples of monetary co-operation – among the thirteen members of the CFA zone – that go far beyond what any regional grouping with the exception of SACU has achieved in terms of regional trade (including the CFA countries themselves).
- In contrast to most African trade initiatives, the examples of successful monetary integration rely on a strong link with a dominant external partner (here treating South Africa as external).
- Monetary disintegration has prevailed over monetary integration in the postwar period. This was dramatically the case at independence but has also prevailed more recently in the weakening of vertical ties in the three African currency unions.

With this overview of monetary integration as background, there are two main views of the linkages between monetary integration and regional trade. In one view, the potential gains from regional trade provide a central – perhaps the central – rationale for increases in monetary co-operation between regional partners. Full monetary union, in this view, is the culmination of a gradual process of economic integration that begins with the establishment of mutual convertibility and the granting of regional trade preferences. The objective at each stage is to expand the regional market and thereby capture a larger share of the potential gains from regional specialization and exchange. This view was characteristic of the classic literature on optimum currency areas, which took the existence of substantial gains to enhanced regional exchange as axiomatic and focused on the costs of monetary union. Regional trade promotion was an important objective in most stages of European monetary integration in the postwar period, and the notion of accelerated development through increased regional trade appears central to the ECA's vision for its African sub-regions and ultimately for Africa as a whole.

In the second view, the main purpose of monetary integration is to contribute to investment and growth by supporting low and stable inflation and a competitive and stable real exchange rate. In short, the purpose of integration is to help enforce the *policy restraint* necessary for macroeconomic stability. Such restraint may underpin a more open trade regime by supporting a more competitive real exchange rate and releasing trade policy from a preoccupation with external balance. But trade gains are not central to this view, and macroeconomic policy restraint is valued even in their absence. And with respect to regional trade in particular, there is no presumption of greater gains from openness *vis-à-vis* regional partners than non-regional ones.

Which view or combination of views is appropriate for thinking about the interaction between monetary integration and trade in Africa? My view is that the establishment of convertibility for current account purposes is extremely important for Africa's international trade. It is probably even relatively more important for non-traditional trade, including regional trade in locally-manufactured goods, than for trade in traditional products with hard-currency partners outside of Africa. There are two important points to consider here, however. The first is the familiar one that regional trade is unlikely to be an important engine of African growth in the near term. African countries lack the income levels and structural complementarities that would generate large gains from regional specialization, whether within or across industries. In particular, promotion of regional trade at the expense of non-regional trade is nearly certain to favour trade diversion and therefore to fail a standard cost-benefit test; if arguments along the lines of Romer (1994) are correct, the losses would be many times those indicated by standard calculations. The main argument in favour of convertibility is a non-discriminatory one, which in practice applies first and foremost to developed country markets.

Second, convertibility does not require monetary integration. In fact, it does not even require co-operation, since it suffices for each country to unify its exchange rates *vis-à-vis* non-regional hard currencies. What it does require is (1) at least in the short run, a willingness to abandon the use of the exchange rate as a nominal anchor (and/or a mechanism for delivering rents to favoured groups); and (2) over the longer run, a willingness to exercise the fiscal restraint consistent with low inflation.

Both of these requisites of sustained exchange rate unification are currently being enforced by the international financial institutions and bilateral donors through the mechanism of policy conditionality, a situation I have characterized as one of 'restraint without co-operation'. This situation has clear advantages over the opposite extreme of 'co-operation without restraint' epitomized by the regional clearing mechanisms that cover most of Africa and the (less prevalent) bilateral countertrade agreements between regional partners. But traditional macroeconomic conditionality is not designed to obtain macroeconomic restraint over anything but the short term. In response to this, donors and the IFIs are now turning increasingly towards institutional interventions in the monetary and fiscal sectors, in the hope of putting self-restraint on a more durable domestic footing. If monetary integration has a role to play in underpinning convertibility and trade openness, therefore, that role must stem from its advantages over new-fangled policy condition-ality – or home-grown versions of the same institutional reforms, for that matter – as an 'agency of restraint' over the medium to long term. The terminology is Collier's (1991), along with the argument that the vertical and horizontal links in the CFA zone generate a 'participatory, supra-national agency of restraint' with major advantages over the es-sentially alien, unidirectional, and unreliable conditionality of donors and the IFIs.

Establishing convertibility is important, therefore, although more for overall trade than for regional trade in particular. Assuming mutual convertibility, what about the other benefits of monetary integration for regional trade, those assumed by the literature on optimum currency areas? In my view, these benefits – associated with reductions in intra-union exchange rate variability and currency transactions costs – do not in themselves provide a strong case for further monetary integration, given the relatively limited prospective gains from intra-African trade. Integration with a northern partner or set of partners, in contrast, is more appealing since stabilization of the exchange rate with major hard-currency partners would affect a much larger share of African trade.

A final topic touched on is the co-ordination of tariffs and export taxes on trade with non-regional partners. A large share of intra-Afri-can trade is motivated by differences in domestic taxes (or implicit taxes) on such trade. The transport costs, enforcement expenditures and trade conflicts associated with such trade are inefficient for the region as a whole. Morover, the implicit competition for trade tax rev-enues can lead to suboptimal outcomes, either by producing external tariffs that are 'too low' or by increasing the uncertainty of private traders and investors about the trade policy regime. External tariffs and export taxes therefore represent a potentially promising area for co-operation.

APPENDIX

This appendix derives the IB, EB and AB schedules from dynamic equations for the real exchange rate, private stocks of financial assets, and international reserves, and indicates how illegal trade and foreign exchange black markets can be incorporated into the analysis. The model simplifies in a number of respects: for example, making no distinction between regional and 'external' trade, assuming away intermediate imports, ignoring capital accumulation and growth, and adopting a non-optimizing specification for private saving.

Consider the real exchange rate first. The economy produces exports and domestic goods and consumes imports and domestic goods. Domestic goods include not only pure non-traded goods but also 'semi-traded' goods that compete with the export sector for resources and are imperfect substitutes for imports in consumption. Since the stance of trade policy can change, there are two real exchange rates to keep track of, one for imports and one for exports. Only the real exchange rate for exports, e, affects production decisions, since imports are not produced domestically.

The dynamics for e come from the labour market. Labour is perfectly mobile between sectors, so there is a single economy-wide nominal wage ω for employed workers. There is a benchmark level of employment, L, that constitutes 'full employment', but in the short run employment is determined by the demand for labour at a sticky nominal wage. Domestic goods are produced with a constant average (and therefore marginal) product of labour α_D. With competitive labour and product markets this means that the product wage ($\omega/P_D \equiv \alpha_D$) is constant and output is demand-determined in this sector. Output in the export sector, in contrast, is subject to diminishing returns to labour and therefore depends on the product wage in that sector, ω/P_X. This real wage is flexible in the long run but predetermined (given the export tax rate) in the short run, given the sticky nominal wage and the small country assumption. Unemployment emerges when low aggregate demand reduces output and employment in the domestic goods sector and the real wage for exportables is too high for exporting firms to absorb the unemployed labour.

The nominal wage (and therefore the price of non-traded goods) responds gradually over time to labour market slack, along an expectations-augmented Phillips curve of the form:

$$\hat{P}_N = \pi^e + \beta[L_D(Q_D) - L_X(e) - L], \quad \beta > 0, \tag{3A.1}$$

where $Q_D = D_D + G_D$ is the (demand-determined) output of domestic goods and π^e is the expected rate of inflation in the overall price level. Defining $S_D(e)$ as the output of domestic goods consistent with full employment, the excess demand for labour (XDL) in (3A.1) is directly proportional to the excess demand for domestic goods (XDG), $D_D + G_D - S_D$. The story is simplest when the exchange rate is pegged and expecations of inflation are zero, since in this case,

$$\hat{e} = \delta[D_D(e,h) + G_D - S_D(e)], \quad \delta \equiv \beta/\alpha_D > 0. \tag{3A.2}$$

The internal balance schedule (eq. (3.1)) is given by $XDL = XDG = 0$, which in turn implies a constant real exchange rate for exports by (3A.2). The real exchange rate is appreciating when there is excess demand for domestic goods and labour, and depreciating when there is excess supply.

A second dynamic equation is for the overall current account, which is the sum of the change in international reserves and the change in private holdings of foreign assets, $f*$:

$$\dot{r}* + \dot{f}* = S_X(e) - \tau*[D_M(\theta\tau*,h) + G_M - a]$$ (3A.3)

In the absence of capital flows ($\dot{f}* = 0$), the current account is just the change in international reserves, and the external balance schedule (eq. (3.2)) is just (3A.2) with the left-hand side set equal to zero. Away from this schedule, a trade surplus means rising reserves and a deficit means falling reserves.

A third dynamic equation describes the evolution of private wealth (and therefore spending, given the constant velocity assumption). One component of wealth is domestic money balances, which evolve according to the sum of domestic credit expansion and the balance of payments surplus. Thus

$$\dot{h} = -\pi_E h + d - a + \left(\frac{E}{P_X}\right)\dot{r}*$$ (3A.4)

where the fiscal deficit d may itself be a function of e, h and θ. The simplest case is when domestic money is the only asset, since in this case (3A.4) completely describes the evolution of private wealth. The asset balance schedule (eq. (3.3)) sets $\dot{h}$ equal to zero.

More generally, wealth will be include foreign assets, $f*$, valued at the exchange rate relevant for capital account transactions. With the additional asset comes a portfolio equilibrium condition of the form

$$h = \lambda(\pi_E)w,$$ (3A.5)

where $w \equiv h + (E/P_X)f*$ is total real wealth and π_E is the opportunity cost of holding wealth in the form of domestic real balances. With an open capital account and a fixed rate of crawl, the IB/EB/AB analysis goes ahead as in the text (see Khan and Lizondo, 1987). In the background, the private sector continuously exchanges the two assets with the central bank to maintain a constant desired proportion of domestic to foreign assets. Total spending is now governed by total wealth $w \equiv h + (E/PX)f*$, not just domestic real balances, and the EB schedule now refers to net foreign assets $r* + f*$ rather than just to reserves. With w replacing h on the horizontal axis, however, the IB and EB schedules are unchanged. The AB schedule is altered only through the replacement of $\pi_E h$ by $\pi_E \lambda(\pi_E)w$.

With illegal trade and foreign exchange black markets, the analysis is more complicated. Black markets introduce an additional variable, the parallel premium, defined as (1 +) the ratio of the black market exchange rate, B, to the official rate: $z \equiv B/E$. Private holdings of foreign assets now evolve according to the parallel trade balance, which is governed by the parallel premium and the other determinants of illegal trade:

$$\dot{f}^* = f^*(h, e, \theta, \tau^*, t_X, t_M, z). \qquad (3A.6)$$
$$\phantom{\dot{f}^* = f^*(}? - - ? \ + - +$$

The signs of derivatives in (3A.6) stem from the theory of illegal trade with black markets. A rise in the export tax, for example, diverts exports from official to parallel channels, increasing the flow supply of foreign exchange into the parallel market. A rise in the parallel premium increases the reward for smuggled exports and the cost of smuggled imports, increasing the parallel trade balance. A real appreciation reduces aggregate exports; given the share smuggled, this in turn reduces the flow supply of illegal foreign exchange.

The opportunity cost of holding domestic assets is now the rate of depreciation in the parallel market. The portfolio equilibrium condition becomes:

$$h = \lambda(\hat{B}^e, v)w = \lambda(\hat{z}^e + \pi^e_E, v)w, \qquad (3A.7)$$
$$+ \ -$$

which under perfect foresight gives us a dynamic equation for the parallel premium. The parameter v is a measure of the success (if any) of capital controls in creating a captive demand for domestic assets.

The Fiscal Deficit with Trade Taxes

With trade taxes at rates t_M and t_X and other taxes in amount T, the fiscal deficit is given by

$$D = P_N G_N + P_M G_M - (T + E t_M P^*_M D_M + E t_X P^*_X S_X) \qquad (3A.8)$$

Deflating by $P_X \equiv (1 - t_X)P^*_X$ and using the fact that with $a = 0$, the change in reserves is the trade balance $S_X - (D_M + G_M)$, we get (after some rearranging) eq. (3.5).

Notes

1. This paper was prepared for the AERC/CEPR/Oxford Collaborative Project on African Trade Liberalization and Regional Integration. It is a revised and expanded version of a draft presented at the conference in Nairobi, December 1993. I thank conference participants, and especially my discussant Paul Collier, for helpful comments, and colleagues at the Centre for Study of African Economies for providing a stimulating environment in which to do the initial work. The material in section 3.2 reflects discussions with Chris Adam, David Bevan, Mohsin Khan, Saul Lizondo, Chris Milner,

Norman Gemmel, Charles Soludo, and Larry Westphal; I thank them all without implicating them in the results. I am grateful to Mark Henstridge, Mohsin Khan and Karim Nashashibi for providing data and to Swarthmore College for supporting my leave at Oxford through a Lang Faculty Fellowship. Sampriti Ganguli and Jude Uzonwanne provided excellent research assistance.

2. What follows is not a full treatment of the macroeconomics of protection and liberalization. The focus is on the 'fundamentals' of trade, exchange rate and fiscal policy, and particularly on the question of what motivates the stance of trade policy and what policies are needed to make a liberalization technically feasible or 'compatible' in the language of Bevan *et al.* (1990). A full discussion would also have to consider the role of speculative behaviour in rendering even a compatible liberalization unsuccessful.

3. The private demand for imports is in general a function of P_M/P_X as well as of e, but the domestic relative price of traded goods drops out if there are constant expenditure shares.

4. Devaluation would be contractionary if the elasticities of demand and supply of domestic goods were low enough that the switching effect of the devaluation – generated on the demand side by the fall in the real exchange rate for importables and on the supply side by the fall in the real exchange rate for exportables – were smaller than the contractionary spending effect coming from the fall in real balances. This possibility is ruled out by our assumption of constant expenditure shares, but it can be reinstated by allowing a more general specification of demand (or incorporating other features like imported intermediate goods).

5. The inflation tax term is really $\pi_X h$, where π_X is the rate of inflation of domestic export prices. But as long as export taxes are at a constant *ad valorem* rate, we can replace π_X with π_E.

6. Assume throughout that there are no quantitative restrictions on the export side, so that t_x is predetermined.

7. The direct proportionality between e and the real consumption wage comes from the assumption that labour has a constant marginal product in the domestic goods sector. If the marginal product of labour were diminishing, a real depreciation would generally raise the real wage measured in terms of domestic goods (while lowering it in terms of traded goods). The real consumption wage would fall only if the share of imports in consumption were sufficiently large.

8. There is no import-substituting production here, so the improvement in the trade balance comes from a substitution effect in consumption, and a reduction in real balances measured in importables. In a richer model an additional effect would come from an increase in import-substituting production.

9. Recall that we are assuming in this section that any revenue impact of trade restrictions is returned to the private sector via lump-sum transfers.

10. Government spending and aid can easily be incorporated. Government spending would simply shift the origin for the private sector's indifference curves in quadrant 1 to the point (G_M, G_D) instead of $(0,0)$. Aid would shift the 'External Balance' line in quadrant 3 downwards by the amount of aid measured in imports; this would shift the consumption

possibilities locus in quadrant 1 to the right along the horizontal axis.
11. A kind of Lerner symmetry continues to operate here, in the sense that trade taxes enter only through θ. This is because with the overall trade balance – the last term in eq. (3.5) – held constant, a rise in D_M implies an equal rise in S_X.
12. With regard to the diversion of resources, Bhagwati and Srinivasan (1983) categorize illegal trade as an example of 'directly unproductive, profit-seeking' (or DUP) activity. Deardorff and Stolper (1990) argue convincingly that illegal trade was welfare-improving in most African countries in the 1970s and 1980s, given the highly distortionary policy regimes that encouraged it (see also Berg, 1985). At the heart of this view is the assertion that the 'resource cost' effect of illegal trade in SSA has usually been dominated by the trade liberalization effect. One can imagine a strong form of this in which illegal trade takes place at rising *private* marginal costs, but at a social opportunity cost of zero. This would be approximately true if the private costs of engaging in illegal activity primarily involved transfer payments to the government, in the form of bribes or expected penalties.
13. While capital controls can also drive trade underground, their influence through this channel is (mostly) transitory. The analysis in this section – which continues to ignore capital flows – therefore remains appropriate as a description of the long run even when we incorporate asset trade and foreign exchange black markets.
14. While the monetary disequilibrium in Figure 3.1 could be called an 'inconsistency' between private nominal wealth and the nominal exchange rate (and could have been produced by a temporary money-financed fiscal deficit), the macroeconomic imbalance at point 2 is short-run in nature. Real balances are too high to support convertibility without a loss in reserves, but since the fiscal deficit is zero, this loss is finite.
15. Illegal trade can undercut this potency to some degree, by reviving the trade tax Laffer curve even when convertibility restrictions are binding (see below).
16. The sustainable level of the real exchange rate for exports also rises, however, and this may worsen the fiscal deficit. Nashashibi and Bazzoni (1993) argue that real appreciation tends to worsen the fiscal deficit in SSA by shifting the allocation of resources away from the tax-intensive traded good sector. Holding the stance of trade policy constant in eq. (3.5), this effect is apparent in the increase in the real value of spending on nontraded goods when e rises. In Figure 3.2, the effect of a positive relationship between the fiscal deficit and the real exchange rate is to make the AB schedule steeper or even positively sloped. This further undercuts the role of trade policy in resolving macroeconomic inconsistencies on the margin, since trade interventions appreciate the real exchange rate and worsen the external balance problem from the fiscal deficit side. If this effect is strong enough, a tightening of trade policy may no longer be capable of substituting for fiscal adjustment or an increased rate of crawl in restoring long-run equilibrium.
17. Capital controls are restrictions on trade in foreign assets. Foreign exchange rationing systems require such restrictions, given the ease with

which official foreign exchange obtained for portfolio purposes could be converted to trade finance. Thus foreign exchange rationing is not used in the CFA countries, for example, where the currency has been freely convertible for capital account transactions, at least until recently.

18. The other main role is to insulate the balance of payments from short-run volatility in the capital account. This role of capital controls has been studied extensively in the literature (see the surveys by Agénor, 1992 and Kiguel and O'Connell, 1995) and we will not dwell on it here.

19. This should be applied cautiously, since other variables can intervene, such as the strength of the enforcement effort. And the premium can be extremely volatile in the short run, since the parallel exchange rate is a forward-looking variable that is driven by portfolio equilibrium in the short run (Kiguel and O'Connell, 1995).

20. We saw above that illegal trade and foreign exchange black markets may undercut the leverage of convertibility restrictions over the actual stance of trade policy. When they do, the trade liberalization 'implied' by a restoration of convertibility is smaller than if the restrictions had been fully enforced. In extreme cases, the stance of trade policy may even tighten as import tariffs and export taxes that were 'infra-marginalized' by direct controls and illegal trade regain their influence over domestic prices.

21. The African Heads of State, in the 1980 Lagos Plan of Action and Final Act of Lagos, saw monetary integration as an essential component of the economic union to be attained by the year 2000. The objective of eventual monetary union was explicitly underscored in the Abuja Treaty (June 1991) that created the African Economic Community. In that treaty, monetary union is envisioned as occurring in the last stage of a process that would be completed by roughly 2025.

22. Berg (1988) provides a comprehensive review of African regional organizations, including all the organizations listed in Table 3.1 with the exception of the EAEC and EACM.

23. There have been minor changes in membership, and Equitorial Guinea (joined 1985) is not a former French colony. See Boughton (1991) for further details and a list of references.

24. This is not to claim that macroeconomic divergence led to the demise of the EAC. Long-standing differences over ideology, Tanzanian resentment over the distribution of gains from cooperation and Tanzania's open repudiation of the Idi Amin regime in Uganda were undoubtedly more important in ultimately destroying the possibility of cooperation.

25. The Treaty for East African Co-operation (signed 1967) included a formal agreement to harmonize monetary policies with the objective of maintaining convertibility at least for current account purposes (see Resnick, 1972).

26. Mundell (1972) anticipated the later literature by arguing that the adoption of a common African currency would help shelter monetary policy from the pressure of large domestic interest groups, like labour unions or monopoly firms in the manufacturing sector, that might otherwise force devaluation and money growth by raising prices.

27. The rand still circulates freely in Swaziland, Lesotho and Namibia, and South Africa pays compensation for the implied loss of seigniorage. Lesotho

and Namibia cannot change their exchange rates against the rand without advance consultation with South Africa. See Chipeta and Davies, 1993 and Davies *et al.* (1993).

28. The CFA countries as a whole are roughly the size of Nigeria, and competition for regional influence between France and Nigeria has probably been a constraint on regional integration of all types in West Africa. In this sense, a waning of French influence in the CFA countries opens up new possibilities, for example for a currency area based on the naira. But the political and economic instability of Nigeria would appear to rule this out in the foreseeable future.

29. Krugman (1993) argues that understanding the microeconomic benefits of currency union is the overriding analytical task facing international economists. See Melitz (1993) for work in this direction.

30. The optimum tax argument is simply that in the absence of non-distortionary means of raising revenue, the optimum vector of tax rates equates the marginal distortion associated with each tax. The low administrative costs of the inflation tax suggest that it would be prominent among those used. The political economy argument stems from the observation that the inflation tax is a 'hidden' and widely-spread tax and therefore less likely, per unit of revenue raised, to provoke highly focused opposition.

31. Useful recent discussions include de la Dehesa and Krugman (1993), Corden (1993), Bayoumi and Eichengreen (1994) and, for subSaharan Africa in particular, Cobham and Robson (1994).

32. The same colonial history that created the nations and unions of the CFA zone also separated pairs like Senegal and The Gambia or Niger and Nigeria that would appear to be more natural partners by at least some of these criteria.

33. Evidence on growth performance in the CMA is less useful given the difficulty of disentangling the preformance of Lesotho and Swaziland from that of South Africa.

34. Unlike the other studies mentioned, Boughton (1991) does not control for other determinants of output variability than zone membership.

35. In fact, the possibility of free-riding on the common resources of the union – international reserves, for example, or creditworthiness in international financial markets – may make the incentive for national fiscal self-discipline lower in a monetary union than it would be otherwise.

36. Dollar (1992) makes this distinction in analysing the relationship between outward orientation and growth. Section 3.5 below discusses Dollar's measures of outward orientation.

37. This is not to say that trade controls and exchange rate policy are perfect substitutes. While at first blush it might appear possible to mimic an exchange rate change through the use of uniform trade taxes and subsidies, without changing the overall fiscal stance or pattern of trade protection, illegal trade undercuts this possibility in practice (O'Connell, 1992). A tax-subsidy scheme that is designed to be revenue-neutral will produce an adverse fiscal shock, and one that is designed to be non-discriminatory is likely to end up introducing an inadvertent export subsidy. Moreover, trade policies tend to leave more room for discriminatory application than the equivalent exchange rate policies. Of course, the use of trade taxes as

proxies for devaluation in any case re-introduces many of the uncertainties that the stabilization of intra-union cross rates was intended to remove.

38. This is the essence of the view that commodity price stabilization has limited microeconomic benefits. The technical point is that indirect utility functions and profit functions are convex in prices.

39. The required levels of aversion, using standard utility functions, appear to be extremely high (Gagnon and Gagnon, 1993).

40. This is all the more important if the capital account is open.

41. Lipumba and Kasekende (1991) report that the share of intra-PTA imports cleared increased from 8.8 per cent in 1984 to 29.7 per cent in 1988; net settlement in foreign exchange declined from 70.4 per cent to 41.3 per cent in 1989.

42. The argument is that neither the condition-imposing institutions nor their country-by-country clients are able to pose the credible threats or make the credible promises that would cement a long-term relationship.

43. Note that the analysis in section 3.2 suggests that there are conditions under which exchange controls actually lower inflation relative to what would prevail under unified exchange rates. In such cases domestic prices fully reflect the parallel exchange rate, but the spread between the parallel and official rates provides financing that reduces money growth relative to the unified counter factual.

44. The real effective exchange rate is defined as REER $\equiv$ NEER . RELP, where RELP $\equiv$ CPI/WPI* is the ratio of the home consumer price index to a trade-weighted geometric average of trading partner wholesale price indexes. NEER is the nominal effective exchange rate, expressed as the (similarly trade-weighted) foreign currency price of a unit of local currency. There is an exact decomposition in logs: log (REER) = log(NEER) + log(RELP).

45. I am indebted to Paul Collier for suggesting this point.

46. The fact that Africa is simultaneously the poorest and most inward-looking region makes it difficult to control for level of development in calculating a 'norm' for domestic price levels. The data in Table 3.6 should probably be regarded as an upper bound on the relative inward-orientation of African countries. See Dollar (1992) for further discussion.

47. Dollar (1992, p. 532) states that 'in Africa inward orientation results from exchange rates that are overvalued as a result of protection but are rather stable'. The Heston–Summers data are well worth more work along these lines; there are other readily-measured variables, like aid inflows, that could help explain the stability of an overvalued real exchange rate independently from the orientation of trade policy. Van Wijnbergen (1986) provides both theory and empirical evidence on the role of aid in African exchange rate over-valuation.

48. While the overall results are similar across studies, the results can vary substantially for individual countries depending on the variables being investigated and the data and methodology employed. Leamer (1988), for example, finds Côte d'Ivoire to be very open, and certainly more open than, for example, Ethiopia; Dollar (1992) places Côte d'Ivoire well below the median in terms of openness and Ethiopia at the median; and Greenaway and Nam categorize Ethiopia as well below the median and

Côte d'Ivoire as roughly at the median.
49. The seigniorage argument would have to be examined empirically. The CFA countries have enjoyed seigniorage from the general acceptability of the CFA franc in regional transactions, a phenomenon tied to the convertibility guarantee.

References

Adam, C., B. Ndulu, and N. Sowa (1993) 'Efficiency Gains versus Revenue Losses: Liberalization and Seigniorage Revenue in Kenya, Ghana and Tanzania' (Oxford: University Centre for the Study of African Economics; Institute of Economics and Statistics) processed.

Agénor, P.-R. (1992) 'Parallel Currency Markets in Developing Countries: Theory, Evidence, and Policy Implications', *Princeton Essays in International Finance*, 188 (Princeton, NJ: Princeton University).

Ariyo, A. and M.I. Raheem (1991) 'Enhancing Trade Flows within the ECOWAS Sub-Region: an Appraisal and Some Recommendations', in A. Chhibber and S. Fischer (eds), *Economic Reform in Sub-Saharan Africa* (Washington: World Bank) 245–58.

Azam, J.-P. (1991) 'Cross-Border Trade between Niger and Nigeria, 1980–87: The Parallel Market for the Naira', in M. Roemer and C. Jones (eds), *Markets in Developing Countries: Parallel, Fragmented, and Black* (San Francisco: ICS Press) 47–62.

Bahmani-Oskooee, M. and N. Ltaifa (1992) 'Effects of Exchange Rate Risk on Exports: Crosscountry Analysis', *World Development* 20(8): 1173–81.

Balassa B. (1961) *The Theory of Economic Integration* (Homewood, Ill.: Richard D. Irwin).

Barro, R. and J.-W. Lee (1993) 'Losers and Winners in Economic Growth', *World Bank Economic Review, Annual Conference on Development Economics*.

Bates, R. (1981) *Markets and States in Tropical Africa: The Political Basis of Agricultural Policy* (Berkeley: University of California Press).

Bayoumi, T. and B. Eichengreen (1994) 'Monetary and Exchange Rate Arrangements for NAFTA', *Journal of Development Economics*, 43(1): 125–65.

Berg, E. (1985) *Intra-African Trade and Economic Integration*, report by Elliot Berg Associates, distributed by Development Alternatives, Inc., Bethesda, Md.

—— (1988) *Regionalism and Economic Development in Sub-Saharan Africa*, report prepared for USAID, contract no. AFR–0458–A–00–7062–00, distributed by Development Alternatives, Inc., Bethesda, Md.

Bevan, D., P. Collier and J. Gunning (1990) *Controlled Open Economies: A Neoclassical Approach to Structuralism* (Oxford: Clarendon Press).

Bhagwati, J. and B. Hansen (1973) 'A Theoretical Analysis of Smuggling', *Quarterly Journal of Economics*, 87(2): 1972–87.

—— and T.N. Srinivasan (1983) *Lectures in International Trade* (Cambridge, Mass.: MIT Press).

Boughton, J.M. (1991) 'The CFA Franc Zone: Currency Union and Monetary

Standard', International Monetary Fund working paper WP/91/133, Dec.

Caballero, R.J. and V. Corbo (1989) 'The Effect of Real Exchange Rate Uncertainty on Exports: Empirical Evidence', *World Bank Economic Review*, 3(2): 263–78.

Central Bank of Kenya (1986) *The Central Bank of Kenya: Its Evolution, Responsibilities and Organization* (Nairobi: Government Printer).

Chipeta, C. and R. Davies (1993) *Regional Relations and Cooperation Post-Apartheid: A Macro Framework Study Report* (Gaboreone: SADC).

Chhibber, A. and N. Shafik (1991) 'Exchange Reform, Parallel Markets and Inflation in Africa: The Case of Ghana', in A. Chhibber and S. Fischer (eds), *Economic Reform in Sub-Saharan Africa* (Washington: World Bank).

Cobham, D. and P. Robson (1994) 'Monetary Integration in Africa: A Deliberately European Perspective', *World Development*, 22(3): 285–99.

Collier, P. (1989) 'Exchange Rates and Exchange Controls in Developing Countries', *Greek Economic Review*, 12: 132–47.

—— (1991) 'Africa's External Economic Relations: 1960–90', *African Affairs*, 90: 339–56.

Corden, W.M. (1987) 'Protection and Liberalization: A Review of Analytical Issues', Occasional Paper no. 54 (Washington, DC: International Monetary Fund) Aug.

—— (1993) 'European Monetary Union: The Intellectual Pre-History', in de la Dehesa, G.A.G., M. Guitan, and R. Portes (eds), *The Monetary Future of Europe*, Report of a CEPR Conference, London.

Davies, R., D. Keet, and F. Nkuhulu (1993) 'Reconstructing Economic Relations with the Southern African Region: Issues and Options for a Democratic South Africa', Macroeconomic Research Group, Centre for Development Studies, University of the Western Cape, Sep.

Deardorff, A.V. and W.F. Stolper (1990) 'Effects of Smuggling Under African Conditions: A Factual, Institutional and Analytic Discussion', *Weltwirtschaftliches Archiv*, 126: 116–40.

de la Dehesa, G.A.G., M. Guitan and R. Portes (eds) (1993) *The Monetary Future of Europe*, report of a CEPR conference (London: CEPR).

—— and P.R. Krugman (1993) 'Monetary Union, Regional Cohesion, and Regional Shocks', in de la Dehesa, G.A.G., M. Guitan, and R. Portes (eds), *The Monetary Future of Europe*, Report of a CEPR Conference (London: CEPR).

DeRosa, D.A. (1992) 'Protection and Export Performance in Sub-Saharan Africa', *Weltwirtschaftliches Archiv*, 128: 88–124.

Devarajan, S. and J. de Melo (1987) 'Evaluating Participation in African Monetary Unions: A Statistical Analysis of the CFA Zones', *World Development*, 15: 483–96.

—— and —— (1991) 'Membership in the CFA Zone: Odyssean Journey or Trojan Horse?', in A. Chhibber and S. Fischer (eds), *Economic Reform in Sub-Saharan Africa* (Washington: World Bank).

——, J. Lewis, and S. Robinson (1993) 'External Shocks, Purchasing Power Parity, and the Equilibrium Real Exchange Rate', *World Bank Economic Review*, 7(1): 45–63.

—— and D. Rodrik (1992) 'Do the Benefits of Fixed Exchange Rates Outweigh Their Costs: The Franc Zone in Africa', in I. Geldin and A. Winters (eds), *Open Economies: Structural Adjustment and Agriculture* (Oxford University Press).

Dixit, A.K. and R.S. Pindyck (1994) *Investment Under Uncertainty* (Princeton University Press).

Dollar, D. (1992) 'Outward-Oriented Developing Economies Really Do Grow More Rapidly: Evidence from 95 LDCs, 1976–1985', *Economic Development and Structural Change*, 40(3): 545–66.

Elbadawi, I. and N. Majd (1992) 'Fixed Parity of the Exchange Rate and Economic Performance in the CFA Zone: A Comparative Study', Country Economics Department Working papers series no. 830, The World Bank.

Foroutan, F. (1993) 'Regional Integration in Sub-Saharan Africa: Past Experience and Future Prospects', in J. de Melo and A. Panagariya (eds), *New Dimensions in Regional Integration* (Cambridge University Press).

—— and L. Pritchett (1993) 'Intra-Sub-Saharan Trade: is it too Little?', *Journal of African Economies*, 2(1): 74–105.

Frimpong-Ansah, J. (1990) 'The Prospects of Monetary Union in the context of ECOWAS', in *The Long Term Perspective Study of Sub-Saharan Africa, Vol. 4: Proceedings of a Workshop on Regional Integration and Cooperation* (Washington, DC: The World Bank) 52–8.

Gagnon, J.M. (1993) 'Exchange Rate Variability and the Level of International Trade', *Journal of International Economics*, 34(3–4), May: 269–87.

Gemmell, N. (1993) 'Fiscal Dependence on Trade Taxes and Economic Development', *Scottish Journal of Political Economy*, 40(1): 56–68.

Greenaway, D. and C. Milner (1991) 'Fiscal Dependence on Trade Taxes and Trade Policy Reform', *Journal of Development Studies*, 27(3), April: 95–132.

—— and C.H. Nam (1988) 'Industrialization and Macroeconomic Performance in Developing Countries Under Alternative Trade Strategies', *Kyklos*, 41(3): 419–35.

Guillaumont, P. (1988) 'L'Ouverture Commerciale sur l'Extérieure Mesurée à Partir du Taux d'Exportation', in P. and S. Guillaumont (eds), *Stratégies de Développement Comparées: Zone Franc et Hors Zone Franc* (Paris: Economica).

—— and Guillaumont, S. (1988) *Stratégies de Développement Comparées: Zone Franc et Hors Zone Franc* (Paris: Economica).

—— and —— (1989) 'The Implications of European Monetary Union for African Countries', *Journal of Common Market Studies*, 28: 139–53.

——, —— and Patrick Plane (1988) 'Participating in African Monetary Unions: An Alternative Evaluation', *World Development* 16(6): 569–576.

Honohan, P. (1991) 'Monetary Cooperation in the CFA Zone', in A. Chhibber and S. Fischer (eds), *Economic Reform in Sub-Saharan Africa* (Washington: World Bank) 1991: 148–60.

Hopkins, A.G. (1973) *An Economic History of West Africa* (New York: Columbia University Press).

Johnson, O.E.G. (1987) 'Trade Tax and Exchange Rate Coordination in the Context of Border Trading', *IMF Staff Papers*, 34(3): 548–64.

Kamin, S. (1993) 'Devaluation, Exchange Controls, and Black Markets for Foreign Exchange in Developing Countries', *Journal of Development Economics*, 40(1): 151–69.

Khan, M.S. and J.S. Lizondo (1987) 'Devaluation, Fiscal Deficits, and the

Real Exchange Rate', *The World Bank Economic Review*, 1(2): 357–74.

Kiguel, M. and S.A. O'Connell (1995) 'Parallel Exchange Rates in Developing Countries', *World Bank Research Observer* 10(1): 21–52.

Kitchen, R. (1992) 'Problems of Regional Integration in Africa: The Union Douaniere et Economique de l'Afrique Centrale (UDEAC)', in C. Milner and A.J. Rayner (eds), *Policy Adjustment in Africa: Case-Studies in Economic Development, vol. 1* (London: Macmillan).

Krugman, P.R. (1993) 'What Do We Know About the International Monetary System?', Princeton Essays in International Finance no. 190 (International Finance Section, Department of Economics, Princeton University).

Leamer, E. (1988) 'Measures of Openness', in R. Baldwin (ed.) *Trade Policy Issues and Empirical Analysis* (University of Chicago Press) 147–199.

Leith, J.C. (1992) 'The Static Welfare Effects of a Small Developing Country's Membership in a Customs Union: Botswana in the South African Customs Union', *World Development*, 20(7): 1021–8.

Lipumba, N.H.I. and L. Kasekende (1991) 'The Record and Prospects of the Preferential Trade Area for Eastern and Southern African States', in A. Chhibber and S. Fischer (eds), *Economic Reform in Sub-Saharan Africa* (Washington: World Bank) 233–44.

Lizondo, J.S. (1991) 'Alternative Dual Exchange Rate Regimes', *IMF Staff Papers*, 38(3): 560–81.

Medhora, R. (1990) 'The Effect of Exchange Rate Variability on Trade: The Case of the West African Monetary Union's Imports', *World Development*, 18(2): 313–24.

Melitz, J. (1993) 'The Theory of Optimum Currency Areas, Trade Adjustment, and Trade', CEPR Discussion Paper no. 847 (London: CEPR).

Morris, S. (1995) 'Inflation Dynamics and the Parallel Market for Foreign Exchange', *Journal of Development Economics*, 46(2), April: 295–316.

Mundell, R. (1961) 'A Theory of Optimum Currency Areas', *American Economic Review*, 51:657–65.

—— (1972) 'African Trade, Politics, and Money', in R. Tremblay (ed.), *Africa and Monetary Integration* (Montreal University Research Center in Economic Development).

Nashashibi, K. and S. Bazzoni (1993) 'Alternative Exchange Rate Strategies and Fiscal Performance in Sub-Saharan Africa', IMF working paper WP/93/68, Fiscal Affairs Department, Aug.

O'Connell, S.A. (1991) 'Short and Long Run Effects of an Own-Funds Scheme', *Journal of African Economies*, 1(1): 131–50.

—— (1992) 'Uniform Commercial Policy, Illegal Trade, and the Real Exchange Rate: A Theoretical Analysis', *World Bank Economic Review*, 6(1): 459–79.

Ogunkola, E.O. (1993) 'An Evaluation of Trade Potential in the Economic Community of West African States' (AERC Interim Report, University of Ibadan) processed.

Pinto, B. (1989) 'Black Market Premia, Exchange Rate Unification, and Inflation in Sub-Saharan Africa', *World Bank Economic Review*, 3(3): 321–38.

Pitt, M. (1981) 'Smuggling and Price Disparity', *Journal of International Economics*, 11(4): 447–58.

Resnick, I.N. (1972) 'East African Economic Cooperation: The Impact on a

Less-Developed Participant', in S.P. Schatz (ed.), *South of the Sahara* (London: Macmillan) 317–45.

Rodrik, D. (1993) 'Trade Liberalization in Disinflation', CEPR discussion paper no. 832 (London: CEPR) Aug.

Romer, P.M. (1994) 'New Goods, Old Theory, and the Welfare Cost of Trade Restrictions', *Journal of Development Economics*, 43(1): 5–38.

van Wijnbergen (1986) 'Aid, Export Promotion, and the Real Exchange Rate: An African Dilemma' (Macroeconomics Division, Development Research Department, The World Bank) processed.

4 Regional Integration in SubSaharan Africa: A Review of Experiences and Issues*

William Lyakurwa, Andrew McKay,
Nehemiah Ng'eno and Walter Kennes

4.1 INTRODUCTION

In the late 1980s and early 1990s regional integration has again become an attractive policy option, in both the developed and developing world. Regional integration arrangements initially became fashionable in the 1960s, following the formation of the European Economic Community in 1957 and the European Free Trade Area in 1960. These were followed by a large number of regional integration agreements in the developing world. Such arrangements started to fall out of fashion in the 1970s, in part because the first experiences were not successful. At the moment, considering, *inter alia*, the deepening of European Integration in 1992, the formation or prospective formation of free trade arrangements involving the United States (most significantly the NAFTA agreement), and the difficulties encountered in concluding the Uruguay Round of the GATT negotiations, regional integration is again very much on the policy agenda in the developing world.

At the first two post-colonial meetings in April 1958 and in June 1960 African leaders adopted regionalism as a vehicle for overcoming the economic constraints imposed by the smallness and fragmentation of national markets. At the inaugural meeting of the OAU in May 1963 regionalism was enshrined in the OAU Charter.

* We gratefully acknowledge the comments of participants at the AERC Collaborative Research Project Workshop on 'Regional Integration and Trade Liberalization in Sub-Saharan Africa' at which an earlier draft of this chapter was presented. We especially would like to thank David Greenaway for his comments on the earlier draft. However, full responsibility for the contents of this paper rests with the authors.

Current thinking and debate in many official African circles on the subject of regional integration is centred around the Abuja Treaty of 1991 and the Lagos Plan of Action of 1980. The Lagos Plan of Action (LPA) called for the formation of an African common market by the year 2000. This was to be achieved in stages, starting with the formation of free trade areas followed by a common market and an economic union. The LPA divided subSaharan Africa (SSA) into three sub-regions: West Africa, Central Africa, and Eastern and Southern Africa. Each of the sub-regions was to go through the stages of integration before an African common market could be formed. In 1991 the OAU Heads of State and Government judged the progress made in sub-regional co-operation enough to justify the signing of the treaty to establish a Pan African Economic Community (PAEC). The Treaty establishing the PAEC provides for the existing sub-regional groupings to serve as the building blocks for the new Community, and that the first five years of the new institution will be devoted to the strengthening of these sub-regional groupings.

The PAEC provides a broad, long-term perspective on regional economic integration in Africa. However, the relevance of PAEC for addressing practical current issues of integration appears limited. The LPA led to the establishment of the PTA. The other regional integration (RI) groupings, ECOWAS in West Africa and ECCAS in Central Africa and most other RI organizations in SAA had been established before 1980. A treaty aimed at transforming PTA into a Common Market for Eastern and South African States (COMESA) was signed in November 1993. A movement towards a common market in West Africa has hardly started.

On theoretical grounds, small countries can expect more benefits from integration and co-operation than large countries. It has been argued that given any targeted level of import substitution, SSA countries, with their small markets, could reduce the cost of this industrialization by exploiting economies of scale through preferential opening of markets with one another. However, to date, attempts at forming regional free trade areas and customs unions along these lines have not achieved any significant progress. A problem has been that, instead of using trade liberalization and hence prices to guide industrial allocation, such arrangements sought to allocate industries by bureaucratic negotiations and tied trade to such allocations (Bhagwati, 1993). Another problem has been the lack of effective implementation of integration measures and the spread of various non-tariff barriers.

From the political perspective, SSA countries have advanced regional integration as a means of enhancing political cohesion to overcome intra-regional problems. Regional integration has been seen as a means of alleviating political tensions, promoting closer political co-operation and building a common consensus on issues of mutual concern in areas that go beyond trade in goods and services.

A recent OECD study (OECD, 1993), has argued that many developing countries pursued regional integration strategies to enhance the security of access to markets of their important trading partners. In addition many developing countries hold the notion that regional integration is a precondition for long-run growth since national markets are incapable of providing the necessary size to exploit economies of scale and specialization. For these countries, trade arrangements are intended to give smaller economies access to larger markets in order to achieve these goals. Protective regional barriers are also seen as necessary for nurturing infant industries into efficient and competitive producers.

The objective of this chapter is to review the main issues pertaining to regional integration covering the theoretical underpinnings and experiences with regional integration in subSaharan Africa and outside Africa. It concludes by raising issues for future research in this area.

The chapter is organized as follows: section 4.2 presents the theoretical and methodological analysis of RI schemes. First, the definition and classification of different integration schemes is set out. Then the next two sub-sections survey the theoretical literature on the desirability of integration based on static issues of resource allocation and the dynamic issues (embracing economies of scale, efficiency, bargaining power and capital formation). Other issues discussed in Section 4.2 include: economic geography; lessons for regional integration; and other dynamic factors that relate to regional integration arrangements. Finally, the important question of the policy environment in which regional integration takes place is addressed. This is done in order to assess its desirability in the context of a policy of import substitution or of export promotion.

Section 4.3 presents a brief review of regional integration experiences in subSaharan Africa, including a discussion of the experiences, problems and prospects, then Section 4.4 draws on the lessons and experiences of RI arrangements outside Africa, specifically the European Community, Latin America and South East Asia. Section 4.5 presents some major researchable issues in the area of regional integration arrangement with particular reference to subSaharan Africa.

4.2   THEORETICAL AND METHODOLOGICAL ISSUES

Definitional Issues

The term 'integration' in fact covers a wide variety of possible schemes. Given the differences in nature and objectives of these different schemes, it is important that they are clearly distinguished at the outset. The following classification of different degrees of integration (based on Balassa, 1961; and Jovanovic, 1992) is useful as a starting point:

(1) *Preferential tariff agreement*   In this case customs duties on trade among member countries are reduced relative to those on trade with non-member countries. An example of such an arrangement in the African context is the Preferential Trade Area for Eastern and Southern African States (PTA).

(2) *Free Trade Area (FTA)*   Here member countries remove tariffs and quotas on trade between members in goods originating within the FTA, but retain control over their own restrictions on trade with non-member countries. The tariffs and other restrictions applying to external trade will vary from one country to another. For this reason an FTA will normally also embrace rules of origin agreement.

(3) *Customs Union*   In this case members not only abolish restrictions on internal trade (as in the FTA) but also impose a common external tariff (CET) on trade with non-member countries. Rules of origin are then no longer required. The Southern African Customs Union (SACU) is an example of such an arrangement in the African context.

(4) *Common Market*   This is a customs union which has, additionally, free movement of factors of production. Common restrictions apply to the movement of factors with non-member countries. In the African context, ECOWAS was intended to achieve a common market, though it has so far fallen far short of this objective.

(5) *Economic Union*   This goes further than a common market in that major economic policies are (for example, fiscal, monetary, industrial) co-ordinated, and monetary union may be introduced. Examples of monetary union exist in the African context (for example, the CFA and the Rand zones), but these are rather special in nature (because of the role played by France or South Africa). These arrangements, therefore, do not really qualify as true economic unions in the sense defined here.

As can be seen, this classification of schemes is hierarchical with each level embracing that before it. The schemes actually implemented in Africa (as opposed to proposed) do not go further than level (3), the exception being the defunct East African Community. Hence the focus on this survey is on trade integration schemes, though factor market integration will be referred to tangentially. The focus in the next three sub-sections will therefore be predominantly on customs unions as representing the most general of (1), (2), (3) above, and as representing the case which has been analysed in most detail in the theoretical economics literature.

The Case for Regional Integration: Static Issues

Entry into a regional integration scheme can have both static effects, resulting from once and for all resource reallocation in response to changing relative prices, and dynamic effects, resulting *inter alia* from changes in efficiency, in the ability to exploit economies of scale, and in levels of investment and growth. Much of the theoretical literature relates to the static effects of trade integration, in particular in the context of a customs unions; however, it is likely that dynamic effects are more significant given that the changes they represent are cumulative rather than simply once and for all adjustments (Hine, 1994). This lack of treatment of the dynamic effects is because they are more difficult to model, although recent theoretical developments help us to identify some of the key issues. These will be surveyed in the next sub-section. The present sub-section confines itself to the static, resource reallocation effects.

The question to be addressed is the desirability of two countries entering into a customs union. This immediately raises the issue of the criterion of desirability.

Two such issues need to be addressed:

(1) *What is the counterfactual?*   Generally the comparison is between a pre-union situation of non-preferential tariffs and a prospective union with a common external tariff equal to the average pre-union rate. However, the question arises as to whether there is an alternative change in trade policy (such as a unilateral, non-preferential tariff reduction) which is preferable.

(2) *Whose welfare is to be considered? – Each individual member country, the union as a whole, or the world?*   This will depend on the question being addressed. In asking about the desirability

to its members of participating in a union, the joint union welfare level may be used as the criterion on the assumption that countries gaining from the prospective union can make non-distortionary compensation payments to those losing (a standard assumption in the customs union literature). However, even if this latter assumption is valid, this approach ignores the possibility of retaliation by non-member countries. Given that retaliation is highly likely, it seems desirable to consider the welfare effects on both prospective member and non-member countries. In many theoretical models used in the literature, the joint welfare of the prospective union members and world welfare move in the same direction, but of course this need not apply in the less-stylized 'real world' situation.

The pioneering study of the theory of customs unions by Viner (1950), focused on the production effects and resultant changes in trade structure. According to Viner, the formation of a customs union would lead to increased trade between the union members; however, the desirability of this (from the point of view of the union members or of the world as a whole) would depend on the balance between the two following effects:

- *trade creation*, the shifting of production of some goods from a less efficient member to a more efficient member; and
- *trade diversion*, the shifting of production from an efficient non-member to a less efficient member.

Both effects are likely to occur as a result of the tariff changes implicit in the formation of a customs union.[1] The former represents a move towards freer trade and greater efficiency at both the union and world level, and so is welfare-improving at both these levels. Within the union it enables more efficient resource allocation. The latter effect, however, leads to reduced efficiency and to an adverse movement in the member countries' terms of trade (the partner country representing a more expensive source), and so has an adverse effect on welfare at both the union and the world level. The overall impact of the customs union will depend on the balance between trade creation and trade diversion, with prospective unions being assessed as desirable or not depending on whether or not total trade creation outweighs total trade diversion. In a general theoretical case, of course, this will be ambiguous.

The foregoing discussion is based on the assumption that the average tariff level remains unchanged after the formation of the customs union. By relaxing this assumption (and continuing to allow for the existence of non-distortionary compensation payments) it is possible to make a more definitive statement (Vanek, 1965; Kemp and Wan, 1976).

McMillan (1993) argues that it is always possible for a regional integration arrangement, formed among an arbitrary group of countries, to structure itself in such a way as to make the member countries better off without making any of the non-member countries worse off. In other words, by setting the external tariff optimally, it is always possible for an integration arrangement to be welfare-improving. Given the likely difficulty in calculating the optimal tariff level in any particular case, this proposition may seem to be only of theoretical interest; however, McMillan uses it as the basis for an elegant and straightforward test of the welfare effects of an integration arrangement. We will return to this point in more detail in section 5.1.

A vast literature on the theory of customs unions followed Viner's original contribution, mostly focusing on the static effects; it ultimately continued to offer ambiguous conclusions. One key omission from Viner's analysis, identified by Lipsey (1957), was his failure to take the consumption effects of a custom's union into account. These effects, which result from the changes in relative prices when a customs union is formed, may lead to welfare benefits through enabling more efficient consumption. Taking these effects into account it becomes possible for a trade-diverting union to be welfare-improving. This can happen, in spite of the loss in tariff revenue due to the trade diversion, because relative prices will tend to move closer to their international values than in the pre-union situation.

Subsequent literature offers a more complete taxonomy of the welfare effects of custom union formation. Lipsey (1970) classified these (static) effects into three categories:

(1) inter-country substitution, in other words changes in the sources of commodities, which may be trade creating or trade diverting, each of which can have both production and consumption effects;
(2) inter-commodity substitution, as a result of changes in tariff adjusted relative prices, even if the sources remain unchanged; and
(3) changes in the terms of trade between union members and between union members and outsiders.

In the context of a more general, five-commodity, model, which encompasses most of the models in the then-existing literature, Collier

(1979) argues that the simple Vinerian notions of trade creation and trade diversion do not carry over to the general situation. He offers an alternative classification of the welfare effects of customs unions as follows:

(1) terms of trade effects, which may be import-diverting or export-diverting;
(2) substitution effects in production, which may take the forms of intra-export substitution and export–import substitution; and
(3) substitution effects in consumption, which may be classified in an analogous way to the substitution effects in production.

In introducing a wider variety of effects these theoretical developments represent a significant step closer to reality; however, the complexity that they introduce makes the ambiguous conclusions about the desirability of integration more deeply entrenched. In the African context (and in many others), problems of data availability make it very unlikely that the relative importance of the various effects could be quantified empirically. Does the theoretical literature offer any general guidelines as to circumstances which make it more likely that a particular integration scheme is likely to be welfare-improving, at least in the static sense? While not theoretically rigorous, perhaps at this more practical level Viner's model can offer some intuitive guidance. Gunter (1989) argues that it remains the case that it is likely that the extent of trade created by an integration scheme is positively correlated, and the amount of trade diversion negatively correlated, with the resultant change in welfare.

Consequently, integration schemes characterized by factors which are likely to enhance trade creation and those likely to minimize trade diversion are the most likely to be welfare-improving. Thus, following Hazelwood (1987), the following factors increase the likelihood that a given integration scheme is welfare-improving:

(1) *Factors tending to enhance trade creation:*
    (a) an extensive overlap among union members in activities protected by the tariff; and
    (b) large differences between member countries in the cost of producing the commodities subject to protection.
(2) *Factors tending to minimize trade diversion:*
    (a) many union members;
    (b) pre-union trade being a small proportion of members' production;

(c) a high proportion of pre-union trade being with members; and
(d) a low common external tariff compared with the members' pre-union tariff.

This suggests that customs unions are likely to be most successful between countries which are currently competitive but potentially complementary (Hine, 1994). The final point 2(d) highlights the importance that customs unions are not used as a surreptitious means of increasing protection; this will increase their trade-diversionary impact.

The Case for Regional Integration: Dynamic Issues

The effects considered in the previous sub-section are the purely static responses of producers (and consumers in the more general models) to changes in relative prices as a result of the changing pattern of tariffs. The associated welfare changes are once and for all effects which in principle have their impact shortly after the integration scheme is introduced. On top of these static effects, however, there is also a variety of potential dynamic effects. These may be felt more gradually but will be longer lasting and in some cases continued. For example, an increase in the growth rate made possible by integration will have a continued effect as long as it is sustained. In the end, dynamic effects, if present, are likely to dominate static effects.

Trade integration can potentially bring a number of dynamic effects into play to a greater extent than in the pre-union situation, including the following:

(1) the larger market offers greater possibilities for the exploitation of economies of scale;
(2) integration is likely to lead to increased competition within the union, with consequent efficiency benefits;
(3) there is an impact on capital formation, possibly through several channels: reduction on barriers to diffusion; technology transfer; externalities from export growth; increased marginal product of capital, and so on; and
(4) the union members, acting as a group, may be more able to influence the terms of trade they face.

Each of these points are consequences of the increase in effective size following integration. If they apply, they will potentially have positive effects on growth. They are likely constitute a stronger argument for regional integration than the static arguments based on resource allocation arguments addressed above. They also represent some of the issues to be considered in assessing the relative desirability of non-preferential tariff reduction versus regional integration. It should also be noted that some of these dynamic effects could also result from non-preferential tariff reduction.

To discuss the likely influences of these dynamic factors requires different models from those used in addressing the static issues, which typically do not incorporate the time dimension and are based, implicitly or explicitly, on assumptions of perfect competition and constant or decreasing returns to scale. However, despite the potential importance of these dynamic factors, there is no consensus as to a single adequate model to treat these issues.

Economic Geography

Recent theoretical developments in the theory of international trade, which lay increasing emphasis on increasing returns to scale and imperfect competition, may offer some guidance. In particular, in the context of looking at regional integration, recent work by Krugman (1991a, 1991b, 1991c), stressing the importance of geographical considerations, in trade is likely to be helpful in identifying some of the key issues. While 'economic geography' models are, by Krugman's own admission, somewhat stylized in their assumptions, and not as yet empirically testable, they do, however, offer a useful framework for thinking about a number of key issues: the desirability of integration; appropriate member countries for an integration scheme; how integration schemes might be made successful; and the possible adverse effects of integration.

The key model for present purposes is the so-called 'core–periphery' model developed by Krugman (1991a, 1991b, 1991c). Stressing the importance of geographic considerations in economics, he claims that one of the key geographic features to be explained is the *concentration* of economic activity. In the United States for example, for many decades in the late nineteenth century and the first half of the twentieth century, manufacturing activity was highly concentrated in a small part of the north-east and eastern mid-west states. Similar examples of industrial concentration in small geographic areas exist elsewhere. Krugman sets out a model, focusing essentially on economies of scale in production and their interaction with demand externalities and transport costs, to explain this observed concentration in economic activity.

This model can also offer some useful insights for thinking about regional integration. It seeks to explain, within a sufficiently large geographic area, the existence of a core region, in which manufacturing activity and population is highly concentrated and a periphery region, much less densely populated and with a much lower level of manufacturing activity.

Following Krugman, consider a country comprising of two regions, and engaged in two types of economic activity, agriculture and manufacturing. By its very nature, agriculture is location-specific, and so this can be expected to take place throughout the country. Manufacturing, however, does not need to be specific to a particular location, because it does not rely on factors of production which are geographically fixed. The possibility of transporting both inputs and outputs give manufacturers much more flexibility in selecting the most advantageous location. If one of the two regions is better suited to manufacturing activity than the other, for example, because of better infrastructure, then manufacturers may prefer to concentrate in this region rather than being equally distributed between the two. The advantages derived from concentration are:

(1) the ability to exploit economies of scale by locating in one region rather than being divided between two;
(2) the existence of demand externalities from the fact that other firms, who may be suppliers or demanders of intermediate inputs, are located in the same region; and
(3) the concentration of production, which will constitute increased local demand (another form of demand externality).

The disadvantage is, of course, the increased transport costs involved in serving the market in the periphery.

Thus, whether or not the concentration for manufacturing activity takes place, the extent of the concentration will depend on the balance of these different factors. Manufacturing activities which are 'footloose', to use Krugman's term (in other words those not tied to a particular locality – for example, by reasons of natural resource requirements so that they may have to concentrate where the natural resource is extracted), and which therefore have low transport costs, are more likely to concentrate in a single or small number of localities. Manufacturing activities which use or produce intermediate manufacturing inputs on a large scale are more likely to concentrate, and activities with large economies of scale are more likely to concentrate, other things being equal.

Krugman sets out a stylized model of the interaction of these different factors, and shows that there are a number of possible equilibria, depending on the balance of forces tending toward concentration:

(1) the extent to which economies of scale can be exploited;
(2) the desire of firms to locate closer to a larger market; and
(3) the desire of workers to have access to goods produced by other workers; and dispersion:
(4) the desire to locate closer to the peripheral markets (and so save on transport costs).

Depending on the characteristics of the industry, the equilibrium may be:

(1) concentration in a single location;
(2) concentration in a small number of locations; or
(3) no concentration.

In cases in which the equilibrium involves concentration, what factors will determine where this concentration takes place? This may be a historical or geographic 'accident' which gives certain regions initial advantages. For example, regions which were developed earlier due to the pattern of colonization, or regions rich in key natural resources (oil, coal), or regions with a better transport infrastructure, may be better placed to attract manufacturing activity. Once the process of concentration begins, the advantages of these regions, initially arising as a result of natural or historical reasons, for example, may cumulate.

The ability to exploit economies of scale may be a key issue in economic development. Recent growth theory give a key role to increasing returns to scale (Romer, 1986, 1987). Geographic concentration in manufacturing may be necessary to exploit these economies of scale.

Lessons for Regional Integration?

Many manufacturing activities involve significant fixed costs, and consequently have significant economies of scale. Many developing countries are too small, in terms of population and effective demand, to be able to exploit fully economies of scale. Regional integration may allow a way of doing this, this being achieved by increased concentration in manufacturing production.

If economies of scale are large enough relative to intra-regional transport costs, then a group of countries may benefit from concentrating their manufacturing activities. The localities in which the concentration takes place might not necessarily be the same for each sector, though the extent to which it would be desirable to have different centres of concentration for different sectors would depend on the extent of the demand externalities between sectors.

Herein, of course, lies the difficulty. Regional integration enlarges the unprotected domestic market, and so potentially allows the exploitation of economies of scale. Within countries, the exploitation of the economies of scale is likely to result in geographic concentration in production. Indeed, increased geographic concentration may be *necessary* to enable economies of scale to be fully exploited. The same argument applies between countries within the RI arrangement. To exploit the benefits of regional integration, it will also be necessary to allow increased concentration between countries. Only then is it possible to exploit efficiently the increased possibilities of scale economies offered by the regional integration scheme. In other words, in any particular manufacturing industry, and perhaps in the manufacturing sector as a whole, the benefits of regional integration are unlikely to accrue equally to participating countries. While the union as a whole may gain, some individual countries may lose, introducing the likely requirement for an appropriate compensation.

The potential benefits of concentration for the union as a whole have been pointed out. If such concentration does occur, two sets of factors can be expected to influence where it occurs:

• the strength of demand externalities in different regions; and
• cost considerations (production and transport costs).

Demand externalities can be expected to be stronger in core than in periphery countries. The reverse may apply for production costs if wage costs are lower, but this may be offset by higher transport costs.

If an important element of demand for manufacturing production is expected to come from the domestic market, then the level of transport costs will be an important factor determining the extent to which concentration, and hence the further exploitation of economies of scale, can take place. As a result, high transport costs within a group of countries in a regional integration scheme which may be viewed as equivalent to non-rent creating, non-tariff barriers, may prevent the realization of this potential benefit of regional integration. Measures to improve transport networks need therefore to be given a high priority in the development of regional integration schemes. Such measures to reduce transport costs will also increase the possibilities for competition between the member countries, with consequent gains in efficiency and international competitiveness.

The importance of transport costs means that integration schemes between geographically proximate countries are more likely to be successful in realizing scale economies and increasing efficiency through competitiveness. In order to achieve these scale economies and competitiveness gains, it is also desirable that the economies of the integrating countries be similar in structure prior to integration. The static analysis above suggests that integration arrangements between economies which are currently competitive but potentially complementary are most likely to be successful. This conclusion is reinforced by the consideration of the dynamic factors.

Other Dynamic Factors

Besides the possibility of further exploiting economies of scale, three other potential benefits of integration have been noted. These are the possibility of increased competitiveness; the greater bargaining power of the union over its terms of trade than individual (and competitive countries) can achieve individually; and the possibility of increased levels of capital formation. The first benefit arises because firms in the member countries have free access to their partners' markets. This greater competition can be expected to lead to reduction in x-inefficiency relative to the pre-union situation of protection by non-discriminatory tariffs. However, as noted above, one effect of integration is that it may result in greater geographic and economic concentration in production, which by itself will reduce competition within the union. Whether or not this will lead to inefficiency or not will depend on whether or not the market in question is contestable or not and on whether the concentrated firms are subject to effective international competition or not. If integration is simply used as a means of developing import-substituting industries behind tariff walls, then this economic concentration in production in conjunction with the protection can be expected to lead to a loss in efficiency and greater exploitation of market power by firms. On the other hand, if regional integration is used as a means of promoting manufacturing exports to compete on world markets, the international competition provides a greater incentive to firms to produce efficiently.

The terms of trade argument is straightforward. If by participating in an effective regional integration scheme, a group of countries is able to function as a single block, then it has increased market power. If the group is a significant seller in its key export markets and/or significant buyer in its import markets, then it is more able to influence its terms of trade in its favour than in a situation in which each country acts non-cooperatively. This, of course, assumes no retaliation. The importance of these arguments in the African context is an empirical question. Given the very small proportion of world manufacturing trade represented by Africa (especially as an exporter), the ability to influence her terms of trade in manufacturing by acting as a bloc may be very limited. On the other hand, the terms of trade benefits from co-operative behaviour may be greater in agriculture. Unlike the other dynamic factors previously identified (economies of scale, competitiveness and capital formation) which apply more to manufacturing than agriculture, this third factor is potentially of more relevance to Africa (if at all) in agriculture than in manufacturing.

Regional Integration and Outward Orientation

The issue of regional integration cannot be considered in isolation of the policies to be pursued by the union thereby formed; for some strategies regional integration may be desirable, for others not. In the present context the key issue is whether regional integration is seen as a means of enhancing an import substitution strategy or alternatively, as an export promotion strategy. Mansoor and Inotai (1991) argue that the failure of many of the regional integration schemes in the 1970s (as measured for example, by the failure to stimulate intra-union trade) was due to the fact that such schemes pursued an import substitution strategy, which they argue was inefficient. They view regional integration in the 1990s as a means of enhancing an export promotion strategy.

The arguments set out in the previous sub-section suggest that regional integration may enhance the success for the union as a whole (though not necessarily for each individual country), of either an import substitution or an export promotion strategy relative to the equivalent policy pursued unilaterally by each individual member. This is because in each case regional integration will allow greater exploitation of economies of scale, if countries are willing to accept a geographic concentration of production in particular localities. The effectiveness is likely to be further enhanced by factor mobility (labour and capital) between countries. This will enlarge the benefits to be derived from the concentration of production, though it may also increase the inequality in the distribution of the benefits from integration.

While regional integration may potentially be beneficial to both import substitution and export promotion strategies, this does not mean that both are equally desirable. There are two strong arguments based on the above analysis for preferring an export promotion strategy rather than an import substitution strategy. They both relate to the fact that, however large the size of the regional integration in subSaharan Africa, the size of the internal market will always be small. This means, first, that in sectors in which the economies of scale are sufficiently large, there will be potentially less possibility for exploiting them in the inward-oriented strategy relative to the outward-oriented strategy. The second, and more compelling, argument has already been referred to briefly above. Given the size of the domestic market, internal competition in many industries is likely to be limited. The international competition provided by an outward-oriented policy is likely to give rise to result in the attainment of higher levels of efficiency. Of course, the conventional argument against an import substitution policy, that an import tariff designed to protect domestic import-substituting industry has adverse welfare consequences for consumers, continues to apply.

These arguments suggest that an export promotion strategy, especially one in which manufacturing exports play a significant role, may be enhanced by regional integration, at least for the group as a whole. The extent to which this is realized in practice, however, will be dependent on the extent to which economies of scale and international competitiveness are achieved as a result, and on the feasibility of agreeing on an appropriate compensation scheme by which the gainers from regional integration can compensate the losers. Given the likelihood that an *effective* RI scheme is likely to result in geographic concentration in production, the issue of compensation is a key one. Mansoor and Inotai (1991, pp. 228–9) discuss possible compensation schemes.

Summary

The above brief survey has highlighted many of the issues arising in considering the desirability of regional integration schemes from a theoretical perspective. It is clear that the theoretical arguments do not give an unambiguous conclusion about the desirability of regional integration schemes even when the counterfactual is clearly stated. In the static perspective, the conclusions of theory are clearly ambiguous in general. Even in the simple Vinerian model, the desirability of an integration scheme depends on the balance of opposing forces, in this case trade creation and trade diversion. Moving to a more general static framework, such as that of Collier (1979), only heightens the complexity. Nevertheless, as McMillan (1993) argues, it is always possible for an RI arrangement to be structured in such a way as to make the member countries better off without making non-member countries worse off.

Taking dynamic factors on board, the case for regional integration appears to become stronger, particularly in the context of an export promotion strategy, but only if the participating countries are prepared to accept the possibly adverse distributional consequences for some members or alternatively to set in place an appropriate compensation scheme. Setting in place such a scheme is likely to be difficult and may introduce distortions. The relative importance of the benefits of integration compared to the costs (administrative and distortionary) of the compensation scheme becomes an issue that needs to be addressed.

4.3 REGIONAL INTEGRATION IN SUBSAHARAN AFRICA

Regional integration in subSaharan Africa is not a recent phenomenon. At least two unions, the Southern African Customs Union and the East African Community have existed since 1910 and 1919 respectively. However, the majority of the regional economic integration schemes were established in the 1970s. There are currently ten such schemes and the revival of the EAC is being pursued seriously.

The motivations behind the establishment of RI schemes in SSA have been both political and economic. Most schemes were formed as a result of disillusionment with the international political and economic systems, which were viewed as being unfavourable to developing countries. Some RI schemes such as the EAC and those in the CFA Zone were formed at the instigation of the former colonisers with the view of maintaining closer links.

The formation of most of the unions also coincided with the era of export pessimism. This school of thought argued that the world trading system was not favourable to developing countries as a result of declining commodity terms of trade against LDC exports, export earnings instability, low trade elasticities and unfair protectionism against LDC exports in developed countries. These arguments led to the conclusion that the trade could not promote development in developing countries. These arguments were therefore used to justify import substitution industrialization (ISI) policies.

Most of the RI groupings in SSA were formed on the basis of import substitution strategies. The hope was that by widening the market, together with protection of important sectors, economies of scale would ultimately lead to increased intra-union trade and promotion of overall development. History has shown that the ISI policies not only failed in individual countries but also in the RI groupings.

Despite the failures, the glamour for RI in SSA has not diminished. It is hoped that, with a population of about half a billion people, SSA forms a potentially large market if only per caput incomes could be raised. It is, however, evident that the region has been experiencing economic decline since the 1970s. Moreover with the economy predominantly agricultural and a trade structure dominated by exports of fuels and other primary products (92 per cent) and imports of machinery and other manufactures (69 per cent), the conditions for successful RI appear to be lacking (Table 4.1).

De Melo and Panagariya (1992) argue that, because of past failures, RI among LDCs should be discouraged. For RI arrangements to be beneficial in LDCs they must be coupled with Unilateral Trade Liberalization (UTL). Foroutan (1993), however, notes that with trade liberalization taking place in most SSA countries RI is more promising than ever before.

In reviewing the experiences of RI in SSA, this section will examine the objectives and achievements of the main RI schemes. On the basis of current political and economic conditions this section will also examine the problems and prospects of RI in SSA. The major reasons which have been given for the failure of RI in LDCs include:

- failure to implement reduction in trade barriers;
- inability to devise fair arrangements for distributing the benefits arising from RI;
- restrictions on factor mobility;
- ineffectiveness of industrial planning, especially failure to agree on methods to distribute industries;
- ineffectiveness of CET arising from member countries requesting exemptions to avoid the revenue constraint;
- general failure of import substitution policies;
- lack of a strong and sustained political commitment; and
- macroeconomic instability.

Many of these issues have already been referred to in conceptualised form in the previous section. The conditions under which RI schemes could be effective in SSA will also be discussed.

Table 4.1 Economic indicators for SSA

	1991	1970–80	1980–91
Population	488.9[a]	2.8[b]	3.1[b]
Per capita GNP	350.0[c]		
Annual growth of GDP (%)		4.0	−1.2
Agriculture (%)		1.5	2.1
Manufacturing (%)		3.5	1.8

	1970	1991
GDP	40.1[c]	104.3[c]
Agriculture (%)	35	31
Manufacturing (%)	8	–
Services (%)	41	40
Imports	–	35.2[c]
Food (%)	10	16
Fuels (%)	8	10
Other primary products (%)	10	8
Machinery (%)	34	35
Other manufactures (%)	35	36
Exports	–	38.1[c]
Fuels (%)	41	58
Other primary products (%)	51	34
Machinery (%)	0	1
Other manufactures (%)	7	7
Textiles and clothing (%)	1	2

Note: [a]millions; [b]percentage change; [c]billion US dollars.

Source: The World Bank, 1993, *World Development Report*.

An Evaluation of RI Schemes in SSA

A substantial literature on RI schemes in SSA exists. Recent studies include World Bank (1991), Mansoor and Inotai (1991), Lipumba and Kassekende (1991), Ariyo and Raheem (1991), de la Torre and Kelley (1992), Foroutan (1993) and OECD (1993).

This section expands on the reviews on RI schemes by Foroutan (1993). The reviews will summarize the basic characteristics and trade pattern of the schemes. However, the major objectives of this section is to enumerate the objective of the RI schemes in the SSA and assess their achievement and prospects.

Table 4.2 presents, in a summary form, the membership, objectives, instruments and achievements of some regional integration arrangements in SSA.

Table 4.2 Regional integration arrangements among SSA countries: membership, objectives, instruments and achievements

Regional integration arrangements	Membership	Objectives	Instruments	Achievements
ECOWAS Economic Community of West African States Formed in 1975	Benin, Burkina, Faso, Cape Verde, Côte d'Ivoire, Gambia, Ghana, Guinea, Guinea Bissau, Liberia, Mali, Mauritania, Niger, Nigeria, Senegal, Sierra Leone and Togo	Promote cooperation and development in economic, social and cultural activity; raise the standard of living of the people in member countries; maintain economic stability; eliminate tariffs and other barriers to trade and establish a common market by 1990	Elimination of tariffs and other non-tariff barriers on intra-trade in 10 years; adopt a common external tariff by 1990; fund for labour compensation and development; abolish obstacles to free movement of factors of production; harmonize monetary and fiscal policies	Trade liberalization programme not implemented to date; no national allocations to the fund for compensation and development; no labour mobility
CEAO West African Economic Community Formed in 1972	Benin, Burkina, Faso, Côte d'Ivoire, Mali, Mauritania, Niger and Senegal	Promote cooperation and economic development through trade and community projects; establish a common external tariff	A single tax on intra-trade (replaces customs duties); harmonization of investment rules; a fund to finance regional projects	Common market not achieved: only 428 products receive regional preferences; some labour mobility
MRU Mano River Union Formed in 1973	Guinea, Liberia and Sierra Leone	Promote economic cooperation through the establishment of a customs and economic union	Elimination of tariffs on intra-trade; common external tariff	Common external tariff implemented in 1977; industrial projects in agriculture & energy
CEPGL Economic Community of the Great Lakes Countries Formed in 1976	Burundi, Rwanda and Zaire	Promote economic cooperation and development	Reduce tariff barriers and free factor mobility; joint industrial projects	Slow progress towards trade liberalization and factor mobility; industrial projects in agriculture and energy

Organization	Members	Objectives	Institutional features	Progress
UDEAC Central African Customs and Economic Union Formed in 1964	Cameroon, Central African Republic, Chad, Congo, Equatorial Guinea and Gabon	Promote economic development in order to increase living standards, establish a customs union	A single tax on intra-trade (replaces customs duties); elimination of non-tariff barriers; common investment rules: policy harmonization and factor mobility	No common external tariff; no labour mobility; substantial barriers to intra-trade remain
PTA Eastern and Southern African Preferential Trade Area Formed in 1981	Angola, Burundi, Comoros, Djibouti, Eritrea, Ethiopia, Kenya, Lesotho, Madagascar, Malawi, Mauritius, Mozambique, Namibia, Rwanda, Seychelles, Somalia, Sudan, Swaziland, Tanzania, Uganda, Zambia and Zimbabwe	Improve commercial and economic cooperation; transform the structure of production in national economies; promote intra-trade by removing tariff and non-tariff barriers on some products; develop industry; cooperate in agriculture; improve transportation links; establish a common market by 1992	Multilateral clearinghouse; tariff reductions; a PTA Trade and Development Bank	Multilateral clearinghouse; UAPTA traveller's cheques; some tariff reductions introduced in 1988 to facilitate monetary transactions trade facilitation measures
SADC Southern African Development Community Formed in 1992 (formerly SADCC, formed in 1980)	Angola, Botswana, Lesotho, Malawi, Mauritius, Mozambique, Namibia, South Africa, Swaziland, Tanzania, Zambia and Zimbabwe	To promote cooperation and integration in the region, sectoral coordination and improve transport links	Sector coordination units in each member state	Significant improvement in transport links, little progress on intra-regional trade flows

Source: OECD (1993); for SADC, various sources

West Africa

There are three major RI schemes in West Africa. These are: the Economic Community of West African States (ECOWAS), the Economic Community of West Africa (CEAO) and the Mano River Union (MRU).

ECOWAS: This arrangement was formed in 1975 and comprises 16 member countries. It had a population of about 186 million in 1991 and an estimated per caput income of $383 (Table 4.3). The economies of the ECOWAS countries are very diverse. The dominance of Nigeria, with 53 per cent of the region's population and 48 per cent of the GNP, however, stands out. The importance of Nigeria in the success of the union is vital.

ECOWAS started with the aim of becoming a free trade area with the objective of promoting industrialization and economic development among the member states. It was expected to be a complete customs union fifteen years after the treaty came into effect. Trade within the union was to be fully liberalised by 1989 and a common external tariff was to be in place by 1994. Harmonization of fiscal and monetary polices were also important areas of co-operation. A compensatory financing scheme, the Fund for Co-operation Compensation and Development, was to be established to reduce the costs of integration to the least developed members of the union. The Dakar agreement of 1979 also allowed for free movement of labour across the ECOWAS countries.

None of the objectives of ECOWAS has been met. This failure is clearly manifested by the low intra-ECOWAS trade. The share of intra-ECOWAS exports has grown marginally from 3 per cent in 1975 to 6 per cent in 1991 (Table 4.4). The growth of the share of intra-regional imports has followed a similar trend. It is noticeable however that the share of the region in world trade has been declining in the 1980s. This has been as a result of unfavourable conditions in international markets and import compression in the member countries. Low intra-ECOWAS trade has been a result of strict rules of origin and trade barriers.

The prospects for ECOWAS are not bright. Political instability remains a problem in many of the member states. Many countries of ECOWAS belong to more than one RI grouping and this has led to conflicts. International markets are not favourable to the region's major exports. Apart from Senegal, Benin and Sierra Leone, whose share of manufactures in total exports is greater than 20 per cent, the other countries have a very low share of manufactures in total exports (Table 4.5).

CEAO: This union was established in 1972 but became effective in 1974. All the members of this union are also members of ECOWAS. The union brings together West African states who belong to one monetary union (UMOA) under the CFA zone and Mauritania, but without Togo.

The CEAO has a population of 53 million and per caput income of $462 (Table 4.3). Although the per caput income is above the subSaharan average, the CEAO economy is dominated by Côte d'Ivoire and Senegal, which together constitute about 56 per cent of the regional GDP. Foroutan (1993) argues that this has been a source of polarization in the union.

The CEAO started out to become a free trade area with the objective of moving towards a customs union through reduction in the trade barriers, free movement of factors and the establishment of a common external tariff. A monetary union has been in existence in the region since the colonial period (Mauritania is not part of this).

Trade liberalization in the CEAO has been slow. Existence of quantitative restrictions and high tariff protection by the least developed members of the union have contributed to the slow growth in intra-regional trade. Intra-regional exports have stagnated at around 7 per cent (Table 4.4) of total exports. The region's share in world trade is also very small and has been declining in recent years. Moreover, the share of manufactures in total exports was only 12 per cent in 1990 (Table 4.5).

The CEAO has been more successful in the other areas of co-operation. There has been success in factor mobility, although the movement of labour is restricted. A Community Development Fund has been established to compensate those countries which lose tariff revenues. A Solidarity Fund financed mainly by Côte d'Ivoire and Senegal has also been established to finance projects in the least developed areas of the region. A CET has, however, not been established.

MRU: This union was formed in 1973 and its membership comprises Guinea, Liberia and Sierra-Leone. All these countries are also members of ECOWAS. MRU is the smallest RI grouping in SSA. The countries of this region have faced political instability in the last few years.

One of the reasons for low intra-regional trade is the existence of NTBs and tariff equivalent barriers to regional trade. Intra-regional trade has also been restricted by political instability and non-complementarily in production among the member states.

The union was formed to promote economic co-operation and increased trade among the member states. Trade among these countries is tariff free and a CET has been established. However, Table 4.4 shows

Table 4.3   Economic indicators for regional groupings in SSA

	Population 1991 (millions)	GDP 1991($M)	GNP 1991 ($M)	GNP per capita ($)	Average annual GDP growth rate (%) 1980–91
ECOWAS					
Burkina Faso	9.3	2629	2697	290	4.0
Benin	4.9	1886	1862	380	2.4
Cape Verde	0.4		285	750	
Côte d'Ivoire	12.4	7283	8556	690	−0.5
Gambia	0.9		324	360	
Ghana	15.3	6413	6120	400	3.2
Guinea	5.9	2937	2714	460	
Guinea Bissau	1.0	211	180	180	3.7
Liberia	2.6				
Mali	8.7	2451	2436	280	2.5
Mauritania	2.0	1030	1020	510	1.4
Niger	7.9	2284	2370	300	−1.0
Nigeria	99.0	34124	33660	340	1.9
Senegal	7.6	5774	5472	720	3.1
Sierra Leone	4.2	743	882	210	1.1
Togo	3.8	1633	1558	410	1.8
ECOWAS	185.9				
CEAO					
Benin	4.9	1886	1862	380	2.4
Burkina Faso	9.3	2629	2697	290	4.0
Côte d'Ivoire	12.4	7283	8556	690	−0.5
Mali	8.7	2451	2436	280	2.5
Mauritania	2.0	1030	1020	510	1.4
Niger	7.9	2284	2370	300	−1.0
Senegal	7.6	5774	5472	720	3.1
CEAO	52.8	23337	24413	462	1.7
MRU					
Guinea	5.9	2937	2714	460	
Liberia	2.6				
Sierra Leone	4.2	743	882	210	1.1
MRU					
UDEAC					
Cameroon	11.9	11666	10115	850	1.4
CAR	3.1	1202	1209	390	1.4
Chad	5.8	1236	1218	210	5.5
Congo	2.4	2909	2688	1120	3.3
Gabon	1.2	4863	4536	3780	0.2
Equatorial Guinea	0.4		132	330	
UDEAC	24.8		19898	460	
CEPGL					
Burundi	5.7	1035	1197	210	4.0
Rwanda	7.1	1579	1917	270	0.6
Zaire	38.6				
CEPGL	51.4				

PTA					
Angola	9.5				
Burundi	5.7	1035	1197	210	4.0
Comoros	0.5		250	500	
Djibouti	0.5				
Ethiopia	52.8	5982	6336	120	1.6
Kenya	25.0	7125	8500	340	4.2
Lesotho	1.8	578	1044	580	5.5
Malawi	8.8	1986	2024	230	3.1
Mozambique	16.1	1219	1288	80	−0.1
Mauritius	1.1	2253	2651	2410	6.7
Rwanda	7.1	1579	1917	270	0.6
Somalia	8.1				
Sudan	25.8				
Swaziland	0.8	5774	840	1050	3.1
Uganda	16.9	2527	2873	170	1.1
Tanzania	25.5	2223	2550	100	2.9
Zambia	8.3	3831			0.8
Zimbabwe	10.1	5543	6565	650	3.1
PTA	224.4				
SADC					
Angola	9.5				
Botswana	1.3	3644	3289	2530	9.8
Lesotho	1.8	578	1044	580	5.5
Malawi	8.8	1986	2024	230	3.1
Mozambique	16.1	1219	1288	80	−0.1
Namibia	1.5	1961	2190	1460	1.0
Swaziland	0.8		840	1050	
Tanzania	25.5	2223	2550	100	2.9
Zambia	8.3	3831			0.8
Zimbabwe	10.1	5543	6565	650	3.1
SADC	83.7				
SACU					
Botswana	1.3	3644	3289	2530	9.8
Lesotho	1.8	578	1044	580	5.5
Namibia	1.5	1961	2190	1460	1.0
South Africa	38.9	91167	99584	2560	1.3
Swaziland	0.8		840	1050	
SACU	44.3		106947	2414	
IOC					
Comoros	0.5		250	500	
Madagascar	12.0	2488	2520	210	1.1
Mauritius	1.1	2253	2651	2410	6.7
Reunion	0.6				
Seychelles	0.07		358	5110	
IOC	14.27				
EAC					
Kenya	25.0	7125	8500	340	4.2
Uganda	25.2	2223	2520	100	2.9
Tanzania	16.9	2527	2873	170	
EAC	67.1	11875	13893	207	

Source: World Bank, 1993, *World Development Report*.

Table 4.4 Share of trade in intra-regional exports and imports and world exports and imports by trading schemes in selected years (1970–91) (%)

	1970	1975	1980	1985	1990	1991
ECOWAS						
Share in intra-regional exports	2	3	3	5	5	6
Share in total world exports	1.05	1.45	1.62	1.08	0.68	0.62
Share in intra-regional imports	2	2	3	7	7	6
Share in total world imports	0.94	1.27	1.36	0.67	0.59	0.61
CEAO						
Share in intra-regional exports	6	7	6	7	7	8
Share in total world exports	0.29	0.24	0.29	0.26	0.16	0.16
Share in intra-regional imports	5	7	6	7	8	9
Share in total world imports	0.29	0.30	0.34	0.23	0.18	0.17
MRU						
Share in intra-regional exports	0.2	0.3	0.6	0.4	0.01	0.03
Share in total world exports	0.13	0.08	0.07	0.06	0.08	0.04
Share in intra-regional imports	0.2	0.4	0.7	0.6	0.02	0.02
Share in total world imports	0.11	0.08	0.06	0.04	0.14	0.14
UDEAC						
Share in intra-regional exports	5	4	3	2	2	2
Share in total world exports	0.16	0.24	0.26	0.25	0.18	0.17
Share in intra-regional imports	5	5	5	2	4	3
Share in total world imports	0.16	0.20	0.18	0.16	0.11	0.10
CEPGL						
Share in intra-regional exports	0.4	0.5	0.2	0.8	0.4	0.4
Share in total world exports	0.28	0.14	0.13	0.07	0.05	0.95
Share in intra-regional imports	0.5	0.3	0.3	0.6	0.5	0.7
Share in total world imports	0.20	0.16	0.09	0.07	0.05	0.04
PTA						
Share in intra-regional exports	8	7	8	5	6	7
Share in total world exports	1.1	0.58	0.46	0.39	0.32	0.31
Share in intra-regional imports	9	6	5	4	4	5
Share in total world imports	0.98	0.77	0.63	0.54	0.44	0.42
EAC						
Share in intra-regional exports	17	13	9	6	8	8
Share in total world exports	0.30	0.16	0.13	0.09	0.05	0.05
Share in intra-regional imports	15	8	5	4	4	4
Share in total world imports	0.31	0.24	0.22	0.15	0.11	0.09
SADC						
Share in intra-regional exports	3	3	2	5	5	NA
Share in total world exports	0.67	0.31	0.27	0.21	0.19	0.19
Share in intra-regional imports	6	3	2	4	5	NA
Share in total world imports	0.53	0.35	0.25	0.23	0.19	0.18

SACU						
Share in intra-regional exports						
Share in total world exports	NA	NA	0.71	0.43	0.36	0.37
Share in intra-regional imports						
Share in total world imports	NA	NA	0.78	0.64	0.42	0.41
IOC						
Share in intra-regional exports	8	6	3	3	4	5
Share in total world exports	0.09	0.08	0.05	0.05	0.06	0.05
Share in intra-regional imports	5	4	1	1	2	2
Share in total world imports	0.14	0.12	0.12	0.10	0.14	0.12

Note: NA = not available.

Source: International Monetary Fund, *Direction of Trade Statistics*.

that intra-regional trade and the share of the regional trade in world trade is negligible.

MRU in general has no future. The countries are too small and competitive to merit forming a union.

Central Africa

The RI groupings in Central Africa are the Customs and Economic Union of Central Africa (UDEAC) the Economic Community of the Countries of the Great Lakes (CEPGL) and the Economic Community of Central African States (ECCAS).

UDEAC: This union was formed in 1973 and its members are Cameroon, Central African Republic, Chad, Congo, Gabon and Equatorial Guinea. It is dominated by Cameroon with 48 per cent of the union population and 51 per cent of its GNP. The union also has one of the highest per caput GNPs in SSA. Congo and Gabon have per caput GNP above $1000.

The UDEAC was formed with the objectives of facilitating free trade and free movement of factors. As a customs union, it was intended to establish a common external tariff and maintain a monetary union, which has been in existence since 1948.

The union has failed to increase trade. Indeed the intra-regional trade shares have declined since the formation of the union. The region's share in world trade is also very low (Table 4.4). Low intra-regional trade is a result of trade barriers. Existence of a monetary union implies free movement of capital but this has not been sufficient to generate increased trade flows.

Table 4.5 Manufacturing output and exports for regional groupings in SSA

	Share of manufactured goods in merchandise exports 1990 (%)	Value added in manufacturing 1991 ($ millions)
ECOWAS		
Benin	32.0	162
Burkina Faso	14.0	325
Cape Verde	–	–
Côte d'Ivoire	13.0	–
Gambia	–	–
Ghana	1.0	575
Guinea	–	123
Guinea Bissau	–	18
Liberia	–	–
Mali	1.30	286
Mauritania	5.0	–
Niger	2.0	219
Nigeria	1.0	–
Senegal	25.0	775
Sierra Leone	32.0	52
Togo	12.0	162
CEAO		
Benin	–	–
Burkina Faso	14.0	325
Côte d'Ivoire	13.0	–
Mali	13.0	286
Mauritania	5.0	–
Niger	2.0	219
Senegal	25.0	775
CEAO	12.0	
MRU		
Guinea	–	123
Liberia	–	–
Sierra Leone	32.0	52
UDEAC		
Cameroon	–	1363
CAR	43.0	–
Chad	5.0	250
Congo	3.0	220
Gabon	4.0	264
Equatorial Guinea	–	–
CEPGL		
Burindi	2.0	99
Rwanda	–	316
Zaire	–	–

PTA		
Angola		
Burundi	2.0	99
Comoros	–	–
Djibouti	–	–
Ethiopia	4.0	614
Kenya	22.0	862
Lesotho	–	64
Malawi	7.0	227
Mozambique	–	–
Mauritius	54.0	496
Rwanda	–	316
Somalia	–	–
Sudan	1.0	772
Swaziland ˙	–	–
Tanzania	14.0	86
Uganda	0.0	107
Zambia	1.0	1180
Zimbabwe	38.0	1508

SADC		
Angola	–	–
Botswana	–	128
Lesotho	–	64
Malawi	7.0	227
Mozambique	–	–
Namibia	–	77
Swaziland	–	–
Tanzania	14.0	86
Zambia	1.0	1180
Zimbabwe	38.0	1508

SACU		
Botswana	–	128
Lesotho	–	64
Namibia	–	77
South Africa	–	23197
Swaziland	–	–

IOC		
Comoros	–	–
Madagascar	11.0	–
Mauritius	54.0	496
Reunion	–	–
Seychelles	–	–

EAC		
Kenya	22.0	862
Tanzania	14.0	86
Uganda	0.0	107
EAC	12.0	1055

Source: World Bank, 1993, *World Development Report*.

The abolition of a common external tariff in 1974 means that the union has failed to develop into a customs union, despite its name. The membership of three countries with high per caput incomes has been a source of potential polarization in the region.

CEPGL: The scheme was established in 1976 and comprises of Burundi, Rwanda and Zaire. The countries are relatively poor and have experienced serious political instability in recent years. The objectives of the union were the removal of trade barriers, free movement of labour and co-operation in the development and implementation of joint projects. None of these objectives have been achieved. Intra-CEPGL trade is very low and the region's share in world trade is negligible (Table 4.4). Competitiveness among these countries implies little possibility of increased trade in the union. Success in other areas is also limited by the political uncertainty in the countries of CEPGL.

Eastern and Southern Africa

This region has the highest population and number of RI groupings in SSA. The existing RI groupings include: the Preferential Trade Area for Eastern and Southern African States (PTA), the Southern African Development Community (SADC), the Southern African Customs Union (SACU) and the Indian Ocean Commission (IOC). The revival of the East African Community (EAC) is being seriously considered. In this chapter the experiences, especially the reasons for the failure of EAC, are reviewed in order to provide lessons for existing RI groupings.

PTA: The scheme was formed in 1981 but became operational in 1984. It presently comprises twenty-two countries. It is the largest RI scheme in SSA (in terms of population). It is also the poorest, with a per caput income of about $200.

The PTA was established with the purpose of promoting trade in the region. Intra-regional trade was to be promoted by tariff reduction and removal of NTBs. Tariffs were to be gradually reduced, with total elimination by 1992. Other objectives of PTA included co-operation in other economic areas, harmonization of policies across member countries and regional economic development.

There has been some movement towards freer trade in the PTA. However, tariff reduction is behind schedule and total elimination is now expected by the year 2000. NTBs have also been relaxed in several countries. Nevertheless intra-PTA trade remains low. Intra-PTA exports declined in the 1980s but have recently began to show signs of revival. The shares of PTA exports in world trade have also declined over the years.

Co-operation exists in many areas in the PTA. These include customs, immigration, trade, trade information and transport policies. A Clearing House and a Development Bank have been established and are functioning. A treaty on a common market (COMESA) was signed in November 1993.

However, there seems to be developing a rift between the Southern and Eastern African states. The formation of SADC and the reluctance by some SADC members to sign the COMESA treaty is a manifestation of this. East African countries are currently negotiating to re-establish the East African Community.

SADC: This arrangement was established in 1980 by Southern African states. Namibia joined the organisation when it attained independence in 1990. SADCC now SADC, was formed with the main purpose of reducing dependence on South Africa through economic co-operation. This was to be achieved mainly through regional development projects.

SADC has been reasonably successful in promoting regional development projects, especially in the areas of transport, communication, industry and environment. It has also been successful in securing donor funding for the projects.

In 1992 SADC was transformed from a project co-ordinating body into an RI scheme. Although intra-SADC trade is low, there are possibilities of increased flows. The shares of trade in the region has gone up since 1980 (Table 4.4). However, following a common trend in SSA, the share of the region's world trade has declined since the 1980s.

Most members of SADC belong to the PTA and/or SACU. South Africa joined the organization in August, 1994 to bring the total SADC member states to eleven.

SACU: This is the oldest customs union in SSA. It comprises Botswana, Lesotho, Namibia, South Africa and Swaziland, and it currently operates under agreements reached in 1969. SACU is the richest RI scheme in SSA with per caput income of $2414. However, it is dominated by South Africa with 88 per cent of the union's population and 93 per cent of its GNP.

The union has broadly achieved its objectives. All trade barriers have been removed and there is free movement of factors. A common external tariff with a common customs organisation exists. All SACU members, except Botswana, also belong to the Rand Monetary area. A consolidated Revenue Fund was established to distribute the gains from the union. On balance, South Africa has been compensating the other members of the union. The small member states complain that they have to buy expensive South African products, that industries have favoured locating in South Africa and that they have not been involved in decision-making.

Given the advanced nature of the South African economy, the union would seem to have great potential. However, economic realignments which may be necessary in the post-apartheid South Africa may distabilize the union.

IOC: The commission was established in 1982, but the secretariat was only set up in 1989. IOC comprises Comoros, Madagascar, Mauritius, Réunion (France) and Seychelles, the islands in the Indian Ocean. It is the only RI scheme which includes a developed country.

The Commission was set up with the purpose of promoting regional co-operation in trade and industrial development. Most of the projects in IOC are funded by UN agencies and regional funds under the Lomé Convention.

The prospects for this organisation are low. Intra-IOC trade, although rising after 1985, is low. Economies of IOC members are too small to allow for economies of scale. Co-operation with larger economies would be the most viable alternative.

EAC: Before collapsing in 1977, the EAC was the second-oldest RI in SSA and one of the most advanced customs union in LDCs. It was started as a currency board in 1919 and was reconstituted into the East African High Commission in 1948. The Commission had legislative and administrative bodies charged with co-ordinating policies and activities in the whole of East Africa on behalf of the British Government. The commission was reorganized in 1961 and renamed the East African Common Services Organisation.

The EAC became a customs union under the treaty of 1967, with the objective of promoting co-operation in all fields. Table 4.4 shows that intra-EAC trade, which had stagnated with the collapse of the Community in 1977, has picked up since the mid-1980. These figures however hide intra-EAC inequality of trade. Kenya maintains a large trade surplus with both Tanzania and Uganda.

The East African countries are currently negotiating to revive EAC.

The prospective union has one of the lowest per caput incomes among the RI schemes in SSA. The three East African countries account for about 14 per cent of SSA population and 7 per cent of its GDP.

A new treaty by the East African countries should avoid the problems which led to the earlier collapse. Chief among the problems was the failure to share the gains from the union equitably. The fear of this problem has led to a reluctance among the negotiators to go for a full customs union.

4.4 INTEGRATION EXPERIENCE OUTSIDE AFRICA

In order to clarify and better understand the African regional integration experience, it is useful to examine integration experiences in other parts of the world. It is beyond the scope of this section to present a thorough review of integration experiences outside Africa. The emphasis is on outlining the main characteristics of experiences that were instrumental in the success or failure. Describing experience outside Africa is not meant to suggest that such experience is transferable: the circumstances of a group of countries will always be specific in terms of history, culture, political system and economic resources. However, it is still possible to draw useful lessons, especially on the way certain problems were overcome.

European Integration Experience

The European integration process is often referred to as one of the few successful integration experiences. More than forty years have passed since the process started in the period just following the Second World War. Presently, the European integration experience is often considered to be synonymous with the experience of the European Community. However, there have been a variety of integration initiatives preceding the Treaty of Rome that established the European Economic Community in 1957. Some of this early European integration experience is relevant for the present debate on integration in Africa.[2]

It should be recalled that the European co-operation and integration experience received significant support from outside through the Marshall plan. Recent analysis of the Marshall plan by De Long and Eichengreen (1992) concludes that the plan amounted to a highly successful programme to adjust the European economies and to avoid the inward-looking approach that characterized these economies during the interwar period.

The main effect of the Marshall plan according to this view was not the physical deliveries of goods that were in short supply (capital goods, fuel, food, and so on), but the policy reforms that were enforced through conditionality. The Marshall plan strengthened the credibility of these economic reforms. Among the conditionalities figured the abolition of trade quotas and other non-tariff barriers (NTBs). Negotiations on these matters took place in the *Organization for European Economic Co-operation* (OEEC) that was created in 1948. The Marshall plan also promoted the convertibility of the European currencies by providing support for the European Payments Union (EPU) that was set up in 1950. It is interesting to observe that both organizations ceased to exist once their main task was carried out. The EPU was replaced by the European Payments Agreement in 1958 when convertibility was restored. The OEEC was transformed into the Organization for Economic Co-operation and Development (OECD) in 1961. The OECD continues to play an important role as a think tank and forum for the industrial countries on international economic matters.

Presently, the African countries are confronted with a number of problems that were also prevalent in postwar Europe: widespread use of non-tariff barriers and non-convertibility of the currencies. A lesson of the early European co-operation experience is that NTBs should be abolished and currency convertibility should be restored before more ambitious integration initiatives can be successfully started.

Before turning to the European Community, it is useful to recall the experience of the *European Free Trade Association* (EFTA) that was founded in 1959. The countries joining EFTA were those that did not wish to pursue the deeper integration programme of the European Community. EFTA was very successful in quickly achieving its main objective of establishing a free trade area. It is interesting to observe the incompatibility of EFTA and EC membership, because the EC right from the start aimed at a customs union as well as common policies in certain areas. On the other hand, membership of Benelux (the association of Belgium, the Netherlands and Luxembourg) has remained compatible with EC membership because the Benelux countries subscribed to all the EC requirements, but went further in some respects. Even today, Benelux still functions in a number of areas that are not (yet) handled by the European Community.

Turning to the *European Community* (EC), or more precisely the European Union, since the ratification of the Maastricht Treaty in 1993, there is a collection of factors that help to explain its success. European integration would probably not have gone very far without a strong and original set of *institutions*. The institutions that were put in place represented a reconciliation between national and community (that is, European) interests. There are four basic institutions: The Council of Ministers, the Commission, the Parliament and the Court of Justice. The Council is composed of the ministers of the member states and its composition changes according to the subject that is dealt with, for example, the agriculture ministers deal with matters of agriculture and rural development. The Commission of the EC (CEC) consists of seventeen commissioners who are nominated by the member states, two commissioners for each large member state and one for each small member state. The commissioners must always act jointly, even though each of them has an area of competence. The European Parliament has been elected directly for a five-year mandate since 1979. The Court of Justice comprises thirteen judges who are appointed for a six-year term by common agreement between the member states.

The functioning and interaction of these institutions can be briefly summarised as follows. The Commission represents the Community interest, it has the right to propose legislation to implement the different Treaties. The Commission often has a role as well in the implementation of approved legislation. After consultation with the Parliament and with possible amendments, the Council formally decides on legislation. In the Council, ministers naturally take into account their national interest, however, they can only act upon a proposal that reflects the Community- wide interest. Decisions can be adopted by unanimity, simple majority or qualified majority.

There has been a gradual shift towards more use of simple or qualified majority, especially in the legal framework for the single European market, in order to speed up the process of legislation. Nevertheless, on a matter of vital interest to a member state, unanimity remains the rule. In addition to its role in amending proposed legislation, the Parliament has a crucial role in approving the annual Community budget. In the event of disputes about the application or interpretation of European legislation, the Court of Justice intervenes.

A central feature of the institutional set-up is the *legal framework*, which represents a careful balance between the interest of the community as a whole and the interests of the member states, with a safeguard on vital national interests. As a rule, European legislation prevails over national legislation. An important requirement for successful integration is that the legal structures in the different member states should be compatible with each other. It is difficult to conceive integration between a country that is governed by executive decree and another that has a parliamentary system. Similar compatibility is necessary for fundamental personal rights.

A characteristic of the European institutional system that is not often mentioned, because it is taken for granted, is the constant dialogue and communication that takes place between national and community institutions. This dialogue fulfils two crucial functions: first information and sensitivities from within the member states are transmitted to the European Commission and second it constitutes a channel to implement European legislation at the national level. This system of dialogue is costly, because of the need to organise frequent meetings and to translate documents into several languages. However, the system evolved gradually over a long period, it was not build from scratch at a particular moment. Only a small part of the total cost is covered by the Community budget. At the centre of the system is the Committee of Permanent Representatives grouping ambassadors of the member states to the Community. The main task of this committee is to prepare the sessions of the Council of Ministers. This is done through various working groups covering the main aspects of Community policy.

It would not be easy to set up a similar dialogue system in the African context, if only because of its high cost. In this respect it should be kept in mind that the cost rises more than proportionately with the number of participants in a regional arrangement.

Another feature of the EC institutions is the system of *'own' resources*. Institutions to promote integration need to have a certain independence from the participating governments so that they can effectively pursue 'community' interests rather than the sum of national interests. This independence requires a claim to financial resources to carry out the community tasks. Otherwise the institution will have constantly to solicit funding and will not be able to formulate and implement a coherent integration policy. This is what is often happening in the African context. A logical start may be to consider customs receipts as community resources, because in a customs union it should not matter where a product is imported from and which country happens to collect the duty. However, in the African context this may be very difficult because customs duties make up a very large share of government receipts. Clearly, access to 'own' resources does not imply that an integration organization needs an apparatus to collect taxes, rather it means transparency and clarity on rules to finance the implementation of integration measures.

The successful introduction of a system of 'own' resources again requires a basic compatibility and harmony of the member states, so that they all accept the rules of the game. Otherwise there will be frequent disputes that will block the integration process or worse, there could be back-tracking. Needless to say that there have been disputes in the EC about the transfer of resources from the member states to the Community. However, these disputes have been resolved within the existing legal framework and have not prevented sustained progress.

Another lesson to be learnt from the European experience is the importance of *co-ordinating macro-economic policies*. In the area of monetary policy, the European experience demonstrates that, even though a full monetary union is not at all necessary for progress on market integration, a satisfactory degree of *currency convertibility* is indeed required. As economic integration proceeds, there is gradually a greater need for co-ordination of monetary policy. This ultimately leads to the desirability of a full monetary union. Convertibility of the currency generally implies a separation of the responsibility of the treasury and the central bank. Convertibility makes it possible for traders and investors to plan their operations and to avoid costly barter operations. Payments arrangements through clearing houses are generally a step towards convertibility. There should also be sufficient co-ordination of fiscal policies. For example, indirect tax rates within the member states are fixed within agreed common margins. Progress on integration also requires a competition policy that helps to ensure that companies in different member states operate within similar conditions. A competition policy helps to establish a level playing field and calls for a high degree of compatibility of the member states.

The European experience also demonstrates the importance of regional and social policies to *reduce welfare disparities* between different zones in the integration area. The creation of a larger market tends to benefit first the areas of great economic potential, because supply response to comparative advantage is quicker in such areas. Even though less favoured areas may not be worse off as a result of integration, the increased disparities are typically perceived as a cost for such areas. Compensatory regional policies should preferably attack the root causes for the relative backwardness of certain zones. In the African context, the financing of such policies certainly poses problems, because the more advanced areas have a lot of problems of their own. However, not all compensatory policies should cost money. In some cases one could try to protect the market for products for which the poorer area has a comparative advantage (for example, protection of livestock products in coastal West Africa could help the Sahel area).

The recent discussions on European integration have underlined the importance of the principle of *subsidiarity*, which implies that the responsibility for dealing with an issue should shift from a lower to a higher level only if the issue can be more effectively handled at the higher level. According to the principle, decentralization should be the rule, centralization should apply only where it has been shown to be more effective. This principle provides a way to distribute responsibility over various levels of government such as communes, provinces, countries, groups of countries. For example, the running of primary schools can probably be best organized at a more local level, whereas environmental problems which transcend borders are better handled at a regional level. The subsidiarity principle may help in determining a reasonable division of labour between different regional bodies and/or national administrations.

The European experience also shows that a certain pluralism of organizations can be compatible with integration. The continued existence of Benelux as being compatible with wider European integration has already been mentioned. Several EC policies have been implemented by sub-groups of the twelve member states. Such cases of 'integration at different speeds' are to be expected and might even be common once the number of participating countries becomes relatively large. Without such *'variable geometry'* progress will be determined by the pace of the slowest member country. In the African context, such an approach of variable geometry could, for example, mean making genuine progress at ECOWAS level while maintaining the achievements and benefits of UMOA. Similarly, the concepts of variable geometry and subsidiarity could also be useful in Southern Africa in relation to the PTA, SADC and SACU. However, even though variable geometry may justify a certain pluralism of organizations, it should not be used as a pretext for wasteful duplication of functions.

Another aspect of the European integration process is that it has not been a purely government affair. It has benefited a lot from *civil society participation* through a wide variety of socioeconomic groupings, including trade unions, employers' organizations and consumers groups. The pressure of such groups ensured that certain issues remained high on the agenda.

Many of the characteristics of European integration outlined above can be considered to have been made possible by a *strong, sustained political will*. The European integration process was a long-term process with realistic objectives. Progress over time has certainly been uneven, with periods of great difficulties sometimes alternating with periods of successive breakthroughs. However, there has been no reversal on what has been achieved because the political will has been sustained.

In trying to relate the above characteristics of the European experience to the African context one should avoid the trap of simply advocating a transfer of the European model. What counts is to learn from the mechanisms that were used to overcome problems that arise when sovereign states engage in beneficial co-operation. There is certainly a danger of superficial copying of an experience or of copying selected aspects before crucial preconditions have been met. As an example one might refer to the implementation of policies to reduce regional disparities. If such policies are attempted in the absence of a system of 'own' resources within a sound legal framework, they will not work. This illustrates the importance of having a thorough understanding of the issues at stake in relation to regional integration and hence of training on the subject. Such understanding should help to avoid unrealistic ambitions for regional integration schemes which lead to disappointment, wastage of resources and possibly to a rejection of integration. Furthermore, ambitions should be matched with human and other resources.

Integration Experience in Latin America

In a certain way, the integration and co-operation experience in Latin America is comparable to the African situation. An overview of the evolution of regional integration in Latin America can be found in Bataller (1992). There was a strong drive towards regional integration in the 1960s when several institutions were created, including:

- the Latin American Free Trade Association (LAFTA), created in 1960, comprising Mexico and the whole of South America, except Guyana, Suriname and French Guyana who are oriented towards the Caribbean;
- the Central American Common Market (CACM), also created in 1969, comprising Costa Rica, El Salvador, Guatemala, Honduras and Nicaragua; and
- the Andean Pact, created in 1969, formed by Bolivia, Chile (until 1976), Colombia, Ecuador, Peru and Venezuela.

LAFTA never became a free trade area and was transformed in 1980 into the Latin American Integration Association, best known by its Spanish abbreviation: ALADI. The lack of achievements of ALADI illustrates the difficulty of integration involving a large group of countries that are diverse in levels of development and socioeconomic strategy. To some extent, the origin of the Andean Pact was a reaction of the smaller LAFTA countries to the larger LAFTA countries (Mexico, Brazil and Argentina). The smaller countries felt that the larger, more industrialised, countries were mainly interested in expanding their regional market. In another sub-region, ALADI's policy objectives have recently have been taken over by Mercosur.

After making rapid progress and reaching nearly a full customs union, the integration process in Central America came to a halt and even reversed as a result of political and economic crises (including civil wars and armed conflicts between some of the member states). It is not difficult to draw parallels with the situation in parts of Africa. The Andean Pact is a sophisticated integration scheme, mainly focused on import substitution. It has been characterized by an unsuccessful attempt at regional investment planning and an inward-looking economic policy.

The late 1980s and early 1990s have witnessed a revival of regional integration in Latin America and a significant rise in intra-regional trade (see Nogués and Quintanilla, 1992). The current approach contrasts with the attempts of the 1960s and 1970s as it is largely based on an outward-oriented strategy (Edwards, 1993). Mercosur was established in 1991 by Argentina, Brazil, Paraguay and Uruguay. It originated from a desire toward more economic co-operation between Brazil and Argentina. However, even though Mercosur introduced a new approach, its objectives tend to be very ambitious and it is too early to make a judgement. The wide disparities (for example, in size, macroeconomic policies) between its member states make it difficult for Mercosur to reach its targets within the short period foreseen. The revival of integration in Central America appears to be promising. The economic outlook of the countries in the region has improved. A characteristic of this new integration drive is its reliance on low tariffs and the abolition of non-tariff barriers. There have also been recent changes in the strategy of the Andean Pact towards a more outward-looking approach. This is in line with policy changes at the national level in the direction of a more liberal economy (especially in Bolivia and Peru).

The most significant recent development in relation to integration in Latin America has been the approval in 1993 of the North American Free Trade Area (NAFTA), including Mexico in addition to the USA and Canada. Countries such as Argentina and especially Chile are now also reflecting on becoming part of or being associated with NAFTA.

The recent relative success of integration in Latin America contains some important lessons for Africa. The lack of success of a continent-wide scheme illustrates the difficulties that can be expected in the way of making concrete progress towards the Pan-African Economic Community as envisaged by the Abuja Treaty that was signed in 1991. The failure of regional investment planning in combination with high tariff protection, as was the case in the Andean Pact, is also relevant for some of the sub-regional African integration schemes. The Latin American experience furthermore illustrates the importance of peace and stability to make progress with integration.

Integration Experience in Asia

Whereas in the case of integration in Latin America there are some immediate similarities with the African situation, this is not the case for Asia. In Asia, there are only few organizations concerned with regional integration or co-operation and there does not exist a Pan-Asiatic ideal. Also, in comparison to Africa, the economic size of the countries is much larger, so that the immediate advantages of a regional approach (for example, in terms of scale economies) are less obvious. Nevertheless, as in the case of Europe, there seem to be some relevant lessons to be drawn.

The best known integration organisation in Asia is the Association of South East Asian Nations (ASEAN) with the following member states: Indonesia, Malaysia, the Philippines, Singapore, Thailand and Brunei. The creation of ASEAN in 1967 was mainly in order to stabilise the political environment in the region. It has a light institutional structure: an ASEAN secretariat was established only in 1976, in Jakarta. The secretariat played a small role until 1992 when the decision was taken to develop an ASEAN Free Trade Area (Pelkmans and Alburo, 1993). For most of its existence, ASEAN focused on regional co-operation in various areas rather than on trade integration.

In the area of industrial co-operation ASEAN set up a number of investment co-ordination programmes. These programmes, which were established during the late 1970s and early 1980s, involved joint planning and allocation of large scale industrial investments, combined with protection. In line with the experience in Latin America, the current assessment of the joint industrial planning programmes is that they were not successful (DeRosa, 1993). It was not possible to strike a balance between many national public and private sector interests.

In the area of trade, ASEAN started the implementation of preferential trading arrangements in 1977. Under these arrangements, limited preferences (around 10 per cent) were exchanged first on a product-by-product basis. In many cases, the products selected involved little trade among the ASEAN countries. Restrictive rules of origin provisions required a minimum ASEAN content of 50 per cent and the need for the final production stage to occur within the ASEAN region. During the 1980s the arrangements were broadened, covering more products and a wider preference margin (around 20 per cent). Nevertheless, exclusions to safeguard national interests made the system ineffective.

Only recently, with the decision in 1992 to establish an ASEAN Free Trade Area (AFTA), did the ASEAN countries embark on a more ambitious programme towards trade integration. The objective is to establish a free trade area by the year 2008. This is to be done by gradual, across-the-board tariff reductions. AFTA also plans to abolish remaining non-tariff barriers. Two sectors are excluded: unprocessed agricultural products and services.

It is remarkable that despite ASEAN's modest achievements, at least in the economic field, it is often considered a successful experience of regional co-operation and integration. To some extent, considering ASEAN as a success is derived from the impressive economic advances of its member states, who all followed a general export-orientated strategy. However, there are other reasons for the success of ASEAN. A significant result of ASEAN has been to provide a useful framework for dealing with the large trading countries or groups in the world. Furthermore, intra-ASEAN trade and cross-border investment have expanded along with trade and growth in general. The present move towards market integration can be expected to provide further encouragement of intra-regional trade and factor movements.

ASEAN provides some useful references for the debate on regional integration and co-operation in Africa. ASEAN has on the whole been pragmatic and with limited objectives focusing on co-operation in certain areas before tackling more far-reaching across-the-board market integration. With respect to market integration, objectives and results have been very limited so far, so that there has not been any quick disappointment or reversal.

4.5 MAJOR RESEARCHABLE ISSUES

The ambiguity of the theory means that it was important to undertake an evaluation of past regional integration schemes in Africa, especially as these are widely viewed as having been unsuccessful (Mansoor and Inotai, 1991; Langhammer, 1992; Foroutan, 1993). If this conclusion is accepted, then there are a number of possible explanations.

(1) Regional integration in itself is undesirable, at least in the African context.

(2) Many past regional integration experiences in Africa have been unsuccessful, because they have been ill-conceived (for example, by being viewed as a means of pursuing inward-orientated policies), but this does not necessarily mean that all regional integration schemes in Africa would be unsuccessful.

(3) The supposed regional integration was not in fact properly implemented, so that it is not possible to draw conclusions about regional integration schemes in general, but only about those elements actually implemented. This conclusion in turn raises an important political economy question about why the proposed integration scheme was not implemented.

A major objective of the case studies in the regional integration dimension of this project is to establish whether regional schemes were unsuccessful and, in such cases, which of the explanations (1) – (3) are most applicable in explaining failure. This allows lessons to be drawn in order to inform current policy discussion.

The question of how to undertake an evaluation of a particular regional integration scheme is not straightforward. It is desirable that the particular case studies follow broadly similar approaches, at least initially, to allow the possibility of conclusions which can be generalized, and so used in assessing the question of regional integration in Africa more generally.

Issues

Based on the survey above, the following is a proposal for a minimum set of questions to be addressed in a case study. They are not intended to be definitive.

A. The Conception of the Regional Integration Scheme

(1) What was the nature of the intended regional integration arrangement? What measures were to be undertaken? On what time scale? What was the ultimate economic objective of the scheme?

(2) Were the countries involved appropriate for participating in a union? Were their structures of production compatible?

(3) Was any redistribution mechanism included in the scheme?

B. The Implementation of the Regional Integration Scheme

(1) To what extent were the intended measures implemented? Which measures were not implemented and why?
(2) To what extent were the effects circumvented by other measures taken by the member countries?
(3) What exclusions were there?

C. The Impact of the Regional Integration Scheme

(1) What was the impact of the scheme on intra-regional trade flows (level, direction, composition)? On external trade flows?
(2) What was the impact of the scheme on the structure of production in member countries?
(3) Is there any evidence that the scheme led to concentration of production in particular countries and the exploitation of economies scale?
(4) Is there any evidence that the scheme led to increases in production efficiency or in competition?
(5) What were the distributional impacts of the scheme? How well did the compensation scheme (if any) work?
(6) Were there any important asymmetric shocks?
(7) Is there any evidence that the scheme led to increased foreign investment?

The major constraint in undertaking the economic evaluation of the scheme is inevitably that of data availability, which places severe limits on the methodology which can be applied. Many of the methods used to evaluate the impact of trade integration in the European Community or North America, such as convergence measures or general equilibrium modelling, will not be feasible in the African context. It is necessary therefore to devise methods which are sensitive to the data constraints but can still provide some answers (however tentative) to at least some of the above questions. Given, however, that a sophisticated modelling approach will not be feasible in most cases, the problems of attribution (what causes given changes?) and counterfactual (what would have happened in the absence of regional integration?) will always arise. Use of more naïve 'before and after' comparisons may be needed in many instances, despite the weaknesses of such an approach.

The most productive avenue is likely to be in terms of the study of trade flows, given that data is more complete, regular and detailed in this area than in many others. The issue is how participation in a regional integration scheme, and the implementation of the various measures of internal trade liberalization and changes in external protection levels impacted on trade flows. The key point is to identify when these major trade policy changes took place and to see what was their effect (if any) on the volume and commodity composition of exports and imports between member countries and between member countries and non-members. Note that in general changes in both internal and external trade policy can affect both internal and external trade.

The problem is, of course, that many other factors, besides participation in a regional integration scheme, can account for changes in trade flows – for example, income levels and prices. In principle it is desirable to distinguish such factors from the trade policy changes resulting from participating in the integration scheme. If these latter changes are implemented at one or two specific points in time, it may be possible to distinguish these changes from other factors using simple (if not very robust) econometric methods, testing for structural changes in econometric equations for each country for the determination of export and import volumes in terms of appropriate explanatory variables (Adam, 1993). Clearly it would be desirable to conduct this analysis at the most disaggregated level permitted by data availability. Another problem is the prevalence of unrecorded trade. There should be some attention to the size of this as well as to the likely effects of RI on this trade.

The straightforward test of the welfare effects of integration proposed by McMillan (1993) can be conducted. Based on the Kemp–Vanek Theorem, McMillan argues that a simple test of whether an integration arrangement is welfare-improving for both the members (jointly) and the world as a whole is to examine what happens to the exports and imports of the group as a whole with the rest of the world. If in each commodity category the volume of imports and exports increases after the entry into the integration scheme then the scheme is welfare-improving relative to the pre-integration situation. This represents an elegant and straightforward test for the welfare effects of an integration scheme, though it is subject to the same objection as before; that changes in trade volumes may have other causes besides the entry into an integration arrangement – in other words, there remains a problem of counterfactuals (Bhagwati, 1993).

The other issues listed under C above will be much more difficult to test statistically due to the fact that the likely data may not exist. Available data on the structure of production is unlikely to be detailed enough to see the types of sectoral changes which might take place following

Table 4.6 Summary of Membership of regional trade arrangements in SSA

Country	ECOWAS	CEAO	MRU	UDEAC	CEPGL	PTA	SADC	SACU	IOC	EAC
Angola						x	x			
Benin	x	x								
Botswana							x	x		
Burkina Feso	x	x								
Burundi						x				
Cameroon				x						
Cape Verde	x									
Central Africa				x						
Chad				x						
Comoros									x	
Congo				x						
Côte d'Ivoire	x	x								
Djibouti						x				
Equatorial Guinea				x						
Ethiopia						x				
Gabon				x						
Gambia	x									
Ghana	x									
Guinea	x		x							
Guinea Bissau	x									
Kenya						x				x
Lesotho						x	x	x		

	1	2	3	4	5	6	7	8	9
Liberia	x								
Madagascar			x		x	x		x	
Malawi					x	x			
Mali	x	x							
Mauritania	x	x							
Mauritius					x	x		x	
Mozambique					x	x			
Namibia					x		x		
Niger	x	x							
Nigeria	x								
Reunion								x	
Rwanda				x	x			x	
Sao Tome									
Seychelles						x			
Senegal	x	x							
Sierra Leone	x	x							
Somalia					x				
South Africa						x			
Sudan					x				
Swaziland					x	x			
Tanzania					x	x	x		x
Togo	x								
Uganda					x				x
Zaire				x					
Zambia					x	x			
Zimbabwe					x	x			

entry into an integration scheme. Similar points apply to the concentration of production in particular countries, though this might be detectable to some extent in trade statistics. Where statistics are inadequate, anecdotal evidence may be all that is available.

Similar remarks apply to the distributional effects of integration schemes. While differences between countries in growth rates of output and trade volumes may be attributable to the differential impact of the integration scheme, they may have a number of other explanations. However, where a compensation scheme exists, information may be available on flows between member countries depending on the nature of that scheme.

Given the informational problems it is clear that the conclusions of the case studies can only be tentative, and counterfactual scenarios cannot be thoroughly evaluated. In spite of these difficulties, however, it is important to learn the lessons of past regional integration schemes, especially given the widespread view that these were not successful. If this latter view is sustained, then it is critically important to try to assess which of the three explanations considered applies. This will help determine whether regional integration is desirable in the specific context of Africa, and, if it is, in which form.

Further Issues

In addition to the issues raised in the previous sub-section the following issues would need to be addressed.

(1) Most countries in SSA belong to more than one RI area (Table 4.6). It is also evident that several RI do not meet the simple de Melo and Panagariya (1992 p. 15) test of viability (Table 4.4). The test is that the share of (recorded) intra-regional exports in total exports should be above 4 per cent in any one or more of the reported years.

The observations would seem to establish a prima-facie case for rationalization of RI groupings in SSA. This however would need to be rigorously established. There is also a need to:
(a) establish the degree of complementarity and competitiveness among the integrating countries;
(b) determine the gains and losses of integration and how to share out optimally the gains to avoid polarization; and
(c) determine what type of co-operation to adopt; customs union, free trade area or economic union?

(2) With the recent changes in South Africa there is a need to establish the impact this will have on regional co-operation in Eastern and Southern Africa.

(3) There is also a need to determine the effect of increased regionalism in world trade on RI in SSA. This should include the impact of EC-92, NAFTA and similar trade arrangements. Empirical analysis of Unilateral Trade Liberalization should also be done. This should include the impact of SAPs related unilateral trade liberalization in SSA on regional integration efforts.

Notes

1. In practice, whether both trade creation and trade diversion occur will depend on a number of factors, including the levels of pre-union and post-union tariffs, and the composition of trade.
2. It is not possible in this short text to describe the functioning of the European Community institutions in detail, only some key features are given. No reference is made to the Court of Auditors nor to the Economic and Social Committee. There is also no separate reference to the institutional differences between the European Economic Community and the European Coal and Steel Community. There is also no coverage of some of the recent changes or prospective changes that result from the completion of the single market programme or from the Maastricht Treaty which came into force in November 1993.

References

Adam, C. (1993) 'Testing for Regime Shifts in Short-Sample African Macroeconomic data: A survey of some Monte Carlo evidence', Centre for the Study of African Economies WP5/93.1

Ariyo, A. and M.I. Raheem (1991) 'Enhancing Trade Flows within the ECOWAS sub-Region: An Appraisal and some Recommendations', ch. 23 in A. Chhibber and S. Fischer (eds), *Economic Reform in Sub-Saharan Africa* (Washington DC: World Bank).

Balassa, B. (1961) *The Theory of Economic Integration* (London: George Allen & Unwin).

Bataller, F. (1992) 'Economic Integration and the Strengthening of Economic and Political Pluralism in Latin America', in *Development and Democracy: Aid Policies in Latin America* (Paris: OECD).

Bhagwati, J. (1993) 'Regionalism and Multilateralism: An Overview', ch. 2 in J. de Melo and A. Panagariya (eds) *New Dimensions in Regional Integration* (Cambridge University Press for CEPR).

Collier, P. (1979) 'The Welfare Effects of Customs Unions: An Anatomy', *Economic Journal*, 89: 84–95.

de Melo, J. and A. Panagariya (1992) *The New Regionalism in Trade Policy* (Washington DC: World Bank).

De la Torre and M.R. Kelley (1992) 'Regional Trade Arrangements', IMF Occasional Paper no. 93 (Washington DC).

De Long, B. and B. Eichengreen (1992) 'The Marshall Plan: History's Most Successful Structural Adjustment Programme', CEPR Discussion Paper no. 634 (London: CEPR).

DeRosa, D. (1993) *Regional Trading Arrangements Among Developing Countries: the ASEAN Example* (Washington DC: IFPRI).

Edwards, S. (1993) 'Latin American Economic Integration: A New Perspective of an Old Dream', *The World Economy*, 16(3).

Foroutan F. (1993) 'Regional Integration in Sub-Saharan Africa: Past Experience and Future Prospects', ch. 8 in J. de Melo and A. Panagariya (eds), *New Dimensions in Regional Integration* (Cambridge University Press for CEPR).

Gunter, F.R. (1989) 'Customs Union Theory: Retrospect and Prospect', ch. 1 in D. Greenaway, T. Hyclak and R.J. Thornton (eds), *Economic Aspects of Regional Trading Arrangements* (Hemel Hempstead: Harvester Wheatsheaf).

Hazelwood, A. (1987) 'Customs Unions' in J. Eastwell *et al.* (eds), *The New Palgrave: A Dictionary of Economics* (London: Macmillan).

Hine, R.C. (1994) 'International Economic Integration', ch. 9 in D. Greenaway and L.A. Winters (eds), *Surveys in International Trade* (Oxford: Blackwell).

Jovanovic, M.N. (1992) *International Economic Integration* (London: Routlege).

Kemp, M.C. and H.Y. Wan (1976) 'An Elementary Proposition Concerning the Formation of Customs Unions', *Journal of International Economics*, 6: 95–7.

Krugman, P.R. (1991a) *Geography and Trade* (Leuven: Leuven University Press and Cambridge, Mass.: MIT Press).

—— (1991b) 'History and Industry Location. The Case of the U.S. Manufacturing Belt', *American Economic Review*, 8(2): 80–83.

—— (1991c) 'Increasing Returns and Economic Geography', *Journal of Political Economy*, 99(3): 483–99.

Langhammer, R. (1992) 'The Developing Countries and Regionalism', *Journal of Common Market Studies*, 30: 211–31.

Lipsey, R.G. (1957) 'The Theory of Customs Unions: Trade Diversion and Welfare', *Economica* (NS), 24: 40–6.

—— (1970) *The Theory of Customs Unions: A General Equilibrium Analysis* (London: Weidenfeld & Nicolson).

Lipumba, N.H.I and L. Kasekende (1991) 'The Record and Prospects of the Preferential Trade Area for Eastern and Southern African States', ch. 22 in A. Chhibber and S. Fischer (eds), *Economic Reform in Sub-Saharan Africa* (Washington DC: World Bank).

Mansoor, A. and A. Inotai (1991) 'Integration Efforts in Sub-Saharan Africa: Failures, Results and Prospects – a suggested Strategy for Achieving Efficient integration', ch. 21 in A. Chhibber and S. Fischer (eds), *Economic Reform in Sub-Saharan Africa* Washington DC: World Bank).

McMillan, J. (1993) 'Does Regional Integration Foster Open Trade? Economic Theory and GATT's Article XXIV', ch. 13 of K. Anderson and R. Blackhurst (eds), *Regional Integration and the Global Trading System* (Hemel Hempstead: Harvester-Wheatsheaf).

Nogués, J. and R. Quintanilla (1992) 'Latin America's Integration and the Multilateral Trading System', paper presented at the conference on *New Dimensions in Regional Integration* (Washington DC: World Bank).

OECD (1993), *Regional Integration and Developing Countries* (Paris).

Pelkmans, J. and F. Alburo (1993) 'Regional Integration in the Pacific Asia Area', paper prepared for OECD working party on *Trade Relations with Developing Countries.*

Romer, P. (1986) 'Increasing Returns and Long-run Growth', *Journal of Political Economy*, 94: 1002–38.

—— (1987) 'Growth Based on Increasing Returns due to Specialization', *American Economic Review*, 77: 56–62.

Vanek, J. (1965) *General Equilibrium of International Discrimination: The Case of Customs Unions* (Cambridge, Mass.: Harvard University Press).

Viner, J. (1950) *The Customs Union Issue* (London: Stevens and Sons Ltd. for the Cargegie Endowment for International Peace).

World Bank (1991) 'Intra-Regional Trade in Sub-Saharan Africa', report no. 7685–AFR (Washington, DC: World Bank).

5 The Impact of Regional Trade and Monetary Schemes on Intra-subSaharan Africa Trade*

Ibrahim Elbadawi

5.1 INTRODUCTION

A rather varied menu of regional integration (RI) schemes spans almost the entire space of subSaharan Africa (SSA). The stated objectives of these schemes range from co-operation between neighbouring states in a limited set of policy areas, as in the case of the Southern African Development Co-ordination Conference (SADCC); to complete trade and monetary integration, for example, the Communauté Economique de l'Afrique de l'Ouest (CEAO) and the Customs and Economic Union of Central Africa (UDEAC); or to currency union and capital and labour market integration, as in the case of Southern Africa Customs Union (SACU).[1] More recent developments aimed at reforming and further deepening these schemes include: the accession of South Africa to SADCC to form the Southern African Development Community (SADC); the integration of CEAO with the West African Monetary Union (UMOA) in a new bloc, the Economic and Monetary Union of the West African States (UEMOA), that as before will be externally anchored by France; and preparation for similar arrangements for francophone Central Africa, through the merger of the Central African Monetary Union (BEAC) and UDEAC and the revival of the defunct East African Community.[2] There is a further, but at this stage conjectural, arrangement involving the extension of SACU to include other countries in Southern Africa. (Fine and Yeo, 1994).

Another major distinguishing characteristic stems from the extent of

* The views expressed in this chapter do not necessarily represent the official view of the African Economic Research Consortium. The author would like to acknowledge the research assistance of Claudio Montenegro and Sheila Nyanjui.

Table 5.1 Selected economic indicators and intra-bloc trade flows 1980–4 and 1986–90

Bloc	GDP[a] (millions)		GDPPC[c] (millions)		RERVAR[a]		REROVER[a]		Intra trade[b] (millions)		% Intra-Trade to total trade[c]	
	1980–4	1986–90	1980–4	1986–90	1980–4	1986–90	1980–4	1986–90	1980–4	1986–90	1980–4	1986–90
ECOWAS	6404	7035	534	484	2.781	2.742	0.109	0.015	399	152.3	4.95	2.70
CEAO	4460	4711	650	570	2.084	1.559	0.101	0.178	99	81.6	1.65	1.25
UDEAC	5136	5882	2222	1936	1.631	2.601	0.251	0.128	37	51.6	0.80	1.15
CEPGL	3807	4359	219	221	2.973	2.173	6.817	6.759	1.9	2.4	0.15	0.05
PTA	3396	3941	368	397	2.875	2.938	0.293	0.535	255	277.7	2.15	1.75
SADCC	2501	2876	284	267	2.075	3.131	2.107	2.121	75.3	105.2	1.55	1.40
SSA	3494	3885	376	371	2.403	2.524	1.613	1.645	867.4	670.8	1.20	1.6
LAFTA	64535	72407	1909	1860	3.178	3.172	0.657	0.582	4323	7190	5.30	6.15
CACM	4562	4880	1153	1058	2.192	4.483	0.027	0.391	514.5	551.5	7.55	6.55
ASEAN	39397	52440	910	1048	2.027	1.754	0.080	0.068	5725	12099	8.10	8.85

Notes:
[a] These entries represent the mean for the countries in the bloc and are based on the GDP constant at 1987 prices
[b] Refers to intra-bloc trade
[c] The percentage of 'intra-bloc trade' to 'total bloc exports'

GDPPC: GDP per capita
RERVAR: real exchange ratte variability
REROVER: real exchange rate overvaluation

Trade Blocs
ECOWAS: Benin, Burkina Faso*, Cape Verde*, Côte d'Ivoire, Gambia*, Ghana-Guinea*, Guinea Bissau*, Liberia, Mali*, Mauritania, Niger, Nigeria, Senegal, Togo
CEAO: Benin, Burkina Faso*, Côte d'Ivoire, Mali*, Mauritania*, Niger, Senegal
UDEAC: Cameroon, CAR*, Chad*, Congo, Equatorial Guinea*, Gabon
CEPGL: Burundi, Rwanda*, Zaire
PTA: Angola, Burundi, Comoros*, Djibouti*, Ethiopia, Kenya, Lesotho*, Malawi, Mauritius, Mozambique, Rwanda*, Swaziland*, Somalia, Sudan, Uganda. Tanzania, Zambia, Zimbabwe
SADCC: Angola, Botswana*, Lesotho*, Malawi, Mozambique, Namibia*, Swaziland*, Tanzania, Zambia, Zimbabwe
LAFTA: Argentina, Bolivia, Brazil, Chile, Colombia*, Ecuador*, Mexico, Peru, Paraguay, Peru, Uruguay, Venezuela
CACM: Costa Rica, Guatemala, Honduras, Nicaragua, El Salvador
ASEAN: Indonesia, Malaysia, Philippines, Singapore, Thailand

* denotes countries that belong to the trade bloc, but were not in the sample.

geographical coverage of the RI schemes. For example, the Economic Community of the West African States (ECOWAS) and the Preferential Trade Area for Eastern and Southern African States (PTA) represent the vision of the UN Economic Commission for Africa (ECA), which argues that regional grouping in Africa should comprise a large number of countries in order to allow development of sufficiently large internal markets, necessary to support the process of Africa's industrialization.[3] On the other hand, the rest of the schemes are based on a strategy of promoting regional objectives among smaller and, it is hoped, more homogenous neighbouring countries.

Unfortunately, trade data pertaining to the two decades of the 1970–90 period, which encompasses the life span of most of the existing RI schemes in SSA, reveals that intra-SSA trade and even most intra-scheme trade has not only been minuscule but nearly stationary as well.[4] This 'apparent' failure of regionalism in SSA can at least in part be attributed to the highly protectionist national trade policies in the region. Other related factors include: fiscal revenue constraints; the very skewed nature of costs and benefits of integration across countries in the schemes; and the associated difficulty in devising sustainable compensation schemes from the gainer to the losers (Foroutan, 1993). A further reasoning (Fine and Yeo, 1994) is that the dominant role of the state in African regional initiatives resulted in the marginalization of an already weak private sector, and hence its potentially critical contribution to the success of regional integration could not be realized. Some argue that the notable exceptions to the above have been the cases of SADCC, SACU and to some extent CEAO. All of the three cases have been distinguished either by the availability of substantial external support as in the case of SADCC, or the participation of a dominant regional or Northern partner as in the cases of SACU and CEAO.[5] However, the above conclusion remains largely indicative since without conditioning for other determinants of bilateral trade flows, it will be difficult to ascribe the evolution of intra-scheme trade flows only to the scheme effect (see section 5.2).

The perceived disappointing performance of RI schemes in enhancing intra-SSA trade has caused a considerable degree of anxiety and concern in various echelons of African economic policy-making institutions. Low intra-African trade was seen by African policy-makers as an unavoidable indicator of the failure of African economic integration, a goal that has been consistently pursued by African governments and African regional organizations over the last thirty years.[6] The basic arguments for economic integration as an engine of growth are now sufficiently articulated in the new growth literature and the more recent models of economic geography (for example, Krugman, 1991a).[7] Deeper economic integration in a given region could permit expansion of the regional economy to generate the threshold scales necessary to trigger the much-needed strategic complementarity, and to attract adequate levels of investment (especially DFI) necessary for the development of modern manufacturing cores and the transfer of technology within the region. Given the relatively small scale (both in terms of output level and population size) of the typical African economy, there seems to be a strong a priori case for regional integration on pure 'normative' economic grounds.[8]

The empirical evidence from the endogenous growth literature suggests important implications for country-specific growth of regional spill-over effects of investment, both on physical and human capital; in addition, the level of regional instability was shown to have had significant impact on individual country growth performances. In fact, when these regional spill-overs are taken into consideration, the 'African dummy' ceases to be significant in the usual endogenous growth cross-country regressions (Chua, 1993 a,b; Ades and Chua, 1993). Also, Fine and Yeo (1994) argue that while there is at best mixed evidence directly linking regional integration to economic growth, the experiences of postwar Europe and the more recent one of East Asia suggest that RI has conferred policy credibility at the national level as well as fostered direct foreign investment initially and then higher saving and investment within the region at a later stage. Both policy credibility and broad capital accumulation were credited for the stellar growth performance of East Asia (Young, 1994).

Indeed, any number of 'normative' approaches – based on growth or welfare considerations – could be marshalled to derive the conclusion that SSA is not sufficiently integrated and that intra-SSA trade is 'too little'. For example, Baldwin (1993) outlined a simple model that classifies African trade relations in terms of a 'hub-and-spoke' arrangement, where Europe and North America are the hub (or centre of the wheel) and the African nations are the spokes. The basic argument is that despite SSA's advantage in terms of lower labour cost for example, the rather high cost of trade within Africa (due to lack of adequate transportation, banking and insurance services, and so on) makes it less profitable for manufacturing firms to locate in SSA. He argues that

the hub-and-spoke free trade arrangements have a tendency to marginalize the 'spoke' economies, since production facilities located in the 'spoke' have artificially lower market access than factories in the hub. Consequently, hub-and-spoke free trade arrangements (FTAs) render an artificial deterrent to investment in the outer economies. Filling in the gaps with spoke–spoke FTAs removes this policy-induced investment deterrent.

However, as pointed out by Foroutan and Pritchett (1993):

> aside from the desirability of greater trade and economic integration among SSA countries, namely from a strictly positive view, the claim that intra-SSA trade is too little implicitly assumes that such trade encounters specific obstacles that do not affect the trade of SSA countries with the outside world or the trade of other countries with similar economic characteristics with each other.

This study will attempt to contribute to the positive strand of this literature, by formally modelling the determinants of intra-SSA trade in the context of an extended traditional 'gravity model', focusing on the role of African regional integration schemes (especially monetary unions) in regional trade. In addition to controlling for the standard factors that reflect absolute trade potential in a given country and the factors that affect the trade attraction between any two trading partners (see section 5.2), the model will attempt to account for the following potential determinants:

- the effects of the RI schemes (including currency unions) in SSA and in other regions pertaining to the other countries in the sample;
- the trade diversion (or creation) effects of the RI schemes; and
- the further marginal effects of RI schemes after controlling for real exchange rate volatility and real exchange rate over-valuation.[9]

To our knowledge, there exists only one study to date that formally applies the gravity model to estimate the determinants of bilateral trade in SSA (Foroutan and Pritchett, 1993).[10] However, this study was confined to addressing only the first effect stated above, for a sample containing only nineteen SSA countries and covering just the period 1980–3. In this chapter, we intend to expand the coverage to twenty-eight SSA countries (see Appendix Table 5A.1) as well as to estimate the model for two periods, 1980–4 and 1986–90.[11] Section 5.2 posits an extended gravity model for SSA, while section 5.3 discusses data issues and describes some salient features of the estimation results pertaining to the basic gravity model variables. Section 5.4 provides a detailed analysis of the estimated effects due to exchange rate policy variables and RI schemes. Section 5.5 contains a review of the debate on the regional integration schemes (especially monetary unions) in SSA, and drawing from this review provides some interpretations of the results pertaining to the incremental effects of these schemes. Section 5.6 concludes.

5.2   AN EXTENDED GRAVITY MODEL FOR SSA

The standard empirical model for investigating patterns of bilateral trade is the gravity model. The basic intuition that gave these econometric models the name 'gravity models' came from the analogy with gravitational force (total trade) between two objects, that depends on the masses of the objects (size of the economies) and the distance between them (transportation cost). Despite lack of formal theoretical background at its inception (for example, Tinbergen, 1962; Poyhonen, 1963; Linneman, 1966), following the above basic intuition, the standard gravity model specifies the volume of trade (T_{ij}) between any two countries (i, j), as a function of each country's trade potential and their mutual trade attraction.

The absolute trade potential of a country depends on its total economic size (nominal GDP) and the trade intensity (the ratio of trade to GDP). In turn, the trade intensity is determined by economic factors (such as the level of development, proxied by nominal GDP per capita [GDPPC]) and geographic characteristics (such as the area size or whether the country is an island). Whereas GDP and GDPPC are expected to have positive effects on bilateral trade, the impact of size should be negative. The greater the area of the country, the smaller the size of economic activity expected to cross its borders. However, the impact on trade of whether or not a country is an island cannot be signed a priori. On the one hand, if a country is an island, lack of borders can be expected to reduce trade, but to the extent that islands are poorly endowed they may tend to engage in more trade.

The trade attraction between two trading partners is determined by a host of factors that influence the cost of trade, such as – transport cost (proxied by the distance between the economic centres of gravity in the two countries and whether or not the two countries share a common border); policy and political inducements (or barriers) to trade, such as trade, currency or regional co-operation schemes; and cultural or historical ties such as a common language or colonial relationships.

An additional variable frequently included in recent versions of gravity models (for example, Foroutan and Pritchett, 1993 Havrylyshyn and Pritchett, 1991; Montenegro and Soto, 1994; among others) is designed to test two hypotheses related to the effect of the differences between two countries' levels of per capita income. On the one hand, countries with similar living standards could realize a higher level of intra-industry trade to the extent that they share a broader range of goods to trade (the so-called Linder Hypothesis). On the other hand, to the extent that GDP per capita differences are highly correlated with differences in factor endowments, inter-industry trade driven by comparative advantage could be smaller between countries with similar levels of income.

Various guises of the gravity model have been widely and successfully used in the empirical literature on international trade.[12] This success of the model is attributed to its ability to explain intra-industry trade and, in particular, the dramatic reallocation of resources that normally follows trade liberalization, which conventional factor endowment theory cannot easily accommodate (Deardorff, 1984).[13] Following the earlier attempt of Linneman (1966), the empirical success of the gravity model has triggered more research aimed at establishing some theoretical foundation for the model. For example, more recently Anderson (1979) and Bergstrand (1985) have shown the gravity model to be consistent with a broad class of structural trade models.[14]

An expanded version of the above model is stated formally in eq. (5.1). The model accounts for three extensions: two channels of exchange rate effects (exchange rate variability and exchange rate misalignment, relative to a notional equilibrium) and a trade diversion effect of an RI scheme (in addition to the usual within-scheme trade effect).

$$T_{ij} = \beta_0 + \beta_1 \log(GDP_i \cdot GDP_j) + \beta_2 \log(GDPPC_i \cdot GDPPC_j)$$
$$+ \beta_3 \log(AREA_i \cdot AREA_j) + \beta_3 \log(ISLAND_i)$$
$$+ \beta_5 \log DISTANCE_{ij} + \beta_6 BORDER_{ij} + \beta_7 \log |GDPPC_i$$
$$- GDPPC_j| + \beta_8 LANGUAGE_{ijl} + \beta_9 RI(1)_{ijk}$$
$$+ \beta_{10} RI(2)_{ijk} + \beta_{11} RERVAR_{ij} + \beta_{12} REROVER_{ij} \qquad (5.1)$$

In this equation, *Island$_i$* is a dummy variable equal to one if i is an island; *Border$_{ij}$* is a dummy equal to one if i, j share a common border;

$LANGUAGE_{ijl}$ is a set of dummy variables equal to one if countries i, j share a similar language l; $RI(1)_{ijk}$ is a dummy reflecting trade diversion effect of RI^{15} scheme k between countries i, j and is equal to one if *only* one country belongs to the scheme. $RI(2)_{ijk}$ is a dummy reflecting trade creation effect of scheme k and is equal to one if *both* countries i, j belong to the scheme k. Finally, *RERVAR* and *REROVER* stand for real exchange rate variability and real exchange rate overvaluation, respectively. *RERVAR* and *REROVER* are defined as follows:

RERVAR = Standard deviation of the change of log RER_{ij}

$REROVER_{ij}$ = log ((average $(RER_i/RER_i)^*$ (average (RER_j/RER_j))), where

$RER_{ij} = RER_i/RER_j$, RER, is defined as the relative price of tradables to non-tradables, and average (RER) is the average for the 1970–2 period.[16]

The multiplicative forms of GDP and GDP per capita in the equation are empirically well established in bilateral trade regressions. The justification for this specification can be provided from the modern theory of trade under imperfect competition, which implies that trade between two equal-sized countries (say, of size 0.5) will be greater than trade between a large country and a small country (say, of size 0.9 and 0.1) (Frankel and Wei, 1993). The property of models based on imperfect competition, such as gravity models that include only multiplicative terms on incomes, does not account for the classical Heckscher–Ohlin theory of comparative advantage, however.[17] Fortunately, this limitation does not apply to the model used in this analysis since the added terms of the per capita income differences allow for the estimation of a Heckscher–Ohlin type comparative advantage effect.

Our model accounts for both the potential trade creation effects within the trade/currency union scheme and their possible trade diversion influences (*vis-à-vis* non-members). The trade creation effect within the union is rather straightforward. It derives from proactive preferential trade arrangements in the case of trade schemes, while currency unions confer on their members the benefits of currency convertibility (at least within the union) and monetary and exchange rate stability (that is, low levels of bilateral RERVAR). However, to the extent that macroeconomic policy is not sufficiently restrained to support the currency peg, substantial real exchange rate appreciation and possibly real exchange rate overvaluation (that is, high REROVER) may ensue. Furthermore, attempts to defend the union in the face of this adversity can lead to restrictive trade policy (O'Connell, 1994).[18] Hence, just as in trade integration schemes, currency unions can lead to trade diversion. The model accounts for this possibility as well. Finally, it is interesting to test the incremental trade creation/diversion effects of trade/ currency union schemes after controlling for the real exchange rate effects (RERVAR and REROVER) that reflect the incompatibility of macroeconomic policy for a given trade regime.[19]

Given that trade flows (the dependent variables) are bounded from below by zero, estimation by OLS will produce inconsistent parameter estimates and may generate negative predicted trade flows. Also, as noted by Montenegro and Soto (1994), alternative OLS procedures based on eliminating zeros, or replacing them with arbitrary small values, tend to bias the results. Inclusion of zeros is desirable since these observations may contain information on reasons why low levels of trade are sometimes observed. This could be of particular importance in SSA, where many countries within and outside Africa do not trade extensively with SSA.[20] The appropriate estimation method in this case is the Tobit model, which allows consistent estimation of censored dependent variables as in our case.[21] To minimize the effect of extreme observations on the estimates, we use the double logarithmic specification, which also yields direct elasticity estimates for the quantitative independent variables.[22] Following Montenegro and Soto (1994), we rewrite eq. (5.1) in the following compact form:

$$\text{Log } y_i = -\tau_y + \theta'\mathbf{Z}_i + \mu_i \quad with \ \mu \sim N(0, \sigma_\mu^2) \tag{5.2}$$

where y_i represents alternatively imports and exports, $-\tau_y$ is an ancillary parameter, θ is a vector of parameters, $\mathbf{Z}$ is the vector of exogenous variables and μ_i is an i.i.d. random shock. Given the censored nature of the data, we have:

$$Prob(y_i = 0) = Prob(u_i < \tau_Y - \theta'\mathbf{Z}_i) = (1 - F_i) \tag{5.3}$$

$$Prob(y_i > 0) \cdot f(y_i | y_i > 0) = F_i \frac{f(y_i - \theta'\mathbf{Z}_i, \sigma_\mu^2)}{F_i}$$

$$= \frac{1}{\sqrt{2\Pi\sigma_\mu^2}} e^{-1/2\sigma_\mu^2(y_i + \tau_y - \theta'\mathbf{Z}_i)^2}$$

where $f(y_i | y_i > 0)$ is a density function, and F_i is the normal cumulative density function. The log-likelihood function is then:

$$\text{Log } L = \sum_{y=0} \log(1 - F_i) + \sum_{y>0} \log\left(\frac{1}{\sqrt{2\Pi\sigma_\mu^2}}\right)$$

$$- \sum_{y=0} \frac{1}{2\sigma_\mu^2} (y_i + \tau_y - \theta'\mathbf{Z}_i)^2 \tag{5.4}$$

The maximum likelihood estimates of τ_y and θ maximize Log $L(y,\mathbf{Z},\tau_y,\theta)$.

As eq. (5.4) suggests, the intuition behind the Tobit method is straightforward: countries first determine whether to trade with one other, and if they do the value of trade is determined by economic, geographic and other characteristics (for example, see Havrylyshyn and Pritchett, 1991; and Foroutan and Pritchett, 1993).

5.3 EMPIRICAL ESTIMATION AND DATA ISSUES

This study covers a sample of sixty-two *reporting* countries,[23] of which 28 are in SSA. The sample of reporting countries was restricted to include only those non-SSA countries with per capita GDP less than US$3000[24] (see Appendix Table 5A.1). Furthermore, the above model was estimated for two periods (1980–4) and (1986–90), where trade flows are represented by import flows (however, for comparison, Appendix Tables 5A.3 and 5A.4 contain estimates for both export and import flows). In principle, bilateral trade flows (whether import or export flows) should be influenced by the same set of determinants.[25] We chose not to run separate regressions for SSA in view of the evidence that in terms of bilateral trade flows, African countries do not seem to exhibit special characteristics that distinguish them from other low-income countries (Foroutan and Pritchett, 1993). More importantly, joint estimation of the determinants of bilateral trade flows in SSA and other low-income countries allows comparisons of African and non-African RI schemes. Also it is obvious that the expansion of the African sub-sample is desirable because it permits the assessment of the impacts of a larger number of African RI schemes. On the other hand, the benefit derived from extending the sample to 1990 might not seem to be obvious, given the stationary nature of intra-SSA trade during the 1980s (see Table 5.1 and Figure 5.1). However, between the two periods the performance of the currency unions in West Africa, for example, deteriorated quite considerably. This is because the *numeraire* currency (the French franc) has appreciated steadily against the dollar since 1986 in the face of worsening terms of trade and

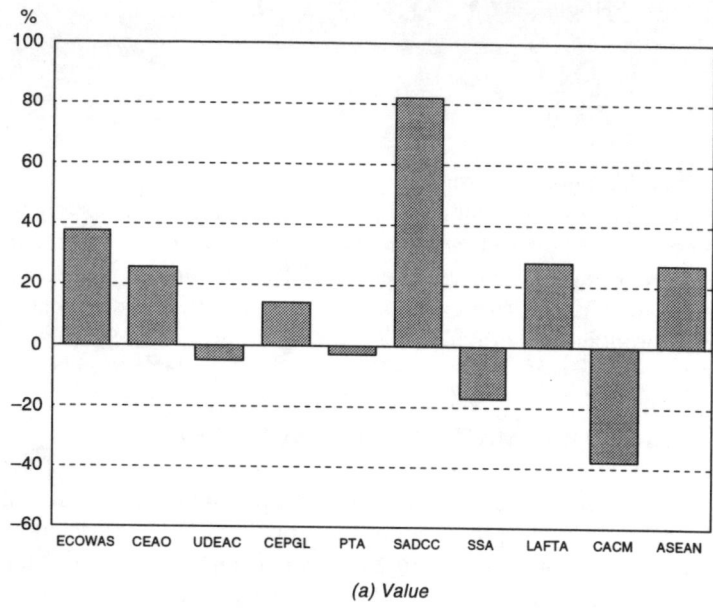

(a) Value

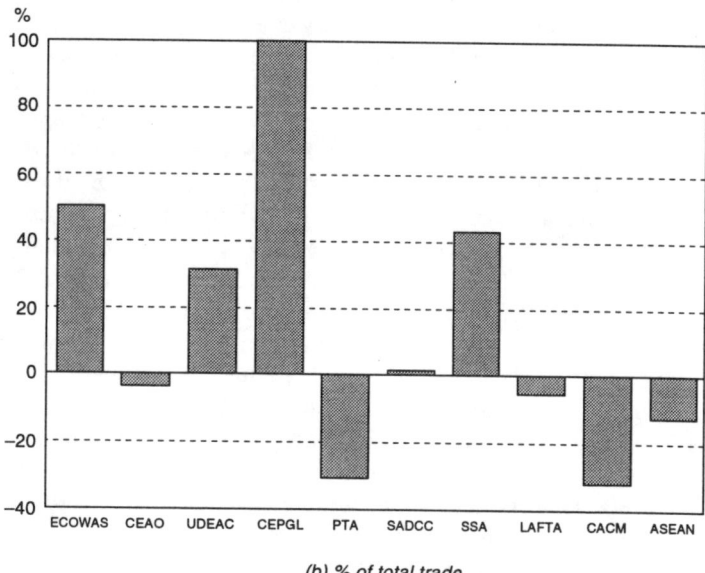

(b) % of total trade

Figure 5.1   Rates of change of intra-bloc trade flows 1980–4 and 1986–90

accumulating fiscal imbalances in the CFA. What makes the adjustment all the more difficult, is that the fixity of the exchange rate eliminates it from being available as an instrument of policy, thus leaving
only the option of deflating the economy. But since inflation is already
very low, internal adjustment is an extremely limited option. It is widely
believed that though the West African currency union countries achieved
exchange rate stability without causing real over valuation in the first
period, these two objectives could not be achieved in the second period.[26]
In the context of the gravity model, we expect these developments to
affect the estimated coefficients reflecting the effectiveness of the currency unions both in relation to trade creation and trade diversion.

The results of the Tobit estimation for the full model are presented
in Table 5.2. Estimation results for two smaller versions of the model,
one confined to the traditional gravity model variables (that is, without
RI schemes and exchange rate effects) and another that adds the effects of RI schemes (but not the exchange rate), are reported in Appendix Tables 5A.2 and 5A.3, respectively. As expected, the empirical
performance of the model is consistent with its reputation in this literature.[27] The increase in the degree of fit and the significance of individual coefficients of the RI and exchange rate variables clearly indicate
that after controlling for traditional determinants of bilateral trade flows,
both of the RI schemes and the exchange rate variables have significant effects on trade flows (compare the results of Appendix Table
5A.2, Appendix Table 5A.3, and Table 5.2). Based on the above, we
will mainly confine ourselves to the results in Table 5.2 for further
analysis.

According to the results in Table 5.2, almost all the traditional variables of the gravity model are significant and have plausible signs.
However, there are some interesting differences across time. For example, only four variables show across-the-board robustness in terms
of both sign and significance. The four are the two basic gravity variables, distance and economic size (GDP); the indicators of cultural
affinity for some influential languages (English, Spanish and French as
opposed to Arabic, Portuguese and Swahili);[28] and the GDP per capita
differential. In the case of distance even the size of the elasticity remains the same. As expected, whereas the distance between two trading partners negatively affects their bilateral trade flow, economic size
tends to enhance it. The results pertaining to the GDPPC differentials
support the traditional comparative advantage effect on trade, and not
the Linder intra-industry type source of trade. The results also suggest
the obvious in that cultural similarity could also enhance bilateral trade,

Table 5.2   Gravity model estimates: SSA and other low-income countries
(Averages 1980–4 and 1986-90)

| | Imports[a] | | | |
| | 1980–84 | | 1986–90 | |
Variables	Coef.	t-Stat.	Coef.	t-Stat.
Standard gravity model				
Constant	−6.93	−6.79	−9.08	−9.23
$\log(Distance_{ij})$	−1.79	−19.43	−1.72	−19.42
$Border_{ij}$	1.02	2.73	0.18	0.49
$Island_i$	0.06	0.26	−0.11	−0.5
$\log(Area_i \cdot Area_j)$	−0.35	−12.29	0.37	17.04
$\log(GDP_i \cdot GDP_j)$	1.60	39.7	0.26	13.52
$\log(GDPPC_i \cdot GDPPC_j)$	0.01	0.24	1.26	24.2
LINDER: $\log|GDPPC_i - GDPPC_j|$	0.14	2.66	0.51	10.01
$Language_{ij}$				
English	0.35	1.58	0.36	1.72
Spanish	1.70	5.83	1.42	5.13
French	1.95	4.89	1.49	3.81
Arabic	0.49	1.14	−0.26	−0.63
Portuguese	1.89	0.55	0.83	0.25
Swahili	1.79	1.23	2.06	1.43
Regional trade/monetary schemes				
Within Bloc$_{ij}$:				
ECOWAS[b]	0.13	0.67	−0.22	−1.2
CEAO	3.56	2.44	1.31	0.93
DEAC	2.37	0.96	−2.61	−1.09
CEPGL	3.7	1.48	3.73	1.48
PTA	2.29	4.58	0.35	0.74
SADCC	−1.83	−1.2	0.38	0.26
LAFTA	0.73	1.41	0.04	0.08
CACM	−1.69	−1.96	0.81	0.98
ASEAN	−0.36	−0.45	2.03	2.68
Bloc Members$_{ij}$:				
ECOWAS[b]	–	–	–	–
CEAO	0.36	1.64	−1.44	−6.89
UDEAC	−0.23	−0.89	−2.94	−12.48
CEPGL	−1.98	−7.79	−1.53	−6.38
PTA	−0.00	−0.02	−0.64	−4.12
SADCC	−0.33	−1.4	0.39	1.79
LAFTA	−0.53	−3.32	−1.12	−8.19
CACM	−2.08	−11.74	−0.92	−5.36
ASEAN	0.66	4.31	2.1	14.27
Macroeconomic policy stance				
$RERVAR_{ij}$	−0.36	−4.86	−0.41	−7.61

| Pseudo R-square | 0.1537 | 0.1495 |
| No. of observations | 5104 | 5104 |

Notes:

[a] The dependent variables are estimated in logs (for values > 0)

[b] Because of multicollinearity, the effects due to ECOWAS could not be decomposed into Within Bloc and Bloc Members; therefore the estimated coefficient for ECOWAS reflects the net effect

$Border_{ij}$ = 1 if countries i and j share the same border

$Island_i$ = 1 if country i is an island

$Language_{ij}$ = 1 if countran i and j share the same language

$Within\ Block_{ij}$ = 1 if both countries belong to the same bloc

$Bloc\ Member_{ij}$ = 1 if either country i or j (*not* both) belong to the same bloc

$$RERVAR_{ij} = Var\left[\Delta\log\left(\frac{RER_i}{RER_j}\right)\right] \text{ and } REROVER_{ij}$$

$$= \log\left[\frac{avg(RERi)}{RER_i} \cdot \frac{avg(RER_j)}{RER_j}\right]$$

where $RER = \dfrac{E.P^*}{P}$ and $avg\ (RER)$ is for (1970–2).

at least for some globally influential cultures. The robustness, significance and estimated appreciable effects of these four factors clearly suggest the strength of the two traditional variables of the gravity model (proximity[29] and economic size), the role of cultural similarities and the importance of comparative advantage as a determinant of bilateral trade for low-income countries (which constitute almost all the reporting countries considered in this study, see Appendix Table 5A.1).

The other indicator of proximity (common border) was shown to lead to increased trade by a very high elasticity (about 3.13) for the first period (1980–4), but in the second period (1986–90) it ceases to be significant. In the first period, the GDP per caput (GDPPC) effect was insignificant while its estimated effect for the second period is highly significant and as expected, suggests that countries tend to trade more as they industrialize.[30] The effects due to the last two traditional variables of the gravity model (land size and island) also show relative lack of robustness. For example the effect of island was insignificant in both periods. On the other hand, the effect of land size is highly significant for both periods; however, it has the negative and plausible sign only in the first period.

Having analysed the estimation results pertaining to the basic gravity model variables, in the next section we turn to the incremental effects of macroeconomic policy and RI schemes.

5.4   THE ESTIMATION RESULTS FOR EXCHANGE RATE POLICY AND REGIONAL INTEGRATION SCHEMES

The derived elasticity estimates of the impact of RI schemes on trade flows for both of the first and second halves of the 1980s – controlling for traditional gravity model variables but not for exchange rate policy – are reported in panel (i) of Table 5.3. Panel (ii) of the table reports the corresponding derived estimates when the effect of exchange rate policy was accounted for as well. The estimates of panel (i) were based on Appendix Table 5A.3, while those of panel (ii) were based on Table 5.2. The analysis of this section has the following objectives: to establish some evidence on the relative effectiveness of the African RI schemes compared to other schemes over time; to compare and contrast performances of some selected RI schemes; to assess the independent effect of exchange rate policy over time, and the implied effect through the RI schemes; and to assess the incremental effect of currency union within trade blocs, by comparing the performances of ECOWAS to that of CEAO (which is a sub-ECOWAS trade and currency bloc), and the performances of UDEAC (a currency and trade bloc in central Africa) to that of CEPGL (a trade but not a currency bloc within the central Africa region).

The Incremental Effects of Regional Schemes

In this sub-section we describe the derived incremental elasticity estimates of the regional integration schemes, controlling for the traditional gravity determinants (analysed in Section 5.3 above) but not for the effects of exchange rate policy.

Starting with the 1980–4 period, the estimates of panel (i) of Table 5.3 suggest that in general the African RI schemes fared better than LAFTA and CACM. On median, the presence of African schemes enhanced intra-scheme imports by about 31 per cent without causing trade diversion effects. This compares with negative trade diversion effects for LAFTA (by more than 100 per cent) and CACM (by more than 700 per cent), including a further negative effect on intra-scheme trade that in the case of CACM led to a total negative effect on trade of about 1300 per cent![31] The exception was ASEAN, which despite the lack of evidence for enhanced import trade within the bloc, did lead to import trade creation with partners outside the bloc by more than 100 per cent. Further, there was also considerable diversity within the African regional schemes, with CEAO increasing import flows within the

Table 5.3 The marginal contribution of RI schemes and exchange rate policy in the determination of bilateral trade flows: 1980–4, 1986–90 (derived elasticities)[a]

		1980–84			1986–90	
RI schemes	Within scheme	Scheme effect	Total effect	Within Scheme	Scheme effect	Total effect
(i) *RI only*						
(Appendix Table 5A.3 estimates)						
ECOWAS	1.32	–	1.32	–1.95	–	–1.95
CEAO	32.07	NS	32.07	NS	–2.59	–2.59
UDEAC	NS	NS	NS	–NS	–13.20	–13.20
CEPGL	NS	–7.61	–7.61	NS	–4.22	–4.22
PTA	3.50	–NS	3.50	–NS	–1.90	–1.90
SADCC	–3.89	–NS	–3.89	–NS	–NS	–NS
LAFTA	NS	–2.08	–2.08	NS	–2.53	–2.53
CACM	–5.96	–7.77	–13.73	–NS	–3.97	–3.97
ASEAN	–NS	2.14	2.14	11.82	12.81	24.63
(ii) *RI and exchange rate policy*						
(Table 5A.2 estimates)						
ECOWAS	NS	–	NS	–NS	–	–NS
CEAO	35.16	1.43	36.60	NS	–4.22	–4.22
UDEAC	NS	–NS	NS	–NS	–18.92	–18.92
CEPGL	NS	–7.24	–7.24	NS	–4.62	–4.62
PTA	9.97	–NS	9.97	NS	–1.84	–1.84
SADCC	–NC	–NC	–NC	NS	–1.48	–1.48
LAFTA	NS	–1.70	–1.70	NS	–3.06	–3.06
CACM	–5.42	–8.00	–13.42	NS	–2.51	–2.51
ASEAN	–NS	1.93	1.93	7.61	8.17	15.78
$RERVAR_{ij}$	–	–	–0.36	–	–	–0.41
$REROVER_{ij}$	–	–	–0.03	–	–	–NS
TOTAL *RER*	–	–	–0.39	–	–	–0.41

Notes:
[a] The elasticity estimates of this table for the RI effects are derived as exponentials of the estimated coefficient of Table 5.2 and Appendix Table 5A.3.

bloc by a staggering 32 times without creating trade diversion, compared to CEPGL, which caused significant trade diversion by 7.6 times without enhancing intra-CEPGL import flows, and SADCC, which reduced intra-SADCC imports by about 4 times. In between, ECOWAS (PTA) enhanced total (intra-bloc) imports by 32 per cent (250 per cent), while UDEAC had completely neutral effect.

During the second half of the 1980s, however, the story changed dramatically. The performance of four African regional blocs worsened considerably, especially the two currency blocs, CEAO and UDEAC, which diverted import trade by 160 per cent and 1200 per cent, respectively, without positively enhancing intra-bloc trade. Compared to the first period, the performance of ECOWAS and PTA also deteriorated, albeit less dramatically, with the first reducing total ECOWAS imports by 95 per cent and the latter diverting import trade by 90 per cent without leading to increased intra-PTA imports. The exceptions were SADCC, which had a neutral effect on import flows, and CEPGL, which reduced its trade diversion effect from 660 per cent to 320 per cent between the two periods. On the other hand, even though the total effect on import trade of LAFTA and CACM was still negative, it worsened only slightly for the case of LAFTA and improved for the case of CACM. However, the most dramatic improvement happened in the ASEAN bloc, which increased total trade by a staggering 25 times, more than 50 per cent of which was due to trade creation with partners outside the bloc.

The Incremental Effects of Exchange Rate Policy and Regional Schemes

To the extent that exchange rate policy should influence bilateral trade flows as we argued in Section 5.2, the results discussed above may overstate the effects of regional schemes. Therefore in this sub-section we describe the derived incremental elasticity estimates of exchange rate policy and of the regional integration schemes, controlling for the traditional gravity determinants.

The Exchange Rate Policy Effects

The estimates of panel (ii) of Table 5.3 include the effects of exchange rate policy as well as those due to the regional blocs. Quantitatively, the direct effects of the two components of exchange rate policy (RERVAR and REROVER) are rather small. The elasticity estimates for RERVAR were -0.36 for 1980–4 and -0.41 for 1986–90; for REROVER they were only significant for the first period and were much smaller at -0.03. These results are consistent with those estimated by Frankel and Wei (1993) for trade flows between major regional trade and currency blocs in Europe, North America and Asia.[32]

However, as argued by Frankel and Wei (1993), the direct effect of real exchange rate policy on trade flows may not tell the whole story about the potential role of exchange rate policy. Also, as we argued above, the full effect of RERVAR or REROVER may be confounded by the effects of regional blocs, especially currency unions. For example, intra-bloc RERVAR and REROVER is much smaller in CEAO and UDEAC compared to the SSA-wide median average (see Table 5.1). Indeed, accounting for the exchange rate policy does lead to changes in the order of magnitudes of the regional blocs effects, and in some cases the changes are quite substantial.

The Regional Schemes Effects

Subscribing to the above discussion, when controlling for exchange rate policy the estimates of the regional schemes effects suggest the following broad observations.

First, if anything, in the first period the median performance of the African regional blocs relative to the others was even more impressive. For example, CEAO slightly improved its performance, UDEAC remained neutral as before, the bias against trade estimated for CEPGL remained virtually the same, while PTA's effect on intra-bloc import flows was much higher (it increased imports by 10 times) and SADCC's effect on trade was in fact neutral rather than negative. The exception was ECOWAS, for which the small but positive effect on total import flows appears to be accounted for by exchange rate policy. On the other hand, the effects of the non-African regional blocs did not change much. It is clear from this evidence that once we control for the effect of exchange rate policy, some of the African regional blocs had significant positive influence on intra-bloc import flows (PTA) or at least a neutral effect (SADCC). The evidence is consistent with the relatively sizable RERVAR found in these two blocs during the 1980–4 period (see Table 5.1).

Second, during the second half of the 1980s, accounting for exchange rate policy results in some interesting differences from the pattern of changes observed for the first half of the decade. The performance of two African trade blocs (ECOWAS and SADCC) was actually better when we controlled for exchange rate policy effect, while the performances of PTA and CEPGL remained similar to the case when exchange rate policy was not accounted for. On the other hand, when controlling for exchange rate policy, the already bad performance of the two African monetary unions deteriorated further in the second period, with CEAO and UDEAC reducing total imports by more than 4 times and by about 19 times, respectively. As for the three non-African blocs, controlling for exchange rate policy led to a slight reduction (increase) in the negative effect of import trade diversion of CACM (LAFTA), while the performance of ASEAN was still remarkable though its total positive effect reduced to about 16 times. The evidence suggests that the effect of exchange rate policy (especially RERVAR) was much higher in ECOWAS, SADCC and CACM than the other blocs. Hence, exchange rate policy had deleterious effects on import flows in these blocs, while in CEAO, UDEAC and ASEAN some of the credit should go to exchange rate policy, which successfully produced relatively more stable exchange rates.[33]

Third, the comparison of the estimates of regional bloc effects across the two periods, when adjusting for exchange rate policy, reveals that the performance of the African blocs generally worsened, especially the performance of CEAO and UDEAC, the exception being SADCC. On the other hand, to some extent CACM negative impact on import flows declined, but the most dramatic change was the increase of the total trade creation effect of the ASEAN from about 2 times in 1980–4 to a spectacular 16 times in 1986–90, 50 per cent of which was due to trade creation with trading partners outside the ASEAN bloc.

5.5   THE ROLE OF THE REGIONAL SCHEMES IN SSA: INTERPRETING THE RESULTS

Three fundamental conclusions can be drawn from the analysis in the preceding section. First, the experience of regional integration in SSA has by and large been a failure. However, the African experience is by no means unique and there are parallels to it in other developing regions (namely Latin America). Second, ASEAN has significantly enhanced both intra-regional and inter-regional trade, even though it was not explicitly designed to be a deliberate trade creating scheme. Third, the two monetary unions (CEAO and UDEAC), especially CEAO, have displayed very extreme patterns of performance, where their effects on both intra-scheme and inter-scheme trade flows were very positive (negative) and substantial during the first (second) half of the 1980s.

For the remainder of this section, we will attempt to explain these findings in light of the known characteristics of the RI schemes and their records of implementation of stated goals.

The Failure of the African Regional Integration Schemes

A brief review of the literature on African economic integration reveals a record of failures and unfulfilled expectations.[34] As such, the results of this chapter in this regard are neither new nor surprising.

The novelty of our results stems from the fact that they obtain even after controlling for key policy variables (such as exchange rate variability and exchange rate overvaluation) in addition to the traditional trade flow determinants (such as economic size, distance, and so on). It is clear, therefore, that the failures of these schemes can be at least partially explained by their own characteristics and the constraints they face. It is also pertinent to add that the similar performance observed for the two Latin American regional schemes (LAFTA and CACM) is also consistent with their own comparable problems and constraints (see Langhammer and Hiemenz, 1991; Fine and Yeo, 1994; Lyakurwa *et al.* 1993; and Foroutan, 1993 for more details on the experiences of regional integration schemes in SSA and other developing regions).

Take three African RI schemes, ECOWAS, PTA and CEPGL, to illustrate this point.[35] The first two schemes represent the vision of large-scale integration. However, due to their huge sizes, these two schemes were hampered by immense diversities in economic size, historical experiences and cultural background. In the case of ECOWAS, this reflected itself in wide divergence between Nigeria (which showed considerable commitment to the scheme) and the smaller partners, especially the francophone countries. Therefore, despite its ambitious treaty, ECOWAS remains a largely ineffective (refer to the results in Table 5.3) and dormant integration scheme; with 'trade liberalization not yet achieved, CET does not exist, labour movement restricted, fiscal and monetary harmonization far away, and limited cooperation in other areas' (Foroutan, 1993). Similarly, PTA has been biased toward trade diversion due to numerous uncoordinated and often arbitrarily applied non-tariff barriers (again this is consistent with the results in Table 5.3). As explained by Langhammer and Hiemenz (1991), the trade-diversion bias is precipitated by the requirement that

> member states must document an 'import interest' to qualify for preferential treatment, an interest that is likely to be expressed only if intra-regional imports do not compete with local production. Furthermore, preference margins increase with the amount of equity capital. This procedure aimed at containing the strong position of Kenya- and Zimbabwe-based firms, but it discriminates against just those foreign investors with the strongest intra-PTA networks for expanding intraregional trade.[36]

Like ECOWAS, the PTA so far has only managed to achieve partial tariff concessions to partners on a limited number of goods, while its agenda calls for free trade area and complete trade liberalization by the year 2000.[37] Finally, CEPGL – which comprises Zaire, Burundi and Rwanda – aimed at achieving a currency union; free movements of capital, labour and goods; and co-operation among member states. However, except for some few joint projects, negligible progress has been made on its stated objectives. This particular grouping has not only been beset by the huge disparity between Zaire and the other two members, and the often conflicting loyalties to more than one regional groupings (both Rwanda and Burundi belong to PTA, with which they conduct the greatest share of their African trade), but all three countries (and hence their regional grouping) have been substantially affected by political instability and civil strife, especially since the mid-1980s.

Fine and Yeo (1994) argue against renewed regional integration efforts in SSA along the traditional lines, where the existing regional schemes are called upon to attempt to promote regional trade directly despite repeated failures. In their view, these schemes are inappropriately structured, since they were designed to pursue the now ill-fated and out-moded import-substitution development strategy. They propose a new paradigm for regional integration in SSA inspired by the experiences of post-Second World War Europe and the recent 'miracle' experience of East Asia. They suggest that regional integration initiatives in SSA should be designed to achieve the twin objectives of fostering national policy credibility, and rapid accumulation of physical and human capital – the latter being initially triggered by enhanced direct foreign investment and by saving and investment surges within the region in subsequent stages. They provide an exhaustive review of the evidence linking regional integration to these two objectives, which are now being accepted as the two main fundamentals behind the East Asia's economic miracle. The key element of this strategy adopts the Collier (1991) and Collier and Gunning (1993) proposal of 'participatory supranational agencies of restraint' in which national economic policy will be tied in a reciprocal threat-making arrangement to a Northern anchor (the European Union). Fine and Yeo then ask the question as to why might the EU be interested in playing such a role; they argue that unlike the case of Eastern Europe, enhancement of trade, fears of mass migration or imminent security concerns could not be major factors. However, they suggest that the precedent of UEMOA, the vast interest of the EU in South Africa, the realization that the African, Caribbean and Pacific (ACP) agreement – which is administered by the European Commission – has met with limited success, and the growing EU concerns with political stability as a prerequisite for economic growth may prompt a more active policy toward SSA. (Cobham and Robson (1994) adopt similar arguments for the EU as an external anchor in the context of monetary integration in SSA.)[38]

The High Performance of the ASEAN and Lessons for SSA

After controlling for other traditional and policy determinants of bilateral trade flows, the ASEAN regional scheme increased trade with the rest of the world in the period 1980–4 by 93 per cent. During the following period (1986–90) its performance turned from fair to spectacular: the presence of the ASEAN increased trade within the bloc by 7.6 times, and with the rest of the world increased by 8 times (see Figure 5.2 for the comparison with SSA).

An equally interesting fact is that the ASEAN was not explicitly designed to be a deliberate trade-creating scheme.[39] The story behind the ASEAN is summed up by Langhammer and Hiemenz (1991), who argue that 'ASEAN owes its worldwide reputation not to any progress in internal integration or industrial cooperation, but to other factors. These include its role as a representative of the common interests of its members in foreign affairs and in continuing dialogues with the major OECD countries on market accessibility.' It was also noted that 'ASEAN has achieved some success in increasing its collective bargaining power in dialogues with OECD members (Langhammer, 1985). In addition, ASEAN members have established strong internal networks for business consultation and software cooperation without surrendering national sovereignty with respect to major economic policies.'

Taking into consideration as well the stellar performances of the ASEAN countries in the areas of economic growth and economic development in general over the last two and a half decades,[40] three interrelated factors behind the success of the association can be identified: first and foremost, a strong country-specific and regional economic performance in terms of economic growth, which in turn was substantially enhanced by collective policy credibility and investment spillovers brought about by regional co-operation; second, measured but effective regional co-operation; and third, policy co-ordination in the area of external economic relations. It is interesting that Collier and Gunning (1993) identified country-specific multilateral trade liberalization, policy harmonization and regional co-operation in a limited set of areas (such as infrastructure, power and communication), and a strong and co-ordinated strategy for external relations as the best options for

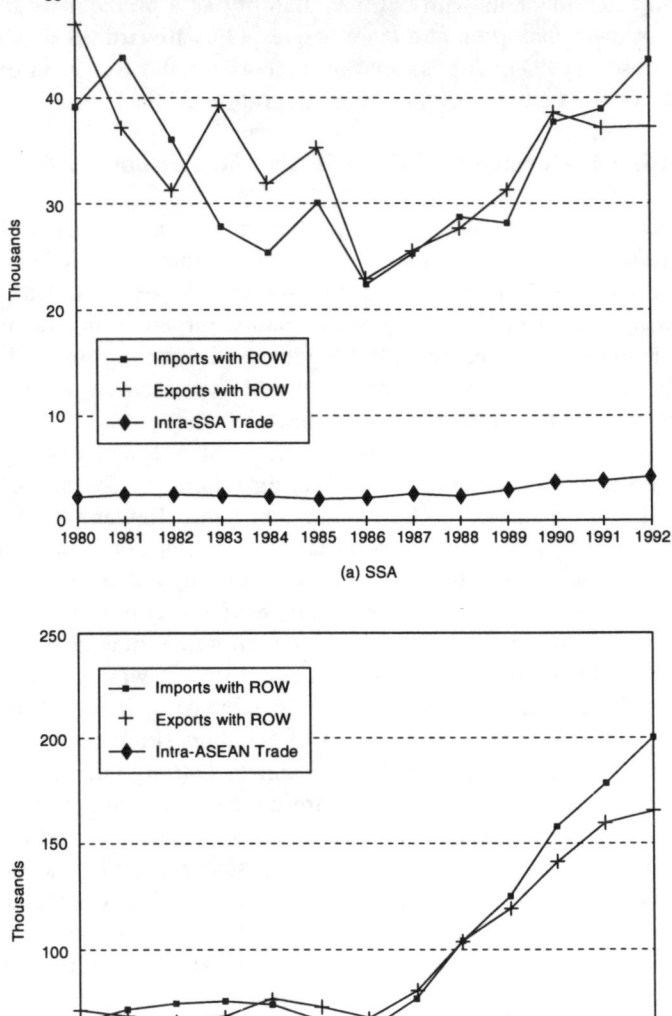

(a) SSA

(b) ASEAN

Figure 5.2 Evolution of trade: region versus the rest of the world

subSaharan Africa to use to foster both growth and regional integration (without actively promoting it), as well as to avoid marginalization in the global economy.

SADCC is the only African regional scheme that comes close to the ASEAN, given that its main objectives are in the areas of co-operation and joint projects in transport, communication, agriculture, industry and energy. Given the strong political appeal of SADCC when it was formed in 1980 and until recently,[41] it has been successful in generating strong external support – which has translated into relatively generous external funding for its regional projects. For example, 85 per cent of a total cost of $6.6 billion for 216 projects in the areas of transport and communication will be financed by foreign aid, as will the entire cost of energy projects (African Development Bank, 1993). However, external support cannot be a substitute for genuine internal co-operation. In fact, as pointed out by Langhammer and Hiemenz (1991),

> SADCC clearly lacks defined objectives and efficient instruments of regional policy. While these deficiencies are in part attributable to external shocks and internal problems such as famine, drought, civil disorder and conflict with [pre-democratic] South Africa,[42] ideological differences between members have played a large role. Because of the lack of consensus, objectives are defined in increasingly broad and vague terms and policy instruments are subject to so much negotiation and compromise as to render them nearly ineffectual.

Their analysis suggests that it was not just the lack of strong economic growth in SADCC, but also inadequate commitment to internal co-operation, and by implication the inability of the group to develop an effective and co-ordinated strategy for external economic relations, that all conspired to prevent SADCC from being the African equivalent of the ASEAN.

The Role of Monetary Unions in SSA

Before attempting to interpret the results of Section 5.4 on the effects of monetary unions in SSA, we provide a brief account of the salient features of monetary integration schemes in francophone West Africa as well as a brief review of the main debates on the rationale for monetary integration in SSA.

The Structure of Monetary Integration in SSA

Tables 5.4 and 5.5 (taken from Cobham and Robson, 1994) give, respectively, a description of the salient features of various forms of monetary integration, including the two West African monetary unions; and the matrix of cost and benefits of different monetary integration arrangements. As shown in Table 5.5, fixed exchange rates and full convertibility (current and capital accounts) among the members' currencies are the common denominators in all forms of monetary integration. However, the table also indicates three forms of integration: informal and formal exchange rate unions, where the crucial difference is that the latter has a central agency co-ordinating the national central banks, and full monetary union, which is a deeper form of integration compared to the formal exchange rate union because it has a single currency and a single (supranational) central bank. As indicated in the table, both of the African monetary integration schemes are full monetary unions.

Based on the matrix in Table 5.5, Cobham and Robson argue that

> higher forms of monetary integration are more desirable: the main cost involved – the loss of exchange rate as an instrument of adjustment among members, the initial disinflation required to enter the union, and the loss of seigniorage and inflation tax revenue – are the same for each form of monetary integration. But the benefits tend to be greater for the 'higher' forms.

The benefits include further improvements in resource allocation and greater dynamic gains with deeper integration; in addition, full monetary integration should reduce the cost of public debt and of reserve holding (due to reserve pooling).

Therefore, they concluded that the African monetary integration is optimal in terms of structure and design. However, the actual performance will ultimately be determined by the outcome of the trade-offs, especially the fundamental one involving the loss of exchange rate as an instrument of adjustment policy in return for monetary and price stability, policy credibility and currency convertibility.

The Monetary Integration Debate in SSA

According to orthodox theory, SSA could neither constitute optimal trade blocs nor optimal currency areas, since it is characterized by low recorded intra-regional trade, heavy dependence on external trade, limited

Table 5.4 Characteristics of different types of monetary integration

	Current account convertibility	Capital market integration	Between members		banks	Central pooling	Reserve undertaken	Foreign exchange market intervention
			Exchange rate fixity of parities	Ex-ante credibility Currencies				
Informal exchange rate union	Yes	Yes	Yes	No	Separate	Multiple, independent	No	Separate
Formal exchange rate union	Yes	Yes	Yes	Yes	Separate	Multiple, strongly co-ordinated	Yes	By single
Full monetary	Yes	Yes	Yes	Yes	Single	Single	Yes	By single agency
UMOA and BEAC	Yes	Yes	Yes	Yes	Common	Single	Yes, but individual accounts	By single agency

Source: Cobham and Robson (1994).

Table 5.5　Costs and benefits of different forms of monetary integration

	Informal ERU	Formal ERU	Full MU
Costs			
(1) Loss of exchange rate as instruments vis à vis other members	Yes	Yes	Yes
(2) Initial disinflation where necessary	Yes	Yes	Yes
(3) Loss of segniorage and inflation-tax revenue from lower inflation	Yes	Yes	Yes
Benefits			
(1) Improved price stability (and actual expected) leading to better resource allocation	Partially	Yes	Yes
(2) Reduced exchange rate variability (actual and expected) leading to increased trade and investment flows within the union	Partially	Partially	Yes
(3) Reduced transaction costs and improved price transparency leading to increased trade and investment flows within the union	—	Partially if zero margins	Yes
(4) Interest savings on government debt from lower nominal interest rates and reduced exchange rate risk premium	Partially	Partially	Yes
(5) Resource saving from pooling of foreign exchange reserves	—	Partially	Yes
(6) Resource saving from centralization of monetary policy	—	Partially	Yes
(7) Dynamic gains	—	Partially	Yes

Source: Cobham and Robson (1994).

cross-border flows of capital (though not of labour for some countries), relatively small economic size, marked disparities in fiscal policies, and so on. This theory – which emphasizes the direct trade benefits of integration – suggests that these characteristics of regional blocs in SSA set them apart from those in developed countries. The result is problems of sequencing, selection of instruments and distributional stresses, especially where net benefits were demonstrably significant. Thus, effective regional integration and suitable regional policies have been difficult to devise and implement (Cobham and Robson, 1994).

This view is challenged by the modern approach to monetary integration (De Grauwe, 1992), which emphasizes two considerations: the ineffectiveness of repeated devaluations as a means to correct balance of payments problems and enhance competitiveness in the long run, and the time consistency literature (initiated by Kydland and Prescott,

1977, and developed by Barro and Gordon, 1983), which emphasizes the importance of credibility and reputation in monetary policy. As suggested by Cobham and Robson (1994), two conclusions can be derived from this approach:

(a) that the loss of the exchange rate as a policy instrument within the existing African monetary unions (or, more exactly, its permanent assignment to the control of inflation via the peg to the French franc) is less of a disadvantage than might at first appear; and (b) that the assignment of monetary policy to a supranational central bank has clear advantage in terms of reputation and credibility.

Clearly the performance of monetary integration in francophone West Africa – and which, of the two approaches, is a more accurate description of reality – will very much depend on the outcome of the trade-offs outlined in Table 5.5.

Interpreting the Results

The estimation results in Section 5.4 suggest that the two African monetary unions studied in this paper (CEAO, UDEAC),[43] especially CEAO, have displayed very extreme patterns of performance. Their effects on both intra-scheme and inter-scheme trade flows were very positive (negative) and substantial during the first (second) half of the 1980s. According to the estimates of Table 5.3, the presence of CEAO increased intra-bloc trade flows by 35 times in the first half of the 1980s, while still managing to increase trade flows with the rest of the world by 43 per cent. During the same period UDEAC was not as spectacular, with basically neutral effects on trade. However, in the second half of the 1980s the story changed very dramatically. While failing to generate any positive effects on intra-bloc trade, both CEAO and UDEAC caused significant trade diversion with the rest of the world, where CEAO reduced inter-bloc trade flows by 4.2 times, while UDEAC reduced it by 19 times. This very drastically different performance of the CFA zone (the two monetary unions constitute the CFA zone) between the first and second half of the 1980s is consistent with the pattern of the overall economic performance of the zone between the two periods. For example, Elbadawi and Majd (1992)[44] apply a modified-control-group model that controlled for the initial conditions, internal and external shocks and the policy stance to test for the impact of zone membership on key endogenous macroeconomic performance indicators. They concluded that between the second and first halves of the 1980s, the CFA members were outperformed by the groups of comparators – other SSA, other SSA and low income countries – in terms of output growth as well as export, investment, and savings performance, except for inflation.

In my view, the main factor behind these findings is that the outcome of the fundamental trade-off entailed by the monetary union is very much dependent on the interplay of the policy stance and the external environment, especially the behaviour of the French franc. As we noted above, the fundamental trade-off is that individual members of the union have essentially lost the use of the nominal exchange rate as an instrument of policy, in return for currency convertibility and freedom of capital and factor movement, in addition to the stability and credibility brought about by the supranational rules of monetary co-operation such as credit controls and budgetary disciplines. These rules, while offering some hope for low inflation, appear not to have been sufficiently forthcoming in bringing the necessary adjustment to the CFA economies at times of domestic macroeconomic laxity and severe exogenous shocks. As early as the second half of the 1970s, the CFA franc zone started to show signs of economic difficulties as the accumulated effects of laxity in the implementation of the zone fiscal/monetary regime began to materialize, especially for the bigger countries.[45]

The problems of the zone, however, did not assume crisis proportions until after 1985, when the French franc began to appreciate *vis-à-vis* the US dollar in the face of deteriorating terms of trade for the CFA zone. This period also witnessed the onset of considerable real depreciation in several subSaharan African countries (including key export-competitors of the zone in West Africa). This acted like an added adverse exogenous shock to the economies of the zone. With nominal devaluation not available as an instrument of policy, adjustment by deflating the economy has so far proven to be slow, costly and politically difficult. This analysis clearly explains the results of Table 5.3, where the CEAO union generated significant intra-union trade as well as modestly enhanced trade with the rest of the world in the first period, while both CEAO and UDEAC caused considerable trade diversions without being able to increase intra-union trade during the second period, when external economic environments and economic policy distortions worsened considerably.[46]

Moreover, there are other influences particular to these unions that interact with the macroeconomic environment to shape trade performance in the zone. In addition to the positive feature of high capital and factor mobility in the zone – especially CEAO – by African standards, there are three other positive features of CEAO, and to a lesser extent UDEAC:

- a high degree of complementary production structure – for example, there appears to be a significant intersectoral division of labour in the trade between smaller countries such as Burkina Faso and Mali (potential agricultural product exporters) and Côte d'Ivoire and Senegal, the two relatively industrialized members;
- natural barriers to trade, such as prohibitive transportation costs, are lower in CEAO than elsewhere in SSA; and
- the availability of funds, from outside the union in the case of CEAO, to finance development in the less developed areas (Langhammer and Hiemenz, 1991).

Despite these positive features, efficient intra-regional specialization never emerged in the zone due in large measure to the macroeconomic constraints and the vulnerability of the zone to external shocks, but also because of a policy-induced impediment to trade. In the CEAO this impediment was the *taxe de coopération régionale*, which was designed to secure a complicated and sometimes conflicting menu of distributional and allocational objectives. Similarly, in UDEAC there is the 'single tax', which was imposed on regionally traded goods and differed according to origin, product, enterprise, and consumer country. Both measures 'promoted regional import substitution and sheltered marginal suppliers against competition from member countries' (Ravenhill, 1985). Also, Langhammer and Hiemenz (1991) observe that, by favouring products from poorer member countries over those from more advanced ones, the costs of this policy in the context of CEAO 'have affected both groups of countries in CEAO – keeping inefficient industries alive in the poorer countries and protecting industries in the more advanced countries against outside competition, thereby crippling their international competitiveness'.

5.6 CONCLUSIONS

This study is concerned with formally modelling the determinants of intra-SSA trade in the context of an extended traditional 'gravity model'. As stated in the introduction, in addition to controlling for the standard factors that reflect absolute trade potential in a given country and the factors that affect the trade attraction between any two trading partners, this model also accounts for the following potential determinants:

(1) the effects of the RI schemes (including currency unions) in SSA and in other regions pertaining to the other countries in the sample;
(2) the trade diversion (or creation) effects of the RI schemes; and
(3) the further marginal effects of RI schemes after controlling for real exchange rate volatility and real exchange rate overvaluation.

The model was estimated for a sample of sixty-two reporting countries of which twenty-eight are in SSA, and for the two periods of 1980–4 and 1986–90. Consistent with other evidence in this literature, the estimation results were generally sensible and they strongly corroborate the main predictions of the model.

Starting with the traditional variables of the gravity model, our results show very robust and strong influences for four factors (distance, economic size, cultural similarity and income per capita differentials), but there was no equally compelling evidence for the others. The robustness, significance and estimated appreciable effects of these four factors clearly suggest the strength of the two traditional variables of the gravity model (proximity and economic size), the role of cultural similarities (at least for some globally influential cultures) and the importance of comparative advantage as a determinant of bilateral trade for low income countries (which constitute almost all the sample of reporting countries considered in this study).

Our estimates suggest that the direct effects of the two components of exchange rate policy (RERVAR and REROVER) are rather small, with estimated elasticities ranging from −0.36 to −0.41 for RERVAR and a minuscule 0.00 to −0.03 for REROVER. These results are consistent with those estimated for RERVAR by Frankel and Wei (1993) for trade flows between major regional trade and currency blocks in Europe, North America and Asia. However, as argued by Frankel and Wei, the direct effect of real exchange rate policy on trade flows may not tell the whole story about the potential role of exchange rate policy. Moreover, the full effect of RERVAR or REROVER may be confounded by the effects of regional blocs, especially currency unions. For example, intra-bloc RERVAR and REROVER are much smaller in CEAO and UDEAC compared to the SSA-wide median average (see Table 5.1). Indeed, accounting for the exchange rate policy does lead to changes in the order of magnitudes of the regional blocs effects, and in some cases the changes were quite substantial (compare the results of Appendix Table 5A.3 to those of Table 5.2).

After controlling for the traditional gravity variables and exchange rate policy, our results suggest three fundamental conclusions on the effects of regional schemes in SSA and other developing countries.

(1) By and large the experience of regional integration in SSA has been a failure. However, our results also show that the African experience is by no means unique and there are parallels to it in other developing regions (namely Latin America).
(2) ASEAN has significantly enhanced both intra-regional as well as inter-regional trade, even though it was not explicitly designed to be a deliberate trade-creating scheme.
(3) The two monetary unions (CEAO, UDEAC), especially CEAO, have displayed very extreme patterns of performance, where their effects on both intra-scheme and inter-scheme trade flows have been very positive (negative) and substantial during the first (second) half of the 1980s.

In attempting to explain the findings on the performance of the regional schemes in SSA, it is pertinent to point out that our conclusion that the record of African economic integration has been one of failures and unfulfilled expectations is neither novel nor surprising, given that it agrees with previous evidence on this literature. It can be argued, however, that this conclusion is interesting because it obtains even after controlling for key policy variables (such as exchange rate variability and exchange rate overvaluation) in addition to the traditional trade flow determinants (economic size, distance, and so on). It is clear, therefore, that the failures of these African schemes (like CACM and LAFTA in Latin America) can at least be partially explained by their own characteristics and the constraints they face, most notably the development strategy upon which they were created.

Our analysis also attempted to explain the stellar performance of the ASEAN and to compare it to the largely ineffective role of SADCC – which is arguably the closest African regional scheme to the concept of the ASEAN. Our main conclusion in this regard is that in addition to lack of strong economic growth in SADCC, inadequate commitment to internal co-operation and, by implication, the inability of the group to develop an effective and co-ordinated strategy for external economic relations have conspired to prevent SADCC from being the African equivalent of the ASEAN.

Finally, on the role of the CFA monetary unions of West Africa (both the UEMOA and the prospective successor to BEAC), our analysis suggests that the success of these unions in enhancing bilateral trade within and outside the schemes depends on three prerequisites:

- respecting static macroeconomic balances (especially fiscal balance) on a sustained basis to ensure a positive outcome in terms of economic performance (including trade performance) of the fundamental policy trade-off facing the zone (that is, loss the exchange rate as an instrument of national policy in return for monetary stability);
- reforming the inherently trade-impeding zone-wide distributional/ allocational arrangements before the potentially positive effects on trade of the zone monetary discipline can be realized; and
- favourable external environments, especially a reversal or moderation of the French franc appreciation *vis-à-vis* the US $ and the worsening terms of trade for primary commodities.

However, it is pertinent to note that given the recent and anticipated appreciation of the French franc *vis-à-vis* the US $, the continued pegging of the CFA franc to it is bound to generate problems for the zone in the not too distant future, despite the huge devaluation of the CFA franc in 1994.

Notes

1. Table 5.1 gives the country groupings and key economic indicators for African and other RI schemes. For a more detailed account containing additional information of the objectives and record of achievements of various schemes see Table 8.2 of Foroutan (1993) and Table 1 of Lyakurwa *et al.* (1993).
2. In terms of membership, the mergers in francophone West Africa are not that consequential: CEAO and UMOA are almost identical in terms of member countries, since the former includes in addition to Mauritania all the members of the latter except Togo (Togo and Guinea are observers in CEAO); and UDEAC is identical to BEAC. However, Fine and Yeo (1994) argue that the UEMOA arrangement 'is more than cosmetic, and marks a radical departure from the past'.
3. According to this view, no more than four such regional groupings should exist in Africa: North, West, Central, and East and South. Thus the PTA, like its West African counterpart, ECOWAS, received the active support of the ECA (for example, Foroutan, 1993).
4. See Table 8.3 of Foroutan (1993) and Tables 4 and 5 of Lyakurwa *et al.* (1993), also see Table 5.1 in this chapter, which focuses on the 1980s.

continued on page 244

Table 5A.1   Reporter and Partner Countries in the Sample

Reporter countries	Partner countries
Sub-Saharan Africa	Argentina
Angola	Australia
Benin	Austria
Burundi	Belgium/Luxembourg
Cameroon	Burma
CAR	Canada
Chad	Chile
Congo	Denmark
Côte d'Ivoire	Finland
Equatorial Guinea	France
Ethiopia	Germany
Gabon	Greece
Ghana	Haiti
Kenya	Hong Kong
Liberia	Iraq
Malawi	Ireland
Mauritania	Israel
Mauritius	Italy
Mozambique	Japan
Niger	Korea
Nigeria	Kuwait
Senegal	Lebanon
Somalia	Libya
Sudan	Malaysia
Tanzania	Mexico
Togo	Netherlands
Uganda	New Zealand
Zambia	Norway
Zimbabwe	Oman
Other	Panama
Algeria	Portugal
Bangladesh	Saudi Arabia
Benin	Singapore
Bolivia	Spain
Botswana	Sweden
Brazil	Switzerland
Bulgaria	Syria
Colombia	Trinidad & Tobago
Costa Rica	United Arab Empirates
Dominican Republic	United Kingdom
Ecuador	Uruguay
Egypt, Arab Rep.	USA

continued on page 244

Table 5A.1 *Continued*

Reporter countries	Partner countries
El Salvador	
Guatemala	
Honduras	
India	
Indonesia	
Iran, Islamic Rep.	
Jamaica	
Jordan	
Madagascar	
Morocco	
Nicaragua	
Pakistan	
Papua New Guinea	
Paraguay	
Peru	
Philippines	
South Africa	
Sri Lanka	
Thailand	
Tunisia	
Turkey	
Yemen, Rep.	

5. The 'frontline' countries of SADCC received significant external support in their bid to minimize their economies' dependence on pre-democratic South Africa. Furthermore, the success of SADCC is also credited to the limited set of objectives set forth for the scheme. In the other two schemes the willingness of South Africa to provide adequate compensation to other weaker countries in SACU, and of France to guarantee convertibility in the case of CEAO, are among the major factors behind their relative success (Foroutan, 1993).

6. The creation of an African Common Market by the year 2000 is the ultimate objective of the Abuja Treaty.

7. A review of a wide range of views on the potential role of regional integration as an engine of growth for SSA is provided in Elbadawi and Ndulu (1994).

8. The fact that many African countries have equated 'increased intra-African trade with self-reliant policies required to break from the economically "dependent" trading patterns established during the colonial period' (Berg and Associates, 1988), provides an additional political consideration attached to increased intra-African trade and deeper African economic integration.

9. The possible adverse effects of substantial real exchange rate variability or real exchange rate overvaluation on trade flows (especially exports) is

continued on page 245

Table 5A.2   Gravity model estimates: SSA and other low-income countries (averages 1980–4 and 1986–90)

	Imports[a]			
	1980–84		1986–90	
Variables	Coef.	t-Stat.	Coef.	t-Stat.
Standard gravity model				
Constant	−6.72	−8.11	−11.92	−13.80
log(*Distance*$_{ij}$)	−2.04	−24.09	−1.92	−21.62
Border$_{ij}$	1.39	4.21	0.57	1.64
Island$_i$	0.65	2.61	1.08	4.13
log (*Area*$_i$ · *Area*$_j$)	−0.45	−18.67	70.24	11.12
log (*GDP*$_i$ · *GDP*$_j$)	1.84	53.74	0.44	23.18
log (*GDPPC*$_i$ · *GDPPC*$_j$)	−0.23	−4.35	1.22	24.35
Linder: log |*GDPPC*$_i$−*GDPPC*$_j$|	0.20	4.18	0.62	11.96
Language$_{ij}$:				
English	1.10	5.31	1.53	7.06
Spanish	0.95	3.59	1.28	4.68
French	2.70	7.97	0.33	0.91
Arabic	0.81	2.48	−1.04	−3.01
Portuguese	2.62	2.02	0.25	0.18
Swahili	−0.49	−0.42	0.04	0.03
Pseudo-R-square	0.1383		0.1133	
No. of observation	6386		6386	

Notes:
[a] The dependent variables are estimated in logs (for values > 0)
Border$_{ij}$ = 1 if country *i* and *j* share a common border
Island$_i$ = if country *i* is an island
Language$_{ij}$ = 1 if countries *i* and *j* share the same language

well documented in the literature (for example, see Caballero and Corbo, 1989; Balassa, 1985,1988).
10. Three other specialized studies include Ogunkola (1994), which evaluates intra-ECOWAS trade potential; Foroutan, Montenegro and Pritchett (1994); and Foroutan, Jenkins and Montenegro (1994), which analyse bilateral trade in South Africa and Zimbabwe, respectively.
11. The possible implications of these extensions for the analysis will be articulated in Section 5.2.
12. Examples of empirical gravity model-based studies that were corroborated by subsequent evidence include: Aitken (1973), which predicts that the formation of the EC will substantially influence trade volume and patterns of its member countries; Havrylyshyn and Pritchett (1991), which shows that trade between Eastern and Western Europe was much less

continued on page 250

Table 5A.3 Gravity model estimates: SSA and other low-income countries (averages 1980–4 and 1986–90)

| | Imports[a] | | | | Exports[a] | | | |
| Variables | 1980–84 | | 1986–90 | | 1980–84 | | 1986–90 | |
	Coef.	t-Stat.	Coef.	t-Stat.	Coef.	t-Stat.	Coef.	t-Stat.
Standard gravity model								
Constant	−6.92	−7.20	−8.67	−8.81	−6.91	−6.99	−11.15	−11.20
log $(Distance_{ij})$	−1.88	−21.17	−1.90	−20.98	−1.82	−19.83	−1.88	−20.39
$Border_{ij}$	1.14	3.26	0.16	0.45	0.98	2.74	0.49	1.36
$Island_i$	0.23	0.94	0.05	0.21	−0.52	−2.00	−0.32	−1.24
$\log(Area_i \cdot Area_j)$	−0.45	−17.13	0.30	13.65	−0.48	−17.59	0.17	7.72
$\log(GDP_i \cdot GDP_j)$	1.78	47.06	0.30	15.07	1.78	45.27	0.63	31.26
$\log(GDPPC_i \cdot GDPPC_j)$	−0.21	−3.67	1.16	21.70	−0.23	−3.97	0.93	17.03
Linder: $\log |GDPPC_i - GDPPC_j|$	0.20	4.02	0.62	11.93	0.17	3.34	0.67	12.51
Language$_j$:								
English	0.66	3.10	1.11	5.14	1.08	4.94	1.35	6.22
Spanish	2.06	6.69	1.80	5.81	1.94	6.15	1.75	5.58
French	2.20	5.92	1.30	3.38	2.59	6.73	2.11	5.44
Arabic	0.68	2.07	−1.42	−4.21	1.11	3.27	−0.65	−1.91
Portuguese	2.99	2.35	0.94	0.71	2.80	2.16	0.16	0.12
Swahili	0.29	0.25	0.65	−0.76	−0.62	0.56	0.45	
Regional trade/monetary schemes								
Within bloc$_{ij}$[b]								
ECOWAS[b]	0.27	1.56	−0.67	−3.66	−1.36	−7.38	−0.66	−3.51
CEAO	3.47	3.06	0.91	0.77	5.07	4.36	1.14	0.96
UDEAC	3.19	1.21	−1.60	−0.59	1.17	0.43	−2.47	−0.91
CEPGL	3.85	1.44	4.43	1.53	5.09	1.86	−23.26	—
PTA	1.25	2.96	−0.28	−0.66	0.93	2.13	−0.49	−1.13
SADCC	−1.36	−1.61	−0.59	−0.69	−0.60	−0.70	−0.09	−0.11

LAFTA	0.70	1.29	0.35	0.64	1.62	2.91	0.86	1.53
CACM	-1.79	-1.95	-0.20	-0.22	-1.31	-1.39	0.43	0.46
ASEAN	-0.52	-0.61	2.47	2.87	0.26	0.30	2.01	2.32
Bloc members$_{ij}$:								
ECOWAS^b	—	—	—	—	—	—	—	—
CEAO	0.28	1.38	-0.95	-4.73	1.27	6.12	-0.63	-3.11
UDEAC	0.35	1.35	-2.58	-10.25	0.64	2.42	-1.97	-7.66
CEPGL	-2.03	-8.01	-1.44	-5.59	-1.86	-7.12	-1.34	-5.08
PTA	-0.20	-1.22	-0.64	-3.97	-0.42	-2.49	-0.58	-3.57
SADCC	-0.06	-0.29	-0.26	-1.35	0.09	0.44	0.14	0.71
LAFTA	-0.73	-5.04	-0.93	-6.46	-0.17	-1.16	-0.67	-4.56
CACM	-2.05	-11.39	-1.38	-7.93	-1.59	-8.67	-1.34	-7.47
ASEAN	0.76	4.92	2.55	16.40	1.01	6.37	2.23	14.13
Pseudo-R-square	0.1479		0.1304		0.1436		0.1407	
No. of observations	6386		6386		6386		6386	

Notes:

^{a} The dependent variables are estimated in logs (for values > 0)

^{b} Because of multicollinearity, the effects due to ECOWAS could not be decomposed into within bloc and bloc members; therefore the estimated coefficient for ECOWAS reflects the net effect

$Border_{ij} = 1$ if countries i and j share the same border

$Island_i = $ if country i is an island

$Language_{ij} = 1$ if countries i and j share the same language

$Within\ bloc_{ij} = 1$ if both countries belong to the same bloc

$Bloc\ member_{ij} = 1$ if either county i or j (*not* both) belongs to the bloc

Table 5A.4 Gravity model estimates: SSA and other low-income countries (averages 1980–4 and 1986–90)

Variables	Imports[a]				Exports			
	1980–84		1986–90		1980–84		1986–90	
	Coef.	t-Stat.	Coef.	t-Stat.	Coef.	t-Stat.	Coef.	t-Stat.
Standard gravity model								
Constant	−6.93	−6.79	−9.08	−9.23	−6.84	−6.36	−10.76	−10.4
$\log(Distance_{ij})$	−1.79	−19.43	−1.72	−19.42	−1.72	−17.73	−1.70	−18.27
$Border_{ij}$	1.02	2.73	0.18	0.49	0.98	2.5	0.62	1.64
$Island_i$	0.06	0.26	−0.11	−0.5	−0.55	−2.21	−0.40	−1.7
$\log(Area_i \cdot Area_j)$	−0.35	−12.29	0.37	17.04	−0.46	−15.43	0.24	10.66
$\log(GDP_i \cdot GDP_j)$	1.60	39.7	0.26	13.52	1.73	40.35	0.58	28.25
$\log(GDPPC_i \cdot GDPPC_j)$	0.01	0.24	1.26	24.2	−0.21	−3.3	0.99	18.16
Linder: $\log \lvert GDPPC_i - GDPPC_j \rvert$	0.14	2.66	0.51	10.01	0.15	2.73	0.6	11.07
Language$_{ij}$*:*								
English	0.35	1.58	0.36	1.72	0.67	2.86	0.68	3.08
Spanish	1.70	5.83	1.42	5.13	1.8	5.9	1.56	5.37
French	1.95	4.89	1.49	3.81	2.54	6.07	1.96	4.76
Arabic	0.49	1.14	−0.26	−0.63	0.98	2.19	0.27	0.63
Portuguese	1.89	0.55	0.83	0.25	3.34	0.93	1.31	0.38
Swahili	1.79	1.23	2.06	1.43	0.43	0.27	1.68	1.11
Regional trade/monetary schemes								
Within bloc$_{ij}$[b]								
ECOWAS[b]	0.13	0.67	−0.22	−1.2	−1.33	−6.44	−0.32	−1.62
CEAO	3.56	2.44	1.31	0.93	5.39	3.52	1.66	1.13
UDEAC	2.37	0.96	−2.61	−1.09	0.93	0.36	−3.12	−1.26
CEPGL	3.7	1.48	3.73	1.48	4.94	1.89	−21.29	—
PTA	2.29	4.58	0.35	0.74	1.9	3.62	−0.05	−0.11

SADCC	-1.83	-1.2	0.38	0.26	-0.96	-0.6	1.02	0.66
LAFTA	0.73	1.41	0.04	0.08	1.67	3.06	0.67	1.31
CACM	-1.69	-1.96	0.81	0.98	-1.16	-1.29	1.69	1.96
ASEAN	-0.36	-0.45	2.03	2.68	0.34	0.41	1.52	1.93
Bloc members$_{ij}$: ECOWAS^b	—	—	—	—	—	—	—	—
CEAO	0.36	1.64	-1.44	-6.89	1.41	6.03	-0.91	-4.15
UDEAC	-0.23	-0.89	-2.94	-12.48	0.43	1.58	-2.25	-8.99
CEPGL	-1.98	-7.79	-1.53	-6.38	-1.94	-7.22	-1.4	-5.48
PTA	-0.00	-0.02	-0.64	-4.12	-0.3	-1.71	-0.55	-3.34
SADCC	-0.33	-1.4	0.39	1.79	0.31	1.25	0.78	3.38
LAFTA	-0.53	-3.32	-1.12	-8.19	-0.05	-0.3	-0.8	-5.52
CACM	-2.08	-11.74	-0.92	-5.36	-1.6	-8.63	-0.72	-3.94
ASEAN	0.66	4.31	2.1	14.27	0.91	5.65	1.89	12.2
Macroeconomic policy stance								
REERVAR$_{ij}$	-0.36	-4.86	-0.41	-7.61	-0.09	-1.16	-0.6	-10.52
REROVER$_{ij}$	-0.03	3.96	0.00	0.54	-0.02	2.77	0.01	1.63
Pseudo-R-square	0.1537		0.1495		0.1446		0.1535	
No. of Observations	5104		5104		5104		5104	

Notes:

^{a} The dependent variables are estimated in logs (for values > 0)

^{b} Because of multicollinearity, the effects due to ECOWAS could not be decomposed into within bloc and bloc members; therefore the estimated coefficient for ECOWAS reflects the net effect

$Border_{ij} = 1$ if countries i and j share the same border

$Island_i = 1$ of country i is an island

$Language_{ij} = 1$ if countries i and j share the same language

$Within\ bloc_{ij} = 1$ if both countries belong to the same bloc

$Block\ member_{ij} = 1$ if either country i or j (not both) belongs to the same bloc

$$RERVAR_{ij} = \text{Var}\left[\Delta\log\left(\frac{RER_i}{RER_j}\right)\right] \text{ and } REROVER_{ij} = \log\left[\frac{avg(RER_i)}{RER_j} \cdot \frac{avg(RER_j)}{RER_j}\right]; \text{ where } RER = \frac{E.P^*}{P} \text{ and } avg\,(RER)\ (1970\text{-}2)$$

Notes cont.

than predicted by the model; and Foroutan and Pritchett (1992), which shows that the rather low intra-SSA trade appears consistent with the model predictions. Other versions of the gravity model focus on specific issues such as the effect of exchange rate variability (for example, Frankel and Wei, 1993); the role of political variables in trade flows (for example, Srivasta and Green, 1986); or the determinants of trade diversion effects of regional blocks (for example, Eichengreen and Irwin, 1993).

13. For example, Foroutan and Pritchett (1993) note that 'although the gravity model is unwieldy, the basic logic is straightforward. For example, although Belgium's ($192 bn) and Mexico's ($236 bn) GDPs are roughly the same, the model employs other factors to predict correctly that the trade between Belgium and France will be larger than the trade between Mexico and France'.

14. However, the above models use restrictive assumptions to derive the gravity equation, such as: identical preferences; identical production technologies; perfect substitutability of goods in production and consumption; perfect arbitrage; and constant transportation costs. More recently, Asilis and Rivera-Batiz (1994) have derived the gravity equation from a general equilibrium model that relaxes technological assumptions and allows for externalities (pollution and congestion).

15. Various RI schemes are listed in Table 5.1, which includes all trade arrangements as well as currency union arrangements: CEAO, UDEAC and Rand Monetary Area (which includes all SACU countries except Botswana).

16. For a review of the concept of real exchange rate overvaluation and its calculation relative to a behavioral empirical model of the equilibrium real exchange rate see Elbadawi (1994). This particular measure is a simple Purchasing Power Parity (PPP)-based approach which assumes the actual rate for 1970–2 to be consistent with equilibrium behaviour for the entire period.

17. See Helpman (1987) and Helpman and Krugman (1985, section 1.5).

18. See section V.3 for a detailed discussion of monetary integration schemes in SSA.

19. While Frankel and Wei (1993) include a measure of real exchange rate variability in their gravity model, ours is perhaps the first application of the model that also adds a measure of real exchange rate overvaluation as well (see sections 5.2 and 5.5 for a discussion on the relevance of this to SSA's monetary unions).

20. Eichengreen and Irwin (1993) noted the relevance of this issue for the case of inter-war trade.

21. Another advantage of Tobit specifications is the use of maximum likelihood technique yield parameters, which are extremely reliable even when the sample is rather small (Sen and Matuszewski, 1991). In our case, the relatively large sample of 5104 observations should enhance the confidence in the estimation results.

22. The elasticities for the qualitative variables are given as the exponential of the estimated coefficients.

23. The total of sixty-two reporting countries and forty-two partner countries generated $62 \times (62 - 1) + 42 \times 62 = 6386$ observations on bilateral trade flows (see Appendix Tables 5.2 and 5A.3). However, due to data

unavailability for some right-hand side variables in the extended model (Table 5A.2), only 5104 observations were available for Table 5A.2's regressions.

24. We follow Foroutan and Pritchett (1993) to make this restriction to ensure that the set of *reporting* countries includes mostly low-income countries that we hope share the same economic characteristics.

25. However, Forouton and Pritchett (1993), for example, see otherwise. They estimate separate models for exports and imports and give the following two reasons for doing so. 'First, bilateral imports patterns may be determined differently from export patterns, especially for gross, as opposed to net, flows. Second, and importantly in the SSA case, using both imports and exports attenuates the problem of unrecorded trade as one reporter's recorded imports are a partners's exports and vice versa.' Also see the data appendix of Foroutan and Pritchett for a discussion of the problem posed by the extent of unreported trade in SSA.

26. For example, see Elbadawi and Majd, 1992; Devarajan and de Melo, 1987a, b.

27. An imperfect measure of the empirical performance of the model is the degree of fit given by the derived Pseudo R2, which ranges from 0.133 for the smaller model of Appendix Table 5A.2 to 0.154 for the full model of Table 5A.2. This, of course, is not exceptional, but it remains admissible for cross-sectional regressions. However, the key test is the ability to corroborate the predictions of the model in terms of the significance of individual – effects which was met by our empirical results.

28. Obliviously these effects are confounded by historical colonial ties.

29. For example, Krugman (1991b) emphasizes the role of simple geographical proximity in explaining the bias toward intra-regional trade, and Frankel and Wei (1993) argue that to the extent that regional groupings are influenced by this effect, they should be welfare-improving natural groupings.

30. However, an opposite (and rather suprising) result for the case of exports was found by Foroutan, Montenegro and Pritchett (1994) and Montenegro and Soto (1994), who argue that the GDPPC may not be a very good proxy for industrialization.

31. These estimates may appear implausible; however, they are consistent with other estimates in the literature (for example, Frankel and Wei, 1993; Foroutan and Pritchett, 1993; Montenegro and Soto, 1994; among others).

32. However, Frankel and Wei (1993) only consider the effect of real exchange rate variability.

33. The fact that the 'incremental' trade performance of CEAO and UDEAC as regional blocs was even worse in the second period when we control for the effects of exchange rate policy, could have three – not necessarily mutually exclusive – explanations: (1) that RERVAR, which remains low in CEAO and UDEAC, is more important as a bilateral trade determinant than REROVER, which was very substantial in both blocs during the second period (see Table 5.1); (2) that there were factors influencing the observed overall worsening of economic conditions in the two blocs in the second period that are also confounded with the bloc effects; and/or (3) that the PPP-based measure of REROVER used in the paper is not a good measure of the true real exchange rate overvaluation in the two blocs during the 1986–90 period.

34. See for example Foroutan (1993), Foroutan and Pritchett (1992) and Langhammer and Hiemenz (1991).
35. The cases of SADCC; CEAO and UDEAC will be addressed in points two and three, respectively.
36. Clearing arrangements through the Harare-based PTA Clearinghouse did not solve the trade-diversion either, since only products eligible for preferential treatment have access to the clearing facility. Also, licensing by local authorities tends to favour 'essential' goods imported from outside the PTA over goods originating within PTA that are deemed to be nonessential.
37. As pointed out by Langhammer and Hiemenz, 'Despite these shortcomings, member governments have launched new integration plans, two of them recently. One calls for intra-PTA liberalization through annual 10-percent reduction in tariffs among members between 1988 and 1996. The second introduced and mandated the use of travellers checks denominated in PTA Currency Units for all travellers from within the region in order to facilitate commercial exchanges and free local businesses from existing exchange restrictions.'
38. In addition, Fine and Yeo propose that the new regional schemes in SSA should also: take into account the incentives facing the government bureaucracy and the private sector; address the issues of concentration and agglomeration, and the distribution of gains and losses; attempt to deal creatively with the problems of 'hub-and-spoke'; and create strong institutions that can effectively implement integration measures.
39. In fact, as pointed out by Langhammer and Hiemenz (1991), most intra-ASEAN trade is in primary commodities, which are not eligible for preferential trade treatment, or in manufactures that do not meet rules-of-origin requirements (Rieger, 1985). Furthermore, according to recent empirical evidence, many tariffs are not binding (Langhammer, 1988), and NTBs are considered more serious obstacles to trade by ASEAN traders (Sanchez, 1987).
40. See for example the World Bank (1993) for a comprehensive review.
41. SADCC was founded in 1980 by five frontline states: Angola, Botswana, Mozambique, Tanzania and Zambia, and was joined later by Malawi, Lesotho, Swaziland and Zimbabwe. The main objective of SADCC is to foster economic co-operation between its member countries in order to reduce and eventually eliminate their dependence on apartheid South Africa.
42. The distinction between pre-democratic and current democratic South Africa is mine.
43. Unfortunately, due to lack of data, we could not include the case of SACU. This monetary union – which includes Botswana, Lesotho, Namibia, Swaziland and South Africa is judged to be the most successful in Africa, with the objectives of currency union, capital and labour market integration as well as CET having all been achieved (Foroutan, 1993).
44. See also Devarajan and de Melo (1987a, b; 1990).
45. The larger economies of the zone such as Côte d'Ivoire, Senegal and Cameroon, which dominate the process of credit distribution, tended to have the most inflationary monetary policies and hence the most appreciated exchange rate.

46. The 100 per cent devaluation in 1994 of the CFA franc relative to the French franc appears to have eliminated at least temporarily the competitiveness problem of the CFA.

References

Ades, A. and Chua, H. (1993) 'Regional Instability and Economic Growth: Thy Neighbor's Curse', Center Discussion Paper no. 704 (Yale University, Economic Growth Center).

African Development Bank (1993) *Economic Integration in Southern Africa*, vol. 2 (Oxford: Biddles).

Aitken, N.D. (1973) 'The Effects of the EEC and EFTA on European Trade a Temporal Cross-Section Analysis', *American Economic Review*, 63(5): 881–92.

Anderson, J. (1979) 'A Theoretical Foundation for the Gravity Equation', *American Economic Review*, 69 (Mar.): 106–16.

Asilis, C. and L. Rivera-Batiz (1994) 'Geography, Trade Patterns and Economic Policy', IMF working paper, Feb.

Balassa, B. (1985) 'Exports, Policy Choices and Economic Growth in Developing Countries After the 1973 Oil Shock', *Journal of Development Economics*, 18 (2).

—— (1988) 'Outward Orientation', in H. Chenery and T.N. Srinivasan (eds), *Handbook of Development Economics* (Amsterdam: North-Holland).

Baldwin, R. (1993) 'Review of Theoretical Developments on Regional Integration', a paper presented at an AERC conference on *Trade Liberalization & Regional Integration in SSA*, Nairobi, Dec.

Barro, R. and R. Gordon (1983) 'Rules, Discretion and Reputation in a model of Monetary Policy', *Journal of Monetary Economics*, 12 (1): 101–22.

Berg, E. and Associates (1988) 'Regional and Economic Development in Sub-Saharan Africa', a study prepared for USAID, Alexandria, Virginia, USA.

Bergstrand, J. (1985) 'The Gravity Equations in International Trade: Some Microeconomic Foundation and empirical Evidence', *Review of Economics and Statistics* 67 (Aug.): 474–81.

Caballero, R. and V. Corbo (1989) 'The Effects of Real Exchange Rate Uncertainty on Exports: Empirical Evidence', *World Bank Economic Review*, 3 (2): 263–78.

Chua, H. (1993a) 'Regional Spillovers and Economic Growth', Discussion Paper no. 700 (Economic Growth Center, Yale University).

—— (1993b) 'Regional Public Capital and Economic Growth,' unpublished mimeo (Economic Growth Center, Yale University).

Cobham, D. and P. Robson (1994) 'Monetary Integration in Africa: A Deliberately European Perspective', *World Development*, 22 (3): 285–99.

Collier, P. (1991) 'Africa's External Economic relations: 1960–90', *African Affairs*, 90 (360): 339–56.

—— and J. Gunning (1993) 'Linkages Between Trade Policy and Regional Integration', a paper presented at an AERC conference on *Trade Liberalization & Regional Integration in SSA*, Nairobi, Dec.

De Grauwe, P. (1992) *The Economics of Monetary Integration* (Oxford University Press).

Deardorff, A. (1984),'Testing Trade Theories and Predicting Trade Flows', in R. Jones and P. Kenen (eds), *Handbook of International Economics*, vol. 1 (Amsterdam: North-Holland).

Devarajan, S. and J. de Melo (1987a) 'Evaluating Participation in African Monetary Unions: A Statistical Analysis of the CFA Zones', *World Development*, 15 (4): 483–96.

―― and ―― (1987b) 'Adjustment with a Fixed Exchange Rate: Cameroon, Côte d'Ivoire, and Senegal', *World Bank Economic Review*, 2 (2).

―― and ―― (1990) 'Membership in the CFA Zone: Odyssean Journey or Trojan Horse?', paper presented at World Bank Conference on *Africa Economic Issues*.

Eichengreen, B. and D. Irwin (1993) 'Trade Blocs, Currency Blocs and the Disintegration of World Trade in the 1930s', Discussion Paper no. 837 (London: Centre for Economic Policy Research).

Elbadawi, I. (1994) 'Estimating Long-run Equilibrium Real Exchange Rates', in J. Williamson (ed.), *Essays on the Estimation of Equilibrium Exchange Rates* (Washington, D.C.).

―― and B. Ndulu (1994) 'Long term Development and Sustainable Growth in SSA', a paper presented at the SAREC International Colloquium on *New Directions in Development Economics*, Stockholm, Mar.

―― and N. Majd (1992) 'Fixed Parity of the Exchange Rate and Economic Performance in the CFA Zone: A Comparative Study', Policy Research Working Paper no. 830 (Washington, DC: World Bank).

Fine, J. and S. Yeo (1994) 'Regional Integration in Sub-Saharan Africa: Dead End or a Fresh Start?', a paper prepared for the AERC project *Regional Integration and Trade Liberalization in SSA*, Nairobi.

Foroutan, F. (1993) 'Regional Integration in Sub-Saharan Africa: Past Experience and future Prospects', in J. de Melo and A. Panagariya (eds), *New Dimensions in Regional Integration* (Cambridge University Press).

――, C. Jenkins and C. Montenegro (1994) 'Zimbabwe's Regional Trade: An Evaluation', unpublished mimeo (CSAE, University of Oxford).

――, C. Montenegro and L. Pritchett (1994) 'South Africa's Pattern of Bilateral Trade', unpublished mimeo (Washington, DC: World Bank).

―― and L. Pritchett (1993) 'Intra-Sub-Saharan African Trade: is it too little?', *The Journal of the African Economies*, 2 (1).

Frankel, J. and S. Wei (1993) 'Trade Blocs and Currency Blocs', in *The Monetary Future of Europe* (Centre for Economic Policy Research).

Havrylyshyn, O. and L. Pritchett (1991) 'European Trade Patterns After the Transition', World Bank Working Paper WPS748, Aug.

Helpman, E. (1987) 'Imperfect Competition and International Trade: Evidence from Fourteen Industrial Countries', *Journal of the Japanese and International Economics*, 1: 62–81.

―― and P. Krugman (1985) *Market Structure and Foreign Trade* (Cambridge, Mass.: MIT Press).

Krugman, P. (1991a) *Geography and Trade* (MIT Press).

―― (1991b) 'The Move Toward Free Trade Zones', in *Policy Implications of Trade and Currency Zones*, a Symposium sponsored by the Federal Reserve Bank of Kansas City, Jackson Hole, Wyoming, 7–42.

Kydland, F. and E. Prescott (1977) 'Rules Rather Than Discretion: the Inconsistency of Optimal Plans', *Journal of Political Economy*, 85 (3): 473–92.

Langhammer, R. (1985) 'The Economic Rationale of Trade Policy Cooperation between ASEAN and the EC: Has Cooperation Benefitted ASEAN?', *ASEAN Economic Bulletin* 2: 107–17.

—— (1988) 'Tariff Reductions and Tariff Redundancy in the ASEAN Countries', *ASEAN Economic Bulletin*, 4: 252–70.

—— and U. Hiemenz (1991) 'Regional Integration Among Developing Countries: Survey of Past performance and Agenda for Future Policy Action', Occasional paper no. 7 (Washington, DC: UNDP-World Bank Trade Expansion program, World Bank).

Linneman, H. (1966) *An Econometric Study of International Trade Flows* (Amsterdam: North-Holland).

Lyakurwa, W., A. McKay, N. Ng'eno and W. Kennes (1993) 'Regional Integration in Sub-Saharan Africa: A Review of Experiences and Issues', a paper presented at an AERC conference on *Trade Liberalization & Regional Integration in SSA*, Nairobi, Dec.

Montenegro, C. and R. Soto (1994), 'How Distorted is Cuba's Trade? Evidence and Predictions From Gravity Model', unpublished mimeo (Washington DC: Georgetown University)

O'Connell, S. (1994) 'Macroeconomic Harmonization, Trade Reform, and Regional Trade in SubSaharan Africa', A paper prepared for the AERC Collaborative project on *Regional Integration and Trade Liberalization in SSA* (Nairobi: African Economic Research Consortium).

Ogunkola, E.O. (1994) 'An Empirical Evaluation of Trade Potential in the Economic Community of West African States', final report (Nairobi: The African Economic Research Consortium).

Poyhonen, P. (1963) 'A Tentative Model for the Flow of Trade Between Countries', *Weltwirtschaftliches Archiv*, 90 (1).

Ravenhill, J. (1985) 'The Future of Regionalism in Africa', in R.I. Onwuka and A. Sesay (eds), *The Future of Regionalism in Africa* (New York: St. Martin's Press).

Rieger, H.C. (1985) 'ASEAN Cooperation and Intra-ASEAN Trade', ASEAN Economic Research Unit, Research Notes and Discussion Paper no. 57 (Singapore: Institute of South East Asian Studies).

Sanchez, A. (1987) 'Non-Tariff Barriers and Trade in the ASEAN', *ASEAN Economic Bulletin*, 4 (1).

Sen, A. and Z. Matuszewski (1991) 'Properties of maximum Likelihood Estimates of Gravity Model Parameters', *Journal of Regional Science*, 31 (4): 460–86.

Srivastava, R.K. and R.T. Green (1986) 'Determinants of Bilateral Trade Flows', *Journal of Business*, 59 (4): 623–40.

Tinbergen, J. (1962) *Shaping the World Economy: Suggestions for an International Economic Policy* (New York: The Twentieth Century Fund).

World Bank (1993) *The East Asian Miracle: Economic Growth and Public Policy* (New York: Oxford University Press).

Young, A. (1994) 'The tyranny of Numbers: Confronting the Statistical realities of the East Asian Growth Experience', presented at the CEPR Workshop on Growth, Les Arcs, Jan.

6 Regional Integration and the Bias Against Agriculture and Other 'Disadvantaged' Sectors in SubSaharan Africa*

Dean A. DeRosa

6.1 INTRODUCTION AND THE ECONOMIC SETTING

With few exceptions, the economic performance of subSaharan African countries during the past decade has been poor relative to other countries. Whereas the world economy grew at an average rate of about 3.0 per cent per annum and the developing countries at an average rate of about 3.3 per cent per annum, the mainly low-income countries of subSaharan Africa (SSA) grew at only about 2.1 per cent per annum (World Bank 1993b). In per capita terms, economic growth in the region was negative, about −1.2 per cent per annum (compared to 1.2 per cent for the world economy and 1.0 per cent for other developing countries), giving rise to the 'lost decade' as an epitaph describing the economic record of the region during the 1980s.

As mainly exporters of agricultural and other primary commodities, the SSA countries also witnessed considerable deterioration in their international terms of trade during the past two decades. In the minds of many, the adversities of the international economic environment, coupled with 'structural' impediments such as weak or inadequate physical and other social infrastructure, bear much of the blame for the dismal economic growth and development record of the countries in the region.

* This chapter was prepared as a paper for the Workshop on *Regional Integration and Trade Liberalization in Sub-Saharan Africa*, organized by the African Economic Research Consortium, 2–4 December 1993, Nairobi, Kenya. The assistance of Marcelle Thomas and helpful comments received from Richard Baldwin, Ibrahim Elbadawi, and David Greenaway, among other workshop participants, are gratefully acknowledged.

Other views of the countries' poor performance emphasize the equal, if not greater, importance of domestic economic policies that have misguided the allocation of resources in these countries and have limited their ability to adjust to new circumstances in the world economy. The SSA region, it is contended, is no less well endowed with productive resources than other regions where, under more liberal and 'open' economic policies, developing countries have faced the same adversities and yet prospered.

Prodded in many cases by the Bretton Woods institutions, policymakers in many African countries have begun to look to the more outward-orientated policies of the major industrial nations, as well as increasing numbers of developing countries, as prototypes for guiding reforms in their own economies. Combined with the adoption of more stable and prudent monetary and fiscal policies, 'structural adjustment' programmes are now widespread in SSA countries and typically share the primary goal of instituting greater reliance on competitive markets, unrestricted entry of producers and intermediate agents (for example, traders), and freely determined prices, to provide for the allocation of resources to more efficient uses and for greater consumer choice and sovereignty in the market place.

A frequent cornerstone of these programmes is the liberalization of the international trade and payments regime. The tariffication of quantitative restrictions, the lowering and unification of import (and export) tariff rates, and the elimination of exchange controls and administrative procedures governing imports and access to foreign exchange are viewed as essential ingredients for achieving greater economic efficiency and national welfare. In addition, reduced protection is expected to spur exports of non-traditional as well as traditional goods, by increasing the relative price of exportables to both importables and non-traded goods sufficiently to achieve external equilibrium at a higher level of import consumption.

Notwithstanding the expected benefits of trade liberalization and related economic reforms, achieving greater openness in SSA countries is still circumscribed by political considerations. Resistance to change is marshalled by vested economic interests in sheltered industries, as well as large government bureaucracies and parastatals. In the minds of policymakers there also remains substantial uncertainty about the magnitude of the expected benefits of economic reforms and unresolved issues concerning the optimal implementation of reform programmes. Reservations include, for instance, the proper 'timing' and 'sequencing' of trade policy changes in relation to one another, plus major reforms to domestic regulation of agriculture, industry and service sectors including commercial banking.

Appreciable uncertainty also surrounds the international environment in which the external economic relations of subSaharan countries are to be liberalized. Trade liberalization is politically easier to initiate when the global trading system is expanding at a faster rate. With the recent slow growth of the world economy and the failure of the Uruguay Round of multilateral trade negotiations, begun in 1986, to be concluded sooner than seven years after its initiation, circumstances have not been particularly favourable for undertaking unilateral trade liberalization.

Recent waning support for multilateralism, however, has renewed interest in possibilities for regional economic co-operation. This is true in both industrial countries (for example, the new European Union and the North American Free Trade Agreement) and less developed countries (namely, the new ASEAN Free Trade Area and plans for similar preferential trading areas in Latin America, South Asia and subSaharan Africa). In something of a challenge to the multilateral trading system, regional economic arrangements present a competing institutional setting, or 'paradigm', in which the liberalization of restrictive trade policies in developing countries might unfold (for example, see Bhagwati, 1991, 1992).

This chapter concerns the implications for the SSA countries of fostering closer economic relations with one another. The comparison is of regional trading arrangements as envisioned by established regional organizations for economic co-operation (Table 6.1) with non-discriminatory trading arrangements that underlie the normative theory of international trade and most-favoured-nation (MFN) principles of the General Agreement on Tariffs and Trade (GATT).[1] Of particular interest are the implications of regional economic integration for agriculture and other sectors whose comparative advantage lies in the relative abundance of arable land and other resources in the SSA countries. Incentives for greater production and exports in these sectors are often repressed by the indirect effects of inappropriate fiscal, monetary and foreign exchange policies. Also, industrialization and other import substitution policies distort relative prices of tradables and the real exchange rate between non-traded goods and exportables (for example, Krueger *et al.*, 1988).

Table 6.1   Organizations for economic co-operation in developing regions

Region	Organization (Member Countries)

SubSaharan Africa
Central African Customs and Economic Union (UDEAC – Cameroon, Central African Republic, Chad, Congo, Equatorial Guinea, Gabon)
Common Market for Eastern and Southern Africa (COMESA – Angola, Burundi, Comoros, Djibouti, Ethiopia, Kenya, Lesotho, Madagascar, Malawi, Mauritius, Mozambique, Namibia, Rwanda, Somalia, Sudan, Swaziland, Tanzania, Uganda, Zambia, Zimbabwe)
Economic Community of West African States (ECOWAS – Benin, Burkina, Cape Verde, Côte d'Ivoire, Gambia, Ghana, Guinea, Guinea-Bissau, Liberia, Mali, Mauritania, Niger, Nigeria, Senegal, Sierra-Leone, Togo)
Southern African Customs Union (SACU – Botswana, Lesotho, Namibia, South Africa, Swaziland)
Southern African Development Community (SADC – Angola, Botswana, Lesotho, Malawi, Mozambique, Namibia, South Africa, Swaziland, Tanzania, Zambia, Zimbabwe)

Asia
Asia Pacific Economic Co-operation (APEC – Australia, Brunei, Canada, China, Hong Kong, Indonesia, Japan, Korea, Malaysia, New Zealand, Philippines, Singapore, United States, Taiwan, Thailand)
Association of Southeast Asian Nations (ASEAN – Brunei, Indonesia, Malaysia, Philippines, Singapore, Thailand)
South Asian Association for Regional Co-operation (SAARC – Bangladesh, Bhutan, India, Maldives, Nepal, Pakistan, Sri Lanka)

Latin America
Andean Common Market (ANCOM – Bolivia, Colombia, Ecuador, Peru, Venezuela)
Caribbean Community (CARICOM – Antigua-Barbuda, Bahamas, Barbados, Belize, Dominica, Grenada, Guyana, Jamaica, Montserrat, St Kitts-Nevis, St Lucia, St. Vincent, Trinidad–Tobago)
Central American Common Market (CACM – Costa Rica, El Salvador, Guatemala, Honduras, Nicaragua)
Latin American Integration Association (LAIA – Argentina, Bolivia, Chile, Colombia, Ecuador, Mexico, Paraguay, Peru, Uruguay, Venezuela)
Southern Cone Common Market (MERCOSUR – Argentina, Brazil, Paraguay, Uruguay)

Middle-East
Co-operative Council for the Arab States of the Gulf (GCC – Bahrain, Kuwait, Oman, Qatar, Saudi Arabia, United Arab Emirates)
Council of Arab Economic Unity (CAEU – Egypt, Iraq, Jordan, Kuwait, Libya, Mauritania, Somalia, Sudan, Syria, United Arab Emirates, Yemen Arab Republic, Yemen P.D.R.)
Economic Co-operation Organization (ECO – Iran, Pakistan, Turkey)

Source: Union of International Associations (1987) and Torre and Kelly (1992).

The African Economies

In terms of their resource endowments and economic structures, the SSA countries bear a close resemblance to other low-income developing countries (Table 6.2). Particularly noteworthy in subSaharan Africa is the importance of agriculture and the still rather limited contribution of manufacturing to total output. At the same time, the SSA countries are distinct from other developing countries, as well as the major industrial countries. For example, they tend to be less densely populated, and they appear on the bottom (international) rungs of the education ladder. Finally, the low per capita income levels of the countries in subSaharan Africa may be taken as an indicator of the still limited accumulated stock of physical and human capital in the region, including physical and other social infrastructure.

These indicators of fundamental economic factors point to the importance in subSaharan Africa of arable land in particular, certain other natural resources and, to a somewhat lesser extent, unskilled labour in the vector of primary resource endowments. Thus, from both positive and normative perspectives, attempts to assess the implications of trade liberalization for these countries must take account of the extent to which production and exports are stimulated in goods and possibly tradable service sectors that employ intensively the primary factors that are relatively abundant.[2]

Emphasis in this chapter is given to the implications of trade liberalization for the agricultural sector following the contributions of Valdés (1973), Cavallo and Mundlak (1982), Krueger *et al.* (1988), Krueger (1992) and Bautista and Valdés (1993). These studies point to the special importance of agriculture for the economic growth and development of most low-income developing countries, and hence to the unfortunate bias against agriculture that import substitution and other inappropriate trade and macroeconomic policies have etched in the economic and political landscape of these countries. Thus, an important issue in assessing the implications of preferential (that is, regional) versus general (that is, non-discriminatory) approaches to trade liberalization is the extent to which policy-induced distortions to production and export incentives in agriculture and other potentially internationally-competitive sectors are reduced under these alternative approaches.

Table 6.2 Indicators of fundamental economic factors, 1989

| | Population (millions) | Population density (Pers/km²) | Education Index[a] | Per caput income ($US) | Structure of production (% of GDP) | | | | | |
| | | | | | Industry | | | Other Services | Merchandise trade | |
					Agriculture	All industries	Manu-facturing		Exports	Imports
Developing countries	4053	53	63	600	19	38	—	44	16	16
Low-income	2948	80	52	330	32	27	17	31	12	14
Middle-income	1105	27	142	2 040	12	36	—	50	18	18
subSaharan Africa	480	21	28	340	32	27	11	38	19	19
Low-income[b]	397	22	29	270	33	25	8	37	22	25
Middle-income[b]	54	14	34	870	27	30	—	44	30	23
Six most-populous economies[b]	253	30	31	270	34	30	8	35	23	26
Sahelian economies[b]	39	7	13	270	24	20	13	44	24	25
Oil-exporters[b]	130	40	41	460	27	38	9	35	31	27
East Asia[c]	1552	100	71	540	24	44	33	34	23	24
ASEAN, excl. Singapore	310	101	87	759	20	37	20	42	31	32
South Asia	1131	219	62	320	32	26	17	41	6	9
Europe, Middle East, North Africa	433	37	130	2 180	—	—	—	—	15	17
Latin America	421	21	133	1 950	—	—	—	—	14	10
Industrial countries	830	25	293	18 330	2[d]	34[d]	23[d]	64[d]	16	17

Notes

[a] Harbison-Myers index of human resource development calculated as the secondary enrolment rate plus five times the university enrolment rate, both calculated in their respective age cohorts.

[b] 1986 for education statistics and 1987 for all others

[c] Includes China.

[d] 1988

Sources: Harbison and Myers (1964), World Bank (1989, 1991), and UNCTAD (1991).

Plan of the Chapter

The remainder of this chapter is organized in three sections. Section 6.2 sets out a simple analytical framework for beginning to assess the sectoral impacts of protection, and reviews some quantitative evidence on protection in SSA countries and its implications for these countries' exports of agricultural and other goods. Section 6.3 considers the basic elements of co-operative economic policies to promote greater regional integration and trade, focusing on how these policies might contribute to lessening the bias against agriculture and other sectors. By way of drawing insights from the experiences of developing Asia, the main findings of a recent study of the economic implications of the new free trade area among ASEAN members are also reviewed. Finally, Section 6.4 offers a summary of the chapter and some final remarks.

6.2. PROTECTION AND THE BIAS AGAINST AGRICULTURE AND OTHER SECTORS

Economic Theory

The neo-classical theory of international trade is often represented by simple analytical models, such as the celebrated Heckscher, Ohlin and Samuelson (HOS) model. These models are often capable of providing profound insights into the determinants of international trade, the implications for production, trade and economic welfare of alternative economic policies and the political economy of who 'gains' and who 'loses' from protection and trade liberalization (for example, see Stolper and Samuelson, 1941).

In the context of economic development, early applications of the HOS model emphasized the abundance of unskilled labour, relative to physical and human capital, in the less developed countries. While the SSA countries may certainly be regarded as relatively scarcely endowed with physical and other accumulated capital, their relative abundance of primary resources is not strictly limited to basic labour. Along with many Latin American countries, the SSA countries are, broadly speaking, more abundantly endowed with arable land than with labour. Thus, the production of agricultural goods, including especially many tropical food commodities and agricultural raw materials, should be regarded as lying strongly within their comparative advantage.

Recent studies by Krueger, *et al.* (1988), Krueger (1992) and Bautista and Valdés (1993), among others, have found that restrictive import policies in combination with inflexible exchange rate regimes and the pursuit of unsustainable fiscal and monetary policies have systematically repressed market incentives (that is, domestic relative prices) for greater specialization in agricultural production and exports in many developing countries. This is over and above considerations for possible weaknesses in international markets for agricultural and related commodities of either a periodic or secular nature.[3]

These studies focus principally on the bias against agriculture arising from policy-induced distortions to the so-called real exchange rate, defined as the relative price of non-traded goods to exportables. In the analytical models underlying these studies, industrial protection and inappropriate monetary and fiscal policies result in 'overvalued' levels of the real exchange rate, causing the traded goods sector to be smaller than otherwise and the production and overseas sales of agricultural (and other) exportables to decline.[4] Notably, the external imbalances that arise with some regularity under managed foreign exchange regimes must frequently be controlled by additional administered restrictions on imports (and capital outflows). This gives rise to 'import compression' and further appreciation of the real exchange rate if policy-makers do not correct the unsustainable macroeconomic policies or do not allow the nominal exchange rate to adjust fully.

Industrial protection leads to similar repression of economic incentives to agricultural production and trade in the familiar HOS model.[5] Consider Figure 6.1, which depicts the production and consumption possibilities of a 'small' agricultural-exporting country. The country produces both manufactures (M) and agricultural goods (A), but its stock of both natural and accumulated primary factors of production – land, labour, and capital (inclusive of human capital, technology and social infrastructure) – is assumed to support greater production of food and other agricultural goods than manufactures over a wide range of possible relative prices. At the given international terms of trade Pa/Pm^*, the country produces at point P^* and consumes at a point such as C^*. This involves the (balanced) international exchange of the country's excess supply of agricultural goods (exports, Y^*Z^*) to meet its excess demand for manufactures (imports, X^*W^*).

Introducing import substitution policies (in the form of an *ad valorem* tariff on imports of manufactures) results in production and consumption occurring at points such as P and C, respectively. More specifically, in protecting local industry the import substitution policy causes

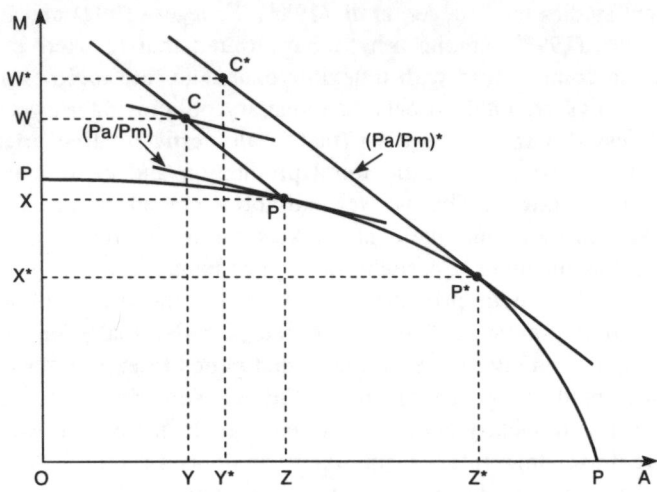

Figure 6.1   Equilibrium under free trade and protection

the domestic terms of trade *Pa/Pm* to decline and thereby provides the incentive to produce and consume a greater quantity of local manufactures. It also reduces the domestic terms of trade to a point below the international terms of trade for agriculture *Pa/Pm** and thus has the indirect effect of 'repressing' production (and exports) in the agricultural sector, as emphasized in the economic literature on the bias against agriculture.[6,7]

In variants of the HOS model featuring greater numbers of producing sectors, the implications of protection for other disadvantaged sectors might also be investigated. It is not always possible in such models to predict the commodity composition of trade based on familiar notions about the relative resource endowments of countries, on the one hand, and the factor intensities of efficient production of different goods, on the other hand (Vanek, 1968; Dixit and Norman, 1980; Deardorff, 1984; Ethier, 1984; Leamer, 1984). Nevertheless, protection of especially capital-intensive industries might still be expected to repress incentives for greater production and trade by other sectors as well as agriculture. These are sectors that rely importantly upon primary factors of production, such as basic labour and natural resources other than arable land, which are in greater relative abundance in subSaharan Africa than accumulated physical and human capital.

In the wider context of international flows of productive resources as well as goods, in which trade between countries especially in labour services may be regarded as a substitute for trade in goods (Mundell, 1957), restrictive trade policies often motivate unwelcome pressure for greater labour migration (and goods smuggling). Although hindered in varying degrees by natural physical obstacles to transporting resources across national boundaries and by the enforcement of criminal penalties against illicit trade, these pressures do alleviate some of the economic costs of domestic distortions resulting from protection.[8]

Quantitative Evidence

Protection

The relevance of the basic theory just reviewed may be seen in (nominal) protection statistics for a broad sample of African countries, from a data base on trade control measures in developing countries compiled by the United Nations Committee on Trade and Development (UNCTAD, 1987, 1988, 1989; DeRosa, 1992). The UNCTAD data are collected from official national sources, GATT documents and commercial reporting systems. They catalogue both tariff measures and major forms of non-tariff barriers as they existed in the late 1980s.[9] While tariffs and 'para-tariffs' (other fiscal charges applied to imports) are presented in familiar *ad valorem* terms, in what follows non-tariff measures are presented in terms of frequency ratios that measure the percentage of tariff-line items within an aggregate goods category affected by a given import regulation.

Overview Table 6.3 summarizes the average rates of nominal protection enforced in twenty-three subSaharan African countries. Together these accounted for nearly 60 per cent of the region's total exports and imports in 1987. The statistics for the countries are reported by income group, using population levels as weights in the computation of the group averages. The middle-income subSaharan countries are those with per caput income levels greater than $500. The low-income countries are sub-divided into two groups, with the dividing line being a per caput income level of $300.[10]

The low-income countries typically enforce the highest rates of protection, and the frequency of non-tariff measures is especially high. Because of widespread use of discretionary licensing of imports and monetary exchange controls (mainly advanced import deposit schemes and restrictive foreign exchange practices), the average frequency of

Table 6.3 Import restrictions in SSA countries, 1987 (%)[a]

Country	Tariff and para-tariffs		Frequency of non-tariff barriers[b]						
	Mean tariff	Total charges[c]	All NTBs	Quantitative restrictions			FER[d]	DCV	STM
				licence	quota	prohib.			
Low-income	30	34	89	51	3	3	40	—	14
Lowest-income	24	29	95	64	—	2	39	—	21
Zaire	22	22	100	3	—	—	100	—	—
Malawi	17	22	96	96	—	—	—	—	—
Mozambique	16	26	100	100	—	—	—	—	57
Tanzania	32	32	100	100	—	—	—	—	62
Burkina Faso	61	77	81	80	—	1	—	x	x
Madagascar	6	42	100	38	—	19	100	—	—
Burundi	37	37	100	100	—	—	17	—	—
Zambia	30	30	100	100	—	—	100	—	—
Uganda	20	20	100	100	—	—	—	—	14
Guinea	9	9	38	—	—	—	—	—	38
Upper-low-income	41	43	77	28	9	6	43	—	—
Somalia	31	31	100	5	—	1	100	—	—
Sierra Leone	26	26	100	100	—	—	100	—	—
Benin	37	49	100	100	5	4	—	x	x
C. African Rep.	32	39	5	2	—	1	—	x	x
Kenya	39	40	67	37	31	—	100	—	—
Sudan	57	57	100	9	—	1	100	—	—
Ghana	30	33	48	17	—	28	x	—	x

Middle-income	22	30	48	29	1	1	18	—
Senegal	34	34	7	4	1	1	—	x
Zimbabwe	9	26	100	100	—	—	100	x
Côte d'Ivoire	23	25	7	6	3	1	—	x
Congo	32	33	100	100	1	1	—	x
Cameroon	32	42	21	19	—	1	—	x
Angola	12	21	100	1	—	—	—	100
All countries	29	33	81	47	3	3	36	14

Notes:

FER = Foreign exchange restrictions

DCV = Decreed customs value

STM = State trading monopoly

[a] Statistics by country are simple averages of rates of protection across trade categories. Averages for country groups are computed using 1987 population levels as weights. Frequency ratios of NTBs denoted by 'x' are assumed equal to zero in computations of weighted averages.

[b] Percentage of tariff lines affected by NTBs, excluding restrictions on imports of alcohol and tobacco. Positive-valued NTB frequency ratios whose precise values are not possible to compute from the source document are denoted by 'x'.

[c] Customs duties plus customs surcharges and surtaxes, stamp taxes, certain other fiscal charges, and tax on foreign exchange transactions

[d] Advance imports deposits, multiple exchange rates, and licensing or other restrictions on the acquisition and use of foreign exchange.

Sources: UNCTAD Secretariat, Handbook of Trade Control Measures of Developing Countries, 1987 and Handbook 'Supplement, 1987 (Geneva, 1988).

NTBs is over 90 per cent in the lowest-income countries and over 75 per cent in the upper-low-income countries. By comparison, the frequency of NTBs is substantially lower in the middle-income countries, about 50 per cent.

Both tariff protection and the frequency of foreign exchange controls are highest in the upper-low-income countries. Whereas the middle and lowest-income countries enforce rates of tariff and total fiscal charges in the range of 20 per cent to 30 per cent, the group of upper-low-income countries enforces an average protection rate of about 40 per cent. This is due mainly to the high rates enforced in the two most populous countries in the group – Kenya and, particularly, Sudan. A similar pattern of protection is seen with respect to the application of foreign exchange controls. Among the seven upper-low-income countries, Somalia, Sierra Leone and Sudan impose exchange controls on all imports. Only Madagascar and Zambia among the larger sample of ten lowest-income countries and Zimbabwe among the sample of six middle-income countries impose exchange controls against imports so extensively.

Discretionary licensing of imports is by far the most widely applied quantitative restriction. Some countries, however, rely importantly on quotas (Kenya) and prohibitions (Madagascar and Ghana) to restrict imports. Other frequently encountered forms of non-tariff barriers include minimum import prices (decreed customs value) and state trading monopolies. Administered pricing of imports is most commonly practised in the higher-income countries, whereas state trading is widely practised throughout the countries examined. Except in Angola, Mozambique and Tanzania, where state monopolies controlled imports of nearly all goods in 1987, regulation of import prices and state trading generally occurs at appreciably lower frequency than either quantitative restrictions or foreign exchange controls.

While the economic implications of tariffs and other trade taxes are relatively straightforward, those of non-tariff barriers are more indirect and difficult to assess (for example, Deardorff and Stern, 1985).

Nonetheless, NTBs have been regarded traditionally as particularly trade-distorting and hence very costly in economic terms, both to individual countries and to the global trading system.[11] To individual countries, they are costly because they limit the extent to which the price system operates to allocate resources for production and consumption in the economy. They are also costly because they tend to be associated with highly discretionary administrative systems that encourage rent-seeking activities.[12] From a multilateral perspective, the economic costs of non-tariff barriers are magnified when large numbers of countries adopt administered protection systems, either in retaliation or through imitation.

Structure of protection Table 6.4 provides a view of protection in SSA countries in several broad categories of primary commodities and manufactures: foods, agricultural raw materials, fuels, minerals and nonferrous metal ores, chemicals, iron and steel products, machinery and equipment and a residual category of other manufactures. For expository purposes, the data are presented solely in aggregate terms for the three groups of countries defined previously.

With regard to tariffs and para-tariffs, the structure of nominal protection is remarkably similar among all three groups of countries. This is despite the fact that generally the upper-low-income countries enforce the highest tariff rates among the sample SubSaharan countries. Except perhaps for the lowest-income countries, the sample countries tend to apply higher tariff rates against manufactures than against primary commodities, with labour-intensive manufactures typically the most highly protected category.

This pattern of protection is not unusual in developing countries; like many industrial countries, developing countries tend to enforce escalating rates of protection against labour-intensive products.[13] Why labour-intensive products are so heavily protected, especially by comparison with other manufactured goods in which African and other developing countries have a lower comparative advantage, is sometimes puzzling. An explanation frequently given is that organized labour in the 'modern sector' of these countries enjoys a wage rate higher than its social opportunity cost. This encourages the adoption of more capital-intensive technologies than otherwise and reduces competitiveness except behind high tariff walls.[14]

High tariff rates are also applied to imports of food in the subSaharan countries. Presumably reflecting concerns for food security, these high rates of protection are enforced in order to encourage sufficient domestic production to meet domestic demand as fully as possible. Notably, however, food security policies are often coupled with administered price systems to ensure low prices of agricultural staples especially for urban dwellers, and therefore self-sufficiency is not always achieved.

Across other categories of traded goods, there is less apparent variation in the tariff rates enforced by the subSaharan countries. Mineral fuels and chemicals tend to enjoy the lowest rates of tariff protection, because imports of these goods are widely regarded as essential inputs

Table 6.4 Import restrictions in SSA countries by traded goods category, 1987 (%)^a

Commodity^b	Tariffs, para-tariffs			Frequency of non-tariff barriers^c					
	Mean tariff	Total charges	All NTBs	Quantitative restrictions			Foreign exchange restr.	Decreed import value^d	State trading monopoly^d
				licence	quota	prohib.			
Lowest-income countries									
Primary commodities	26	31	94	61	—	2	39	—	19
Food	34	41	94	59	—	4	39	BF	22
Agr. raw materials	21	26	95	64	—	1	38	—	12
Mineral fuels	18	22	94	61	—	—	39	BF	18
Mineral, metal ores	17	21	92	62	—	—	38	—	19
Manufactures	23	28	96	64	—	1	39	—	22
Chemicals	16	21	95	62	—	—	38	—	25
Iron and steel	17	20	96	70	—	—	38	—	30
Mach. and equip.	19	23	97	68	—	—	38	—	24
Oth. manufactures	30	36	97	66	—	2	39	—	21
All goods	24	29	95	64	—	2	39	—	21
Upper-low-income countries									
Primary commodities	39	41	80	26	12	10	43	BE	BE
Food	46	47	89	34	17	10	43	CF(s)	GH(r,s)
Agr. raw materials	38	43	75	12	13	11	43	CF(t)	—
Mineral fuels	25	26	64	22	2	5	43	—	—
Mineral, metal ores	32	34	72	24	4	8	43	—	—
Manufactures	42	43	76	28	8	4	43	—	—
Chemicals	29	30	56	15	1	1	43	CF(p)	—
Iron and steel	35	36	81	29	5	9	43	—	—
Mach. and equip.	32	34	72	31	2	2	43	—	BE(26)
Other manufactures	52	55	86	33	15	6	43	BE, CF(t)	CF(t), GH
			77	28	9	6	43	—	

				Middle-income countries[c] [d]					
Primary commodities	20	27	48	28	1	1	18	—	—
Food	23	29	49	29	2	1	18	SE, CI, CG(s), CM(s)	AG* ZW(m, w), SE(r), CG(s)
Agr. raw materials	18	29	49	29	2	1	18	SE	AG*, CG(t)
Mineral fuels	16	23	49	29	6	—	18	SE, CI	AG*
Mineral, metal ores	19	26	43	24	1	—	18	—	AG*
Manufactures	23	31	48	28	1	—	18	—	—
Chemicals	16	23	46	27	1	—	18	CG(p), CM(p)	AG*
Iron and steel	20	28	44	24	2	—	18	CI	AG*
Mach. and equip.	17	24	44	26	1	—	18	—	AG*, CG
Oth. manufactures	30	39	51	31	—	1	18	SE(t), CI(t), CG(t), CM(t)	AG*, SE, CG
All goods	22	29	48	29	1	1	18	—	—

Notes:

a Averages for a sample of twenty-three subSaharan countries, using 1987 population levels as weights.

b Commodity sectors are defined according to the Standard International Trade Classification (SITC) system as follows: food (0 + 1 + 22 + 4), agricultural raw materials (2 less (22 + 27 + 28), mineral fuels (3), mineral and non-ferrous metal ores (27 + 28 + 68), chemicals (5), iron and steel (67), machinery and equipment (7), other manufactures (6 + 8) less (67 + 68).

c Percentage of tariff lines affected by NTBs, excluding restrictions against imports of alcohol and tobacco. Country abbreviations are reported in cases where it is not possible to compute the appropriate value of the frequency ratio from the source document.

d Country abbreviations in the column refer to Angola (AG), Ghana (GH), Zimbabwe (ZW), Benin (BE), Burkina Faso (BF), Cameroon (CM), Central African Republic (CF), Congo (CG), Côte d'Ivoire (CI), and Senegal (SE). Letters in parentheses refer to specific commodities and goods: maize (m), rice (r), sugar (s), wheat (w), soap (p), and textiles and apparel (t), and asterisks denote frequency ratios of 100 per cent.

to local production (and frequently exports) and face little competition from local producers. At the other end of the spectrum, agricultural raw materials and iron and steel products frequently enjoy higher rates of tariff protection (after foods and labour-intensive manufactures).[15]

With regard to non-tariff barriers, the subSaharan countries appear to enforce quantitative restrictions with considerable frequency across all categories of primary commodities and manufactures, following much the same commodity pattern revealed by the data on tariffs and other fiscal measures. Thus, non-tariff barriers tend to reinforce the structure of protection defined by fiscal measures, but at considerably higher economic costs in terms of the limited transparency of the import controls and extensive involvement of official bureaucracies.[16]

Despite their pervasiveness, some selectivity is apparent in the enforcement of NTBs in the statistics describing the frequency of import price-control measures and state trading monopolies. Imports of cereals (maize, rice and wheat), sugar and, among manufactures, textiles, apparel and toiletries (mainly soaps and household detergents) are frequently singled out for regulation by national authorities. Many of these goods have high profiles in international trade disputes and negotiations. As mentioned previously, food imports are frequently regulated in connection with the food security interests of countries, raising objections from more resource-abundant countries that export foods and related agricultural commodities. Textiles and apparel also have a long history of engendering trade restrictions because they are among the first manufactures countries produce and export.[17]

Trade liberalization

The levels of protection revealed in the data for the subSaharan countries are appreciably higher than those for other developing countries as well as the major industrial countries. SSA countries enforced average tariff rates of about 30 per cent and NTB frequency ratios of about 80 per cent during the late-1980s. Developing countries as a group enforced average tariff rates of about 20 per cent and NTB frequency ratios of about 40 per cent. Average protection levels in the industrial countries were lower still. The industrial countries enforced average tariff rates of less than 5 per cent and NTB frequency ratios of about 20 per cent (Erzan *et al.* 1989).

The quantitative implications of protection for the export performance of SSA countries have been considered previously by the author, using a simple multi-commodity trade model that incorporates a non-

Table 6.5 Price elasticity values

	Foods	Ag. raw materials	Mineral fuels	Minerals, metal ores	Manufactures
Import demand	−0.75	−0.75	−0.50	−0.75	−1.25
Export supply	1.00	1.00	0.50	0.50	1.50

traded goods sector and hence determines changes in the real exchange rate as well as relative prices of exports and imports (DeRosa, 1992). The analysis gauged the effects of reducing tariffs and other fiscal charges to a uniform rate of 10 per cent, while simultaneously increasing administered imports (that is, those restricted by NTBs) by 25 per cent in quantity terms. Estimates of medium-term import demand and export supply price elasticities are shown in Table 6.5.

The simulation results indicate that general trade liberalization by the twenty-three sample countries would increase their combined total exports by about $2.7 billion per annum, at 1985 prices (Table 6.6). In proportional terms, total exports of the countries increase by about 33 per cent on average, in both value and volume terms.[18] Because of their higher rates of protection, the low-income countries experience the greatest (proportional) increase in total exports, about 37 per cent. Though protection is lower in the middle-income countries, these countries also experience an appreciable increase in total exports, about 12 per cent.[19]

Consistent with the bias against agriculture hypothesis, producers of primary commodities are found to have the largest absolute gains in export earnings. At the same time, the multi-sector model also predicts that import liberalization would promote greater proportional expansion of non-traditional than traditional exports. This prediction follows from the model's assumption of a higher elasticity of export supply for manufactures than for primary commodities, and smaller base-period level of non-traditional than traditional exports. Nonetheless, it illustrates that protection inhibits possibilities for subSaharan countries to achieve their often-stated economic goal of achieving greater export diversification.

The gains in economic welfare, computed on the basis of familiar Harberger triangles for consumer and producer surpluses (for example, Harberger, 1971), are significantly less than the potential value of expanded trade. The largest part of the welfare gains is associated with the expansion of trade in primary commodities. Indeed, the detailed

Table 6.6 Effects of import liberalization in SSA countries

	Real exchange rate[a]	International trade						Value	Economic welfare: Gain in consumer and producer surplus		
		Volume (%)						All goods			
		Primary commodities		Manufactures		All goods		All goods Exports (imports) ($USm.)[b]	Primary commodities ($USm.)[b]	Manufactures ($USm.)[b]	All goods (% GDP)
		Exports	Imports	Exports	Imports	Exports	Imports				
Low-income	-27.80	34.5	21.7	57.8	22.6	37.3	21.8	1670.0	405.5	158.7	1.2
Lowest-income	-27.27	32.6	21.9	56.3	23.5	36.1	22.0	976.1	209.4	106.5	1.3
Zaire	-19.22	14.2	25.0	35.7	25.0	16.5	25.0	252.2	41.3	23.2	1.3
Malawi	-21.69	27.6	20.3	41.5	24.0	28.3	20.4	68.5	11.1	6.0	1.8
Mozambique	-39.06	57.1	25.0	96.1	25.0	75.0	25.0	113.8	28.0	26.2	1.7
Tanzania	-33.99	47.6	25.0	77.3	25.0	49.7	25.0	165.5	45.3	17.2	1.1
Burkina Faso	-44.20	79.1	1.0	118.8	17.8	82.4	2.4	30.8	13.3	3.7	1.8
Madagascar	-28.72	38.2	25.0	60.4	25.0	40.5	25.0	116.0	28.5	11.1	1.7
Burundi	-33.86	50.2	25.0	76.8	25.0	51.9	25.0	56.3	17.1	5.0	2.3
Zambia	-21.63	14.2	25.0	41.4	25.0	14.8	25.0	93.4	13.2	9.5	1.0
Uganda	-13.57	15.7	25.0	23.5	25.0	15.7	25.0	62.8	9.8	4.2	0.3
Guinea	-6.37	3.5	-1.2	10.2	6.0	3.6	-1.1	16.6	1.9	0.3	0.1
Upper-low-income	-28.72	37.9	21.2	60.4	20.9	39.5	21.3	693.8	196.0	52.2	1.1
Somalia	-58.26	133.6	25.0	209.3	25.0	137.8	25.0	57.7	41.7	6.4	2.1
Sierra Leone	-16.53	14.5	25.0	29.7	25.0	19.5	25.0	28.5	3.0	3.4	0.5
Benin	-41.86	57.6	25.0	108.0	25.0	58.9	25.0	94.6	38.3	8.1	4.8
Central African Rep.	-8.17	8.8	8.2	13.3	22.0	10.3	12.7	11.0	0.4	0.8	0.2
Kenya	-16.11	17.2	18.8	28.8	15.8	18.5	18.4	176.8	21.6	11.0	0.6
Sudan	-34.98	53.7	25.0	80.7	25.0	54.8	25.0	264.3	85.4	19.9	1.5
Ghana	-10.87	11.1	17.8	18.3	18.0	11.5	17.8	60.9	5.6	2.7	0.2

Middle-income	−13.12	10.7	13.9	22.6	17.7	11.7	13.9	984.9	119.1	74.5	0.6
Senegal	−11.82	11.8	8.4	20.0	0.6	12.7	7.5	42.2	4.2	1.8	0.2
Zimbabwe	−17.97	19.2	25.0	32.8	25.0	23.2	25.0	217.8	31.0	24.2	1.2
Côte d'Ivoire	−5.03	5.0	7.0	7.9	11.5	5.3	7.4	139.0	6.6	5.1	0.2
Congo	−19.48	12.5	25.0	36.3	25.0	13.3	25.0	145.1	22.0	12.7	1.6
Cameroon	−9.91	7.1	4.2	16.5	21.5	7.2	4.4	178.6	10.2	11.8	0.3
Angola	−19.74	12.4	25.0	36.8	25.0	12.4	25.0	262.2	45.0	18.8	0.9
All countries	−25.43	30.0	20.2	51.1	21.7	32.5	20.3	2654.8	524.5	233.2	1.1

Notes: Effects are simulated by a multi-sector model for each country under the assumption that import duties are reduced to 10 per cent and non-tariff barriers are liberalized to increase the volume of administered imports by 25 per cent.
[a] Price of non-traded goods relative to exportables
[b] Per annum at 1985 prices

Source: DeRosa (1992).

multi-sector model results underlying those reported in Table 6.6 reveal that the welfare gains to commodity exporters (producers) are about twice the magnitude of those of importers (consumers) of manufactured goods. By comparison, the welfare gains associated with imports of primary commodities are appreciable but smaller in magnitude, and those associated with exports of manufactures are the smallest.

The quantitative data and empirical results summarized here, on the magnitude of protection in subSaharan Africa and the potential economic gains from trade liberalization, support many important aspects of the basic theory presented at the outset of this section. In particular, they support the contention that the high rates of protection found in many subSaharan countries during the late-1980s were an important factor in the low productivity of agriculture and poor performance of exports observed for these countries during the previous decade.

6.3. REGIONAL INTEGRATION

Policy-makers in subSaharan Africa have a keen, and long-standing, interest in promoting regional integration, derived from their view that the global trading system is unfavourable to producers of primary commodity exports. The system could become even more unfavourable in the wake of the conclusion of the Uruguay Round of multilateral trade negotiations for two reasons. One reason is the erosion of trade preferences extended by the industrial countries to sub-Saharan African countries under bilateral and multilateral accords. The second is the expected increase of international prices for food commodities under the terms of the agreed liberalization of world trade in agriculture. In addition, SSA has an extensive history of co-operation efforts, manifest today in the number of regional organizations for promoting regional economic co-operation (Table 6.1).[20] Thus, the implications of regional trading arrangements among sub-Saharan countries, featuring the liberalization of trade within the region on a preferential rather than general (that is, nondiscriminatory) basis, are of widespread interest.

Economic Theory Once Again

As reviewed by Lyakurwa *et al.* (1993), a vast economic literature on theoretical and applied analytical aspects of economic integration has emerged from the seminal work on the 'customs union issue' by Viner (1950) and, later, Meade (1955), Lipsey (1957, 1960) and Balassa (1961).

Using two original concepts that have come to be familiar, trade creation and trade diversion, Viner succeeded in demonstrating that customs unions and free trade areas need not always be welfare-improving.

The present discussion considers regional trading arrangements through the simple neoclassical framework introduced in the previous section.[21] Figure 6.2(a) depicts a regional trading arrangement in which the country specified in Figure 6.1 forms a free trade area with a second country from the same region. The production possibilities of the second country are represented by the *PP*-curve, which portrays the second country as identical to the first country in terms of *relative* resource endowments. The production possibilities of the two countries differ in scale, however, reflecting an underlying difference in the absolute size of their respective endowments of primary factors of production. Like the first country, the second country is assumed to forgo production at the free trade point P^* and to enforce import restrictions that promote greater domestic production of manufactures. Thus, equilibrium production under protection occurs at point P at the domestic terms of trade *Pa/Pm*, which are lower than the international terms of trade Pa/Pm*.

The terms of trade governing production and consumption in the first and second countries, Pa/Pm and *Pa/Pm*, are not necessarily the same. Their relative magnitudes depend upon the restrictiveness of the trade measures enforced in the first versus the second country. If protection levels are the same in both countries, relative prices will be the same in both countries, and there will be no incentive for intraregional trade. If the first country, however, maintains a higher (lower) level of protection than the second country, the relative price of agricultural goods will be lower (higher) in the first country than the second country, and there will be some incentive for trade between the two countries, on either an official or unofficial basis. Specifically, the first country will tend to exchange exports of agricultural goods (manufactures) for imports of manufactures (agricultural goods) accordingly as Pa/Pm $<(>)$ *Pa/Pm*.

Under a free trade arrangement between the two countries, trade with third countries (that is, countries outside of the regional trading bloc) would be diverted in some measure, if not substantially. Assuming no other barriers to trade than political ones, the domestic terms of trade in the two countries would converge at a level between Pa/Pm and *Pa/Pm* in order to accommodate the adjustment of production, consumption and trade. Economic welfare in the two countries, however, would not necessarily be improved. In Figure 6.2(a), the well-being of

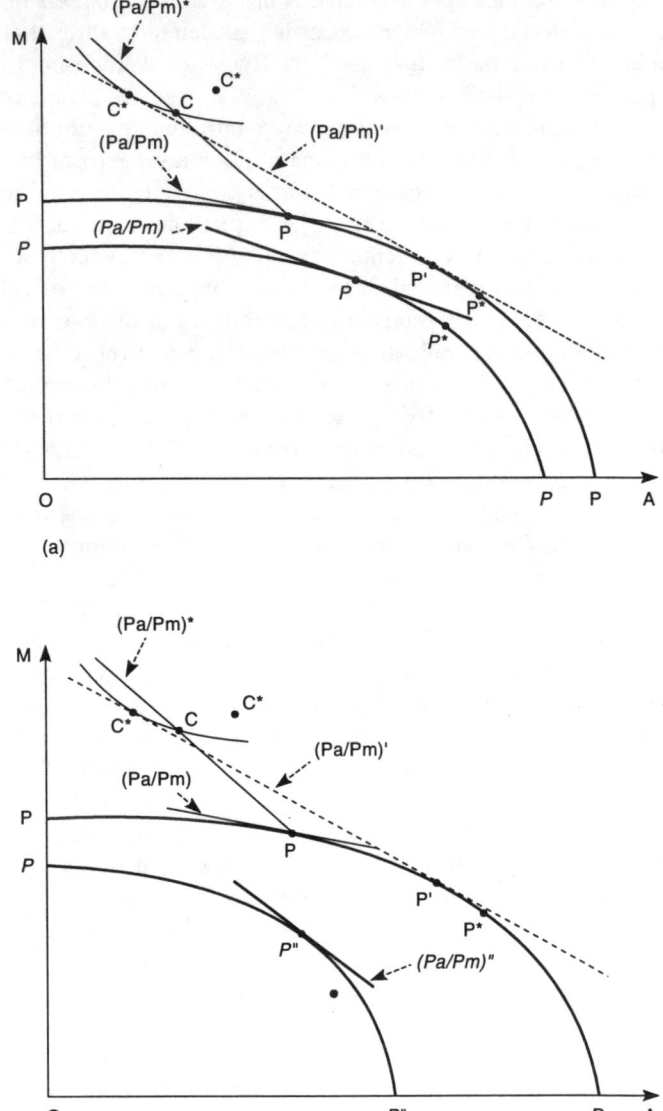

Figure 6.2   Equilibrium under a regional trading arrangement

the first country is not improved unless the intra-bloc terms of trade are greater than the terms of trade depicted by the dashed line (Pa/Pm′). In this case, the new equilibrium point for production would lie between P′ and P*, and the new equilibrium point for consumption would occur at a higher level of national economic welfare than that corresponding to point C.

These results demonstrate the fundamental importance of the complementarity of relative factor endowments, and hence differences in comparative advantage, among the countries forming a preferential trading arrangement. If the first country allies itself with one or more countries that have relative factor endowments very similar to its own – that is, other agricultural exporting countries – the intra-bloc terms of trade are unlikely to exceed Pa/Pm′. Only if the alliance is one in which members are marked by considerable complementarity of natural and accumulated factor endowments would the regional trading arrangement be likely to result in a significant reduction in the bias against agricultural production and trade and to yield an appreciable improvement in the economic welfare. This is ironic, because in such circumstances the members of the trading alliance would be more likely to enjoy terms of trade approximating those available to them under free trade – that is, Pa/Pm*.

Foreign Trade Barriers, Structural Impediments and Other Considerations

During an earlier period of widespread interest in economic co-operation among developing countries, Cooper and Massell (1965) and Johnson (1965) emphasized that countries often have non-economic objectives in establishing regional trading and other economic arrangements, thus transcending the normative focus of much of the literature on economic integration. Notwithstanding this, recent policy discussions and economic research have both pointed to some substantive reasons why regional trading arrangements among developing countries might deserve greater consideration. These include the existence of important barriers to trade outside of the region, 'structural bottlenecks' and uncertainty surrounding especially year-to-year levels of production of staple foods within the region. Another reason cited is the complementary nature of resources among neighbouring countries seeking to establish closer economic relations.[22]

With regard to extra-regional trade barriers, increased protection in the major industrial countries or, in the case of commodity-exporting developing countries, the 'dumping' of agricultural surpluses on world markets by industrial countries, sustains the view that greater integration with the world economy does not offer clear advantages to less developed countries. In this vein, Wonnacott and Wonnacott (1981, 1992) point out that at the margin, foreign protection and its contribution to weaker international terms of trade for developing (or other) countries make membership in regional trading arrangements more attractive, namely, by lowering the critical terms of trade Pa/Pm' in Figure 6.2(a). Similarly, significant natural barriers to extra-regional trade, reflected for instance in high transportation costs for either exports or imports, would increase the likelihood that regional trading arrangements might improve the welfare of countries forming co-operative economic blocs.[23]

Recent studies of the possibilities for greater integration of food grain and other markets for farm products in subSaharan Africa (Koester, 1986; Badiane, 1991; Delgado and Badiane, 1992; Valdés and Muir-Leresche, 1993) suggest that uncertainties of nature surrounding the production and trade of primary commodities and structural impediments found in many low-income African countries provide substantive bases for the establishment of welfare-enhancing regional trading arrangements.

With regard to uncertainty, drought and other natural calamities often result in periodic, but geographically random, shortfalls in annual harvests of food and other agricultural commodities. In Figure 6.2(b), the possibility of such adverse developments befalling the second country is represented by the alternative production possibilities schedule PP". In the calamitous state of nature, equilibrium production under protection in the second country occurs at P" at a sharply higher level of domestic relative prices (Pa/Pm" > Pa/Pm). Accordingly, in the circumstances depicted, a greater probability arises that a free trade area between the two countries would result in intra-bloc terms of trade that are sufficiently high to be welfare-improving in the first country. In the second country, economic welfare might still be expected to decline, but less precipitously because the free trade area would afford the country the security of access to ample food supplies, at lower relative prices than otherwise during drought and other adverse harvest times.

Structural bottlenecks and, more generally, differences in physical and other social infrastructure between countries with otherwise similar economies might also give rise to greater intra-regional trade. In Figure 6.2(b), with structural bottlenecks the possibilities for agricultural production in the second country are again 'foreshortened' in relation to their potential.[24] The factors contributing to lower output of agricultural and other primary commodities are important to note. As documented in 'studies of impediments to greater agricultural productivity, important components of the infrastructure serving production, distribution and marketing of agricultural products are often inadequate in many low-income and other developing countries (for example, Lele, 1991). This infrastructure has many facets, including transportation and communications networks, rural credit markets and institutional arrangements. These involve not only the organization and regulation of agricultural input and output markets, but also the tenure and property rights of individual economic agents over agricultural lands, waterways and irrigation systems.

Poor rural roadways and parastatal marketing boards for primary commodities provide two specific examples of structural impediments that in Figure 6.2(a) would be expected to impair economic incentives for agricultural production in the second country. These impediments would give rise (again) to the production possibilities curve PP'' and the wide difference in the relative price of agricultural goods between the two countries illustrated. In this case, however, whether the creation of a free trade area would result in greater intra-regional trade would depend upon whether the inadequacies of the infrastructure serving the rural economy in the second country were less binding upon the possibilities for intra-regional trade than wider international trade. If overland routes from surplus agricultural areas to markets in neighbouring countries were shorter or more passable than, say, trunk routes to port facilities for overseas trade, or if intra-regional trade in agricultural commodities were not required to pass through the parastatal marketing system, the free trade area would expand intra-bloc trade and tend to eliminate the differences in the relative price of agricultural goods between the two countries. In other circumstances, the creation of the preferential trading area would lead to no expansion of intra-regional trade or adjustment in domestic relative prices without the simultaneous elimination of the underlying structural impediments.

Finally, with regard to resource complementarities, the probability that a preferential trading arrangement among developing countries will be welfare-improving increases if the countries forming the arrangement are more dissimilar in their relative endowments of primary resources than depicted in Figure 6.2(a). This might be the case, for example, if the countries are drawn from completely different developing regions, as emphasized by Lewis and the Group of 77 in proposals for expanding South–South trade (Lewis, 1980; UNCTAD, 1985).

Still more favourable circumstances occur if the countries differ substantially in their level of economic development, as in the case of NAFTA (for example, Saborio, 1992), proposals for an Asia-Pacific free trade area (APEC, 1993), and the increasingly important case of South Africa and its neighbouring countries in the Southern Africa region (Aspen Institute, 1993; Davies *et al.*, 1993). In such cases, the relative resource endowments of the countries forming the free trade area are more complementary and thus would be expected to result in gains from trade more closely approximating those that the countries would enjoy by reducing their levels of protection on a non-discriminatory basis.

Beyond the possibilities just enumerated, other opportunities for expanded, welfare-enhancing trade among developing countries in close proximity to one another may exist. Indeed, not unlike the expectation that opportunities for mutually benefical exchange of services exist among most groups of individuals, beneficial opportunities for expanded trade among most groups of neighbouring countries are likely to abound, especially where the countries enforce high levels of protection. In this vein, an excellent example is provided by Pearson and Ingram (1980) who investigated the opportunities for greater intra-industry trade between Ghana and Côte d'Ivoire arising from the existence of unrealized internal economies of scale and hence domestic divergences between private and social costs in the highly sheltered markets of the two countries. In the context of the analysis here, however, at greater issue is whether the gains from expanded intra-regional trade are of comparable magnitude to those available from greater integration with the world economy.[25]

A final caveat is that the analysis here is predominantly static in nature. Longer-term considerations related to the dynamic process of investment, changes in international comparative advantage and agricultural (and general economic) growth are also undoubtedly important in the context of regional integration. Recent advances have been made in regard to the economic theory of 'dynamic gains' from trade, contributed mainly by Baldwin (1989) – with important inspiration from the new endogenous growth theory (Lucas, 1988; Krugman, 1988; Romer, 1990; Mankiw *et al.*, 1992) as discussed by Baldwin (1993). Nevertheless, there is still little consensus on how to treat dynamic factors in quantitative models of intra-regional or international trade. Traditionally, however, applied static analysis of international trade relations has not been far divorced from concerns for dynamic gains from international trade. Specifically, static economic gains in production and consumption have frequently been held to be necessary precursors for realizing greater economic gains related to investment and long-term economic growth. This is particularly the case with the observed economic vitality of developing countries that have maintained more open trading regimes, such as the countries of East and South-east Asia (World Bank, 1993a).[26]

The ASEAN Free Trade Area: Quantitative Estimates

While insights from economic theory are important, policy-makers are often influenced more by 'tangible' estimates from applied economic analysis. Unfortunately, little quantitative work of a comprehensive nature has been undertaken to assess the implications of closer economic relations in subSaharan Africa. For comparison with regional trading arrangements in other developing regions, the remainder of this section considers the results of a recent quantitative analysis of the new free trade area of the ASEAN, whose members consists of Brunei, Singapore, and four countries abundant in natural resources and labour – the so-called ASEAN-4 – Indonesia, Malaysia, the Philippines, and Thailand (DeRosa, 1995).

The basic elements of the ASEAN Free Trade Area (AFTA) plan are straightforward.[27] Under what is termed the common effective preferential tariff scheme, each ASEAN country is to reduce its import tariff walls, beginning in 1995. During the first five years of the plan, tariff levels are to be reduced substantially. Then, during the remaining three years of the plan, each member country will reduce its tariff levels to a range of 0–5 per cent. Although the scheme makes provisions for safeguard measures in cases of 'serious injury' to domestic producers, it explicitly calls for the simultaneous elimination of quantitative restrictions and other non-tariff barriers.

In an important institutional innovation, the plan singles out ten to fifteen categories of goods for accelerated reductions in protection (Table 6.7). The group of products is an important mixture of industrial products of keen interest to exporters and policy-makers in the ASEAN countries, but notably does not include agricultural or other primary commodities. The levels of protection associated with the products identified for accelerated trade liberalization are similar, on average, to protection for all manufactures in the ASEAN countries. Also, in many cases non-tariff barriers are enforced with appreciable frequency, reinforcing the importance of explicitly liberalizing NTBs as well as tariff measures.

Table 6.7 Manufactures for accelerated trade liberalization under the AFTA plan and ASEAN import restriction

Selected manufactures	SITC[a]	Indonesia	Malaysia	Philippines	Singapore	Thailand
				Average rate of tariffs plus para-tariffs, 1987 (frequency ratio of non-tariff barriers) (%)		
Vegetable oils	22 + 42	29.3 (100.0)	4.6 (0.0)	31.4 (26.0)	0.0 (4.0)	49.7 (96.0)
Cement, ceramic and glass products, and gems and jewelery	66	26.1 (100.0)	18.3 (13.4)	40.5 (33.5)	0.0 (0.0)	48.1 (8.0)
Chemicals, plastics	5	11.0 (100.0)	9.4 (3.0)	23.4 (47.7)	0.0 (49.0)	35.5 (6.0)
Pharmaceuticals	54	4.8 (100.0)	3.3 (0.0)	17.5 (95.0)	0.0 (95.0)	30.5 (0.0)
Fertilizers	56	0.0 (100.0)	0.6 (0.0)	22.6 (100.0)	0.0 (0.0)	10.0 (0.0)
Rubber products	62	10.3 (66.1)	32.6 (0.0)	33.7 (46.3)	0.0 (0.0)	52.0 (0.0)
Leather products	61 + 83	28.2 (100.0)	27.5 (0.0)	38.9 (29.4)	0.2 (0.0)	64.1 (0.0)
Pulp	64	29.4 (84.5)	16.4 (0.0)	40.5 (57.9)	0.0 (0.0)	40.7 (21.5)
Textiles	65 + 84	32.7 (87.5)	28.9 (0.5)	48.2 (12.8)	1.7 (8.5)	61.5 (0.9)
Electronics, copper cathodes	76 + 77	25.2 (80.5)	20.5 (5.4)	37.4 (98.1)	0.0 (11.8)	43.3. (15.6)
Wooden furniture	82	42.2 (100.0)	40.4 (0.0)	52.1 (46.4)	2.2 (0.0)	63.6 (0.0)

Memorandum items:						
Primary commodities	(0 – 4) + 58	14.7	8.7	31.9	0.1	38.0
		(98.9)	(4.5)	(40.5)	(15.3)	(24.4)
Manufactures	(5 – 8) – 68	19.6	16.2	33.5	0.4	42.5
		(93.1)	(3.2)	(46.3)	(14.1)	(7.8)
Selected manufactures	—	22.8	19.3	36.3	0.4	46.4
		(92.0)	(1.9)	(54.5)	(12.0)	(14.3)
All goods	0 – 9	18.2	14.3	33.1	0.3	41.2
		(94.7)	(3.7)	(44.9)	(14.7)	(12.4)

Note. [a] Standard International Trade Classification divisions.

Source: Singapore Declaration of 1992 (Singapore: Fourth ASEAN Summit, January 1992).

The AFTA plan discriminates against goods imported from outside of the ASEAN region. Moreover, in emphasizing the liberalization of intra-bloc trade in manufactures, it may presage eventual reluctance on the part of the ASEAN countries to implement the plan with respect to agriculture. To investigate the implications of these aspects of the plan, and especially whether the new trading pact should be expected to expand economic relations among the ASEAN countries in a manner consistent with reducing the bias against agriculture and other sectors with strong comparative advantage in the ASEAN countries, the ASEAN trade simulation model was developed to gauge empirically the medium-term to long-term effects of the new free trade area on economy-wide and sectoral variables (Table 6.8).

The ASEAN trade simulation model is patterned after the specifications of the 'Michigan model' of world production and trade (Deardorff and Stern 1986) and is similar in a number of regards to other multisector CGE models applied widely in analysing trade and development policy issues (for example, Dervis *et al.*, 1982). Notably, the model accounts explicitly for the incidence of non-tariff as well as tariff barriers in the ASEAN countries, thereby enabling quantification of the effects of simultaneously reducing these barriers on either a preferential or non-discriminatory basis.[28]

Four scenarios are considered using the simulation model, depicting three variants of the AFTA plan plus a fourth policy option, namely, pursuing general trade liberalization in the ASEAN countries on a non-discriminatory rather than preferential basis.

The first two scenarios represent basic variants of the AFTA plan announced in January 1992, namely, complete removal of tariffs and non-tariff barriers against intra-ASEAN trade in the categories of manufactures identified in Table 6.7 (Scenario I) and all categories of manufactures (Scenario II). The third scenario (Scenario III) represents the variant of the AFTA plan endorsed by the ASEAN economic ministers in late-1994, in which barriers to intra-ASEAN trade are removed against all categories of trade, including trade in agriculture and other primary commodity sectors.

The fourth scenario depicts an alternative policy of non-discriminatory liberalization of ASEAN trade relations, covering all traded goods. The trade and welfare effects of this last scenario are intended to indicate the potential effects of adopting more liberal ASEAN trade relations on an MFN basis. The MFN scenario is expected to yield the largest improvements to ASEAN trade and economic welfare, because it would integrate the ASEAN economies fully into the global trading system. Of greater interest here is the extent to which, by comparison, the AFTA plan might promote agriculture as well as provide other economic'gains, in either quantitative or qualitative terms.

Under each scenario, import tariffs in the ASEAN countries are reduced to zero, on an *ad valorem* basis. The elimination of non-tariff barriers, on the other hand, is represented by an increase in the volume of administered imports by 25 per cent, on the assumption that NTBs restrict imports to levels in the neighbourhood of 80 per cent of their free trade levels.[29]

The simulation results, summarized in Table 6.9, indicate the adjustment in economy-wide variables and sectoral variables for each ASEAN country. The former variables include the aggregate level of expenditures on final demand, wage rate, and real exchange rate, while the latter variables include prices, production, consumption, and trade in each sector of the model. The economic benefits of the variants of the AFTA plan and MFN liberalization can be considered in terms of (net) trade creation. Following neoclassical economic theory, however, national welfare is mainly evaluated here with reference to variations in real absorption (expenditures on final demand), following the Hicksian approach to measuring changes in welfare applied widely in CGE modeling (Shoven and Whalley 1984, 1992).

The simulation results indicate that the AFTA plan is mainly trade-creating, with intra-ASEAN trade estimated to expand by as much as 19 per cent ($2.9 bn). In addition, the sectoral details (not presented) of the simulation results indicate that the expansion of production and exports under the AFTA plan bears a close similarity to that under the shadow scenario. Specifically, the simulated expansion of production and exports tends to follow the widely acknowledged comparative advantage of the ASEAN countries in natural resource-intensive and labour-intensive goods.

With regard to agriculture, the simulation results by sector indicate that the bias against the sector in the ASEAN countries is reduced under the AFTA plan. Specifically, the domestic terms of trade for agriculture (relative to non-traded goods) are widely improved, giving rise to expanded agricultural production. Moreover, with the depreciation of the exchange rate in several ASEAN countries and the preferential trade liberalization itself, increased exports of agricultural commodities also occur. The improved circumstances of agriculture, however, are substantially less than those found under MFN liberalization. Whereas the most liberal variant of the AFTA plan (Scenario III) results in expanded agricultural output in the ASEAN-4 of between

Table 6.8 The ASEAN trade simulation model: goods categories and elasticity of substitution values

Goods category	SITC[1]	Elasticity of substitution Consumption[2]	Production[3]
Primary commodities	(0 – 4) + 68	—	—
Foods	0 + 1 + 22 + 4	—	—
Cereals (1)	041 – 045	4.0	0.6
Vegetable oils & oil seeds (2)	22 + 42	4.0	0.6
Other foods (3)	—	4.0	0.6
Agricultural raw materials	2 less (22 + 27 + 28)	—	—
Textile fibres (4)	26	4.0	0.6
Other raw materials (5)	—	4.0	0.6
Other primary commodities	27 + 28 + 3 + 68	—	—
Crude fertilizers & mineral ores (6)	27 + 28	4.0	0.8
Mineral fuels (7)	3	4.0	0.8
Non-ferrous metals (8)	68	4.0	0.8
Manufactures	(5 – 8) less 68	—	—
Chemicals	5	—	—
Pharmaceuticals (9)	54	3.0	0.8
Toiletries & perfumes (10)	55	3.0	0.8
Manufactured fertilizers (11)	56	3.0	0.8
Other chemicals (12)	—	3.0	0.8
Iron & steel (13)	67	3.0	1.0
Machinery & equipment	7	—	—
Non-electrical machinery (14)	71 – 75	2.0	0.6
Electrical machinery (15)	76 + 77	2.0	0.8
Transport equipment (16)	78 + 79	2.0	0.8
Other manufactured goods	(6 + 8) less (67 + 68)	—	—
Leather & travel goods (17)	61 + 83	2.0	0.8
Rubber products (18)	62	3.0	0.8
Wood products (19)	63	2.0	0.8

Paper products (20)	64	2.0	1.0
Textiles & clothing (21)	65 + 84	3.0	1.0
Non-metal mineral products (22)	66	3.0	1.0
Furniture (23)	82	3.0	0.8
Footwear (24)	85	3.0	1.0
Professional equipment (25)	87 + 88	2.0	1.0
Other manufactures (26)	—	3.0	1.0
Other			
Non-traded goods (27)	—	—	1.0

Source: DeRosa (1995).

Notes: In addition to the ASEAN countries (Indonesia, Malaysia, Philippines, Singapore, and Thailand), twenty-one countries and country groups are covered in the model. Other developing Asian countries include China; Hong Kong; Republic of China. and Republic of Korea (East Asia); and Bangladesh, India, Pakistan, and Sri Lanka (South Asia). Industrial countries include Australia and New Zealand; Belgium, France. Germany, Italy, Netherlands, Switzerland, and United Kingdom (Europe); and Canada, Japan, and United States. Other developing and industrial countries are grouped into the rest of the world.

[1] Standard international trade classification.
[2] Elasticity of substitution in demand for similar traded goods differentiated by country of origin.
[3] Elasticity of substitution in value-added primary factors of production (ASEAN countries only).

Table 6.9 Changes in economywide variable, international trade, and economic welfare

Import liberalization scenario	Economywide variables			International trade (m. US$)					Economic welfare
				Exports (Imports)	Exports		Imports		
	Expenditures	Wage rate %	Exchange rate %	World	ASEAN	Industrial countries	ASEAN	Industrial countries	Real absorption %
I. AFTA – Selected manufactures									
Indonesia	0.09	0.43	-0.28	130.29	102.01	26.80	134.12	-3.33	0.13
Malaysia	0.66	1.78	-0.39	213.06	239.13	-20.90	396.27	-144.61	0.78
Philippines	0.14	0.32	-0.47	69.91	55.62	13.95	103.25	-19.95	0.18
Singapore	0.96	2.09	1.34	426.64	594.97	-96.68	179.03	179.65	1.69
Thailand	0.14	1.11	-0.30	112.04	95.77	12.24	274.84	-118.63	0.20
ASEAN[b]	—	—	—	951.94	1,087.51	-64.58	1,087.51	-106.87	—
				(0.89)	(7.26)	(-0.11)	(7.26)	(-0.19)	—
II. AFTA – All manufactures									
Indonesia	0.20	0.97	-0.83	212.94	127.48	76.55	222.77	-8.35	0.21
Malaysia	0.79	2.19	-0.39	273.01	314.88	-33.13	508.07	-180.76	0.97
Philippines	0.16	0.83	0.14	104.31	113.27	-6.27	140.70	-21.47	0.32
Singapore	1.56	2.82	2.43	679.57	1,002.45	-207.36	226.34	330.52	2.85
Thailand	0.33	0.93	-1.21	189.16	128.88	48.91	589.08	-306.42	0.36
ASEAN[b]	—	—	—	1,458.99	1,686.96	-121.30	1,686.96	186.47	—
				(1.36)	(11.25)	(-0.20)	(11.25)	(-0.33)	—

III. AFTA – All goods

Indonesia	0.21	1.26	-0.79	341.71	257.19	77.16	351.36	-8.15	0.23
Malaysia	0.76	3.07	0.49	535.82	715.80	-134.58	752.83	-167.02	1.30
Philippines	0.32	0.96	-1.15	170.57	127.62	36.75	261.75	-42.60	0.41
Singapore	2.09	6.32	3.18	592.64	1,520.19	-314.36	418.16	377.52	3.86
Thailand	0.62	4.16	-1.96	405.35	274.09	106.28	1,110.79	-393.38	0.56
ASEAN[b]	—	—	—	2,446.09	2,894.89	-228.75	2,894.89	-233.63	—
				(2.29)	(19.31)	(-0.39)	(19.31)	(-0.41)	

IV. MFN – All goods

Indonesia	3.77	22.91	-23.22	3,102.22	212.79	2,484.29	287.91	2,004.45	2.33
Malaysia	5.79	22.39	-11.85	1,263.46	528.86	585.82	437.70	554.51	4.87
Philippines	4.83	4.58	-34.73	1,437.61	96.46	1,201.26	141.53	729.59	4.58
Singapore	0.24	7.10	-6.74	685.72	550.58	59.48	539.72	185.90	-2.05
Thailand	5.62	13.59	-26.75	2,572.19	343.58	1,836.30	325.40	1,374.39	4.36
ASEAN[b]	—	—	—	9,061.20	1,732.27	6,167.15	1,732.27	4,848.84	—
				(8.47)	(11.56)	(10.38)	(11.56)	(8.56)	

Notes: [a] Per annum, measured in 1988 U.S. dollars.
[b] Values in parentheses are percentage changes in ASEAN trade relative to baseline 1988 trade levels. The percentage changes in ASEAN trade with the world are average changes of ASEAN exports and imports with the world.

Source: DeRosa (1995). Simulations of the ASEAN trade simulation model using 1988 trade flows and circa-1987 import control measures data as baseline data and assuming ad valorem customs duties are reduced to zero and nontariff barriers are liberalized to increase the volume of administered imports by 25 percent, on a preferential basis (AFTA plan) and, alternatively, on a most-favored-nation basis (MFN liberalization).

0.1 per cent (Indonesia) and 0.6 per cent (Thailand), MFN liberalization results in expanded agricultural output in the ASEAN-4 of between 2.3 per cent (Indonesia) and 8.7 per cent (the Philippines).

The limited potential of the AFTA plan to reduce the bias against agriculture in the ASEAN countries points to concerns for other qualitative and quantitative aspects of the expected effects of the plan. In particular, the sectoral adjustment of consumption and imports under the AFTA plan diverges importantly from that under MFN liberalization, owing to the discriminatory nature of the trade liberalization. Overall, the AFTA plan is estimated to yield appreciable, but mainly small, improvements in economic welfare measured in terms of changes in real expenditures on final demand (less than 0.5 per cent), except in Singapore and, to a lesser extent, Malaysia, which by virtue of their relatively open economies stand to gain substantially from expansion of intra-bloc trade under the AFTA plan. Most important, in effectively targeting imports from the major industrial countries for trade diversion, the AFTA plan sacrifices important gains to ASEAN consumers from trade with the principal trading partners of the South-east Asian countries – the major industrial countries, imposing economic costs in terms of forgone consumption opportunities on the ASEAN economies.

Although circumscribed by political obstacles, liberalizing ASEAN trade relations on a non-discriminatory basis results in significant gains in economic welfare for the four natural resource-abundant ASEAN countries, ranging between about 2.0 per cent (Indonesia) and about 5.0 per cent (Malaysia and Philippines) in terms of real absorption. For Singapore, however, real absorption is estimated to decline, by nearly 2.0 per cent. In the case of the ASEAN-4, economic welfare is improved more substantially because the adjustment of consumption and imports, as well as production and exports, in the lower-income ASEAN countries is more complementary to their underlying comparative advantage in efficient sub-sectors of agriculture and industry under MFN liberalization. In the case of Singapore, the results reflect the reduced hegemony of the country in regional markets for manufactures under MFN liberalization.[30]

Finally, with regard to aggregate trade, the simulation results indicate that although the liberalization of ASEAN trade relations on an MFN basis results in smaller gains in intra-ASEAN trade ($1.7 bn), the estimated gain in total ASEAN trade with the world ($9.1 bn) is more than three times larger than under the AFTA plan ($2.4 bn). The improvement of ASEAN trade in agriculture is even more dramatic.

Whereas ASEAN exports of agricultural commodities expand by \$621 m. under the AFTA plan, they expand by \$3765 m., or six times more, under MFN liberalization.

These findings cast substantial doubt on the desirability of pursuing the ASEAN Free Trade Area plan, especially if it threatens continuation of the heretofore *de facto* policy of 'open regionalism' in the ASEAN countries. The latter policy emphasizes non-discriminatory trade relations, to the point of undertaking trade liberalization unilaterally (Arndt 1993). Indeed, the pursuit of open regionalism is often offered as an important explanation for the robustness and vitality of the ASEAN economies, and especially the economies of the newly industrialized countries of East Asia: Hong Kong, Korea, Singapore and Taiwan.[31] As Drysdale and Garnaut (1993, p.187) have put it, open regionalism has given developing countries in Asia, and elsewhere, an alternative to being caught in the prisoner's dilemma of negotiated trade 'concessions'. Specifically, it has given them the 'prisoner's delight' of observing the highly beneficial effects of each country's liberalization on its own trade expansion.

6.4. SUMMARY AND CONCLUDING REMARKS

Despite its increasing prominence in international relations today, regionalism has a history of mostly unfulfilled goals for co-operative economic growth and trade in subSaharan Africa as well as other developing regions, and unanswered questions about its consistency with the most-favoured-nation principle underlying normative economic theory, GATT, and the new World Trade Organization.

This paper has sought to highlight important sectoral aspects of regional integration in subSaharan Africa, emphasizing especially the implications for agriculture – the region's primary source of employment as well as output. Beginning with an examination of the importance of protection and widespread recourse to non-tariff barriers in the region during the late 1980s, the analysis identified how this protection resulted in a bias against agricultural production and exports. The implications of general (that is, non-discriminatory) trade liberalization were also examined. These were supported by quantitative estimates indicating that thoroughgoing trade liberalization in subSaharan Africa should be expected, in the medium to long run, to reduce substantially the bias against agricultural production and trade. Additionally, the theoretical and empirical analyses indicated that general trade liberalization would also benefit other disadvantaged sectors. Among these should be counted industrial and service sectors that would contribute more to increasing the factor content of SSA exports in the services of relatively abundant minerals, other natural resources and unskilled labour than many 'politically-advantaged', capital-intensive and parastatal sectors that today are sheltered by government policies from import competition.

While the importance of trade liberalization for economic performance is increasingly widely understood in Africa, the relative merits of preferential versus non-discriminatory approaches to trade liberalization remain somewhat less clear in the minds of many policy-makers, especially against the background of slow growth and resurgence of regionalism in the world economy.

With regard to regional economic integration, the mainly neoclassical analysis of preferential (that is, regional) versus non-discriminatory approaches to trade liberalization presented in the paper points to the importance of assessing the complementarity of national economies. This involves considering especially the relative natural resource endowments and accumulated stocks of physical and human capital of countries, in order to assess the implications of trade and other economic co-operation initiatives for agriculture and other internationally-competitive sectors, as well as national economic welfare. The analysis indicates that the more 'competitive' the economies of the countries forming a preferential trading bloc are, the less likely it is that intra-bloc trade flows will be stimulated along efficient lines and will result in significant gains in national welfare.

These precepts were illustrated with reference to the results of a recent quantitative study of the ASEAN Free Trade Area in South-east Asia. The study finds that the disincentives to greater ASEAN production in agriculture and other sectors with strong potential for comparative advantage in international trade are reduced under AFTA, but to an extent that is substantially less than under non-discriminatory trade liberalization, or 'open regionalism'. This results because open regionalism goes the longest way towards dismantling the industrialization and other import substitution policies that have repressed production in agriculture but also industrial sectors that would employ greater numbers of low-wage workers under more liberal import regimes in the ASEAN countries.

These findings were based on rudimentary methods in theoretical and applied analysis, without taking into account the importance of political economy considerations. More comprehensive studies of the experiences of co-operative economic arrangements among developing countries, including in subSaharan Africa, are needed to assess the economic benefits and costs of such arrangements, but also to identify the nature and variety of institutional elements underlying past and ongoing regional trade, investment and monetary arrangements, and how they have succeeded or failed. These studies are also likely to reveal in fuller measure the importance of differences in political power among domestic interest groups for shaping the external economic relations of developing countries.

In subSaharan Africa, understanding the reasons for the past failure of regional economic pacts and illuminating what institutional arrangements, or other economic and political conditions, might be counted upon to promote greater intra-regional or international trade are essential. From a purely normative perspective, closer attention should also be paid to institutional arrangements that might be expected to bring the greatest economic benefit to the subSaharan African countries, especially in agriculture and other repressed economic sectors. The results would have potential to be of direct benefit to the impoverished rural and urban populations, whose livelihoods are often closely bound up with the fortunes of those same 'disadvantaged' sectors.

Notes

1. Wider issues surrounding economic co-operation in subSaharan Africa, which involve the co-ordination of country policies in areas of common interest in the region, are not addressed explicitly. These issues include the development of transcontinental communications and transportation networks, scientific research and extension activities related to the problems of African agriculture and dialogues with countries outside of the region and international organizations concerning foreign aid, market access, and resource management. For an introduction to these wider issues, see, for instance, Langhammer (1993).
2. In the real world of many sectors producing different traded goods and a smaller number of primary factors of production, such an analytical methodology might not always yield reliable predictions (Vanek, 1968). From a theoretical perspective, what is ultimately more certain is that the net factor content of a country's trade flows will reflect its underlying relative factor endowments (for example, see Dixit and Norman, 1980).
3. On the export performance of the SSA countries in relationship to the deterioration of the external trading environment facing commodity-exporting countries worldwide during the 1980s compared with earlier decades, see Svedberg (1991). More generally on the relationship between price instability in international commodity markets and economic growth

in sub-Saharan Africa, see Deaton (1993). With regard to the repression of economic incentives in the agricultural sector in SSA countries owing to the indirect effects of trade and macroeconomic policies, see Krueger, Schiff, and Valdés (1991), Oyejide (1986 1993) and Valdés and Muir-Leresche (1993).

4. See, among others, Salter (1959), Swan (1960), Corden (1971), Dornbusch (1974) and Edwards (1989).

5. In the remainder of the chapter, only the implications of protection are considered, in keeping with the primary focus of the analysis on the implications of regional versus general trade liberalization for 'disadvantaged' economic sectors in subSaharan Africa.

6. Also, national welfare associated with consumption at point C is inferior to that associated with consumption under free trade at point C^*, and total consumption as well as total production of farm goods is reduced, from OZ^* to OZ and from OW^* to OW, respectively, in the equilibrium under protection.

7. In part, this outcome also has origins in important political economy considerations, as expounded by Olson (1965), Tullock (1967) and Krueger (1974), among others, in the context of rent-seeking economies and by Anderson and Hayami (1986) in the context of agriculture in Asia. The political economy of agriculture in industrial countries differs importantly from that in less developed countries, mainly because the farm sector comprises typically only a small proportion of domestic output in the former countries. See, for instance, Petit (1985).

8. Labour migration in the Southern Africa region, for instance, can be viewed as a response to restrictive trade policies found widely in the region, in combination with the effects of regional and international sanctions against trade with the Republic of South Africa enforced. On the theory of illegal international transactions, see Bhagwati and Hansen (1973) and Bhagwati (1974).

9. The UNCTAD data pre-date important reforms to trade and other economic policies, announced in connection with recent adoption of structural adjustment programmes in a number of SSA countries. Unfortunately, in the intervening years the UNCTAD data have not been updated, and therefore no independent analysis has been completed to verify the extent of the implementation of the announced trade liberalization measures.

10. The distinction between the two groups of low-income countries, termed here lowest-income countries and upper-low-income countries, is somewhat artificial given that considerable margins of error surround per capita income estimates. None the less, as the tables accompanying this section demonstrate, this division of the low-income countries reveals some interesting and notable differences in protection between the three groups of subSaharan countries.

11. See, for instance, Baldwin (1970).

12. On the economics of rent seeking and so-called directly unproductive profit-seeking activities, see Tullock (1967 and 1980), Krueger (1974) and Bhagwati (1982).

13. Similar evidence of high rates of tariff protection against imports of labour-intensive manufactures is reported for the Asian developing coun-

tries by DeRosa (1986). A comprehensive review of tariff escalation in developing countries is presented by Laird and Yeats (1987), whereas tariff escalation in developing and industrial countries is compared in Finger and Laird (1987) and Yeats (1987).

14. See, for instance, Power (1972) and Papanek (1985). A further explanation for high rates of protection against imports of labour-intensive manufactures is that these goods are predominantly consumer goods. Because the interests of consumers are typically less concentrated than those of manufacturers in less-developed countries, consumers may enjoy little effective political power to promote their economic interest in the adoption of more liberal trade regimes. On this possibility, see Olson (1965).

15. The pattern of protection afforded by statutory tariffs is not altered appreciably by the addition of other fiscal charges. Para-tariffs, however, appear to be applied more widely in the lowest-income and middle-income countries, where they contribute about 5 to 7 percentage points, on average, to total charges as a percentage of import value.

16. Erzan *et al.* (1989) report that complementarity between tariffs and NTBs is commonly found in developing countries, especially middle-income developing countries.

17. See, for instance, GATT (1984). The interest of developing countries in liberalizing world trade in textiles and apparel is considered recently in Hamilton (1990) and Trela and Whalley (1990).

18. Because the international terms of trade are exogenously determined in the empirical analysis, proportional increases in exports measured in US dollars and quantity terms are equal in magnitude.

19. The 'incidence' of protection on exports can be considered more formally, with reference to the substitutability in production and consumption between non-traded goods and importables measured by so-called shift parameters, which may range in value between zero and unity (for example, Clements and Sjaastad 1984; Greenaway and Milner 1993). The greater the value of the shift parameter (w), the greater is the incidence of import tariffs and other protection measures on exports, in export tax-equivalent terms. For a sample of five African countries, Greenaway and Milner (1993, p. 130) report w-values between 0.55 (Côte d'Ivoire) and 0.86 (Mauritius), derived from econometric estimates. W-values derived from the multicommodity model simulation results considered here indicate that for the sample of twenty-three African countries in Table 6.6 the mean value of the shift parameter is 0.55, with a somewhat higher mean value found for the low-income countries (0.57) and an appreciably lower mean value found for the middle-income countries (0.41).

20. Among other references, see OAU (1981), Mansoor and Inotai (1991), Lipumba and Kasekende (1991), Ariyo and Raheem (1991), Foroutan (1993), Lyakurwa *et al.* (1993) and Mwase (1993). After subSaharan Africa, Latin America has the most extensive history of regional co-operation agreements among developing countries. On the experiences of Latin America, see recent reviews by Edwards (1993) and Nogués and Quintanilla (1993). On the experiences of developing countries more generally, see Langhammer and Hiemenz (1990) and de Melo and Panagariya (1992, 1993).

21. Though pathbreaking, Viner's analytical framework has some important

shortcomings and therefore is not applied here. Lipsey (1960), for instance, pointed out that Viner's analysis does not take into account possible differences in marginal rates of substitution in the consumption between countries, and considers only the case of constant-cost production technologies. More recently, Collier (1979) demonstrated that Viner's concepts of trade creation and trade diversion cannot be identified meaningfully in more general economic models admitting terms of trade effects and important dimensions of substitution in production and consumption of exportables and importables.

22. In relationship to the present study, Collier and Gunning (1993) provide a complementary analysis of the strategic role that regionalism in sub-Saharan Africa might play in expanding trade relations with other blocs of countries (for example, the European Union) and, ultimately, in advancing general trade liberalization in African countries.

23. On the importance of international transportation costs for subSaharan African countries, see Yeats (1990).

24. The representation of structural impediments in Figure 6.2(b) is highly stylized, and in particular assumes that although agricultural production falls short of its potential, competition prevails in the economy and prices of the services of primary factors of production as well as goods for consumption are perfectly flexible. The result is that, as portrayed in Figure 6.2(b), optimization of output occurs at a point determined by the tangency of the marginal rate of transformation along the (foreshortened) production possibilities frontier and the domestic terms of trade of agriculture Pa/Pm. See, for instance, Haberler (1950).

25. In regard to the Pearson–Ingram analysis, possibilities for intra-regional rationalization of industrial production to realize the efficiencies of greater economies of scale can presumably be found in numerous regions of subSaharan Africa and other developing areas. As noted by Greenaway and Milner (1990), however, of fundamental importance is whether the cost reductions resulting from intra-industry specialization compare favourably with those implicit in prices of goods that might be imported from third countries where scale economies in production might be still greater, owing to the orientation of production in the latter countries to larger, and more competitive, world markets. For further consideration of scale economies in connection with customs unions and free trade areas, see Corden (1972).

26. Recent advances in the economics of geography, poineered by Krugman (1991a, 1991b), point to another possibly important area for theoretical and applied research related to regional integration. For a discussion of this possibility, see Baldwin (1993).

27. The AFTA plan is outlined in the Singapore Declaration of 1992, signed by the ASEAN heads of state in January 1992 (ASEAN, 1992). Originally, the plan was slated to begin during 1993, but technical problems and political differences between member countries were encountered that could not be resolved before 1995. Also originally, the plan excluded the liberalization of intra-bloc trade in agricultural and other primary commodities, contradicting GATT Article xxiv that requires members forming a regional trading arrangement to reduce barriers to trade on substantially

all goods exchanged. For further discussion of the AFTA plan, see Imada and Naya (1992). On the history of ASEAN economic co-operation, see Wong (1985), Lim (1987), and Meyanathan and Haron (1987).

28. Drawing on information about the frequency of NTBs in other developing countries (UNCTAD, 1987 and 1989) and the major industrial countries (Nogués *et al.*, 1986), the ASEAN trade simulation model also accounts for the incidence of non-tariff barriers in the principal trading partners of the ASEAN countries. For further details regarding the specifications of the model and its sensitivity to alternative parameter values, see DeRosa (1995).

29. In reality, non-tariff barriers in the ASEAN countries might be either more or less restrictive. In particular, where trade is strictly prohibited or quantitative controls are especially stringent, the liberalization of administered imports might imply increases in trade much greater than 25 per cent.

30. They also suggest that Singapore's greater economic interest lies in successful multilateral rather than regional liberalization of trade on an MFN basis.

31. See, Hughes (1991), Drysdale and Garnaut (1993), Panagariya (1993) and World Bank (1993a).

References

Anderson, K. and Y. Hayami, with associates (1986) *The Political Economy of Agricultural Protection: East Asia in International Perspective* (Boston: Allen & Unwin).

APEC (Asia–Pacific Economic Co-operation) (1993) *A Vision for APEC: Towards an Asia Pacific Economic Community*, report of the Eminent Persons Group to APEC Ministers (Singapore: Asia–Pacific Economic Co-operation).

Ariyo, A. and M.I. Raheem (1991) 'Enhancing Trade Flows Within the ECOWAS Subregion: an Appraisal and Some Recommendations', in A. Chhibber and S. Fischer (eds), *Economic Reform in Sub-Saharan Africa: a World Bank symposium* (Washington, DC: The World Bank).

Armington, P.A. (1969) 'A Theory of Demand for Products Distinguished by Place of Production', *IMF Staff Papers*, 16: 159–78.

Arndt, H.W. (1993) 'Anatomy of Regionalism', *Journal of Asian Economics*, 4(2): 271–82.

ASEAN (Association of South-East Asian Nations) (1992) *Singapore declaration of 1992* (Singapore: Fourth ASEAN Summit).

Aspen Institute (1993) *South Africa's International Economic Relations in the 1990s: Conference Report* (Washington, DC).

Badiane, O. (1991) 'Regional Agricultural Markets and Development Strategies in West Africa', *Quarterly Journal of International Agriculture*, 30(1): 37–50.

Balassa, B. (1961) *The Theory of Economic Integration* (London: George Allen & Unwin).

Baldwin, R.E. (1989) 'Measurable Dynamic Gains from Trade', *Journal of Political Economy*, 100(1): 162–74.

—— (1993) 'Review of Theoretical Developments on Regional Integration', Workshop on *Regional Integration and Trade Liberalization in Sub-Saharan Africa* (Nairobi: African Economic Research Consortium).

Baldwin, R.E. (1970) *Nontariff Distortions in International Trade* (Washington, DC: The Brookings Institution).

Bautista, R.M. (1993) 'Development Strategies, Industrial Policies, and Agricultural incentives in Asia', in Romeo M. Bautista and Alberto Valdés (eds), *The Bias Against Agriculture: Trade and Macroeconomic Policies in Developing Countries* (San Francisco: ICS Press).

—— and Alberto Valdés (1993) *The Bias Against Agriculture: Trade and Macroeconomic Policies in Developing Countries* (San Francisco: ICS Press).

Bhagwati, J. (ed.) (1974) *Illegal Transactions in International Trade* (Amsterdam: North Holland).

—— (1982) 'Directly Unproductive Profit-seeking (DUP) Activities', *Journal of Political Economy*, 90: 988–1002.

—— (1991) *The World Trading System At Risk* (Princeton, NJ: Princeton University Press).

—— (1992) 'Regionalism versus multilateralism', *The World Economy* 15(5): 535–56.

—— and B. Hansen (1973) 'A Theoretical Analysis of Smuggling', *Quarterly Journal of Economics*, 87(2): 172–87.

Brown, D.K. (1987) 'Tariffs, the Terms of Trade, and National Product Differentiation', *Journal of Policy Modeling*, 9: 503–26.

Buehrer, T.S. and S. Devarajan (1993) 'Why the Welfare Gains from Trade Liberalization are So Small' (Cambridge, Mass.: Harvard Institute for International Development) mimeo.

Cavallo, D. and Y. Mundlak (1982) 'Agriculture and Economic Growth in an Open Economy: the Case of Argentina', Research report 36 (Washington, DC: International Food Policy Research Institute).

Clements, K.W. and L.A. Sjaastad (1984) *How Protection Taxes Exporters*, Thames Essays 33 (London: Trade Policy Research Centre).

Collier, P. (1979) 'The Welfare Effects of Customs Unions: an Anatomy', *Economic Journal*, 89: 84–95.

—— and J. Gunning (1993) 'Linkages Between Trade Policy and Regional Integration', Workshop on *Regional Integration and Trade Liberalization in Sub-Saharan Africa* (Nairobi: African Economic Research Consortium).

Cooper, C.A. and B.F. Massell (1965) 'Toward a General Theory of Customs Unions for Developing Countries', *Journal of Political Economy* 73: 461–76.

Corden, M.W. (1971) *The Theory of Protection* (Oxford University Press).

—— (1972) 'Economies of Scale and Customs Union Theory', *Journal of Political Economy*, 80(3): 465–75.

Davies, R., D. Keet and M. Nkuhlu (1993) *Reconstructing Economic Relations with the Southern African Region: Issues and Options for a Democratic South Africa* (Belville, South Africa: The Centre for Development Studies, University of Western Cape).

Deardorff, A.V. (1984) 'Testing Trade Theories and Predicting Trade Flows', in R.W. Jones and Peter B. Kenen (eds), *Handbook of International Economics* (Amsterdam: North-Holland).

—— and R.M. Stern (1985) *Methods of Measurement of Nontariff Barriers* (New York: UNCTAD) (ST/MD/28).

—— and —— (1986) *The Michigan Model of World Production and Trade: Theory and Applications* (Cambridge, Mass.: The MIT Press).

Deaton, A.S. (1993) 'Commodity Prices, Stabilization, and Growth in Africa' (Princeton, NJ: Princeton University Research Program in Development Studies) mimeo.

Delgado, C. and O. Badiane (1992) 'Strategies for Regional Integration of Agricultural Markets in West Africa: Issues for Policy and Research', paper presented at the IFPRI/ISRA Conference on *The Regional Integration of Agricultural Markets in West Africa: Issues for the Sahelian Countries and Their Trading Partners*, 2–4 December, Saly Portudal, Senegal.

de Melo, J. and A. Panagariya (1992) *The New Regionalism in Trade Policy: an Interpretive Summary of a Conference* (Washington, DC: The World Bank).

—— and —— (eds) (1993) *New Dimensions in Regional Integration* (Cambridge: Cambridge University Press for the Centre for Economic Policy Research).

DeRosa, D.A. (1986) 'Trade and Protection in the Asian Developing Region', *Asian Development Review*, 4: 27–62.

—— (1992) 'Protection and Export Performance in Sub-Saharan Africa', *Weltwirtschaftliches Archiv*, 128 (1): 88–124.

—— (1995) 'Regional Trading Arrangements Among Developing Countries: The ASEAN example', Research Report no. 103 (Washington, DC: International Food Policy Research Institute).

Dervis, K., J. de Melo and S. Robinson (1982) *General Equilibrium Models for Development Policy* (Cambridge University Press).

Dixit, A.K. and V.D. Norman (1980) *The Theory of International Trade: a Dual General Equilibrium Approach* (Cambridge University Press).

Dornbusch, R. (1974) 'Tariffs and Nontraded Goods', *Journal of International Economics*, 4: 177–85.

Drysdale, P. and R. Garnaut (1993) 'The Pacific: An Application of a General Theory of Economic Integration', in C.F. Bergsten and M. Noland (eds), *Pacific Dynamism and the International Economic System* (Washington, DC: Institute for International Economics).

Edwards, S. (1989) *Real Exchange Rates, Devaluation, and Adjustment: Exchange Rate Policy in Developing Countries* (Cambridge, Mass.: The MIT Press).

—— (1993) 'Latin American Economic Integration', *World Economy* 16(3): 317–38.

Erzan, R., and H. Kuwahara, S. Marchese and R. Vossenaar, (1989) 'The Profile of Protection in Developing Countries', *UNCTAD Review*, 1: 29–50.

Ethier, W.J. (1984) 'Higher Dimensional Issues in Trade Theory', in R.W. Jones and P.B. Kenan (eds), *Handbook of International Economics* (Amsterdam: North-Holland).

Finger, J.M. and S. Laird (1987) 'Protection in Developed and Developing Countries – an Overview', *Journal of World Trade Law*, 21 (6): 9–24.

Foroutan, F. (1993) 'Regional Integration in Sub-Saharan Africa: Past Experience and Future Prospects', in J. de Melo and A. Panagariya (eds), *New*

Dimensions in Regional Integration (Cambridge: Cambridge University Press for the Center for Economic Policy Research).

GATT (General Agreement on Tariffs and Trade) (1984) *Textiles and Clothing in the World Economy* (Geneva).

Greenaway, D. and C. Milner (1990) 'South–South Trade: Theory, Evidence, and Policy', *World Bank Research Observer*, 5(1): 47–68.

——— (1993) *Trade and Industrial Policy in Developing Countries* (Ann Arbor, Mich.: University of Michigan Press).

Haberler, G. (1950) 'Some Problems in the Pure Theory of International Trade', *Economic Journal*, 60(238): 223–40.

Hamilton, C. (ed.) (1990) *Textiles Trade and the Developing Countries: Eliminating the Multi-fibre Arrangement in the 1990s* (Washington, DC: The World Bank).

Harberger, A.C. (1954) 'Monopoly and Resource Allocation', *American Economic Review*, 44: 77–87.

——— (1971) 'Three Basic Postulates for Applied Welfare Economics', *Journal of Economic Literature*, 9: 785–97.

Harbison, F. and C. Myers (1964) *Education, Manpower and Economic Growth* (New York: McGraw-Hill).

Hughes, H. (1991) 'Does APEC Make Sense?', *ASEAN Economic Bulletin*, 8: 125–37.

Imada, P.Y. and S. Naya (eds) (1992) *AFTA: the Way Ahead* (Singapore: Institute of Southeast Asian Studies).

Johnson, H.G. (1965) 'An Economic Theory of Protectionism, Tariff Bargaining, and the Formation of Customs Unions', *Journal of Political Economy*, 73: 256–83.

Koester, U. (1986) 'Regional Cooperation to Improve Food Security in Southern and Eastern African countries', Research Report 53 (Washington, DC: International Food Policy Research Institute).

Krueger, A.O. (1974) 'The Political Economy of the Rent-seeking Society', *American Economic Review*, 80: 48–62.

——— (1992) *The Political Economy of Agricultural Pricing Policy, vol. 5, A Synthesis of the Political Economy in Developing Countries* (Baltimore: The Johns Hopkins University Press).

———, M. Schiff and A. Valdés (1988) 'Agricultural Incentives in Developing Countries: Measuring the Effect of Sectoral and Economywide Policies', *World Bank Economic Review* 2(3): 255–72.

———, M. Seriff and A. Valdés (eds) (1991) *The Political Economy of Agricultural Pricing Policy, vol. 3, Africa and the Mediterranean* (Baltimore: The Johns Hopkins University Press).

Krugman, P.R. (1988) 'Endogenous Innovation, International Trade and Growth', in Paul Krugman (ed.), *Rethinking International Trade* (Cambridge, Mass.: The MIT Press).

——— (1991a) *Geography and Trade* (Cambridge, Mass.: The MIT Press).

——— (1991b) 'Increasing Returns and Economic Geography', *Journal of Political Economy*, 99(3): 483–99.

Laird, S. and A. Yeats (1987) 'Empirical Evidence Concerning the Magnitude and Effects of Developing Country Tariff Escalation', *The Developing Economies*, 25: 99–123.

Langhammer, R.J. (1993) 'Integration "Through the Market"': High Costs and Risks', *Courier*, Nov.–Dec., 56–9.

—— and U. Hiemenz (1990) *Regional Integration Among Developing Countries: Opportunities, Obstacles and Options* (Boulder, Colo.: Westview Press).

Leamer, E.E. (1984) *Sources of International Comparative Advantage: Theory and Evidence* (Cambridge, Mass.: The MIT Press).

Lele, U. (ed.) (1991) *Aid to African Agriculture: Lessons from Two Decades of Donors' Experience* (Baltimore, Md: The Johns Hopkins University Press for The World Bank).

Lewis, W.A. (1980) 'The Slowing Down of the Engine of Growth', *American Economic Review*. 70(4): 555–64.

Lim, Ch.P. (1987) 'ASEAN Co-operation in Industry: Looking Back and Looking forward', in N. Sopiee, Ch.L. See and L.S. Jin (eds), *ASEAN at the Crossroads* (Kuala Lumpur, Malaysia: Institute of Strategic and International Studies).

Lipsey, R.G. (1957) 'The Theory of Customs Unions: Trade Diversion and Welfare', *Economica*, 24: 40–6.

—— (1960) 'The Theory of Customs Unions: A General Equilibrium Analysis', *Economic Journal*, 70: 498–513.

Lipumba, N.H.I. and L. Kasekende (1991) 'The Record and Prospects of the Preferential Area for Eastern and Southern African States', in A. Chhibber and S. Fischer (eds), *Economic Reform in Sub-Saharan Africa: a World Bank Symposium* (Washington, DC: The World Bank).

Lucas, R.E. Jr. (1988) 'On the Mechanics of Economic Development', *Journal of Monetary Economics*, 22: 3–42.

Lyakurwa, W., A. McKay, N. Ngeno and W. Kennes (1993) 'Regional Integration in Sub-Saharan Africa: a Review of Experiences and Issues', Workshop on *Regional Integration and Trade Liberalization in Sub-Saharan Africa* (Nairobi: African Economic Research Consortium).

Mankiw, N.G., D. Romer and D.N. Weil (1992) 'A Contribution to the Empirics of Economic Growth', *Quarterly Journal of Economics*, 107(2): 407–38.

Mansoor, A. and A. Inotai (1991) 'Integration Efforts in Sub-Saharan Africa: Failures, Results and Prospects – a Suggested Strategy for Achieving Efficient Integration', in A. Chhibber and Stanley Fischer (eds), *Economic Reform in Sub-Saharan Africa: a World Bank symposium* (Washington, DC: The World Bank).

Meade, J.E. (1955) *The Theory of Customs Unions* (Amsterdam: North-Holland).

Meyanathan, S. and I. Haron (1987) 'ASEAN trade Co-operation: a Survey of the Issues', in N. Sopiee, Ch.L. See and L.S. Jin (eds), *ASEAN at the Crossroads* (Kuala Lumpur, Malaysia: Institute of Strategic and International Studies).

Mundell, R.A. (1957) 'International Trade and Factor Mobility', *American Economic Review*, 47(3): 321–35.

Mwase, N. (1993) 'Economic Integration for Development in Eastern and Southern Africa: Assessment and Prospects', *African Development Review*, 5(2): 20–37.

Nogués, J., A. Olechowski and L.A. Winters (1986) 'The Extent of Nontariff Barriers to Imports in Industrial Countries', World Bank staff working paper 789 (Washington, DC).

—— and R. Quintanilla (1993) 'Latin America's Integration and the Multilateral Trading System', in J. de Melo and A. Panagariya (eds), *New Dimensions in Regional Integration* (Cambridge: Cambridge University Press for the Centre for Economic Policy Research).

OAU (Organization of African Unity) (1981) *Lagos Plan of Action for the Economic Development of Africa: 1980–2000* (Geneva: International Institute for Labour Studies).

Olson, M. (1965) *The Logic of Collective Action: Public Goods and Theory of Groups* (Cambridge, Mass.: Harvard University Press).

Oyejide, T.A. (1986) 'The Effects of Trade and Exchange Rate Policies on Agriculture in Nigeria', Research Report 55 (Washington, DC: International Food Policy Research Institute).

—— (1993) 'Effects of Trade and Macroeconomic Policies on African Agriculture', in R.M. Bautista and Alberto Valdés (eds), *The Bias Against Agriculture: Trade and Macroeconomic Policies in Developing Countries* (San Francisco: ICS Press).

Panagariya, A. (1993) 'Should East Asia Go Regional? No, No and Maybe', Policy Research Working Paper 1209 (Washington, DC: The World Bank).

Papanek, G.F. (1985) 'Industrialization Strategies in Labor-Abundant Countries', *Asian Development Review*, 3: 43–53.

Pearson, S.R. and W.D. Ingram (1980) 'Economies of Scale, Domestic Divergences, and Potential Gains from Economic Integration in Ghana and the Ivory Coast', *Journal of Political Economy*, 88: 994–1008.

Petit, M. (1985) 'Determinants of Agricultural Policies in the United States and the European Community', Research Report 51 (Washington, DC: International Food Policy Research Institute).

Power, J.H. (1972) 'The Role of Protection in Industrialization Policy with Particular Reference to Kenya', *East Africa Economic Review*, 4 (1): 1–20.

Romer, P.M. (1990) 'Endogenous Technological Change', *Journal of Political Economy* 98: 71–102.

Saborio, S. (ed.) (1992) *The Premise and the Promise: Free Trade in the Americas* (New Brunswick: Transaction Publishers).

Salter, W.E. (1959) 'Internal and External Balance: the Role of Price and Expenditure Effects', *Economic Record*, 35: 226–38.

Shoven, J.B. and J. Whalley (1984) 'Applied General-Equilibrium Models of Taxation and International Trade: an Introduction and Survey', *Journal of Economic Literature*, 22: 1007–51.

—— (1992) *Applying general equilibrium* (Cambridge University Press).

Stolper, W.F. and P.A. Samuelson (1941) 'Protection and Real Wages', *Review of Economic Studies*, 9: 58–73.

Svedberg, P. (1991) 'The Export Performance of Sub-Saharan Africa', *Economic Development and Cultural Change*, 39(3): 549–66.

Swan, T. (1960) 'Economic Control in a Dependent Economy', *Economic Record*, 36: 51–66.

Torre, A. de la and M. Kelly (1992) 'Regional Trade Arrangements', Occasional paper no. 93 (Washington, DC: International Monetary Fund).

Trela, I. and J. Whalley (1990) 'Global Effects of Developed Country Trade Restrictions on Textiles and Apparel', *Economic Journal*, 100: 1190–1205.

Tullock, G. (1967) 'The Welfare Costs of Tariffs, Monopolies and Theft', *Western Economic Journal*, 5: 224–32.
—— (1980) 'Efficient Rent Seeking', in J.M. Buchanan, R.D. Tollison and G. Tullock (eds), *Towards a Theory of the Rent-seeking Society* (College Station, Texas: Texas A&M Press).
UNCTAD (United Nations Conference on Trade and Development) (1985) *Ministerial Declaration on the Global System of Trade Preferences Among Developing Countries* (Geneva).
—— (1987) *Handbook of Trade Control Measures of Developing Countries 1987* (New York: United Nations).
—— (1988) 'The UNCTAD Data Base on Trade Measures', *UNCTAD Bulletin*, (244): 1–4.
—— (1989) *Handbook of Trade Control Measures of Developing Countries 1987: Supplement* (Geneva).
—— (1991) *Handbook of International Trade and Development Statistics 1990* (New York: United Nations).
Union of International Associations (ed.) (1987) *Yearbook of International Organizations 1987/88* (Munich: Saur).
Valdés, A. (1973) 'Trade Policy and its Effects on the External Agricultural Trade of Chile, 1945–1965', *American Journal of Agricultural Economics*, 55(2): 154–64.
—— and K. Muir-Leresche (eds) (1993) *Agricultural Policy Reforms and Regional Market Integration in Malawi, Zambia, and Zimbabwe* (Washington, DC: International Food Policy Research Institute).
Vanek, J. (1968) 'The Factor Proportions Theory: The n-factor Case', *Kyklos*, 21: 749–56.
Viner, J. (1950) *The Customs Union Issue* (New York: Carnegie Endowment for International Peace).
Wong, J. (1985) 'ASEAN's Experience in Regional Economic Cooperation', *Asian Development Review*, 3 (1): 79–98.
Wonnacott, P. and R. Wonnacott (1981) 'Is Unilateral Tariff Reduction Preferable to a Customs Union? The Curious Case of the Missing Foreign Tariffs', *American Economic Review*, 71: 704–14.
—— (1992) 'The Customs Union Issue Reopened', *The Manchester School*, 60(2): 119–35.
World Bank (1989) *Sub-Saharan Africa: From Crisis to Sustainable Growth* (Washington, DC).
—— (1991) *World Development Report 1991* (New York: Oxford University Press).
—— (1993a) *The East Asian Miracle: Economic Growth and Public Policy* (New York: Oxford University Press).
—— (1993b) *World Development Report 1993* (New York: Oxford University Press).
Yeats, A. (1987) 'The Escalation of Trade Barriers', in J.M. Finger and A. Olechowski (eds), *The Uruguay Round: a Handbook on the Multilateral Trade Negotiations* (Washington, DC: The World Bank).
—— (1990) 'Do African Countries Pay More for Imports? Yes', *World Bank Economic Review*, 4(1): 1–20.

7 Evaluating Trade Liberalization: A Methodological Framework*

Paul Collier, David Greenaway and
Jan Willem Gunning

7.1 AN OVERVIEW OF EXPERIENCE WITH LIBERALIZATION

Throughout the post-Second World War period there has been enormous and sustained interest in trade policy in developing countries. Analysts have addressed three sets of issues: Should developing countries follow inward or outward-orientated trade strategies? What are the consequences of a particular trade strategy for the structure of protection and overall economic performance? What has been the experience of developing countries that have undertaken reform programmes? The first two of these questions have been very intensively studied. Although they remain controversial, some level of consensus has been reached; the costs of indiscriminate intervention have been well documented, and a positive association between growth of exports and growth of output has gained a lot of empirical support, although the strength and direction of causality remains problematic. Indeed, a greater consensus on these issues has in part been responsible for the extensive reforms we have observed in the last decade. This is the third issue referred to above, and the one on which we focus in this chapter.

What is Liberalization?

The regime changes that we will discuss are programmes targeted at more open policies – programmes that are often referred to as 'liber-

* A first draft of this chapter was presented as a paper at the AERC workshop in Nairobi in December 1993, and benefited from helpful comments, especially those of the paper's discussant, Dean DeRosa.

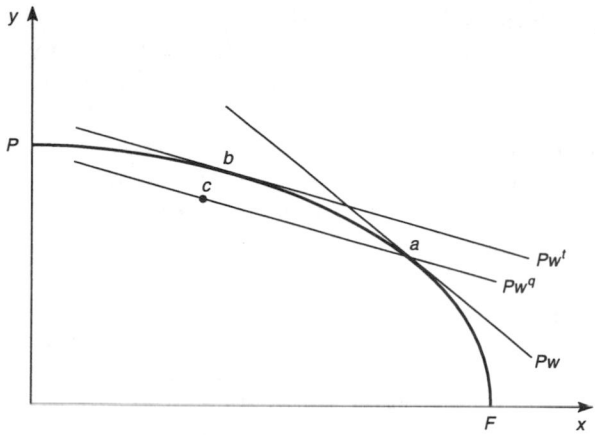

Figure 7.1   Import distortions

alization'. What, however, is liberalization? In a simple two-sector trade model this is a trivial question that is easily answered. In Figure 7.1 the free trade (production) equilibrium is at *a* where the terms of trade line is tangential to the production frontier. Point *b* represents a tariff distorted equilibrium. If the import tariff is the only distortion in place, its removal constitutes a clear act of liberalization – returning the economy to point *a*. Theory gives us a clear lead on what constitutes liberalization and on the potential benefits of such a policy change.

There are, however, a number of obvious problems in operationalizing this concept. First, we may have a range of imported inputs and final products rather than only one. Although theory is more ambiguous in its guidance here, we can develop rules for liberalization (reducing the mean) and harmonization (reducing the variance) that are consistent with welfare gains in a wide range of circumstances (see Greenaway and Reed, 1990). Indeed, this has clearly been the way in which liberalization has been pursued in the Kennedy, Tokyo and Uruguay Rounds. Frequently, liberalization is defined (implicitly) in this narrow sense of reducing the average level of protection. This is a rather inadequate approach as we could envisage reforms that reduced the mean tariff, for example, but increased the variance and therefore increased domestic price distortions.

A second complication is that intervention may be targeted at exports as well as imports. Using the Lerner symmetry theorem, for a given tariff we can always find an equivalent export subsidy, where equivalence is defined in relative price terms. Referring again to Figure 7.1, point a could be consistent with a relative price ratio of Pm/Px, or $Pm(1 + t)/Px(1 + s)$ where $t = s$. We can think of Pw as a *neutral* set of relative prices. Whether secured by free trade or by the introduction of equivalent taxes and subsidies, relative prices are neutral in the sense that they do not provide a net incentive to agents to invest in one sector rather than another. When some analysts are discussing liberalization, they clearly have in mind this notion of neutrality. In a recent study of thirty-six liberalization episodes in nineteen countries, Papageorgiou *et al.* (1991, vol. 7, p. 13) define liberalization as 'any act that would make the trade regime more neutral'.

The notion of neutrality has obvious intuitive attractions. In relative price terms it is equivalent to free trade, and, in that sense, policy actions that move the economy towards neutrality would superficially appear to be liberalizing. The great difficulty with the concept is that, although we can identify equivalence in relative price terms across an infinite set of tariffs and offsetting subsidies, the resource allocation effects will only be equivalent at one unique set of relative prices, when $t = s = 0$, that is, free trade. This is so in part because as t and s increase it is likely that they become more distortive, and in part because once we introduce a non-tradables sector we have to allow for a second set of relative prices. As Greenaway and Milner (1987) show, what happens to the price of non-tradables relative to tradables has a profound effect on resource allocation. For example, Hong Kong and South Korea would have had similar computed values for Krueger's bias index in the early 1970s, but these numbers came from quite different trade regimes that had different allocative effects.

A third complication is that tariffs are not the only instrument of import protection, nor in many developing countries are they even the most important instrument. Since Bhagwati (1969), equivalences and non-equivalences between tariff and non-tariff barriers have been extensively analysed. What theory shows us is that although we can always identify the tariff equivalent of a given non-tariff distortion, in relative price terms, there are clear (static and dynamic) non-equivalences in allocative and distributional terms. The proposition that a tariff is generally more efficient than an equivalent quota is well established and needs no elaboration here. In the context of Figure 7.1 the excess costs of the quota (due to rent seeking, for example), may mean that we end up at c rather than b. For this reason many analysts view the substitution of more efficient for less efficient instruments of protection as liberalization. Indeed, as we shall see later, this particular policy change has been a key ingredient in policy-based lending programmes.

Thus, in framing reform programmes, it is not a straightforward matter to map from the simple unambiguous notion of liberalization that comes out of the two-sector trade model to an operational measure. In practice, 'liberalization' could refer to import liberalization and/or a move towards neutrality in the structure of relative prices and/or the substitution of less distorting for more distorting forms of intervention. As we shall see later, reform programmes sponsored by the World Bank often incorporate ingredients of all three. Table 7.1, summarizes the policy reforms associated with the liberalizations evaluated by Papageorgiou *et al.* (1991). This illustrates nicely the menu of reforms that can be construed as comprising 'liberalization'.

It is clear from Table 7.1 that the majority of the reforms fall within the import liberalization or instrument substitution definitions. Export promotion measures were included in six of the seventeen cases, which is potentially consistent with the 'neutrality' approach. It is worth noting that most cases also included exchange rate adjustments, usually devaluation. This would not normally be considered a trade reform although it has important trade effects. In particular, exchange rate adjustments alter relative price incentives between importables and exportables. We will return to this issue in the next section.

What Form Has Liberalization Taken?

In a world where there are multiple instruments of intervention, and self-interested agencies to defend their use, policy reform tends to be incremental rather than comprehensive. Bold across-the-board liberalization like that implemented in Chile in the 1970s is the exception rather than the rule. Papageorgiou *et al.* (1991) define an episode of liberalization as commencing 'at a point at which a significant policy change towards liberalization was implemented. It ends with a reversal or when no further policy trend in either direction is apparent' (vol. 17, p. 29). They use this criterion to define thirty-six liberalization episodes across nineteen countries in a study that is particularly ambitious. As well as identifying the episodes, the authors also attempt to evaluate various characteristics such as speed, intensity and duration.

The ingredients of the liberalization episodes in their sample are listed in Table 7.1, which reveals that tariff reductions are a recurring component, as is liberalization/reduction of quantitative restrictions. Such acts would be consistent with a rotation of Pw' towards Pw in Figure 7.1. Note, however, that some form of export support is also common:

Table 7.1   Components of liberalization episodes: the Papageorgiou *et al.* study

Country	Features of liberalization episode
Argentina 1967–70 1976–80	Average tariff reduced from 94 to 49 per cent Increased variance of tariffs Increase in effective exchange rate Exchange rate devaluation Export promotion
Brazil 1965–73	Tariff reductions Duty drawback scheme Tax exemptions and subsidies for exports Exchange rate devaluation
Colombia 1964–6 1968–82	Tariff reductions Prohibited import list abolished Reduced variance of tariffs Differential export subsidies
Peru 1979–80	Maximum tariff reduced from 355 to 60 per cent Some increase in tariff escalation Most imports go on quota free list
Uruguay 1974–82	Tariff reductions QRs eliminated Unification of foreign exchange market
Indonesia 1950–1 1966–72	Rationalized tariff structure Elimination of import licence restrictions Reduced use of QRs, but pervasive controls remained Simplification of export restrictions Exchange rate devaluation and unification of foreign exchange market
South Korea 1965–7 1978–9	Reduced tariffs to average of 22 per cent Reduced use of QRs, but 1200 items remained controlled Export incentives Exchange rate adjustment
New Zealand 1951–6 1964–81 1982–4	Tariff reductions Import licence reductions Tariff compensation Greater exchange rate flexibility
Pakistan 1959–65 1972–8	Exchange rate devaluation Abolition of export bonus scheme
Philippines 1960–5 1970–4	Liberalized foreign exchange system Reduction in peak tariffs Piecemeal reductions in import controls Increase in effective tariffs

Table 7.1 Continued

Country	Features of liberalization episode
Singapore 1968–73	Tariff reductions QR liberalization
Sri Lanka 1968–70 1977–9	Removal of Import licences Increased tariffs Increased export taxes Greater exchange rate flexibility Free trade zone incentives
Turkey 1970–3 1980–4	Tariff reduction QR reduction Export incentives Exchange rate devaluation
Israel 1952–5 1962–8 1969–77	Replacement of QRs with tariffs Some tariff reduction to hit target effective protection rate Exchange rate adjustment
Spain 1960–6 1970–4 1977–80	Tariff reductions Export incentives Exchange rate adjustment
Yugoslavia 1965–7	Average tariffs reduced from 23 to 10.5 per cent Shift of products from restricted to liberal lists Abolition of export subsidies Exchange rate devaluation
Chile 1956–61 1974–81	QRs largely eliminated Tariffs reduced to uniform rate of 10 per cent Exemptions reduced

export promotion, export subsidies, duty drawback arrangements and so on. Other things being equal, these kinds of policy innovations result in greater neutrality in relative prices. Note also that, in a number of cases, the replacement of quotas with tariffs is mentioned.

Whalley (1991) reports the results of an evaluation of liberalization in eleven developing countries. He acknowledges the difficulties of identifying a liberalization episode and refrains from any attempt to do so. Instead, he infers that liberalization has occurred from the scale and intensity of reforms. The components for his sample are listed in Table 7.2. There is some overlap in country coverage between Tables 7.1 and 7.2. However, it should be noted that even where this occurs the liberalization episodes are actually different. Table 7.1 effectively

Table 7.2 Components of liberalization in 11 developing countries: the Whalley study

Country	Features of liberalization episode
Argentina 1987–8	Coverage of QRs reduced Reduction in import licensing Reduction in average tariffs Reduction in variance of tariffs
Brazil 1988	Lowered tariff rates Elimination of tariff exemptions Reduction of non-tariff measures
China 1978–87	Creation of export processing zones Reduced taxes on exports
Costa Rica 1982–3	Reform of foreign exchange market Creation of export-processing zones
India 1985–8	Reduced tariffs on agricultural items Auxiliary customs duty abolished Open General Licensing extended
Kenya 1980–6	Reduction in import duties Reduction in non-tariff barriers Exchange rate depreciation
Mexico 1985–8	QR liberalization Tariff reductions Reduced variance of tariffs Reformed customs valuations procedures
Nigeria 1986–7	Import licensing system abolished Import levy discontinued Cuts in import tariffs Import deposits abolished Exchange rate reforms
Philippines 1981–7	Import controls liberalized Reduction in tariffs
South Korea 1978–81 1989	Elimination of discretionary import licensing Reduction in tariffs
Tanzania 1984–9	Exchange rate adjustment Reduction in import restrictions Rationalization of tariffs Export promotion

Source: Adapted from Whalley (1991), Appendix 10.1.

ends in 1984, while for the most part Table 7.2 begins around then. What is clear, however, is that the ingredients taken by Whalley as signalling liberalization are, with the exception of export promotion measures, similar to those of Papageorgiou *et al.* Although both studies have some difficulty in defining liberalization, they seem to be able to recognize it when it occurs.

The same can be said of the World Bank evaluations. We noted earlier that the advent of policy-based lending was a crucial ingredient in explaining liberalization in developing countries; around four-fifths of SALs incorporate trade policy conditions. This conditionality has resulted in actual or intended trade policy reforms of a liberalizing nature in some sixty or so developing countries. The type which are typically proposed are outlined in Table 7.3, which is drawn from a detailed analysis of forty SALs. The pattern one observes in Tables 7.1 and 7.2 is repeated here. Some reform proposals have been directed at 'pure' liberalization, some at moving relative prices towards neutrality; still others aim at replacing more costly with less costly instruments.

7.2 MEASURING TRADE POLICY AND IDENTIFYING LIBERALIZATION EPISODES

Introduction

In principle there are three approaches to ensuring trade liberalization: by changes in policies, by changes in prices, or by the resulting changes in quantities. Many different methods have been used. In this section we review the most important ones and evaluate their attractiveness both on theoretical grounds and in terms of the practical difficulties involved in applying them.

Unfortunately, there are theoretical or practical difficulties with all methods. One response to this is to use several methods in the hope that the results will confirm each other. Cross-country analysis has ranked countries according to a large number of different measures of trade policy. The correspondence between pairs of methods, as measured by rank correlations, turned out to be extremely low. In other words, the measurement of trade restrictiveness appears to be extremely sensitive to the choice of method. The same conclusion could, but need not, apply when the focus is not on differences between countries, but on differences over time for the same country, the focus of

Table 7.3   Trade policy reform proposals in 40 SAL countries

	Intensity of reforms[a]			Presence	
Item	Strong	Medium	Weak	Yes	No
Overall import policy	14	15	11		
Non-protective QRs	14	16	10		
Protective QRs[b]	14	15	11		
Tariff level[b]	7	21	12		
Schedule of future reduction	6	29	5		
Overall export policy	15	15	10		
Imports for exports	17	15	8		
Overall reduction in anti-export bias	17	12	11		
Exchange rate flexibility[c]				38	2
Export promotion measures[d]				33	7
Studies of effects of trade policy					
reform				28	12

Notes:
The assessments refer to proposals supported by the Bank. They do not refer to policy implementation (experience with which is very varied).
[a] Totals are 40 in all cases.
[b] Reforms which replaced QRs with tariffs are included in both lines.
[c] Often these were not explicit conditions, but constituted understandings made under the programme, usually as part of a standby agreement.
[d] Includes such schemes as export credits, insurance, guarantees and institutional development.

Source: Thomas and Nash (1991) Table 1.

the AERC country studies. As yet, there has not been much work in this area. The work of Reinikka (1993) on Kenyan trade policy is a notable contribution and we shall refer to it frequently.

Before discussing the various methods, we need to establish what a trade liberalization index is supposed to measure, in particular whether it should be restricted to changes in trade policy. This is less trivial than it may seem to be. Consider the following two examples. In the first case imports are subject to quotas and these quantitative restrictions are binding. Domestic producers of import substitutes enjoy protection as the ex-factory prices of their products are higher than the c.i.f. prices of competing imports. When quotas are not auctioned and domestic prices are market-clearing, changes in real income will be reflected in the value of quota rents (QR). An income increase, for example, as a result of a commodity boom, will drive up the domestic price of importables. The market will continue to clear (with an unchanged import volume) as the income effect on import demand is precisely offset by a substitution effect: the domestic price will rise just enough to keep import demand constant. In this example there has been no change in trade policy but a common measure of protection, the implicit tariff rate (the ratio of the domestic price of importables and the c.i.f. price in domestic currency), has risen.

In the second case, imports are again subject to QRs that are not changed. Prior to the period of analysis there have been investments in the import substitutes sector. These investments now come on stream, resulting in an increase in production and a fall in the domestic price. As in the first example, there has been no change in trade policy, but the implicit tariff measure falls, suggesting a trade liberalization. (In an extreme case an economy can 'float off' the QRs: the restrictions remain in force but cease to be binding, so that trade policy becomes irrelevant.)

Should the fact that the implicit tariff changes in both examples in the absence of changes in trade policy be considered as a disadvantage of that measure? Obviously, there are arguments either way. The essence of trade policy consists of the substitution effects it induces in production and consumption through changes in prices. It seems artificial to accept some and to disqualify other price changes, depending upon whether or not they can be deemed to be the direct result of a change in trade policy. In addition, in practice it will often be impossible to make such distinctions. We therefore accept changes in prices of tradables (or the resulting quantity changes) as 'trade liberalization' (or increased trade restrictiveness, as the case may be) irrespective of whether or not they are caused by trade policy changes. One implication of this position is that quantitative measures of trade reform may well fail to correspond with a policy-based account.

Changes in Policies

Policy Accounts

Nevertheless, an account of major trade policy changes is obviously a useful first step towards the identification of periods of trade liberalization or trade restriction. Constructing such an account is usually unproblematic. Such an account of changes in policy is useful for dating liberalization episodes, but will, obviously, not generate a quantitative indicator (unless one is willing to admit the subjective judgements of country authors, as was done in the recent World Bank study). At the very least an account of policy changes serves as a check on the quantitative measures discussed below. Policy accounts should cover not just changes in trade policy narrowly defined (tariffs, quotas and other NTBs), but also changes in the system of foreign exchange allocation (for example, the introduction of foreign exchange certificates or the introduction of a forex auction).

Incidence Measures

These measures typically count non-tariff barriers (including quotas) as the number or percentage of SITC line items covered by NTBs. This approach (used in some UNCTAD publications) is clearly extremely crude. It has no theoretical appeal since the severity of trade restrictions is not taken into account. For example, the removal of a large number of quotas would be measured as trade liberalization even if none of them were binding. Conversely, with binding quotas in place (and unchanged), theory would suggest that as real income rises the trade regime becomes more restrictive: the implicit tariff rate would have to rise to choke off the increase in import demand. But, obviously, the incidence measure would not register a change in trade restrictiveness. We do not therefore regard this as an indicator to be commended for the cross-country comparisons.

Changes in Prices

Implicit Tariff Measures

The domestic price (ex-factory) of an importable good i may be written as:

$$p_{mi} = p_m^*.e.\,(1 + t_i) \tag{7.1}$$

where p_m is the c.i.f. import price (in dollars), e the exchange rate (domestic currency per dollar) and t the (implicit) tariff rate. Given observations on world prices, domestic prices and the exchange rate, eq. (7.1) may be used to derive an implicit tariff index. Trade liberalization can then be measured as a reduction in this index.

The implicit tariff calculation is appealing since it directly measures differences between world and domestic prices. There are, however, three problems involved with it. First, it is not a measure of incentives for producers (or consumers). For example, in an economy in which only tradables were produced, a proportional increase of all producer prices (both for importables and exportables) would be registered as an increase in protection while producers would still face the same relative prices. Second, it may be extremely difficult to find a level of aggregation on which world prices and domestic prices could be compared directly. The two aggregates (domestic and foreign) for which prices are compared may differ radically in composition and this difference may change over time. In many cases, one may not be able to do better than match SITC categories (for imports) and ISIC categories (for domestic production) as carefully as possible.

The most serious problem involved in differences in composition concerns inputs. Unless one works at a very low level of aggregation, domestic production and imports may differ substantially in their composition in terms of final and intermediate goods. For example, in many African countries a tightening of trade policy has resulted in an increased share of consumer goods in domestic production of importables and an increased share of intermediate and capital goods in imports. If tariffs on intermediate inputs are raised and tariffs on final goods are kept constant, the implicit tariff measure (which corresponds to the nominal, not the effective, rate of protection) will register an increase in protection when in fact domestic producers of import substitutes are being squeezed as the prices of their imported inputs rise.

Changes in c.i.f. prices (unless reported separately by category of end use) may therefore be quite misleading indicators of changes in protection. In the limit (approached by Tanzania in the early 1980s) imports consist entirely of intermediate inputs and capital goods for which no domestic substitutes exist. Obviously, in such cases the implicit tariff calculation makes no sense.

Third, reported c.i.f. prices are likely to reflect over-invoicing. Again, this need not be serious if the focus is on changes in t_i rather than on its level, but the degree of over-invoicing is most unlikely to remain constant over the period of analysis. For example, Bevan *et al.* (1990) show that for given tax and trade policies the incentive to over-invoice is greater under a system of cost-plus price control. The Tanzanian trade liberalization coincided with the gradual abandonment of such a price control system, so that the extent of over-invoicing probably fell. This would tend to lead to an *underestimate* of the extent of trade liberalization, since the calculation would pick up an artificial fall in the reported c.i.f. price p_{mi}. One way to deal with this problem is to use price data as reported by partner countries (see Yeats, 1991) rather than customs data.

Fourth, to aggregate individual t_i estimates requires a weighting procedure. Sometimes base-year import values are used as weights. This is clearly wrong since it would give a weight of zero to goods for which imports were banned and, more generally, it would be biased; the lower the weights, the more successful the trade policy would have been in suppressing imports of a particular category. The alternatives are to use weights either based on the composition of domestic production or on the composition of expenditure. Use of these two methods will give very different results and both should be used since they address different questions. Trade liberalization induces substitution effects both in production and in demand. Clearly, production weights are appropriate for the former and expenditure weights for the latter.

Which prices should be used for p_{mi}? Implicit GDP deflators for sectors producing import substitutes are *not* appropriate: these deflators correspond to the concept of effective protection and are therefore not consistent with the nominal protection formulation of eq. (7.1). Ideally one uses ex-factory gross output prices when the focus is on incentives for producers. These are not always reported; they may have to be derived from output series in current and constant prices. One can also use consumer prices using CPI components for importables. In general this is more difficult; it is easier to match ISIC and SITC categories than to map from CPI components to imports categories. If CPI data are used, care must be taken to use consumption rather than production or import weights.

As a check, it is useful to try to measure both producer and consumer prices. When indirect taxes change, the two will not move in parallel. This is as it should be. Conceivably production is not protected at all while consumers do face a higher price and vice versa. Both should be measured since they are indicators of the extent to which there might be substitution effects in production and in consumption, respectively.

Relative Price Changes

While the implicit tariff rate has an intuitive appeal because of its similarity to the nominal tariff rate, it is a poor measure of changes in the incentives facing either producers or consumers since it ignores alternatives. It can be supplemented by relative price indicators. In the small open economy (SOE) model three aggregates are used: importables (M), exportables (X) and non-tradables (N). Incentives can then be summarized by two relative prices, that is, p_X/p_M (the domestic terms of trade index) and p_M/p_N. Measuring trade policy by the ratio of the domestic to the world terms of trade:

$$(p_X/p_M)/(p^*_X/p^*_M)$$

and writing, in analogy with eq. (7.1), the domestic price of exportables as:

$$p_X = p_X^*.e.(1 + t_e)$$

where t_e measures net export subsidies. The ratio of the two terms of trade indexes then reduces to:

$$(1 + t_e)/(1 + t_m)$$

This indicates that in the absence of export taxes or subsidies ($t_e = 0$) or when t_e is at least constant, the implicit tariff rate is an appropriate indicator of changes in p_X/p_M (corrected for changes in the world terms of trade). However, in some of the country studies t_e may be subject to substantial change. For example, in Nigeria in the late 1980s there was a large reduction in export crop taxation. This should be counted as trade liberalization but is, obviously, not picked up by the implicit tariff measure.

As in the case of imports, the issue of weighting arises in the construction of a p_X price index. However, the issue is likely to be much less serious, since in many countries there is little domestic consumption of exportables (oil in Nigeria and coffee in Ethiopia are notable exceptions). Nevertheless, care must be taken to use production weights in the construction of an aggregate price index p_X.

Parallel Market Premium

This indicator has the advantage of being easily measured in most countries. It is appropriate if the supply of imports through smuggling is so substantial that domestic prices of importables reflect not the official exchange rate e but the parallel rate. In other cases, for example, if border controls are reasonably effective, then the parallel market premium is an inappropriate indicator of trade restrictiveness. If smuggling is very difficult, demand for foreign exchange in the parallel market will largely be asset demand and the premium can then not be used as an indicator of trade restrictiveness.

Foreign Exchange Certificates

For about a year, starting in October 1991, Kenya operated a system of Foreign Exchange Bearer Certificates (FEBCs). Effectively these certificates amounted to a circumvention of exchange control. They were denominated in foreign currency and could be freely purchased at face value by Kenyan residents. The certificates could be used to purchase imports, including goods otherwise subject to QRs. While the certificates could be bought at face value, they effectively represented an import licence for goods subject to quotas and therefore the FEBCs were traded at a premium. This premium can be used as a measure of the QR part of the implicit tariff rate.

Changes in Quantities

Trade Intensity Measures

Trade intensity is measured as the ratio of trade (imports plus exports) to GDP. In cross-country work, trade intensity has been regressed on explanatory variables such as per caput GDP and country size in terms of population or area. The regression is then interpreted as establishing a 'normal' pattern (in the tradition of gravity models and of Chenery's cross-country work), with the residuals taken as an indicator of that country's trade policy.

One objection to trade intensity measures is that imports are financed both by export revenue and by capital flows. Therefore, a change in the trade intensity measure $(M + X)/GDP$ may simply pick up an increase in aid flows. Also, the use of the GDP variable is difficult to defend. For example, an increase in real income as a result of a terms of trade improvement will lead to an increase in trade intensity. The measure will then indicate trade liberalization even if there have been no policy changes and no substitution effects, either in production or in demand.

Changes in Factor Use

For some countries it will be possible to measure changes in the allocation of production factors between sectors (for example, the broad X, M and N-aggregates of the SOE model) directly. This might provide a leading indicator of production changes. For example, it may be possible to measure shifts of labour and capital into the export sector before a change in the volume of exports. Some countries publish data on the sectoral allocation of investment, and labour force surveys can be used to measure labour shifts.

Import Counter-Factuals

This is a variant of trade intensity measures. The effect of trade policy is measured by comparing actual import volumes with counterfactual volumes given by an import demand function with real income and some price variable as the explanatory variables. In practice (Narasimhan and Pritchett; 1993; Reinikka, 1993) fixed income and price elasticities are imposed. Given the counterfactual defined by the import demand function one can then derive a measure of trade restrictiveness either in price or in quantity space. In quantity space the measure is simply the difference between actual and counterfactual; if actual imports are found to be lower than the demand function predicts, then the difference is deemed to be the result of trade policy. If a measure in price space is desired, the import demand function is in fact inverted to derive (given the chosen values of the elasticities) the implicit price change from the observed changes in real income and in the volume of imports. For example, for an income elasticity of 1.25 and a price elasticity of -1 (these are the values preferred by Pritchett) an import volume increase of 20 per cent would, if accompanied by a 5 per cent real income increase, be interpreted as the result of a 14 per cent reduction in the price variable and this would be the indicator of trade liberalization.

This method has two disadvantages. First, the empirical basis for the two coefficients (the price and income elasticities) is often extremely weak. Narasimhan and Pritchett simply impose plausible values for the elasticities and normalize by designating the 1970–9 period as a free trade period. However, in country applications it may be possible to estimate the coefficients econometrically. Second, the specification is crude: while a constant price elasticity might apply to consumption demand, imports (the difference between consumption and domestic production) are unlikely to be iso(price)elastic.

A more sophisticated approach is to estimate a demand system, thereby allowing explicitly for substitution in demand between importables and non-tradables. However, as before, the problem is that this yields a counterfactual demand for importables but not for imports. Implicitly, imported and domestically produced goods are treated as complements. There is little justification for ignoring changes in domestic production by focusing on the estimation of a demand system.

A drawback of all quantity-based measures is that they are likely to pick up changes in the extent of illegal trade. For example, a trade liberalization might result in a large increase in official imports at the expense of smuggling, with little change in total imports. Unlike a price-based measure, a quantity-based measure would then give an unrealistic indication of the change in incentives for consumers and producers.

Trade Reform Measurement and Policy Compatibility

The literature on the measurement of trade liberalization is usually not based on a theoretical model. When there is such a link, either implicit or explicit, the model is invariably a barter model and issues of policy compatibility do not arise.

These two points are related, since trade reform raises a compatibility issue only in a monetary economy. Trade liberalization lowers the domestic price of importables, either by relaxing (or removing) quotas or by lowering (or abolishing) tariffs. In a barter economy this has the usual substitution effects in production and demand, tending to increase import demand. But, unless export production responds immediately, this will be exactly offset by income effects: the reduction in income from tariffs and quota rents will have a negative effect on import demand. As long as there is no change in world prices, in capital flows and in the volume of exports, trade liberalization will not affect imports (measured in world prices). The short-run effect will be a change in the composition of imports (a better allocation), not a change in the aggregate level. Hence there is no change in the trade deficit since substitution effects on import demand are offset by income effects.

However, in a monetary economy there is, in addition, a real balance effect. The reduction in the domestic price of importables lowers money demand, an effect that is potentially important in African economies where money demand tends to be dominated by transactions demand. Without offsetting policy changes, trade liberalization makes the government's set of policies incompatible. Private agents will attempt to run down their excess money balances. But in doing so they will raise import demand and (assuming a fixed exchange rate regime) there will be a run-down of reserves: the trade deficit increases and this is financed by a fall in reserves.

This may be sustainable, depending upon whether or not the initial level of reserves is sufficient to finance the central bank's purchase, at the given exchange rate, of the private sector's excess money balances. In Africa the combination of low reserves and large trade liberalizations is common, so that trade reform is likely to be unsustainable if not co-ordinated with other policies.

In Section 7.3 we consider offsetting policy changes that eliminate the excess money supply so that the trade liberalization becomes sustainable. Here we need to consider the consequences of such policy changes for the measurement of trade liberalization.

These are potentially serious. As an example, consider a trade liberalization made sustainable by an increase in indirect taxes. If trade liberalization is measured by the change in the domestic consumer price of importables, the measure will understate the extent of trade reform since the negative effect on the price of the liberalization itself is off-set by the price-raising effect of the tax increase. Indeed, in the extreme case when consumption demand consists entirely of importables (that is, there are no non-tradable consumer goods and there is no domestic demand for exportables) the two effects will exactly offset each other: the indirect tax increase keeps the consumer price constant. Hence, using this measure, the researcher will conclude that no liberalization has taken place. As a second example, suppose that indirect taxes were raised, but this time only for non-tradable consumer goods. This time the measure would indicate a trade liberalization. But the two examples differ, not in the extent of the trade policy change but only in the method chosen to ensure compatibility.

Obviously, this could have absurd consequences. Suppose trade liberalization was measured (now by a quantity measure, say the volume of imports) for a sample of countries where some had made reform sustainable through a liberalizing exchange rate adjustment while in others no offsetting policy measures were taken so that reform had to be abandoned once reserves were exhausted. The researcher would then conclude that reform took place in the latter group of countries, those in which reform failed since in those countries imports would rise. Similarly, for the countries in which reform was successful, the conclusion would be that no liberalization had occurred since imports would remain constant in the short run and would rise only in the long run, when resources had shifted to the export sector.

Whether or not the measure of trade liberalization is affected by policy changes introduced to ensure compatibility depends on what those changes are. For example, if in the previous example compatibility was ensured by an increase in aid rather than by a tax increase, then the trade liberalization would be correctly measured, either by a quantity measure or by a price measure such as the implicit tariff rate – the domestic price of importables would fall.

The implication of this discussion is not that trade liberalization cannot be measured. Rather, it is that, while trade liberalization and the policy change introduced to ensure sustainability are analytically distinct, they have to be considered simultaneously in empirical work. This issue of measurement will be considered further in Section 7.3.

Conclusion

As noted above, the comparison of different methods of measuring trade policy in cross-country work is rather disquieting. There is no correlation between the rankings of countries produced by different methods. In a single-country, time-series context, Reinikka's work on Kenya is more promising.

7.3   MEASURING INCREDIBILITY AND ITS CONSEQUENCES

Introduction

Several African trade liberalizations have been reversed. This section considers the circumstances in which private agents might reasonably expect that there is a risk of policy reversal, and how they will respond if they hold such expectations.

Causes of Incredibility and Diagnostics

Clearly, there is a myriad of circumstances that might cause a policy reversal, most of which are not analysable, so that there is an irreducible level of uncertainty. However, there are some circumstances in which reasonably alert private agents can predict policy reversal with a fairly high probability of being correct and this is what will concern us here. The sufficient conditions for policy reversal to be predictable follow from the necessary conditions for a liberalization to be sustainable. That is, if the necessary conditions are not met, then policy change is predictable and so the liberalization is incredible. There are three necessary conditions for a trade liberalization to be credible: *macroeconomic compatibility*, the absence of *systematic forecastability*, and *time consistency*. We now review each of these, showing how a breach in the conditions will make a reversal of a trade liberalization a predictable event.

Macroeconomic Compatibility

Macroeconomic compatibility has two components, balance of payments and fiscal. Of these the former is generally the more important in the African context. A trade liberalization without any other policy changes almost invariably worsens the balance of payments in African circumstances, whereas it might worsen or improve the budget deficit.

Payments compatibility A good way of seeing the effect of a trade liberalization on the balance of payments is through the monetary approach to the balance of payments. The balance of payments is in equilibrium when the supply of money is willingly held by private domestic agents. Abstracting from the dispersion in tariff equivalent rates, the domestic prices of importables and exportables are related to world prices as described in eq. (7.1) above.

A trade liberalization that lowers implicit tariffs without changing other policies lowers the domestic price of importables, which then lowers the price level since importables are part of expenditure. This in turn reduces the transactions demand for money, which is a function of the price level and the quantity of expenditure. The resulting excess supply of money is a payments deficit. There are many strategies that can restore compatibility, but they work by one of two approaches. Either the excess supply of money is eliminated by policy changes that raise the demand for money, or it is eliminated by policies that reduce the supply of money.

Money demand-raising policies Money demand-raising policies work by offsetting the reduction in the price level brought about by the trade liberalization. The most notable of such policies is exchange rate depreciation. Let us take a couple of examples. First, suppose that there is no export tax ($t_x = 0$), whereas there is an import restriction ($t_m > 0$). The trade liberalization lowers the price of importables unless it is offset by a rise in e (exchange rate depreciation). If the price of imports is permitted to fall then the demand for money falls, producing a payments deficit. Secondly, suppose that trade restrictions are all on the exportables side; there is an export tax, $t_x > 0$, but no import restrictions, $t_m = 0$. Further, to simplify, suppose that exportables are not consumed domestically (Zambian copper), and that whatever is raised from the export tax is given to other private agents. Then the trade liberalization has no impact effect on the domestic price level and so no impact effect on the balance of payments. Gradually, however, as resources relocate into the export sector, real income in the economy rises, since the exporters gain more than the beneficiaries of the transfer payments financed by the export tax revenue have lost. Hence, as real income rises, real expenditure rises, and this raises the demand for money. The trade liberalization therefore gradually improves the balance of payments. Usually in Africa, trade restrictions are more severe on the import side than on the export side ($t_m > t_x$) and importables are more important in expenditure than the exportables. As a result, trade liberalization has an impact effect that worsens the balance of payments.

The second strategy for raising the demand for money is to raise indirect taxes on expenditure. Note that this does not need to be on tradable goods. Taxes levied on non-tradables will still raise the price level and so raise the demand for money. The objective is simply to raise the demand for money by raising any part of the price level sufficiently to bring the average price level back to its pre-liberalization level. This was tried, for example, in Kenya during the 1989 trade liberalization.

Money supply-reducing policies   If neither of the above strategies is adopted then a trade liberalization that lowers t_m will lower the demand for money. It will therefore worsen the balance of payments unless the money supply is correspondingly reduced. Several policies work in this way, but they fall into three groups, each of which reduces the money supply through a different mechanism.

- *Asset strategies* involve the government in selling some claim to private agents in return for currency. The government can sell foreign currency. For this, it must either run down its reserves, receive extra foreign aid, or borrow from abroad. This is the underpinning to the notion that a balance of payments deficit is self-correcting. A deficit implies that the private sector is net selling domestic currency to the central bank in return for dollars and so the domestic money supply is falling. Once it has fallen to match the fall in money demand the balance of payments is again in equilibrium. The problem with this strategy is that the government must have sufficient foreign exchange to sustain it to the point at which the money supply has fully adjusted. For a large trade liberalization this will require either large initial reserves or an assured supply of programme aid. If these conditions are not met, then the strategy will be perceived as incompatible. Other than foreign exchange, the government can sell real assets such as equity in public enterprises, or it can sell claims against itself, such as bonds. The scope for these is very variable across Africa. In all cases, for these sales of claims to reduce the money supply there must be no offsetting increase in government expenditure.

- *Savings strategies* involve the government in improving the budget. This can be done either by increasing revenue or reducing expenditure. Necessarily, these strategies work slowly since they work through flows whereas the previous policies have worked through stock-adjustment. Nor has the government any very obvious way of signalling that such a policy change will be sustained for a sufficient duration to reduce the money supply to some target level; government statements of intent on future budget deficits have virtually no informational content and are perceived as such. Hence, budget-based strategies seem singularly ill-suited to maintain compatibility in the face of a quantum change in trade policy. Rather, to be credible, trade liberalization would need to creep in arrears of revealed improvements in the budget. The one exception to this in Africa may be the switch to a *cash budget rule*. Since this is not just a target but a procedure, it has greater durability. In both Uganda and Zambia the adoption of such a rule produced a very rapid end to high inflation and changed expectations may have played some part in this.

- The final strategy is to reduce the money supply only by *reducing financial intermediation*. That is, the government does not attempt to reduce the monetary claims outstanding against it (M_0), but rather the claims between private agents (for example, M_1–M_0). To do this it must force banks to reduce their lending. It can directly regulate lending by imposing a 'corset' (such as the British government used to do), or it can reduce it indirectly by raising the minimum required ratio of cash or liquidity relative to bank deposits. One problem with this strategy is that it achieves compatible trade liberalization at the price of intensifying financial repression and there is no presumption that there will be net efficiency gains. A limit to the strategy is evidently when private financial intermediation has been completely crowded out of the banking system (as was virtually the case in Tanzania during the 1980s). If the country starts from this position then there is no scope for attaining compatibility in this way.

As stated above, the direct impact effect of a trade liberalization that lowers t_m is generally to worsen the balance of payments. Since the

whole point of trade liberalization is to secure gains in terms of improved allocative efficiency, there will at some stage be an increase in
real income. However, these gains are likely to take some years to
accrue. The gain in real income will raise real expenditure and hence
raise the demand for money, so that gradually the balance of payments will improve. This alone implies that the need for offsetting
policies to cope with the impact effect of a trade liberalization exceeds
that in the long term. If, for example, trade liberalization is made compatible by devaluation, then the devaluation needed in the short term
will exceed that needed in the long term (see Collier and Gunning,
1992). Further, because the income gains are slow to come through,
the short-term effect of trade liberalization is to raise permanent income without raising current income, so inducing dissavings. In part
the resulting attempt to deplete assets will simply lower their price
until they are again willingly held. However, in part there will be an
attempt by the private sector in aggregate to convert some of its claims
upon the government into foreign exchange. The claim of the private
sector on the government is money, and so the dissaving will reduce
the demand for money and so worsen the balance of payments. This
reinforces the tendency for the impact effect to be worse than the long-
run effect. Few of the strategies for restoring compatibility are capable
of achieving a large impact effect. As discussed above, working through
the budget is inevitably slow, and relying upon the sale of claims is
only feasible if the government is initially quite asset-rich or not heavily
in debt. The exchange rate is likely to be the main policy option and
if this is politically infeasible then a large trade liberalization will not
be compatible with debt payment obligations.

Diagnostics of Payments-Incompatibility

Private agents have an incentive to diagnose payments-incompatibility. Here we consider the diagnostic that they are likely to use. Ideally,
the researcher wishing to predict speculative responses to payments-
incompatibility should use the same diagnostics as the private agents
whose behaviour is to be predicted. Private agents can diagnose incompatibility by monitoring outcomes, policies and 'states of the world'.

Monitoring outcomes   The most obvious diagnostic of incompatibility
is the change in the level of reserves. What private agents can infer
from this depends both on whether and how the government attempts
to ensure compatibility. If the trade liberalization is not co-ordinated

with other policy changes then the reserves will start to fall immediately. This may, but need not, indicate that the policy stance is unsustainable. Private agents must form a judgement as to whether the level of reserves is sufficient to accommodate the reduction in money demand. Since the running down of excess real money balances will not occur instantaneously, private agents must try to judge from the flow (the reduction in the level of reserves) whether the stock will be sufficient. However, in the African context this may be a distinction without a difference; typically reserve levels are so low that almost any reduction in the level will be interpreted as a threat to sustainability.

When the government does introduce policies to eliminate the effect of trade liberalization on money demand, the chosen method may affect predictability. If liberalization is combined with a devaluation then sustainability can be judged instantaneously; if reserves do not fall after the devaluation, sustainability is ensured. Conversely, when aid is supplied to enable the government to purchase excess money balances from private agents it will take time before the sufficiency of the package can be determined. Hence, the information conveyed by the reserves diagnostic depends on the nature of co-ordinating policy changes.

Let us look at Kenyan foreign exchange reserves from 1976 to 1991. The trade liberalization attempt of 1980, in which t_m was lowered without offsetting changes in the exchange rate, would be predicted to yield an unsustainable payments deficit. This evidently happened in no uncertain terms. There was a catastrophic loss of reserves of a magnitude quite outside the range of experience before or since, and at a rate that could not be sustained for more than about a year. In September 1980, the liberalization was reversed. Although the reversal was not fully predictable, what was predictable was that either there would have to be some major policy change (such as reversal) or there would need to be a rare stroke of good fortune such as a repeat of the coffee boom.

A related diagnostic is the current account of the balance of payments. A trade liberalization made compatible by aid or commercial borrowing will initially deteriorate the current account but raise the reserves, culminating, if successful, in a depletion of the reserves back to their initial level at which point the current account reverts to its initial level.

A third diagnostic is the value of merchandise imports and exports. The impact effect of a trade liberalization on the volume of exports is likely to be minimal because supply response takes time (except in the case where there is initially substantial smuggling). Hence, in the short term, except where compatibility is achieved by reserve depletion or aid, a compatible trade liberalization will not increase imports but simply change the process by which a given value is allocated and hence their composition. An increase in merchandise imports associated with the liberalization is therefore *prima facie* a diagnostic either that the liberalization is incompatible or that it is reliant upon the reduction in the money supply by the use of foreign exchange.

Each of these diagnostics should be measured in units of foreign exchange. Because speculation will tend to overwhelm payments-incompatible liberalizations rather rapidly, the reserves and the current account should be reported on a monthly or quarterly basis for the period of the liberalization attempt.

A fourth diagnostic is the impact of the liberalization on the price level. Where possible this should show the part of the consumer price index that is composed of importable goods. There should be some discussion of whether this part of the CPI truly reflects market-clearing prices of importables, or whether it is contaminated by price controls or biases in statistical coverage. If the liberalization lowers the price, or more likely, lowers it relative to some counterfactual trend increase, then it is either incompatible or has been made compatible by some compensating reduction in the money supply.

Monitoring policies   The two money-demand-increasing strategies are easily monitored, namely the average rate of indirect taxes and the nominal exchange rate. Asset-based strategies of money supply reduction can be monitored by the government's net receipts of programme aid, commercial borrowing and sales of domestic debt. The government's savings stance can be monitored through the budget deficit as a percentage of GDP. Finally, monetary policy is readily monitorable through the minimum cash (or liquidity) ratio imposed by the central bank on the commercial banks.

Monitoring 'states of the world'   A policy configuration can be made compatible or incompatible by exogenous shocks. The most common of such shocks are changes in the terms of trade. An improvement can validate an otherwise incompatible liberalization attempt, while a deterioration will require macroeconomic policy change even in the absence of a trade liberalization. The terms of trade is usually a readily available series, at least on an annual basis. Because imports usually exceed exports, terms of trade shocks originating from higher import prices have a more serious effect than those originating from lower export prices for equivalent deteriorations in the terms of trade. Hence, where possible, it is useful to decompose changes in the terms of trade during a trade liberalization episode into changes in the dollar prices of exports and changes in the dollar prices of imports. In a few cases external shocks occur independent of the terms of trade. For example, Nigeria in 1981 faced a sharp drop in oil sales despite no deterioration in the world price of oil. Similarly, in the tightly controlled world diamond market, all producers faced sharply reduced sales at given prices during 1981. Finally, there are periodic domestic shocks, most commonly climatic, reducing agricultural output below normal. One example would be the drought in Zambia during the liberalization attempt in 1992. The objective in monitoring states of the world is not to build up an exhaustive narrative account of the economy, but simply to check whether during key episodes of trade liberalization there were exogenous factors influencing outcomes and, if necessary, to quantify the importance of those factors.

Budget compatibility Trade liberalization on the export side, that is, lowering t_x, is always liable to lower government revenue in the short run. By contrast, reductions in t_m are ambiguous. In many cases a large part of t_m is in the form of the tariff-equivalent of quotas. These trade restrictions generate intra-private transfers rather than revenue for the government. The conversion from quotas to tariffs is likely to be revenue-raising. Further, quotas tend to be set closest to zero on those products that carry the highest tariffs. The liberalization of quotas therefore probably changes the composition of imports in favour of revenue-yielding items. Because of the very detailed nature of tariff schedules it will not generally be possible to disentangle the effects of the trade liberalization. Therefore the best feasible approach is likely to be to monitor government revenue from tariffs as a percentage of GDP.

In addition to the direct effects of changes in the composition of imports and tariff rates on tariff revenues, the compensating policy changes needed to maintain payments-compatibility will have revenue effects. For example, if the exchange rate is depreciated, the impact on the budget will depend upon whether the government is a net buyer or net seller of foreign exchange. This can generally be found from the central bank's 'foreign exchange budget', which will show sources and uses of foreign exchange.

The overall budget deficit is already to be monitored as an indicator of the government's savings effort. Recall that an improvement in the budget is one strategy for making a trade liberalization compatible.

However, a sharp deterioration in the budget, especially one triggered by a collapse in revenue that could be related to trade policy, would be a symptom of fiscal incompatibility. Whereas payments-incompatibility is manifested in an unsustainable loss of reserves, fiscal incompatibility is manifested by an unsustainable budget deficit relative to GDP. In the short run, almost any budget deficit is sustainable at the price of accelerating inflation, but this in turn triggers policy change.

In principle, fiscal incompatibility can give rise to incredibility during a trade liberalization in just the same way as payments-incompatibility. However, in practice this is much less likely. First, the link of trade policy changes with the budget deficit is far weaker than the link with the balance of payments deficit. A deterioration in the budget is more likely to be due to other factors; trade policy would not be high on the list of 'usual suspects'. Consequently, it would not be high on the list of policies liable to be changed in response to an unsustainable budget deficit. Finally, in many cases the fiscal position is neither revealed nor corrected with anything like the speed of a payments deficit. For speculation based on an assessment of policy incompatibility to be profitable, enforced policy change within a fairly short time span must be forecastable. This is because the costs of speculation are broadly linear in the time in which the speculator must wait between betting on policy change and the implementation of the change, whereas the gains are broadly linear in the magnitude of policy change. Betting on a change in the exchange rate or trade restrictions when it can be seen that the reserves will be exhausted in a further three months on current policies is likely to be more profitable than betting on an increase in tariff rates because the budget deficit and with it the inflation rate have increased to 'unacceptable' levels. The exhaustion of reserves is a harder constraint than the unacceptability of an inflation rate, and the policy response to it is more predictably likely to provide opportunities for speculation. For this reason, the analysis of speculative responses to macroeconomic incredibility should focus on payments incompatibility rather than on fiscal incompatibility.

Systematic Forecastability: Endogenous Trade Policy

The notion that some aspects of macroeconomic policy might be systematically forecastable, and that this would alter the efficacy of policy, is due to Lucas. In the Lucas model the government varies monetary policy systematically in response to an unemployment target. That is, monetary policy is changed not in some *ad hoc* fashion but according to some systematic criteria, which could be described as a policy *rule*: 'When the "state of the world" is *y*, policy will be *x*'. However, private agents know that the government is operating according to this policy rule and so can to an extent predict monetary policy.

In Africa, the equivalent policy predictability would be with respect to trade restrictions and the balance of payments. Although not universal, it has been common for governments (and their central banks) to ration foreign exchange according to its availability. When little foreign exchange comes into the central bank, instead of its price being raised, its rationing has been intensified, raising the implicit tariff rate. Conversely, when foreign exchange becomes abundant, instead of the price being lowered, allocations are increased. This is termed an *endogenous trade policy*.

A change in trade policy might therefore reflect either of two types of decision. First, it could simply be a *response* according to an existing policy rule: the state of the world has changed and so, maintaining the policy rule, trade policy is altered. Second, the change in trade policy could represent an initiative, a change in the rule. The type of trade liberalizations this study is mainly interested in are policy initiatives. However, quantitative measures of trade policy do not distinguish between initiatives and responses. For example, quantitative measures will show that there were trade liberalizations in Kenya in 1978 and 1980, in the sense that in these years the average implicit tariff rate fell. We need to look behind these figures to see how policy was actually being made in order to discover that the liberalization of 1978 was a response to the favourable state of the world (the coffee boom), whereas that of 1980 was an initiative.

Liberalizations that are responses under an endogenous trade policy rule can in certain circumstances be predicted to be reversed and are therefore incredible. Policy is predictable to the extent that the events influencing the supply of foreign exchange to the central bank are predictable. By definition, 'states of the world' that are shocks are not predictable. No one can predict a coffee boom or a drought with any accuracy. However, once such a shock has occurred, it is sometimes reasonably clear that it will not persist. Hence, while the arrival of such a state of the world is a shock, its departure is not. In these circumstances, if the government is known to be operating an endogenous trade policy, then private agents can infer from the expected change in the state of the world that trade policy is likely to be changed. For example, it was reasonably predictable that the Kenyan liberalization of 1978 would be reversed as the coffee boom faded.

The methodological implication is that liberalizations should be categorized according to whether they are responses or initiatives. If they are responses, then the nature of the change in the state of the world that triggered the response should be discussed with a view as to whether it was predictably temporary. To take three examples, a liberalization following an oil discovery would be likely to be a policy response but it would not be predictably temporary; a liberalization during a cocoa boom would be likely to be a policy response and in that case would be predictably temporary; a liberalization without a change in the state of the world but following a debate on whether to change policy would be likely to be a policy initiative (for example, the introduction of a foreign exchange auction). Only the second of these three examples would be a candidate for incredibility due to systematic forecastability. Of course, the other two examples might also be incredible, but for different reasons.

Time Inconsistency

The third and final necessary condition for credibility during a trade liberalization is time consistency. The problem of time inconsistency is best understood in the context of a two-period game (see Persson, 1988, for a review). The game is between the government and the private sector. The government must choose trade policies in each period. Let us take the example of an export tax on coffee that the government can choose in each period, t_{x1} and t_{x2}, and which the government needs for revenue. The private sector has two decisions, both of which must be taken in the first period. It must decide whether to plant coffee trees and whether to use 'fertilizer' in period 1. 'Fertilizer' in this story has the effect not so much of raising yields as of shifting them between time periods: if fertilizer is applied in period 1, it raises the yield in period 1 at the cost of reducing it in period 2.

The problem worrying the government is that by levying an export tax it discourages the planting of coffee trees. This is socially inefficient and reduces its own revenue in period 2. The 'first-best' would be if the government could in some way fool the private sector into expecting that the export tax would be zero. The private sector would then plant coffee and the government could then tax it, since once the coffee trees are planted there is (by assumption) nothing that the private sector can do about it. The government might in this situation be tempted to liberalize trade in period 1 (that is, set $t_{x1} = 0$), in the hope that private agents would then expect that the policy would be maintained in period 2. If this strategy worked it would be superior to setting the export tax at the same positive rate in both periods ($t_{x1} = t_{x2} > 0$), which could therefore be described as the 'second-best' strategy.

However, private agents know the structure of the game and so know that the government has no incentive to maintain the export tax at zero in period 2. Once the private sector has planted coffee then the government will tax it because the tax then causes no distortion. The trade liberalization in period 1 is therefore incredible because the maintenance of the policy would be against the government's own interests. The maintenance of free trade in this example is said to be *time inconsistent*. If the government ignores the problem of time inconsistency and sets $t_{x1} = 0$, then private agents know that in period 2 the export tax will be positive. Knowing this, they not only have an incentive not to plant coffee, but they have an incentive to use 'fertilizer'. The fertilizer enables private agents to bring their output forward from period 2 to period 1, thereby avoiding the anticipated period 2 tax. However, since the fertilizer merely shifts output, it is socially costly. The government's attempt to achieve the first-best has therefore resulted in the 'third-best': no coffee planting and excessive fertilizer.

Time inconsistency may well be a major problem in African trade liberalizations. The export tax example could easily be modified into something fairly realistic. Initially, the government had an incentive to have high taxes on the export sector. Over time, this persistent high taxation (explicit or implicit) has gradually withered the export sector to the point where the tax yields little revenue. The government has therefore little to lose from reducing the taxation, that is, embarking upon trade liberalization. However, if private agents respond by making irreversible investments in the export sector restoring it to its initial size, the government's decision problem is exactly as it was initially, and so it will again choose to impose high taxation. A second important way in which an African trade liberalization might be viewed as time inconsistent is if it is supported by programme aid from donors. The government might simply be adopting the liberalization in order to get the aid, after which it will revert to trade restrictions.

In the above situations it is the structure of incentives rather than the government's actual intentions that is the cause of the problem. That is, the government might genuinely want to liberalize permanently, but it cannot escape from the problem that the private sector knows that it, or a future government, has an incentive to change its mind.

It is quite difficult to research time inconsistency empirically, but a good approach is to ask three questions:

- Why did the government adopt and maintain trade restrictions: that is, what were the benefits for it, or for the interest groups that it might have represented?
- Why did it liberalize: that is, how did the balance of interests change so as to produce the liberalization episode?
- Were private agents to have acted on the assumption that the policy would be permanent (for example, by investing in the export sector), how would this have further changed the balance of interests?

From these answers comes the concluding question to be addressed: was there, at the time of the liberalization episode, good reason to expect that the future political equilibrium trade policy would be different from that in the past? If the answer to this fourth question is 'no', then the trade liberalization episode was probably viewed as time inconsistent by private agents.

Consequences of Incredibility and Diagnostics

The basic theory of how private agents respond to incredible trade liberalization is due to Calvo (1987) and Dixit (1989). Calvo's idea is that, if an agent anticipates that implicit tariffs will be increased, the appropriate strategy is to hoard imports, selling them once their price has been increased by the reimposition of the implicit tariffs. Dixit's idea is that faced with uncertainty about how relative prices will evolve, agents will defer irreversible investment until the uncertainty is resolved, preferring liquid assets because the uncertainty creates a premium on keeping options open. Collier and Gunning (1994) bring these arguments together, so that the drop in fixed investment provides the finance for the hoarding of imports. There are several strategies that private agents can adopt in order to hoard imports and the full range of options will vary according to the details of the control regime. The range below is representative.

First, agents might choose to stockpile import licences. In many African trade control regimes imports require a licence that entitles the possessor to purchase foreign exchange for the specified import good. The stockpiling of these licences is the cheapest way of stockpiling imports because the goods themselves are not purchased and put in storage. Hence, the agent does not incur interest and storage costs. If the private expectation is that trade controls will be tightened by making licences harder to get, but that existing licences will be honoured, then the stockpiling of licences is the most profitable response to incredibility. Governments often regulate licence-holding, for example, making them time-specific, and having easier or harder procedures for renewal.

Second, agents might choose to stockpile imports in bonded warehouses. This is more costly than just holding the licences, since the imports must be paid for and so interest and storage costs are incurred. The advantage over licences is that in the event of the government exhausting its reserves the licences cannot be honoured.

Third, agents might store imports in unbonded warehouses. The disadvantage of this as compared with holding them in bonded warehouses is that the import duty is paid only once the goods leave bond. Hence, holding in bonded warehouses is cheaper because the agent does not need to finance the cost of the import duty. Imports will only be stored duty-paid if there is an expectation that the cost of import duty will increase. This could happen either if the rate of duty is increased, or if the exchange rate is devalued. The amount of duty payable is sensitive to the exchange rate because the duty is levied on the domestic currency value of the goods at the official exchange rate. That is, the duty charged is $t_m.e.P_m$.

The goods stored could either be consumer durables or intermediate inputs. If the expectation is that foreign exchange will become more severely quantity-rationed and that this rationing will discriminate against consumer goods, then the storage of consumer goods may be more profitable. If the expectation is that the exchange rate will be depreciated, then stockpiling of intermediate inputs may be more profitable, since all imports will cost more as a result of the devaluation while intermediate inputs may be less costly to store than consumer goods.

Each of the above responses can be the most profitable depending upon the nature of the incredibility. If the trade liberalization is payments-incompatible, then in all likelihood imports are temporarily cheap: either the exchange rate will be devalued to make the liberalization compatible or the liberalization will be reversed. It is therefore no use to stockpile import licences, because once policy has been changed in either way imports will be more expensive. The licence must actually be used in order to take advantage of the temporary cheapness of imports. Hence, if the diagnosis by private agents is payments incompatibility then the expected response would be to run down any previous stockpiles of import licences. If agents expect an increase in implicit tariffs but no change in actual tariffs or the exchange rate then holding in bonded warehouses is the most profitable response. If they anticipate devaluation or tariff increases then there is a case for paying duty in advance of sale and so storing in unbonded form.

If, by contrast, the diagnosis is of time inconsistency, then imports on average are not temporarily cheap. Once the government reimposes trade restrictions the exchange rate will appreciate (relative to its counterfactual). What is anticipated then is not a general increase in the price of imports but a change in their composition: those imports that become rationed will sell for a higher price, those that acquire privileged access will become cheaper. Hence, the appropriate response is to stockpile licences for those goods that will be rationed. The licences only get converted into imports of these goods once the restrictions have been re-imposed.

Finally, consider a liberalization that is incredible because it is recognized as the response to an endogenous trade policy rule. Once the favourable state of the world ends then implicit tariffs will again rise. However, the timing of this is less predictably imminent than if the diagnosis is payments incompatibility. The latter policy is unsustainable even on current terms of trade: reserves are being exhausted and so the agent needs to get hold of cheap foreign exchange before others do so. While with an endogenous trade liberalization imports are indeed temporarily cheap, the policy is sustainable for as long as the terms of trade boom lasts. Hence, agents might well stockpile import licences, only converting them into bonded imports once the terms of trade deteriorate.

Stockpiles of import licences are usually not directly observable but can be estimated by comparing the time series of actual imports with that of licences issued. Usually, data on licences issued must be obtained from the central bank since they are not published. The unknown is what the normal non-speculative lag is between the issue of the licence and the entry of goods into the country. Typically, this will be around three or four months. On any of these lags there was a sizeable stockpiling of licences during 1977, consistent with the prediction that under an endogenous trade policy agents would stockpile licences during a temporary terms of trade boom. There was a more dramatic de-stocking of licences during 1980, consistent with the notion that this was recognized as a payments-incompatible liberalization during which imports were temporarily cheap.

Data on goods held in bonded warehouses can be obtained from customs information although again they are not usually published. Data for Kenya shows the extraordinary stockpiling in bonded warehouses that took place during 1980. Evidently, agents decided to switch from holding licences to holding goods in bond.

Data on overall stocks, whether in bond or not, are available partly as a component of the National Accounts ('changes in inventories') but more accurately from surveys of manufacturing. For example, Kenya has a quarterly survey of business expectations that includes questions on inventories. This confirms the enormous inventory spike that occurred in late 1980, just as the 1980 liberalization attempt was reversed.

Whereas firms are in a position to speculate through storing intermediate goods and holding consumer goods in bond, private households may also speculate. To do so they must purchase consumer durables. Imports of consumer durables reveals two spikes 1978 and 1980, which might be interpreted as speculative responses to endogenous trade liberalization and payments-incompatible liberalization, respectively.

If private agents store imports then they must finance them. This provides a further opportunity for diagnostics. Data on bank lending are often broken down by the purpose of the loan or the category of the borrowing agent. Bank loans to the commercial and manufacturing sectors are the pertinent aggregate for the financing of inventories of imports. Speculation against a trade liberalization episode should therefore manifest itself as an increase in this source of borrowing.

A final diagnostic of incredibility is private investment. If agents anticipate that liberalization may be reversed, they will hold off irreversible investment in the export sector. While this series is well worth producing, so many other factors influence investment that it is hard to interpret.

Conclusion

A trade liberalization need not encounter a credibility problem. However, since several African trade liberalizations have been reversed, it is worth investigating whether private agents were able to anticipate the reversal. We have suggested three sets of circumstances in which such an anticipation would be held by rational and reasonably well-informed private agents. A variety of diagnostics is available to the researcher for identifying whether these circumstances characterize any particular liberalization attempt. We then turned to the speculative consequences of various types of incredibility, illustrating with Kenyan data. The data suggested that in Kenya speculation against trade liberalization attempts had been substantial. This is important because a liberalization attempt that is reversed and induces speculation may well be worse than no liberalization attempt: the pursuit of the first-best ends up with the third-best.

7.4   WHAT ARE THE EFFECTS OF LIBERALIZATION?

Trade policy reform in developing countries over the last twenty years or so has been pervasive, although, as we shall see, we need to qualify this statement somewhat. Not all intended liberalizations are implemented and, moreover, many of those that are implemented subsequently collapse. Despite these qualifications, we have observed widespread liberalization. Has it been successful in some sense? Has it 'worked'? Theory leads us to believe there are gains to be realized from successful liberalization. Have these gains been reaped?

Problems of Evaluation

Evaluating liberalization is demanding, for several reasons. First of all, one needs to have some reasonable counterfactual, that is, some picture of what the economy would have looked like in the absence of the reforms. One response to this may be to assume that the paths various indicators were on would have continued in the absence of reform. The problem with this is that trade liberalization is not always implemented in the most auspicious of circumstances. Indeed, in the context of SAL-based reforms, the opposite is frequently the case – reform against a background of difficult, and possibly unsustainable, conditions. Related to this there is also the problem of disentangling the effects of trade policy reforms from other policy changes. Many of the liberalizations studied by Papageorgiou *et al.* (1991) were not accompanied by other major reforms, but others were. The hallmark of the SALs is a package of reforms aimed at several targets simultaneously. Thus, at the same time as tariffs are reduced, or QRs eliminated, agricultural prices may be reformed, privatization promoted, the financial sector reformed and so on. For obvious reasons it then becomes difficult to conduct anything that resembles a controlled experiment!

A third complication is one of timing – how long should a liberalization programme have been in place before we evaluate its success? Theory gives us no clear guidance on this. It would depend, among other things, on the ingredients of the programme, the circumstances in which it was implemented, whether it was single-stage or multi-stage, whether other reforms were simultaneously implemented or not and so on.

Finally, there is the issue of performance criteria – what indicators do we use to evaluate success or failure? One possibility is to compare outcomes with targets. If the reform set out to reduce the average nominal tariff to 10 per cent, and its upper bound to 50 per cent, was this achieved? Superficially this is an attractive option because it focuses on the instruments of reform. In the case of policy-based lending reforms, it is also a relatively straightforward strategy to implement, since the World Bank uses compliance with conditionality as a performance criterion. However, one has to show some caution, in part because these criteria are inputs to the reform process rather than outputs from it, and in part because it is not unusual to find that instrument substitution occurs. In other words, the average nominal tariff may be reduced to the stated target; if at the same time, however, new anti-dumping or safeguard provisions are introduced, the overall impact on protection may be unchanged. Rather than inspecting the target indicators, one could try and evaluate the impact of reforms on overall economic performance, for example on exports, investment or growth. This is where the counterfactual problem can be seen most clearly. What would have happened to exports, investment, growth in the absence of the reforms? How do we disentangle the effects of trade policy changes from other reforms?

Evaluation of Outcomes

Studies of the process of implementation outnumber studies of the impact of liberalization. This is partly a function of time, that is, the liberalization experience is fairly recent, partly due to the problems of evaluation adumbrated in the previous paragraph. The most comprehensive study of outcomes is Papageorgiou *et al.* (1991), which supersedes Krueger (1978) in terms of coverage and breadth. In addition there have been a number of studies of the experience with SALs, notably World Bank (1988, 1990), Mosley, Harrigan and Toye (1991) and Thomas *et al.* (1992), as well as a series of individual country case studies. These, however, are assessments of adjustment programmes overall, and not just the experience with trade policy reform.

As noted earlier, Papageorgiou *et al.* (1991) is a cross-country assessment of the process and outcomes of twenty-six liberalization episodes in nineteen countries. In terms of scale, it is unrivalled. The methodology employed involves detailed documentation of the experiences of seventeen of their sample countries, the output of which then forms the raw material for a comparative analysis. The key conclusions reached are:

- liberalization that is initiated at a time of crisis (as defined by the authors) tends to be radical and sustained: moreover, liberalization that is launched as a bold step tends to be more sustainable than one that is staged;
- radical removal of quotas is conducive to sustainability;
- exchange rate devaluation is crucial to sustainability, but expansionary demand management is associated with abortion of liberalization;
- liberalization appears to affect the balance of payments favourably;
- the impact of liberalization on unemployment is minimal;
- liberalization tends not to lower production, nor inhibit economic growth; and
- liberalization leads to rapid and sustained export growth.

Thus, the analysis provides insights on timing, sequencing and adjustment problems, as well as on 'performance indicators'. Timing/ sequencing/adjustment lessons will be evaluated more fully in the next section. For the time being we will concentrate on performance indicators.

As we saw in Section 7.2, the objective of liberalization is to 'get (relative) prices right' in the tradable sector, with a view to improving efficiency in the allocation and utilization of resources, increasing exports and increasing growth. Judged in these terms, the Papageorgiou *et al.* (1991) evidence seems to suggest that liberalization has worked. Tables 7.4 and 7.5 report the results for growth rates and exports before and after liberalization. In the case of the former it seems that average growth three years after liberalization was 35 per cent higher than the average for the three years prior to liberalization (6 per cent as opposed to 4.45 per cent). In some case, the increases are quite spectacular, as in the case of Korea and Spain. The results for real export growth are even more impressive, with average real growth rates being 150 per cent higher for the three-year period following liberalization than they were for the three years prior to liberalization (11 per cent rather than 4.4 per cent). Again, the performance of some countries stands out as particularly striking – Korea and Turkey for example.

These results appear to be very favourable to the case for liberalization, not only because of the absolute magnitude of the changes, but also because they appear to reflect the experience of a large number of countries with different initial conditions, different programmes and so on. There are, however, problems with the evidence. In particular, there are some fairly fundamental problems with the way in which liberalization episodes are identified and measured. These are discussed at length in Greenaway (1993) and Collier (1993) and need not detain us

Table 7.4 Performance of GDP (real annual rate of growth)

Episode	PtL	T	T+1	T+2	T+3	AVG-T	AVG
Argentina 1 (1967–70)	6.70	2.60	4.40	8.50	5.40	6.10	5.23
Argentina 2 (1976–80)	2.90	−0.60	6.50	−3.10	6.90	3.43	2.43
Brazil (1965–73)	3.23	2.70	5.10	4.80	9.30	6.40	5.48
Chile 1 (1956–61)	2.30	1.20	7.90	2.80	0.53	3.74	3.11
Chile 2 (1974–81)	−1.50	8.50	−12.90	3.50	9.86	0.15	2.24
Colombia 2 (1968–82)	3.87	2.67	4.93	6.59	6.50	6.04	5.17
Greece 1 (1953–5)	4.90	13.06	3.10	6.81	8.70	6.20	7.92
Greece 2 (1962–82)	6.13	0.58	10.07	7.54	9.25	8.95	6.86
Indonesia (1966–72)	0.80	2.72	1.41	10.89	6.83	6.38	5.46
Israel 2 (1962–8)	9.80	10.10	11.40	9.80	9.10	10.10	10.10
Israel 3 (1969–77)	5.77	12.60	7.90	11.0	12.60	10.40	10.95
New Zealand 2 (1962–81)	4.02	5.84	6.57	5.54	−2.16	3.32	3.95
New Zealand 3 (1982–4)	4.32	4.66	0.48	2.78	3.29	2.18	2.80
Pakistan 1 (1959–65)	21.5	1.47	4.34	5.23	5.92	5.16	4.24
Pakistan 2 (1972–8)	0.30	3.78	3.07	3.14	0.74	2.32	2.68
Peru (1979–80)	0.30	3.78	3.07	3.14	0.74	2.32	2.68
Philippines 1 (1960–5)	5.88	7.55	6.39	9.49	11.48	9.12	8.73
Philippines 2 (1977–80)	5.32	4.84	5.72	5.23	8.48	6.48	6.07
Portugal 1 (1970–4)	5.88	7.55	6.39	9.49	11.48	9.12	8.73
Portugal 2 (1977–80)	16.0	5.30	3.20	4.50	4.90	4.20	4.48
Singapore (1968–73)	10.10	14.27	13.50	13.65	12.61	13.25	13.51
South Korea 1 (1965–77)	6.97	5.80	12.70	6.60	11.30	10.20	9.10
South Korea 2 (1978–9)	13.80	3.31	6.36	−6.20	6.36	2.17	2.46
Spain 2 (1970–4)	6.67	4.89	5.54	8.59	8.06	7.40	6.77
Spain 3 (1977–80)	3.30	3.72	2.50	0.16	1.48	1.38	1.97
Sri Lanka 1 (1968–70)	3.57	7.57	4.25	3.50	−0.52	2.41	3.70
Sri Lanka 2 (1977–9)	2.80	4.87	8.69	6.28	5.47	6.81	6.33
Turkey 1 (1970–3)	5.69	5.28	9.00	6.00	4.10	6.37	6.10
Turkey 2 (1980–4)	2.90	−1.07	4.10	4.61	3.25	4.00	2.73
Uruguay (1974–82)	−4.69	3.37	5.28	1.62	2.75	3.22	3.26
Yugoslavia (1965–7)	7.90	1.40	5.00	0.90	3.50	3.13	2.70
Average	4.45	4.69	5.45	5.26	6.00	5.57	5.35

Notes:
PtL: Average of three years up to liberalization: *T*: year of liberalization; *T* + *1*: one year after liberalization; *T* + *2*: two years after liberaliztion; *T* + *3*: three years after liberalization; *AVG-T*: average of three years after trade liberalization; *AVG*: average of *T* plus three year after liberalizations.

Source: Papageorgiou *et al.* (1991) vol. 7, Table 12.4.

here. The point that comes out of that evaluation is that it is not always clear that 'liberalization' in any of the various senses discussed above has occurred. In some instances it is only stabilization combined with devaluation that has been implemented. This is important because these may be key causal ingredients in stimulating export and output growth. Thus, for example, Whalley (1988) has argued that an

Table 7.5 Export performance (real annual rate of growth)

Episodes	T-3	T-2	T-1	PtL	T	T+1	T+2	T+3	AVG	AVG-T
Argentina 1 (1967–70)	-6.4	9.8	6.8	4.4	-1.2	-1.4	16.1	7.2	5.2	7.3
Argentina 2 (1976–80)	16.8	2.2	-22.7	-1.2	-31.5	42.2	5.2	0.7	19.9	1.6
Brazil (1965–73)	-7.2	28.8	-14.1	2.5	4.0	11.7	-2.9	15.2	7.0	8.0
Chile 1 (1956–61)	-23.6	15.3	13.3	1.7	-7.3	1.9	0.7	16.4	3.0	6.4
Chile 2 (1974–81)	8.6	-13.0	-0.4	-1.6	49.4	7.9	25.4	7.4	22.5	13.6
Colombia 2 (1968–82)	6.5	-1.7	8.7	4.5	8.3	4.7	0.9	-0.2	3.4	1.8
Greece 1 (1953–5)	-21.7	13.3	17.6	3.1	7.5	17.8	20.4	3.8	12.4	14.0
Greece 2 (1962–82)	-3.5	11.7	9.3	2.5	8.2	2.5	7.7	8.8	6.8	6.3
Indonesia 2 (1962–8)	-6.0	11.9	3.1	3.0	-1.1	-0.2	10.5	14.0	5.8	8.1
Israel 2 (1962–8)	44.4	23.1	15.5	56.7	15.3	20.5	6.0	10.4	13.0	12.3
Israel 3 (1969–77)	12.2	9.0	26.9	16.0	7.6	7.5	19.0	14.9	12.2	13.8
New Zealand 2 (1962–81)	17.4	3.1	-6.4	4.7	0.6	14.0	18.1	-6.3	6.6	8.6
New Zealand 3 (1982–4)	-7.7	13.1	6.8	4.1	3.3	-1.1	9.3	9.7	5.3	6.0
Pakistan 1 (1959–65)	26.3	-13.2	-20.0	-2.3	10.0	49.1	-23.8	4.8	10.0	10.0
Pakistan 2 (1972–8)	-3.3	13.9	-3.4	-6.4	-21.6	-5.3	17.8	-3.9	-3.0	2.9
Peru (1979–80)	-14.4	17.0	19.6	7.4	44.7	-2.7	-9.8	16.0	12.0	1.2
Philippines 1 (1960–5)	-6.2	9.9	-1.0	0.9	8.2	-3.7	9.7	23.8	9.5	9.9
Philippines 2 (1977–80)	-1.5	-3.9	-3.5	-3.0	23.1	9.0	-13.5	11.6	7.5	2.4
Portugal 1 (1970–4)	8.9	5.0	10.0	-3.0	12.0	1.2	5.9	7.8	6.7	5.0
Portugal 2 (1977–80)	1.7	-22.8	-0.7	-7.9	9.0	3.0	21.4	10.1	10.8	11.5
South Korea 1 (1965–77)	12.6	7.4	23.6	14.5	40.6	52.3	35.7	41.6	42.6	43.2
South Korea 2 (1978–9)	10.6	35.5	27.9	24.7	13.8	-0.3	10.0	19.0	10.6	9.6
Spain 1 (1960–66)	1.0	3.1	11.0	5.0	51.4	1.2	-7.1	-0.6	11.2	-2.2
Spain 2 (1970–74)	1.5	-3.9	-3.5	-3.0	23.1	9.0	-13.5	11.6	7.5	5.4
Spain 3 (1977–80)	0.9	-1.4	10.0	3.2	8.5	10.7	6.4	0.6	6.6	5.9

	$T-3$	$T-2$	$T-1$	T	$T+1$	$T+2$	$T+3$	AVG	PtL	AVG-T
Sri Lanka 1 (1968–70)	6.1	-6.0	6.2	2.1	2.1	-2.6	3.1	0.1	0.7	0.2
Sri Lanka 2 (1977–9)	-13.4	20.1	2.2	3.0	-13.3	9.5	13.8	3.6	3.4	8.9
Turkey 1 (1970–3)	9.3	-1.8	8.1	5.2	8.0	7.4	29.7	15.6	15.2	17.6
Turkey 2 (1980–84)	-17.7	14.1	-9.6	-4.4	4.2	85.5	10.0	13.7	35.8	46.4
Uruguay (1974–82)	-12.9	-19.5	-1.3	-11.3	20.4	13.9	28.2	6.8	17.3	16.3
Yugoslavia (1965–7)	17.0	15.0	8.4	13.5	11.1	12.6	5.2	4.9	8.4	7.6
Average	1.6	6.5	5.1	4.4	12.6	11.8	9.6	9.9	11.0	10.5

Notes:
$T-3$: three years prior to liberalization; $T-2$: two years prior to liberalization; $T-1$: one year prior to liberalization; PtL: average of the three years prior to liberalization; T: year of liberalization; $T+1$: one year after liberalization; $T+2$: two years after liberalization; $T+3$: three years after liberalization; AVG: average of T plus the three years after liberalization; $AVG-T$: average of the three year liberalization.

Source: Papageorgiou et al. (1991) vol. 7, Table 12.4.

ability to stabilize quickly when faced with exogenous shocks is a crucial element in explaining Korean growth in the 1960s and 1970s.

Related to the previous point, as we noted at the start of this section, trade liberalization may be only one of a number of factors that affect growth. To isolate the effect of trade policy reform is complicated, but the starting point is some explicit counterfactual model. This is not the methodology adopted by Papageorgiou *et al.* (1991). They simply compare performance before and after liberalization, and attribute the differences to trade policy reforms. The changes may indeed be attributable to trade policy reforms, but then again they may not. In the absence of an explicit model and rigorous statistical testing, we cannot be entirely certain. In fact, given their vague definition of liberalization, we can barely accept the evidence as a test of the effect of trade liberalization. Greenaway and Sapsford (1994) use time series data to investigate the relationship between liberalization, exports and growth in the PMC sample. They find it in only four cases between liberalization (as defined by PMC) and exports. This of course may say as much about the identification of liberalization episodes by PMC as about the relationship between liberalization and exports.

World Bank (1988, 1990) and Mosley *et al.* (1991) use similar performance indicators to evaluate the impact of policy-based lending programmes overall. The problem here is that although trade policy conditions figure very prominently in SALs (accounting for around 80 per cent of all conditions), they are typically not the only reforms that are implemented. When we observe a particular set of results, therefore, we cannot be sure of the precise contribution of trade policy reform. Nevertheless, the results are interesting, and are reported in Table 7.6. The methodology used is 'with/without' i.e., a comparison of the performance of adjustment lending with non-adjustment lending countries. The studies suggest that adjustment lending may improve real export performance, and also lead to an improvement in the current account. On the other hand, they also suggest that the impact on real GDP growth is more or less neutral, while the impact on real investment is adverse. There is some consistency with the Papageorgiou *et al.* results, that is, on real export growth, but not so on others, such as real output growth and investment.

What can we make of these results? The stock of cross-country evidence is unfortunately limited, and the studies we have evaluated use different methodologies, and methodologies that are not free of problems. They suggest that successful liberalization may have encouraged real export growth, and may be associated with real output growth. If

Table 7.6 Comparison of results on effectiveness of SALs

Study	Percentage of SAL countries which outperformed non-SAL countries			
	Growth of real GDP	*Investment (% of GDP)*	*Growth of real exports*	*Current account (% of GDP)*
World Bank (1988)	53	37	57	70
Mosley *et al.* (1991)	50	36	65	79

	Effect of SAL on variable*		*Effect of compliance**	
	Growth of real GDP	*Growth of real exports*	*Growth of real GDP*	*Growth of real exports*
All (19)	−	−	+	+
SSA (8)	−	−	+	?
MIC (14)	−		+	+

Notes:
* Summary of econometric results in Mosley *et al.* (1991, Vol. 1, pp. 212–14); only those coefficients estimated as statistically significant are reported. Numbers in parentheses are number of countries in subSaharan Africa (SSA) sample and middle-income countries (MIC) sample.
Both SAL and compliance variables were lagged – the one case where lags gave conflicting significant estimates is denoted '?'.

so, this is not only consistent with what theory would predict but also potentially encouraging to policy-based lending, which has a strong element of trade policy reform. However, alongside this evidence, we also have to recognize that many liberalization attempts have failed and, as we shall see in Section 7.5, failed liberalization may be more damaging than no liberalization.

7.5 A FRAMEWORK FOR EVALUATING THE CONSEQUENCES OF CREDIBLE TRADE LIBERALIZATION

In discussing the target of trade liberalization, a distinction must be made between primary and secondary targets and between outcomes recorded in the transition, the medium run and the long run. The first distinction is easier to make than the second, which may vary from one economy to another depending upon supply responses. The targets themselves are, however, controversial. Fundamentally, the objective of liberalization is to alter the utilization, allocation and accumulation of factors and there are a number of indicators of these processes that we can rely on. In the short run it may generate unemployment and/or fiscal imbalances; over the longer term, it may affect income distribution and fiscal diversification.

A common methodology requires three ingredients: a set of performance indicators that can be measured across countries; a time-frame within which the assessment is based; and a methodology for assessment.   Let us take each in turn.

Performance Indicators

This was relatively straightforward. Each country study was asked to aim to link liberalization to:

- aggregate unemployment
- composition of GDP by broad economic aggregate
- composition of employment
- composition of trade
- current account balance
- gross domestic capital formation
- growth of trade
- growth of real output
- fiscal profile
- distribution of income

Data for most of these series can be obtainable relatively easily, though one or two are more difficult (income distribution being the one that is most problematic).

Time Frame

It was not possible to lay down precise guidelines on the time-frame for investigation, because both transmission lags and data constraints vary across countries. The principal objective here was to obtain data points for as many observations as possible before and after a given liberalization episode.

Methodology

Devising a methodology for a multi-country study that is both credible and robust poses real challenges. As we noted in Section 7.2, the counterfactual problems are especially intractable, not only because we can never be entirely certain about what would have happened in the absence of liberalization, but also because of the difficulties of disentangling the effects of liberalization from other influences, such as terms of trade changes or stabilization efforts. In addition, the absence of a coherent underlying model leaves us without a clear theoretical steer. We do not actually have a 'consensus' growth model that leads us to make firm theoretical predictions about the impact of liberalization on accumulation processes.

There are three ways of dealing with this: CGE modelling, cross-section analysis or time-series analysis. The first has the virtue of allowing systematic evaluation of alternative liberalization scenarios. Depending upon the dimensionality of the model, it offers the prospect of an assessment of a given liberalization on all of the targets identified above. Although there were opportunities to inform particular country studies with CGE methods, (for example, there is a Côte d'Ivoire model available), reliance on this methodology was not feasible. Quite apart from the fact that we lack the capacity for a multi-country model building exercise, the approach is fundamentally experimental; it investigates the impact of possible liberalization scenarios, rather than actual liberalizations. It is the latter we are interested in.

As we saw in Section 7.2, cross-section analysis has already been extensively used in evaluating SALs. This is the so-called with/without approach. World Bank (1988, 1900) and Harrigan-Mosley (1991) have implemented this methodology. It involves comparing the experience of countries that have undergone liberalization with those that have not. World Bank studies used pooled data, Harrigan-Mosley use pairwise comparisons. This type of methodology has a long tradition in applied economics. It is not ideal for present purposes, however, largely because of the difficulties of finding reliable comparators for the African countries in which we are interested. The diversity of experience in terms of liberalization episodes leaves us with severe problems in finding a suitable control. Besides which, it is essential that the results for different country studies be comparable across countries in Africa.

This then leaves us with time-series analysis. Depending upon the availability of data this is potentially the most fruitful. This is essentially a 'before and after' methodology, that is it tracks the series concerned up to liberalization and after liberalization. This approach was followed by Papageorgiou, *et al.* (1991) who, as we saw earlier, compared the performance on exports and growth three years after liberalization with that three years before liberalization. In principle this makes sense. In practice one needs to be more pragmatic. We do not have strong priors on the transmission channels between liberalization and the various target variables, having regard to the fact that we are dealing with a general equilibrium issue; nor do we have strong priors on the lag structures involved.

7.6 CONCLUSIONS

In this chapter we have set out a framework for the analysis of trade liberalization in Africa. Our approach has been to survey indicators, diagnostics and methodologies used in previous work and to use this as a basis for framing our approach. In our cross-country study we aimed to do three things: identify liberalization episodes; confirm whether or not those episodes were credible; and assess the impact of the liberalizations on economic performance. With respect to identification, our analysis points to a combination of policy accounts, a quantity-based, counterfactual analysis and a (relative) price-based analysis. Diagnostics of incredibility are more difficult to identify but we have been able to isolate a menu of four or five that should be informative. We have also assessed the impact and medium-term or long-term effects of liberalization and used this analysis to inform the discussion of performance indicators. Finally a framework for monitoring performance has been set out.

References

Anderson, J.E. and J.P. Neary (1991) 'A New Approach to Evaluating Trade Policy', University College Dublin, Department of Economics, Working Paper 91/5.
Balassa, B. (ed.) (1982) *Development Strategies in Semi-Industrialised Countries* (Baltimore: Johns Hopkins University Press).
Bevan, D.L., P. Collier and J.W. Gunning (1990) *Controlled Open Economies: a Neoclassical Approach to Structuralism* (Oxford University Press).
——, ——, and —— (1992) 'Anatomy of a Temporary Trade Shock: the Kenyan Coffee Boom of 1976–9', *Journal of African Economies*, vol. 1, pp. 271–305.
Bhagwati, J. (1969) 'On the Equivalent of Tariffs and Quotas', in *Trade, Tariffs and Growth* (London, Weidenfeld & Nicolson).
Calvo, G. (1987) 'Costly Trade Liberalizations', *IMF Staff Papers*, 35:461–73.

Collier, P. (1993) 'Higgledy-Piggledy Liberalization', *The World Economy*, 16:503–11.
—— and J.W. Gunning (1992) 'Aid and Exchange Rate Adjustment in African Trade Liberalizations', *Economic Journal*, 102:925–39.
—— and —— (1994) 'Trade and Development: Protection, Shocks and Liberalization', in D. Greenaway and A.L. Winters (eds), *Surveys of International Trade* (London: Macmillan).
Dixit, A. (1989) 'Intersectoral Capital Reallocation under Price Uncertainty', *Journal of International Economics*, 26:309–25.
Donges, J. (1974) 'A Comparative Survey of Industrialisation Policies in Fifteen Semi-Industrialised Countries', *Weltwirtschaftliches Archiv*, 112:626–59.
Greenaway, D. (1993) 'Liberalising Foreign Trade Through Rose Tinted Glasses', *Economic Journal*, 103:208–22.
—— and C.R. Milner (1987) 'True Protection Concepts and the Role in Eliminating Trade Policies in LDCs', *Journal of Development Studies*, 23:200–19.
—— and C. Nam (1988) 'Industrialisation and Macroeconomic Performance in Developing Countries Under Alternative Trade Strategies', *Kyklos*, 41:419–36.
—— and G.V. Reed (1990) 'Empirical Evidence of Trade Orientation and Economic Performance in Developing Countries', in C. Milner (ed.), *Export Promotion Strategies* (London: Harvester Wheatsheaf).
—— and D. Sapsford (1994) 'Exports, Growth and Liberalization: An Evaluation', *Journal of Policy Modeling*, 16(2):165–86.
—— and A.L. Winters (eds) (1994) *Surveys of International Trade* (London: Macmillan).
Gunning, J.W. (1993) 'Trade Reform in Africa: the Role of Donors', in J.W. Gunning *et al.* (eds), *Trade, Aid and Development Essays in Honour of Hans Linnemann* (London: Macmillan).
—— and M.A. Keyzer (1993) 'Applied General Equilibrium Models for Policy Analysis', in J.R. Behrman and T.N. Srinivasan (eds), *Handbook of Development Economics, vol. 3* (Amsterdam: North-Holland).
Harrigan, J. and P. Mosley (1991) 'Evaluating the impact of World Bank Structural Adjustment Lending – 1980–1987', *Journal of Development Studies*, 27(3):63–94.
Jung, W.S. and P. Marshall (1985) 'Exports, Growth and Causality in Developing Countries', *Journal of Development Economics*, 18:1–13.
Krueger, A. (1978) *Foreign Trade Regimes and Economic Development: Liberalization Attempts and Consequences* (Cambridge: MIT, NBER).
—— (1981) *Trade and Employment in Developing Countries* (University of Chicago Press).
Lal, D. (1984) *The Poverty of Development Economics* (London: Institute of Economic Affairs).
Leamer, E. (1988) 'Measures of Openness', in R. Baldwin (ed.), *Trade Policy Issues and Empirical Analysis* (University of Chicago Press) pp. 147–200.
Little, I.M.D. (1982) *Economic Development* (New York: Basic Books).
Mosley, P., J. Harrigan and J. Toye (1991) *Aid and Power: The World Bank and Policy-based Lending. vols 1 and 2* (London: Routledge).

Mussa, M. (1976) 'Tariffs and the Balance of Payments', in J.A. Frenkel and H.G. Johnson (eds), *The Monetary Approach to the Balance of Payments* (London: George, Allen & Unwin).

Narasimhan, B. and L. Pritchett (1993) 'The Evolution of Import Restrictions in Sub-Saharan Africa in the 1980s: an Empirical Analysis', draft.

Papageorgiou, D., M. Michaely and A. Choksi (1991) *Liberalising Foreign Trade*, 7 vols (Oxford: Basil Blackwell).

Persson, T. (1988) 'Credibility of Macroeconomic Policy: an Introduction and a Broad Survey', *European Economic Review*, 32:519–32.

Reinikka, R. (1994a) 'The Welfare Cost of Speculation During Kenyan Trade Reforms', CSAE Working Paper, no. 10.

—— (1994b) 'How to Identify Trade Liberalization Episodes: an Empirical Study on Kenya', CSAE Working Paper no. 11.

Rodrik, D. (1989) 'Credibility and Trade Reform: a Policy Maker's Guide', *The World Economy*, 12:1–16.

—— (1993) 'Trade and Industrial Policy Reform in Developing Countries: A Review of Recent Theory and Evidence' (mimeo).

Salvatore, D. and R. Hatcher (1991) 'Inward Oriented and Outward Oriented Trade Strategies', *Journal of Development Studies,* 27:7–25.

Thomas, V. and J. Nash (1991) 'Reform of Trade Policy: Recent Evidence from Theory and Practice', *World Bank Research Observer*, 6(2):219–40.

Thomas, V., A. Chibber, M. Dailami and J. de Melo (1992) *Restructuring Economies in Distress* (Oxford University Press).

Whalley, J. (1991) 'Recent Trade Liberalization in the Developing world: What is Behind it and Where is it Headed?', in D. Greenaway *et al.* (eds) *Global Protectionism* (London: Macmillan).

World Bank (1988) *Report on Adjustment Lending*, Document R88–199 (Washington, DC: Country Economics Department, The World Bank).

—— (1990) *Report on Adjustment Lending II: Policies for the Recovery of Growth*, Document R90–99 (Washington, DC: The World Bank).

Yeats, A.J. (1990) 'On the Accuracy of Economic Observations: Do SubSaharan Trade Statistics Mean Anything?', *World Bank Economic Review*, 4:135–56.

8 Trade Liberalization and Regional Integration in Africa

Charles D. Jebuni

As the world seems to be evolving towards a possible tripolar trading bloc, the issue of an African trading bloc or region becomes more urgent. A number of integration schemes have been arranged in Africa, including trade integration, labour market integration, capital market integration, monetary integration and integration of government activity and regulations. Thus regional integration can imply a number of things. For the purposes of this chapter we shall concentrate on trade integration. For, as de Melo and Panagariya (1993, p. 12) put it:

> Whatever the ultimate goal of a regional arrangement increased intra-regional trade ranks high among the priorities. It is also the yardstick to measure how deep integration actually is.

We do not examine the issues of the desirability of intra-African trade. Our concern is mainly for the relationship between trade liberalization and trade integration. Trade liberalization is conceived here as the process by which the total volume of imports is determined and how that total is allocated within the economy. Using this definition, a customs union is a preferential trade liberalization scheme. This is to be distinguished from a general trade liberalization, which does not discriminate according to the source of imports.

The fundamental issue raised in this chapter is that, among African economies at the national level, general trade liberalization is more likely to increase regional integration in terms of trade integration than preferential trade liberalization schemes. Many of these schemes have failed to generate the relevant response because they are accompanied by national trade policies that tend to discourage exports, particularly of the non-traditional type. The structure of African imports and exports shows that preferential trade liberalization cannot generate the relevant incentives and competition required to induce entrepreneurs to export, which is a necessary condition for trade integration. As long as exports remain concentrated on traditional exports, the level of regional trade integration will remain low, as these exports will continue to flow to the industrial countries.

8.1 PREFERENTIAL TRADE LIBERALIZATION, DOMESTIC POLICIES AND TRADE INTEGRATION

In the past three decades a large number of regional integration schemes of all sorts have been adopted by almost all countries in subSaharan Africa. At present there are seven or eight groups in subSaharan Africa aimed at full-fledged integration.

Most assessments of these schemes, however, conclude that they have failed to increase intra-union trade flows. In a recent assessment, Foroutan (1993) concluded that 'if intra-group as a proportion of total trade is a good indicator of trade integration, it can be concluded that trade integration in SSA has failed'. Foroutan's data showing intra-group trade since 1970 are presented in Table 8.1.

The data show that the formation of the union did not increase intra-group trade for most of the groupings.

For MRU, UDEAC, CEPGL and PTA, the share of intra-group trade remained stagnant or actually declined. For groups where the share increased, Foroutan attributed the gain to a decline in the terms of trade, reducing the value of traditional exports. In the case of ECOWAS, for instance, the increased intra-group trade between 1980 and 1990 is attributed to the decline in oil prices over the same period, which caused Nigerian and ECOWAS dollar exports to the world to decline by 47 per cent and 35 per cent, respectively.

In an earlier study, Mansoor and Inotai (1991) conclude of integration attempts in subSaharan Africa: 'In general the results of integration schemes in sub-Saharan Africa have been more disappointing than elsewhere in terms of generating regional trade'.

Lipumba and Kasekende (1991) observe for the Preferential Trade Area for Eastern and Southern African States (PTA) that the statistics do not show evidence of an increase in intra-PTA trade arising out of the implementation of the PTA programme.

While Ariyo and Raheem (1991) see some room for optimism, they admit that the level of intra-regional trade in West Africa is still very low. Their analysis does not take into consideration the point made by

Name of grouping	Average intra-group trade imbalance index[b]		GNP[a] per caput in 1989 $US			Share of manufactures in GDP in 1989			Share of intra-group export trade in total exports				
	1980	1990	Min.	Max.	Min. as % of max.	Min.	Max.	Min. as % of max.	1970	1975	1980	1985	1990
SAA groupings													
ECOWAS	52	54	180	790	23	3	20	15	2.9	4.0	3.5	5.3	5.7
CEAO	66	68	290	790	37	5	20	20	6.3	12.7	8.9	8.7	10.5
MRU	100	26	200	430	46	3	6	50	0.2	0.4	0.5	0.4	0.1
UDEAC	99	92	190	2 270	7	0	16	0	4.8	2.7	1.6	1.9	3.0
CEPGL	33	18	220	310	67	10	15	66	0.4	0.3	0.1	0.8	0.2
PTA	59	47	80	1 950	4	4	25	16	8.0	9.3	7.6	5.5	5.9
SADCC[c]	31	57	80	1 600	5	4	24	17	2.6	3.7	2.1	3.9	4.8
SACU[c]	n.a.	n.a.	470	2 470	19	4	24	17	n.a.	n.a.	n.a.	n.a.	n.a.
Other groupings													
LAFTA/TAIA	16	17	600	2 620	23	16	35	46	10.1	13.4	13.0	8.0	10.6
CACM	21	20	250	1 790	14	14	27	62	26.2	23.4	25.4	15.5	14.2
NAFTA[d]	6	5	1 990	21 100	9	13	17	76	36.3	35.0	33.6	39.7	41.5
ASEAN	13	23	490	10 450	5	17	26	65	14.8	11.2	18.3	18.4	18.5
EEC[e]	6	8	4 300	20 800	20	18	32	56	53.2	52.5	55.7	54.7	60.6

Notes:

[a] SSA is uniformly defined to exclude South Africa:

[b] The index for individual countries is calculated as total exports to the group minus total imports from the group expressed as a percentage of trade with the group. The average for the group is a weighted average of each member country's index where weights are equal to the sum of the share of exports and imports.

[c] Data for SADCC and SACU exclude Namibia

[d] Canada, Mexico, United States.

[e] The average trade imbalance index for EC(6) in 1958, when the European Community was formed, was equal to 8. The 1980 and 1990 data refer to EC(12). Data on the share of manufacturing excludes Ireland.

Source: Foroutan (1993) Table 8.3.

Foroutan (1993) that the increase observed could be due to the decline in the terms of trade.

Several reasons have been given for the failure of these arrangements. Most of these reasons are perhaps captured by Foroutan (1993, p. 239):

> The structural characteristics of the SSA economies, the pursuit of import substitution policies, and the very uneven distribution of costs and benefits of integration arising from economic differences among partner countries have thus far prevented any meaningful trade integration in SSA.

A fundamental issue raised in all these is whether inward-looking preferential liberalization can increase intra-African trade.

The institution of general controls on international trade in terms of tariffs and non-tariff barriers tends to adversely affect overall exports and intra-African trade. The burden of these taxes is to a large extent borne by the export sector. For Ghana it is estimated that 74 per cent to 85 per cent of the import tax is shifted to the export sector (Jebuni *et al.*, 1992). Oyejide (1986) obtained an estimate of between 55 per cent and 90 per cent for Nigeria. Similar estimates were obtained for Zaire by Tshibaka (1986).

In examining the extent and structure of nominal protection in a large sample of sub-Saharan African countries, DeRosa (1992) estimates the effects of this protection on exports of these countries. He bases his estimates on simulations of a simple partial equilibrium model of trade and real exchange rate adjustment. His results suggest that protection reduces the value of these countries' exports by between 15 per cent and 33 per cent per annum and inhibits export diversification.

Preferential/discriminatory trade liberalization within the context of import-substitution with high protection does not generate the type of competition required to induce firms to export. Firm-level analysis shows that it is stiff competition within the domestic market that tends to induce firms to export. In Zimbabwe, for example, exporting was a means of increasing capacity utilization within the context of depressed domestic demand (Riddell, 1991). In Ghana, firms cited competition arising from imports and other domestic firms as reasons pushing them to take advantage of external demand (Jebuni, *et al.*, 1992). This was also an important shift factor in the case of Turkey in the 1980s (Milanovic, 1986).

Table 8.2   Intra-African exports by commodity

	1970	1975	1980	1985	1989
Food Items	32.3	33.9	25.9	27.1	23.7
Agricultural raw material	4.9	4.4	3.7	5.0	7.0
Ores and metals	3.0	5.3	5.6	5.1	5.1
Fuels	11.5	30.5	40.9	35.9	28.3
Manufactured goods	48.1	25.3	18.9	24.6	34.9

Source: *Handbook of International Trade of Development Statistics.*

The fundamental issue raised by all these is the limited role for preferential trade liberalization in raising the level of trade integration in SSA. Preferential trade liberalization that is not anchored in appropriate domestic policies of the participating countries is unlikely to succeed. For most African countries political rhetoric is at variance with domestic policy positions. While governments extol the virtues of regional integration and enter arrangements that will promote greater intra-regional trade, their domestic policies discourage exporting. It is also doubtful that preferential trading arrangements have reduced effective trade barriers among them.

The structure of intra-African trade is dominated by trade in manufactures (See Table 8.2). In 1989, 34.9 per cent of intra-African exports consisted of manufactured goods, followed by exports of fuels at 28.3 per cent. Intra-African exports in traditional agricultural raw materials and ores and metals were only 7 per cent and 5.1 per cent, respectively. Even though fuels ranked second, this was only 3.6 per cent of total African fuel exports. A critical factor in this change was the rise in oil prices.

Given this structure of intra-African exports, there appears to be potential for greater intra-regional trade in manufactures and food exports – the non-traditional exports. Yet it is precisely these types of export activities that are discouraged by national protective measures.

The Heckscher–Ohlin theory provides the basic predictive guide in terms of the composition and direction of trade. The extension of this theory to a multi-country world by Krueger (1977) and Baldwin (1979) suggests that a country may trade in both directions. A country could therefore export labour-intensive products to countries relatively more endowed with capital while exporting capital-intensive goods to countries more generously endowed with labour.

The stages approach to this model implies that comparative advantage changes as a country develops. Growing economies gain comparative advantage overall in skill and capital-intensive goods while losing comparative advantage to slower growing countries in labour-intensive goods. Evidence supporting these hypotheses is provided in Havrylyshyn and Wolf (1981), Balassa (1979) and Jebuni (1983). Havrylyshyn and Wolf (1981) note that developing countries' manufactured exports to developed countries are, on balance, more labour-intensive than those to other developing countries. Balassa (1979), using a sample of thirty-six economies, including both developed and developing countries, finds evidence that comparative advantage changes with development. Jebuni (1983), using a sample of seventeen developing countries, finds that even among this subset comparative advantage changes with indicators of development, including levels of per capita income, industrialization, and so on.

Variations in natural resource endowments across countries could generate trade in food and non-food raw materials, including cotton, rubber, timber, minerals, livestock, and so on. In global terms it is not clear that such differences are significantly different from differences in capital relative to labour.

But since most African economies started their industrialization via import-substitution, Linder-type exports could develop among them as a result of liberalization within their economies. Linder (1961) considers international trade as an extension of domestic trade. In this formulation the greater the similarity of domestic demand, the higher the trade between two countries.

It has been argued that because African countries produce similar products, in particular primary products, there is little basis for trade. However, the new trade theories of imperfect competition and economies of scale suggest a potential for trade in manufactured goods.

8.2 GENERAL TRADE LIBERALIZATION

From the previous sections we have raised some issues as to why preferential trade liberalization may not increase exports and intra-Africa trade. From that analysis it seems that through trade liberalization and subsequent removal of distortions, some positive response can be expected. One thing is certain: trade liberalization increases the openness of the economy. Whether this leads to increased exports without the accompanying macroeconomic policies and intra-Africa trade is an empirical question.

Analysis must start with the question of whether trade liberalization leads to an increase in exports. This should then be followed by the second question, whether the increased exports will increase trade integration within the sub-region or continent.

General trade liberalization is expected to affect exports positively and increase intra-African trade. This is supposed to work by reducing the distortions in the structure of relative prices and by directing resources to sections that can make the best use of them.

This is subject to test by individual country studies comparing the country's trade with the rest of Africa or a particular group prior to general trade liberalization and during or after trade liberalization. However, the liberalizations experienced so far have usually been accompanied by devaluation of the currency in the context of structural adjustment. Thus, disentangling the effects of trade liberalization from the other macroeconomic policies becomes difficult.

The general pattern of trade flows seems to support the idea that general trade liberalization tends to increase regional integration in terms of trade integration within the continent. Tables 8.3 and 8.4 present the trends in intra-African trade. Since the data show the share of intra-African trade before the general movement towards trade liberalization in Africa with structural adjustment, it is possible to detect whether the increasing general trade liberalization had any impact on intra-African trade.

The data indicate that intra-African trade has increased, with increasing openness since 1987. During that period a large number of African economies began pursuing structural adjustment programmes, of which trade liberalization is one of the key elements. On average, intra-African trade increased faster than total trade and trade with the industrial countries between 1987 and 1992. For instance, whereas Africa's total exports during the period increased by 54.3 per cent and exports to industrial countries increased by 52.7 per cent, intra-African exports increased by 75.6 per cent (see Table 8.3). This constrasts with the earlier years, when intra-African exports declined: by 3.1 per cent in 1984, 1.7 per cent in 1985 and 0.7 per cent in 1986.

This trend is reflected in the increasing proportion of intra-African exports to the total of African exports. The share of intra-African exports increased from 5.7 per cent in 1987 to 7.1 per cent in 1992.

A similar pattern can be observed for imports (Table 8.4). The proportion of intra-African imports to total imports increased from 6.2 per cent in 1987 to 7.3 per cent in 1992.

From the theoretical framework, one might expect traditional exports to follow the lines of exports established by the colonial system.

Table 8.3   Exports by Africa to and from the countries listed

	1984	1985	1986	1987	1988	1989	1990	1991	1992
% Distribution									
Industrial countries	72.0	71.6	67.3	67.4	67.8	69.3	70.6	68.8	65.7
Developing countries	13.4	14.6	15.0	14.2	15.8	15.3	15.6	16.6	18.7
Africa	4.9	4.9	5.8	5.7	5.9	5.9	6.3	6.5	7.1
Asia	2.9	3.1	4.4	3.8	4.6	4.2	4.1	5.2	6.5
Europe	1.6	2.2	1.9	1.7	1.7	1.7	1.7	1.0	.9
Middle East	1.3	1.1	1.4	1.3	1.5	1.6	1.5	1.6	1.8
Western Hemisphere	2.6	3.4	1.5	1.8	2.1	1.9	2.0	2.3	2.4
USSR & selected other countries n.i.e.	0.9	1.6	1.4	1.0	0.9	0.9	0.7	0.6	0.6
Annual % change									
World	3.2	-0.8	-16.7	18.2	1.7	8.9	20.8	2.6	2.1
Industrial countries	3.4	-1.4	-21.6	18.3	2.3	11.4	23.0	0.1	-2.4
Developing countries	2.9	8.6	-15.4	11.9	13.2	5.5	23.2	9.1	15.0
Africa	-3.1	-1.7	-0.7	15.0	5.5	9.3	29.8	5.7	10.3
Asia	5.7	5.4	11.4	1.8	24.8	-0.9	17.3	32.3	27.4
Europe	33.6	32.6	-27.4	7.3	3.9	5.6	22.3	-41.6	-9.0
Middle East	-8.1	-15.0	9.3	10.3	17.7	15.3	13.3	9.5	15.1
Western Hemisphere	3.2	28.3	-62.8	36.6	19.0	2.1	25.2	15.8	10.1
USSR & selected other countries n.i.e.	28.3	70.1	-21.1	-11.6	-9.8	3.3	-5.6	-5.9	2.0

Source: Direction of Trade Statistics, Yearbook 1991 and 1993 (IMF).

Table 8.4 Imports by Africa to and from the countries listed.

	1984	1985	1986	1987	1988	1989	1990	1991	1992
% Distribution									
Industrial countries	73.5	73.9	72.9	73.6	73.2	73.2	71.7	68.9	68.5
Developing countries	19.9	20.2	19.4	19.7	20.2	20.3	22.2	24.7	24.9
Africa	5.8	5.7	5.8	6.2	5.4	6.7	7.2	7.2	7.3
Asia	5.3	4.9	6.1	6.1	7.3	6.5	7.9	11.3	11.3
Europe	1.9	2.0	2.3	2.0	2.4	2.1	1.8	1.6	1.6
Middle East	4.3	4.4	3.2	3.1	2.7	2.9	3.3	2.7	2.6
Western Hemisphere	2.7	3.2	2.2	2.4	2.5	2.1	2.0	1.9	2.0
USSR & selected other countries n.i.e.	1.4	1.5	1.6	1.4	1.2	1.2	1.2	1.2	1.1
Annual % change									
World	-6.8	-6.9	-0.5	7.1	16.9	2.8	18.3	3.1	9.3
Industrial countries	-6.4	-6.4	-1.5	8.1	16.2	2.8	15.9	-0.7	8.6
Developing countries	-2.8	-5.7	-4.7	8.6	20.0	3.1	29.2	14.9	10.3
Africa	-1.0	-8.5	0.5	14.8	2.3	28.3	26.3	2.7	11.1
Asia	-6.1	-13.7	23.5	7.5	40.0	-8.2	44.5	47.0	9.6
Europe	-4.7	-1.7	6.8	-6.5	39.2	-10.5	1.2	-4.4	7.8
Middle East	0.6	-3.7	29.1	4.2	3.1	10.5	33.4	-16.5	8.7
Western Hemisphere	-3.8	9.5	-31.4	17.5	20.4	-13.0	12.3	0.6	15.7
USSR & selected other countries n.i.e.	-36.3	2.0	4.2	-7.5	0.7	3.9	16.0	4.0	-2.7

Source: Direction of Trade Statistics: Yearbook: 1991 and 1993 (IMF)

Even with liberalization, the share of these exports in intra-African trade is limited and may decrease. The limited experience of Ghana, however, shows that the share of these exports to industrial countries increased. For example, the share of Ghana's cocoa exports going to the UK, USA and EEC increased from 49 per cent in 1984 to 54.8 per cent in 1987, and to 62.8 per cent and 72.2 per cent in 1988 and 1989, respectively.

Within non-traditional exports these limited data also showed that those products in which Ghana had revealed comparative advantage went to industrial countries. Those in which it had no comparative advantage went to developing countries, including Africa (Oduro, 1994). One possible reason is that such products are Linder-type exports with characteristics suitable for other developing countries. It is also possible that these exports are made under the competitive pressures generated by trade liberalization and would not have occurred without it. It is not clear that preferential trade liberalization would generate such exports. One could also argue that intra-African trade is based on exports of non-competitive products. But benefits of learning by doing or possibilities of scale economies associated with higher levels of production could increase the competitiveness of these products with time. Indications of the relationship between direction of trade and comparative advantage for different product categories in individual country studies should provide generalizable conclusions on these issues. It is important that analysis decomposes exports into traditional and non-traditional exports.

Frequently these levels of intra African-trade are said to be low without indicating the yardstick for the judgement. Applying a gravity model to address this issue, Foroutan and Pritchett (1993) conclude that 'contrary to popular belief, the gravity model produces no evidence that inter SSA trade is below expectation'.

In the gravity model, the volume of trade between any two countries, i and j, is a function of each country's trade potential and their mutual trade attraction, so that:

$$T_{ij} = f(TP_i, TP_j, TA_{ij})$$

where: T_{ij} is the volume of trade between i and j
   TP_i is the trade potential of i
   TP_j is the trade potential of j
   TA_{ij} is the trade attraction between i and j.

The trade potential of a country in these models is determined by its economic size as measured by GDP and its trade intensity, measured by the ratio of trade to GDP.

In Foroutan and Pritchett, trade intensity is determined by geographic and economic characteristics proxied by the area of the country, whether the country is an island and per caput GDP.

Trade attraction is determined by distance between the pair of trading countries, whether they share a common language, and so on,[1] so that the model estimated is specified as:

$$T_{ij} = f(GDP_i, \ GDPPC_i, \ Area_i, \ GDP_j, \ GDPPC_j,$$

$$Area_j, \ ID_j, \ Distance_{ij}, \ BD_{ij}, \ /GDPCC_i - GDPPC_j/,$$
$$PAD_{ijk} - LD_{ij})$$

where GDPPC is GDP per caput. *ID* is a dummy if i is an island, *BD* is a dummy variable if *i* and *j* share a common border. *PAD* is a set of dummy variables for a set of *K* different preferential trade arrangements and is equal to 1 if both *i* and *j* are members of the particular arrangement. *ID* is a set of dummy variables if countries share a similar language (= 1 if *i* and *j* share the same language).

Since the dependent variable in this model can be zero, when there is no trade between any two countries, the value of the dependent variable is censored at zero. Foroutan and Pritchett therefore use Tobit estimates.

This model is then used by Foroutan and Pritchett to test for possible gaps between potential and actual trade among subSaharan African countries. Their results show that the levels of intra-SSA trade are identical to those that are predicted by the model.

The model could be modified to examine the effects of trade liberalization on intra-African trade by including the trade intensity variable in estimating T_{ij} and specifying the trade intensity as a function of some indicator of trade liberalization, size, island and GDP per caput. This will give a two-equation model as in

$$T_{ij} = f(GDP_i, \ GDP_j, \ TI_i, \ TI_j, \ Distance_{ij},$$

$$BD_{ij}/GDPPC/, \ PAD_{ijk} - LD_{ij}).$$
$$TI = g(Trade \ lib, \ size, \ ID_i, \ ID_j, \ GDPPC_i,)$$

where *TI* is trade intensity measured as Imports + Exports/GDP.

8.3   CONSTRAINTS AND PROBLEMS OF MARKET ACCESS

We have noted that general trade liberalization could improve the prospects for regional trade integration. A number of constraints to regional integration have been identified. These include government revenue repercussions, balance of payments, employment and transportation. Here we discuss these constraints as impediments to market access and examine how trade liberalization may affect them.

Government Revenue

A major consideration in discussions of regional integration in Africa is the role of government tax revenues. A large number of African governments depend heavily on taxes on international trade. In some cases, revenue considerations have led countries to prefer trade with the outside world to other African countries. Countries take advantage of policy disparities among the countries of the region: trade policy, price policy, monetary policy. Some traders also benefit from the complicity of politicians and civil servants. In many countries it has proved easier to cream off rents from relations with the outside world. This has led some observers to speak of *rentier* states.

These considerations have also led governments to revenue sharing arrangements that tend to restrict trade among African countries. Given the low levels of intra-regional trade, revenue losses to government under preferential trade liberalization should be low, depending on the extent to which member countries can be induced to take advantage of the preferences and the size of the preferences.

Under general trade liberalization these considerations become more important. But this consideration may be hypothetical.

At the theoretical level, the effect of trade liberalization on tax revenues depends on the direct impact on trade tax revenues and the economy's response to the changes in relative prices. Liberalization may have a positive effect on tax revenue through:

- the imposition of tariffs to replace quotas and other quantitative restrictions;
- reduction of duties from the prohibitive to a more normal range;
- putting low tariffs on previously exempted goods (in a situation where exempted goods form a large share of imports, perhaps due to import substitution industrialization policy, this change is potentially very important in terms of revenue yield);

- the likely reduction in smuggling;
- changes in the composition of imports in favour of the decreased incentive to bias imports towards imports of raw materials and intermediate products;
- improvements in tradable output, especially over the medium run, associated with the liberalization policy (Tanzi, 1989).

At the practical level, a 'serious trade liberalization is as likely to increase revenues as it is to reduce them: the elimination of tariff exemption and quantitative restrictions and the ensuing import boom, may more than outweigh the reduction in (statutory) tariffs in practice' (Rodrik, 1993 p. 2).

Even though Greenaway and Milner (1991) find no evident relationship between trade reform and the amount of revenue collected from trade taxes, dependence on trade taxes has decreased for a number of African countries pursuing liberalization programmes. For Malawi, the share of taxes on international trade and transactions in tax revenue declined from 22 per cent in 1980 to 17.7 per cent in 1991. In Côte d'Ivoire, the share declined from 42.8 per cent in 1980 to 27.8 per cent in 1991; while in Kenya it decreased from 18.0 per cent to 15.0 per cent over the same period. In Botswana, also, the share decreased from 39.1 per cent to 13.4 per cent in the same period.[2]

The experience of Ghana suggests that trade liberalization may increase total tax revenues from international trade and transactions but the share in total tax revenues may decline (Jebuni *et al.*, 1993). This has to be set against the extra efforts made by the government to increase tax revenue collection.

Individual country studies will have to establish the link between trade liberalization and government tax revenue. But since this analysis will be *ex post*, there is the problem of ascertaining the extent to which the changes in revenues are due to trade liberalization. Most recent trade liberalizations in Africa have occurred in the context of overall structural adjustment programmes, which include exchange rate policies as well as fiscal and monetary reforms. Furthermore, in a number of countries the structural adjustment programmes have also involved substantial inflows of external assistance that has shored up imports and tax revenues from imports. The analysis will therefore have to adjust for exchange rate policy, external resource flows and elements of macroeconomic policy.

Balance of Payments

An issue of considerable concern in trade liberalization among African countries is the balance of payments effects of such liberalization. It has been argued that because trade liberalization may be expected to worsen the trade balance, at least in the short run, it may not be a viable policy option for countries with foreign exchange or borrowing constraints.

The importance of this argument for the sustainability of such efforts is captured by the World Bank's nineteen-country study, which notes: 'These considerations may lead individual countries to begin to roll back the liberalization effort'.

But both the theoretical and empirical literature indicate that the effect of trade liberalization on the external balance is ambiguous. The current account is identically equal to the difference between national savings and investment. Liberalization can therefore be expected to affect the current account if it induces a differential response of savings and investment flows.

Using this savings-investment approach and considering a model that involves reduction of restrictions on imported intermediate inputs, Ostry (1991, p. 476) concludes that:

> if tradables use both capital and intermediate inputs intensively relative to the rest of the economy, liberalization leads to an increase in the level of saving and a decline in the level of investment and, hence, unambiguously to an improvement in the external current balance.

Of course the reverse could occur under alternative assumptions.

The use of balance of payments considerations to deny access to products from other African countries may be based on short-term trade balance and revenue considerations. Typical of this attitude are the trade relations among Ghana, Nigeria and Côte d'Ivoire. All three belong to the same customs union, ECOWAS, and all three have embarked on trade liberalization. The manufactured goods to be exported among them and other ECOWAS members are approved and certified by the ECOWAS secretariat. Yet customs officials deny duty-free access of these goods to each other's markets.

While this may indicate the disparities between politically agreed regulations and the intepretation by implementing agencies, it also reflects concerns about revenues, trade balance and employment effects of intra-African trade.

Case studies will have to establish the reality of these fears.

Transportation

According to the gravity model, the trade attraction between any two countries also depends on the distance between the countries. The distance in the model reflects a number of things, including transportation costs. While in this model distance affects the volume of trade, in reality it also affects the type of goods that are traded.

Intra-African trade is hampered by transportation costs in both absolute and relative terms. In absolute terms, the causes are due to the costs arising from, among other factors, the lack of shipping services – especially for intra-African trade. Most shipping arrangements are north-bound with primary raw materials and south-bound with manufactured goods. Ships of the roll-on-roll-off type from coast to coast along Africa are absent. Most trade has to go by road, which is more expensive. It is therefore likely that only high-value goods will use this mode of transport and low-value goods, which are much more suitable for shipping, will be excluded.

Intra-African trade may also be hampered by transport costs in relative terms because of the lower transportation costs for South–North imports of goods competing with African imports from other African countries.

8.4 LIMITATIONS OF TRADE LIBERALIZATION

The development of exports on which this paper is based is more complex than simple trade liberalization. In the East Asia experience, the maintenance of macroeconomic stability and the avoidance of overvalued exchange rates were combined with specific export incentive packages in order to develop their export potential. These countries did not all liberalize their trade regimes at the initial phases of this effort.[3] Thus it could be argued that trade liberalization is not necessary for export development and trade integration. At the same time, trade liberalization has implications for changes in the real exchange rate. In a model that incorporates imported intermediate inputs, and where the traded goods sector uses these inputs more intensively, trade liberalization may cause their relative price to fall – a real appreciation. The real income effects of the liberalization may also work in the same direction by increasing the demand for non-tradables and putting upward pressure on their prices.

Thus there are issues about the accompanying macroeconomic and sector specific policies that need to be studied to ensure that trade liberalization does lead to diversification of exports and trade integration in Africa.

Notes

1. See Foroutan and Pritchett (1993) for detailed discussion.
2. The data are obtained from *World Development Report 1993*.
3. See World Bank (1993) and Wade (1990) for detailed discussion of East Asian experience.

References

Ariyo, A. and M.I. Raheem (1991) 'Enhancing Trade Flows Within the Ecowas Sub-Region: An Appraisal and Some Recommendations', in A. Chhibber and S. Fischer (eds), *Economic Reform in Sub-Saharan Africa* (Washington, DC: The World Bank).
Balassa, B. (1979) 'The Changing Pattern of Comparative Advantage in Manufactured Goods', *Review of Economics and Statistics*, 61:259–66.
Baldwin, R. (1979) 'Determinants of Trade and Foreign Investment: Further Evidence', *Review of Economics and Statistics*, 61(1):40–8.
Chhibber, A. and S. Fischer (eds) (1991) *Economic Reform in Sub-Saharan Africa* (Washington, DC: The World Bank).
de Melo, J. and A. Panagariya (1993) *New Dimensions in Regional Integration* (London: Centre for Economic Policy Research).
DeRosa, D.A. (1992) 'Protection and Export Performance in Sub-Saharan Africa', *Weltwirtschaftliches Archiv*, 128(1): 88–124.
Foroutan, F. (1993) 'Regional integration in Sub-Saharan Africa: past experience and future prospects', in J. deMelo and A. Panagariya (eds), *New Dimensions in Regional Integration* (London: CEPR).
——— and L. Pritchett (1993) 'Intra-Sub-Saharan Trade: is it Little?', *Journal of African Economies*, 2(1):74-105.
Greenaway, D. and C. Milner (1991) 'Fiscal Dependence, on Trade Taxes and Trade Policy Reform', *Journal of Development Studies*, 27:96–132.
Havrylyshyn, O. and M. Wolf (1981) 'Trade Among Developing Countries: Theory, Policy Issues and Principal Trends', World Bank Staff Working Paper no. 479 (Washington, DC).
International Monetary Fund (1991, 1993) *Direction of Trade Statistics* (Washington, DC).
Jebuni, C.D. (1993) 'Domestic Market Structure, choice of Technology and Manufactured Export Performance in Less Developed Countries', University of Strathclyde, Glasgow, unpublished thesis.
———, A. Oduro, Y. Asante and G.K. Tsikata (1992) *Diversifying Exports: The Supply Response of Non-Traditional Exports to Ghana's Economic*

Recovery Programme (London: Overseas Development Institute).

Krueger, Anne O. (1977) 'Growth, Distortions and Patterns of Trade among Many Countries', Princeton Studies in International Finance, no. 40.

Linder, S.B. (1961) *An Essay on Trade and Transformation* (Chichester: John Wiley & Sons).

Lipumba, N.H.I. and L. Kasekende (1991) 'The Record and Prospects of the Preferential Trade Area for Eastern and Southern African States', in A. Chhibber and S. Fischer (eds) *Economic Reform in Sub-Saharan Africa* (Washington, DC: The World Bank).

Mansoor, A. and A. Inotai (1991) 'Integration Efforts in Sub-Saharan Africa: Failures, Results and Prospects – A Suggested Strategy for Achieving Efficient Integration' in A. Chhibber and S. Fischer (eds), *Economic Reform in Sub-Saharan Africa* (Washington, DC: The World Bank).

Milanovic, B. (1986) 'Export Incentive and Turkish Manufactured Exports, 1980–84' World Bank Staff Working Paper no. 768 (Washington, DC).

Oduro, A. (1994) 'The Direction of Ghana's Export Trade in the Nineteen Eighties', *African Journal of Economic Policy*, 1 (1):125–39.

Ostry, J.D. (1991) 'Trade Liberalization in Developing Countries: Initial Trade Distortions and Imported Intermediate Inputs', *IMF Staff Papers*, 38 (3):447.

Oyejide, A.T. (1986) 'The Effects of Trade and Exchange Policies on Agriculture in Nigeria', Research Report no. 55 (Washington, DC: IFPRI).

Riddell, R. (1991) 'Zimbabwe: The Expansion of Non-Traditional Exports: General Explanation', *The Courier*, 127:78–80.

Rodrik, D. (1993) 'Trade Liberalization in Disinflation. Discussion Paper Series' 832 (London: Centre for Economic Policy Research).

Tanzi, V. (1989) 'The Impact of Macroeconomic Policies on the Level of Taxation and the Fiscal Balance in Developing Countries', *IMF Staff Papers*, 36(3).

Tshibaka, T.B. (1986) 'The Effects of Trade and Exchange Rate Policies on Agriculture in Zaire', Research Report no. 56 (Washington, DC: IFPRI).

UNCTAD *Handbook of International Trade and Development Statistics*, various issues (Geneva).

Wade, R. (1990) *Governing the Market: Economic Theory and the Role of Government in East Asian Industrialization* (Princeton, NJ: Princeton University Press).

World Bank (1993) *The East Asian Miracle: Economic Growth and Public Policy* (Oxford University Press).

9 The Uruguay Round and SubSaharan Africa's Trade Policies

Piritta Sorsa

9.1 INTRODUCTION

Participation in a multilateral trading system can foster trade liberalization in a number of ways. Multilateral rounds of tariff negotiations allow countries to bargain their own liberalization against lower trade barriers in their export markets. Bindings of reforms in the multilateral framework can increase stability of reform and predictability of policies, factors that are essential for attracting foreign investments. International binding of reform is also a way to confront lobbies against change and reform at home.

The Uruguay Round (UR), the eighth multilateral round of trade negotiations, was the first in which developing countries were active participants. Their closer integration into the multilateral trading system reflected changes in development strategies in the 1980s towards greater openness and outward-orientation. Instead of emphasizing special and differential treatment as in the past, many were willing to bind unilateral liberalization in the multilateral set-up and comply with the rules. In return, two sectors of major export interest to them were brought under the multilateral rules – textiles and agriculture. However, most of subSaharan Africa participated only marginally in the negotiations and with an emphasis on the special and differential treatment.

The impact of the Uruguay Round on poorer and especially African countries has been a subject of much controversy since the conclusion of the round in April 1994. A number of recent papers have raised concerns about the high costs for developing countries of complying with the new obligations from the round and the limits these may put on development strategies (UNCTAD, 1994b; Weston, 1994; Agosin *et al.*, 1994; Konate, 1994). Other concerns relate to potential market losses for Africa from the erosion in the value of its preferences in its export markets as overall cuts in tariffs will reduce the value of the preferences (Davenport *et al.*, 1994), and from terms-of-trade losses from potentially higher food prices to net importers of food (GATT, 1994) as export subsidies are reduced. More recent estimates of the results have reduced (Goldin and van der Mensbrugghe, 1995), if not eliminated, the latter fears as agricultural protection will be decreased less than expected.

This chapter will assess SSA's own commitments in the Uruguay Round. It concludes that the UR, by continuing to exempt many trade restrictions applied in developing countries from the general rules, requires few binding commitments from SSA in the near future. Moreover, most of SSA did not make meaningful liberalization commitments in the Uruguay Round. Thus, by resisting liberalization and the opportunity to anchor domestic reform in an international framework, SSA has forgone an opportunity to reap substantial gains from the UR, and to promote foreign investment.

9.2 SUBSAHARAN AFRICA AND THE MULTILATERAL TRADING SYSTEM – A BRIEF HISTORY

Two countries were original signatories of the GATT in 1948 (South Africa, and Zimbabwe as successor to Rhodesia). Most SSA countries (twenty-five) joined in the 1960s upon independence. The third phase of accessions took place during the Uruguay Round when another ten became contracting parties. As former colonies they were able to join by a simple declaration to the GATT Director-General (Article XXVI:5(c)). In August 1995, thirty-eight out of the forty-eight subSaharan African countries were members of the GATT and twenty-six of them had ratified the World Trade Organization agreement.[1]

SubSaharan African countries have not been the most active members of the multilateral trading system and many do not have delegations in Geneva at its headquarters to participate in the regular business of the organization. This reflects both cost and traditionally the relatively smaller importance of world trade rules or market access constraints to Africa's commodity-dominated exports. In most of SSA commodity exports account for 65 per cent–99 per cent of total exports. Apart from temperate agriculture, barriers on many primary goods tend to be lower than those on manufactures.[2]

The GATT has had a long tradition of non-reciprocity *via-à-vis* developing countries.[3]

In the past, developing country efforts in the system were concentrated on getting preferential treatment in access to industrial country markets, and being exempted from many of the GATT rules on trade or other policies. Special and differential (S&D) treatment was their main objective in the negotiations and the yardstick for judging their links to the multilateral trade rules. During the Tokyo Round in the 1970s special and differential treatment was included in the multilateral codes on rules and in the enabling clause legalizing the generalized system of preferences (GSP). Much of this was influenced by the inward-orientated import substitution policies prevalent in many developing countries in the 1960s and 1970s and the mercantilistic view of GATT negotiations. GATT compliance of many developing country trade or other policies was also overlooked by their trading partners and few policies have been challenged in the GATT.

The change in interest of many developing countries in the GATT in the Uruguay Round is related to the increased importance of their role in the world economy and of trade and openness in their development strategies. This was reflected in their active participation in the Uruguay Round negotiations and resulted in commitments either in binding a substantial share of tariff lines or in complying with the rules. Unilateral liberalization increased the stakes of developing countries in the orderly functioning of the world trading system and in access to industrial country markets. The increased willingness to comply with the multilateral disciplines may also reflect disappointments with the past 'exemptions approach', and reliance on regional or other preferences for trade development. For small players, such as many developing countries, the multilateral rules are often the only way to make their voice heard in the world trade scene dominated by the rich and powerful traders, and against unilateral action by larger countries. The Uruguay Round still maintained much of the special and differential treatment in the obligations, but differentiated it more between the least developed and other developing countries (Harmsen and Subramanian, 1994).

SubSaharan African interest in the multilateral system has remained more marginal. Some African countries, such as Nigeria, Senegal and Tanzania, participated relatively actively in the UR. But their motivation was more dominated by attempts at safeguarding old preferences or getting compensation for potential adverse effects from higher world food prices on their import bills, than by efforts at liberalizing their own trade policies.

The Uruguay Round is expected to bring important benefits to the world economy, although most preliminary estimates have been revised downwards since the final results were known. While early estimates put annual income gains between $US213 billion and $US270 bn (in 1992 dollars) per year over the next ten years, more recent estimates by the same and similar models are of the order of $US40–100 bn (in 1992 dollars) mostly due to lower than expected liberalization in agricultural trade.[4] Estimates of gains differ substantially across countries – depending on estimated reductions in existing distortions or ability to take advantage of the new export opportunities. Many models show that most gains for developing countries would come from their own liberalization commitments (World Bank, 1994b).

9.3 MARKET ACCESS COMMITMENTS BY AFRICAN COUNTRIES IN THE URUGUAY ROUND

Market access commitments are made by binding tariffs to an agreed or negotiated level.[5] Market access also covers reductions in non-tariff measures (NTM).[6] In successive negotiations bound tariffs are reduced. Although bindings may differ from applied rates, they have a number of important economic benefits. Apart from potential efficiency gains from lower import barriers, bindings can improve the security given to tariff commitments and help reduce policy reversals. Before the Uruguay Round, developing countries had bound very few of their tariff lines[7] (for examples in SSA see Table 9.1 on industry). During the Uruguay Round all countries were required to make some commitments in the three main sectors: agriculture, industry and services.

Agriculture

The commitments required and made by SSA suggest that they did not undertake substantial liberalization commitments. This is because the agreed rules do not cover most frequent policy distortions in SSA and SSA countries made few commitments within the rules. Moreover, many of the GATT/WTO exemptions available for developing countries to deviate from the general rules remain available or many new rules are subject to long transition periods and exemptions.

Liberalization in developing countries is first limited by the nature of the agreed rules for liberalization, which are more relevant for agricultural policies in industrial countries.[8] While the agreement clearly addresses the worst distortions in world agriculture, it leaves many agricultural distortions especially in low-income developing countries,

Table 9.1 Summary of Uruguay Round (UR) commitments in agriculture and industry

Country	GATT status (%)	Agriculture							Industry		
		Average[a] bound duty (%)	Average[a] bound ODC (%)	Average appl. rates (%)	Domestic support	Export subsidies	Previous bindings (% of lines)	Share of lines bound in UR (%)	Average[a] bound duty (%)	Average[a] bound ODC (%)	Average appl. rates (%)
Angola	LD	80	0.1	—	—	—	0	3.8	80	0.1	
Benin	LD	60	18	—	—	—	29[g]	1.4	50	19	
Botswana	LD	40[e]	—	—	—	—	31[h]	68	17[d]	—	
Burkina Faso	LD	100	50	—	—	—	29[g]	1.2	100	50	
Burundi	LD	100	30	—	—	—	n.a.	2.3	100	30	
Cameroon	D	80	24–70	24.5[b]	—	-	0	0.1	50	22–35	18.5[b]
CAR	LD	30	16	—	—	—	0	56	38	16	
Chad	LD	80	—	—	—	—	0	0.0	75	0	
Congo	D	30	0	—	—	—	0	3.2	15	0	
Côte d'Ivoire	D	15	0–50	20	(c)	—	29[g]	0.4	7	28	27[i]
Djibouti	LD	42	100	—	—	—	29[b]	71	40	100	
Gabon	D	60	19	—	—	—	0	1.3	59	18	
Gambia	LD	102	10	—	—	—	0	0.5	56	10	
Ghana	D	98	0.2	22[b]	—	—	0	1.1	33	0	16[b]
Guinea	LD	38	24	—	—	—	29	1.3	26	23	
Guinea-Bissau	LD	40	26	—	—	—	0	97	50	50	
Kenya	D	100	0	44[b]	—	—	0	1.6	54	0	35[b]
Lesotho	LD	200	—	—	—	—	0	100	60	—	
Madagascar	LD	30	250	39[i]	—	—	n.a.	11.1	30	250	
Malawi	LD	124	20	—	—	—	n.a.	3.6	47	20	41[i]
Mali	LD	60	50	—	(c)	—	29[g]	2.8	60	50	
Mauritania	LD	37	15	—	—	—	29[g]	1.3	30	15	
Mauritius	D	120	17	52[i]	—	—	0	1.6	65	17	63[i]

Country											
Mozambique	LD	100	300		—		0	1.9	80	300	
Namibia	D	40[e]	0		—		31[h]	68	17[d]	0	22[f]
Niger	LD	80	50		—		29[g]	65	50	50	
Nigeria	D	150	80	47[b]	—		0.1	7.0	48	80	36[b]
Rwanda	LD	80	—		(c)		n.a.	100	100	—	
Senegal	D	30	150	44[b]	—		29[g]	2.4	30	44	34[b]
Sierra Leone	LD	40[e]	20		—		0	100	49	20–50	
South Africa	IND	40[e]	—	7[b]	by 2000	by 2000	31[h]	68	17[d]	—	22[d]
Swaziland	D	40	—	34	—		31[h]	68	17[d]	—	22[d]
Tanzania	LD	120	120		—		0	0.1	120	120	28[i]
Togo	LD	80	7		—		0	1.0	80	7	
Uganda	LD	80	0		—		0	2.7	50	—	
Zaire	LD	98	—		—		n.a.	100	96	—	
Zambia	LD	124	0		-		n.a.	4.0	42	—	
Zimbabwe	D	146	15		—		8	0.8	38	29	31[b]

Notes:

[a] Simple averages of bound rates as reported in countries' UR schedules; assumes that base for both duties is the same

[b] From GATT Trade Policy Reviews, latest available

[c] List of domestic programmes permitted, no subsidy commitment

[d] Reduced from 24 per cent to 17 per cent

[e] Reduced from 70 per cent to 40 per cent

[f] Trade weighted average.

[g] Assumes countries applied same schedule as Senegal as former French colonies

[h] Assumed same as South Africa

[i] UNCTAD (1994) latest available

outside its scope. Many African countries do not subsidize, but tax agriculture either implicitly by giving higher protection to industry, or more explicitly by taxing exports of many commodities, or by maintaining government-controlled domestic prices below world prices (Schiff and Valdés, 1992). These distortions were not part of the Uruguay Round agenda, and some of them are not even covered by the GATT/WTO rules (export taxes or domestic pricing policies that 'tax' agriculture). Actual liberalization of industrial tariffs in Africa within the round is also modest (see below) and unlikely to reduce the existing bias against agriculture.

African trade policies have also suffered from frequent policy reversals and from the impact of exchange restrictions on trade flows. Some of these policies have been addressed in the countries' structural adjustment programmes over the past decade (World Bank, 1994a; Schadler *et al.*, 1993).

As the rules were flexible with SSA policies, liberalization in agriculture in the Uruguay Round was left to the willingness of the participants to undertake commitments and that of their trading partners to accept these in the bargaining process. While most SSA countries are small markets for most agricultural exporters, relatively little was requested from them by other participants. South Africa is the exception.

Tariffication

Though all African participants bound 100 per cent of their tariff lines in agriculture as required, the bindings by many countries were at prohibitive levels (100 per cent – 300 per cent) (Table 9.1). The only 'reasonable' bindings (less than 50 per cent) were by Congo (30 per cent ceiling binding), the Central African Republic (ceiling binding at 46 per cent), and four of the five countries of the Southern African Customs Union (Botswana, Namibia, South Africa, Swaziland). In the last, bound duties on average will decline by 43 per cent from about 70 per cent to 40 per cent) over a six-year period.[9] Few of the developing countries that are not least developed countries offered to make reductions from their ceiling bindings, although this was required by the agreement.[10] Only Côte d'Ivoire, Ghana and Zimbabwe offered minor reductions on a few items. Only South Africa made minimum access commitments.

The bindings consist of a customs duty and other duties and charges ODC. The use of these rates is particularly frequent in Africa.[11] In some countries, such as Côte d'Ivoire, that had old bindings, reduction commitments in the round were made on the customs duty only. To this an ODC rate is added. For example, in Côte d'Ivoire a 7 per cent bound duty on fresh milk (HS 040110) will be reduced to 6 per cent over a ten-year period, but an ODC will be added to this item.[12]

The high levels of bindings resulting from the Uruguay Round may have a number of unexpected effects on protection of agriculture in Africa and amount to a lost opportunity to liberalize. First, the results indicate that the round will not liberalize agriculture in Africa in the sense of reducing actual tariff rates. It is likely (and to be hoped) that most countries will not apply the high bound rates. Available data indicate that applied rates are in general lower (Table 9.1). The policy implications of this are that rationalization of protection in agriculture in SSA will have to rely on continued unilateral liberalization.

Second, the high bindings do not impose an effective constraint on policy reversals. The high level of the bindings can by itself undermine their stability objective and the transparency objective of tariffication in general. In principle, countries can continue to change tariffs within the margins provided by the bindings (duties and ODCs). The likelihood of this depends on whether the recent trend of unilateral liberalization continues. Most of the maximum rates are too high to provide a meaningful cap on rates to improve the security of market access.

Third, the high level of bindings is unlikely to serve the objective of removal of all non-tariff barriers in agriculture. Countries can charge duties at varying levels within the margins of the bindings, which could be linked to a domestic threshold price. The duty can be set as the difference of the given domestic price and the world price as long as the duty charged does not exceed the binding. In practice this can work like a variable levy or a minimum price. However, the levies might be challenged as such under the agreement. A footnote to the agriculture agreement states that variable levies, and so on, are forbidden and will be converted to tariffs. Furthermore, the Agreement on Customs Valuation forbids the use of minimum prices, except for developing countries that make a special reservation for it.[13] Clarification of the issues may require recourse to the dispute settlement proceedings.

Subsidies

Except for South Africa, the commitments on domestic agricultural policies or on export subsidies required by SSA in the Uruguay Round are likely to have little if any impact on their domestic agricultural policies.[14] The main reason is that most of SSA does not subsidize agriculture or its exports. As mentioned, many traditional export commodities are taxed, not subsidized, in many SSA countries. Only Côte d'Ivoire, Mali and Senegal have submitted lists of domestic agricultural programmes that they consider permissible – that is, not subject to cuts – and that may have some subsidy elements.

Industry

The main impact of the Uruguay Round on industry in SSA is likely to be some increase in transparency of policies from increased notification requirements (if followed). The round will not liberalize protection of industry in SSA, which made few meaningful bindings in industrial goods and well above applied rates. The UR will set few new constraints on existing non-tariff measures in SSA in the near future, as tighter rules on non-tariff measures concerned mostly industrial countries. The adoption of any new policy obligations by developing countries is subject to long transition periods and can be extended in many cases indefinitely. Old exemptions in the GATT 1994, such as Article XVIII:B, continue to be available to justify border restrictions.

As in agriculture, the case of South Africa (and some members of the Southern African Customs Union) is different and stands out from the rest of SSA. Southern Africa made substantive commitments in terms of increased bindings and cuts in existing bindings, which are close to applied rates. Southern Africa used the UR to bind domestic unilateral reform, which can work as a powerful argument against domestic lobbies resisting change.

In many African countries existing tariff and non-tariff barriers on industrial goods vary substantially and accurate information on existing policies is at times difficult to get. Policies in a sample of SSA countries[15] reviewed in the GATT's Trade Policy Review mechanism indicate that, apart from tariffs and fiscal duties, applied border measures include an array of bans and prohibitions on imports and exports, licensing, exchange rate rationing, quantitative import restraints and minimum prices.

In many countries the structure of the tariff is quite dispersed as high duties co-exist with numerous exemptions. A recent World Bank study on African trade policies underlined the importance of exchange controls in restricting imports and exports in many SSA countries (Nash, 1993). Over the past decade many of these issues have been addressed by adjustment programmes supported by multilateral donor agencies resulting in some improvements (World Bank, 1994a; IMF, 1994). However, reforms have suffered from credibility problems due to frequent reversals[16] and slow implementation.

Tariffs

In the Uruguay Round there was no uniform rule for making tariff commitments apart from having to achieve the stated (voluntary) goal of a 33 per cent reduction in tariffs over a 5 to 10-year period. This made actual cuts dependent on the results of bilateral negotiations, which tended to bias them in favour of cuts on products of interest to main industrial country partners. Developing countries were encouraged to make either ceiling bindings, as many had no previous bindings (Table 9.1), or some reductions in previously bound items. As in agriculture, the ODC rates were to be included in the new schedules (see above).

Most commitments in SSA are ceiling bindings on a handful of tariff lines (Table 9.1). Twelve countries made broader bindings (50 per cent to 100 per cent of tariff lines), while the majority bound less than 2 per cent of tariff lines. As a result only eleven countries will have bindings on over 90 per cent of tariff lines after the Uruguay Round (Djibouti, Guinea-Bissau, Niger, Rwanda, Sierra Leone, Zaire and the five countries of the Southern African Customs Union). Only four members of the Southern African Customs Union and Côte d'Ivoire offered to reduce previously bound rates.[17]

In many cases the resulting bound rates are prohibitive at rates over 100 per cent. Only in ten countries were the few duties bound at levels below 50 per cent. This includes four of the five countries of the Southern African Customs Union, in which bound duties will decline to an average of 17 per cent.[18] As applied rates, at least in countries for which data are available, are in general lower, the bound rates may not be applied in practice and will only serve as upper bounds.

Apart from the countries of the Southern African Customs Union, tariff commitments on industrial goods by SSA do not represent meaningful liberalization and are unlikely to address any of the key distortions in SSA trade policies in industry. First, as with agriculture, the high level of bindings can undermine their impact on security of market access, as duties can readily be changed within the maximum bounds. Security is further reduced by the small number of lines bound. Second, credibility of policies is unlikely to improve: SSA countries have not taken advantage of the opportunity offered by the Round to bind domestic reforms to an international anchor to improve credibility of reform. Third, the Uruguay Round in most cases will not change existing levels of protection as applied rates will not change in most of SSA. Therefore, it will do little to promote, for example, regional trade, or competition in domestic market.

Non-tariff Measures

Most of the agreed liberalization commitments in non-tariff measures were designed to reduce distortions in existing policies in industrial countries.

The main obligations from the Uruguay Round in industrial non-tariff measures are that all countries are to remove voluntary export restraints within four years,[19] and to eliminate all GATT-inconsistent restrictions on textiles and clothing imports within a ten-year phase-in period.[20] As industrial countries are the main users and developing countries the main targets of these measures there was no need to foresee different rules for developing countries. A number of other agreements such as that on balance of payments restrictions and customs valuation deal with non-tariff measures, but resulted in few new binding obligations to developing countries.

The agreement on balance of payments mostly reinforces earlier recommendations for greater transparency by public announcements of plans to terminate the measures and preference for the use of price-based measures over quantitative restrictions. Apart from some tightening, the agreement does not create new obligations to reduce existing measures or limit the use of balance of payment restrictions in the future.

The Agreement on Customs Valuation in the WTO (see Table 9.2), in principle requires countries to eliminate official minimum prices at the border as customs valuation is to be based on the price actually paid or payable for the imported good. The single undertaking means that all countries will have to adopt these rules. However, developing countries that so notify the Director-General of the WTO have five years to comply with this agreement.[21] Developing countries that wish to retain the use of minimum prices during a transition period can make a reservation for this.[22] The adoption of the rules can be further postponed if trading partners approve such a request to the WTO. In practice, this means that, although developing countries have undertaken the new obligations, the long transition periods and potential for their extension require little change in policies in the near future. Im-

Agreement	Notification	Transition period (years)		Extensions or exemptions
		Developing countries	Least-developed countries	
1. *BOP restrictions* Public announcement of removal, preference for price based measures	Four months after measure introduced	n.a.	n.a.	Can be extended
2. *Customs valuation* Agreement	If delay	5	5	Additional three years to use computed value
Removal of minimum prices	If reservation made	Can be maintained for limited unspecified time, if reservation made.		Five-year deadline can be extended upon request
3. *Subsidies* Prohibited export subsidies	By 1 April 1995	8[a]	—	Can be extended subject to annual review
Prohibited local content subsidies		5	8	No extension.
Other specific subsidies	By July every year	—	—	
4. *TRIMS* Remove measure such as content and trade balancing req.	By 1 April 1995	5	7	Can be extended; Art. XVIII exemption possible
5. *TRIPS* Adopt protection and enforcement	—	5	11	Can be extended for LLDCs Developing countries have additional five years to introduce protection for new product patents.

Note: [a] If GDP per caput > $US1000.

plementation of the new obligations therefore depends on the will of trading partners to grant exemptions or on the countries themselves to implement the obligations.

A review of submitted schedules indicates that, so far, in textiles the only commitment in SSA is by four of the five countries of the Southern African Customs Union, which have agreed to reduce barriers (high specific duties in local currency) in textiles and clothing imports over a ten-year period. The only other commitments in non-tariff measures were made by Senegal and Cameroon. Senegal offered to remove prior authorization requirements on a number of tariff lines (paper products and some machinery). Cameroon agreed to eliminate import quotas on a number of products (paper products and miscellaneous items).

If applied, the new rules on customs valuation may imply changes to existing laws in SSA. At present many of them use the so-called Brussels Definition of Value at the border.[23] Compliance may imply more stringent administrative requirements, but the removal of minimum prices could increase efficiency. The use of an international standard for valuation could also imply lower trading costs for importers by reducing discretion in valuation at the border, and hence reducing rent-seeking opportunities.

A main impact of the UR agreements on non-tariff measures in industry for countries in SSA is likely to be an increase in the transparency of policies. This will arise from the increase in notification requirements (textile restrictions, minimum prices, voluntary export restraints). The conduct of trade policy reviews confirmed in the UR will also add to the transparency of policies. This is reinforced by the general trend in recent years, for example, to require developing countries to list and justify more carefully all measures maintained under the balance of payment exceptions. In the past, many developing countries have not notified their non-tariff measures to the GATT as required and their trading partners have not actively challenged the GATT consistency of applied policies. For example, only South Africa and Nigeria of the SSA countries have followed GATT procedures and notified their import restrictions and held consultations in the GATT Balance of Payments Committee. The increased pressure for transparency may be less for the very small and poor countries with a minor role in international trade, but may affect the larger traders of SSA.

Services

In services most commitments by SSA are likely to reflect the status quo, with little additional liberalization. All developing countries were required to make market access commitments (liberalization) in services and accept the framework agreement (the rules). The General Agreement on Services (GATS) obliges countries to give most-favoured-nation (MFN) treatment to foreign service providers in sectors and modes of supply,[24] in which liberalization commitments have been made. A one-time exemption from MFN treatment could be made at the time of making the market access commitments.[25]

Services was an area that developing countries initially were reluctant to include in the negotiations. Many felt that they had no comparative advantage in services or that liberalization of this sector would be of little relevance for their development strategies. But as the Uruguay Round progressed developing countries started to see a new potential in the sector both directly for their exports, and indirectly as liberalization of services may have an important impact in improving the competitiveness of many export industries. Openness and competition are likely to improve efficiency in local provision of services, which often are important inputs to manufacturing or other economic activities (banking, transport).

Very little information is available on the structure of protection in the services sector in SSA. A large part of the sector is likely to be dominated by state enterprises with privileged market positions or government monopolies often raising prices of services. Government-provided services are not covered by GATS. Many international transport routes are subject to cargo-sharing arrangements, which have a tendency to maintain the price of freight at high levels. Provision of professional services is often subject to aid tied to a specific country, which limits competition on potential suppliers. Liberalization in the sector could bring substantial efficiency gains, although in Africa competition in transport or other sectors is also restricted by many natural factors such as the small size of the markets.

The nature of the liberalization commitments in the UR vary substantially among the thirty-eight SSA countries. The extent of the liberalization in the submissions is difficult to estimate for the complex nature of the market openings in the different modes of delivery. One rough measure can be the number of sectors in which commitments were made. According to this measure the range of sectors opened varied from one in seven countries (Chad, Burkina Faso, Madagascar,

Mauritania, Mozambique, Tanzania, Uganda) to twelve in one country (Gambia) of the twelve sectors and thirty-eight countries covered (Table 9.3). The sectoral breakdown indicates that most commitments were in tourism (35 countries), business (19 countries) and communication (13 countries). Twelve countries had made reservations to the MFN obligation, mostly in maritime transport. Commitments in financial, business and communication services, which are important 'input sectors' to exports, were made by less than half of the countries. This can reduce the potential for efficiency gains or transfer of technology in many of these countries in sectors that are inputs in export production. Most of the commitments are likely to reflect the status quo with little additional liberalization.

9.4   OTHER OBLIGATIONS

The single undertaking of the Uruguay Round means that all countries had to adopt all the agreements. As only a few SSA countries were signatories to the Tokyo Round Codes on subjects such as anti-dumping, subsidies and import-licensing,[26] they may have to review their present laws in light of these revised or new rules. However, apart from anti-dumping, most of the new or revised old obligations have relatively long transition periods, which in some cases can be further extended. The most important obligations with a potential impact on domestic policies in SSA are likely to be the revised rules on subsidies, the agreement to eliminate GATT-inconsistent trade-related investment measures (TRIMs) and the new rules on intellectual property (TRIPs). (See Table 9.2.)

Export and Other Subsidies

The new subsidy rules cover essentially trade in industrial goods. In the Uruguay Round, developing countries agreed to new rules on prohibited export subsidies,[27] and to remove prohibited local content subsidies,[28] as well as to continue to submit other domestic subsidies to the revised international rules.[29]

In principle, existing export subsidies cannot be increased in those countries that are not LLDCs that have per caput income below $US1000.[30] To increase transparency and reduce the potential for trade friction, all countries have to notify the prohibited subsidies to the WTO by April 1995 and all other specific subsidies, that is, actionable and non-actionable, annually by July. Failure to notify does not, however, affect rights and obligations under the agreement.

The revised disciplines on subsidies in the UR can reduce their economic costs, although the rules remain stricter on trade-related subsidies, which may not be those with highest economic costs. Export subsidies are forbidden, while more lenient rules apply to more general subsidies to industry. However, the criteria for disciplining subsidies in WTO are their trade effects, not the size of the potential economic distortions created by subsidies. It is also paradoxical that the poorest countries (which might least afford them either in economic or fiscal terms) are given the most flexibility to subsidize. From the point of view of the trading system, least developed countries are allowed to do this because their subsidies are deemed to have no trade effects on their partners.

SSA has few obligations from *forbidden subsidies* in the near term. In SSA, prohibited subsidies were only notified by South Africa, which has to eliminate them in three years. In the higher income developing countries (income above $US1000 per caput) special guarantees or credits to exports, or tax breaks for exporters, will be forbidden *after* the eight-year transition period, if these policies carry a subsidy element conditional upon export (for example, if they are given at below market rates) and extension is not sought. Existing subsidies cannot be increased or new ones introduced, in this group. Currency retention schemes or any similar practices that involve a bonus upon export will in principle fall into this category.[31] Botswana, Gabon, Mauritius, Namibia and Swaziland should review their existing export subsidy policies, if any, and make them WTO-compatible within the eight-year transition period (unless they apply for an extension of the transition period). In other SSA developing countries, the use of export incentives (old and new) can continue.

According to GATT trade policy reviews, Ghana, Kenya, Nigeria, Senegal and Uganda have or have had some kind of export subsidy/ incentive programme.[32] But as they presently fall into the low-income category in the WTO agreement, they are not obliged to remove these policies until their income per caput reaches $US1000. None of these programmes was notified to the WTO.

Two aspects of the agreement can insert some discipline on existing or new export subsidy policies. The first is that export subsidies can be challenged by countervailing duties, if they cause injury to trading partners. If this is likely, SSA countries may want to review existing export subsidy programmes. For most SSA countries this risk is likely

Table 9.3 Overview of initial commitments in services by sector

Country	Total	Business	Communications	Construction	Distribution	Education	Environmental	Financial	Health	Tourism	Recreation	Transport	Other	MFN exemptions
Angola	2							x		x				x
Benin	3	x						x		x		x		x
Botswana	3		x							x				
Burkina Faso	1									x				
Burundi	5	x		x	x				x	x				x
Cameroon	2	x			x					x				
Chad	1									x				
CAR	5	x	x				x			x	x			
Congo	2	x	x	x				x						x
Côte d'Ivoire	4	x	x	x				x		x		x		x
Djibouti	3		x							x	x			
Gabon	4	x		x				x		x		x		
Gambia	12	x	x	x	x	x	x	x	x	x	x	x	x	x
Ghana	5			x	x	x	x	x	x	x		x		
Guinea	5	x					x		x	x		x		
Guinea Bissau	2									x	x			
Kenya	5		x					x		x		x	x	
Lesotho	10		x		x	x	x	x		x		x	x	
Madagascar	1	x									x			
Malawi	5	x		x					x	x	x			
Mali	2				x					x				x
Mauritius	2		x						x	x				x
Mauritania	1													
Mozambique	1							x						

Namibia	2	x												
Niger	2									x		x		x
Nigeria	4		x							x		x		
Rwanda	5					x	x	x		x				
Senegal	6	x	x		x					x	x			
Sierra Leon	10	x	x	x		x	x	x	x	x	x	x		x
South Africa	9	x	x	x	x		x	x		x	x	x	x	x
Swaziland	2								x			x		x
Tanzania	1									x				
Togo	3			x							x	x		
Uganda	1										x			
Zaire	6	x	x	x		x				x				
Zambia	4	x		x						x	x			
Zimbabwe	3		x					x		x				
Total by sector		19	13	12	5	7	7	12	7	35	11	12	4	12

to be minimal as they are small exporters.[33] However, the possibility of accumulating injury among exporters may open SSA countries to challenges by trading partners, a procedure which can be costly for small exporters in terms of legal fees. The second is the limits put on existing or new export subsidies for countries subject to transition periods. But as no existing programmes (apart from South Africa) were notified, it will be difficult to monitor whether existing programmes are increased or new ones introduced.

On actionable *domestic subsidies*, the main immediate obligations for SSA is their notification to the WTO. Only if policy-makers want to avoid any risk of being subject to countervailing duty investigations in their export markets would a review of domestic subsidy policies be warranted. Policies that may be subject to countervailing duties can be, for example, tax credits or other tax benefits given to specific industries, if they can be shown to cause injury to an industry in the importing country.

TRIMS

The agreement on trade-related investment measures mainly enforces existing GATT disciplines.[34] Local content or trade balancing requirements can act as a tax on imports without the revenue accruing to the government. The agreement itself, with long transition periods and the possibility for their extension, puts few immediate obligations on SSA countries. But as notification is also a requirement for benefiting from the transition periods, it remains up to the SSA countries to take advantage of this. By May 1995, only Mauritius, South Africa and Zambia among the SSA countries had submitted a notification to the WTO, and only South Africa stated that they have any TRIMs (to be eliminated by 1997). If other SSA countries maintain TRIMs, they can now be challenged in the WTO.

According to GATT trade policy reviews trade balancing and especially local content rules are likely to be relatively frequent in SSA.[35] In principle, by not notifying its TRIMs, most of SSA has forgone a right to gradual adjustment and, in principle, should now eliminate these programmes. If maintained, the possibility of WTO challenge can create uncertainty for investment incentives. Although the likelihood of a challenge for SSA is small, SSA countries should review their policies in this regard. As many of these measures are likely to allocate resources inefficiently and act as a quantity restraint or tax on imports, their elimination can bring efficiency gains.

TRIPS

The agreement on intellectual property requires countries to put into place the agreed minimum standards of protection, and administrative capacities to enforce them. Developing countries have five years and least developed countries eleven years to do this.[36] Least developed countries may have the eleven-year transition period extended further; this applies to two-thirds of SSA countries. For them the only immediate obligation is to provide for a procedure to file an application for patents in pharmaceutical, and agricultural chemicals.

For most SSA countries the long transition periods and their extension are likely to postpone both the negative and positive effects of TRIPs for several years. The expected benefits of the TRIPs agreement are higher returns to innovation, increased investment and transfer of technology as patents would be protected. The potential for these gains in most of SSA, even in the longer run, is likely to be small.

The main impact in the short run can be some additional administrative costs from the filing procedures, which in countries with scarce administrative capacities can have a high opportunity cost. In the medium run these will increase in non-LLDC developing countries in SSA. These thirteen countries should have administrative procedures in place in five years' time and changed laws to correspond to the international standard.[37] These, coupled with the potential rent transfers, will increase the economic costs of complying with the agreement in this group.

9.5   SUMMARY AND POLICY CONCLUSIONS

The Uruguay Round will have a limited impact on trade liberalization in SSA. First, most SSA countries made no substantial liberalization commitments on border protection in agriculture, industry or services. This was partly a reflection of the nature of the agreements concluded. As many of the reductions in non-tariff barriers were designed for the types of policies applied in industrial countries, the often different policies in developing countries will be less affected. For example, many developing countries do not subsidize agriculture, but tax it, which is not covered by the agreement. It also reflected the unwillingness of SSA to make meaningful commitments to bind protection to reasonable levels (applied rates will not change).

Second, the agreements offer much flexibility in the adoption of the obligations. The adoption of many new rules is subject to long transition periods, which in most cases can be further extended. Many of the general exemptions or those for balance-of-payments support remain available for unwilling liberalizers wishing to seek legal cover for trade restrictions. Apart from the increase in transparency from the notification requirements (if followed), few changes to policies are required by SSA countries in the short run. Some review may be required in export subsidies, and local content requirements. In the medium run, SSA countries should review their TRIPS obligations. While the benefits of the TRIPs agreement can be questionable for most of SSA in the short run, the rules in subsidies in most cases should promote sound economic policies.

SSA has not used the UR to support domestic efforts at trade policy reform. The round provided an opportunity for countries to go beyond their unilateral liberalization efforts in exchange for multilateral concessions, or to bind their domestic reforms to an international framework. As most models showed that most gains from the UR would come from countries' own liberalization efforts, SSA, by not making liberalization commitments in the round, may have thereby lost one opportunity for gains. The exceptions were the four out of the five members of the Southern African Customs Union that used the UR to consolidate ongoing domestic reform programmes. In the end, this means that structural change and trade liberalization in most of SSA will depend on unilateral initiatives taken independently or in the context of World Bank/IMF adjustment operations. Unless these are pursued, the ability of SSA to take advantage of the emerging opportunities in their export markets may also be lost. It may also mean a lost opportunity for more foreign investments.

Table 9A.1   GATT status of SSA countries

Country	Year of accession	Pre-UR schedule	Development status
Angola	1994	no	LD
Benin	1963	S[b]	LD
Botswana	1987	no	D
Burkina Faso	1963	S[b]	LD
Burundi	1965	S	LD
Cameroon	1963	no	D[c]
CAR	1963	no	LD
Chad	1963	no	LD
Congo	1963	no	D[c]
Côte d'Ivoire	1963	S[b]	D[c]
Djibouti	1994	S[b]	LD
Gabon	1963	?	D
Gambia	1965	no	LD
Ghana	1957	no	D[c]
Guinea	1994	S[b]	LD
Guinea Bissau	1994	no	LD
Kenya	1964	no	D[c]
Lesotho	1988	no	LD
Madagascar	1963	S	LD
Malawi	1964	S[a]	LD
Mali	1993	S[b]	LD
Mauritania	1963	S[b]	LD
Mauritius	1970	no	D
Mozambique	1992	no	LD
Namibia	1992	S	D
Niger	1963	S[b]	LD
Nigeria	1960	S	D[c]
Rwanda	1966	S	LD
Senegal	1963	S[a]	D[c]
Sierra Leone	1961	no[b]	LD
South Africa	1948	S	IND
Swaziland	1993	no	D
Tanzania	1961	no	LD
Togo	1964	no	LD
Uganda	1962	no	LD
Zaire	1971	S[a]	LD
Zambia	1982	S[a]	LD
Zimbabwe	1948	S	D[c]

Notes:
[a] = Schedule under waiver for HS
[b] = Schedule inherited from France upon accession; not updated to HS
D[c] = Income per caput < $US1000.
D = Developing
LD = Least developed
IND = Industrial

Notes

1. About two-thirds (24) are members as least developed countries as defined by the United Nations, while South Africa traditionally has been a member as an industrial country. The remainder are developing countries (See Appendix to this chapter). Development status in GATT is self-proclaimed and has an impact on the level of obligations within the international trading rules. Cape Verde, Comoros, Equatorial Guinea, São Tomé and Príncipe and Seychelles apply the GATT *de facto*, and Ethiopia, Liberia, Somalia and Sudan are observers. Among them only Sudan has applied for WTO membership. Eritrea has no links to the system.
2. For example, the share of duty free imports of natural resource-based or tropical products to the EU and United States in 1988 was around 50–70 per cent, while in textiles and clothing it was 0–1 per cent (UNCTAD 1994b). Non-tariff barriers have in general affected very few exports from SSA (Erzan and Svedberg, 1991).
3. Over the years the General Agreement was modified to give legal effect to these claims. Part IV was added in 1965; it recognizes the special needs of developing countries and enforces the principle of non-reciprocity (see McGovern, 1986). Article XVIII also offers exemptions for developing countries from their GATT obligations either under its balance of payments provisions (B) or under the development provisions (A, C, D), of which the former has been more frequently used. The latter, which in principle require prior notification, consultation and in some cases compensation, has only been invoked by Cuba, Greece, Haiti, India, Indonesia, Malaysia and Sri Lanka during the early years of GATT. The last annual report on its use by Sri Lanka dates from 1968. Other GATT exemptions available (for all countries) to justify non-confirming trade-restrictive measures are general safeguards (Article XIX), general and public policy exemptions (Article XX) or exemptions with general shortages (Article XI) and state enterprises (Article XVII). Many restrictions are maintained by developing countries without recourse to specific provisions.
4. Recent estimates with general-equilibrium models put the annual welfare gain between 0.2 per cent and 1.1 per cent of world income over the next ten years, depending on sectoral coverage, different model structures and calibrations. Most estimates are in the lower range, that is, 0.1–0.2 per cent of world GDP. See Harrison *et al.* (1995), Francois *et al.* (1995) or Goldin and van der Mensbrugghe (1995).
5. This means that countries can apply tariffs at or below the bound maximum, but not raise them above this unless it is renegotiated in the WTO and compensation is given to affected trading partners.
6. Their negotiation is complex, as many NTMs were outside the GATT rules such as grey area measures, or existed against the GATT, or are closely linked to the rules negotiations. During the Uruguay Round negotiations they were covered in several negotiating groups
7. The share of tariff lines bound for a sample of twenty-six developing countries (including two from SSA) before the round was 21 per cent in industry and 17 per cent in agriculture compared to 78 per cent and 58 per cent for industrial countries (GATT 1994). Twenty SSA countries had

a schedule in GATT prior to the Uruguay Round (see Appendix to this chapter).

8. In agriculture the Uruguay Round agreement required participants:

   (1) to eliminate all quantitative restrictions, establish bound, tariff-based protection and reduce existing border protection (1986–8 level) by 36 per cent on average over a six-year period and to open tariff quotas (in products previously subject to non-tariff barriers) to guarantee existing or minimum access for at least 3–5 per cent of domestic consumption;

   (2) to reduce certain domestic subsidies by 20 per cent; and

   (3) to reduce, from a 1986–90 base, the value of mainly direct export subsidies by 36 per cent and the quantity of subsidized exports by 21 per cent.

   Special safeguards are allowed for items with past quantitative restrictions, provided their potential use is notified initially. For developing countries, reductions of tariffs, selected domestic supports and export subsidies were set at two-thirds of the level of industrial countries. Developing countries were allowed to use ceiling bindings (a binding at an arbitrarily chosen maximum level), and were given a longer transition period (ten years) to make the commitments. Only least developed countries were exempt from the tariff cut, but not from the bindings. A number of agricultural subsidies in developing countries (food security, investment, inputs, export transport and marketing) are exempt from the cuts. The maximum level of domestic subsidization (*de minimis*) for developing countries that need not be reduced was set at 10 per cent of the value of the product per item.

9. This is a simple average based on information in their Uruguay Round schedules. This excludes ODC rates, which are mostly specific duties.

10. Only least developed countries were exempt from cuts in bound rates. The lack of reduction commitments was accepted by SSA trading partners tacitly during the verification process.

11. According to the Understanding on Article II:1(b), the ODC rates that are bound and listed as part of the schedule should reflect actually applied rates on 15 April 1994. Contracting parties can challenge these levels during a three-year period after the entry into force of the WTO or of the commitment creating some additional uncertainty on the level of the bindings negotiated. Before the Uruguay Round ODC rates were not listed in schedules.

12. Some of the high ODC rates have been questioned by Africa's trading partners during the verification process. Cameroon, Côte d'Ivoire, Gabon and Senegal have until mid April 1995 to clarify the high rates proposed (230 200, and 150 per cent, respectively). Mozambique has also been requested to provide further information to justify its 300 per cent ODC. These were subsequently reduced.

13. Notification, however, does not affect the rights and obligations under the agreement; that is, it is not a prerequisite for benefiting in the transition periods.

14. Countries that have made no reduction commitments will have to notify

annually (every two years for LLDCs existing [allowable] support programmes by type or state that no support exists. Developing country, net-
food-exporters of a product will have to notify the WTO of export
prohibitions and restrictions on that product.

15. Trade policy review reports for Cameroon, Côte d'Ivoire, Ghana, Kenya,
    Nigeria, Senegal, South Africa, Uganda and Zimbabwe.
16. Of the ten countries studied recently by the World Bank only four were
    able to sustain trade reforms (Collier, 1993).
17. Bound tariffs in the former will declined on average from 24 per cent to
    17 per cent (Hoda, 1994). Côte d'Ivoire offered to cut duties on about
    twenty tariff lines to an average of 7 per cent, but added a 250 per cent
    ODC to these rates (Schedule LII – Côte d'Ivoire).
18. Many negotiators consider 20 per cent to be a commercially meaningful
    maximum level for tariffs (naturally subject to potential exchange rate
    distortions).
19. One measure per country can be maintained for five years. The EU is the
    only member that notified one voluntary export restraint with Japan on
    automobiles within the set time limits.
20. Should developing countries maintain quantitative restrictions in textiles
    and clothing, they have to be removed within the ten-year transition pe-
    riod. All restrictions have to be notified to the relevant WTO body at the
    start of the transition period.
21. In SSA only Côte d'Ivoire, Gabon, Ghana, Kenya, Mauritius and Senegal
    have notified this.
22. Only three countries in SSA (Côte d'Ivoire, Gabon and Kenya) did so.
23. Only five countries in SSA had signed the Tokyo Round Code on Cus-
    toms Valuation, most with reservations (Botswana, Lesotho, Malawi, South
    Africa, Zimbabwe).
24. A service can be delivered via four different modes of supply: cross-bor-
    der supply, consumption abroad, commercial presence, presence of per-
    sons.
25. For example, a country could state that a bilateral navigation treaty will
    remain outside the scope of the agreement.
26. Subsidies: none; anti-dumping: none; import-licensing: Nigeria, South Africa.
27. The least developed countries (see Appendix to this chapter) and coun-
    tries with income per caput below $US1000 (Cameroon, Congo, Côte
    d'Ivoire, Ghana, Kenya, Nigeria, Senegal, Zimbabwe) are exempted from
    the commitments on export subsidies (until the latter reach that income
    level). Another threshold is if a developing country reaches export com-
    petitiveness in a product measured as 3.25 per cent of world market in
    two consecutive years. 'Product' as a relatively broad definition (a sec-
    tion head in the HS nomenclature). As very small exporters, SSA coun-
    tries are unlikely to be affected by this provision.

    Other developing countries have eight years to remove their export sub-
    sidies, which in SSA at present concerns only Botswana, Gabon, Mauri-
    tius, Namibia and Swaziland. The eight-year transition period can be
    extended, if the prohibited export subsidies are deemed necessary by a
    WTO committee.
28. '*Subsidies* contingent, . . ., upon the use of domestic over imported *goods*'

(Art.3.1(b)). This seems to cover local content rules that are a condition for a subsidy (a financial advantage). Some local content rules are also covered by the TRIMs agreement. The main difference in implementation is that the TRIMs agreement allows two years rather than three for industrial countries and seven years rather than eight for least developed countries in the subsidies agreement, and that in the TRIMs agreement the transition period can be extended for developing countries. For other developing countries the transition period is the same in the two agreements.

29. General subsidies and those given for three enumerated purposes (regional, R&D, environmental) are allowed under certain criteria. Other specific subsidies are allowed to the extent that they do not have serious trade effects (challenge in GATT/WTO or by countervailing duties by trading partner). For example, subsidies given to small enterprises can be allowable, but subsidies given to a specific industry can be subject to challenge.

30. The exact meaning of this in the text is not clear. It is not specified what 'level' or 'increase' mean – total of subsidies by product or by industry.

31. According to one interpretation, multiple currency practices or currency retention scheme would be allowed, if approved by the Fund (Article xv).

32. Ghana has had an export retention scheme and has given export tax credits for exporters; Kenya has given subsidies for exports with over 30 per cent domestic value-added and with an export retention scheme; Nigeria has provided an export retention scheme and given subsidies to exporters that export over 50 per cent of sales with 40 per cent local content and 35 per cent of domestic value-added; Senegal has subsidized exports; Uganda has export performance requirements as conditions for investment benefits

33. On actionable subsidies the agreement allows for some exemptions for developing countries from an eventual countervailing duty challenge. Serious prejudice challenge in the GATT for a developing country has to be based on positive evidence. This can arise, for example, if a subsidy displaces imports from a partner country of a product that is subject to a bound concession. In countervailing duty cases a minimum subsidy of 2 per cent of value of production (3 per cent for low income countries) is allowed, or investigations are to be terminated, if the share of the subsidizing country is less than 4 per cent of the complainant's imports, or the share of similar small developing countries is below 9 per cent. Direct forgiveness of debt and subsidies to cover social cost when applied on a one-time basis in connection with privatization programmes (and notified) is non-actionable in developing countries.

34. Discriminatory measures such as local content rules, or trade or foreign exchange balancing that are against the national treatment provision (Article III) or prohibition of quantitative restrictions. (Article XI) have to be eliminated in five years by developing countries and within seven years by the least developed countries after the establishment of the WTO. The transition period can be extended upon request for both developing and least developed countries. In some cases the line between TRIMs and local content subsidies falling under the subsidies agreement can be very fine.

35. According to GATT/WTO trade policy reviews Ghana, Kenya, Nigeria, Senegal and South Africa have maintained local content rules as conditions for some investments incentives. Zimbabwe may impose local content rules as conditions for investment approval.
36. An additional grace period of five years is granted for developing countries to establish patent law on products that are not presently protected. that is, in which they do not have existing patent laws. However, all countries must have a system in place whereby all patentable inventions on pharmaceutical and agricultural chemical products made after the entry into force of the WTO must be protected.
37. An additional grace period of five years is granted for developing countries to establish patent laws on products that are not presently protected, i.e. in which they do not have existing patent laws. In SSA at least five (Cameroon, Congo, Cote d'Ivoire, Gabon, Senegal) of the thirteen have existing patent and other intellectual property laws under the Bangui Convention, which have to be revised to correspond to the TRIPs requirements.

References

Agosin, M.R., D. Tussie and G. Crespi (1994) 'Developing Countries and the Uruguay Round. An Evaluation and Issues for the Future', seminar on *Trade Prospects for Developing Countries up to the Year 2000 and Beyond*, 27–9 September (UNCTAD).

Collier, P. (1993) 'African Trade Reform', in F. Foroutan and J. Nash (eds), *Trade Policy and Exchange Rate Reform in Sub-Saharan Africa: What Went Right?, What Went Wrong? What Lessons for the Future?* (Washington, DC: World Bank).

Davenport, M., A. Hewitt and A. Koning (1994) *The Impact of the GATT Uruguay Round on ACP States* (London: Overseas Development Institute and Maastricht: European Centre for Development Policy Management).

Erzan, R. and P. Svedberg (1991) 'Protection Facing Exports from SSA in the EC, Japan and the US', in J. Frimpong-Ansah *et al.* (eds), *Trade and Development in SSA* (Manchester University Press).

François, J.F., B. McDonald and H. Nordstrom, (1995) 'Assessing the Uruguay Round', paper presented at *The Uruguay Round and the Developing Economies*, a World Bank Conference, 26–7 January.

GATT, *Trade Policy Reviews* on: Cameroon, Ghana, Kenya, Nigeria, Senegal, South Africa, Zimbabwe.

—— (1989) *GATT. International Trade 1988–89* (Geneva).

—— (1994) 'The Results of the Uruguay Round of Multilateral Trade Negotiations. Market Access for Goods and Services: Overview of the Results', (Geneva).

Goldin, I. and D. van der Mensbrugghe (1995) 'Uruguay Round Reforms: Emphasizing Agricultural Reforms', paper presented at *The Uruguay Round and the Developing Economies*, a World Bank Conference, 26–7 January.

Harmsen and Subramanian (1994) 'Economic Implications of the Uruguay Round', in Kirmani *et al.* (eds) *International Trade Policies, The Uruguay Round and*

Beyond, Vol. 2. Background papers, World Economic and Financial Surveys (Washington, DC: IMF).

Harrison, G.W., T.F. Rutherford and D.G. Tarr (1995) 'Quantifying the Uruguay Round', paper presented at *The Uruguay Round and the Developing Economies*, a World Bank Conference, 26–7 January.

Hoda, A. (1994) 'Trade Liberalization Results of the Uruguay Round', a paper presented to an OECD workshop on *The New World Trading System* (Paris).

IMF (1994) Comprehensive Trade Paper – 'Trade Reforms in Fund-Supported Programs', SM/94/192 Supplement 2.

Konate, T.M. (1994) 'The Implications of the Uruguay Round for Africa', mimeo.

Martin, W. and J. François (1994) 'Bindings and Rules as Trade Liberalization', a paper presented at the *festschrift* conference for Professor R. Stern (Ann Arbor, Michigan, 18–20 November).

McGovern, E. (1986) *International Trade Regulation* (Globefield Press).

Nash, J. (1993) 'Trade Policy Reform Implementation in Sub-Saharan Africa: How Much Heat and How Much Light?', in F. Foroutan and J. Nash (eds), *Trade Policy and Exchange Rate Reform in Sub-Saharan Africa: What Went Right?, What Went Wrong? What Lessons for the Future?* (Washington, DC: World Bank).

Pohl, G. and P. Sorsa (1993) 'European Integration and the Developing World', Policy Research Paper no. 161 (Washington, DC: World Bank).

Schadler, S., F. Rozwadowski, S. Tiwari and D. Robinson (1993) 'Economic Adjustment in Low-Income Countries. Experience Under the Enhanced Structural Adjustment Facility', Occasional Paper no. 106 (Washington, DC: IMF).

Schiff, M. and A. Valdés (1992) *The Plundering of Agriculture in Developing Countries* (Washington DC: World Bank).

UNCTAD (1994a) *Directory of Import Regimes* (Geneva).

—— (1994b) *Trade and Development Report* (Geneva).

Weston, A. (1994) 'The Uruguay Round: Unravelling the Implications for the Least-Developed Countries and Low-Income Countries', UNCTAD, mimeo.

World Bank (1994a) 'Adjustment in Africa, Reforms, Results and the Road Ahead', A Policy Research Report (Washington, DC: World Bank).

—— (1994b) 'Preliminary Assessment of the Uruguay Round for Developing Countries', mimeo.

10 Changing Political and Economic Conditions for Regional Integration in SubSaharan Africa

H.M.A. Onitiri

10.1 INTRODUCTION

Some thirty years ago, when regional integration in Africa became a major subject of reflection and debate, the world could not have been more different from what it is today. On the political front, the cold war was in full swing; relations with one or the other of the great powers were major factors in African politics. Quite often, they were sources of serious friction among African countries themselves. Central and Eastern Europe was firmly in the Soviet camp, and Germany was divided between East and West. Relations with Israel and the Arab countries were key factors in African diplomacy.

Disengagement from the structures of the colonial economy was then a major preoccupation of African politicians and economic researchers. What is now the European Union (EU) was just beginning to take shape, and Africa was split between countries associated with the new organization and those that were not. At the first UNCTAD conference in 1964, the developing world had established a common front, in the Group of 77. The aim was to press for reforms in the international economic system that were relevant to the interests of the developing nations. Two of the major issues being hotly debated at that time were the stabilization of commodity prices and improved terms of trade for developing countries.

At the national level, there was concern with the diversification of exports, the expansion of industrial production behind tariff protection and the improvement of economic and social infrastructure. African economists were already elaborating the importance of economic integration for a badly fragmented continent, although some major international institutions, such as the World Bank, were not yet convinced that integration was a viable policy option in the African situation.

The changes that have taken place in these three decades have been profound. That is putting it very mildly. What has happened in the world, and in subSaharan Africa (SSA), can only be described as a political and economic revolution. While the consequences of this revolution on development policy, and on regional integration in SSA, will take many years to work themselves out, some effects are already apparent.

This chapter examines the likely impact of these developments on regional integration in subSaharan Africa. Following this introduction, Section 10.2 looks briefly at the political changes in the world that have had, or are likely to have, significant effects on regional integration in SSA, while Section 10.3 considers the effects of developments in the world economy on the integration process. Section 10.4 looks at the impact of changing political and economic conditions in SSA on regional integration in the region. Sections 10.5 and 10.6 examine new perspectives and future prospects, and Section 10.7 concludes with a discussion of the implications of the discussion for future research on regional integration in SSA.

10.2 POLITICAL CHANGES IN THE WORLD OF SIGNIFICANCE FOR INTEGRATION IN SSA

There has been much discussion of the impact of the end of the cold war on African development. In particular, there has been concern about the effect on subSaharan Africa of the decided shift of emphasis in resource transfer in favour of the Soviet Union and Eastern Europe. While it is not easy to quantify the effects of this development, several observers have drawn attention to some of the consequences. For example, Edward Jaycox of the World Bank[1] has noted that in the course of the world-scale political and economic changes currently underway, Africa risks being marginalized, and that obtaining aid and foreign investment has become an increasingly competitive process and is much more unsure than in the past.

The UN magazine, *Africa Recovery*,[2] has also reported that evidence is mounting that the international strategy to boost aid flows to Africa is in crisis. Both the World Bank and the IMF have reported downturns in lending to Africa during the latest financial year (1993). These sources have also noted that the fall in Bank lending to Africa has coincided with a large surge in commitments to Eastern Europe, which have increased from $US1.7 bn to $US3.8 bn.

The current situation is aptly summed up by Henry Louis Gates:[3]

> Africa . . . is probably worse off after the cold war. With the loss of socialist allies in international organizations, Africa has become more marginalized. The resources available for solving its problems are beginning to decline in the face of competing claims on the West and on international lending institutions – claims from the former members of the Warsaw Pact and, increasingly, from Vietnam.

In response to this trend, Africa's development partners have continued to stress the continuation of present structural reforms, with particular emphasis on regional integration, an increased role for the private sector and liberalization of macroeconomic policies. These prescriptions, including the need for good governance and peaceful resolution of conflicts, also feature in the Tokyo Declaration on African Development – 'Towards the 21st Century' – adopted by the Tokyo International Conference on African Development (TICAD), 5–6 October 1993. In particular, the declaration underlined the role of the private sector, the importance of regional co-operation and integration and the lessons to be drawn from the development experience of East and South-East Asia.

These prescriptions now constitute what can be regarded as the emerging consensus, on the part of Africa's development partners, on how Africa should respond to current world developments. However, many observers are doubtful that these measures will achieve substantial results without greater effort by the international community to ease the debt burden of African countries.

The role of regional integration in Africa's response to current world trends is particularly important. In an increasingly competitive world, where it will be ever more difficult to resort to protective measures, a high level of productivity is undoubtedly the key to improved competitiveness of African products in world markets. Therefore, if one of the principal objectives of regional integration is to contribute to this objective. To that end, the process must go beyond the mere integration of markets. It must deal as well, and effectively, with the integration of production at the regional and continental levels. This will encourage and facilitate the participation of African countries in the global trend towards the integration of production processes on a worldwide basis, involving the establishment of linkages between production units in different countries.

10.3 DEVELOPMENTS IN THE WORLD ECONOMY AND THEIR IMPLICATIONS FOR INTEGRATION IN SSA

It should be evident that the most profound pressures on SSA originate from the changes in the international environment, which are generally of a nature requiring collective and co-ordinated action at the regional and continental levels. They range from the technological to the growth of trading blocs.

The Effect of Rapid Changes in Technology

The tremendous speed of technological change calls for swift response by trading nations to changing situations in the world market. It also calls for urgent measures to improve efficiency and maintain a high level of productivity in the use of resources. Rapid adaptation will be difficult without the capacity for swift response, and African countries must ensure that they are part of this development rather than its victims.

All aspects of life will be touched by new technologies. Some examples are information technology, synthetic substitutes for a growing list of natural products and the use of robotics performing complex manufacturing functions. Others are new processes economizing on the use of raw materials and the extensive application of biotechnology techniques in agriculture and other spheres. These changes will have profound effects on international competitiveness and those who are not effectively in the race will be pushed further to the margin of world development and prosperity. Since the march of technology cannot be stopped, trading countries must develop the capacity to respond with maximum speed to changing situations in world markets.

Such rapid response is now beyond the capacity of most African countries. It would require a high level of productivity and far more success with integration programmes than is currently evident. African countries must face the reality that, in a world of free markets and fierce competition, productivity is king. They must draw lessons from the examples of countries with few raw materials but highly skilled and productive labour, which have succeeded in achieving sustained high standards of living for their peoples. On the other hand, some countries that are at the opposite end of the scale are those well endowed with abundant raw materials but lacking in the skill and productivity necessary to transform those materials into high-value-added products. Regrettably, many African countries fall at this end of the scale. Therefore, one major task facing African integration groupings is to improve the productivity of African industries, and to promote regional trade in raw materials and intermediate products.

The Possible Impact of the Uruguay Round

There are fears that the Uruguay Round of Multilateral Trade Negotiations under the GATT (UR), concluded in Geneva on 15 December 1993, will saddle SSA countries with new obligations in many areas without easing the old problems, such as falling commodity prices and restricted market access for processed commodities, that have bedeviled their development. On the other hand, the new situation created by the UR calls for even more across-the-board trade liberalization beyond what most African countries have already implemented under their respective SAPs. Under the UR, African countries also have to accept a number of new obligations: an undertaking to liberalize their trade in services, under the General Agreement on Trade in Services (GATS), new constraints on their investment policies, under the agreement on Trade-Related Investment Measures (TRIMs), and new obligations, under the agreement on Trade-Related Aspects of Intellectual Property Rights (TRIPs), which may severely constrain their acquisition of technology. Few African countries will benefit from tariff reductions on tropical products. Most will suffer a net loss of advantage because the general extension of liberalization will erode the margin of preference that they now enjoy under the Lomé Convention. Lumping together various issues in a single final act, to be administered by an umbrella organization – the World Trade Organization (WTO) – will pose several problems for SSA. For example, it may result in cross-retaliation between trade in goods and trade in services, or between these and policies on TRIMs and TRIPs.

SSA, like the rest of Africa, seems to have been guided by three main considerations during its participation in the negotiations. First, because the present structure of its trade is heavily concentrated on tropical products and natural resource-based products, it pressed for the removal of trade restrictions and greater market access for such products. Second, mindful of their limited capacity to take advantage of new opportunities under the agreements on the new issues (services, TRIPs and TRIMs), the countries were concerned with ensuring that these agreements were compatible with their development needs. Third, SSA had been conscious of the fact that, in spite of the UR agreement, regional economic blocs were likely to play an increasing role in world trade relations, and that in trading blocs they would be in a stronger position to defend their interests.

The final results of the UR negotiations have confirmed Africa's fears and anxieties that implementation of the agreement will have a major impact on the continent's trading position in the world and with the other trading blocs.

(1) Africa is expected to sustain substantial losses and make few gains from the UR agreement. Most of the assessments of the impact of the round on Africa show that the continent may lose up to $US3 bn per annum during the initial years of implementation, while other trading countries share benefits that could amount to $US500 bn per annum. The losses will result mainly from the loss of the special preferences at present enjoyed under the Lomé Convention, as well as the increase in the food import bills of the net food importing countries.

(2) Although theoretically Africa should gain from the expansion of trade that would result from the lowering of tariffs in non-European markets, including the USA and Japan, not previously covered by special preferences, it is unlikely that Africa's competitive position will be strong enough to take advantage of this potential.

(3) African countries are at present not well placed to take advantage of the opportunities in the new areas, such as services and intellectual property, while their dealings with foreign investors may be constrained by the provisions on TRIMs.

(4) The UR agreement is of such magnitude and complexity that it would require a far more effective mechanism for the management of trade policy than many African countries have at present.

(5) The principles of progressive liberalization and freer markets that the agreement seeks to underline will obviously favour those countries that have been able to achieve a high level of productivity and competitiveness, and penalize those that still have a long way to go to achieve that status. Therefore, the limited period many African countries will have under the agreement to adjust to full implementation of the various measures would have to be used most constructively to prepare the ground for more competitive production structures.

The Growing Importance of Services in World Trade

Under the General Agreement on Trade in Services (GATS), SSA countries may now have to accept new obligations for the liberalization of their trade in services. The conclusion of GATS is itself an acknowl-edgement of the growing importance of services in world trade and in national production and consumption, particularly in the developed countries. It is a trend that is already exerting a great influence on international economic relations. It explains why, during the prepara-tions for the Uruguay Round, the developed countries pressed for a special negotiating group to work out new rules under the GATT for trade in services. If developing countries were generally lukewarm to the inclusion of services in the negotiating agenda, it was not for lack of recognition of its importance. Their concern was that, given the asymmetric position between them and the developed countries in the production of services, developing countries would be at great disad-vantage if this sector were to be thrown open to free international competition.

As events have turned out, the developed countries have had their way, and GATS is already a part of the final act of the Uruguay Round. Since this is an area where the transnational corporations (TNCs) are particularly active and well entrenched, it is unlikely that SSA will be able to protect its interests without effective co-ordination of its pro-grammes through regional and continental integration.

Possible Impact of the Formation of Major Trading Blocs

It is becoming increasingly clear that a few major trading blocs will dominate the future trading world. The main actors are likely to be the European Union (EU), substantially enlarged with the accession of Sweden, Norway, Finland and Austria, the North American Free Trade Area (NAFTA) or most likely the all-embracing Free Trade Area of the Americas (FTAA), the Association of South-East Asian Nations (ASEAN), and the Asia–Pacific Economic Cooperation forum.

Opinion is divided about the impact of such blocs on non-member countries, but discussions within GATT and during the Uruguay Round negotiations reflect the anxieties of such countries about the possible negative impact of trading blocs on non-members.

Although the rules about regional economic blocs, under the UR agreement, are much more stringent than those under the old GATT, it is still likely that large and viable economic blocs will be able to claim, or get away with, a number of advantages and exceptions. This ex-plains why, even as the UR negotiations proceeded, many countries accorded great priority to consolidating their programmes for regional economic integration. It was during this period that the EU was further consolidated, NAFTA established, the idea of FTAA was broached, the AEC was established, ASEAN accelerated implementation of its free trade area and APEC agreed to achieve free regional trade and investment by the decade 2010–2020.

Though Article XXIV of the GATT was expected to protect the interests of non-members of trading blocs, the general view is that the article had never been effectively implemented. Although trade blocs are supposed to be non-discriminatory, this is, in fact, a contradiction in terms, since the very basis of their existence is discrimination in favour of their members. The crucial issue is that trade blocs had some privileges, under Article XXIV of GATT and the 1979 enabling clause, that they could use to by-pass the MFN principle and discriminate against non-members. Under the WTO, Article XXIV of GATT 1994 has not explicitly removed these privileges, but it has reaffirmed that

> the purpose of such agreements should be to facilitate trade between the constituent territories and not to raise barriers to the trade of other Members with such territories; and that in their formation or enlargement the parties to them should to the greatest possible extent avoid creating adverse effects on the trade of other Members.[4]

In spite of this safeguard, it is generally believed that powerful trading blocs will still be able to circumvent the MFN rule and the principles of free trade and unfettered competition, in the interest of their members.

While regionalism is not necessarily incompatible with multilateralism, there are fears that the blocs may, in fact, develop into 'fortresses'.[5] In any case, an objective assessment of the impact of a trading bloc would have to be made with reference to the circumstances of the particular situation. In their recent historical study of trade blocs, Barry Eichengreen and Douglas Irwin have argued that 'the implications for the multilateral trade system of emerging regional arrangements, like NAFTA and Europe's Single Market, will depend on the specific structure of these initiatives and on accompanying policies'.[6] A more recent study by UNCTAD has argued that 'continued trade liberalization and intensified disciplines at the multilateral level are the most effective way of integrating regional groupings into the multilateral trading system'.[7]

Although African integration groupings will also be free to take advantage of whatever privileges survive for trading blocs under the new WTO rules, their position in this regard will not be particularly strong. For one thing, the heavy dependence of African countries on external markets would make it more difficult for them to utilize those privileges effectively. For another, the situation of heavy external dependence will continue for a very long time, unless they make more rapid progress with their programmes for regional and continental union.

As a basis for developing an effective response to regional trade blocs, it is important that African integration groupings should study very carefully the possible effects of particular trading blocs on their trade, and review various options for special relationships that they could develop with particular blocs. Because most of the large trade blocs now have mixed memberships of developed and developing countries, there is little chance that the kind of special relationship developed between the ACP and the EU, under the Lomé Convention could be widely utilized in the future. It is most likely that future relationships between SSA and the emerging trade blocs will be guided largely by commercial considerations, with little or no concessionary elements. It is important therefore that SSA should consider that the most important response would be an effective mobilization of Africa's own regional and sub-regional economic groupings to achieve rapid structural transformation and a high level of productivity and competitiveness.

Effects of New Global Linkages and Interdependence

An effective response to the prevalence of regional economic blocs should be regarded as an important component of a comprehensive strategy by SSA to cope with the implications of the current trend towards the global linkages and interdependence of production units the world over. This trend is perhaps the most important aspect of the major changes in the international environment to which African economies, with their present inadequate structures and orientations, are still ill-adapted to adjust. It has been accelerated, among others, by the rapid development of technology and the adoption of free market policies. A few such developments need to be mentioned. The rapid development of technology has brought about profound changes in the organization of world production, and this has significantly altered the environment for competition. The attainment of a high level of productivity now requires, even more than before, the organization of production across national borders. In short, the internationalization of production has become an indispensable basis for maintaining competitiveness in international markets. The process has gathered increased momentum in the past three decades, and it will accelerate considerably with the conclusion of the Uruguay Round. The global process will undoubtedly accelerate with the extension of the internationalization of markets to the realm of services, such as banking, insurance and transportation.

The emergence of an integrated international production system, the growing interdependence of the world economy and the extensive linkages between production processes and ownership of enterprises present African countries with both problems and opportunities. While this global process has undoubtedly contributed to world economic growth, the benefits have largely by-passed those countries, including most SSA countries, that have not been able to join in the process. Improvements in infrastructure, particularly transport and communications, an enabling environment for foreign investment and the capacity to adjust rapidly to sudden changes in the external environment are prerequisites for effective participation in the new global linkages of production processes. Indeed, the trend towards market economies in Africa as elsewhere requires the restructuring of national economies so that they can respond swiftly to market forces.

The 1993 United Nations *World Investment Report* has noted that:

> Those developments make it more important than ever for developing countries to build up their own human and physical infrastructure. In addition to providing the basis for industrialization and development of the domestic economy, it would allow national enterprises to join up with TNCs on a more equal basis. It would raise the quality and sophistication of the foreign direct investment (FDI) a host country could attract and would strengthen the prospects for technology acquisition. It would also enable host developing countries to build up supplier capabilities which are sometimes a precondition for the location of TNC activities and which, moreover, add to the economic and technological spillovers from affiliates. The building up of such facilities has been an essential feature in the developing countries, including those in Asia and Latin America, that have succeeded in restructuring both their international and domestic production sectors towards higher-value-added activities.[8]

The same source has noted further that:

> Other developing countries that do not offer the locational advantages required by regionally or globally integrated firms, such as a skilled labour force, an open trading and investment environment, a developed communication and transport infrastructure and networks of local suppliers on which TNCs can draw, risk being further

marginalized. Those countries need to consider how to formulate
and co-ordinate policies so as to maximize the benefits to them from
the emerging integrated international production system as well as
from FDI in more traditional organizational forms which they may
be in a better position to obtain.[9]

The TNCs provide a vital link between this global development and
economic integration. As noted by UNCTAD,

> TNCs are increasingly organizing themselves into multi-tier networks
> including parent firms, foreign affiliates, firms linked through sub-
> contracting, licensing and similar contractual arrangements, and firms
> tied together through alliances. These networks include all major cor-
> porate functions – R&D, procurement, manufacturing, marketing, finance,
> accounting, human resource development, etc. – and occur in both de-
> veloped and developing countries. Such changes in TNC strategies and
> organization are fostering world-wide economic integration.[10]

SubSaharan African countries have to face the reality that sharing in
future world growth and prosperity now requires effective participation in the new global linkages and interdependence. Their integration
programmes have to be geared to take advantage of the opportunities
presented by this development. If such programmes emphasize growing linkages of production units among member countries of their integration groupings, this can provide a valuable basis for their eventual
participation in the new global linkages of production processes.

Implications of the New Concern About the Environment

For the rest of the 1990s and beyond, environmental concerns will be
major factors in world development and will have major implications
for development at the national and regional levels. By their very nature, environmental issues require very close co-operation at the regional level, and several inter-governmental organizations would have
to work in close harmony to carry out the programmes and projects
identified in Agenda 21 agreed at the World Conference on Environment and Development (UNCED) in Rio de Janeiro in 1992.

The unprecedented African drought of the 1980s and the untold
hardship and misery that it brought to the populations of several
subSaharan African countries kindled great interest in the protection
and preservation of the environment. For millions of the affected

populations, famine became the order of the day; tens of thousands died of starvation, and millions of those who survived were destined to endure life-time scars from the effect of famine. There was awareness that the drought was the result of misguided policies and the misuse and abuse of natural resources that were dangerously altering the ecological balance in many areas. Millions of hectares of forest cover were being destroyed annually, and the Sahara Desert had expanded southward by a belt at least 150 kilometres wide.

The experience underlined the importance of implementing the African Convention on the Conservation of Nature and Natural Resources adopted in Algiers in 1968. The OAU Pan-African Conference on Environment and Sustainable Development held in Bamako (Mali) in January 1991 culminated in the Bamako Commitment on Environment and the Bamako Convention on the Transboundary Movements of Hazardous Wastes. To enhance environmental awareness, the OAU declared 1991–2 African Year of the Environment.

The AEC treaty reflects the environmental concerns of African countries. Under Articles 58, 59 and 60 of the treaty, member states undertake to co-operate in:

- promoting a healthy environment;
- adopting national, regional and continental policies, strategies and programmes and establishing appropriate institutions for the protection and enhancement of the environment;
- taking the necessary measures to accelerate the reform and innovation process leading to ecologically rational, economically sound and socially acceptable development policies and programmes;
- banning the importation and dumping of hazardous wastes in their respective territories; and
- co-operating in the trans-boundary movement, management and processing of such wastes produced in Africa.

The OAU participated fully in UNCED and is committed to the implementation of Agenda 21 within the context of the African Common Position on Environment and Development. The task for the future is to mobilize the integration organs to establish a long-term programme of activities for the implementation of Agenda 21. To this end, it will be necessary to build capacities within the AEC and the RECs to implement environmental objectives. This should include mechanisms for consultation at the continental and regional levels on environmental matters.

Implications of the Worldwide Increase in Demand for Foreign Investment

The slowing of foreign investment to Africa is not likely to be reversed soon, even if the political situation becomes more stable. Africa's share in the global total of inflows of foreign direct investment has remained at an average of 2 per cent since 1986.[11] The share of all developing countries in the global total in 1992 was 32 per cent. Real improvement in inflows to Africa will require a concerted effort by African countries to make a more productive use of investment generally, and to improve the basic infrastructure of transport and communication, energy supplies and water resources. Greater regional co-ordination and harmonization of policies in these spheres within the RECs will accelerate this process and provide greater incentives for foreign investment.

According to the Global Coalition for Africa,

Africa has been largely left outside these fast growing capital markets. Since 1980, foreign direct investment in Africa has remained below US$1 billion, in a period in which direct foreign investment in Latin America has ranged between US$3.5 billion and 14 billion. US$570 million of direct foreign investment flowed into Africa in 1990, compared with US$2.7 billion in China and US$964 million in Indonesia. During the 1980s, direct foreign investment in Africa was about 1% of the world total, and in 1991 Africa received only 6% of the private investment flows to developing countries.[12]

Other figures show that Africa's relatively small share of foreign investment inflows to the developing regions declined from an average of 12.9 per cent for the period 1981–85 – already a strikingly low figure when compared with the 37.6 per cent share for South, East and South-East Asia – to 5.9 per cent in 1992. On the other hand, the share of South, East and South-East Asia increased from 37.6 per cent to 57.1 per cent during the same period. A continuation of these disparate trends will be certain to translate into wider disparities in future rates of economic growth between SSA and most of the developing world. Indeed, World Bank projections for 1995-2000 show that average growth of real GDP in SSA of 3.8 per cent during this period will be lower than the 4.95 per cent for all developing countries.[13]

The failure of Africa to share significantly in the current boom in private investment flows to developing countries is underlined in a recent UN report, which drew attention to the effort made by African countries to attract foreign investment, the many profitable opportunities waiting to be explored and the relatively high rates of return on foreign investment in Africa.[14]

10.4 POLITICAL AND ECONOMIC TRENDS IN SSA AND THEIR IMPLICATIONS FOR ECONOMIC INTERGRATION

Political Trends

The political upheavals that Africa has witnessed during the past decade in internal and inter-state relations have had dire consequences for economic integration. They have absorbed substantial resources that could have been devoted to development. They have created an atmosphere of instability and uncertainty that has been detrimental to foreign investment and favourable to capital flight. And they have eroded that mutual trust and confidence among countries which are essential for the implementation of integration programmes.

African countries are aware that the successful implementation of economic programmes requires the creation of an enabling political environment. They also believe that the current political situation calls for urgent measures to establish appropriate mechanisms for the peaceful resolution of internal and inter-country conflicts that are detrimental to development and the attraction of foreign investment.

This explains why in Article 3 of the treaty establishing the AEC, they solemnly affirm their adherence to the following principles, among others:

- peaceful settlement of disputes among member states, active cooperation between neighbouring countries and promotion of a peaceful environment as a prerequisite for economic development;
- recognition, promotion and protection of human and peoples' rights in accordance with the provisions of the African Charter on Human and Peoples' Rights; and
- accountability, economic justice and popular participation in development.

The OAU has now established a mechanism for conflict prevention and resolution and is playing a vital role in several conflict situations in SSA. Because of the disruptive effects of political conflicts, it is now generally believed that regional efforts to prevent and resolve conflicts should be accorded no less priority than measures to promote development.

Economic Trends

The economic trends have not been less worrying. Though there are now indications that the growth prospects may be much better than they looked a few years ago, the global projections referred to above show that there is little cause for much optimism. The main sources of concern are deteriorating economies and limited progress with structural adjustment.

Continuing Deterioration of SubSaharan African Economies

SSA countries have continued to experience serious problems carried over from the last decade. In many SSA countries, GDP growth rates, which are below 2 per cent in many cases, are still below the rates of population growth. Large fiscal deficits and high rates of inflation are still the rule rather than the exception. The terms of trade have continued to deteriorate. Interest on foreign debts continues to climb.[15]

Limited Progress with SAPs

The results of the current structural adjustment programmes have been mixed. All the assessments so far show very few successes. According to the ADB's Africa Development Report 1993, the experience to date points to the following conclusions.

(1) Very few adjusting countries have recorded appreciable growth rates after a decade of adjustment. In many countries, adjustment policies have depressed the incomes of large segments of society.

(2) Adjustment programmes seem to have accorded greater priority to short-term objectives of maintaining sound fiscal balance sheets and balance of payments improvement and less to long-term growth.

(3) Adjustment policies have fallen short of expectations in stimulating growth. Many adjusting countries have had to cope with the burden of overwhelming debt. Resources absorbed by debt payments have left little room for growth.

(4) Many countries have faced the problem of limited institutional capacity to manage reforms. Apart from the problem of managing macroeconomic objectives, many countries face major problems

in key sectors. These are evident, in particular, in education, health, transport, infrastructure, the environment and urban development.

(5) SAPs have continued to rely predominantly on concessional lending by international financial institutions. The expected increase in foreign investment counted upon to make adjustment self-sustaining has not been forthcoming.

(6) The experience of countries with fixed exchange rate parities (mostly countries belonging to monetary zones) has shown the importance of macroeconomic flexibility for the success of adjustment programmes. Unable to adjust the exchange rate, and with little scope for the pursuit of an active monetary policy, they have had to rely predominantly on fiscal policy in responding to external economic disruptions. In this regard, the devaluation of the CFA franc on 12 January 1994 was of particular significance as it was the first change of parity with the French franc since 1948. This development has introduced a new flexibility into the monetary system of the franc zone countries, which should help to promote the process of monetary co-operation in West Africa.

(7) Because little attention was given in the early years to the social consequences of SAPs, deteriorating social situations in many adjusting countries did not create a favourable environment for the implementation of the programmes. Therefore, special programmes have had to be designed to alleviate the impact of SAPs on the poor. The recent report on adjustment in Africa by the World Bank, has drawn attention to some of the pitfalls in the adjustment process and suggested the paths to faster progress.[16]

Need to Improve Interactions Between Structural Adjustment and Economic Integration

The policy implications of current economic trends for regional integration have not been lost on the integration organs. In particular, they have become increasingly aware of the need to ensure that structural adjustment programmes and economic integration objectives will be mutually reinforcing. Both are important instruments in the strategy for organizing and focusing economic policy for mobilizing and allocating resources, and have become central elements of the development policies of most SSA countries.[17] Improving interactions between the two objectives requires closer economic co-ordination and harmonization at the regional level, as well as joint action at the regional level to improve the efficiency of their national SAPs. For example, improvement of infrastructure – in particular transport and communication – and power supplies will improve the productivity of domestic industries, and therefore generally promote beneficial interactions between structural adjustment and regional integration.

It is also necessary to reduce possible conflicts between structural adjustment and regional integration. For example, the impact of the rapid adjustment of the exchange rate by a member country of an integrated market may be disruptive to other member countries in the short run. However, this may be beneficial eventually if it stimulates a general, and desirable, realignment of exchange rates of the integrated market in relation to external currencies. A good example is the experience of ECOWAS countries. The rapid devaluation of some non-CFA currencies in the region in the second half of the 1980s undoubtedly exerted major pressures on the CFA franc and contributed to its devaluation in January 1994.[18]

It has become evident from this experience that serious economic integration requires the harmonization of national macroeconomic policies and the establishment of an effective regional mechanism for this purpose. In particular, with the movement towards greater convertibility of currencies, co-ordination and consultation could be useful to exchange experience, reduce uncertainties and increase mutual confidence among the member countries of a regional grouping. Although some RECs have made a start on an *ad hoc* basis on fiscal policy co-ordination, a more systematic approach is necessary.

ECOWAS has attempted to explore the regional dimensions of SAPs in its Economic Recovery Programme, but the effort has not achieved much so far. It is unlikely that much progress will be made on the issue until there is more success with the co-ordination of fiscal and monetary policies among the member countries.

The experience so far leads to the conclusion that more conscious efforts are necessary to ensure that SAP policies and integration objectives reinforce each other. Such efforts should include an assessment of the expected regional impact of national macroeconomic measures. Furthermore, because sectoral strategies and policies have macroeconomic and inter-sectoral implications, it is also necessary to examine the regional impact of national sectoral programmes. Because the improvement of the regional dimensions of structural adjustment has such wide implications, the RECs need to give more serious thought to the idea of regional structural adjustment programmes.

Promotion of Multinational Projects

The difficulty of promoting multinational enterprises has been one major impediment to the rapid integration of African economies. The ADB has devoted much attention to this question since its establishment. Although its mandate required it to devote most of its resources to the financing of multinational enterprises, it has had great difficulties in fulfilling this mandate. This problem requires in-depth research to help the bank to develop new approaches and strategies. Such research should concentrate on the following questions, among others: What have been the successful experiences? What are the examples of failure? What lessons can be learned from these experiences? In the light of these experiences, what are the new options for policy? What new institutional arrangements will facilitate the financing and operation of multinational projects?

Since industrial development holds the key to the economic transformation of sub-Saharan Africa, including the transformation of the vital agriculture sector, industrial programming on a regional scale is imperative in the economic integration strategy of these countries. Given the small size of most of the economies, failure to harmonize national industrial programmes at the regional level has obviously retarded structural transformation. Harmonization will promote inter-linkages among industrial units in the region and contribute to balanced industrial development.

10.5 NEW PERSPECTIVES

Implications of New Institutional Developments at the Regional Level

Four major developments that need to be followed very carefully in the next few years are:

- relations between PTA and SADC;
- implementation of the revised ECOWAS treaty;
- the West African Economic and Monetary Union (UEMOA); and
- the impact of a democratic South Africa on economic integration in SSA.

Little should be said at present on relations between PTA and SADC until the high-powered committee established on the subject has completed its work. In the same vein, the major study on South Africa soon to be published by the ADB should provide a good factual basis for a discussion of the possible impact of a democratic South Africa on economic integration in subSaharan Africa. The results of these two developments will undoubtedly have a major impact on the integration arrangements in subSaharan Africa. The discussion here therefore concentrates on the revised ECOWAS treaty, and the proposed West African Economic and Monetary Union.

The Revised ECOWAS Treaty

The recent reform of the ECOWAS treaty, following the proposals put forward by the Committee of Eminent Persons for the Review of the ECOWAS Treaty in June 1992, promises to put new life into the organization. Most of the recommendations of the committee have been incorporated into the revised ECOWAS Treaty, which has extensive provisions for the strengthening of ECOWAS. The aim, as provided for in Article 2 (1) of the revised treaty, is that the organization 'shall ultimately be the sole economic community in the region for the purpose of economic integration and the realisation of the objectives of the African Economic Community'.

The West African Economic and Monetary Union (UEMOA)

The treaty establishing UEMOA was published in December 1993.[19] However, the formation of the new organization had been under discussion for most of the year.

During the Seventh Conference of Heads of State and Government of UEMOA held in Dakar in July 1992, the governor of BCEAO submitted an orientation paper for the establishment of the new Union.[20] The meeting mandated the governor to 'deepen the sectoral studies required for an implementation as soon as possible, of the proposed integration strategy'. The sponsors of the new organization have given many reasons for their proposal. According to information available, the aim is to build on the advantages of the present monetary union by transforming the arrangement into an economic and monetary union. The sponsors believe that this transformation will reinforce the economic integration of the member states of UEMOA and arrest the present drift of their economies towards marginalization. They explain the move by drawing attention to historical factors and the compelling need to match monetary union with economic integration.

The view of the BCEAO head office is clearly set down in a paper presented at the International Conference on West African Integration held in Dakar in January 1993.[21] It emphasized the need to match monetary integration and economic integration. It noted that, at present, UMOA is characterized by a double centre of decision: (1) monetary, falling within the competence of community institutions, and (2) economic and budgetary, falling under the authority of member states. The creation of UEMOA, the paper explains, will resolve this duality; for example, by harmonizing the management of public finance, debt and external payments, pricing policy, and so on, in the member states.

Seen against the background of the revised ECOWAS treaty, the establishment of UEMOA is obviously a development of profound significance for the economic integration of the West African region. The creation of what looks like a permanent organization will be difficult to reconcile with the implementation of the revised ECOWAS treaty. In particular, it may be inconsistent with Article 2 of the revised treaty, which provides that ECOWAS 'shall ultimately be the sole economic community in the region for the purpose of economic integration and the realisation of the objectives of the African Economic Community'. It is particularly interesting that in the first paragraph of the preamble to the treaty, establishing UEMOA signatories reaffirmed their faith in the objectives of the AEC and ECOWAS. How this will be reconciled with the implementation of the parallel programmes of UEMOA will be watched with great interest.

In any case, with the establishment of UEMOA, West African leaders would have to make a great effort to ensure that this development does not constitute a major setback to regional integration in West Africa.

Possible Impact of the African Economic Community

The establishment of the AEC opens a new chapter in Africa's integration, and could have beneficial effects on the integration process, in particular by providing a continental framework for the rationalization of integration organs and institutions. The implementation of the AEC treaty therefore poses a major challenge to African organizations and institutions concerned with integration at all levels. Since the treaty embraces all aspects of African economic and social life, it also provides a convenient framework for re-examining and streamlining the activities of the existing African international government organizations, and mobilizing them more effectively to address the pressing problems of African economic and social development. While experience suggests that, in the African context, reforming, restructuring or rationalizing institutions is an extremely difficult task, it is nevertheless a task that needs to be accomplished if the continent is to face the challenges of a rapidly changing world.

The successful implementation of the AEC treaty would depend in large measure on several crucial factors, among which are the following:

- the structure and capability of the single OAU/AEC secretariat that is yet to be determined;
- the co-ordination arrangements between the AEC and the RECs;
- the effectiveness of the efforts to mobilize the activities of other African institutions and organizations (IGOs, NGOs, and so on) for the implementation of the treaty;
- the mechanisms established at the national level to focus attention on the regional and continental dimensions of national programmes and on the implementation of regional and continental programmes at the national level; and
- the effectiveness of international support for Africa's integration programmes.

The Single OAU/AEC Secretariat

While the AEC treaty provides for a large number of implementing mechanisms and subsidiary bodies, the task of administering and managing the community will devolve largely on the secretariat, which will have the main responsibility for servicing the Economic and Social Commission and other specialized bodies of the community. However, since the OAU secretariat is also expected to be the secretariat of the AEC, the structure of the single secretariat is of crucial importance to the success of the organization.[22]

The creation of a single OAU/AEC secretariat involves a radical transformation of the OAU's traditional structure. The new structure will have two basic functions: the implementation of the AEC treaty; and the prevention, management and resolution of conflicts and monitoring of the transition to multi-party democratic systems. How the single OAU/AEC secretariat should be structured is still under discussion by the organization.

Four basic considerations will be important in the search for a structure that will enable the OAU to fulfil its new responsibilities effectively. First, the secretary-general of the OAU is also the secretary-general of the AEC, and has responsibilities for the implementation of the AEC treaty as well the pursuit of the expanded political functions of the OAU. Second, with the establishment of the single OAU/AEC secretariat, the activities of the OAU will now fall under two clear divisions – implementation of the AEC treaty and performance of the political functions. Therefore, within the framework of the division of labour in the OAU/AEC secretariat, a senior functionary of the organization (assistant secretary-general or deputy-secretary-general of the OAU) will probably be in charge of matters relating to the AEC. Third, since the AEC deals with social and also economic matters, some reorganization of the present structure will be necessary so that all activities now falling under the Economic Co-operation Department (EDECO) and the Social Affairs Department (ESCAS) will come under the senior official who will be responsible for the implementation of the AEC treaty under the overall direction of the OAU secretary-general. Finally, because of the new role of the OAU in conflict prevention, management and resolution, it will be necessary to enlarge the political department to take on these new duties, under another senor functionary who will be responsible to the OAU secretary-general.

One other mechanism is expected to supplement the capacity of the OAU secretariat to cope with the new tasks of implementing the treaty. This is the provision for regular meetings of the chief executives of the OAU, ECA and ADB, who are the primary actors in the implementation of the AEC treaty. At the official level, the three organizations constitute the 'Joint Secretariat', whose main purpose is to co-ordinate the efforts of the three organizations in the implementation of the treaty. A suggestion that the Joint Secretariat should be given a more formal structure is now under discussion.

The Relationship Between the AEC and the RECs

The AEC Treaty provides that the RECs will serve as the building blocks for the new community. The relationships between the AEC and the RECs are to be governed by a protocol to the AEC treaty that is now under discussion by the Permanent Steering Committee of the OAU. The protocol is expected to make a positive contribution to the institutional framework for African economic integration.

It is expected that the substantial strengthening of the RECs will provide a strong foundation for the implementation of the AEC treaty. Therefore, the treaty provides that the first five years of its operation should emphasize the strengthening of the RECs. What are the options for policy in this area? The answer to this question should consider that strengthening implies essentially three main activities:

- support for the efforts of the RECs to rationalize and strengthen their institutional structures;
- assistance with the implementation of REC programmes; and
- new initiatives to promote co-operation among the RECs in areas where more rapid progress requires extensive inter-regional linkages.

The Role of IGOs, NGOs, and Others

The AEC treaty provides (in Article 90) that the community shall establish relations of co-operation with African non-governmental organizations, with a view to encouraging the involvement of the African peoples in the process of economic integration and mobilizing their technical, material and financial support. It also provides (in Article 91) that the community shall establish relations of co-operation with socioeconomic organizations and associations, mainly including producers, transport operators, workers, employers, youth, women, artisans and other professional organizations and associations, with a view to ensuring their involvement in the integration process of Africa. To this end, the community is required to set up mechanisms for consultation with such non-governmental and socioeconomic organizations and associations.

The structure of the AEC secretariat should therefore enable it to mobilize these institutions for the task of implementing the treaty. The situation calls for minimum centralization of activities and a good deal of devolution and delegation, such as would enable the NGOs and other organizations to play an effective role. One idea under consideration for this purpose is the establishment of a network of relationships between the AEC and such organizations. At least two sensitization programmes involving some of these organisations have already been held.

Mechanisms at the National Level

The involvement of NGOs and other organizations in the implementation of integration programmes also underlines the necessity of establishing appropriate mechanisms at the national level to sensitize socioeconomic groups on the advantages of regional solutions to Africa's socioeconomic problems. Some new initiatives under consideration in this connection will start to unfold with the ratification of the AEC treaty.

Increasing the Effectiveness of International Support for African Integration

Most of the international institutions important for African development have now accepted the fundamental importance of economic integration to African development. Therefore, their future activities will no doubt respond to the programmes and projects of the integration groupings. To make the most effective use of this opportunity, however, African integration organs should clearly articulate their needs and priorities for the implementation of their objectives. The reason is that the approaches to African economic integration favoured by donors may not always coincide with the approaches that African countries wish to follow. Already there are differences of opinion on how much emphasis should be placed on market integration and how much on the integration of production structures.

Another area where differences may be emerging is on the institutional framework for integration. For example, the idea of 'variable geometry' that has now crept into the vocabulary of African economic integration may be at variance with the approach favoured in the AEC treaty. The debate on this concept has gathered momentum at a time when the establishment of the AEC has added a new dimension to the geometry of existing integration groupings and provided a continent-wide framework for rationalizing the activities of these groupings. The concept of variable geometry has been interpreted in different ways. One view argues that the approach to integration most likely to succeed 'will be pragmatic and incremental, allowing two or more countries to move forward with co-operative arrangements wherever opportunities arise'.[23]

Another view interprets this approach as the setting up of new institutions, such as the UEMOA. The former interpretation is not necessarily inconsistent with the provisions of the AEC treaty, or those of the existing regional economic communities. In fact, many bilateral agreements have been signed between countries belonging to different RECs. For example, Nigeria and Cameroon, which belong to different RECs, have an agreement on free movement of persons. It should also be noted that the AEC treaty envisages 'co-ordination and harmonization of activities among the existing and future economic communities'. The real disagreement is whether such co-operation requires the establishment of new institutions. Given the difficulties of rationalizing the existing IGOs, there is considerable scepticism in encouraging the establishment of still more integration organs.

It is obvious from these developments that the way international financial support for African integration is disbursed, and the underlying priorities guiding the allocation of such resources, could have a major impact on the implementation of the AEC treaty. Considering the major difficulties facing existing integration organs, it could be said that international aid for integration would go a long way if devoted largely to the rationalization of existing institutions, the development of multinational projects and the improvement of regional infrastructure relevant to raising the level of productivity and increasing the competitiveness of African products in world markets.

The Distribution of the Costs and Benefits of Economic Integration

It is acknowledged that economic integration cannot be viable unless member states perceive themselves to be net beneficiaries. In several RECs, measures have been tried to achieve the objective of fair distribution of costs and benefits, and a good many lessons have been learnt from the experience. The expectation for the future is that a combination of fiscal transfers with measures to mobilize resources for priority projects, particularly in the less developed members of the integration groupings, may be more successful than fiscal transfers alone.

10.6   FUTURE PROJECTS

Where will all this lead by the turn of the century? What will Africa's political and economic map look like at that time? In a situation fraught with so many uncertainties, it would be unusually brazen to attempt predictions of such magnitudes. A more modest exercise could assess how the political and economic map would change if the measures already adopted by the various RECs were to be implemented. Not only will the implementation of such measures change the political and economic map by the end of the decade, it will also increase the credibility of African countries as to their readiness to implement their integration programmes. That credibility at the moment has ebbed very low. Edward Jaycox is reported to have made the following remarks at a luncheon speech during the annual World Bank meeting in September of 1993:[24]

We are very supportive of African integration but we are very skeptical too. Africa has been talking about integration for 30 or more years and they haven't done very much because they haven't gotten from rhetorics to the implementation phase.

Accelerating the Implementation of Liberalization Programmes

The impact of implementing the programmes already elaborated by the RECs and the AEC in a few critical areas, such as trade liberalization, freedom of movement, rights of residence and establishment, and the establishment of multinational projects, will be tremendous. It will alter the economic picture significantly and provide a strong foundation for further progress on integration. The modest action programme could consist of elements from the present programmes of the RECs and the AEC that would be accomplished by the end of the decade, with the assistance of the international community. One such programme could comprise elements at both the regional and the continental levels.

At the Regional Level

Action at the regional level could include:

- removal of all duties and non-tariff barriers on regional trade in originating products;
- removal of all restrictions on freedom of movement, rights of residence and establishment.

At the Continental Level

A continental programme could involve adoption of the AEC protocols on:

- relations between the AEC and the RECs
- free movement of persons, rights of residence and establishment
- transport and communications
- elimination of customs duties
- elimination of non-tariff barriers
- rules of origin
- energy
- the environment.

New Drive to Promote Multinational Projects

Although experience suggests that there are great difficulties in promoting multinational projects, the opportunities for such projects are still immense and new attempts should be made to explore them. The RECs themselves are the best focal points for the development of multinational projects, but they would need assistance in building the necessary capacity for this purpose. The ADB, the African Capacity Building Foundation (ACBF) and the World Bank should explore the possibility of helping the RECs to utilize existing regional research networks to develop options for the establishment of multinational projects, paying particular attention to industry, energy and the environment.

An example of the options that could be examined is the link between energy development and the preservation of the environment. In this connection, it is noteworthy that Nigeria, Ghana, Togo and the Republic of Benin, with the involvement of the World Bank, are currently discussing the export of Nigeria's natural gas to the three West African countries through a network of gas pipelines.[25] This project obviously has greater potential than its present conception. Within the framework of Agenda 21, it is not far-fetched to imagine the extension of the gas pipelines to some of the countries of the Sahel region as a way of reducing their dependence on wood for fuel.[26]

Targeting Specific Issues

Regional integration should aim in particular to contribute to the elaboration of policies on these important issues:

- maintaining sustainable agriculture and food security;
- reducing the dependence of industrial production on imported materials;
- ensuring adequate and well-maintained economic infrastructure; and
- ensuring that macroeconomic policies, particularly trade, exchange rate and monetary policies, create a favourable environment for growth and development.

All this will not be easy, but regional integration can help in many ways. For example, as already mentioned, it can rationalize present liberalization policies under the SAPs. It can also co-ordinate whatever efforts are considered necessary to protect particular industries or interests.

The regional groupings have to face three major realities: first, that in a world moving relentlessly towards free markets in goods and services, improved productivity and enhanced competitiveness are indispensable to economic survival; second, that where it is necessary and admissible to protect domestic industries, this is better done within the framework of the regional economic groupings rather than on a national basis; and third, that, in designing support for domestic industries, improvements in infrastructure and services – particularly transport, communications, power supplies and a wide range of ancillary services – would have to be fully explored as the first line of approach before resorting to tariff protection.

10.7 CONCLUSION: IMPLICATIONS FOR FUTURE RESEARCH

The changes in the political and economic conditions in the world and in Africa during the past two decades have been profound. They have underlined the importance of regional integration for strengthening the capacity of SSA to respond to changing situations in the global economy. The rationalization and strengthening of the integration organs in the regions will enhance the capacity of SSA countries to respond to the global changes, and arrest the current trend towards their marginalization in the world economy. A more concerted effort to implement a substantial part of their current programmes will make a major difference to their effectiveness and create a more conducive atmosphere for more decisive accomplishments in the next decade.

If this is to be possible, many critical issues, and several bottlenecks, inhibiting the implementation of present programmes would have to be resolved. It is to these that the current upsurge of interest in economic integration should be directed. This can be turned to great advantage if properly channelled into well-coordinated research that will be of immediate practical application by the integration organs. In recent years, the ECA, ADB, OAU, AERC, the African Academy of Sciences, the EU, the World Bank, the Global Coalition for Africa and others have encouraged a good deal of useful reflection on the subject. The process now has to be carried forward and better focused, in close co-operation with the OAU/AEC secretariat, the RECs and relevant international institutions.

With the ratification of the AEC treaty, the OAU/AEC is already involved in organising a series of consultative meetings with the RECs and other agencies with important roles to play in the implementation of the treaty. One such meeting should be devoted to the research needs for the implementation of the treaty, how they could be met and how the research results can be translated into policy options for consideration by the integration organs. There was some discussion on this topic at the continent-wide seminar on the AEC held by the OAU in July 1993. Future consultations should carry the process forward and lead to the establishment of a network of relationships between the AEC and African IGOs, NGOs, and academic and research institutions geared to the implementation of the AEC treaty and its protocols.

Notes

1. In an address on 'Capacity Building and Utilization for Sustainable Development' to the African Governors of the World Bank in Washington, DC, on 25 September 1993, and in his remarks on 'Partnership in African Development' at the Tokyo International Conference on African Development, 5–6 Oct. 1993.
2. *Africa Recovery*, 7(2), October 1993, in an article 'Africa faces crisis over aid as World Bank lending falls'.
3. In an article, 'Blood and irony – How race and religion will shape the future', published in 'The Future Surveyed', *The Economist*, 11 Sep. 1993.
4. Final act embodying the results of the Uruguay round of multilateral trade negotiations (Understanding on the interpretation of Article XXIV of the General Agreement on Tariffs and Trade 1994).
5. See, for example, the argument by A. de la Torre and M. R. Kelly, 'Risks and limitations of regionalism', in *Regional Trade Arrangements*, IMF Occasional Paper no. 93, Mar. 1992.
6. B. Eichengreen and D. Irwin, 'Trade Blocs, Currency Blocs, and the Disintegration of World Trade in the 1930s', National Bureau of Economic Research, Working Paper no. 4445.
7. UNCTAD (1995) 'Major new developments in large economic spaces and regional integration processes and their implications', Report by the UNCTAD Secretariat, Doc. no. TD/B/SEM.1/2 of 30 Aug. 1995.
8. United Nations (1993) *World Investment Report 1993: Transnational Corporations and Integrated International Production*, p. 177.
9. Ibid.
10. 'TNCs have become a driving force for World-wide economic integration', UNCTAD Press Release no. TAD/INF/2344, 6 Jul. 1993, p. 3.
11. UNCTAD Press Release no. TAD/INF/2344, 6 Jul. 1993, Table 4.
12. Global Coalition for Africa (1995) *Africa: 1990–1995 and beyond*, Document GCA/SC-JS.4/no. 2/06/1995.
13. World Bank, *Global Economic Prospect and the Developing Countries* (Washington, 1995).
14. United Nations (1995) *Foreign Direct Investment in Africa*, New York, Jul. 1995.
15. According to the World Bank Annual Report, 1993.

16. 'Adjustment in Africa: Lessons from Country Case Studies', and 'Adjustment in Africa: Reforms, Results, and the Road Ahead'.

17. The case for establishing a strong linkage between economic integration and structural adjustment in Africa is argued strongly in the article 'Economic Integration and Structural Adjustment', published in the *African Development Report 1993* (African Development Bank, 1993).

18. The pressures leading to the devaluation of the CFA franc are descibed in *Jeune Afrique* 1701–2, 12–25 Aug. 1993. See also *IMF Survey*, 7 Feb. 1994, which describes the rationale for the realignment.

19. Traité de L'Union Economique et Monetaire Ouest Africaine (UEMOA), Banque Centrale des Etats de L'Afrique de L'Ouest, Dec. 1993.

20. UEMOA, 'Rapport du Gouverneur de la BCEAO sur l'Intégration Economique des Etats de l'Union Monétaire Ouest Africaine' (Dakar, 2 Jul. 1992).

21. *'L'Experience et le rôle de la BCEAO en matière d'intégration sous-régionale: Perspectives de l'union économique envisagée au sein de l'UEMOA'*

22. The OAU has commissioned a major study on the options for the structuring of the secretariat to serve the needs of the AEC. This will provide the basis for the eventual decision on this important matter.

23. *Reflections on Africa – The Priority of Sub-Saharan Africa in Economic Development*, addresses by Barber B. Conable, President, The World Bank, Mar. 1991.

24. Reported in The *Guardian* (of Nigeria), 10 Nov. 1993, p. 19.

25. Reported in United Bank for Africa, *Monthly Business and Economic Digest*, 16(5) May 1993.

26. This will be a good example of international co-operation to accelerate sustainable development as envisaged in ch. 2 of AGENDA 21, which recommends that 'the international economy should provide a supportive international climate for achieving environment and development goals by:

   (a) promoting sustainable development through trade liberalization;
   (b) making trade and environment mutually supportive;
   (c) providing adequate financial resources to developing countries and dealing with international debts; and
   (d) encouraging macroeconomic policies conducive to environment and development.

11 Regional Integration in SubSaharan Africa: Dead End or a Fresh Start?*

Jeffrey Fine and Stephen Yeo

11.1 INTRODUCTION

The need for closer ties among the forty-five or so economies of subSaharan Africa appears self-evident. Totalling less than the gross domestic product of Belgium, in many instances lacking direct access to the sea, and vulnerable because of a narrow base of primary exports and inadequate infrastructure to the vicissitudes both of nature and the international economy, these economies should clearly profit from concerted investment as well as a freer flow of goods and services among themselves. None the less, in spite of numerous declarations of intent, the establishment of many sub-regional entities and substantial expenditure on transport and communications, links among the economies of the region are in certain respects even weaker than in colonial times. Whereas travel from Kampala on the northern shore of Lake Victoria to Mwanza at its south-eastern edge was once widely accessible through inexpensive and regular steamer service, the same route now requires at least 36 hours of air travel and is available only twice weekly at substantially higher cost. In West Africa, neither the establishment of the Economic Community of West African States (ECOWAS) nor the West African Economic Community (CEAO) has restored the economically efficient seasonal migration of labour from the interior to the coast of colonial times. In spite of growth in air travel in other developing areas, links across subSaharan Africa remain infrequent, unreliable and expensive.

Declarations of support for forms of 'deeper integration' progressing from the removal of tariff and non-tariff barriers to the establishment of a common external tariff, then to the co-ordination of monetary and

* This chapter was prepared under the auspices of the AERC collaborative research programme on 'Regional Integration and Trade Liberalization in SubSaharan Africa', funded by the Canadian International Development Agency, the European Commission and the Ford Foundation. The opinions expressed in the paper are those of the authors, not those of AERC or the funders.

fiscal policies, and eventually to economic union, are belied by actual achievements over the past 30 years. Indeed, as outlined in Section 11.2 of this chapter, any perceived trend would appear to be in the opposite direction. The proportion of trade, for example, among the members of the Preferential Trade Area for Eastern and Southern Africa (PTA) has actually fallen in recent years from an already low level. It might be argued that other regional groupings, notably the Association of South-East Asian Nations (ASEAN), also display low levels of intra-regional trade. In the case of ASEAN, however, the proportion has been slowly increasing, in line with the overall growth in international trade. This trend suggests that in general the more outwardly-orientated an economy is, the more likely it is to expand transactions with its immediate neighbours as well.

Since structural adjustment policies in subSaharan Africa invariably entail trade liberalization on a multilateral basis, deeper integration is more likely to occur as a consequence of these policies rather than through the efforts of regional and sub-regional entities especially established for this purpose. Indeed, these bodies, suffering from conflicting mandates, overlapping memberships and inadequate support, could well obstruct rather than facilitate promising linkages that would otherwise emerge from trade liberalization undertaken unilaterally by many African countries. Such issues, though, appear more amenable to analysis by political scientists than economists. Similarly, there appears at first glance little that economists can contribute to the study of broader integration. The need for co-ordinated, multi-country investment in large-scale projects in transport, energy and telecommunications is self-evident. Beyond assessments of net economic returns, economists appear to have little to say on the regional integration aspects of such issues *per se*. In short, this chapter begins by questioning the utility of further economic analysis of this issue.

Indeed, our initial scepticism would appear justified by the brief summary, in the following section, of various efforts to achieve deeper forms of regional integration. The fact that African leaders, first in the Lagos Plan of Action of 1980 and then in the Abuja Treaty of 1991, have elected to pursue the quixotic goal of an African Common Market – in spite of their continued failure to begin removing even modest impediments to the flow of goods and services within the region – would suggest that their agenda is driven by political rather than economic considerations, and by domestic rather than regional pressures. Their approach may not be misplaced, since the economic rationale underlying earlier initiatives, namely economic growth through import substitution, is no longer viewed as a serious policy option. Furthermore, as economic theory would postulate, the initial gains from trade liberalization within the region are likely to be modest. None the less, this review, which synthesizes the principal findings of a number of various previous studies, serves two essential purposes in terms of our subsequent discussion. It questions the fundamental premises of the initiatives pursued over the past thirty years and consequently, the utility of retaining the various regional entities in their current forms.

At this juncture, regional integration would appear to be a dead end in terms of its ability to make a significant contribution in any substantive fashion to rapid and sustainable growth in the economies of subSaharan Africa. Section 11.3, however, presents the case for a new approach that offers a fresh start. Our advocacy of it rests on two radically different premises: first, that regional integration has the potential to promote the adoption of sound domestic economic policies and to sustain these policies once adopted; and second, the possibility that regional integration is capable of mobilizing private investment, initially from foreign sources. These arguments draw on the positive experiences of those Asian economies, whose very rapid and sustained growth has been attributed *inter alia* to sound macroeconomic policies and rapid superior accumulation of physical and human capital (World Bank, 1993) and on European experience in the postwar period.

As will be argued in Section 11.3, the African situation will differ in two important respects. First, the historical record indicates that regional agreements alone are not sufficient guarantors of sound macroeconomic management in subSaharan Africa. Collier and Gunning (1993) suggest that an external guarantor is needed in the form of a non-regional entity that anchors commitments on a reciprocally binding basis. We examine both the rationale and content of such arrangements, with particular reference to the possibility that the European Union might act as the external guarantor. Second, neither trade liberalization nor increased investment necessarily ensures fundamental and sustained changes in the structure of African economies over the longer term. As noted by Baldwin (1993 and 1994), the resulting pattern could comprise a hub-and-spoke, with flows directed from African economies comprising the periphery along 'spokes' to the industrialized 'hub', with little deepening of economic links in the periphery itself. We proceed to examine this possibility in terms of the factors most likely to influence flows of private investment, as the principal determinants of the locus of economic activity, and what implications such flows might have in turn for sub-regional arrangements.

This discussion, while intellectually stimulating, would prove barren in terms of its practical bearing on economic policy were it not for actual or potential developments that offer the possibility of anchoring regional integration in an external guarantor. Section 11.4 looks at three such arrangements. The first is francophone West Africa, which has recently merged two separate arrangements, namely the West African Monetary Union (UMOA) and the Community of West African States (CEAO) into a new entity, the Economic and Monetary Union of West African States (UEMOA), that in turn will be anchored externally by France. It presages a similar arrangement for francophone Central Africa, through the merger of the Central African Monetary Union and the Customs Union for Central African States. We argue that this change is more than cosmetic, and marks a radical departure from the past. The second arrangement, although admittedly more conjectural at this stage, involves the extension of existing monetary and customs arrangements (centring on South Africa) to other economies in Southern Africa, along with the establishment of reciprocal economic links with the European Union. The third is in East Africa, where there is renewed interest in reviving the defunct East African Community.

Central to this discussion is the would-be anchor, namely the European Union (EU). Section 11.5 therefore examines these three arrangements from the perspective of the Union. Under what circumstances might the European Union be prepared to assume this role? What type of reciprocal arrangements, covering economic policy, trade, investment and aid, would it be prepared to entertain? How would these affect current agreements, notably those under the Lomé Agreement?

The final section, by way of summary and conclusion, assesses whether such new approaches to regional integration would allow African economies to replicate the Asian experience and achieve rapid, sustained growth through sound economic management and faster accumulation of human and physical capital.

11.2 THE FIRST 30 YEARS: A DEAD END?

The first formal moves toward regional integration, articulated in the establishment of the UN Economic Commission for Africa (ECA) in 1958, the African Development Bank (ADB) in 1963, and the Organisation of African Unity (OAU) in 1963, drew on a century-old tradition of Pan-Africanism, as well as the ideals of leading figures in Africa's struggle for independence from colonial rule. The latter were strongly influenced by contemporary thinking, much of it originating in Latin America, that espoused development through rapid industrialization based on import substitution. It considered the international trading system, then experiencing its postwar boom, as inherently skewed toward entrenching the interests of a developed North and dooming the less developed South through inequitable commodity exchange to perpetual dependency. Since SSA was fragmented into over fifty national economies, closer collaboration was seen as essential to achieve the minimal domestic market size necessary for industrialization.

This process would commence with the creation of four sub-regions, (including one for North Africa), that would eventually merge into an African Economic Union, a goal first articulated in the Lagos Plan of Action and recently reaffirmed (despite the absence of any significant action) in the Treaty of Abuja. In subSaharan Africa, the sub-regions eventually emerged as the Economic Community of West African States (ECOWAS), the Union Douanière et Economique d'Afrique Centrale (UDEAC), and the Preferential Trade Area for Eastern and Southern Africa (PTA) (Lyakurwa *et al.,* 1993; Seydina and Georgiadis, 1993; Foroutan, 1993).

Suspicion of international markets extended to the domestic economy and was reflected in the strong, virtually unquestioned, belief that the state should play the dominant role, not only in mobilizing and allocating resources, but in owning and managing a wide range of activities. Thus regional integration in SSA has historically and perhaps paradoxically been associated with an inward-looking and illiberal development strategy. This linkage was evident, for example, in the ECA's attack on the World Bank's structural adjustment programmes at the end of the 1980s. The ECA proposed instead a policy of African self-sufficiency, designed to insulate economic activity from international shocks and to ensure a continuing dominant role for the state.

To this first tier of regional bodies we can add other sub-regional entities that have built on institutional links from the colonial era. These include the West African Economic Community, the CEAO (1973), which perpetuated the Union Douanière de l'Afrique de l'Ouest (1959) and comprises virtually the same members as the West African Monetary Union, UMOA, and the East African Community. In the case of Southern Africa, analogous bodies remain from the apartheid era: the Southern African Customs Union (SACU) and the Rand Monetary Area (RMA). Finally, there are other regional initiatives that have emerged in response to specific circumstances, the most notable of these being the Southern African Development Co-ordination Conference (SADCC), more recently recast, following the liberation of South Africa, as the Southern African Development Community (SADC). Others include the defunct Senegambia Union, the moribund Mano River Union (MRU) and the non-functioning Economic Community of the Great Lakes States (CEPGL).

All of these entities, whether active or moribund, originated from common historical antecedents and the development strategy closely associated with them. Moreover, despite the widespread adoption of economic reforms predicated on economic liberalization (expressed in export-orientated growth, greater reliance on market forces and a redefined economic role for the state), the compatibility of regional integration, premised on this earlier and now abandoned development strategy, has never been questioned.

The performance of the regional entities has been well documented both by the separate case studies and in other reports (Lyakurwa *et al.*, 1993; Seydina and Georgiadis, 1993; Foroutan, 1993; World Bank, 1989; OECD, 1993). In virtually all cases the volume of intra-regional trade has stagnated or even declined slightly, and there have been no changes in the composition of trade that would suggest that integration has led to any significant structural change in the economies concerned. Indeed, the removal of even minor impediments has been a painstaking and complex process in contrast to the more rapid progress toward multilateral tariff reductions. The institutions themselves are barely functional. In 1991–92 the OAU received only about 20 per cent of the dues necessary to finance its $27.4 m. regular budget and arrears totalled $59.2 m. All of the members of ECOWAS were in arrears on their dues. In one memorable case, staff of a sub-regional entity had been on strike for six months because their salaries had not been paid. This had escaped notice, however, because their one telephone line had been disconnected since the account was long overdue! (Seydina and Georgiadis, 1993)

More significantly, African governments had often shown no compunction in disregarding regional covenants in the pursuit of national goals, as witnessed for example in Nigeria's abrupt reversal of structural adjustment measures without prior consultation with its ECOWAS partners. Even efforts at broad integration, which skirt issues touching on national sovereignty, have seemed mainly motivated by external assistance. The most celebrated example is the recently formed SADC, largely replicating the membership and mandate of the PTA, which has identified a pipeline of projects whose financing depends almost entirely on foreign aid. Finally, we note that the linkages themselves are largely inter-governmental. Despite attempts, such as those fostered by the PTA, to link private chambers of commerce, the principal contacts and loci of integration activities lie within the public sector.

Various studies have noted the absence in Africa of conditions conducive to successful economic integration, such as an already high level of intra-regional transactions; complementarities with regional partners in goods and factors; and a potential for product differentiation, for example through differences in per caput income and hence consumption patterns. Indeed, initial circumstances suggested the opposite: the lack of transparency and predictability, especially in terms of non-tariff barriers and bureaucratic obstruction; very high government reliance on trade-related revenues; and the absence of well-managed mechanisms for redistributing benefits to the more disadvantaged partners. Even if these impediments could be overcome, the underlying rationale of industrialization through import substitution, when combined with rent-seeking proclivities at the national level have still pointed toward growing inefficiencies resulting from trade diversion over the medium and longer term (World Bank, 1994).

Domestic political interests conducive to regional integration have also been conspicuous by their absence. Weak at independence, the private sector in most SSA economies has failed to develop rapidly because of the strong interventionist role of the state in the economy, policies marked by an emphasis on import substitution, active state participation in key sectors through direct public ownership, and controls over key prices and movements of trade. Thus, in contrast to the EU, where private firms, especially in exporting sectors, have comprised a lobby in support of closer economic ties, there has been no comparable pressure group in SSA. Hence discussions of regional integration have been conducted among governments, with very little input from the private sector or consideration of its private sector interests.

Why have efforts at integration persisted in spite of their demonstrated ineffectiveness and more recently, growing irrelevance in terms of achieving sustainable growth? One explanation is bureaucratic inertia, the tendency of all organizations to redefine new roles for themselves. This is clearly the case, for example, with the transformation of the Southern African Development Co-ordination Conference, initially comprising the 'front-line' states confronting South Africa, into the Southern African Development Community, whose mandate and membership clearly overlap those of the PTA. Regional integration has also become a question of competing for increasingly scarce flows of external assistance, especially from donors who have assigned priority to regional integration, often without careful consideration of its underlying assumptions or future relevance. A final explanation is that regional integration has become irrelevant to most national governments. Reaffirming solidarity carries no political or economic cost. On the other hand, questioning the relevance of existing bodies or pressing for their reform could prove politically costly, with little prospect of any tangible benefit.

One theme that runs through this discussion of regional integration is the importance of incentives, political economy and institutional design. Early attempts at regional integration in SSA failed for a variety of reasons, but two proximate causes can be identified: regional integration schemes were based on the premise of import substitution policies and a dominant role for the state, for one, and they were never implemented effectively, for the other. Yet both these proximate causes have a common origin in the failure to take into account the incentives facing the various actors – political leaders and civil servants, as well as the private sector. Import substitution and state-led growth, for example, ignored incentives in assuming that the government could act effectively as an enlightened social planner (which in practice it could not). Ineffective implementation of the regional integration agreements can be traced to the same cause: declarations of regional solidarity and commitment to economic integration were essentially costless and hence popular with political leaders. Implementation of regional integration agreements, on the other hand, brought few if any benefits to other actors in the public or private sectors, and so they lacked any incentive to practice rather than preach regional integration.

This contrasts sharply with the situation in North America, with respect to NAFTA, and especially in Europe, commencing with the Treaty of Rome in the 1950s and 1960s, followed by the Internal Market in the 1980s and the Association Agreements with the Central and East European countries (CEECs) in the 1990s. Political leaders indulged, of course, in ringing declarations, but other actors – in the bureaucracy and private sector – have apparently had incentives to press for and achieve closer economic integration on a regional basis.

Why has regional integration been successful in Europe and North America, but not in subSaharan Africa? There is no simple answer to this question. We still do not, for example, fully understand the political economy of European economic integration in the period since 1945, and in particular the actions of the various actors and interest groups. The relative importance of the bureaucracy, political leadership, firms and workers in sustaining the process of economic integration remains to be clarified, with respect to the political pressures operating during integration episodes, how these pressures have evolved as integration proceeds, and their weight in relation to economic factors.

Other factors clearly played an important role in the success (or failure) of regional integration. Economic structure and income levels, for example, played a role in determining the extent of intra-industry trade, an important aspect of European integration. Economic structure is not the whole answer, of course. In the case of Europe the Cold War provided a geopolitical incentive for regional integration. Western Europe banded together to ward off Communism, with an external power (the United States) providing the political and financial incentives to do so. Another non-economic factor can be found in the desire of the French and German political leadership and electorates in the aftermath of two world wars for close and continuing co-operation between the two countries in order to avoid future conflict. Many commentators stress the importance to the early EC of a deal between the French and the Germans – the French obtained protection for their agriculture in return for German access to French markets for manufactured goods. According to this view, the Common Agricultural Policy (CAP) was the price paid for the Common Market. This argument has been taken further by Giavazzi and Giovannini (1989), who argue that the experience gained by the EC in negotiating a complex system of agricultural price supports CAP during the 1950s and 1960s laid the groundwork for the complicated intergovernmental negotiations necessary during the 1980s to carry out the Internal Market programme and to establish the European Monetary System.

It may be that regional integration schemes, which tend to yield at best modest and highly diffused economic gains, require the existence of such non-economic forces in order to be successful. Without them, there may not exist the political impetus for sustained implementation and the painful adjustments that it entails. Thus, the 'domino' interpretation of regionalism contends that integration is sparked off by isolated, unique political events that have little or nothing to do with economics. Once two or more countries take the first steps towards closer economic integration, other countries have little choice but to join in, lest their competitive position *vis-à-vis* firms in the integrating countries be eroded (Baldwin, 1993b). In short, a political shock may trigger a process that economic forces then amplify through a bandwagon effect.

11.3   A NEW PARADIGM FOR REGIONAL INTEGRATION

Previous attempts at regional integration, at least in SSA, have failed to realize even a modest part of their stated aims. As suggested earlier, this outcome is not entirely surprising, since many of the preconditions for success suggested by economic theory were not present at the outset. Renewed efforts along these traditional lines are not advisable, for two reasons. First, closer integration in terms of freer flows of goods and services is now more likely to result from unilateral tariff reductions that confer most-favoured-nation status on one's neighbours. Second, there are unlikely to be any significant immediate economic gains (at least in the short run) from access to a larger local market and the removal of trade distortions. Certainly such gains would not justify a major effort to shore up existing regional entities that, for reasons argued earlier, are inappropriately structured, since they were designed to pursue a very different approach to economic development.

Ultimately the rationale for closer regional integration rests on its contribution to sustained economic growth. Recent studies of rapid economic development in North-east, East and South-east Asia point to at least two factors that warrant closer scrutiny in the context of subSaharan Africa:, namely effective macroeconomic management, and rapid accumulation of human as well as physical capital (World Bank, 1993 and Young, 1994). The same factors seem to have played an important role in economic growth in Western Europe, whose postwar growth was no less remarkable than that in Asia. During the period from 1950 to 1973, for example, real GDP in almost all Western European countries rose nearly twice as rapidly as in any comparable period before or since (Eichengreen, 1993). Undoubtedly the stimulus of postwar reconstruction proved important, as did technological 'catch up' with the United States but, as in Asia, remarkably high rates of investment also played a key role. Net investment rates in Western Europe were almost twice as high between 1950 and 1973 as in any other period. These high ratios of gross investment to GDP translated into rapid rates of high growth rates: recent estimates suggest that a 10 percentage point increase in the investment share increased the growth rate by 0.5 to 2 per cent annually. These examples suggest that regional integration in SSA could contribute to economic growth in a very different way than envisaged previously, namely by helping underpin stable and sound national macroeconomic policies and rapid accumulation of human and physical capital.

Since integration does, however, also entail sometimes painful adjustments among sectors and locations, the discussion which follows touches on three measures that can help rectify the disparities between apparent 'winners' and 'losers' from regional integration within the region in question, namely:

- accelerated investment in physical and human capital, with a view to the eventual equalization across the region of access to public goods, notably education, health and social services;
- systematic measures to promote greater mobility of labour within the integrated area; and
- interventions to stimulate private investment in specific sectors and locations.

These measures are explored in Section 11.4 in our discussion of three regional groupings in subSaharan Africa. We first examine, in the remainder of this section, how regional integration can promote economic growth through its impact on macroeconomic management and on investment in physical and human capital.

Macroeconomic Management and Policy Credibility

The aforementioned World Bank study (1993) argues that the priority assigned by Asian governments toward rapid economic growth is reflected in their flexible and responsible approach to macroeconomic management. In particular, appropriate combinations of fiscal and monetary policies have resulted in low rates of inflation. More generally, and in contrast to subSaharan Africa and Latin America, policies have generally not been prone to sharp reversals, thereby encouraging high rates of domestic savings, as well as sustained flows of funds for investment, from both local and external sources.

The overriding lesson for SSA is the importance of policy credibility. As argued by Rodrik (1989), credibility is a self-reinforcing process. A correct mix of policies, backed by transparent signals, inspires appropriate responses by economic agents, which in turn reinforce the credibility and hence sustainability of the government policies. Conversely, policy measures deemed to be non-credible by economic agents are unlikely to succeed and may indeed prove positively harmful (Rodrik, 1989).

Existing arrangements, ranging from the Abuja Declaration covering all of subSaharan Africa to the various sub-regional entities, in principle offer a framework for underwriting economic policy reforms through international agreements. In practice, the wholesale non-compliance with even minor provisions of regional treaties and undertakings suggests that they are usually not enforceable or credible. This situation contrasts with experiences elsewhere. One example is Mexico where, it has been argued, the Salinas administration attempted to lock in its economic reforms by joining NAFTA (Perroni and Whalley, 1994). Another is the current set of association agreements between the EU and the countries of Central and Eastern Europe. The agreements represent a means of enforcing liberalization in these countries. The treaties in question are legally binding and each agreement has its own association council and committees of officials (from both the EU and the CEECs) to oversee implementation.

As methods for enforcing domestic policy reforms, these external agreements could prove instructive for SSA. The case of Mexico and NAFTA, for example, involves reciprocal undertakings between Mexico and two more industrialized economies, of which one, the United States, is clearly the dominant partner. Since the bargaining positions have been asymmetric among the three members, Mexico has been obliged to accept the provisions of the previously concluded US–Canada Free Trade Agreement (along with additional side provisions) in order to benefit from closer economic integration and also to lock-in domestic policy reforms (Perroni and Whalley, 1994). A similar negotiating posture is also evident in the association agreements between the EU and the CEECs (Baldwin, 1994).

For SSA, the most plausible partner in such an arrangement would be the European Union for reasons of history, linguistic, historical and cultural ties, as well as existing institutional and economic links. The relationship is, however, unusually asymmetric, since SSA has in recent years become marginal to the EU in economic terms. Over the past thirty years its share of the EU's imports has been halved to only 4 per cent, despite the preferential access it enjoyed under the Lomé Agreements (ACP, 1994). Furthermore, there are growing signs of disillusionment with the Lomé arrangement on the part of Africans as well as the EU. Its aid and trade provisions are being increasingly viewed as having failed to promote structural transformation of the region's economies. Disillusionment with aid within a Lomé-style arrangement is unlikely to be sufficient on its own, however, to persuade the EU to act as an external anchor that would underwrite policy reforms undertaken within sub-regional agreements concluded by African states.

Other issues, such as reciprocity and conditionality, are likely to arise as well. As cogently argued by Collier and Gunning (1993), non-reciprocal agreements, specifically those based on aid conditionality, usually prove inadequate for underwriting the credibility of adjustment policies undertaken by African governments, who are often neither committed to the aims and content of the policies nor convinced as to their efficacy and political sustainability. Indeed, this observation would appear to be confirmed by the very uneven record of structural adjustment programmes over the past five years, climaxing with the dramatic reversal by Nigeria, the region's second-largest economy, of a decade of adjustment policies. Even where these programmes are being implemented diligently, their dependence on non-binding inflows of external assistance can perversely undermine the confidence of economic agents in the viability of reform programmes over the longer term. Thus would-be investors in the Ghanaian economy monitor the actions of multilateral and bilateral donors rather than the far-reaching measures being undertaken by the government, since investors view donor attitudes as a more useful indicator of whether the policies will prove sustainable. In the limiting case, growing dependence on aid, which donors may increase in order to mark their approval of the programme and support for the government, may inadvertently undermine investors' confidence in the programme's sustainability, thereby fashioning self-fulfilling conditions for its ultimate failure!

Non-reciprocal guarantees, in the form of aid conditionality, have therefore not proven effective in sustaining such desirable reforms. By their very nature, they offer the external partner scope for revision or withdrawal because of unfavourable political developments or a lack of resources. A reciprocal international agreement can only guarantee the enforcement of domestic economic policies by abandoning such flexibility, a stance that would clearly involve a major departure from current EU policy. Furthermore, an EU–SSA relationship that involves preferential treatment through what is in effect permanent associate membership of the EU may contravene Article XXIV of the GATT, since such arrangements are only permissible as a step towards full membership. The one existing arrangement of this type, namely between the Maghreb and the EU, is exceptional because of its historical circumstances (Page and Stevens, 1992). The EU would probably be unwilling to contemplate others, especially since it is currently engaged in implementing the association agreements with the CEECs as a prelude to full EU membership (Baldwin, 1994). An EU–SSA relationship is also likely to lead to demands for similar treatment by other countries in the ACP Group. Finally, by cutting across existing regional organizations within SSA, the EU would provoke predictably strong opposition from them, as well as from the Organisation of African Unity and the UN Economic Commission for Africa. African governments may feel obliged to condone such reactions publicly even as they seek special arrangements with the EU in private.

For African governments, participation in African sub-regional entities, with their overlapping memberships and conflicting mandates, has held little practical import. Binding international agreements with reciprocal obligations would be a very different matter. One option for African states is to try to rationalize organizations, in terms of their membership and mandates, prior to commencing negotiations with the EU. This, however, is unlikely to yield any concrete results within a reasonable period. The other option is bilateral negotiations between the EU and the almost 50 governments of SSA, a complex and equally unattractive proposition. Thus, even if the EU were willing to entertain the possibility of acting as external guarantor of sub-regional arrangements aimed principally at sustaining domestic policy reforms, the actual process of negotiating mutually acceptable terms seems likely to render this approach impractical.

Such a pessimistic conclusion may be premature. There already exists at least one such arrangement, namely the recently announced UEMOA, that features support for macroeconomic management by France. A similar arrangement, combining previously separate agreements for monetary union and trade liberalization, is also envisaged for the francophone states of Central Africa (*Coopération Française*, 1993a). While proponents argue that the circumstances of these arrangements are exceptional, in so far as there exists a special relationship with France that predates the Treaty of Rome itself (*Commission Européenne*, 1994), they are none the less significant for two reasons. First, they could pave the way, albeit on a somewhat different basis, for the anchoring of other sub-regional arrangements by the EU. Second, as will be illustrated below, these two agreements provide explicitly for underpinning macroeconomic stability through supranational surveillance and control over monetary and fiscal policies.

In spite of SSA's marginal economic importance to the EU, both as a source of imports and external market, we note that the region's longer-term stability is a major concern for many of the Union's current members. Of particular importance is the future of South Africa. Failure to ensure a smooth transition and sustained growth will doom the southern portion of the continent to economic entropy. Conversely, there is growing recognition that existing monetary and trade arrangements, although historically associated with white-ruled South Africa, do offer an opportunity for a fresh start in terms of regional integration. As will be argued below, these arrangements, although essential for ensuring macroeconomic stability and increased investment, will probably become weak and ineffectual unless they are buttressed by complementary ties between a Southern African Region and the European Union.

Another possible obstacle discussed above is the complexity of multilateral negotiations. The EU's own experience, however, would suggest that not all potential partners need be involved at the outset, but only the key ones. Once the basic agreement has been concluded with the key countries, a 'bandwagon effect' will ensure the adherence of others who fear they will otherwise be excluded (Baldwin, 1993b). Even so, the asymmetry in the bargaining positions of the Africans and EU, as in the case of the Canada–US and Mexico–NAFTA (Perroni and Whalley, 1994) and EFTA–EU negotiations (Baldwin, 1994), will undoubtedly be reflected in separate side agreements to the main treaty.

Private Investment and Rapid Capital Accumulation

Underlying structural adjustment policies is the presumption that growth will be renewed and sustained through increased private investment financed from domestic and external sources. Its importance appears to be confirmed by the experience of rapidly growing Asian economies, where significant public investment in human resources and physical infrastructure has been complemented by sizeable private flows, overwhelmingly financed from domestic sources. Some observers go even further, arguing that most of the remarkable economic growth achieved by the Asian Tigers can be explained by the rapid accumulation of physical and human capital (Young, 1994). Physical capital accumulation also played a key role in postwar European growth (Crafts and Toniolo, 1993 and Eichengreen, 1994).

The contrast with SSA is illuminating: by the beginning of the 1990s, gross fixed capital formation in these Asian economies was equivalent on average to 25 per cent of the GDP and all but 4 per cent of it was financed from local savings. In SSA, investment had fallen to 16 per cent of GDP and only 25 per cent of it was financed locally. Since there is no reason to presume that Africans' propensities to save and invest are significantly lower than those of Asians – an observation that is to a considerable extent supported by trends up to the mid-1970s – the current situation can be largely attributed to poor economic management by African governments (World Bank, 1993). The region's continuing dependence on official development assistance to finance investment is also starkly apparent in the financing of projects aimed at strengthening regional integration. For example, the SADC pipeline for transport and communications comprises 216 projects totalling $6.6 bn, of which 85 per cent would be financed from foreign aid. In the case of energy, virtually the entire amount would have to come from external sources (African Development Bank, 1993c). This dependence could conceivably be justified as a more rational use of official assistance to develop the physical infrastructure necessary to promote higher rates of investment. None the less, there is no reason to presume that higher rates of private investment, in particular from outside the region, will follow automatically.

The examples of East Asia and postwar Europe suggest that the rapid accumulation of human and physical capital plays a key role in sustaining rapid economic growth. How might regional integration affect the process of factor accumulation? Recent European experiences suggest that regional integration arrangements can stimulate investment and capital accumulation by encouraging the pursuit not only of more stable macroeconomic policies, but also the adoption of measures to encourage inward foreign direct investment. As noted in a recent study by Cadot and de Melo (1994), Spain and Portugal grew rapidly after their accession to the EU in 1986, in part because of large FDI inflows. French investment in Spain and Portugal, for example, increased tenfold after 1986. This increase in FDI cannot, however, be attributed to the lowering of trade barriers, since Spain and Portugal had enjoyed duty free access to the EU since 1976. The growth in FDI is attributed instead to more stable economic policies and the adoption of investment codes, which encouraged capital inflows.

The association agreements between the EU and the CEECs may provide another example of this link between regional integration and investment. Cadot and de Melo (1994) conclude that the agreements 'provide at best rather marginal preferential tariff access for trade in non-agricultural goods for the CEECs', and predict that the agreements will result in only a small increase in trade in goods between the EU and the CEECs. The CEECs will benefit for other reasons. In order to encourage inflows of private capital they have committed themselves to allow EU firms to repatriate profits and withdraw capital investments. This commitment will clearly reduce risk and uncertainty for EU firms contemplating investing in the CEECs. The agreements also oblige the CEECs to adopt laws similar to those in the EU, including competition policy, intellectual property and limits on state aid. Such measures are also likely to stimulate inward investment by providing a more favourable and familiar environment for foreign firms.

Empirical evidence also suggests linkages between foreign direct investment and regional integration: the recent examples of Mexico, Morocco, Portugal, Spain and the United Kingdom spring to mind. In Mexico and Morocco FDI has risen sharply in recent years as firms have invested to supply large markets across the Rio Grande and the Mediterranean. The UK in the 1970s and 1980s experienced large inflows of FDI in certain sectors, in particular by Japanese automobile manufacturers. Firms invested in order to supply the more integrated European market from a relatively low-wage site within the EU.

A potentially similar relationship between foreign direct investment and regional integration in SSA has yet to be examined in detail. In a normative vein, investment in essential physical infrastructure – notably transport, communications and energy – more assured access to a larger market, increased productivity through competition and heightened exposure to new technology and methods ought to prove mutually reinforcing. Although we draw comparisons between historical trends in SSA and those in Asia, the results may be of limited relevance. Flows of FDI in the future may be very different because of changes in technology, growing regionalization among industrialized countries and a general slowdown in overall growth in SSA. We therefore proceed to examine the implications of other factors for SSA. Finally, we consider factors operating at the firm and sectoral, as well as national, levels that might affect the concentration of economic activity.

Foreign direct investment at a global level grew rapidly during the 1980s. From an average annual flow of $50 bn between 1980 and 1986, it leaped to $150 bn between 1986 and 1990 (Cockcroft, 1994). Overall, the proportion of global FDI flowing to developing countries dropped from 23 per cent in 1970–9 to 17 per cent between 1986 and 1990, while the share of global FDI directed to East and South-east Asia rose from 4.5 per cent to 9.3 per cent during the same period. From a similar level in 1970–9, the share going to Africa dropped to only 2 per cent by 1990.

The declining proportion of FDI flowing to SSA is reflected in data on capital stock in developing countries. Whereas SSA accounted for 27 per cent of the stock of foreign capital in developing countries in 1975, by 1980 its share had been virtually halved to 14 per cent. Country specific figures confirm this trend: Net productive investment in the Côte d'Ivoire, for example, fell from $63.5 m. annually between 1970 and 1975 to $25 m. by 1980–6. In terms of sources, a Japanese study revealed that SSA's share of Japanese FDI (which, in global terms, had grown in relative importance over the past fifteen years), had fallen from 4.5 per cent in 1983 to less than 1 per cent by 1987. The actual proportion is much smaller, since these figures also include off-shore shipping registrations in Liberia (Cockcroft and Riddell, 1991). Furthermore, they overstate net inflows because of unreported capital flight and involuntary reinvestment due to controls over the remittance of corporate profits and dividends. SSA's diminishing share of the declining proportion of global FDI in developing countries has also been heavily concentrated: at least 50 per cent of the FDI inflows have been in extractive industries, with over 75 per cent in just ten countries.

This trend can be partly attributed to falling commodity prices, which have lowered the return to investment in the primary sector. None the less, it offers an illuminating contrast to the experience of East and South-east Asia. Initially the latter also experienced a heavy concentration in extractive industries. Subsequently, FDI played a major role in developing manufactures and exports as well as services for the local market. The importance of Japanese-sourced FDI varied across Asian countries: where it predominated, there were exports of capital goods to the newly industrializing economies, which in turn exported manufactures to Europe and North America. In the case of the ASEAN countries, investment in manufacturing was orientated toward export, whereas in SSA such investment in the 1970s was often prompted by import substitution policies that are no longer tenable. Hence, such investment is now vulnerable to structural adjustment measures, and trade liberalization in particular. Although there is a tendency to view Pacific Asia and South-east Asia, and ASEAN in particular, as regions in terms of foreign investment as well as trade, the actual proportion of intra-Asian trade among newly industrializing economies has been quite low. The regional links comprise complex flows of trade and investment with the rest of the world as well as among themselves.

Studies of FDI vary in their conclusions (UN Centre on Transnational Corporations, 1992; Riedel, 1991; Chia, 1993; and Dunning, 1988). Investors cite the consistency and soundness of macroeconomic policies as a key factor in choosing among countries for the location of new investments. Such policies have been cited to explain, for example, the very different and negative experience of the Philippines in comparison to the other members of ASEAN. Other policies matter as well, in particular investment codes and other laws governing the repatriation of profits and the withdrawal of capital. Studies at the firm or sectoral level have yielded more ambiguous results, in part because of data limitations and the cross-sectional approach used by many of them. Typically, factors are grouped according to the paradigm developed by Dunning in terms of advantages of ownership, location and internalization (of knowledge and methods within the firm). Overall, the results of such studies suggest that locational factors, such as those associated with export-processing zones, are important but by no means the principal determinants of FDI.

Another set of determinants relates to institutional arrangements. Eichengreen (1994), for example, attributes the high rates of investment experienced in postwar Europe to a combination of wage moderation and export growth. Wage moderation made investment profitable and provided the profits necessary to finance it, while the 8 per cent growth rate of exports in the 1950s and 1960s allowed investment to flow to those sectors where it would make the greatest contribution to productivity growth without regard to the composition of domestic demand. Eichengreen attributes wage moderation to an explicit deal between capital and labour: labour offered wage restraint to capital, capital in turn invested the resulting higher profits productivity and so generated higher productivity and hence higher wages. He argues that 'social and economic institutions disseminated information and monitored the compliance of economic interest groups with the terms of their agreement to moderate wage claims and boost investment'. On the international side, 'institutions were created to coordinate national programmes of economic restructuring along export oriented lines and to lend credibility to European governments' commitment to openness'.

These Asian and European experiences may, however, have only limited relevance because of intervening and far-reaching changes in technology. The importance of locational factors to multinationals – with the significant exception of market size – may have diminished because of streamlined systems for handling information and funds. Patterns of production are also changing for the same reason. Large-scale assembly may no longer be competitive in many industries. Conversely, scale advantages may be realized with smaller production runs. More generally the quality and motivation of the labour force is becoming increasingly important as a major determinant of FDI. Finally, the pace of change itself is increasing, pointing to more rapid obsolescence of skills as well as physical capital in future (Oman, 1994 and Baldwin, 1993a). These trends imply that competitiveness will increasingly come to depend on high levels of qualitatively sound investment in human resources, and upon a highly adaptive and flexible labour force. Development based on an international division of labour, to the extent that it might have been significant in an earlier era, is no longer a credible option. Thus, any advantage accruing to SSA from lower nominal labour costs is unlikely in itself to attract FDI in any sizeable quantity.

A second consideration is the likely supply and distribution of FDI in the future. Recent studies have concluded that its rapid growth during the latter half of the 1980s will not be sustained over the rest of the 1990s because of declining net savings in Japan and Germany (Katseli, 1992). Furthermore, the greater proportion of this increased flow has occurred within the regional triad of Japan, Europe and North America, as multinationals have sought to protect their home markets and penetrate those of their rivals. The overall prognosis is that the proportion of FDI flowing to developing countries will continue to decline. Since over 75 per cent of this amount has been concentrated in only ten countries, including Nigeria as the sole SSA economy among them, we may infer that the actual amounts of FDI that the region can reasonably anticipate will be quite modest, even it were able to compete effectively for them.

A recent World Bank study (1994) suggests that this prognosis might prove unduly pessimistic. Furthermore, given the tiny size of most SSA economies, the size of the inflows needed to induce higher rates of growth may be quite modest. In attempting to attract even this modest inflow, two factors loom large. The first is the need for significant investment in human resources as well as their more efficient utilization, a conclusion that points in turn to the need for greater labour mobility, especially for scarce skills. The second is the continuing importance of sustained and sound macroeconomic policies.

Completing our overview is more recent work on the location of economic activity. In addition to the factors cited by Alfred Marshall, notably the advantages provided by a pooling of labour and the supply of non-traded intermediate goods and spillovers in technology, this research focuses on the importance of increasing returns to scale and trading costs. The distribution of economic activity across space, it is argued, will vary according to the relative importance of these factors (Krugman, 1991 and Baldwin, 1993a, 1994). In this context, two considerations appear especially pertinent to SSA. First, although the initial location of an industry may be the outcome of serendipity, this initial concentration becomes self-reinforcing over time. Thus, the initial presence of economic activity in a particular location could result in further concentration following closer integration. Changes in transport costs, on the other hand, have complex effects on agglomeration.

In the presence of scale economies and imperfect competition, an initial reduction in trading costs, either through improvements in transport and communications or by the removal of administrative and other impediments to transactions, leads to increased concentration and thus may accentuate disparities in income and economic structure. Further declines in trading costs to even very lower levels would, however, reduce the relative advantage offered by agglomeration and thus promote growth in formerly disadvantaged, peripheral locations (Venables, 1993). This two-stage process suggests that the political backlash created by regional integration and consequent need for sectoral adjustment will be most severe during the initial stages of integration, when trading costs first fall from high to intermediate levels.

This approach has been applied recently to suggest a suitable structure for the trade relationships between the EU and the CEECs, as the initial step toward full membership for the CEECs (Baldwin, 1994). It has also been extended, in a more tentative fashion, to speculate on possible links between the EU and SSA (Baldwin, 1993a). Bilateral agreements between the EU and countries seeking an association with it can lead to the hub-and-spoke configuration mentioned earlier, in which economic activity is increasingly concentrated in the EU (the hub). Because of relatively higher trading costs among economies comprising the surrounding periphery, they will continue to relate to each other via the hub, thereby reducing the likelihood that the concentration of economic activity will diminish over time.[1] This scenario for the CEECs contrasts with recent negotiations between the EU and members of the EFTA Group. Having previously established strong links among themselves, EFTA members find themselves better placed to maintain their competitiveness within an expanded EU.

This characterization of regional linkages points to a paradoxical situation in the case of subSaharan Africa. On the one hand, a country that possesses a measure of economic and political strength (such as South Africa) may be essential in order to provide leadership for smaller economies of the sub-region. On the other, regional integration, particularly in its early stages, is likely to widen income disparities and increase the concentration of economic activity. This will almost certainly convince some members that benefits of integration are distributed inequitably and so fuel demands for compensation. Indeed the strength of such reactions is demonstrated by the fate of the East African Community, where perceptions that Kenya was profiting disproportionately contributed to the demise of the Community. A possible solution to this dilemma would be an external anchor that could counterbalance the weight of the dominant regional member. We proceed to apply this insight into the dynamics of regional integration to three emerging possibilities in SSA.

11.4 REDEFINING REGIONAL INTEGRATION: A NEW APPROACH FOR SSA

Regional integration, as argued in the opening section, can be justified in economic terms to the extent that it results in rapid and sustained growth. We depart from traditional approaches to regional integration by suggesting that its virtues lie not in its ability to stimulate new trade, but rather in its ability to provide a framework for locking in sound and stable macroeconomic policies that will in turn induce faster accumulation, and more effective utilization of physical and human capital.

This line of argument might represent only an intellectual curiosity were it not for a number of actual or potential developments within SSA. In this section we look at three regional arrangements. The first is francophone West Africa, where there has been a recent merger of the West African Monetary Union (UMOA) and the Community of West African States (CEAO) into a new entity, the Economic and Monetary Union of West African States (UEMOA), which in turn is being anchored externally by France. The merger presages a similar initiative for francophone Central Africa. The second example would involve extending monetary and customs arrangements centring on South Africa to other economies in Southern Africa in combination with reciprocal economic links between this 'Southern African Economic Region' and the EU. The third explores the possibility of replicating similar arrangements in East Africa through revival of the defunct East African Community.

The West African Economic and Monetary Union

In late 1993, France and the leaders of the seven African states comprising the current West African Monetary Union signed the treaty establishing UEMOA. The agreement brings within a single framework the West African Economic Community, which has attempted (ineffectually) to remove barriers to trade and the West African Monetary Union, which supports a common central bank and currency (CFA) linked at a fixed (and recently devalued) rate to the French franc. The treaty's provisions can be summarized in terms of four principal thrusts, namely:

- harmonization of legislation, regulations and procedures;
- multilateral monitoring of key economic indicators and specific provisions for co-ordinating macroeconomic policy;
- an eventual single market for goods and services, covering factors as well as products; and
- co-ordinated development policies implemented through a revived investment institution (*Commission Européenne*, 1993, 1994).

The treaty provides for an explicit transfer of sovereignty over important areas of national jurisdiction, in particular fiscal policy. It also envisions the establishment of institutions closely analogous to those of the European Union, including a conference of heads of state, a council of ministers, a community secretariat, and an interparliamentary commission as the first stage toward a fully fledged community parliament, an independent revenue authority and a court of justice. These institutions would be financed through independently determined levies.

Before examining its potential implications, both for the sub-region and the rest of SSA, we note that similar measures are planned for the francophone states in Central Africa. Although less advanced than for West Africa, they also envision reform of a virtually moribund trade association (UDEAC); a multilateral surveillance of macroeconomic indicators, in particular fiscal policy; and their enforcement through the joint central bank, the BEAC. These measures and a parallel set of institutions would entail creation of the Communauté Economique et Monetaire de l'Afrique Centrale (CEMAC) (*Commission Européenne*, 1993 and *Co-opération Française*, 1993a,b).

The advent of UEMOA is significant. First, it ends years of speculation regarding the future of the existing monetary union. One aspect has concerned the impact of an overdue devaluation: would the monetary union break up as a consequence or evolve into a looser multilateral arrangement, allowing for the fluctuation of national currencies around an agreed peg? A second has been the continued linkage of the CFA to either the French franc, the ECU or a basket of currencies, as a result of moves toward closer monetary integration within Europe. A third has been whether France or the EU would be willing to maintain convertibility of the CFA and, if so, on what terms.

Using the pretext of Maastricht, France could have commenced withdrawal, through a variety of means, from an arrangement that had proven increasingly costly to maintain in recent years. Instead, it has moved in the opposite direction, embedding an expanded role in a new international treaty for which it acts as the ultimate guarantor. Furthermore, the commitment is open-ended, involving the establishment of new multilateral institutions and surveillance of macroeconomic policies whose credibility ultimately rests on France herself. In short, France's role as guarantor appears significantly greater than under the previous monetary agreement.

We do not intend to speculate at length on the principal motives behind French policy. Some factors do appear important, notably the maintenance of cultural and linguistic influence over a large expanse of the world's second largest continent, as well as an unwillingness to write off years of support for two monetary agreements that in future could yield considerable advantage to French commercial interests. None the less, the new arrangement also appears to address directly some of the perceived weaknesses of the earlier efforts. The treaty provides for independent sources of revenue to support autonomous regional institutions and an independent court to ensure the harmonization of legal systems and administrative procedures. The most far-reaching measure, however, is the explicit provision for surveillance of macroeconomic policies, especially fiscal deficits, with France acting as the ultimate enforcer through its underwriting of the common monetary system. Clearly these measures, along with public investment through a revived development bank, are intended to induce greater investment by lending greater credibility to macroeconomic policies.

For the rest of SSA, UEMOA is significant for three reasons. First, it comprises a direct challenge to the assumptions behind the Ahuja Treaty that have shaped the strategic approach to African regional integration over the past thirty-five years. UEMOA is incompatible with ECOWAS. The UEMOA treaty provides for the accession of other African states in addition to the seven original members of the monetary union. The new arrangement occurs at a moment when ECOWAS, which has never proven effective, has been very badly shaken. Nigeria, its most important member, reversed years of structural adjustment policies, including trade liberalization. The non-francophone members, and Ghana in particular, confront the decision of whether or not to join UEMOA, preferably without inordinate delay, when they can still have some say over the terms of entry and the implementation of the treaty's provisions.

The second is whether UEMOA establishes a precedent that would allow the EU to act as guarantor for other regional arrangements. This possible interpretation had been anticipated by French officials, who argued that the links between France and UEMOA as well as between France and an eventual CEMAC are unique, since they had been explicitly incorporated, during the colonial period, in the Treaty of Rome. These two arrangements, they argue, are successors to the *communauté financière d'Afrique* and hence have always been *une affaire communautaire*. Indeed, France has explicitly suggested that the CFA itself would eventually be incorporated in an ECU Zone (*Commission Européenne*, 1994). Whether this position is in fact likely to take place within an enlarged EU is taken up in Section 10.5.

The third is the nature of the economic development that would ensue from this new arrangement. At first glance, it would seem that it would perpetuate the hub-and-spoke pattern described by Baldwin, and might as a result condemn members indefinitely to a less-developed status *vis-à-vis* the EU (Baldwin, 1994). In the case of UEMOA, one could point to two tiers of hub-and-spoke, the first being a sub-regional hub comprising the Côte d'Ivoire and Senegal, with a rim comprising the other African members, and the second being a French hub with all the UEMOA states on the periphery.

Will this arrangement prove to be politically sustainable over the longer term, in the face of painful sectoral adjustments and the possibility that integration will increase disparities within the UEMOA region? The counterfactual argument, that UEMOA will promote higher levels of FDI and faster economic development than any alternative arrangement (including the earlier UMOA), might not prove sufficiently convincing. Another possible response is to acknowledge that economic activity is geographically concentrated in virtually all industrialized economies (Krugman, 1991). Indeed, programmes specifically targeted toward dispersing such concentrations have proven ineffectual in creating more balanced growth. Hence in countries such as the United States and Canada, characterized by large disparities among regions, one response to unbalanced development has been to ensure comparability in the quality and supply of public goods and services, notably health and education, though a variety of redistributive mechanisms, including transfer payments to second-tier governments (states and provinces) as well as to individuals. A second has been to facilitate labour mobility to more developed regions by ensuring access to comparable educational and training opportunities in the home areas. An analogous approach for UEMOA would involve offering reasonably uniform standards of education and training among its members, as well as enhancing labour mobility, initially among those with skills in high demand. Remittances from those who had migrated to more dynamic advanced locations within UEMOA would help raise living standards in their home areas.

A Southern African Economic Region (SAER)

The second entity to which we apply the new concept of regional integration is a Southern African Economic Region (SAER), comprising members of the Multilateral Monetary Area (MMA), (formerly the Rand Monetary Area, (RMA), the Southern African Customs Union (SACU), and Zimbabwe. Since the sub-region is the study focus of a separate case study, our own discussion examines how an external guarantor, the EU, could help underpin macroeconomic stability and stimulate higher rates of capital accumulation, two essential preconditions for sustained and rapid economic growth. We begin by summarizing briefly those issues most pertinent to the formation of an SAER from the vantage point of South Africa, the dominant economic and political force in the region. We then set out the principal features of the proposed regional entity. Finally, we discuss its main benefits and drawbacks from the perspectives of South Africa, its immediate neighbours and other states in Southern Africa.

The new government in South Africa faces the following major policy choices.

- *Macroeconomic stability and the need for investment* The government will confront very strong demands to increase public expenditure rapidly in order to rectify deeply-rooted economic disparities and begin redressing social injustices. Part of its longer-term response will undoubtedly involve job creation, which in turn will require much higher levels of investment. The latter in turn will depend on sound and sustained macroeconomic management, both to reduce capital flight and to encourage investment from domestic and external sources. Conversely, fears of unsustainable fiscal imbalances will reduce confidence in the government's ability to manage the economy and lead to lower rates of private investment.
- *Trade liberalization and international competitiveness* The previous outgoing South African government presented to GATT far-reaching proposals for rationalizing and liberalizing its current structure of protection. These measures included the reclassification of tariff lines, the removal of non-tariff barriers, the simplification and reduction of nominal tariff rates, and the removal of selective and highly effective anti-dumping measures (Gawith, 1993a,b). These

reforms have been aimed at changing the capital intensity that characterizes much of South African industry and making it more competitive internationally (Page and Stevens, 1992). In this context, we note that although manufactured goods comprise only about 10 per cent of South Africa's total export earnings, these are largely destined for SSA, in particular Eastern and Southern Africa (ADB, 1993c). In reaffirming this earlier commitment, the new government will be seeking to maintain trade liberalization in the face of mounting protectionist pressure and at the same trying to penetrate markets for manufactured goods, including those in SSA.

- *The Lomé Agreement*   South Africa's position with respect to the trade and aid provisions of the Lomé Agreement is anomalous. Its per capita income excludes eligibility for aid. With respect to trade, many of its exports, comprising minerals and output from other extractive industries, enter duty free, with the notable exception of coal (Page and Stevens, 1992). Some of the agricultural and food exports in which it is internationally competitive fall within the EU's sensitive category and are heavily protected under the Common Agricultural Policy. Extension of preferential status to other manufactured exports may provoke a negative response by members of the ACP Group who fear that their own competitive positions would be undermined. Hence negotiations concerning a special form of membership for South Africa within Lomé could prove both protracted and ultimately unsuccessful. On the other hand, a bilateral agreement with the EU would be more attractive, especially if the new government were to secure development assistance comparable to that forthcoming under Lomé to support the transition to majority rule. It would allow not only South Africa but also those members of the EU with strong economic and political interests in it to focus more directly on strengthening those ties of mutual concern to both parties.
- *Southern African Customs Union (SACU)*   Recently South Africa signalled its desire to review the terms of the Union on the grounds that payments to the other members were becoming a major financial burden. More specifically, South African officials noted that their share of customs revenues had declined considerably (SADC, 1993). The other partners contend that these payments compensate for what they consider to be implicit advantages provided to South African industry under the current Union. Moreover, they are seeking the revocation of those provisions that they believe undermine their own potential for industrialization. Neither side wishes to dismantle a

long-established and well-functioning arrangement. The non-South Africans in particular would inevitably suffer from higher transactions costs. On the other hand, any weakening of the arrangement might cause it eventually to unravel unless there is a fresh mandate based on a very different vision of the region's economic development.

- *Multilateral Monetary Area (MMA)* Analogous pressures from both South Africa and the other members have led to a restructuring of the Rand Monetary Area. On the South African side, there is less desire, during a period of intense domestic pressure, for prior consultation on monetary and fiscal policies. The other members, on the other hand, believe they have been adversely affected by inflation imported from South Africa. The new arrangement provides for greater flexibility, but still attempts to maintain currency convertibility, especially for capital movements within the MMA. It is unclear whether the MMA can be maintained in the face of mounting pressures within South Africa itself, as well as a projected severe shortage of credit within the region as a whole (ADB, 1993c). Further weakening of a century-old arrangement, which might even lead to its eventual demise, would adversely affect investor confidence and raise transactions costs within the region.

- *Links to existing regional bodies* For its neighbours, South Africa could provide a major economic stimulus. Among the advantages cited in a recent study are greater access to foreign direct investment, highly developed financial services, educational facilities, transport and communications (ADB, 1993c). While agreeing to join SADC, the new government is likely to decline a similar invitation from the PTA, in part because membership in the latter may pose problems in terms of its agreement with the GATT and ongoing negotiations with respect to SACU. Countries within SADC stand to benefit from collaboration in sectors such as transport, communications and finance as well as focused initiatives, such as those identified in recent studies, that would significantly reduce transactions costs within the region (European Commission, 1992). None the less, historical experience suggests that such agreements, in themselves, are unlikely to offer a major, lasting economic stimulus. Indeed, a more likely scenario is that the more prominent economies, notably Zimbabwe and Kenya, will seek to protect their vital interests through direct bilateral agreements with South Africa.

What would be the principal elements of an emerging Southern African Economic Region?

- South Africa's position at the hub of an SAER would be shaped by two international, reciprocal agreements that would provide mutually advantageous to itself and the other members of this Region. The first would be its agreement with the GATT; in addition to prompting a restructuring of the South African economy that should lead to progressive economic empowerment of the African population, it would bind South Africa in its own trade and industrial policies *vis-à-vis* the other members of SACU, in terms of dismantlement of its own tariff and non-tariff barriers, as well as discriminatory measures that currently impede their own industrialization. The second would be a bilateral agreement with the EU. By encouraging FDI in the rest of SACU as well as in South Africa itself, it would enhance opportunities for intra-regional links and industrial activity.
- A restructured SACU in turn could serve as a focal point for economic integration within much of the area covered by the SADC and the PTA. Here we envisage a two-stage process. The first would entail a bilateral agreement with Zimbabwe, SADC's most important member after South Africa, as an essential move to guarantee its access to South African markets and to attract FDI. Another bilateral agreement, in this case with Kenya, can be anticipated, especially if South Africa formally decides not to join the PTA. These bilateral agreements – and the one with Zimbabwe in particular – would in practice constitute 'associate membership' in SACU. The second stage would involve agreements between South Africa (or a restructured SACU), and the other members of SADC, either on a bilateral basis or possibly under the broader aegis of SADC itself.
- The MMA would be revised to provide for the movement of national currencies, within agreed bounds, around a jointly determined peg. This monetary zone would be characterized by currency convertibility among its members and with the rest of the world, but with controls over large, destabilizing movements of capital. Inclusion of Zimbabwe and Botswana (currently a member of SACU but not of the MMA) would necessitate two major changes in the current arrangement. The first would be the creation of sufficiently large reserves, in a region suffering from an acute shortage of finance, to minimize fluctuations and maintain a credible peg. The second would be an agreement among the participating countries to subject their fiscal and monetary policies to multilateral surveillance of key indicators that would govern access to monetary reserves. In this context the EU could play a role analogous to that of France with respect to

UEMOA, by supplying the necessary reserves and thereby helping to reinforce monetary and fiscal discipline by MMA members.

- The EU, along with other members of the international donor community, would continue to provide assistance to SADC. Of particular importance would be investment in economic infrastructure and continuing pressure for removal of existing impediments to the movement of factors, products and services within the region. This assistance would promote closer economic integration around a restructured SACU and MMA. First, it would reduce the likely dominance of South Africa at the hub of an SAER, by opening up opportunities for investment and industrialization in the other countries. Second, it would lower the reluctance of these other countries to commence negotiations with South Africa because of the significant asymmetry in their bargaining positions.

While this arrangement does appear analogous to UEMOA, it features several significant differences. The first is the dominant position of South Africa. In many respects it already functions as the hub of a southern African region, an asymmetry that threatens to stymie a fashioning of closer links with its neighbours. In acting as the external anchor for the entire arrangement, the EU would help redress this imbalance. A second difference concerns currency convertibility. A monetary arrangement that helped minimize nominal fluctuations and increased convertibility, for financing trade as well as investment, would lower trading costs and help attract FDI. The outcome would, however, entail a regional scheme that is linked in turn to the EU.

For both South Africa and its neighbours, a Southern African Economic Region holds both risks and rewards.

Turning first to South Africa, we note that it will allow the new government to lock-in trade liberalization policies and also to resist populist pressures that might result in economically destabilizing fiscal deficits. The latter stance would rely on two constraints, namely access to short-term external credits, and the need to maintain the value of the nominal exchange rate within the bounds of an agreed peg. Access to a regional market for its manufactured exports would have to be balanced against the need for closer consultation on the customs union and possibly higher than desired compensatory payments. Offsetting the latter would be increased exports of services, including transport, communications and finance. The principal benefit, however, may lie in the higher levels of net private investment. External guarantees through reciprocally binding links may induce an increase in FDI, not only in extractive industries, but in other sectors as well. The flight of human as well as physical capital may be reduced because of these same guarantees.

For South Africa's neighbours, in particular Zimbabwe, the principal concern is whether this new regional arrangement would institutionalize a hub-and-spoke relationship with an industrialized South Africa at the centre and the other partners on the periphery. Our earlier discussion would suggest that this outcome is not inevitable. Initial concentrations of activity do matter (Krugman, 1991), and in this regard Zimbabwe in particular has a potentially robust manufacturing sector. Although only one-twentieth the size of South Africa, recent studies would indicate ample scope for Zimbabwean manufacturing through intra-sectoral and intra-industry trade as well as the capacity to compete in South Africa and other markets. Closer regional ties, especially through currency convertibility, financial services, improved communications and assured transport links, would in fact reduce the likelihood of Zimbabwe remaining on the periphery.

For the other members, the outcome may be less favourable, if only because they already relate to South Africa in terms of a hub-and-spoke arrangement. Weakening such existing links will not, however, increase their chances of attracting FDI. The same observation applies to other schemes associated with the PTA and SADC since neither body has proven effective either in lowering transactions costs or in raising levels of private investment. Returning to the question of economic disparity within an SAER initially comprising SACU and Zimbabwe, we note four strategic responses toward promoting more balanced development over the medium term. The first is accelerated investment, financed from SAER revenues and external assistance, in economic infrastructure, education and training. The second is greater labour mobility, especially for those with skills in high demand, along with more efficient arrangements for the remittance of earnings. The third is a more rapid removal of impediments to movements of goods and services across borders (European Commission, 1992) in order to lower the costs of economic transactions. A final response is selected investment in facilities such as industrial parks, to attract secondary industries and services that might service a particular sub-region. These measures, and in particular those aimed at lowering trading costs, should over time induce a gradual deconcentration of industrial activities and related services (Venables, 1993).

Once an SAER becomes a reality, the other countries in the region will wish to join it, even on less favourable terms, because of the perceived cost of remaining on the outside. Such a bandwagon effect has manifested itself in the adherence of EFTA members to the EU and, more recently, in similar applications by countries in Eastern and Central Europe (Baldwin, 1994 and Perroni and Whalley, 1994). A transitional period of association, as a prelude to full membership, would probably be required, with the necessary adjustments facilitated by development assistance.

An East African Community (EAC II)

Our third example differs from the preceding two in several ways.

First, although the old East African Community may appear to have been highly integrated, this in fact was never the case. Currency convertibility was never a feature. Even the movement of goods was subject to *de facto* tariffs in the form of transfer taxes between countries. In effect, the EAC represented a form of broad integration, comprising common services for ports, air services, rail, electricity and telecommunications; joint revenue collection; and a joint investment bank. Collaboration through a common secretariat and regional organizations extended to sectors such as health and education, as well as professional associations, and also facilitated a limited movement of labour across national frontiers.

Second, perceptions that Kenya benefited inordinately from the earlier EAC have been cited as one of the principal factors behind its demise. At present the three former members appear more evenly matched in terms of their potential contributions to a broader economic entity: Kenya offering a wide range of tradable services; Tanzania endowed with extensive natural resources; and Uganda having potential in agro-industry and food.

A third difference is that there is no immediate pressure to revive the Community in order to accelerate economic development. This situation could, however, change dramatically with the establishment of a UEMOA in West Africa, a CEMAC in Central Africa, and in particular an SAER at the foot of the continent. In this context, a Mark II version of the East African Community is worth examining as an example of a second-generation, sub-regional entity that could emerge in response to the formation of these others.

Renewed interest in a revived EAC would be spurred by three developments associated with the formation of an SAER. The first would be a bilateral agreement between Kenya and South Africa. The second would be a bilateral agreement between Zimbabwe and South Africa, amounting in effect to an associate membership status within SACU. These developments would leave Tanzania in an isolated position in terms of its ties with the dominant economies in the region. Rather than attempting to strengthen its position through a weakened SADC or PTA, Tanzania may elect to pursue a third route of reviving the EAC. Similar considerations, in this case arising from an increasingly less viable PTA, would prompt Uganda to look closely at the same option.

Closer integration would, however, be more problematical for an EAC II because of the lack of a formal external guarantor, as in the case of UEMOA with respect to France; or a natural hub, buttressed by binding bilateral agreements, as envisioned for South Africa with regard to the EU and the GATT. For an EAC II, the principal factor behind closer economic integration would be national structural adjustment programmes. Since these provide for the liberalization of trade on a most-favoured-nation basis, an inevitable consequence would be a lowering of trade barriers among all three countries. There would, however, be less scope than in the other two arrangements for the EU to play the role of external anchor. One possibility might be more liberal cumulation rules, namely for rules of origin that could be modified so that they encouraged joint production across all three countries of products destined for the EU. A second would be a common policy, set out in formal bilateral agreements, toward foreign direct investment. A third would be co-ordinated investment by all three countries in economic infrastructure, spearheaded by a restructured and refinanced East African Development Bank, a vestige of the old EAC. Finally, an EAC II could promote greater labour mobility across the region, beginning with those skills in highest demand.

Currency convertibility would present the most difficult challenge for innovative measures, not least because of erratic macroeconomic management in recent years. In addition, there has been high volatility in nominal exchange movements because of thin and underdeveloped markets for foreign exchange. An initial step toward convertibility would involve the introduction of a multilateral monetary arrangement providing for fluctuation within agreed limits around a common peg. As in the case of an SAER, this arrangement could be backed by joint surveillance of fiscal and monetary policies, and supported by a currency stabilization fund backed by the EU and possibly other interested bodies.

This arrangement would allow governments to resist populist pressures and avoid abrupt destabilizing changes in macroeconomic policy by locking in key instruments, in particular those relating to fiscal, monetary and trade policy. Over time, the benefits of such self-imposed limits would become more apparent in terms of increased levels of investment and economic growth in all three countries. Although the principal rationale for this new form of regional integration is its impact on domestic economic stability and consequently on investment, additional advantages of a more conventional type, resulting from larger domestic markets, more efficient use of scarce human resources and reduced trading costs would emerge over the longer term.

11.5   THE ROLE OF THE EUROPEAN UNION

From the perspective of SSA, the case for an external guarantor, acting within the framework of a reciprocal agreement focusing principally on trade, but also covering other issues of mutual interest, rests on the need to reinforce the credibility and sustainability of sound economic policies. By deliberately agreeing to limit their scope for independent action in fiscal, monetary, trade and exchange rate (and other) policies, African governments can resist strong domestic pressures. As typified by the recent Asian and earlier Western European experiences, sound and sustained macroeconomic management creates the environment needed for more rapid accumulation and more effective utilization of human and physical capital. This in turn results in more rapid economic growth. Benefits would accrue to SSA from such an arrangement, but why should the EU be willing to play the role of guarantor?

To answer this question, we first examine other regional integration and trade liberalization initiatives, specifically the association agreements between the EU and the CEECs, to see whether the principal motivations behind this EU policy might also play a role in creating similar relationships with SSA. We then look at internal changes within the EU itself, in particular the accession of Sweden, Austria and Finland, and whether this expansion is likely to result in shifts in EU policy *vis-à-vis* SSA. Proceeding further, we take up the question of prospective changes in the Lomé Agreement, the principal EU instrument for determining trade and development assistance with the region. Finally, we attempt to identify other emerging EU interests with reference to the three regional sub-groupings presented in the preceding section, and in particular, the one encompassing a Southern African Economic Region. In this context, we draw on recent research into the negotiation of regional trade arrangements, to suggest a form that an association of this type might take.

Stimulating welfare-enhancing trade flows represents one motive behind the EU's association agreements with the CEECs, in so far as these agreements do liberalize trade and constitute an intermediate stage toward full regional integration. The CEECs are geographically close and though moderately poor at present, are potentially much richer in the medium term. Gravity models suggest that natural trade between the EU and the CEECs can grow substantially, even though some of this potential growth is in sensitive sectors (Winters and Wang, 1994). Whether the association agreements will increase trade significantly is, however, unclear. As Cadot and de Melo (1994) note, 'In agriculture, concessions have been minimal and further undermined by subsequent measures like banning meat imports from the CEECs on sanitary grounds. With very few exceptions, agricultural trade is essentially left out of the association agreements'. The agreements do provide preferential access for non-agricultural goods, but as Cadot and de Melo say, 'The preferences will only replicate the GSP status – albeit on a permanent basis – and little liberalization if any will occur during the transition.' If this interpretation of the Agreements is correct, then little new trade will be generated; enhancing the welfare of EU consumers by lowering barriers to trade does not therefore seem to represent an important motivation for EU policy. There are, however, three other important factors to consider.

The first is a desire to maintain EU competitiveness *vis-à-vis* its Japanese and US competitors. One way over the longer term is to integrate the EU economies with their lower-wage neighbours to the East. The reward for short-run problems of adjustment in the EU, as its firms struggle to compete with lower-cost rivals based in the CEECs, is greater competitiveness for Europe (broadly construed) in the longer term. This argument clearly motivates official thinking in the EU, but lacks appeal for European electorates. The second is fear of political and economic instability and even chaos on the EU's eastern borders. Germany in particular is concerned with stability in the Ukraine and the former Soviet Union. Fears of mass migration are the third factor: estimates of potential migration from the East vary, but one suggests 3 million to 6 million potential migrants from the Czech Republic, Hungary, Poland and Slovakia alone. Migration on this scale would cause significant problems since most of the migrants would tend to settle in Austria and Germany. The EU negotiated the association agreements and committed itself to eventual membership for countries with these agreements in large part to preserve stability by underwriting democracy and economic transformation on its eastern borders. Analogous fears of mass migration and political instability in neighbouring countries have played an important function in other regional integration agreements as well, notably in the case of NAFTA, where the Bush administration was clearly anxious to ensure the stability of its southern neighbour.

These three factors are far less likely to be significant, however, in motivating the EU to underwrite new regional integration arrangements in SSA. The first, an increase in competitiveness, is irrelevant. With regard to the second, we observe that the magnitudes of increased trade flows are simply too small and unimportant to the EU. Imports by the EU from the ACP countries are a small and diminishing percentage of total EU trade (as the gravity model might predict). A recent study of the impact of the EC-92 programme on the developing countries suggests that the Single Market will have almost no impact on the Union's trade with the developing countries (Hughes Hallett, 1994). Furthermore, as with the CEECs, many of the most obvious sources of potential trade increases are in sensitive sectors, which the EU will continue to protect. The Common Agricultural Policy (CAP) is also an important obstacle to increased trade between the EU and SSA. Growing economic integration of the EU with the CEECs could eventually lead to collapse of the CAP in its present form, because of the huge increase needed in member state contributions if the CEECs were to join the CAP (Baldwin, 1994). In the short run, however, there seems little prospect of significant further reforms to the CAP. The EU is therefore unlikely to be tempted to underwrite regional integration arrangements in SSA because of any prospect of a major increase in trade, at least over the medium term.[2]

The third factor, namely fear of mass migration and of political instability, is also unlikely to prove an important element in the EU's relations with SSA, although they do play a role in the Union's dealings with the Maghreb (and in particular Morocco). The reason is simple: the Sahara Desert. There is simply no prospect of large numbers of economic or political migrants from SSA appearing on the frontiers of Europe. The fears of migration that motivate EU policy towards Eastern Europe and the Maghreb, and in an analogous way, US policy towards Mexico, are simply too weak to induce the EU to offer comparable arrangements to SSA.

Other factors may come into play, however, that may provide the incentives necessary for the EU to act as an anchor. One such factor may arise from possible shifts in the EU's political centre of gravity to the north and east. The political and economic transformation of Central and Eastern Europe has created a vast area in which Germany, Austria and Switzerland can expand their commercial and political influence. Gravity model estimates (Winters and Wang, 1994) reveal that potential trade between the CEECs and Germany far outweighs that with Japan or the USA. Indeed, Germany has realized more of this potential trade than have other countries. In addition to moving eastward, the EU's political centre is likely to shift northward as a result of the entry of Finland and Sweden. In this broader context, the motives behind French policy toward SSA are more readily understandable as part of an attempt to prevent the EU from tilting too heavily toward the North. Like France's stubborn adherence to a strong link between the franc and the Deutschmark, her support for the CFA zone and the creation of UEMOA, along with the likely advent of parallel arrangements for Central Africa, reflect a desire to counter this emerging shift in the EU's political centre of gravity.

Another potential motivation arises from the current debate over the future of the Lomé Agreement, which provides the framework for EU trade and development assistance with SSA. After two decades, there is a growing perception both within the European Commission, which administers the agreement, and in many member countries, that the arrangement is failing to achieve its stated goals of diversifying production and exports and of promoting rapid economic growth in the ACP countries.[3]

One manifestation of the current unease is the attempt to introduce flexibility into Lomé IV, Part II, slated to run from 1995 to 2000. Under the existing (and previous) agreements, recipient countries in the ACP Group, in addition to receiving preferential access for non-sensitive exports, were allocated a notional five-year amount of development assistance subject to successful negotiation of a National Indicative Programme. Proponents of changes in the structure of the Lomé Agreement argue for greater flexibility in the allocation of assistance at more regular intervals to accommodate adjustments in national priorities; adherence to other stated EU objectives, notably human rights and environmental safeguards; and reallocation of unspent funds. The ACP countries have resisted the introduction of greater conditionality and the withdrawal of assured funds, arguing that the certainty attached to Lomé aid is one of its major virtues. Underlying this more immediate debate, however, is a growing disillusionment with the Lomé framework and the increasing likelihood that the current agreement may be the last one. In this context, the search for an alternative approach that promotes the EU's continuing commitment to regional integration in SSA, and also addresses the overriding concerns of political stability and rapid economic growth, may prompt interest in a more overt role as an external guarantor for sub-regional groupings.

The role played by France with respect to UEMOA, the first of the three regional groupings discussed in the preceding section, may be deemed an exceptional case. First, there is France's long-standing support for the CFA zone and, more tepidly, closer trade links through the CEAO. Second, political motivations are clearly important: a desire to sustain influence in a large portion of the world's second largest continent. These are likely to be reinforced, as suggested earlier, by a tilting of the EU's political centre of gravity to the north and east. A more convincing case for an EU role as an external guarantor, possibly substituting for the current Lomé framework, can be advanced with respect to a Southern African Economic Region, focusing on South Africa, as the dominant economic and political force in the area. The case would rest on two considerations. The first is the strategic importance to the EU of maintaining stability in this part of the continent. It is true, as Cadot and de Melo note, that the end of the Cold War has reduced the 'geopolitical incentives' for European involvement in subSaharan Africa: there is no longer any need to 'attract countries away from socialism'. A number of EU member states do, however, have important commercial interests and investments in South-ern Africa, and this is likely to sustain their interest in the region. The second argument in favour of the EU as a guarantor is its potential ability to stimulate more rapid economic growth through sound economic management, the strengthening of essential regional links and services, and the promotion of investment from domestic and external sources.

Negotiation of an SAER would involve two sets of parties, each with asymmetric bargaining positions. Bargaining would take place not only between South Africa and the other SAER members but also between an SAER, and South Africa in particular, and the EU. At first glance, the likelihood of a successful outcome appears low. Recent research, however, suggests that such asymmetry is far from unique, and has parallels in NAFTA and the association agreements of the EU and the CEECs. As Perroni and Whalley (1994) note, smaller countries appear eager to conclude such agreements, even though they receive very few concessions from the large countries. One possible explanation is that such regional agreements are not primarily concerned with trade liberalization but rather, from the point of view of the small countries, of assuring them market access and providing shelter in the event of trade wars. Non-economic considerations are typically more important for the larger countries. Both aspects were evident in NAFTA, wherein Canada and Mexico sought to limit the application of anti-dumping measures by the United States, while the latter wished to lock-in domestic and political reforms in Mexico. Typically the asymmetry in interests and bargaining positions is evident, not in the main treaty, but rather in the side agreements or payments exacted by the country with the dominant negotiating position. For similar reasons, not all countries that could be members of a sub-regional group need be involved in the initial set of negotiations. Once the sub-regional agreement comes into being, other countries will wish to join it, even on less favourable terms, because of the perceived cost of remaining outside. This bandwagon effect has manifested itself in the adherence of EFTA members to the EU and more recently in similar applications by the CEECs.

We anticipate that both aspects would emerge in any discussions between an SAER and the EU. First, the SAER need not include all the potential members. Once an SAER has been formed and its viability has been underscored by an agreement with the EU, other countries in the region will apply for membership, even on less advantageous terms than the founding members. Second, the asymmetry between the SAER and the EU would undoubtedly be reflected in side agreements reflecting major policy interests of the latter.

11.6 CONCLUDING OBSERVATIONS

This chapter's unifying theme is the need to create the appropriate incentives in order for regional integration to succeed. The old approach to regionalism focused on the wrong set of incentives and so failed. Reviving regional integration is only worth considering in terms of plausible political and economic incentives that will allow it to be implemented effectively and will sustain it politically thereafter.

As argued in Section 11.2, the failure of regional integration in SSA can be closely associated with policies of import substitution pursued during the 1960s and 1970s, and with the dominant role assigned to the state in the operation of the economy. Import substitution politicized the location of industries and made regional integration politically unattractive because it would have encouraged a more rational location of particular sectors and industries and thus threatened the interests of the bureaucracy charged with implementing it. In addition, liberalization threatened to reduce revenue from taxes on trade and so destabilize government finances. At the same time, the dominant role of the state resulted in a weak private sector with little independent political influence and little to gain from the effective implementation of regional arrangements.

We contrast this outcome with the more successful experiences in Europe and North America. Their experiences suggest that economic structure is important, since their economies are more natural trading partners. It is also clear that the private sector plays a more important role in the economy and exercises greater influence over policy in Europe and North America. As a result, the gains from integration are potentially larger and those who benefit are politically stronger. Furthermore, regional integration has not posed the same threat to politicians and civil servants as in SSA: import substitution has not been an important objective, and tariffs and other taxes on trade played only a small role in government revenue in Europe and North America. Broader political forces have also played an important role. A domino interpretation of regionalism suggests that integration may be triggered by political or at least non-economic events that push a few countries into closer integration. This may create a bandwagon effect: once even a small number of countries begin this process, their neighbours will rush to join the scheme for fear of losing competitiveness in the larger, integrated market (Baldwin, 1992). These dynamics seem to have been present in Europe (The Second World War and the Cold War) and in North America (Mexican liberalization in the 1980s), but not in SSA, although we do suggest why the changes in South Africa might set a similar process in motion.

In Section 11.3 we focused on the relationship between integration and more fundamental economic objectives, such as improvements in welfare, real income levels and growth. We argued that even if little new trade would be created within an integrated area, integration would nevertheless be worth pursuing if it had a beneficial effect on domestic policies and on factor accumulation, since these foster growth.

Economic theory suggests channels through which market integration can influence growth rates, but the historical record is mixed. Regional integration has played little or no role in the extraordinary growth of the East Asian newly industrialized nations. Until recently regional arrangements in Asia have been weak or non-existent and intra-regional trade grew less rapidly than trade with the rest of the world. In contrast, regional integration and intra-regional trade seem to have played a more important role in the postwar recovery and subsequent rapid growth in Europe. The historical record is thus ambiguous concerning the relationship between integration and growth.

We therefore examined two other channels through which regional integration *might* matter for economic growth and welfare. The first is the adoption of sensible, stable and credible policies. Both the European and Asian cases suggest that macroeconomic (monetary, fiscal and exchange rate) and trade policies are important for growth. In particular, both historical experience and theoretical analysis highlight the importance of institutional design and the commitment of policymakers for ensuring that policies are consistent and credible to other economic agents. Whereas these arguments have featured prominently in such areas as monetary policy and central bank independence, for example in discussions of the exchange rate mechanism of the European Monetary System, they have been largely absent from the design and implementation of policy in subSaharan Africa.

Rapid accumulation of both physical and human capital has contributed significantly to the rapid growth of East Asian countries and, earlier, of postwar Western Europe. Export-orientated trade and related industrial policies were important as well, because they ensured that investment was not determined solely by the pattern of domestic demand, but channelled to sectors and firms where returns were high on world markets. High rates of domestic savings contributed to rapid factor accumulation, but inflows of foreign capital and in particular foreign direct investment also played important, but as yet imperfectly understood roles.

These observations were used in arguing that regional integration can contribute to growth by helping create a stable economic environment and by encouraging rapid factor accumulation. With respect to the former, we suggested that regional arrangements may lock in monetary and fiscal policies, as well as the open, stable and transparent measures likely to encourage foreign direct investment. We also suggested that regional integration can modify trading relationships between the industrial economies and the developing countries characterized by hub-and-spoke linkages that strongly favour the concentration of economic activity in the hub countries. Market integration on a regional basis, by encouraging stronger linkages among the peripheral countries, may encourage inward investment by firms seeking to supply the entire region from a base in a single country.

Regional integration can thus play a role not envisioned during earlier attempts at regional integration in SSA, namely by sustaining policies necessary for economic growth. In Section 11.3 we began by acknowledging that the experience with regional integration arrangements in subSaharan Africa has been discouraging. Few of the agreements have been implemented and their impact has at best been minimal. Is there any reason to expect renewed attempts to yield better results?

We argued that an approach that takes account of a changing political and economic environment might have a reasonable prospect of success, provided it:

- takes into account the incentives facing politicians, the government bureaucracy and the private sector;
- contributes to the stability and credibility of economic policies;
- addresses the issues of concentration and agglomeration, and the distribution of gains and losses;
- compensates for the weakness of the private sector and its lack of political influence in subSaharan Africa;
- can be structured to avoid the problems of hub-and-spoke systems favour the location of economic activity in hub countries; and
- creates strong institutions that can effectively implementation integration measures.

These conditions are more likely to be satisfied by arrangements resting on an external guarantor that can offer the incentives necessary for implementing agreements and for locking in national policies. The examples of NAFTA and the trade arrangements in Central and Eastern Europe underscore this possibility. It would prove attractive to SSA governments anxious to enhance the credibility of their policies. In addition, guarantees from the industrial economies offer the prospect of greater access to their markets.

We argued that the European Union is the most plausible external guarantor for regional arrangements in subSaharan Africa. Why might the EU be interested in playing such a role? Here we examined the evolution of the EU's economic relationship with the countries of Central and Eastern Europe, which have been motivated by the prospects for enhanced trade, fears of mass migration to the EU and security concerns at the prospect of political instability in the East. We argued that the prospect of enhanced trade is not likely to be important in EU–SSA relations. Fears of mass migration into the EU are a more important issue in relations with the Maghreb than with Africa south of the Sahara. On the other hand, we suggested that a growing EU concern with political stability as a prerequisite for economic growth may prompt a more activist policy toward subSaharan Africa.

A possible precedent for acting as external guarantor is provided by France with respect to UEMOA, where it is the ultimate anchor for an ambitious set of regional links, involving not only a single currency and trade zone, but also supra-national surveillance of national fiscal policies. Curiously analogous to institutional arrangements within the EU itself, UEMOA presages a similar initiative for France's former colonies in Central Africa. France argues that these arrangements do not offer a precedent for similar arrangements by the EU in other parts of SSA (a region of immediate commercial and economic interest to many other members of the Union), since these arrangements are founded on the special status for the former African colonies in the Treaty of Rome. None the less, France's role as an external guarantor will undoubtedly be monitored closely, especially in terms of the maintenance of political stability, increasingly recognized as a precondition for economic progress in a continent racked by civil strife and costly peace-keeping, refugee and humanitarian relief efforts. Coincidentally, the EU's own principal policy instrument for development, the Lomé Agreement, is increasingly viewed as ineffectual in promoting its stated aims of rapid growth and diversification of the structure of production and trade in the ACP countries.

These broader considerations of political economy may prompt a closer look at what we have termed the new paradigm for regional integration. This paradigm is, however, only new with respect to SSA. Regional arrangements are being used elsewhere, notably for Mexico in the case of NAFTA and for the CEECs in the context of their association agreements with the EU, to provide the political framework necessary to lock in desirable essential changes in national economic policies. The extension of the paradigm to SSA might help launch a new wave of sustainable integration efforts across the region.

Notes

1. It is interesting to note in this context that the initial Treaty of Rome Association between the EC and the African 'Associates' tried to avoid a hub-and-spoke structure, since it required the African countries to grant the same preferential trade terms to each other as they granted to the EC. Under the subsequent Yaoundé Convention, however, the Associates were not obliged to grant preferential treatment to each other, thus creating a European hub and African spokes (Cadot and de Melo, 1994). This arrangment has continued under the Lomé Conventions.

2. On the other hand, it should be noted that some observers have predicted the association agreements will have only a small impact on trade between the EU and the CEECs: the main advantages of the association agreements for the CEECs lie elsewhere (Cadot and de Melo, 1994). This is consistent with the Perroni and Whalley argument that such regional trade agreements are motivated by factors other than the desire to increase trade.
3. One reason may be that Lomé in reality offered only very minor trade preferences to the ACP countries. As Cadot and de Melo (1994) note, 50–60 per cent of ACP agricultural exports to Europe consisted of products that were duty-free regardless of their origin, 5–10 per cent were excluded from preferential treatment because they fell within the CAP and the remainder consisted of tropical beverages. ACP manufactured exports enjoyed little if any preferential treatment, since most such developing country products entered duty-free in any event under the GSP.

References

ACP (1994) *The Mid-Term Review of the Fourth Lomé Convention*, memorandum presented by the ACP Group of States to the European Union, ACP/27/003/94 Rev 3, Brussels, Feb.

African Development Bank (1993a) *Economic Integration in Southern Africa, Executive Summary* (Oxford: Biddles Ltd).

African Development Bank (1993b) *Economic Integration in Southern Africa, vol. I.* (Oxford: Biddles Ltd).

African Development Bank (1993c) *Economic Integration in Southern Africa, Vol. II* (Oxford: Biddles Ltd).

Agodo, O. (1978) 'The determinants of US private manufacturing investments in Africa', *Journal of International Business Studies*, Winter 1978: 95–107.

Anderson, K. (1994) 'Trade negotiations and farm policy', *Economic Policy, 18.*

Baldwin, R.E. (1993a) 'Impact of theoretical developments on regional integration', paper presented at the AERC workshop on *Trade Liberalisation, Regional Integration and Growth*, Nairobi, Dec.

—— (1993b) 'A domino theory of regionalism', CEPR Discussion Paper no. 857.

—— (1994) *Towards an Integrated Europe* (London: Centre for Economic Policy Research).

Banque Centrale des Etats de l'Afrique de l'Ouest (1992) *Symposium du Trentième Anniversaire de l'UMOA (Dakar, 30 novembre – 1er décembre 1992)* (Dakar).

Begg, D. *et al.* (1991) 'The impact of Eastern Europe', *Monitoring European Integration*, 1 (London: Centre for Economic Policy Research).

Bossyut, J. (1994) 'Phased programming of Lomé funds: lessons from current EU and ACP experiences', Policy Management Brief no. 2 (Maastricht: European Centre for Development Policy Management).

Brewer, T.L. (1991) 'Foreign direct investment in developing countries: patterns, policies and prospects', IBRD Pre-Working Papers, WPS 712, Jun.

Cadot, O. and J. de Melo (1994) 'The Europe Agreements and EC–LDC Relations', CEPR Discussion Paper no. 1001.

Cassim, R. (1994) 'European economic integration and Eastern Europe: lessons and implications for Southern Africa', Mimeo.

Chia, S.Y. (1993) 'Foreign direct investment in ASEAN economies', *Asian Development Review*, 11: 60–102.

Cockcroft, L. (1994) 'Foreign direct investment in Africa during the 1980s', Mimeo.

—— and R.C. Riddell (1991) 'Foreign direct investment in Sub-Saharan Africa', IBRD Pre-Working Papers WPS 619, Mar.

Collier, P. and J.W. Gunning (1993) 'Linkages between trade policy and regional integration', paper presented at AERC Workshop on *Trade Liberalisation, Regional Integration and Growth*, Nairobi, Dec.

Commission Européenne (1993) *Le programme régional de réformes de l'UDEAC*, Brussels, Oct.

Commission Européenne (1994) *Note de présentation du traité de l'Union Economique et Monétaire Ouest Africaine*, C. Ghymers, Direction Genérale Affaires Economiques et Financières, Feb.

Coopération Française (1993a) 'Le Projet d'une Communauté Économique et Monétaire en Afrique Centrale (CEMAC)', *Les Notes de la Coopération Française*, Nov.

—— (1993b) 'La réforme fiscalo-douanière en UDEAC', *Les Notes de la Coopération Française*, Nov.

Crafts, N. and G. Toniolo (1993) 'Post-war growth: an overview', paper presented at the CEPR conference on *The Economic Performance of Europe After the Second World War*, Oxford, Dec.

de Melo, J. and A. Panagariya (eds) (1993) *New Dimensions in Regional Integration* (Cambridge University Press for CEPR).

Dunning, J.H. (1988) *Explaining International Production* (London: Unwin Hyman).

Eichengreen, B. (1992a) 'The Marshall Plan: history's most successful structural adjustment programme', CEPR Discussion Paper no. 634.

—— (1992b) 'The Marshall Plan: economic effects and implications for Eastern Europe and the former USSR', CEPR Discussion Paper no. 638.

—— (1994) 'Institutions and economic growth: Europe after World War II', CEPR Discussion Paper no. 973.

European Commission (1992) 'Cross border initiative: Eastern and Southern Africa and Indian Ocean', proceedings of a *Workshop to Facilitate Cross Border Trade, Investment and Payments in Eastern and Southern Africa and the Indian Ocean*, Harare, Dec.

Foroutan, F. (1993) 'Regional integration in Sub-Saharan Africa: past experience and future prospects', in J. de Melo and A. Panagariya (eds), *New Dimensions in Regional Integration* (Cambridge University Press for CEPR).

Gawith, P. (1993a) 'South Africa chafes at customs link', *Financial Times*, 17 Aug.

—— (1993b) 'Focus of South Africa reforms shifts to trade', *Financial Times* 20 Aug.

Giavazzi, F. and A. Giovannini (1989) 'Can the EMS be exported? Lessons from ten years of monetary policy co-ordination in Europe', CEPR Discussion Paper no. 285.

Grilli, E. and M. Riess (1992) 'EC aid to associated countries: distribution and determinants', *Weltwirtschaftliches Archiv,* 1992 (2): 202–20.

Hess, R. (1994) 'Rationalization and strengthening of integration institutions in Africa', paper presented to a meeting of the Global Coalition for Africa Sub-Committee on Regional Co-operation and Integration, Dakar, Senegal, 4–5 May.

Hughes Hallett, A. (1994) 'The impact of EC-92 on trade in developing countries', *World Bank Research Observer,* Jan. 121–46.

IDRC/PTA (1992) 'Terms of reference for studies on regional integration in Eastern and Southern Africa' mimeo, Mar.

Jebuni, C. (1993) 'Trade liberalisation and regional integration in Africa', paper presented at AERC workshop on *Trade Liberalisation, Regional Integration and Growth,* Nairobi, Dec.

Katseli, L.T. (1992) 'Foreign direct investment and trade interlinkages in the 1990s: experience and prospects of developing countries', CEPR Discussion Paper no. 687.

Kennes, W. (1994) 'The European Union and support for regional economic integration in Africa', paper presented to a colloquium on *Integration and Regionalism,* Talence, Apr.

Krugman, P. (1991) *Geography and Trade* (Cambridge, Mass.: MIT Press).

Lyakurwa, W., A. McKay, N. Ng'eno and W. Kennes (1993) 'Regional integration in Sub-Saharan Africa: a review of experiences and issues', Paper presented at AERC workshop on *Trade Liberalisation, Regional Integration and Growth,* Nairobi, Dec.

Ministère de la Coopération et du Développement (1991) *Note sur le Zone Franc: de la communauté de monnaie et l'intégration des règles et l'union économique,* Présentations des travaux et des réalisations, Paris, Aug.

Mwase, N. (1993) 'Economic integration for Eastern and Southern Africa: assessment and prospects' *African Development Review,* 5(2): 20–37.

OECD (1993) *Regional Integration and Developing Countries* (Paris: OECD).

Oman, C. (1994) *Globalisation and Regionalisation: The Challenge for Developing Countries* (OECD Development Centre, Jan.)

Ouali, K.S. (1990) Intégration et développement, *CIEREA et Economica* (Paris).

Page, S. and C. Stevens (1992) *Trading with South Africa: the policy options for the EC* (London: ODI).

Perroni, C. and J. Whalley (1994) 'The new regionalism: trade liberalisation or insurance?', NBER Working Paper no. 4626.

Riedel, J. (1991) 'Intra-Asian trade and foreign direct investment', *Asian Development Review,* 9: 111–46.

Rodrik, D. (1989) 'Credibility of trade reform – a policy maker's guide', *World Economy,* 12(1): 1–16.

Seydina, O.S. and N. Georgiadis (1993) 'Study on the institutional framework for regional cooperation and integration in Sub-Saharan Africa' (Brussels: European Commission) Sep.

SADC (1992) *Declaration Treaty and Protocol of Southern African Development Community* (Windhoek, Namibia: Southern African Development Community) Aug.

—— (1992) *Towards Economic Integration,* Proceedings of the 1992 Annual

Consultative Conference, Maputo, Mozambique, Jan.

—— (1993) *Regional Relations and Co-operation Post Apartheid* (Gabarone, Botswana: Southern African Development Community).

UN Centre on Transnational Corporations (1992) *The Determinants of Foreign Direct Investment: A Survey of the Evidence* (New York: United Nations).

Venables, A.J. (1993) 'Equilibrium locations of vertically linked industries', CEPR Discussion Paper no. 802.

Winters, L.A. and Z.K. Wang (1994) *Eastern Europe's International Trade* (Manchester University Press).

World Bank (1989) Intra-Regional trade in the Sub-Saharan Africa region', Technical Department Report no. 7685, Trade and Finance Division, Dec.

—— (1993) *The East Asian Miracle: Economic Growth and Public Policy* (New York and Oxford: Oxford University Press).

—— (1994) *Global Economic Prospects and the Developing Countries* (Washington, DC: The World Bank).

Yannopoulous, G. (1990) 'Foreign direct investment and European integration: the evidence from the formative years of the European Community', *Journal of Common Market Studies*, 38(3): 235–59.

Young, A. (1994) 'The tyranny of numbers: confronting the statistical realities of the East Asian growth experience', presented at the CEPR workshop on *Growth*, Les Arcs, Jan.

Index

Abuja Treaty 1991 160, 199, 429, 432, 451
accelerated implementation 423–4
accumulation effects of RI *see* growth
ADB (African Development Bank) 17, 415, 416, 419, 431
limited progress with SAPs 412–13
adjustment period 60–1
administrative costs 389
AEC (African Economic Community) 17, 405, 409, 411, 417–22, 426, 429
accelerated implementation of liberalization 423–4
international support for African integration 421–2
mechanisms at national level 420–1
possible impact 417–18
relationship with RECs 419–20, 423
role of NGOs and IGOs 420
single OAU/AEC Secretariat 418–19
Africa-Caribbean-Pacific (ACP) countries 406, 454, 464, 470
African Convention on the Conservation of Nature and Natural Resources 409
African Economic Community *see* AEC
AFTA (ASEAN Free Trade Area) 13, 200, 405
quantitative estimates of impact 283–93, 294
agencies of restraint 5–6, 116–19, 145, 230–1
Agenda 21 408
agglomeration *see* concentration; location

aggregate GDP approach 60–3
problems with 62–3
Agreement on Customs Valuation 377, 380–2
agriculture 12–13, 256–305
protection and bias against 262–76; quantitative evidence 265–76
regional integration 276–93; AFTA 287–93; foreign trade barriers and structural impediments 279–83
Uruguay Round 373–8, 389
aid 399
conditionality 128–9, 144–5, 308–9, 313, 346, 440–1
ALADI (Latin American Integration Association) 197–8
allocation efficiency effects of RI 26, 27, 28–46
competitive industries 29–41
imperfectly competitive industries 41–6
see also static effects
anchor countries *see* external guarantor
Andean Pact 197, 198, 199
anti-dumping 384
Ariyo, A. 354
ASEAN (Association of Southeast Asian Nations) 13, 14, 404, 429, 445
experience of integration 199–200
high performance and lessons for SSA 231–3
incremental effects of 224, 226, 228, 241; and exchange rate policy 227–8
Asia
East Asian 'economic miracle' 15, 213, 230
FDI in 445

(Asia *cont.*)
  integration schemes   24, 199–200, 259
Asia-Pacific Economic Cooperation forum (APEC)   404, 405
asset balance (AB)   91–3, 146–8
asset strategies   326–7
Association of Southeast Asian Nations   *see* ASEAN
Azariadis, C.   75–6

balance of payments   366, 380
  policy incredibility   325–32
Balassa, B.   358
Baldwin, R.   61–2, 213–14, 430
'Balkanization'   81–2
Bamako Commitment on Environment   409
Bamako Convention on the Transboundary Movements of Hazardous Wastes   409
bandwagon effect   459, 466, 467
bank loans   339
  policy-based lending   128–9, 144–5, 308–9, 313, 346, 440–1
BCEAO   416, 417
BEAC (Central African Monetary Union)   10, 112, 113, 114, 128, 450
  merger with UDEAC   210, 431
  monetary stability and external dimension   117, 118, 119
  trade openness   138, 139
before-and-after approach   8, 349–50
Benelux   192, 196
Benin, Republic of   424
Bevan, D.L.   95, 317
big push   75–6
bindings   19, 373, 376–7, 378, 379
black markets
  foreign exchange   106–7, 147–8
  premiums   *see* parallel premiums
  see also illegal trade
bonded warehouses   337–9
Botswana   365, 456–7
Brussels Definition of Value   382
budget compatibility   331–2
Burundi   230

Cadot, O.   443, 462
Calvo, G.   336
Cameroon   382, 421
Canada   452
capital accumulation
  effects of RI   *see* growth
  rapid   15, 230, 442–9, 468
capital controls   105–6
  and foreign exchange black markets   106–7
capital formation: induced   57–8, 58–63
capital-intensive goods   357–8
capital–labour ratio   58–60, 64
capital market: international integration   74–5
cash budget rule   327
CEAO (West African Economic Community)   204–5, 210, 212, 428, 431, 432
  evaluation of RI   178, 181, 182, 184, 186
  extreme performance patterns   14, 237–9, 241
  incremental effects   224–5, 226, 227, 228
  intra-African trade   140, 141, 142
ceaseless accumulation   63–76
central banks   112–13
Central African Monetary Union   *see* BEAC
Central American Common Market (CACM)   197, 224, 226, 227, 228, 229
Central and Eastern European countries (CEECs)   70, 399–400
  association agreements with EU   439, 440, 448; bandwagon effect   459; FDI   443–4; motives   462–4
CEPGL (Economic Community of the Great Lakes states)   204–5, 354, 433
  evaluation of RI   178, 182, 184, 186, 188
  failure to meet objectives   229, 230
  incremental effects   225, 227

CFA zone 6, 112, 125, 139, 450
  devaluation of franc in Jan 1994
    413, 414
  ECU Zone 452
  and exchange rate activism
    129–33
  experience of monetary
    integration 121–4, 237–9
  fiscal deficits 134
  impact of anchor on
    inflation 117–19
  trade enhancement 15–16, 242
CGE modelling 349
  see also gravity model
circular causality 49–52, 53
civil society 196
clearing, regional 127–8
clearing (payments) unions 111
CMA (Common Monetary
    Area) 112, 113, 114, 121–2
  inflation 117–19
Cobham, D. 110, 121, 231, 234–7
    passim
Cold War 399–400, 436
Collier, P. 110, 129, 231–3, 336,
    430, 440
  agencies of restraint 5, 6, 15,
    119, 145, 230
  devaluations 135
  welfare effects of customs
    unions 165–6
COMESA (Common Market for
    Eastern and South African
    States) 10, 160, 189
Commission of the EC (CEC)
    193
Committee of Permanent
    Representatives 194
Common Agricultural Policy
    (CAP) 436, 454, 463
common effective preferential tariff
    scheme 283
common markets 162
Communauté Economique et
    Monetaire de l'Afrique Centrale
    (CEMAC) 450
comparative advantage 357–8, 362
compatibility, policy 322–4
compensation schemes 174, 206

competition
  accumulation and 69–70, 72–4
  allocation efficiency effects
    28–46; competitive industries
    29–41; imperfectly competitive
    industries 41–6
  external tariffs and export taxes
    135–7
  for FDI 82–3
competitiveness, international 172,
    294, 453–4
  EU and CEECs 462–3
concentration, industrial 47–52,
    168–72
  trade costs and 52–4
  see also location
concentric circles trade
  arrangements 55, 56–7
conditionality 128–9, 144–5, 308–9,
    313, 346, 440–1
conflict prevention/resolution 411–12
consistency, macroeconomic 103–6
consumer durables 339
consumer prices 316–18
contraction 95
convertibility 5–6, 144–5, 460
  co-operation and restraint 127–9
  protection, fiscal policy and 90–110
convertibility restrictions 97–8,
    105–6, 107–8
co-ordination 18–19, 20, 134–7
  see also multilateralism
core-periphery model 168–70
cost-creating barriers 30–1, 32–3
  removing 38
Côte d'Ivoire 181, 365, 366, 445
Council of Ministers 193
Council for Mutual Economic
    Assistance: Multilateral
    Clearing Arrangement 127–8
counterfactual problem 340–1
creative destruction 69–70
credibility 15, 16, 230, 237, 468
  framework for evaluation of
    credible trade
    liberalization 347–50
  macroeconomic management
    and 438–42
  see also incredibility

cross-section analysis 8, 313, 349
cultural similarity 215, 223, 240
cumulation 40
currency convertibility *see*
    convertibility
currency retention schemes 385
currency unions 111, 113
    see also monetary integration;
    and under individual names
current account 329
customs unions 162, 164–7,
    276–7
    see also under individual names
customs valuation, agreement
    on 377, 380–2

Dakar agreement 1979 180
data availability constraints 202
De Long, B. 191–2
De Melo, J. 176, 206, 353, 443,
    462
demand externalities 171–2
demand side 83–4
DeRosa, D.A. 138, 139, 356
devaluation 95, 107–8, 134–5, 236
developing countries
    GATT status of SSA countries
        390–1
    GATT system and 371–2
    Group of 77 398
    motivation for RI 161
    and services 404
    tariff rates 272
dialogue system 194
discriminatory trade barriers 35–8
distribution 206
distance/proximity 215, 223, 240,
    367
Dixit, A. 336
Dollar, D. 138–9
domestic monopolists 41–2
Drazen, A. 75–6
drought 408–9
Drysdale, P. 293
dynamic effects 282–3
    aggregate GDP approach 60–3
    case for RI 167–73
    see also growth
dynamic efficiency 70

EAC (East African
    Community) 119, 163, 175,
    204–5, 210, 448–9
    evaluation of RI 183, 184, 187,
        190–1
    monetary stability and external
        dimension 115–16
    revival of 431, 449, 459–61
EACA (East African Currency
    Area) 113, 114
East African Common Services
    Organisation 190
East African Development
    Bank 460
East African High Commission
    190
Eastern Europe *see* Central and
    Eastern European countries
ECA (Economic Commission for
    Africa) 10, 17, 110, 212, 431,
    432
ECCAS 160
economic changes 398–427
    deterioration of SSA
        economies 412
    future projects 422–5
    global and implications for
        integration in SSA 410–11
    implications for future
        research 425–6
    limited progress with SAPs
        412–13
    need to improve interactions
        between structural adjustment
        and economic integration
        413–14
    new perspectives 415–22
    promotion of multinational
        projects 415
    trends in SSA 412
economic geography 168–72
    location effects 3, 26, 46–57
economic growth *see* growth
economic integration
    distribution of costs and benefits
        422
    need to improve interactions with
        structural adjustment 413–14
    see also monetary integration

Economic and Monetary Union of
West African States *see*
UEMOA
economic size/GDP 215, 223, 240
economic union 162
ECOWAS (Economic Community of
the West African States) 10,
160, 204–5, 212, 428, 432
balance of payments 366
Economic Recovery
Programme 414
evaluation of RI 178, 180, 182,
184, 186
incremental effects 225, 226,
227, 228
ineffectiveness/failure 229
intra-African trade 140, 354
members' arrears 433
revised Treaty 416, 417
and SAPs 414
UEMOA and 451
education 261
efficiency: trade-off between static
and dynamic 70
EFTA (European Free Trade
Association) 40, 159, 192,
448, 459
Eichengreen, B. 191–2, 405, 446
Elbadawi, I. 237–8
endogenous growth models 4, 63–76
basic logic 63–5
long-run growth effects of trade
arrangements 72–6
main varieties 65–72
endogenous policy approach 77–8
endogenous trade policy 95–8,
109, 332–4
environmental concerns 408–9
environmental standards 33
European Court of Justice 193
European Free Trade Association
see EFTA
European integration 24, 191–7,
435–6
European Monetary Union 124
European Parliament 193
European Payments Agreement 192
European Payments Union
(EPU) 127–8, 192

European Union/Community (EU/EC)
159, 398
association agreements with
CEECs *see* Central and
Eastern European countries
bandwagon effect 459
as external guarantor 20, 230–1,
431, 439, 469–70; EAC II
460; policy credibility 440–2;
role 461–6; SAER 454, 457;
UEMOA 452
global economic impact 404–5
growth effects of 1992
programme 62–3
importance as trade partner for
Africa 25
integration experience 192–7
mutual recognition 33
rules of origin 40–1
evaluation of RI schemes *see*
regional integration schemes
evaluation of trade liberalization
6–7, 306–52
defining liberalization 306–9
form taken by
liberalization 309–13
framework for evaluation of
credible trade liberalization
347–50; methodology 348–50;
performance indicators 348;
time frame 348
incredibility and its consequences
324–39
measuring trade policy and
identifying liberalization
episodes 313–24
of outcomes 341–7
problems of 340–1
exchange controls 98, 266–7, 268,
376, 378–9
exchange rate 7–8, 263, 309, 367
convertibility, protection and
fiscal policy 91, 91–3, 94–5,
141–2; fiscal deficits and
inflation 103–6; foreign
exchange black markets
106–7; liberalization of
macroeconomically motivated
trade restrictions 107–8;

exchange rate *cont.*
  multiple exchange rate
    equivalencies 100
  depreciation and raising money
    demand 325–6, 328
  devaluation 95, 107–8, 134–5,
    236
  extended gravity model 216,
    217, 218, 224–8, 240–1
  monetary integration and trade
    openness 124–7
  policy activism 129–33
  structural adjustment and RI 414
  unification as trade policy
    108–10, 135, 141–2
exchange rate union 111, 113
  costs and benefits 119–24
  see also monetary integration
expectations 51
expenditure changes 84–6
export pessimism 175
export promotion 173–4, 309
export retention schemes 128
export subsidies 377–8, 384–8,
  390
export taxes 99, 356
exporters: effects of import
  barriers 33–5
exports 353–4
  general trade liberalization
    358–62
  growth 342–7
  limitations of trade liberalization
    367–8
  merchandise 329–30
  non-traditional 12, 273, 362
  preferential trade
    liberalization 356–7
  protection and bias against
    agriculture 273–6
  supporting 309–11
  traditional 359–62
external balance (EB) 91–3, 146–8
  protection for 94–8
external guarantor 230–1, 430,
  431, 449–61
  EAC II 459–61
  EU *see* European Union/
    Community

monetary stability 117–19
new paradigm for RI 439–42
SAER 453–9
UEMOA 449–53

factor endowments 277–9, 281–2
factor mobility 52
factor use, changes in 320–1
famine 408–9
financial intermediation: reducing
  327
Fine, J. 230
fiscal balance 98
fiscal deficits 103–6, 130, 134, 148
fiscal incompatibility 331–2
fiscal policy 90–110
food
  imports 269, 272
  uncertainty and production
    279–83
forecastability, systematic 332–4
foreign exchange
  black markets 106–7, 147–8;
    see also parallel premium
  rationing 333
Foreign Exchange Bearer
  Certificates (FEBCs) 320
foreign exchange controls 98,
  266–7, 268, 376, 378–9
foreign investment *see* investment
formal exchange rate unions 111,
  113
Foroutan, F. 11, 25, 46, 176, 181
  gravity model 2, 362–3
  intra-African trade 140–1, 214,
    354, 356
France 40–1, 436
  UEMOA 441, 451, 452, 465, 470
Frankel, J. 226–7, 240
Free Trade Area of the Americas
  (FTAA) 404, 405
free trade areas (FTAs) 162
  reason for failure between
    developing countries 82
  see also under individual names
Frimpong-Ansah, J. 110

Garnaut, R. 293
gas pipelines 424

General Agreement on Tariffs and
Trade (GATT) 81, 371–3,
382, 453–4
Balance of Payments
Committee 382
mercantilistic law of the
jungle 80
SAER 455, 456
status of SSA countries 390–1
trade policy reviews 378, 385,
388
Uruguay Round *see* Uruguay
Round
see also World Trade
Organization
General Agreement on Trade in
Services (GATS) 383–4, 402,
403–4
general trade liberalization 11–12,
358–63
generalized system of preferences
(GSP) 372
geographically discriminatory
barriers 35–8
Germany 41, 71, 436, 462, 464
Ghana 356, 362, 365, 366, 424
Giavazzi, F. 436
Giovannini, A. 436
Global Coalition for Africa 410
global economic change 401–11
global linkages 406–8
global political change 399–400
government revenue *see* revenue
gradualism 54
gravity model 14, 141, 214–55,
362–3
empirical estimation and data
issues 219–23
incremental effects of regional
schemes 224–6; exchange rate
policy and 226–8
for SSA 215–19
Greenaway, D. 308, 346, 365
Grossman, G. 68–9
Group of 77 398
growth 2–3
effects of RI 26, 27, 57–76,
212–13, 437–8, 467–8;
endogenous growth theory 4,

63–76; long-run effects of
trade arrangements 72–6;
medium-term effects 58–63
evaluation of trade liberalization
342–7
SSA region 256, 410
Guillaumont, P. 110
Guillaumont, S. 110
Gunning, J.W. 230, 231–3, 336,
430, 440
Gunter, F.R. 166

Harberger triangles 31
Harrigan, J. 349
Havrylyshyn, O. 358
health standards 33
Heckscher, Ohlin and Samuelson
(HOS) model 13, 262–5
Heckscher–Ohlin theory 357
Helpman, E. 68–9
Herin, J. 40
Hiemenz, U. 229, 231, 233, 239
hoarding 336–9
Hopkins, A.G. 136
hub-and-spoke trade arrangements
3, 25, 430–1, 452
investment deterring aspects
54–7, 213–14
political economy of 80–3
private investment 442–9
see also external guarantor
human capital 70–1, 75–6
see also labour
hysteresis 51

illegal trade 203, 265, 319, 322
co-ordination of trade taxes
135–7
parallel premium 109, 147–8
and stance of trade policy 101–3
imperfect substitutes 42–3
implementation, accelerated 423–4
implicit tariff measures 316–18
import competition 41–4
import counter-factuals 321–2
import licences: stockpiling
336–9
import substitution 173–4, 175–6,
263–4, 314–15, 432, 466–7

imports
  food 269, 272
  general trade liberalization 359,
    361
  merchandise 329–30
  stockpiling 336–9
incentives 435
  repression of economic
    incentives 263–5
incidence measures 316
income elasticity 321
income levels 261
  gravity model 216, 223, 240
  and protection 265–76
incredibility 324–39
  causes of and diagnostics 324–36;
    macroeconomic incompatibility
    325–32; payments
    incompatibility 328–32;
    systematic forecasting 332–4;
    time inconsistency 334–6
  consequences of and diagnostics
    336–9
indirect taxes 323, 326
induced capital formation 57–8,
  58–63
industry
  harmonization of
    programmes 415
  market access and Uruguay
    Round 374–5, 378–82, 389
  standards 33
inflation 130, 133
  fiscal deficits and 103–6, 134
  monetary integration 117, 118,
    121, 122
informal exchange rate unions 111,
  113
infrastructure 281, 407
Ingram, W.D. 282
innovation 66–70, 72–5
innovators: competition among 73–4
Inotai, A. 173, 354
institutional arrangements 446
institutional design 435–6
institutional developments 415–22
intellectual property: TRIPs 381,
  384, 389, 390, 402
interdependence 406–8

inter-governmental organizations
  (IGOs) 420
internal balance (IB) 91–3, 146–8
international capital market
  integration 74–5
international institutions: support for
  African integration 421–2
International Monetary Fund
  (IMF) 123, 399
internationalization of
  production 406–8
intra-African trade 11–12, 17, 429
  general trade liberalization
    359–63
  impact of RI schemes 180–91
    passim, 212–14
  monetary integration and 140–2
  preferential trade
    liberalization 354–8
  transportation costs 367
  see also gravity model
investment 81–2, 437
  global increase in demand for
    foreign investment 410–11
  growth effects of RI 57–8,
    58–63; endogenous growth
    theory 64–76
  hub-and-spoke arrangements 54–7,
    81–2, 82–3, 213–4, 442–9
  irreversible 126
  need for and macroeconomic
    stability 453
  private 339, 442–9; wedge
    between social and private
    investment 65–76
  regional co-operation 4, 82–3
  trade-related investment
    measures (TRIMs) 381, 384,
    388, 402
IOC 183, 185, 187, 190, 204–5
Irwin, D. 405

Japan 71, 445
Jaycox, E. 399, 422–3
Jebuni, C.D. 358
Joint Secretariat 419

Kasekende, L. 354
Kennedy Round 307

Kenya   329, 339, 365
  EAC   449, 459, 460
  FEBCs   320
  and SAER   455, 456
knowledge capital   66–70, 72–5
Korea   342, 346
Krugman, P.R.   168–70
Krugman–Venables theory   47–52,
  52–3

labour   262, 446–7
  migration   52, 265, 462–3
  see also human capital
labour-intensive goods/
  products   269, 357–8
LAFTA (Latin American Free Trade
  Association)   197, 224, 226,
  229
Lagos Plan of Action 1980
  (LPA)   160, 429, 432
Langhammer, R.   229, 231, 233, 239
Latin America   197–9, 259
Lerner symmetry theorem   307–8
Linder, S.B.   358
Linder Hypothesis   216
linkages, global   406–8
Lipsey, R.G.   165
Lipumba, N.H.I.   354
lobbying   78–9
local content subsidies   384, 390
location effects of RI   3, 26, 46–57,
  446–8
  concentration   47–52, 52–4, 168–72
  equilibrium location of
    industry   49–52
  Krugman–Venables theory   47–52,
    52–3
  trade arrangements and   52–7
Lomé Agreement   402, 406, 439,
  454, 464–5, 470
Lucas, R.   70, 332–3

macroeconomic incompatibility
  325–32
  payments incompatibility   328–32
macroeconomic management
  438–42
macroeconomic policy   7–8, 89–158
  consistency   103–6

convertibility, protection and
  fiscal policy   90–110
  co-ordination of in EU   195
  divergence in EAC   115–16
  monetary integration   110–27;
    and African trade   137–42
  piecemeal paths to
    harmonization   127–37
  restraint   143–4
Maghreb   440, 463
Majd, N.   237–8
Malawi   365
Mano River Union   *see* MRU
Mansoor, A.   173, 354
manufacturing   169–72, 261
manufactures
  AFTA   283, 284–5, 286,
    288–91
  intra-African trade   357–8
marginalization: hub-and-spoke
  54–7
market access   80, 81
  Uruguay Round   373–84;
    agriculture   373–8;
    industry   378–82;
    services   383–4
market economies   407
market size   72–3
Marshall, A.   47
Marshall plan   191–2
McMillan, J.   165, 203
medium-term accumulation   58–63
mercantilism   79–80
merchandise imports and exports
  329–30
Mercosur   198
Mexico   439, 444
Michigan model   286
Middle East   259
migration   52, 265, 462–3
Milner, C.R.   308, 365
MMA (Multilateral Monetary Area)
  455, 456–7
'modified-control-group'
  approach   8
monetary integration   5–6, 110–27,
  142–5
  and African trade   137–42;
    intra-African trade   140–2

monetary integration *cont.*
  characteristics of different
    forms 235
  costs and benefits 119–24, 236
  extended gravity model 217–18,
    219–21
monetary stability and the external
    dimension 115–19
  role of monetary integration
    schemes in SSA 15–16, 233–9,
    242; debate in SSA 234–7;
    patterns of performance
    237–9, 241; structure of
    monetary integration 234
  and trade openness 124–7, 137–9
  varied arrangements in
    SSA 111–15
monetary policy
    compatibility 322–4
monetary unions 111, 113
  see also monetary integration;
    and under individual names
money demand-raising
    policies 325–6
money supply-reducing
    policies 326–8
monitoring
  policies 330
  'states of the world' 330–1
monopolists, domestic 41–2
Morocco 444
Mosley, P. 346, 349
most-favoured nation (MFN) 80,
    81, 86, 405
  AFTA 286–93
  GATS 383, 384
MRU (Mano River Union) 204–5,
    354, 433
  evaluation of RI 178, 181–5,
    186
multilateralism 18–19, 258, 370
  history of SSA and 371–3
  see also General Agreement on
    Tariffs and Trade; Uruguay
    Round
multinational projects 415, 424
multiple equilibriums 51
multiple exchange rates 100
Mundell, R. 110, 120

NAFTA (North American Free
    Trade Association) 17, 18, 20,
    198, 404, 405
  Mexico and 439
  USA anti-dumping 466
Nash, J. 378
neutrality 308, 309
Nigeria 331, 356, 366, 382, 421
  ECOWAS 180, 433, 451
  gas exports 424
non-discriminatory trade
    liberalization 11–12, 358–63
non-governmental organizations
    (NGOs) 420
non-reciprocal guarantees 440–1
non-tariff barriers (NTBs)
  AFTA 283, 286–92
  sectoral impacts of
    protection 265–9, 270–1, 272
  and tariff equivalences 308–9
  Uruguay Round 377, 380–2
  see also quantitative restrictions
non-traditional exports 12, 273,
    362
Northern anchor *see* external
    guarantor

OAU (Organization of African
    Unity) 17, 110, 159, 425, 431
  Bamako Conference 409
  conflict prevention/
    resolution 411
  members' arrears 433
  single OAU/AEC
    Secretariat 418–19
ODC rates 377
OECD (Organization for Economic
    Co-operation and Development)
    161, 192
OEEC (Organization for European
    Economic Co-operation) 192
open regionalism 13–14, 293, 294
openness 358
  monetary integration and 124–7,
    137–9
optimum currency areas 119–24
Ostry, J.D. 366
outcomes, evaluation of 341–7

output, aggregate 58–9, 59–60
  aggregate GDP approach 60–3
  and welfare 61–2
outward orientation 173–4
over-invoicing 317
'own' resources system 194–5

PAEC (Pan African Economic
  Community) 160, 199
Pan Africanism 17–18
Panagariya, A. 176, 206, 353
Papageorgiou, D. 8
  liberalization 308, 313;
    episodes 309, 309–11;
    evaluation of outcomes 341–2,
    343, 344–5, 346, 349–50
parallel premiums
  foreign exchange 108, 129, 130,
    141–2, 147–8, 319
  illegal trade 109, 147–8
parastatal marketing boards 281
'passing parade' pandering
  problem 82–3
patents 389
payments compatibility 325–32
  diagnostics 328–32
payments (clearing) unions 111
Pearson, S.R. 282
performance
  economic performance of SSA
    countries 256–7
  indicators 340–1, 342–7, 348
physical capital 71–2
Pitt, M. 101
policy accounts 315–16
policy-based lending 128–9,
  144–5, 308–9, 313, 346, 440–1
policy changes 315–16
  large effects of small changes 52
policy compatibility 322–4
policy credibility *see* credibility;
  incredibility
policy reversals 376, 377
  see also incredibility
policy transparency 382
political changes 398–427
  future projects 422–5
  global and integration in
    SSA 399–400

implications for future
  research 425–6
new perspectives 415–22
trends in SSA 411–12
political economy 435–6
  of creative destruction 69–70
  hub-and-spoke bilateralism 80–3
  of location 52
  of shock treatment
    liberalization 54
  theory and RI 77–9
  trade negotiations 79–80
political instability 462–3
political will 196–7
poverty traps 75–6
power 77
preferential tariff agreements 162
  see also PTA
preferential trade liberalization
  11–12, 353–4
  domestic policies, trade
    integration and 354–8
price elasticity 321
prices
  allocation efficiency effects
    28–46
  changes in 84–6; measuring
    trade policy 316–20; relative
    price changes 318–19
  diagnostic of payments
    incompatibility 330
  measure of openness 138–9
Pritchett, L. 2, 140–1, 214, 313,
  324, 362–3
private sector 434
process-innovation models 68–9
producer prices 316–18
product-innovation models 67–8
production
  interdependence 406–8
  structures 261
production function for
  innovations 67, 68
productivity 401–2
profit: pure profit effect 44–5
protection 90–110, 317
  for external balance 94–8
  for fiscal balance 98
  impact on exports 11–12, 356

protection *cont.*
  macroeconomics of 108–10
  sectoral impacts 262–76, 293–4
  structure of 139, 269–72
proximity/distance 215, 223, 240, 367
PTA (Preferential Trade Area for
    Eastern and Southern
    Africa) 10, 160, 204–5, 212,
    416, 432, 458
  evaluation of RI schemes 179,
    183, 184, 187, 188–9
  failure to meet objectives
    229–30
  incremental effects 226, 227
  intra-African trade 140, 354,
    429
PTA Clearing House
    (PTACH) 113, 114, 127–8
pure profit effect 44–5

quality ladders model 68–9
quantitative restrictions (QRs) 109
  and fiscal deficits 105–6
  liberalization episodes 309–11
  measuring trade
    liberalization 314–15
  non-equivalence to tariffs 43–4
  protection for external
    balance 97–8
  rent-creating barriers 31–2
  sectoral impacts of
    protection 266–7, 268, 270–1,
    272
  and tax revenues 99
  see also non-tariff barriers
quantity-based measures 320–2
quasi-rents 78–9

Raheem, M.I. 354
Rand Monetary Area *see* RMA
real balance effect 322
reciprocity 19–20, 440
redundancy effect 73
regional clearing 127–8
regional disparities 452–3
regional integration (RI)
    schemes 10–11, 210
  AEC and 419–20, 423

Asia 24, 199–200, 259
classification 162–3
in developing regions 258, 259
Europe 191–7
evaluation of SSA schemes
    177–91; Central Africa 185–8;
    Eastern and Southern Africa
    188–91; West Africa 180–5
history of last thirty years
    431–7
impact on intra-SSA trade
    210–55, 354, 355; failure
    228–31; incremental effects
    224–8; lessons from ASEAN
    231–3
Latin America 197–9
membership summary of SSA
    schemes 204–5
new approach for SSA 449–61;
    EAC II 459–61; SAER
    453–9; UEMOA 416–17,
    449–53
possible global impact of major
    trading blocs 404–6
promotion of multinational
    projects 424
researchable issues 200–7
see also under individual names
Reinikka, R. 314, 324
relative price indicators 318–19
rent-creating barriers 30, 31–2,
    36–8
rentier states 364
repression of economic
    incentives 263–5
reputation 237
research and development
    (R&D) 66–70, 72–5
research methodology 348–50
researchable issues 200–7
reserves: change in level as
    diagnostic 328–9
resource allocation efficiency *see*
    allocation efficiency
restraint, agencies of 5–6, 116–19,
    145, 230–1
revenue, government 364–5
  motive 99–100
risk 74–5, 126

RMA (Rand Monetary Area) 112, 117, 119, 432, 455
Robson, P. 110, 121, 231, 234–7 *passim*
Rodrik, D. 124, 438
Romer, P. 63, 66, 71, 109
Rosenstein–Rodan, P. 75
rules of origin: cost of 38–41
Rwanda 230

SACU (Southern African Customs Union) 10, 118, 175, 204–5, 210, 212, 432
  evaluation of RI schemes 183, 185, 187, 189–90
  members and Uruguay Round 379, 382, 390
  SAER 456, 458
  South Africa and 454–5
SADC (Southern African Development Community) 10, 204–5, 210, 416, 433, 434, 458
  evaluation of RI schemes 179, 183, 184, 187, 189
  projects 433–4, 443
  South Africa and 455
  see also SADCC
SADCC (Southern African Development Co-ordination Conference) 10, 210, 212, 433, 434
  comparison with ASEAN 233, 241
  incremental effects 225, 226, 227, 228
SAER (Southern African Economic Region) 449, 453–9, 459–60, 465–6
Sapsford, D. 346
savings strategies for money supply reduction 327
scale economies 47, 48–9, 170–2, 447–8
scale effect 45–6
Schumpeter, J. 69
second-best theory 2
sectoral aspects 12–14, 256–305
  protection 262–76, 293–4
  regional integration 276–93, 294–5
Senegal 181, 382

Senegambia Union 433
services 386–7, 389
  GATS 383–4, 402, 403–4
shock treatment liberalization 54
shocks, exogenous 120–1, 330–1, 333
'single tax' 239
smuggling *see* illegal trade
Solow, R. 58, 66
  growth model 58–9, 63, 64
South Africa 189, 207, 382, 441–2
  and SAER 453–8
  Uruguay Round 19, 378, 385
Southern African Customs Union *see* SACU
Southern African Development Community *see* SADC
Southern African Development Co-ordination Conference *see* SADCC
Southern African Economic Region *see* SAER
special and differential (S&D) treatment 372
spillovers 213
  growth effects 2–3
  technology 27, 66–8, 72–3, 75
  trade and exchange rate policies 135
stabilization 128–9
standards 33
state: dominant role 432, 466–7
static effects 26, 282–3
  case for RI 163–7
  see also allocation efficiency effects
static efficiency 70
stockpiling 336–9
structural adjustment
  loans (SALs) 313, 314; and evaluation of trade liberalization 340, 346, 347
  need to improve interactions with economic integration 413–14
  programmes (SAPs) 257, 376, 378–9; and EAC II 460; ECA and 432; exchange rate activism 129–33; limited progress with 412–13
  stabilization and 128–9

structural bottlenecks 279–83
subsidiarity 196
subsidies 377–8, 381, 384–8, 390
sunk costs 78–9
supply side 84
systematic forecastability 332–4

take-offs 75–6
Tanzania 459, 460
targeting specific issues 424–5
tariff escalation 78
tariffs 272
  AFTA and reductions 283
  bound 19, 373, 376–7, 378, 379
  co-ordination 135–7, 145
  liberalization and 306–9, 309
  non-equivalence to QRs 43–4
  rent-creating barriers 31
  sectoral impacts of
    protection 266–7, 268, 269–72
  Uruguay Round 373, 376–7,
    378, 379–80
taxe de coopération régionale 239
taxes, trade
  co-ordination 135–7, 145
  export taxes 99, 356
  fiscal deficit and 105–6, 148
  indirect 323, 326
  revenue motive and structure of
    trade intervention 99–100
  role of revenues 364–5
technological change 446–7
  global 401–2
  knowledge capital 66–70, 72–5
terms of trade
  RI and 172–3, 277–9
  shocks to 120–1, 330–1, 333
textiles and clothing sector 380, 382
time frame 348
time inconsistency 334–6
time-series analysis 349–50
Tobit model 218–19
Togo 424
Tokyo Declaration on African
  Development 400
Tokyo Round 307, 372, 384
trade arrangements
  and location effects 52–7
  long-run growth effects 72–6

trade barriers 28–9
  foreign and RI 279–83
  geographically
    discriminating 35–8
  impact of import barriers on
    exporters 33–5
  unilateral reduction for small
    country 29–33
  see also under individual forms
trade costs 3, 447–8
  and location 48–9, 52–4
trade creation 36–8, 164–7,
  287–93
trade diversion 36–8, 164–7, 229
trade flows: researching 202–3
trade intensity 363
  measures 320
trade intervention: structure
  99–100
trade negotiations 79–80
  see also Uruguay Round
trade openness *see* openness
trade policy
  endogenous 95–8, 109, 332–4
  measuring 313–24; changes
    in 315–16
  options 16–20
  stance and illegal trade 101–3
trade taxes *see* taxes
traditional exports 359–62
transnational corporations
  (TNCs) 407–8
transparency, policy 382
transport costs 171–2, 367
transportation infrastructure 281
TRIMs (Trade-Related Investment
  Measures) 381, 384, 388, 402
TRIPs (Trade-Related Aspects of
  Intellectual Property
  Rights) 381, 384, 389, 390,
  402
Turkey 356

UDEAC (Central African Customs
  and Economic Union) 10,
  204–5, 210, 431, 432, 450
  evaluation of RI schemes 179,
    182, 184, 185–8

extreme patterns of
performance 14, 237–9, 241
intra-African trade 140, 141,
142, 354
UEMOA (Economic and Monetary
Union of the West African
States) 10, 20, 210, 431, 441,
465, 470
new approach to RI 416–17,
449–53
Uganda 459, 460
UMOA (West African Monetary
Union) 112, 113, 114, 431
monetary stability and the
external dimension 117, 118,
119
openness 138, 139
unbonded warehouses 337–9
uncertainty: food production
and 279–83
under-invoicing 101
unilateral trade liberalization 16–20,
176, 207
United Kingdom (UK) 444
United Nations (UN) 407–8, 411
Committee on Trade and
Development (UNCTAD) 265,
398, 405
Conference on Environment and
Development (UNCED) 408
Economic Commission for Africa
(ECA) 10, 17, 110, 212, 431,
432
United States (USA) 24, 25, 159,
452
unrecorded trade *see* illegal trade
Uruguay Round (UR) 16, 18–19,
159, 276, 307, 370–97
impact on global economy 402–3
impact on trade
liberalization 389–90
market access
commitments 373–84;
agriculture 373–8, 389;
industry 374–5, 378–82, 389;
NTBs 377, 380–2; services
383–4, 404; tariffs 373,
376–7, 378, 379–80
subsidies 377–8, 384–8

TRIMs 388
TRIPs 389

variable geometry 196, 421
variety effect 45–6
Venables, T. 47–52, 52–3
viability test 206
Viner, J. 164, 276–7
volatility, exchange rate 125–7
volume of trade effect 31
voluntary export restraints
(VERs) 380

wage moderation 446
wages 50, 53–4
Wei, S. 226–7, 240
welfare
AFTA plan 287–93
analysis of allocation effects
30–1, 36–8
case for RI 163–4, 165–7
output and 61–2
reduction of disparities 195
sectoral impacts of
protection 273–6
test for welfare effects of
RI 203
West African Clearing House
(WACH) 113, 114, 127–8
West African Economic
Community *see* CEAO
West African Economic and
Monetary Union *see* UEMOA
West African Monetary Union *see*
UMOA
Whalley, J. 311–12, 343–6
with/without approach 346, 349
Wolf, M. 358
Wonnacott, P. 280
Wonnacott, R. 280
World Bank 346, 349, 366, 413,
438, 447
lending to Africa and Eastern
Europe 399–400
reform programmes and trade
liberalization 309, 313
SSA growth projections 410
World Trade Organization
(WTO) 371, 384–5, 388, 402

World Trade Organization *cont.*
  Agreement on Customs
    Valuation 377, 380–2
  see also General Agreement on
    Tariffs and Trade; Uruguay
    Round

Yeo, S. 230

Zaire 230
Zambia 331
Zimbabwe 19, 356, 455, 460
  and SAER 456–7, 458